Adaptation, Resistance and Access to Instructional Technologies:

Assessing Future Trends in Education

Steven D'Agustino
Fordham University, USA

Information Science REFERENCE

INFORMATION SCIENCE REFERENCE

Hershey · New York

Director of Editorial Content:	Kristin Klinger
Director of Book Publications:	Julia Mosemann
Acquisitions Editor:	Lindsay Johnston
Development Editor:	Christina Bufton
Publishing Assistant:	Natalie Pronio
Typesetter:	Natalie Pronio
Production Editor:	Jamie Snavely
Cover Design:	Lisa Tosheff

Published in the United States of America by
Information Science Reference (an imprint of IGI Global)
701 E. Chocolate Avenue
Hershey PA 17033
Tel: 717-533-8845
Fax: 717-533-8661
E-mail: cust@igi-global.com
Web site: http://www.igi-global.com

Library of Congress Cataloging-in-Publication Data

Adaptation, resistance and access to instructional technologies : assessing future trends in education / Steven D'Agustino, editor.
p. cm.
Includes bibliographical references and index.
Summary: "This book captures the current trends in technology integration from PreK-12 to higher education, focusing on the various constituent groups, namely students, teachers, and communities, in education and the effects of educational technology on learning and empowerment"--Provided by publisher.
ISBN 978-1-61692-854-4 (hardcover) -- ISBN 978-1-61692-856-8 (ebook) 1. Education--Effect of technological innovations on. 2. Education and state--United States. 3. Intelligent tutoring systems--United States. 4. Educational change. 5. Computer-assisted instruction. I. D'Agustino, Steven, 1965-
LB1028.3.A7686 2010
371.33--dc22

2010016448

British Cataloguing in Publication Data
A Cataloguing in Publication record for this book is available from the British Library.

Editorial Advisory Board

List of Reviewers

Table of Contents

Section 2
Enabling Students

Section 3
Enabling Communities

Section 5
Training Teachers

Detailed Table of Contents

This chapter explores the gap in information between digital natives and digital immigrants. Advances in computer technology have transformed information, and resulting changes in information behavior clearly mark the digital information divide. These changes in information behavior have affected information literacy instruction, yet educators have opted for quick fix strategies, ignoring the need to develop a comprehensive information literacy curriculum for the digital age. Partnerships—between primary, secondary, and postsecondary teachers and librarians and curriculum designers working to establish a vertically and horizontally scaffolded K-16 information literacy curriculum—may effectively bridge the divide.

This chapter explores factors that enhance and constrain the adoption and sustainability of Information and Communication Technologies in Universities and higher institutions of learning in South Africa. This study examines pedagogical, socio-economic and epistemological aspects of the paradigm shift in higher education delivery in Africa. Adopting and sustaining ICTs for educational improvement is a multifaceted process. As a dynamic process, all the vital elements of technology adoption need to be

This chapter describes a pedagogical approach to engage students in online learning environments, using XNAMEX Becta's model for personalized learning and student engagement (PLEaSE). PLEaSE maximizes learning out comes by supporting students at times and in places that are appropriate to their needs and in ways that suit their personal dispositions In this study, students are encouraged to explore, develop, reflect and construct their own knowledge and create their own learning content, while the instructor plays the role of coach and facilitator. This study is part of an ongoing action research project on the Scholarship of Teaching and Learning (SoTL) in Higher Education, whose purpose is to design and develop the Pedagogy of Engagement Integrating Technology (PoEIT) model. PoEIT engages learners in the use of online tools such as forums and blogs while developing their soft skills using Moodle platform. This study shows that with the right integration of pedagogy and technology students can be transformed to become independent learners.

This study examines peer interaction and peer assistance observed in on an online forum, part of a graduate level instructional design course during the 2008 spring academic term. It incorporates both content analysis and social network analysis techniques. The content analysis results showed that the four types of peer assistance adopted from an existing framework were adequate to categorize the peer assistance that the students received during the study. Students tended to receive more Reflective assistance from their peers if their reading reflections provided high relevance to the course projects. Social network analysis results revealed that while 70% of the students provided peer assistance to one another, they were less likely to go beyond the course requirement of posting toward to end of the semester. Also, a further analysis demonstrated how SNA approach may help examine the influences of actor attributes on their observed communication.

Section 3
Enabling Communities

As educators make greater use of online learning environments and virtual communities, increased attention is being paid to the aspects of computer-mediated communication which facilitate constructive interaction between learners. The benefits of face-to-face cooperative learning are being pursued in the

This chapter takes a novel orientation to understanding adults as learners by arguing that the context rather than age of the learner is more indicative of their approaches to learning to use technologies. Drawing on data from a study of everyday avatars learning to build the online virtual world Second Life®, this chapter argues that learning through recreational activities such as these adults do in Second Life® is adult learning and a kind of 21st century learning that takes place in the wild of virtual worlds. In order to imagine ourselves, students and colleagues or corporate employees engaged by and in world-building, educators must view online technologies as rich social contexts rather than simply educational technologies. The roles of teachers, trainers or support personnel are as designers for learning. They create contexts where the learning objectives they have set can be achieved.

Chapter 13
Using the 3VModel to Explore Virtuality, Veracity and Values in Liminal Spaces.......................... 199
Simon Atkinson, Massey University, New Zealand
Kevin Burden, University of Hull, UK

Adaptation and adoption of immature emergent technologies for instruction fails to account for the challenge to, and creation of, new concepts of self, identity and community both in real and virtual spaces. New insight is necessary to develop social policy responses, including those of educational systems and institutions, to the consequences of these new conceptualisations. This chapter presents an original theoretical model which aims to assist in the interpretation of existing theory, exploring the interrelated dimensions of values, virtuality and veracity disturbed by the adaptation of emergent technologies. It invites an exploration of existing theoretical and methodological instruments available within the broader Social Sciences to examine emerging notions of identity. The emergent theoretical model visualizes a set of complex assumptions within the concepts of the "real-virtual" interface created by emergent technologies; the 3V model represents one means of explore internal structure to this liminal space and invites further empirical study.

Section 4
Enabling Teachers

Chapter 14
Social Networks: Implications for Education.. 216
Mary Hricko, Kent State University, USA

Online social networks (SNs) are dynamic Web 2.0 applications that can be used for teaching, learning, and research activities. These SNs offer a myriad of collaborative features for generating content and fostering interactive communication. Although many K-16 administrators tend to focus on the negative consequences of using such applications, online social networks, if managed effectively as instructional tools, can provide opportunities for educators to help students develop 21st century skills. This discussion provides an overview how online social networks can be used in education and offers guidelines for implementation.

Technological communication advancements in recent years, including, but not limited to, the Internet, cell phones, PDAs and texting, have changed communication, accessing information, and doing business. Unfortunately, education has often lagged behind in the effective implementation of these technological advances. This chapter examines one technological development that has the potential to change the higher educational landscape. The use of online social networking tools can be used to help establish connections student to student, student to faculty, faculty to student and faculty to faculty. These tools can be used to encourage scholarly collaboration in a constructivist manner that builds upon the social learning theories of Albert Bandura and Lev Vygotski.

Oksika, Johnson, and Buteau (2009) state that incorporating new pedagogy into teaching is attributed to the instructor's feelings about themselves and what they have previously learned. In other words, if one has a positive attitude towards technology, one will be more inclined to incorporate it into one's teaching. This chapter discusses changed attitudes and mindsets toward technology, particularly in the mindsets of the secondary education faculty in the author's college. Because technology has been integrated in the college's secondary education courses, the faculty, including the author of this chapter, had to learn about new technologies to teach as well as model to their students. This chapter also discusses the author's personal journey into using technology as a pedagogical tool. Various technology methods taught to secondary education students will be highlighted, with a concluding sampling of students' ideas to illustrate the creative thinking that technology integration can produce.

Through the lens of Technological Pedagogical Content Knowledge (TPCK), this chapter's goal is to understand how commitments affect readiness to innovate and how readiness to innovate affects commitments. Even further, it initiates the conversation on what engages faculty to change and improve their own teaching. Can faculty's commitment to pedagogical quality (CPQ) predict instructional technology adoption? Current Instructional Technology Adoption Models (ITAMs) ignore issues of pedagogy and are mostly developed for an alternative audience and environment, outside the realities and characteristics of higher education. A literature review explores exiting models for factors motivating full-time faculty to incorporate technology. Three audience categories naturally emerge (non-educational, K-12, and higher education), which highlight how each community treats teaching and learning differently. In addition, a study was conducted to analyze relationships between CPQ and adoption. Results indicated

The purpose of this study is to examine the factors to determine the competence of technology integration for teacher candidates. This study utilized data from a 2006 quick-response survey entitled 'Educational Technology in Teacher Education Programs for Initial Licensure.' Only 1,350 institutions that have teacher education programs for initial licensure were selected. The result of a hierarchical regression revealed that the extent of institutional training programs for technology explain most variation (33%) of the competence of technology integration of teacher candidates. In addition, the more variation of technology programs an institution employs in its program, the more confidence the teacher candidates possess. The result supports findings from previous research as well as supporting some emphasis on professional development design considerations that may be of value to those planning the similar technology trainings.

This research studied a professional development technology mentoring program serving approximately 500 K-12 teachers in New York City. The teacher training model, designed to improve student outcomes through the integration of technology into instruction, employed school visits by professional development technology mentors, training workshops and an online collaboration environment for participants. With a theoretical basis in transformative learning, the model focused on developing relationships of trust between teachers and professional developers. Findings in the paper discuss how to improve student performance in mathematics and English Language Arts through technology integration and teacher competence in teaching with technology, and they provide new insights into the potential for professional development initiatives incorporating similar perspectives and practices.

This chapter highlights critical lessons learned during the past six years during the development of a capstone graduate educational technology course, teaching School Library Media (SLMS) pre-service students how to develop learner centered, knowledge centered and assessment centered Web-based learning tools; in short, to enable them to become change agents in their educational communities. A large northeastern University has cultivated educational partnerships that bring together University students with their professional, in-service, PreK-12 counterparts to explore issues of technology in education, pedagogy, theory, curriculum, information literacy, assessment, and evaluation. Unlike traditional courses with prepackaged academic assignments, this course engages school library media specialists with real-world teaching and learning situations that are frequently ill-structured, often chaotic, and collaboratively defined by the learning needs of all participants (PreK-12 through university; in-service

Foreword

Jack Welch, CEO of GE said, "If the rate of change inside an institution is less than the rate of change outside that institution, then the end is in sight." Many would agree that this echoes the sentiments of education technology enthusiasts, those people who are committed to real transformation in our public school classrooms. These are the same individuals who have broken new instructional technology ground through effective deployment and utilization of information communication technologies.

There is no shortage of commentary about U.S. schools lacking focus on the needs of a digital generation and beginning down a path of irrelevancy. Elected officials have responded with urgent calls to develop 21st century skills and drive an information economy—thereby securing the future of not just our kids, but our nation.

We are a long way from meeting the needs and interests of the millennial generation and the post-millennial generation after them. The millennials—touted by many as the next "great generation" because of their similarities to those in the World War II generation—have high-minded values and are keenly interested in social issues and technology. They are exceedingly entrepreneurial, preferring to own their own business rather than working their way toward an executive role in a company.

You may recall that under Jack Welch's leadership, GE grew in value from around $13 billion to several hundred billion dollars during his 20-year tenure. He instituted a culture of change and performance. GE managers were assessed on their ability to change and to be profitable.

He was famous for saying things like, "My main job was developing talent. I was a gardener providing water and other nourishment to our top 750 people. Of course, I had to pull out some weeds, too." He also was quoted as saying, "An organization's ability to learn, and translate that learning into action rapidly, is the ultimate competitive advantage."

What must we do in our schools today to create a competitive advantage for our students, for our communities and for our nation? To plan for this kind of future, we must be prescient to what the future holds. Issues and opportunities facing the world today and the not-too-distant future are complex and exciting. How will problems of energy and the environment be solved? What will farming look like in 10 years? How will health and medicine progress, and in what ways will these two fields merge with information technology? Will vacation options include global high-speed rail routes and space travel? Consider these future trend predictions from the World Future Society (http://www.wfs.org/forecasts.htm):

Tomorrow's inventors will spend their days writing descriptions of the problems they want to solve, and then letting computers find the solutions. Invention programs like Gregory Hornby's "evolutionary algorithm" have been used to invent real-world objects, such as a special space antenna, based entirely on engineering specifications. Continued advances will increasingly rely on cross-fertilization between the fields of biology and computer science. As a result, we will develop not only software that can produce better inventions but also inventions that are able to adapt to their environments. —Robert Plotkin, "The Automation of Invention," July-Aug 2009, p. 24

Ammonia may become the fuel of choice for cars by 2020. As a candidate source for hydrogen used in fuel cells, ammonia (comprising one nitrogen and three hydrogen atoms) is plentiful, easier to liquefy than methane, and emits nitrogen rather than carbon, thus having fewer negative impacts on the climate. —J. Storrs Hall, "Ammonia, the Fuel of the Future," Sep-Oct 2009, p. 10

Algae may become the new oil. According to researchers at a Department of Energy plant in New Mexico, single-celled microalgae, grown in pond water, produce a biofuel that is lead-free and biodegradable, emits two-thirds less carbon dioxide and other pollutants than gasoline, and can run any modern diesel engine. Even better, algae require only a fraction of the land area of biofuel-producing crops. —Robert McIntyre, "Algae's Powerful Future," Mar-Apr 2009, p. 25

Radical methods of altering the planet may be the only way to prevent the worst effects of climate change. Geoengineering may be inevitable because, even if humans could instantly end all greenhouse gas emissions, global temperatures would continue to increase for the next 20–30 years, triggering feedback loops and more warming. Potential megascale geoengineering projects include sending space mirrors into orbit, sequestering carbon in the ground in biomass charcoal, and increasing the amount of carbon that the ocean can absorb by forcing plankton blooms in the seas. —Jamais Cascio, author of Hacking the Earth, reviewed by Bob Olson, July-Aug 2009, p. 51

The World Future Society predicts that the most important job skill for this century is foresight—the ability to see what lies ahead and plan for it. How can we orient our school classrooms to develop foresight in our students? How do we equip teachers and school leaders to lead and plan using foresight?

It doesn't take a special set of skills to know that technology is part of our world's future landscape. It is logical, then, to conclude that technology should be part of the classroom experience. Conversations today must swiftly shift to a serious and focused path, broadly and systematically embracing information communications technologies throughout every student's educational career.

Social networking, mobility, online learning, gaming, peer-to-peer mentoring and tutoring are all part of a rich technology learning environment. Many leading educators have blazed a trail in the practical and appropriate utilization of instructional technology and it's easy to follow in their footsteps.

The answer to Jack Welch's call for a competitive advantage in our schools and for our nation lies in the speed with which we stop talking about "why" we should do things differently and begin diving into "how" we get started.

Marina Leight
Vice President of Education
Converge Media Platform and the Center for Digital Education

Preface

Adaptation, Resistance and Access: Assessing Future Trends In Education is an attempt to capture the current trends in technology integration from Pre-K to K-12 to higher education. It is divided into five sections: Access, Enabling Students, Enabling Communities, Enabling Teachers, and Training Teachers. Each section focuses on the various constituent groups in education and the effects of educational technology on their learning and empowerment.

Section one, Access, considers various issues confronting education when historically underserved populations vary in their ability to access current and emerging technology. The effects of this lack of access and some suggestions for ameliorating these effects are discussed. Chapter One explores the gap between so-called digital natives and digital immigrants and suggests that in most educational environments, the transformation of information has not been acknowledged. The author suggests partnerships among the various educational constituencies from elementary through post-secondary as a solution. Chapter Two examines similar issues of equity and access in postsecondary institutions of learning in South Africa and focuses on technological, socio-economic and political factors. Chapter Three examines improvements in the technological infrastructure and the adoption of and resistance to the use of laptops by teachers in New Zealand, concluding that teacher professional development, a reliable infrastructure, and administrative support are keys to changing instructional practices. Chapter Four examines the perceptions of students and teachers regarding their use of an e-learning/ sharing portal. This chapter provides some promising practices for technology integration and explores the effect of technology on student motivation.

Section Two, Enabling Students, focuses on specific instructional strategies that integrate technology effectively and describes some of the persistent barriers to integration. Chapter Five explores an initiative to develop student-authored textbooks using a web-based collaborative interface. The chapter provides an interesting argument for the use of so-called web 2.0 tools, like wikis, in instructional settings. Chapter Six describes an innovative instructional approach to improving the English Language Arts skills of middle school English language learners by using speech recognition software. The findings describe how the use of the software had a positive effect on pronunciation skills, fluency and text production. Chapter Seven describes engaging post-secondary students in online learning environments with an instructional approach coupling personalized learning and student engagement, which produced positive outcomes for student academic achievement. Chapter Eight's study, conducted as part of a graduate level instructional design course, examines peer interaction and peer assistance in an online forum. The study categorizes online peer assistance and applies social network analysis to examine online interactions in academic settings with social components.

Section Three, Enabling Communities, focuses on the development of technologically mediated learning communities. Rather than focusing on teachers or students in isolation, this section describes strategies for developing communities of learning through the use of technology. Chapter Nine examines the impact of computer supported collaborative learning and offers several best practices for enhancing learners' perceptions of support in digital environments. Chapter Ten presents a case study exploring how collaborative learning may be fostered in a virtual environment. The chapter discusses the necessary components for a successful virtual learning community. Chapter Eleven analyzes the experiences and perceptions of undergraduate students using a three dimensional virtual learning environment. The authors discuss how five forms of collaboration enhanced the learning process. Chapter Twelve identifies a new method for greater understanding of adult learners and their use of technology. The author argues that the learning context rather than the age of the learner is the important factor and that online environments should be considered as social contexts rather than solely educational technologies. Chapter Thirteen presents an original theoretical model designed to explore how adopting emerging technologies impacts values, virtuality, and veracity in learning environments.

Section Four, Enabling Teachers, focuses on promising instructional practices, supports, and training methods for educators working in technologically integrated environments. Importantly, several chapters also address internal and individual learner factors that influence the adoption of technology. Chapter Fourteen examines online social networks and advocates for their use in educational environments, recommending best practices and guidelines for implementation. Chapter Fifteen describes how educational systems have been slow to adopt new and emerging communication technologies with a specific focus on online social networking tools. Chapter Sixteen describes changes in instructor attitudes towards the integration of technology and provides insights into the transformation of educators from instructional technology resisters to instructional technology innovators. Chapter Seventeen examines the factors that contribute to faculty willingness to change and improve instruction in higher education. The author also analyzes motivating factors and their relationship to the integration of technology. Chapter Eighteen discusses the concept of technology momentum and its application to post-secondary education. A case study examines the adoption of online learning managements systems.

Section Five, Training Teachers, the lengthiest section, focuses on promising practices and trends in teacher professional development in technology integration. This section encompasses many of the issues discussed in earlier sections and is optimistic about current and future developments in instructional technology use in teaching and learning. Chapter Nineteen presents a multiple case study that examines the levels of preparation of teacher candidates in using technology in their teacher education program. Resistance to the integration of ICT is discussed. Chapter Twenty examines the competence of teacher candidates in technology integration. The study examines the impact of the variation in technology programs employed by an institution on the competence of teacher candidates. Chapter Twenty-One examines a professional development technology mentoring program designed to improve student outcomes through the integration of technology into instruction. The chapter provides new insights into the potential for professional development initiatives to positively affect student academic outcomes. Chapter Twenty-Two highlights critical lessons learned concerning the development of a graduate course teaching School Library Media pre-service students how to develop learner centered, knowledge centered and assessment centered learning environments. Promising strategies are identified. Chapter Twenty-Three examines the lesson plans of first-year teachers and the relationship between higher-order thinking skills and technology-rich instruction. Findings describe the benefits of indirect instruction for promoting student discovery and higher-order thinking skills. Chapter Twenty-Four describes the effectiveness of an electronic mentoring program for supporting pre-service educators in their transition to the classroom. Chapter Twenty-Five analyzes the use of electronic portfolios in the professional development of teachers. Using a case study-like approach, the chapter details the use of online resources and predicts the beneficial effects of online resources for future educators. The final chapter, Chapter Twenty-Six, presents a blueprint for future faculty development. The authors envision a radically changed role for educators in the future and describe the necessary components of faculty development needed to keep pace with the rapidly advancing ICT environment.

The foreword, written by Marina Leight, focuses the reader's attention on the intended effects of educational programs: their use in developing the skills of learners that result in improvements in the human condition.

This book is intended to provide a way forward for current and future educators. It is impossible to predict what the future of ICT will be–much like it would have been impossible to predict web 2.0 and user-generated content a mere twenty-years ago–but the chapters in this book all present a mode of thinking about the interaction of technology and learning and teaching that is optimistic, empowering and equitable. It is my hope that educators will find this book a valuable resource to guide their own development as teachers and learners.

Acknowledgment

An edited volume is a collaborative effort. I wish to thank the authors who contributed chapters, the members of the Editorial Advisory Board who reviewed and selected submissions, and Monica Palaia, my editorial assistant, who undertook the daunting task of organizing all of the submissions and the attendant paperwork.

Special thanks to Jenny Artnzen for helping get this project off the ground and to Christine Bufton for seeing it through to completion.

Thanks also to Barbara Porco who offered invaluable encouragement during the entire process and to Ron Jacobson for his support and understanding.

Finally, a special thank you to Daniel and Thomas D'Agustino, constant sources of joy, for their inspiration to embark upon and complete this project.

Steven D'Agustino
Fordham University, USA

Section 1
Access

Chapter 1
The Digital Information Divide

Randall McClure
Georgia Southern University, USA

ABSTRACT

This chapter explores the gap in information between digital natives and digital immigrants. Advances in computer technology have transformed information, and resulting changes in information behavior clearly mark the digital information divide. These changes in information behavior have affected information literacy instruction, yet educators have opted for quick fix strategies, ignoring the need to develop a comprehensive information literacy curriculum for the digital age. Partnerships—between primary, secondary, and postsecondary teachers and librarians and curriculum designers working to establish a vertically and horizontally scaffolded K-16 information literacy curriculum—may effectively bridge the divide.

INTRODUCTION

Educational environments have been witness to the widening gap between digital immigrant teachers and digital native students, though many working in higher education in particular are still not quite ready to acknowledge it. This gap is much more than a gap in technological literacy or competency; it is a gap in information that has continued to widen due to the strong resistance in most educational environments to information beyond that found in the library. While digital natives with their increasing reliance and comfort with computer technology are filling classrooms to capacity, the digital immigrant teachers they encounter remain, for the most part, slow and hesitant to join their students in the digital age. These teachers are, as the editor of this collection suggests in his introduction, trapped in a past in which the only way to access information is either to hear it in a lecture or find it on a shelf in the library. These teachers are likely aware that computer technology has radically reshaped the authoring, amount, and access points for in-

DOI: 10.4018/978-1-61692-854-4.ch001

formation, yet many of them, particularly those at the postsecondary level, remain hostile to any information taken from non-traditional sources, especially those on the Web. The information environment of the university—and to a lesser extent the elementary as well as the junior and senior high school—is essentially a traditional one, thus fueling the digital information divide.

In the process of coining the terms in his 2001 article from *On the Horizon*, Prensky divides "digital native" students from "digital immigrant" teachers. In defining students as digital natives, Prensky claims, "Today's students—K through college—represent the first generations to grow up with this new technology. They have spent their entire lives surrounded by and using computers…and all the other toys and tools of the digital age" (p. 1). Students are digital natives and digital consumers, and they are being consumed by the technologies that surround them. In fact, it has been suggested that students could spend up to 10,000 hours on the Web by the time they graduate from college (Bylin, 2009, para. 13). Unlike their digital native students, most teachers are immigrants to digital technologies, adapting to and working with them as needed but valuing and remembering a past that is radically different, according to Prensky. These disparate takes on technology create the digital divide, a separation based on such deep-seated change that Prensky leaves his readers with the provocative claim that "today's students think and process information fundamentally differently" (p. 1).

Prensky uses a linguistic approach in his essay to mark these two groups—claiming they in essence speak different languages—and he maintains that this linguistic divide separates teachers from their students, making it difficult to understand, communicate with, and most importantly teach them. Prensky summarizes this view when he writes, "Today's students are no longer the people our educational system was designed to teach" (p. 1). Prensky goes on to provide several examples of the digital divide, such as networked learning, multitasking behaviors, visual versus print literacy, and "legacy" versus "future" content. Prensky uses these examples to make his argument for new teaching "methodologies for all subjects, at all levels, using our students to guide us" (p. 6).

It should be noted that Prensky's work is certainly not without its critics. Interestingly, most critics focus on the terms of his title, "Digital Natives, Digital Immigrants," his linguistic approach, and the divisive nature of his claims (Flintoff, 2007; Fryer, 2006; Jenkins, 2007; Kennedy and Krause, 2008), thus avoiding the more complicated turn toward the flaws in our educational system, to the possibility that the ways we teach students today do not help them learn[1]. Flaws, I will argue, created by profound changes in information. In this chapter, I detail these changes in information behavior as I comment on the flaws in the current educational system as they relate to the concept that binds as much as it separates teachers and students: information.

Before I begin, however, I must acknowledge the problems with the native/immigrant binary at the center of Prensky's influential work. Certainly, there are some students not interested in computer technologies, just as there are teachers who are not only heavy users but also early adopters of them. It might even be possible to refute the claim that students and teachers process information differently. In other words, teachers and students might not be as different as Prensky makes them out to be. Even if one is at odds with the terms "native" and "immigrant" or other aspects of Prensky's classifications, there seems little room for debate on his idea that students' familiarity, comfort, and proficiency with the "toys and tools of the digital age" are influencing in significant ways students' learning behaviors in the early twenty-first century. There might not be as clear a divide in the computer skills and thought processes of teachers and students as Prensky suggests, but there is in my opinion a divide that is fundamentally reshaping education in the digital age. I call this the digital information divide.

This chapter, therefore, moves in a direction different from those focused on the digital divide. Instead of locating my argument in the area of the toys and tools of digital learning (even though these technologies certainly play a part), I contend that the digital divide is at its core one of information. This chapter shifts the discussion away from those focused on advancements in technology, changes in cognitive processes, or differences in "language" to one centered on the fault line of the digital divide: information. In this chapter, I discuss the information divide that exists between students and teachers in the digital age.

The digital information divide is evident in three ways: the availability of information, information behavior, and approaches to teaching students about information. I begin by detailing the radical changes in information availability in the digital age, looking at everything from the growth in the number of types of websites and online databases, to the development of Web 2.0 applications, to the creation of online journals and presses. I next explain what and why teachers, particularly college and university faculty, must understand about information availability and the information behaviors of today's students, paying particular attention to the behaviors of Google Generation students (those born after 1993) who will soon move with great numbers into postsecondary institutions. I then discuss the problems in current information literacy instruction as I also argue that more research on information behavior and information literacy instruction is needed across the K-16 landscape. I conclude this chapter by suggesting that K-12 teachers are best situated to prepare students to manage this divide, though I concede that only through partnerships among primary, secondary and postsecondary educators can we build a meaningful and cohesive information literacy curriculum for students of the digital age.

BACKGROUND

Citing Frand (2000) and of all things the Wikipedia discussion on the term, researchers from University College London (UCL) define the Google Generation as one in which "constant connectivity is of utmost importance" and "whose first port of call for knowledge is the internet and a search engine, Google being the most popular" (2008, p. 7). While it is common practice in higher education to consider the technological skills and needs of our current group of "millennial" or "Generation Y" students, a generation of students who does not know a world without computers, we have yet to tackle the more difficult challenge of considering how, for example, the search engine and its corresponding access to information has changed not only what we should teach, but also who we are teaching. Badke (2008) writes of the challenges facing higher education in teaching today's students:

We have a whole generation growing up in the cradle of an information world gone wild, where much of the material for research papers comes via Google and hardly anyone even knows for sure what a journal is. We've let this generation find its own way through the information fog, neglecting to teach them even the basics about the nature of the knowledge sources available to them, let alone how to navigate the data that swarms through their lives. (p. 48)

In the above passage, Badke is clearly critical of both the research practices of students and the educational system that he believes must have failed them. This criticism is compounded by the recent suggestion that the information behaviors of students entering postsecondary institutions are largely in place by the time they arrive on campus (UCL, 2008, p. 32). While reading, writing, and researching constitute a significant part of the primary and secondary school curricula in the UK and US, with research a particular emphasis in the high school years, information literacy—or helping students successfully navigate the information fog, using Badke's term above—is still often viewed as solely a postsecondary activity, a skill to be developed and mastered in college.

In fact, colleges and universities across the United States, from California State University Channel Islands to Florida Gulf Coast University, regularly write information literacy skills into their student learning outcomes and general education curricula. Some schools, such as Minneapolis Community and Technical College, even have literacy instruction courses as part of their core curriculum and graduation requirements. Badke (2008), in arguing that the "rarity of for-credit information literacy instruction in higher education is a disgrace," contends that the existing methods for teaching students about research are failing students as the "*information age is too complex and too important to all of us for half measures*" (pp. 47-49). The "half-measured" approach, according to Badke, indicts not only the information literacy curricula at the college level, but also the training students receive prior to entering college.

This view that information literacy is a college-level skill and need could stem from the perceived treatment of research and information literacy skills in the K-12 curriculum. Swanson (2004) presents his version of this assumption when he writes:

Ideally, the students who enter our college classrooms will have experience managing information. Ideally, the students' previous teachers will have...given all students a strong foundation upon which college instructors can build. As most of us know, this is not the case. The reality is that for a variety of reasons most of our students have had little or no experience with research. (emphasis added; p. 263)

Swanson does not suggest what the reasons are that prevent K-12 teachers from building their students' research foundation, opting instead for expected agreement from his readers. If one scans the current literature, this agreement is easy to come by. Gilman (2009), for example, echoes Swanson when he writes, "Students do not come to college armed with [research] skills, nor are they likely to be acquired without guidance" (para. 6), a type of assistance that Gilman later implies is best provided at the college level. Gilman fails to consider that students entering college today might have research skills and information behaviors that work for them, though they may be significantly different than traditionally accepted ones. As such, these skills are therefore in some instances not recognizable or recognized, in others they are vehemently refused. In other words, I believe that most postsecondary educators rebuff the digital information difference.

Gilman, an academic librarian at Yale University, further blames—as many in and out of education seem to do—students' inadequate research and information skills on advances in computer technology: "While college students may be computer-literate, they are not, as a rule, research-literate. And there's a huge difference between the two" (para. 4). In other words, digital natives might be digital literate in a technical sense, but they are not digital information literate. An example of the clear and outright refusal of the digital information difference.

Bauerlein (2008) takes this idea even further claiming that students' technical competency and social literacy with computers hinder their (traditional) intellectual development to the point of stupefication, making our students the "dumbest generation" and jeopardizing our intellectual future to the point that "[t]hey may even be recalled as the generation that lost that great American heritage, forever" (p. 236). In Bauerlein and indeed much of the recent literature of the negative influence of computer technology on students' academic skills and intellectual development, particularly in works focused on college students, rarely is justification provided for such harsh, negative views. A consistent lack of justification suggests the common acceptance of such claims and maintains both a limited definition of information literacy and the separation that exists between postsecondary and pre-college educational environments. It is true that flushing out the treatment of research skills at the K-12 level would be helpful (though it would certainly take another chapter altogether); still, it seems likely that these skills are given more treatment in the K-12 curriculum than most postsecondary educators think.

Much like many college writing teachers believe that students write before they come to college but only learn that writing is a process once they complete college writing courses, it is likely that many college-level teachers and curriculum designers believe that students know very little about conducting research and using information before coming to college and that it is up to those at the college level to teach students to be information literate and research savvy. Both situations, I contend, are not the case.

Just as my first grader asked for my help on his "writing process rainbow" homework, K-12 students are certainly learning research and information literacy skills. In fact, a quick search on the Web reveals a whole host of research and information literacy activities designed for pre-college students, with many aimed at students at the primary school level. For example, the website ReadWriteThink.org—a site sponsored through a partnership of the International Reading Association (IRA), the National Council of Teachers of English (NCTE), and Thinkfinity.org—contains lessons plans such as "Research Building Blocks: Examining Electronic Sources" and "Inquiry on the Internet: Evaluating Web Pages for a Class Collection." In the former, Fink (2009) presents a lesson designed for third through fifth graders to help them "examine and rate the relevance of electronic sources, not only learning another part of the research process but also experiencing it firsthand" (para. 1). In the latter, Gardner (2009) presents a lesson for sixth through eighth graders that asks students to "use Internet search engines and Web analysis checklists and questions to find and evaluate online resources then write annotations that explain how and why the items they have found will be valuable" (para. 1). Both activities rely on active learning strategies and contain reflective components, and as such seem in line not only with best practices in information literacy instruction, but also with the "21st Century Skills" educational reform movement in the US.

Further, both activities are aligned with the NCTE/IRA *Standards for the English Language Arts* (1996), a document designed for pre-college teachers that is similar to the Association of College and Research Libraries (ACRL) *Information Literacy Competency Standards for Higher Education* (2000), widely accepted as the most significant document for information literacy instruction at the postsecondary level. What seems to be missing in the current literature, however, are recent conversations between the disciplines of Library Science and English Studies, and more importantly across all disciplines and educational environments that address the need for a comprehensive K-16 information literacy curriculum designed for students of the digital age. Some literature is available on local partnerships between English departments and their campus libraries, but there is an absence of literature that moves from the inside of these few partnerships out, that considers information literacy instruction on the comprehensive scale I call for in this essay[2].

More research certainly needs to be conducted on the specific ways information literacy instruction common to the postsecondary level is evidenced in primary and secondary education curricula, yet the assumption here is that, much like "writing as a process" pedagogy has influenced writing instruction even at the earliest years of education, methods of teaching research common in postsecondary circles are found in K-12 instruction on information literacy. In fact, K-12 students might even have deeply-rooted research habits and information behaviors by the time they enter postsecondary institutions that are informed to some degree by these methods. Unlike what Swanson, Gilman, Bauerlein and other critics think, students may be as information literate as they are computer literate; however, their information literacy skills are so different due to living in a digital age that postsecondary teachers and librarians fail to recognize or refuse to acknowledge them.

Here is just one feature of the information divide: the belief versus the reality of information behavior, or perhaps better stated the great misconception of information literacy. It is believed that students acquire and hone their information literacy skills in college (since they have failed to do so in elementary and high school); the reality is they have already done so.

INFORMATION LITERACY AND THE REDEFINITION OF INFORMATION

For the purpose of this essay, information literacy is defined as the skill sets students need to successfully form a research question, search for information, evaluate information, and use information critically. This definition provided by the ACRL has become the industry standard for higher education, as evidenced in recent scholarship (Brady et al. 2009; McClure and Clink 2009; Swanson 2004).

Despite an easy definition, information literacy has been made difficult by the rapid growth of information in the digital age. Even just the movement from TV to cable TV to now digital TV, web TV and TiVo has certainly brought more information to people than at any other time in history. Other digital technologies, ones as commonplace as the cell phone and text messaging, have made more information available to more people. Further, the expansion of the Web and the development of Web 2.0 technologies have helped to redefine information.

The development of the Web has certainly changed the traditional notion of information, particularly in the academy. Take, for instance, the rapid growth in the number of online journal databases. We have been witness to the near doubling of online databases over the last decade with now more than 18,000 available (Foster, 2007, para. 3). The national average for expenditures for electronic materials increased by 119% during the period from 2000-2003, with the average research library now spending between 30-50% of its materials budget on e-materials (Mischo, Norman, Shelburne, & Schlembach, 2006, p. 30). For example, one regional state university in the upper Midwest reports expenditures for electronic journals grew from $170,496 in 2000 to $488,609 in 2005, a figure consistent with the 2008 national average of $456,238 (Library Services, 2005, p. 19; Primary Research Group, 2009, p. 47). The increased expenditures are reflected in the use of full-text PDF articles, as Mischo, Norman, Shelburne, & Schlembach (2006) report that PDF downloads at a University of North Carolina regional campus increased 1007% after the school entered the statewide e-library consortium (p. 31). The growth in the number of online databases reflects the exponential growth in the number of sites now on the Web, with Foster (2007) reporting the growth in the number of sites on the Web from 18,000 in 1995 to more than 100,000,000 in 2007 (para. 3). Crum (2008) suggests that the number of sites on the Web was just under 200,000,000 in October 2008, growing at the pace of nearly one million per month (para. 1). Regardless of the true number (and some reports have the number of sites in the billions), the amount of information available today is unprecedented.

It is true that the ease of using the Web to create, disseminate, and store information has also had negative effects on traditional print venues and sources. Over the past decade, there has been a significant drop-off in newspaper readership, a steady decline in library acquisitions of print materials, and a decrease in the number of presses for both commercial and academic works. There also exists an adversarial relationship between educators and digital materials, especially among college professors and librarians, as noted in the introduction to this chapter. The resistance at the postsecondary level to adopting a more open stance toward digital materials exists for a variety of reasons, particularly the continuing emphasis on peer-reviewed publications in tenure and promotion decisions as well as the value of print over electronic publications in teaching, research, and publication. This attitude certainly contributes to the digital information divide, as most students do not share this value for traditional print materials.

In some ways, however, the features of the Web and computer technology in general for the development and retrieval of information have brought these same traditional sources to more people than ever before. Consider the digitization and subsequent enhanced cataloging of print archives; including historical documents, newspapers, books, and other print materials. In decades past, this information was often difficult or even impossible for many to come by. It is possible that some value is lost by viewing electronic versions of print materials and in viewing them in cyberspace as opposed to surroundings for which they were originally intended. Still, these materials are now reaching much larger audiences, creating opportunities for learning not often available prior to the digital age.

In other ways, traditional materials have moved online and been the impetus for the creation of new information. These materials first came to the Web as static pages but have since grown into searchable PDFs, evolved as multimedia texts, and been extended and reformulated in Web 2.0 environments such as wikis, blogs, and multimedia or multigenre compositions. Further, traditional materials have begotten online materials. For example, in my field of study, Rhetoric and Composition, successful print journals such as *Computers and Composition* and *College Composition and Communication* now have online counterparts that publish a set of entirely different works, thus extending the journals to more scholars and larger audiences. Online journals, such as *Kairos* and *Writing Spaces*, create other outlets for research and scholarship to reach audiences beyond those limited by print journal subscriptions. Other technologies—listservs, RSS feeds, social networks—contribute to the now global information economy, thus expanding the definition of information in so many ways that is seems nearly impossible to fully capture. For as quickly as these technologies evolve and reach even newer audiences, the definition of information evolves as well.

All of the positives and negatives aside, there remains one constant relative to information in the digital age: the growth in information and the expanding definition of information has brought issues of students' information literacy into focus. This redefinition of information is perhaps the single greatest contributor to the digital information divide. Head and Eisenberg (2009) summarize the focus on the issues surrounding the expanding definition of information when they write that "no matter what information resources [students] may have at their disposal, and no matter how much time they have, the abundance of information technology and the proliferation of digital information resources make conducting research uniquely paradoxical: Research seems to be far more difficult to conduct in the digital age" (p. 2). In some respects, it can be argued that information literacy has always been difficult for students; however, the information landscape of the digital age has changed information behavior in such distinct ways that only significant changes in curriculum and pedagogy will help today's students become (digital) information literate.

INFORMATION BEHAVIOR

A 2008 study published by University College London, *Information Behaviour of the Researcher of the Future*, evaluates how students of the Google Generation use digital resources. This research identifies several negative search behaviors of young people: lack of understanding of their information needs; preference for basic search engines like Google rather than article databases; use of natural language terms instead of subject terms or key words; quick scanning and skimming of information sites; little or no evaluation of the quality of the information used; and cutting and pasting information into their papers without providing the correct citations (pp. 12-31). The UCL researchers also suggest that most skill development in researching for information occurs in the early teen years. By the time students attend college, argues the UCL researchers, their aptitude for acquiring new skills in information searching may be compromised: "These students have already developed an ingrained coping behaviour: they have learned to 'get by' with Google" (p. 23).

The findings in the UK study are supported by an international study conducted by the Online Computer Library Center (OCLC) from 2005 in which college-age (18-24) students are surveyed on their perceptions of library resources. According to the OCLC report, only 56% of respondents report having ever visited a library web site, 24% have used an online library database and only 17% have used an online book from a digital library catalog (p. 13). In comparison, 78% of college-age respondents and 81% of respondents in the younger group (age 14-17) use a search engine regularly, and a search engine is the preferred information tool for 89% of Google Generation respondents in the UCL study (OCLC, 2005, p. 13; UCL, 2008, p. 7). Findings from other studies, such as those from Project Information Literacy at the University of Washington, suggest that Wikipedia may be replacing search engines like Google as the primary starting point for student research, especially in academic research (Head and Eisenberg, 2009, p. 11). Findings such as these suggest sweeping changes in information behavior.

From the viewpoint of the UCL and OCLC researchers, the information behaviors of young people are largely negative ones. Shifting the lens to students, though, reveals a similar picture best described as an image of frustration. Head and Eisenberg (2009) report from their discussions with groups of college students from seven different US campuses that students believe the challenges of conducting research for both school assignments and personal uses are piqued by digital information. Students in the study acknowledge that the information they need likely exists online, but they are routinely frustrated due to the amount and variety of information on the Web (2009, p. 4). "[Students] also reported having particular difficulty traversing a vast and ever-changing information landscape," note Head and Eisenberg (p. 13). Bauerlein takes this idea a step further, as he believes students' frustration has caused them disconnect from their education. Of this, Bauerlein writes, "With so much intellectual matter circulating in the media and on the Internet, teachers, writers, journalists and other "knowledge workers" don't realize how thoroughly young adults and teens tune it out" (2008, p. 33).

The frustrations and negative behaviors discussed above lend a powerful critique of research in the digital age. Further, there is a clear alignment in much of the recent literature on negative cyber behavior with students as digital natives that subsequently divides them from digital immigrants. Further, the behaviors and frustrations support the belief that students research online, but their research is incorrect, flawed, inadequate. In other words, digital natives are assumed to be information illiterate.

However, students including young people of the Google Generation have also demonstrated several strengths as researchers. According to the UCL study, these strengths include a solid grasp of intellectual property basics, an awareness that the web does not provide for all their information needs, a value for information from authority figures such as teachers and textbooks,

Table 1. Information behaviors of digital natives and immigrants

Digital Natives	Digital Immigrants
Cut-and-paste	Retype from original text
Use information from first available source	Search for information from original source
Search from anywhere, anytime using portable technologies	Search in the library using fixed sources (reference desks, computer workstations, bookshelves)
Begin search in Google or Wikipedia	Begin search in the library (physical or virtual)
View research as another multitasking activity	View research as a focused activity
View information as free	View information as owned
Power browse (finding information quickly)	Scroll-and-mine (taking time to research)
Search using trial-and-error	Search using an organized plan
Conduct basic searches using mainly common words, phrases and questions	Use key words and advanced limiting features to conduct searches
Trust/accept information	Question information
Equate personal opinion (particularly from their peers) with value	Equate personal opinion with bias
Simple/flat definition of information	Complex/layered definition of information
Treat print, audio, video & multimedia texts equally	Preference print texts
Use networks to access information and make meaning before working independently	Work independently before networking or collaborating

and a willingness to spend time on research despite the tendency for instant gratification (pp. 18-20). Another feature of the information divide is the perceived weak information skills of digital native students situated against the assumed information savvy of digital immigrant teachers and curriculum designers. The belief and reality may be in conflict here as well. This and other research suggests the information skills of students are not weak; they may just be different, an idea I will take up later in this chapter.

A graphic might help to illustrate the information behaviors of digital natives and how they differ from digital immigrants. The Table 1 extends the work of Jukes and McCain (2008) and incorporates ideas from Frand (2000), the UCL study as well as from the work of this researcher:

Swanson (2004) argues that "[w]e need to recognize that our students enter our [college] classrooms with their own experiences as users of information" (p. 265). If we concede that our students are, for the most part, digital natives, then the above table attempts to illustrate this very point. However, I argue that we must recognize how *different* these experiences and the behaviors they create and influence are if we hope to bridge the digital information divide. While digital native students and digital immigrant teachers might not be as different in their computer skills and thought processes as Prensky argues, I believe that they are significantly different in how they locate, perceive, and use information.

As I have suggested, the information behaviors of digital natives are perceived as good in some ways and perceived as bad in most others. Whether viewed positively or negatively, they are if nothing else different. Take, for example, digital natives' common use of Wikipedia and Google as the starting point in their research process. Small and Vorgan (2008) illustrate the Google difference in their neurological study of digital natives and immigrants as they use this popular search engine. Digital natives and immigrants, whom Small and Vorgan label "computer-savvy" and "computer-naïve" respectively, were asked to search the Web using Google for an hour each day for five days.

After examining MRI scans of the two groups taken immediately following their search sessions, or as the researchers call it "studying the brain on Google," Small and Vorgan conclude that "the two groups showed distinctly different patterns of neural activation when searching on Google" (p. 16). Interestingly, however, the researchers also find that these differences take very little time to resolve themselves. After only five one-hour Google search sessions, the researchers note, "Digital Immigrants can train their brains relatively quickly…After just five days of practice [with Google], the exact same neural circuitry… became active in the Internet-naïve subjects. Five hours on the Internet, and the naïve subjects had already rewired their brains" (p. 16).

Small and Vorgan dedicate an entire chapter to their study of the "brain gap" in the neural networks between digital natives and digital immigrants as well as the resulting challenges in bridging this gap. The researchers conclude that the gap is caused by differences in interpersonal and technological skills and that both groups need to learn how to work more effectively with each other online and off (p. 46). More importantly, though, the researchers suggest through their work on technologies such as Google that the brain gap can be bridged, just as I believe the information divide can be. In fact, the information behaviors ascribed to digital natives are already influencing the research practices of those on the other side of the divide.

With this thought in mind, let me pause to provide an example of why recognizing these behaviors and their differences is critical to both sides of the digital information divide. Pogatchnik (2009) through his discussion of the "Wikipedia hoax" provides an indication of how the changes in information behavior are not simply behaviors of perceived information illiterate digital natives. Pogatchnik tells the story of University College Dublin student Shane Fitzgerald who "posted a poetic but phony quote on Wikipedia" supposedly by French composer Maurice Jarre in order to test how the "Internet-dependent media was upholding accuracy and accountability" (para. 1). Fitzgerald posted his fake quote on Wikipedia within hours of the composer's death, and later found that several newspaper outlets had picked up and published the quote, even though the administrators of Wikipedia recognized and removed the bogus post. The administrators removed it quickly, "but not quickly enough to keep some journalists from cutting and pasting it first" (para. 4).

It can safely be assumed that these journalists, likely digital immigrants, exhibited nearly all of the behaviors of digital natives, research methods often associated with information illiteracy: starting their search in Wikipedia; power browsing; cutting-and-pasting; viewing information as free, accurate, and trustworthy; treating online information as equal to print information; and so on. Of course, it is impossible to prove the journalists used these behaviors without direct observation of their research processes, but it seems especially likely. This example suggests the divide has been jumped, but not bridged. Hopefully, future research will show that these information behaviors cut across the digital divide in positive ways as well.

TEACHING STUDENTS ABOUT INFORMATION

As the "Wikipedia hoax" example illustrates, information shapes behavior, and behavior shapes the use of information. Unlike the journalists certainly shooting for quick wins, the teachers who are digital immigrants that I have encountered provide instruction on research and information literacy skills in the same ways they learned to value and use these skills as students. Since traditional notions of information have molded teachers' information behaviors, the instruction they provide tends to perpetuate such beliefs. For students who are digital natives, this instruction conflicts with their information behaviors, thus creating a school-specific type of information literacy that students seem to find increasingly unhelpful and unnecessary. The cyber behaviors of today's students—whether we label them as digital natives, millennials, Generation Ys, Generation Zs, Generation DotComs, members of the Google Generation, the Dumbest Generation, or something else—related to information seeking and use have changed and changed in significant ways. However, most of their teachers, librarians, and curriculum designers remain in a world with a closed, traditional definition of information, a definition that no longer suits students and their educational needs.

I believe significant curricular reform will not occur until we acknowledge that digital native students can and do conduct effective research using traditional methods and materials. Further, we must also acknowledge these students have developed new and different information behaviors that now separate them from their digital immigrant teachers. Without such acknowledgement as part of a larger concerted effort to bridge the digital information divide, the traditional information literacy skills students acquire in school will remain in frustrating conflict with the "self-taught, creative workarounds" (Head and Eisenberg, 2009, p. 1) that students have mastered on the Web. At the same time, the information gap continues to widen as the Web continues to evolve.

The resistant and occasionally hostile attitude toward Web-based information continues to play out in many ways inside the postsecondary classroom, including in the types of texts students read and write, the emphasis on the student as an individual, isolated learner, and in the ways teachers expect students to both conduct searches for information and use or rely on certain information. Frand writes of the postsecondary classroom, "Until the nature of the educational relationships change in the classroom and at the institutional level, we will not realize the full value of the computer, communication, and information technology investments we are making" (2000, p. 24). Given the persistent negative attitudes toward digital information in higher education, I contend that K-12 teachers are more open to a digital native-type of information literacy instruction. Through their commitment to continuing education, curriculum development, and assessment along with their attention to fostering skill-based competencies in students much like what was evidenced in the ReadWriteThink lesson plans presented earlier in this chapter, K-12 teachers appear to be more in touch with the information habits and needs of today's students than their postsecondary colleagues. There are many reasons for this, including the amount of contact K-12 teachers have with their students, their regular use of scaffolded curricula and outcomes assessment, and their position in the educational development of student skills like reading, writing, computer literacy and information literacy. However, K-12 teachers are also often limited in what they can do in the classroom, including to what depth they can explore the complex web of information that is commonplace in the lives of today's students.

For this reason, I argue that effective information literacy instruction can occur only if curriculum designers, librarians, and teachers at all educational levels have a clear understanding and appreciation for the digital information divide. Armed with such an understanding, librarians and faculty at the postsecondary level should engage in close collaborations with their counterparts at the primary and secondary level to cross the divide to develop information literacy instruction that acknowledges the information behaviors of today's students and prepares students and their teachers for information literacy in the digital age. Faculty across the university campus should engage in this work since research skills are important to all disciplines and professions, though it seems that faculty involved in teacher certification are best situated to initiate and sustain these partnerships. Given that the US government is "pressing states to get public school and higher education authorities working together" (Dillon, 2009, para. 5), these partnerships seem well timed.

It should be mentioned here that this is one more feature of the information divide: the gap in instruction, a gap evident in the lack of instructional partnerships between K-12 and university faculty. It is true that some partnerships between secondary and postsecondary educators exist, such as those involved in teacher certification, dual enrollment, and programs like the National Writing Project. However, partnerships between schools at different levels, ones even with close connections—such as two- and four-year colleges as well as secondary and postsecondary schools in the same community or region—remain the exception instead of the rule. What partnerships exist are often limited to content areas such as English or Environmental Science; rarely do skills areas like reading or information literacy invite participation across educational environments. It should be mentioned that partnerships between librarians and teachers exist at the postsecondary level and are growing in numbers, albeit slowly, yet these partnerships typically do not reach out to other educational environments, namely K-12 schools. Gilman (2009) and Brady (2009) discuss postsecondary partnerships at their respective universities, for example, yet neither mentions any connections with primary or secondary schools.

If we agree that students today must make "rational decisions in the overloaded information ecology" (Hjorland, 2008, p. 4) and we agree that K-12 teachers can only do so much, it seems necessary that K-12 teachers and librarians and their postsecondary counterparts work together to develop a cohesive information literacy curriculum for the digital age. The UCL researchers suggest that librarians and teachers, at both the high school and college level, could strengthen students information literacy skills if library resources were marketed toward young people and if educators identified student strengths and weaknesses in instructional design when teaching information literacy (p. 31). These ideas taken together suggest that the only way to bridge the information divide between digital natives and immigrants is through the formulation of an entirely new literacy program based on a fresh perspective of information, in every sense of the word, that affects curriculum and pedagogy at every educational level.

FUTURE DIRECTIONS

Future research on information literacy in the digital age must attempt to provide this perspective and map out this program vertically and horizontally across the K-16, curriculum if we are to bridge the digital information divide. Often working with colleagues in Library and Information Science, I have suggested some beginning and basic strategies in some of my other works that might help to jumpstart K-16 partnerships (McClure, 2009; McClure, 2007; McClure and Baures, 2007; McClure and Clink, 2009). However, more research and more collaboration across educational environments are needed before a comprehensive information literacy curriculum for the digital age can be built.

Despite the current breadth and depth of the digital information divide, I remain confident that a comprehensive information literacy curriculum will be built in the near future. In fact, two important research projects are underway in the United States that should help us better understand and solve the digital information divide.

First is the Citation Project, a multi-institution research project led by Sandra Jamieson (Drew University) and Rebecca Moore Howard (Syracuse University). Employing methods of citation analysis developed in information studies and applied linguistics, the project seeks to compile an aggregate description of how college students use the research sources that they cite. Studying papers gathered from a variety of colleges, researchers read the papers and their sources as they pursue answers to a variety of questions, such as what types of sources students choose; how readily those sources can be retrieved by readers; the extent to which students' papers reveal an engagement with the sources being cited; the frequency with which students use quotation, paraphrase, patchwriting, and summary; whether students' choice of quotation, paraphrase, patchwriting, and summary correlates with the difficulty level or genre of the source they are citing; and whether any of these four strategies tend to be used primarily in the early or later part of the student's paper, suggesting that they are strategies to which students resort as they become fatigued or pressed for time.

According to Howard (2009), the purpose of the Citation Project research is to develop educators' understanding of the underlying issues in students' source-based writing so that more effective pedagogy can be developed. The Citation Project researchers question the popular approaches to addressing students' source-based writing, such as instruction in citation systems; installation of honor codes; and/or adoption of plagiarism-detecting software. Therefore, Howard and Jamieson have designed the Citation Project to explore the hypothesis that students' instructional needs are far too complex to be answered by these three responses; that instead students need contextualized instruction in critical reading, building arguments from syntheses of sources, and the rhetorical uses of citation.

Second is Project Information Literacy, led by Alison Head and Michael Eisenberg from the University of Washington. According to the project website (http://www.projectinfolit.org/about/), this is a large-scale study about the research habits of college students whose goal is to "understand how early adults conceptualize and operationalize research activities for course work and 'everyday use' and especially how they resolve issues of credibility, authority, relevance, and currency in the digital age" (para. 2). The project started in 2008 with Head and Eisenberg convening discussion groups with undergraduates on seven college campuses in the US on the topic of how they conduct research in the digital age. The results of these discussions—referenced earlier in this chapter—have led to the development of a web-based student survey currently being administered to more than 30,000 undergraduates on six college campuses. Head and Eisenberg believe the results from this study should reveal more about the habits and behaviors of students as researchers in the digital age. Taken with other recent work on the subject as well as ongoing research like the Citation Project, the findings from Project Information Literacy should help curriculum designers develop better strategies for bridging the digital information divide.

Both of these important projects, however, fail to examine the research skills and information behaviors of primary and secondary school students. Future research in these educational environments seems necessary to develop a complete picture of the digital information divide, including both its challenges and opportunities. Without this research, we are left with a postsecondary definition of information and a curricular agenda limited by this definition. Therefore, it is suggested that research similar to the Citation Project that closely examines student writing along with surveys of students' attitudes and beliefs about research at the center of Project Information Literacy be replicated at the primary and secondary level, hopefully in partnership with faculty, librarians and curriculum designers at the postsecondary level. This research should rely on a national sample if possible as well as include examinations of the existing curricula and surveys of teachers' attitudes and perceptions about students' research practices and information behaviors in the digital age. Such studies would extend beyond the current generation of students to the next generation, thus providing a more complete picture that should allow educators across environments to more effectively engage in the process of a K-16 curriculum design for information literacy.

CONCLUSION

Until the time that such a literacy curriculum is built, there will remain this belief in higher education that students are nothing more than novice researchers (Swanson, 2004, p. 261). Until teachers and curriculum designers change their views on the nature of information in the digital world, on the differences in information skills, behaviors, and areas of expertise common to students of this generation, the teaching of information literacy skills and, borrowing from Gilman, "research education" on the whole will continue to be seen as a set of problems to fix, as symptoms of faulty K-12 curricular planning and the widening digital information divide. Without a redefinition of information that includes information outside of the traditional knowledge stream, many educators will continue to see computer technology as driving students further away from learning.

Information and learning today are profoundly different concepts than they were only a decade ago, and the likelihood that they continue to evolve in new ways is something for which all educators should plan. I agree with Gilman that "students desperately need [research and information literacy] skills if they hope to function effectively in our information-driven economy" (2009, para. 8). However, I disagree with the view of Gilman and others that the research processes and information behaviors of today's students are bad habits, problems in need of a quick fix. Instead, I argue we must plan, implement, and continue to research new models of information literacy instruction—models based on a new definition of information, aware of significant differences in information behavior, and built on partnerships across educational environments.

Frand suggests information literacy is the most important skill college graduates in the early twenty-first century. He writes, "As our students enter the workforce, the ability to deal with complex and often ambiguous information will be more important than simply knowing a lot of facts or having an accumulation of knowledge" (2000, p. 17). Interestingly, Brand made this suggestion nearly a decade ago, long before the Internet became Web 2.0, and years before Facebook, MySpace, Twitter, YouTube and many other social technologies became fixtures in most of our students' lives.

Similarly in Bauerlein's criticism of the current generation of students, the author writes,

We have entered the Information Age, traveled the Information Superhighway, spawned a Knowledge Economy, undergone the Digital Revolution, converted manual workers to knowledge workers... However overhyped those grand social metaphors, they signify a rising premium on knowledge and communications...And yet, while teens and young adults have absorbed digital tools into their daily lives like no other age group, while they have grown up with more knowledge and information readily at hand...young Americans today are no more learned or skillful than their predecessors, no more knowledgeable. (2008, pp. 8-9)

Both Frand's and Bauerlein's statement, albeit in their own ways, call into question how we organize education, especially higher education, around content areas and disciplines, not skills. With the continuing growth and expanding definition of information, with significant changes in information behavior, and without critical reform of our K-16 educational system in the skill area of information literacy, the digital information divide stands to outmode the system designed to prepare students for life after the twelfth or sixteenth grade. In this way, both statements serve as confirmation of Prensky's early twenty-first century declaration, viewed through the rapidly changing lens of information.

REFERENCES

Association of College and Research Libraries. (2000). *Information literacy competency standards for higher education*. Retrieved June 24, 2009, from http://www.ala.org/ala/mgrps/divs/acrl/standards/informationliteracycompetency.cfm#ildef

Badke, W. (2008, November/December). Ten reasons to teach information literacy for credit. *Online*, 47-49.

Bauerlein, M. (2008). *The dumbest generation: How the digital age stupefies young Americans and jeopardizes our future*. New York: Penguin.

Brady, L., Singh-Corcoran, N., Dadisman, J. A., & Diamond, K. (2009). A collaborative approach to information literacy: First-year composition, writing center, and library partnerships at West Virginia University. *Composition Forum, 19*. Retrieved January 29, 2009, from http://compositionforum.com/issue/19/west-virginia.php

Bylin, K. (2009). Minds for the future: Why digital immersion matters. Hypebot. Retrieved October 21, 2009, from http://www.hypebot.com/hypebot/2009/10/minds-for-the-future-why-digital-immersion-matters.html

Crum, C. (2008). How many sites are on the internet? *Webpronews*. Retrieved June 22, 2009, from http://www.webpronews.com/topnews/2008/11/04/how-many-sites-are-on-the-internet

Dillon, S. (2009, May 28). New push seeks to end need for pre-college remedial classes. *The New York Times*. Retrieved from http://www.nytimes.com/2009/05/28/education/28remedial.html

Fink, L. S. (2009). Research building blocks: Examining electronic sources. *Readwritethink.org*. Retrieved June 24, 2009, from http://www.readwritethink.org/lessons/lesson_view.asp?id=149

Flintoff, K. (2007). Digital natives have limits. *Grip, fix, turn [blog]*. Retrieved June 1, 2009, from http://gripfixturn.com/2007/03/31/more-on-grip-fix-turn/

Foster, A. L. (2007). Information navigation 101. *The Chronicle of Higher Education Online*. Retrieved March 9, 2007, from http://chronicle.com/free/v53/i27/27a03801.htm

Frand, J. (2006). The information mindset: Changes in students and implications for higher education. *EDUCAUSE Review, 35*(5), 15–22.

Fryer, W. (2006). Digital refugees and bridges. *Infinite thinking machine: Ideas to help teachers and students thrive in the 21st century*. Retrieved June 6, 2009, from http://www.infinitethinking.org/2006/10/digital-refugees-and-bridges.html

Gardner, T. (2009). Inquiry on the internet: Evaluating web pages for a class collection. *ReadWriteThink.org*. Retrieved June 24, 2009, from http://www.readwritethink.org/lessons/lesson_view.asp?id=328

Gilman, T. (2009). Not enough time in the library. *The Chronicle of Higher Education*. Retrieved May 18, 2009, from http://chronicle.com

Head, A. J., & Eisenberg, M. B. (2009). Finding context: What today's college students say about conducting research in the digital age. *Project information literacy progress report*. Retrieved June 15, 2009, from http://projectinfolit.org/

Hjorland, B. (2008). Information literacy and digital literacy. *Prisma, 7*, 4–16.

Howard, R.M. (2009). Email to author. June 18, 2009.

Jenkins, H. (2007). Reconsidering digital immigrants. *Confessions of an Aca/Fan: The official weblog of Henry Jenkins*. Retrieved June 15, 2009, from http://www.henryjenkins.org/2007/12/reconsidering_digital_immigran.html

Jukes, I., & McCain, T. (2008). Understanding digital kids: Teaching and learning in the new digital landscape. *The Info Savvy Group*. Retrieved October 31, 2008, from http://web.mac.com/iajukes/thecommittedsardine/Articles.html

Kennedy, G. E., & Krause, K. L. (2008). First year students' experiences with technology: Are they really digital natives? *Australasian Journal of Educational Technology, 24*(1), 108-122. Retrieved June 14, 2009, from http://www.ascilite.org.au/ajet/ajet24/kennedy.html

Library Services, Minnesota State University, Mankato. (2005). *Program review self-study, 1999/2000-2003/2004*. Retrieved January 10, 2006, from www.lib.mnsu.edu/intx/ProgRev.pdf

McClure, R. (2007). Digital soapboxes: Understanding the growing presence of advocacy and commercial sites on the web. 8.3. *The Journal of Literacy and Technology, 8*(3). Retrieved June 22, 2009, from http://www.literacyandtechnology.org/volume8/no3/JLT_v8_3.htm

McClure, R. (2009). (forthcoming). Examining the presence of advocacy and commercial websites in research essays of first-year composition students. *WPA: Writing Program Administration*.

McClure, R., & Baures, L. (2007). Looking in by looking out: The DNA of composition in the information age. *Computers and Composition Online*. Retrieved June 22, 2009, from http://www.bgsu.edu/cconline/McClure_and_Baures/

McClure, R., & Clink, K. (2009). How do you know that? An investigation of student research practices in the digital age. *portal. Libraries and the Academy*, *9*(1), 115–132. doi:10.1353/pla.0.0033

Mischo, W. H., Norman, M. A., Shelburne, W. A., & Schlembach, M. C. (2006). The growth of electronic journals in libraries: Access and management issues and solutions. *Science & Technology Libraries*, *26*(3/4), 29–59.

National Council of Teachers of English. (2008). The NCTE Definition of 21st Century Literacies. Retrieved June 15, 2009, from http://www.ncte.org/positions/statements/21stcentdefinition

National Council of Teachers of English/International Reading Association. (1996). *Standards for the English Language Arts*. Retrieved June 24, 2009, from http://www.ncte.org/standards

Online Computer Library Center. (2006). *College students' perceptions of the libraries and information resources: A report to the OCLC membership*. Retrieved February 24, 2009, from http://www.oclc.org/reports/perceptionscollege.htm

Pogatchnik, S. (2009). Student hoaxes world's media on Wikipedia. *msnbc*. Retrieved May 13, 2009, from http://www.msnbc.msn.com

Prensky, M. (2001). Digital natives, digital immigrants. *Horizon*, *9*(5), 1–6. doi:10.1108/10748120110424816

Primary Research Group. (2009). *The survey of academic libraries, 2008-2009 edition*. Retrieved June 21, 2009, from http://www.primaryresearch.com/content-200902049-Libraries--Information-Science.html

Project Information Literacy. (2009). *About*. Retrieved June 15, 2009, from http://www.projectinfolit.org

Reidel, C. (2009, January). Create, collaborate, communicate: Empowering students with 21st century skills. *THE Journal*. Retrieved June 11, 2009, from http://thejournal.com/articles/2009/01/27/create-collaborate-communicate-empowering-students-with-21st-century-skills.aspx

Small, G., & Vorgan, G. (2008). *iBrain: Surviving the Technological Alteration of the Modern Mind*. New York: HarperCollins.

Swanson, T. (2004). A radical step: Implementing a critical information literacy model. *portal. Libraries and the Academy*, *4*(2), 259–273. doi:10.1353/pla.2004.0038

University College London. (2008). *Information behaviour of the future of the researcher: A ciber briefing paper*. Retrieved January 15, 2009, from http://www.jisc.ac.uk/media/documents/programmes/reppres/gg_final_keynote_11012008.pdf

ADDITIONAL READING

Ayers, J. (2006). Looking to the internet for content. *English Leadership Quarterly, 2*(8).

Badke, W. B. (2008). *Research strategies: Finding your way through the information fog*. New York: iUniverse.

Dodge, C. (2005, June/August). Knowledge for sale: Are America's public libraries on the verge of losing their way? *Utne Reader*. Retrieved May 30, 2009, from http://www.utne.com/2005-07-01/knowledge-for-sale.aspx

Palfrey, J., & Gasser, U. (2008). *Born digital: Understanding the first generation of digital natives*. New York: Basic Books.

Tapscott, D. (2009). *Grown up digital: How the net generation is changing your world*. New York: McGraw-Hill.

KEY TERMS AND DEFINITIONS

Digital Divide: The term refers to the gap between people with access to digital technology and those without. It includes the gap in physical access, resources, and skills needed to participate in the digital age.

Digital Immigrant: Coined by Marc Prensky, the term refers to a person not born into the digital world yet has adopted the use of some digital technologies. A digital immigrant is typically not viewed as having regular access to or all of the resources afforded by digital technologies, and he or she is likely not proficient with them.

Digital Native: Coined by Marc Prensky, the term refers to a person for whom digital technologies existed when they were born. A digital native is assumed to have access to and/or the resources to acquire digital technologies and is fluent and proficient with them.

Information Literacy: There are many definitions for this term. In this chapter, the author relies on the definition provided by the Association of College and Research Libraries that maintains information literacy is the set of skills students need to successfully form a research question, search for information, evaluate information, and use information critically.

21st Century Skills: A framework of skills that students need to meet the challenges of the digital information age. Core content areas are combined with interdisciplinary themes such as global awareness and sustainability along with skill areas such as collaboration, information literacy, and critical thinking.

ENDNOTES

1 Though I have not seen literature from the "21st Century Skills" educational reform movement credit the work of Prensky, many iterations of these skills are certainly in line with his views in "Digital Natives, Digital Immigrants." There are countless works on 21st Century Skills now available. See Reidel

(2009) for a quick overview of these skills and NCTE (2008) for a detailed application of these skills in relation to information literacy instruction.

2 See McClure and Baures (2007) for one attempt at coalescing standards for information literacy across K-16 environments. Though this work includes local standards, perhaps it can serve as a model for future attempts at developing a comprehensive K-16 information literacy curriculum. Such attempts will likely need to incorporate the *NCTE definition of 21st Century Literacies* published in 2008 as well.

Chapter 2
The Adoption and Sustainability of Technology-Enhanced Education in Higher Institutions of Learning in Africa

Chijioke J. Evoh
New York City Department of Education, USA

ABSTRACT

This chapter explores factors that enhance and constrain the adoption and sustainability of Information and Communication Technologies in Universities and higher institutions of learning in South Africa. This study examines pedagogical, socio-economic and epistemological aspects of the paradigm shift in higher education delivery in Africa. Adopting and sustaining ICTs for educational improvement is a multifaceted process. As a dynamic process, all the vital elements of technology adoption need to be present in order to meet the goals of technology-enhanced higher education in Africa. It further argues that policy guidelines and strategic plans are essential for the successful adoption and sustainability of ICTs in higher education (HE) institutions in Africa. The chapter argues that the success of ICT-mediated higher education is not only technical but also political in nature.

INTRODUCTION

For centuries self-defining under the rubric of autonomy and academic freedom, universities are seeing their missions being defined by others and having to respond appropriately to visions set for a variety of purposes including the pressures of the market economy and the speed of the information society. –N Barney Pityana

DOI: 10.4018/978-1-61692-854-4.ch002

This chapter focuses on the process of adopting and sustaining Information and Communication Technology (ICT)[1] for learning in universities and other tertiary institutions in Africa. This study examines the pedagogical, socio-economic and epistemological aspects in the shift of paradigm in higher education delivery in Africa. The integration of ICTs into the teaching and learning process is an innovation often needing radical change in the way in which schools operate (Haddad, 2007). As a choice tool of trade and means of academic communication, adopting and sustaining modern ICTs have become essential part of innovation and transformation process in higher education (HE) institutions across the world. As Barney Pityana (2004) expressed in the opening quotation, universities and other higher education institutions in Africa are in a defining moment. This is a time when they have to contend with rapid and imposing change or be swept away by the wind of change. At the center of this change is the application of ICTs in teaching, learning and research. As a complex and challenging process, such innovation requires time and patience to produce sustained results. Socio-economic and political development in Africa depend on a well-educated society and skilled workforce. However, the HE institutions have the responsibility of bringing these lofty expectations to fruition. As Paul Michael (1999, p.5) argued long ago, micro-information technologies have proved "to be powerful forces in shaping the destiny of higher education." Against this backdrop, this study focuses on ICT in education not as a course and subject of study but as a tool of learning in HE institutions across Africa. The increasing role of ICTs in education and the complex nature of integrating technology in education, underscore a closer look at the factors that enhance the adoption and sustainability of such tools in education. Such factors and guidelines will outline when, how and what ICTs can be integrated into the learning process in universities and colleges in the region.

ICT in education policy is either neglected or given inadequate attention in the debate on the use of innovative technologies to expand access to and improve the quality of higher education in Africa. For this reason, ICTs are still on the periphery higher education development in South Africa (SA). Using the actor-network theoretical frameworks (Latour, 1987 and 2004), this chapter puts forward three arguments. First, it argues that the application of ICTs in higher institutions of learning is not driven by the rising demand for higher education in South Africa: it is rather influenced by other social and economic factors in the local context. Some of these factors run along the old social and economic structures/class of the apartheid era. Second, to realize the full potential of e-learning in higher education and ensure the adoption of technology-enhanced HE in Africa; and to avoid mistakes of the past and ensure the sustainability of several ICT in education projects, African countries need clear policy objectives, guidelines and practices. Third, it is argued that the adoption and sustainability of ICTs in tertiary institutions learning in Africa are socio-technical processes. Hence the success of ICT-mediated learning is not only technical but also socio-political in nature. Fourthly, this study argues that collaborative partnerships, which are essential in educational application in the developing world, do not only implement and engage in the provision of e-learning infrastructure and policy processes; they also serve as change agents needed to bring about the paradigm shift in teaching and learning in higher education in Africa. This study seeks to answer the question: What policy measures are essential for the sustainable implementation of ICTs in higher education in Africa? This study is based on qualitative methodology, with particularly emphasis on policy document review.

ICT IN HIGHER EDUCATION IN AFRICA AS AN ACTOR-NETWORK

This study builds on the premise that ICTs have the potential of improving the quality and relevance of HE education in Africa, in the present knowledge economy, if properly integrated. Thus, effective adoption of ICTs by HE institutions involves the strategic deployment of both human and non-human elements crucial for a meaningful integration of ICTs. These efforts involve forging new relationships and strengthening existing connections between individual groups, governments of education, and other human and non-human entities. This perspective stems from the actor-network theoretical framework, which posits that, "a common conception of social reality could not be forged to support successful policy implementation without strategic alliances and support from an encompassing network of intermediaries" (Latour, 1992). Given the nature of technology-enhanced education, the network of intermediaries in the integration of ICT in HE institutions in Africa are many. In line with the actor-network theory, these networks extend beyond the boundaries of the universities and other institutions of higher learning in the region. However, it is the responsibility of institutions to identify and apply non-human actors, called *actants,* (such as computers, policy tools, etc) in ways that serve the interest of HE in Africa. This process of engaging human and non-human partners is called "*translation*" (Callon, 1991; Latour, 1992). This process will co-opt each of the actors in a collective pursuit of a successful integration of ICTs for the transformation of HE in South Africa. It is on this basis of actor-network analysis that ICT intervention in HE in SA will be focused. For, as Moon (2004) argues, the question is no longer "if" ICTs have great potential for educational transformation but rather, which and how these ICTs can be effectively implemented in education?

ICTs have the capacity to contribute to quality and outcome-based education experience by making readily available educational materials accessible to students via the Internet, CD-ROM and satellite broadcast. ICTs can overcome geographic, social, and infrastructure barriers to reach traditional and non-traditional populations that cannot be normally served by conventional delivery systems (Haddad, 2007). Additionally, they provide feasible, efficient, and quick educational opportunities. Therefore, the falling standard of education coupled with the need to expand the reach of HE in Africa call for a change from the traditional didactic, teachers-as-fountain-of-knowledge model of instruction, to a social constructivist perspective of learning (Haddad and Draxler, 2002).

Increased interest in harnessing the potential of modern technologies in HE in Africa has been stimulated by two major factors, namely: 1) the increasing potential functionality of modern ICTs and the desire to understand how best these technologies can support and improve teaching and learning; and 2) as briefly mentioned above, the nature of problems facing HE in Africa (Tinio, 2003; James, *et al*, 2001). Among these problems are:

- Growing pressure on traditional education and training to provide access to far larger numbers of students, of all ages;
- A crisis of confidence in traditional approaches to education, which have often confused education with the transfer of information; and
- Dwindling funding–in real terms–for education and training purposes in the public sector (James, *et al*, 2001. p.92).

Apart from its socio-economic applications, information and communication technology has three forms of application in educational curriculum, namely; learning about ICT, learning with ICT and learning through ICT (Akudolu, 2007). Learning about ICT refers to ICT concept as a subject of learning in the school curriculum, an example is the mastery of computer software such as Excel of PowerPoint. Such skills and training on computers have become essential for gainful employment. On the other hand, learning with ICT is concerned with the use of ICT as a medium to improve instruction. Pelgrum and Law (2003, p.23) maintain that "learning through ICT refers to the integration of ICT as an essential tool into a course/curriculum, such that the teaching and learning of that course/curriculum is no longer possible without it". These forms of applying ICTs have given rise to what Collins and Halverson (2009) called new media literacy, which is not taught in schools. According to Collins and Halverson, "the new literacy extends the symbolic decoding and manipulation skills and traditional print media by integrating video, images and music, and animation comprehension that give rise to the new kinds of production" (p.13). ICT in education (also called e-learning) policy in many African countries approach educational technologies from a holistic perspective by integrating all of the above aspects of ICT in educational curriculum. Thus, ICT in education is considered a discipline, resource and essential skill, which drive the overall development in South Africa.

HIGHER EDUCATION IN POST-APARTHEID SOUTH AFRICA

Education was the first sector to gain greater attention and favor in post-apartheid reconstruction and restructuring of South African society. The apartheid education system was a reflection of the apartheid society. Thus, education in a democratic South Africa is seen as a central factor in the social reengineering geared towards an inclusive society. The end of the apartheid system and the transfer of leadership exposed the huge gap in the availability of manpower and paucity of graduates in the country. The direct impact of this shortage in manpower is that both the public and private sectors in the country lacked sufficient and indigenous human resources and educated workforce to fill administrative positions. This was more important considering that, first: the system of higher education during the apartheid era was not an agent of social transformation (Reddy, 2004); and second, the form of education that was offered to the majority during the apartheid era (under the Bantu education system) was inferior, tainted and insufficient as it was designed to dominate African minds through cultural artifacts, and perpetuate white domination in South Africa. Similar to colonial education offered in other African states, the apartheid education was not meant to bring genuine development to South Africa. This lack of educated personnel created a fierce urgency to address what Thiven Reddy call the "historical backlogs" of educational demand, by training South Africans in higher institutions of learning in post-1994 period by using all modes and means of educational development and delivery. Human resource outputs from higher education institutions were considered strategic to capacity-building, economic development and political leadership in post-apartheid South.

As in many African countries after independence, higher education in post-apartheid South Africa received the utmost priority. The immediate goal was to restructure and de-racialize higher education system in the country. Efforts to restructure and realign higher education in South Africa with national development goals are backed by some national policy initiatives. For instance, the White Paper 3 on Higher Education (Department of Education [DOE] 1997) and the National Plan for Higher Education (NPHE) (2001) have the common goal of expanding access to higher education and matching education outputs with national development needs. The goals of the White paper 3 are to ensure: justice and equality by redressing past injustices in higher education; responsiveness to the needs of the society by shifting enrollment to science/technology and career-oriented fields and programs in higher institutions; and co-operative governance in the higher education system.

Seen as a definitive policy document on higher education restructuring in post-apartheid South Africa, the White Paper 3 on Higher Education attempts to tackle the past problems of inequality and inefficiency of the past by putting forward initiatives aimed at transforming higher education through the development of a "single coordinated system with new planning, governing and funding arrangements" (DOE, 1997, p.3). The policy established one national unit of higher education within the national department of education thereby ending the apartheid system, which fragmented higher education governance by having units and departments that administered different higher institutions of learning such universities and technikons (polytechnics) along racial lines and class (DOE, 1997). As David Cooper argues, "after what might be termed a few years of policy "implementation vacuum," the NPHE in 2001 confronted much more openly than previous documents the crises facing higher education in South Africa" (2001). The NPHE put forward a nuanced and detailed policy framework that addressed some issues overlooked in the 1997 White paper. The policy addressed issues of access, equity, national research output and relevance of higher education in a changing world of globalization. Other issues addressed by the policy are: high dropout rate among first-year students in higher institutions of learning–a trend, which speaks to the quality of students' preparation in secondary schools; underrepresentation of students from some social groups (female and black students) in science and technology disciplines); funding; and the imperative for institutional mergers and regional cooperation. As Cooper (2001) argues, unlike the 1997 White paper 3 on higher education, the NPHE signifies a "'substantive, procedural, and material policy' approaches, incorporating concrete actions, implementation procedures, and resource allocation mechanisms" aimed at enhancing the productivity of higher education institutions in a globalized economic system.

ICTS, HIGHER EDUCATION DEVELOPMENT AND THE KNOWLEDGE ECONOMY

To a large extent, HE is defined by the demands of the economy and the job market. More than ever before, HE has become a means to a more efficient and competitive economy and workforce, known as the "knowledge economy" (Jenson, et al, 2007). The Association of African Universities (AAU, 2000, p.8) maintains that,

> *The ultimate objective of integrating ICT into higher education in Africa, therefore, should be the transformation of the university into a knowledge and information powerhouse, with the ability, capacity, and necessary skills not only to educate students and to generate new knowledge, but also to systematically access, absorb, adapt, and use such information and knowledge for the advancement of national development.*

Thus, HE institutions are better placed to provide the much needed support for knowledge-driven economic growth and socio-economic development through a variety of activities (Magagula, 2005). These institutions engage in socio-economic development process by educating and training researchers, professionals, technicians, teachers and business leaders. Through research activities, Universities and other HE institution generate new knowledge and technological innovations for social development and nation building. The mobility of educational programs, particularly, distance education in the era of knowledge economy, has been made possible by ICTs. Modern information and communication tools have added value to education reform in general, and also transformed the nature of distance education especially, in HE institutions around the world. The massive application of ICTs by some distance education universities to gain a global reach in modern era has turned such institutions into investment attraction, given that some of them are now quoted on the stock exchange (Herselman & Hay, 2003).

Thus, HE institutions are always expected to train and equip the workforce with the essential knowledge and skills needed for economic growth and development. In today's global economy, the production and application of knowledge is the key economic input. Many institutions of higher learning are increasingly converting teaching and learning to online and virtual environments. As an aspect of the new literacy, today's graduates are expected to communicate with people via the Internet in different contexts such as project designs, negotiations, conferences and other forms of problem solving (Collins and Halverson, 2009). This trend in the global market economy poses new expectations on HE institutions in general about the conduct of research, teaching and learning. As Carnoy (1999 cited in Tjeldvoll, *et al,* 2005) argues, the competitive nature of the globalized economy exerts enormous pressure on HE institutions, because 'knowledge is the most highly valued commodity.' This view is further contextualized by Manuel Castells (1994, Tjeldvoll, et al, 2005. p. 58) who posits that: "If knowledge is the electricity of the new informational-international economy, then the institutions of higher education are the power sources on which the new development process must rely." To maintain a competitive edge, HE institutions in African countries need to possess and produce 'value-added intelligence' or knowledge. This was the thesis put forward by Privateer (1999) when he wrote, "...what is clearly going to keep higher education competitive is a balanced strategy that uses technology to invent intelligence and encourage demonstrations of meta-critical reasoning and effective use of symbolic languages and team-based communication skills in solving a range of problems" (Privateer, 1999). Against this background, the suggestion made by Paul Privateer a decade ago, and views expressed by the World Bank in 2002 remain relevant to HE institutions in South Africa today. The World Bank (2002) contends that tertiary institutions perform the following three functions to foster a democratic and knowledge-driven society:

- Supporting innovation by generating new knowledge, accessing global stores of knowledge, and adapting knowledge to local use
- Contributing to human capital formation by training a qualified and adaptable labor force, including high-level scientists, professionals, technicians, basic and secondary education teachers, and future government, civil service, and business leaders
- Providing the foundation for democracy, nation building, and social cohesion. (World Bank, p. 24).

Through expanded and inclusive education, tertiary institutions are expected to produce high caliber human capital formation in form of researchers, managers, and technicians to meet the demands of the knowledge economy. This reality was succinctly express by the Council of Higher Education, South Africa (2001, p. 10) when it argued thus:

In the globalised world lawyers, biotechnologists, engineers, economic editors, software designers, strategic planners are in demand because they contribute to a high 'value added' to their products, whatever that might be. These highly valued knowledge workers are no longer linked to a regional or a national economy but have become functioning and prosperous parts of a borderless world.

The emergence of a borderless world underscores two imperatives in HE system in post-apartheid South Africa and Africa in general, namely: the urgency to increase access to and improving the quality of HE in Africa; and the need to reduce the unit cost of HE in the region. This challenge is well recognized by Eshiwani (1999, cited in Tjeldvoll et al, 2005. p; 55) who argues that "the main challenge for African universities today is the necessity of rapidly expanding their services from the education of elites to mass education despite limited financial resources." Although many HE institutions in SA have dramatically increased their enrollment, but funding for such institutions have not increased at the same rate. For higher institutions of learning in the country to continue in the task of knowledge creation, fundamental changes in education delivery are needed.

THE STATE OF HIGHER EDUCATION INSTITUTIONS IN SOUTH AFRICA

Higher education institutions in Africa such as Universities, Polytechnics, Technikons, Institutes of Technology and research are part of the education sector. These institutions face serious challenges and institutional uncertainties that threaten their existence in a rapidly changing world. While institution-specific solutions are needed in some cases, the set of challenges facing HE and ICT integration in tertiary institutions of learning in South Africa and the solutions to such problems are similar. Despite efforts to centralize HE governance in the post-apartheid period, suffice it to say that tertiary institutions in South Africa are not monolithic entities. These institutions are extraordinarily diverse and unique, reflecting the culture and history its people. Notwithstanding these differences, HE institutions in the country share multiple challenges in common.

In many instances, both the physical infrastructure and academic quality of these institutions are in decline. Among the major challenges facing HE institutions in South Africa are: inadequate funding from government and the inability of institutions to generate private funding; frequent fluctuations in South African economy; erosion of institutional autonomy and the politicization of HE governance; excessive government intervention in HE institution matters and grossly insufficient salary and poor benefit package for university lecturers (Trevor, 1991; Council of Higher Education, South Africa, 2001). Other pertinent challenges facing teaching and learning in institutions of higher learning in South Africa include, large class sizes and inadequate curriculum designs (Jaffer, Ng'ambi, Czerniewicz, 2007). However, most institutions of higher learning in other Africa countries are faced with similar or worst challenges. These poor and unacceptable conditions have made it difficult to retain experienced academic staff and attract young and bright scholars into academia in Africa. Again, because of the lack of sufficient funding, many physical instrastructures in African universities and HE institutions are in a sordid state of decay. In general, challenges facing HE in South Africa and Africa in general can be summed in three word: funding, access and quality (The World Bank, 2009).

While these institutions lack many basic and essential educational infrastructures such as a standard library facility, sufficient seats and desks in lecture rooms and halls, existing facilities are in dire need of maintenance and refurbishment. Paradoxically, while resources for HE institutions are declining, these institutions have experienced astronomical rise in student enrollment over the years. In effect, what the World Bank called the "Massification of Tertiary Enrollment" and lack of adequate funding erode institutional accountability and quality of tertiary education in African countries. As Sutherland-Addy argued, most HE institutions in Africa are nothing but:

"...a mere shadow of their earlier glory drained of teaching staff, lacking in equipment and teaching materials, housed in degenerated infrastructure, surrounded by an air of demoralization and incipient decay. They are at the same time besieged with a growing demand for high quality service and public accountability"(Sutherland-Addy, 1993, cited in Council of Higher Education, South Africa, 2001, p.2).

The mismatch of resources and students population in African HE institutions of learning can be attributed to two factors: political intrusion and poor administrative and management oversight. The deplorable conditions in HE institutions in Africa have compelled well trained academics in such institutions to migrate to advanced countries in search of better working conditions. According to an estimate by the World Bank, 23 000 academic staff leave HE institutions in Africa to Western Europe and North America each year (Blair and Jordan, 1994, cited in Council of Higher Education, South Africa, 2001). This massive brain drain of skilled academics and researchers from African universities has depleted the workforce in such institutions thereby leaving behind unskilled and under-qualified faculty. Consequently, it is becoming more difficult for tertiary institutions in Africa to fill academic positions thereby making vacancy rates in such institutions to run between 25 percent and 50 percent (The World Bank, 2008). For example, in the academic year 2006-2007, the University of Botswana had 465 vacancies that it could not be filled (ibid).

Instructional design theories offer institutions of learning different methods of using ICTs to facilitate learning. Unfortunately, most tertiary institutions in South Africa and Africa in general do not have any given instructional design. Basque, Dore, & Henri (2000, p. 5) suggest five reasons why institutions should adopt instructional design as an institutional practice; "efficiency, profitability, better management of complexity, improved communication and institutional integration of training activities." Too often, the primary pedagogical method in HE institutions in South Africa and other African countries is based on the "chalk-and-talk" model. The domineering influence of rote learning in HE institutions deprive students opportunity for more practical-oriented constructivist methods such as project-based, problem-solving and case study approaches to learning (Basque, Dore, & Henri, 2000). This anachronistic model of education delivery does not provide students with the essential skills in preparation for the realities of the 21st Century workplace and society, where higher-order skills offer students more quality education (such as planning, problem solving, analysis, synthesis, critical thinking search and selection of information) than the mere memorization of "masses of factual knowledge" (Basque, Dore, & Henri, 2000, p. 4). By leveraging the potential of ICTs together with instructional design practices, lecturers in tertiary institutions can enrich their pedagogical skills by having access to more educational resources and by exposing students to 'real-world' problems through simulation models (Baguma & Ssewanyana, 2008). Collective ICT-enhanced pedagogy will assist in the transformation of HE institutions from a place of teaching to a place of learning, with serving as facilitators and supporters of learning.

The challenges facing HE institutions in Africa underscore the need for major changes in the educational practices of Universities and other higher institutions of learning in the region. A major part of this change is the application of ICTs for improved teaching and learning and for organizational management and efficiency. Many see ICTs as solutions to some problems facing HE institution in Africa such as meeting the challenge of rising enrollment and the increasingly diverse demography of students (Adam, 2003). ICTs also have the potential of improving the quantity and quality of HE, which are rapidly declining in many African countries. Thus, a well managed and sustained application of ICTs in HE in Africa promises to challenge the traditional and less productive "chalk and talk" model of education delivery process and encourage a more constructive and inquiry-oriented approach. The traditional pedagogy of face-to-face, lecturer and listener educational model, which characterize postsecondary education in the region, are too expensive to meet the learning needs of students and African countries in a knowledge economy. Besides, these conventional methods can limit the capacities of tertiary institutions in Africa to deliver HE to non-traditional students and expand enrollment (World Bank, 2009). If well planned and implemented, ICT integration can offer lower cost delivery alternative and also enhance the process of decentralizing the source of knowledge creation in HE institutions in Africa. This type of ICT-enhanced education will replace information-based, rote learning with practices such project works and internships, which will enhance students' learning experience.

ICT INTEGRATION AND TRANSFORMATION OF HIGHER EDUCATION IN SOUTH AFRICA

This study strives to understand and elucidate both institutional and national approaches toward technology-enhanced HE in South Africa, by reviewing some extant literature and national ICT in education policies and practices. The massive restructuring of H.E in post-apartheid South Africa from an elite and racially biased to mass and de-racialized system has triggered the demand among South Africa citizens for higher learning. Obviously, the increased demand cannot be met through traditional system of HE provision, which favors face-to-face mode of education delivery. The integration of technology in education is an area of national priority in South Africa. In 1994, the Government of National Unity (GNU) in South Africa points out that:

Unless the types and levels of knowledge and skills available in our society are vastly extended and redirected, the low skill, low wage, racially stratified labor market will persist. An integrated approach to education and training is essential to enable South Africans to broaden their range of knowledge, skills and competencies, and achieve greater mobility in education and training system. (Ministry of education, Republic of South Africa, 1994, p.6, cited in Lewin, 1995, p. 209)

Because of the rising demand, coupled with a more diverse body of student population, HE provision in South Africa needs to be mediated through ICTs and other innovative modes of delivery. This has become more important because many students entering H.E institutions in the country are academically under-prepared; hence, they need remedial support to bridge the gap upon admission into the system (Jaffer, Ng'ambi, and Czerniewic, 2007). The integration of ICTs in the H.E system promises efficiency gains in pedagogy, research and administration (Goddard and Cornford, 2002). Therefore, ICTs have become essential tools for the transformation of H.E in South Africa.

Many factors collectively determine the level of ICT adoption in different institutions of higher learning, and by different provinces in South Africa. Among these factors are: different levels of donor intervention; the level of economic development; the status of ICT infrastructure; and the level of ICT and ICT in education policy processes (Ngugi, 2007; Adam, 2003). As demonstrated by the e-Education policy (DoE, 2004) and other cognate policy issues, South Africa has been at the forefront of ICT in education policy and practice in Africa. Yet, ICT in education policy-making has remained an evolving and to some extent fragmented trend in the country. This overview is meant to provide an initial impression of some important themes and issues in ICT in education policy in South Africa, which have influenced technology adoption in tertiary institutions.

As agents of socio-economic transformation, the expectation is high on HE institutions in South Africa to train students from diverse groups in the society, many of whom were hitherto denied education, and to turnout quality graduates (Jaffer, Ng'ambi, and Czerniewic, 2007). The rationale behind this demand for more quality graduates can be explained in two ways: first, to address the equity needs in post-apartheid South Africa; and second, to equip South African graduates with the necessary skills and know-how to compete in the global employment market with graduates from other countries across the world. This is one of the realities of globalization. To ensure their survival and credibility, HE institutions in Africa are left with no choice but to change their *modus operandi* in the areas of student enrollment and access, pedagogy, research and quality. This underscores the imperative of employing ICTs both as cognitive and management tools in the HE institutions in SA. As a 1996 study by the National Commission on Higher Education in South Africa observed that, "disadvantaged institutions were…

under-resourced with respect to libraries and information technology; (for example), there was only one desktop computer per ten staff members, it was non-existent for students and there was a severe shortage of skilled information technology personnel" (Council of Higher Education, South Africa, 2001. p.9). Although this situation has improved since 1996, the condition of ICTs in tertiary institutions in Africa remains grossly inadequate. This level of modern computer application cannot accomplish the multidimensional objectives of integration ICT in HE in SA.

Generally, very little ICT in education policy development has been undertaken in sub-Saharan Africa. Many countries in the region have rather consolidated educational technology policy into a broader ICT policy framework (James, *et al*, 2001). South Africa played a pioneer role in ICT in education policy development in Africa. As the country's White Paper on e-Education (DoE, 2004, p.15) explains, "The concept of e-Education revolves around the-use of ICTs to accelerate the achievement of national education goals. … It supports larger systematic, pedagogical, curricular and assessment reforms that will facilitate improved education and improved use of educational resources such as ICT." Policy on the use of technologies in education and training exists within a broader education policy framework in South Africa. This makes the country one of the few countries in Africa with a structured and focused policy on educational technology.

The national Draft White Paper on e-Education in South Africa sets government's response to a new information and communications technology environment in education. It is within this policy that the adoption of ICT in HE institutions in the country is located. It also represents a new framework for implementation, particularly about the partnership of government and the private sector in the provision of ICT in education in South Africa (DoE, South Africa, 2003). This policy document recognizes that the objectives of education quality, equity and relevance are embedded in it. Among the targets set by the e-Education White Paper are to:

- Build an education and training system to support ICT integration in teaching and learning and improved management and administration
- Ensure that schools use education content of high quality
- Ensure that schools are connected, have access to the Internet and communicate electronically
- Ensure that communities use and support ICT facilities. (South African Year Book, 2006/07, p. 216).

Although there is no common approach to ICT application in HE institutions, several studies suggest that even with limited resources, HE institutions in Africa use ICTs for developing course material; networking with scholars and institutions abroad; academic research; content delivering and administrative and management support. As Brown *et al* (2008) note, 97 percent of academics in the Western Cape Province in South Africa use ICT in teaching.

In view of the myriad challenges facing HE in SA, it is extremely important to mobilize all resources, including ICTs, for its improvement. However, this expectation has come without a full appreciation, particularly among policy-makers, of the complex nature of such technological innovation in education. For the most part, education policy-makers believe that a set of computers with Internet connectivity in each classroom or in a computer laboratory will transform HE by linking such institution with the world. The extent to which the potential of ICTs are applied in teaching, learning and research in HE institutions in SA is limited by lack of infrastructure and other supporting institutional frameworks.

OBSTACLES TO ICT INTEGRATION IN HIGHER EDUCATION IN SOUTH AFRICA

A sustainable application of ICTs in teaching and learning in tertiary institutions in South Africa is faced with notable challenges. While the diffusion and adoption of various ICTs have risen, especially when compared with what obtains in other sub-Saharan African countries, one can still observe shortage of computer hardware and relevant software in higher education institutions in the country. However, the challenges of ICT adoption and integration in HE goes beyond hardware and software matters.

Within the Africa context, there is the tendency to think that lack of computers is the main obstacle to the integration of technology in education. This has created the mindset, particularly among policy makers, that a computer with internet connectivity in each classroom will solve education problems. As Haddad (2007, p.15) puts it, "no technology can fix a bad educational philosophy or compensate for bad practice. In fact, if we are going in the wrong direction, technology will only get us there faster." This speaks to the systemic nature of successful and sustainable integration of ICT in education. The imperative of non-technical factors in educational technology is underscored when Dede (1998, p. 2) argues that "Unless other simultaneous innovations in pedagogy, curriculum, assessment, and school organization are coupled to the use of instructional technology, the time and efforts expended on implementing these devices produces few improvements in educational outcomes…" Thus, other challenges facing the adoption of ICTs in HE institutions are; insufficient telephone and telecommunication infrastructure, lack of training resources for lecturers, and lack of skilled and experienced information technology specialists and curriculum designers to assist with development, maintenance and support of ICT usage in teaching and learning in higher education institutions.

There is an apparent lack of an ICT in education policy at the institutional levels in South Africa. ICT in education policy frameworks provide road maps for the planning and implementation of effective and sustainable technology application in the HE system. Unfortunately, many HE institutions in the country do not have a plan of action, which is an essential part of ICT adoption. In general terms, the lack of institutional policy guidelines on the integration of ICTs in education is not peculiar to tertiary institutions in South Africa. Writing in the case of Egypt, Said (2001 cited in Ngugi, *et al*, 2007, p.9) argues that "the lack of an overall technology plan, coupled with the short-term funding model and the absence of a clear acquisition and replacement plan, has lead to 'an inconsistent and unproductive approach to IT implementation." Even with sufficient funds and other resources, the lack of ICT integration plans and policy guide in each school is a recipe for the failure of educational technology projects. Adam (2003) observes that different departments and units in different African Universities receive computers and other forms of ICT through donations and purchases with little or no central coordination. The engagement of tertiary institutions in the application of ICTs without a central coordination and oversight of ICT distribution and maintenance, pose difficulties to campus-wide technology integration in such institutions. This trend results in uncoordinated and unsustainable implementation of technology.

As mentioned in the preceding sections, HE institutions in South Africa lack plans to guide ICT integration in teaching and learning, course development, professional development for instructors and lecturers. In effect, these institutions do not have the necessary institutional and collegial support of ICT integration in their day-to-day academic activities (Brown, *et al,* 2008). For these reasons, one can explain the inarticulate nature of course structure and lack of assessment of ICT activities, such as online courses in HE institutions in the country. This situation is particularly critical in most public Universities and Technikons in the country where the practice of "ICT integration in education" is represented by the mere procurement and installation of few computers. This brings up a major misconception among policymakers with regards to ICT in education, not just in South Africa but in many African countries. The misconception stems from the meaning of the acronym "ICT." As Hylton Applebuam remarks, many think that the "C" in ICT stands for computers (Evoh, 2008). Thus, computers have come to be seen as a "vitamin" whose mere presence in schools result in better educational outcomes. Unfortunately, this focus on the computer takes attention away from other non-technical aspects of a sustainable instructional technology practice, which collectively bring about important outcomes in the application of technology in education.

Another major challenge of ICT integration in HE institutions in Africa is the acute shortage of bandwidth connectivity. As many scholars (William, 2008; Jensen, 2006) have observed, bandwidth is the life-blood of today's knowledge economy and ICT-enhanced education. This is because, the major economic impact of increased bandwidth and backbone networks lies in efficient aggregation of connectivity to high-capacity networks and the reduction in costs. Bandwidth is essential for communication, research and collaboration, course and content delivery and academic management of courses (Bateman, 2006). However, the high cost of bandwidth affects HE institutions with limited resources. In effect, students and researchers in these institutions are excluded from the vast knowledge of global research network made possible by internet connectivity. South Africa has the largest number of broadband subscribers with the highest cost in Africa (see Table 1). The unreliable and high cost of bandwidth, which is collectively procured by tertiary institutions in South Africa through the Tertiary Education Network (Brown, *et al*, 2008), pose a barrier to e-learning and ICT integration in HE. The implication of broadband scarcity is that tertiary institutions in South Africa and other African countries spend more financial resources to buy bandwidth (See Figure 1). High cost of broadband translates to high cost of internet access. Brown et al (2008) reports that the cost of internet access in South Africa is the highest in Africa, and the country's cost is four times that in

Table 1. Comparison of South Africa's ICT infrastructure with other sub-Saharan African countries (Source: Brown, C., et al (2008, p. 70))

	SA	SSA Average	Botswana	Namibia	Mozambique	Zimbabwe
Population(million)	47	743	2	20	20	13
% Urban	59%	35%	57%	35%	35%	36%
Per 1000 people						
Fixed Lines	101	17	75	4	4	25
Mobile subscribers	724	125	466	62	62	54
Internet users	109	29	34	7	7	77
Personal Computers (PCs)	85	14	45	6	6	92
Broadband subscribers	3.5	0	0	0	0	0.8
Int Bandwidth (bts pp)	19	2	15	4	1	4
Cost Internet (USD pm)	63	45	21	48	32	24

Figure 1. Comparison of regional average broadband retail prices (Source: William 2008, p. 3)

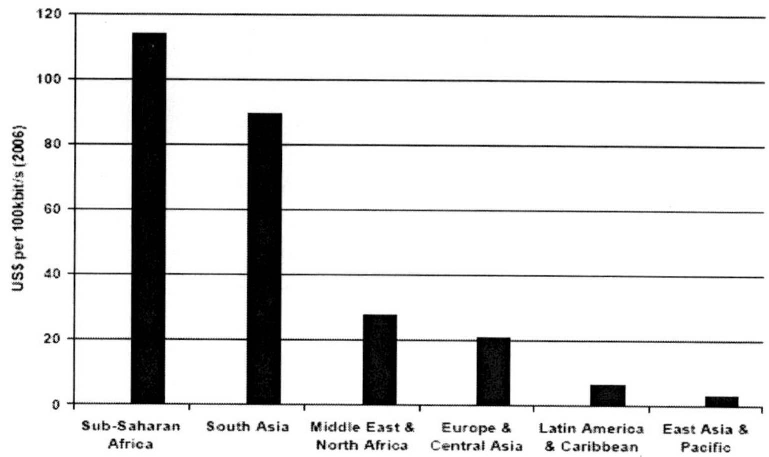

the U.S.A. Among the major causes of expensive bandwidth in Africa are: lack of international optic fiber infrastructure, and the monopoly status of state operators of the first large-scale fiber project in Africa (Jensen, 2006; William, 2008). As Mike Jensen (2006, p.1) puts it, many universities and well-endowed centers of research and academics in Africa "have less bandwidth than a home broadband user in North America or Europe, and it must be shared amongst hundreds or even thousands of users." The statutory monopoly status of state-owned companies in the few existing international optic fiber project, such as the SAT-3/WASC cable[2], discourages free entry of private companies in the market. The implication is that there are few broadband service providers in most African markets to increase supply and competitive pricing in the industries (Figure 2).

As mentioned above, at present, face-to-face lectures remain the dominante mode of delivery in higher education institutions in South Africa. This trend can partly be explained by the chronic lack of infrastructure coupled with the lack of learning and management systems that would enable tertiary institutions to embark on e-Learning. Even if the necessary infrastructure were available, there is yet another obstacle: how to convert the face-to-face lecture materials to digital content. This is a responsibility that many tertiary institutions in South African cannot handle without the help of trained instructional designers. This becomes more important because Instructional Design (ID) is a relatively new field, which is not offered or known in many HE institutions in Africa. In the few Universities where this need had received some attention, the process of ICT in education or e-learning tends to be technocentric in nature. In essence, those in charge of e-Learning are Information Technology experts, and not educators and Instructional Technologists. The implication is that e-Learning in such institution is erroneously perceived primarily as a technical project, and secondly as an educational project. However, it important to emphasize that ICT is a means to an end, and not ends to itself; they are means to improved education.

BEYOND COMPUTERS: A SUSTAINABLE INTEGRATION ICTS IN TERTIARY INSTITUTIONS IN SOUTH AFRICA

This section explores the essentials for effective and sustained ICT Innovation in HE in South Africa. The process of adopting ICTs in HE entails a

Figure 2. Telephones, cellular phones and PCs per 1,000 inhabitants (Source: Haddad, 2007)

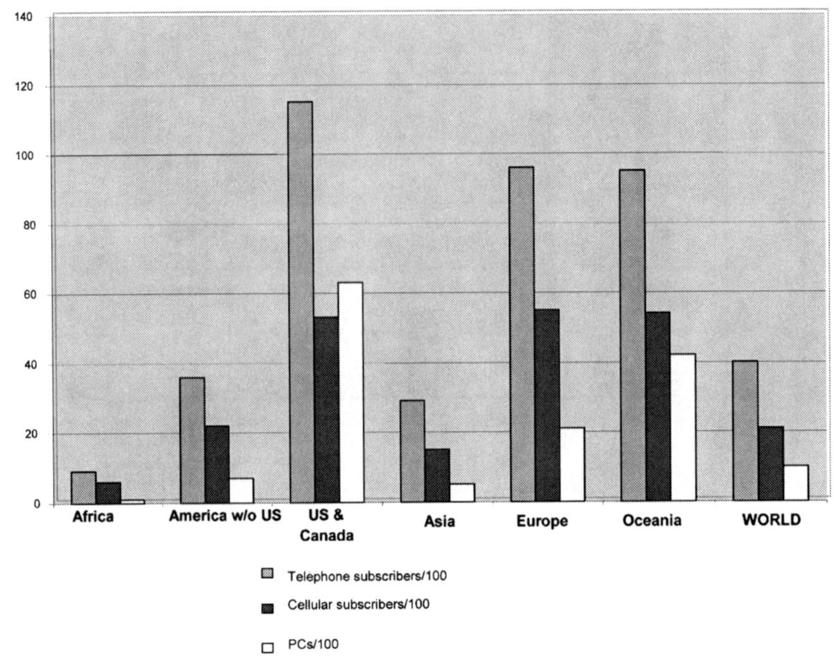

composite compendium of human and technical artifacts including computers, internet connectivity, staff development, policy frameworks and many more. These socio-technical activities recognized by the actor-network theory enable synchronous and asynchronous learning thereby unleashing innovative and borderless education. The primary objective of integrating ICTs in higher education in post-apartheid South Africa is to leverage various technological platforms to provide the right educational contents in the emerging knowledge society. Accomplishing this goal in the complex educational environment in South African is easier said than done. Despite the apparent mushrooming of ICTs such as the Internet, computers and mobile phones in the country; the potential of these technologies as learning objects and educational tools are yet to be realized.

Integrating ICTs in the educational system is not only a technological challenge but also a challenge for national policy and planning within institutions. Given the various ICT in education policy frameworks in South Africa, it is time for the national government to formulate telecommunication policies that will sustain ICT application in tertiary institutions of learning. In regards to using ICT potential to accomplish national educational goals in South Africa, there is a mismatch between ICT in education policies on the one hand, and existing telecommunication policies on the other. This underscores the need for the harmonization of the goals of these policies. This is important because, the pedagogical value of ICTs are determined by educational needs and policy frameworks designed to accomplish those needs. In essence, explicit government actions are required to fully realize the potential benefits of ICTs in HE institutions.

In addition to government policy on educational technology, it is essential for individual HE institutions to development ICT integration master plans. As opined by Peter Bateman (2006), policy is an enabling factor of higher education management. Hence, institutional master plans for ICT integration create the enabling environment in which the adoption of technologies for educational transformation can be sustained over time. In an "ICT Maturity Tool"[3] developed in 2000 for institutions of higher learning in Africa, AAU (2000) stressed the importance of having a formal ICT planning and monitoring functions in individual tertiary institutions. The tool stressed the need for HE institutions to look at the different variables of ICT planning, among which are: institutional strategic plan for technology; derived information policy plan; derived information master plan; and derived information project plan (AAU, 2000). According to AAU, these set of ICT in education plans will create awareness and consensus, which are essential for the effective implementation of the Information Policy Plan (IPP) in such institutions. An IPP can be designed to contain ICT priorities and guidelines, their implementation, monitoring and evaluation strategies (AAU, 2000).

Due to the lack of bandwidth in South Africa, accessibility and availability of internet connectivity is still minimal and expensive. This is partly because, the South African government exercises strict and overwhelming control of the telecommunication sector. The monopoly control of existing bandwidth network by the consortium of African states has stifled competition and innovation in the sector. The South African government needs to use policy instruments to liberalize and encourage private investment in the ICT sector. This policy step will attract more private investments in the sector and eventually reduce cost and improve quality of telecommunication services.

Another policy measure that holds great promise for ICT adoption and sustainability in HE institutions in South Africa is the full implementation of E-rate policy[4], which has been passed in the country. A proper implementation of the E-rate policy will provide tertiary institutions 50 percent discount on approved telecommunication and Internet connection costs (Evoh, 2007). Besides, South African government must demonstrate its commitment to rapid development through the improvement and upgrade of essential infrastructure, which serve as the backbone of the knowledge economy. As Benner (2003, cited in Cross and Adam, 2007, p. 91) contends, national ICT policy "cannot be limited to simply promoting the use of information technology, but must also simultaneously address inequality and the dislocation associated with diffusion of information technology through the economy."

The coordination of government inputs will require an effective alignment of horizontal and vertical policies for the benefit of ICTs in HE institutions in Africa. As Robert Kozma (2008) agues, the role of governments entails the coordination of strategic and operational policies aimed at using ICT programs and projects to meet the economic needs of the nation. He further posits that "strategic policies that emphasize economic development should be matched by operational programs that use ICT to develop new workforce skills, not just purchase new equipment..." (Kozma, 2008). Suffice it to add that the South African government will not be able to accomplish these development goals alone. The adoption of ICTs in HE institutions in the country requires collaborative partnerships. With constrained budgets, African governments cannot unilaterally fund and sustain ICT-based education in tertiary institutions. Therefore, sustaining ICT adoption in HE institution in South Africa would require not only government funding but also inputs, leadership and technical support from the private sector, civil society, and professional organizations. This underscores the need for multiple sources of funding, cost sharing, and partnerships arrangements with the private sector and international donors. Such multi-sectoral efforts will form the pillar for the adoption and sustainability of ICTs to enhance higher education in post-apartheid Africa.

CONCLUSION

As Badat (2007, p.22) reminds us, "higher education institutions exist at the intersection of state, market and civil society, each with its specific, varied and different expectations and demands." With such huge responsibility, the expectations are high on tertiary institutions in South Africa to contribute in realizing the national goal of redressing socio-economic and political injustices of the past. Tertiary institutions are expected exploit the full potential of ICTs in order to accomplish their goals. This form of innovative transformation is needed more if tertiary institutions in South Africa will survive in their mission to teach, research and prepare the needed workforce in the emerging knowledge economy. Many institutions in the country have made sporadic efforts to include e-learning, and web-based learning in their content delivery methods. This study shows that the integration of ICTs in high education in South Africa is challenged at two levels. The first level of challenge is at institutional level: most tertiary institutions of learning in the country do not have strategic plans designed specifically for the integration of ICTs in the educational process. Many of these institutions lack sufficient funding to effectively integrate modern technologies in teaching, learning and research. The second level of challenge is at the national level: despite the professed need for using ICTs in social and economic development, there is the need for policy coherence, particularly in the education and telecommunication sectors. These two levels of related challenges, underscore the need for an effective policy framework and benchmark. Such benchmark will include but not limited to ICT-enhanced course development and delivery (i.e., teaching and learning), students/faculty support, and evaluation/assessment.

Against this backdrop, this study makes the following conclusions. First, the adoption of educational technology in HE institutions in South Africa should occur as a component of a broader effort of reform to improve teaching, learning and research. As illustrated in Figure 3, the adoption of ICT for educational improvement is a multifaceted process. Without other elements of technology adoption, the promise of technology for educational improvement will be lost. Integrating ICTs in education is a change process that can only be sustained if educators are allowed to explore and

Figure 3. Facets of Sustaining ICT adoption in tertiary institutions in South Africa Project

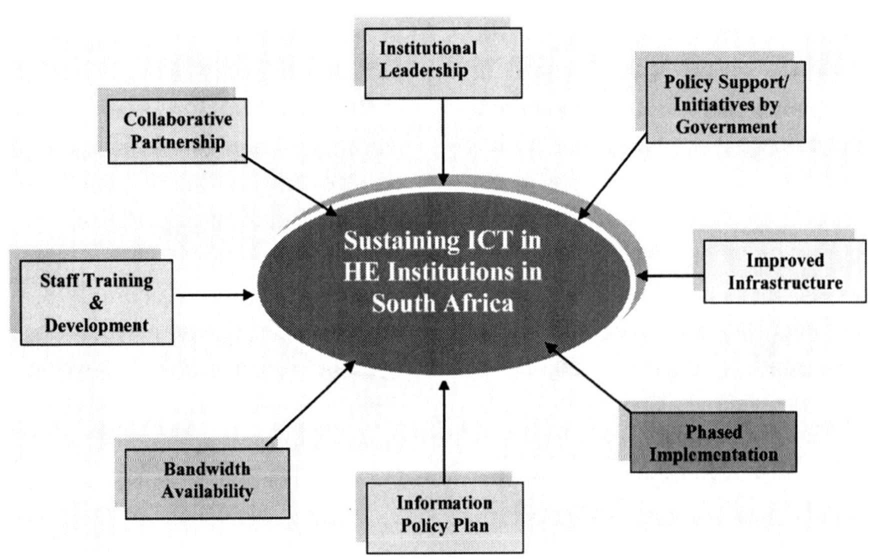

discover the potential of educational technologies. In essence, only educators can meaningfully integrate ICTs in education. Second, it is extremely difficult to integrate ICTs in education without the right policy frameworks, both at the institutional and national levels. Thirdly, ICTs can serve as effective tools for instruction and management in education if used appropriately. However, such technologies are no panacea for challenges facing HE institutions in South Africa. Technologies can only serve as integral part of a larger solution. One cannot overemphasize the imperative for a holistic approach to ICT integration in the HE system. This will involve curriculum, pedagogy, timely evaluation, classroom management, professional development, administration, and an integrated policy implementation at all levels.

REFERENCES

Adam, L. (2003). Information and communication technologies in higher education in Africa: Initiatives and challenges. *Journal of Higher Education in Africa* (JHEA/RESA), *1*(1),195–2210.

Akudolu, L. (2007) The place of ICT in the successful implementation of the education reform under NEEDS and Millennium Development Goals (MDGs). Paper presented at the *ANCOPSS (All Nigeria Conference of Principals of Secondary Schools) 2006/2007 Mandatory Continuing Professional Training (MCPT) for Principals of South East Zone*, Awka, Nigeria, January 2007. Retrieved July 22, 2007, from http://www.lilian-rita.com/lr3/INTRODUCTION%20NATION.pdf

Association of African Universities. (2000). Guidelines for institutional self-assessment of ICT maturity in African universities.

Baguma, I., & Ssewanyana, J. K. (2008). A Simulation Modeling-Based Investigation of the Impact of IT Infrastructure on Business Process Reengineering. [Special Issue]. *International Journal of Computing and ICT Research*, *1*(1).

Basque, J., Dore, S., & Henri, F. (2000). Facilitating a Techno-pedagogical Change in higher education: lessons from the SAVOIR and AMETIST projects. In *Proceedings of the XVIIIth Conference of the International Council for Innovation in Higher Education,* November 5-9, 2000, Quebec, Canada.

Bateman, P. (2006, November 19-2?). Bandwidth Connectivity and Management. Paper presented at the *Frontiers of Knowledge Conference*, University of Cape Town, South Africa. Retrieved on Dec. 27, 2009, from http://www.foundationpartnership.org/pubs/leaders/assets/papers/BatemanSession-7Part1.pdf

Brown, C., et al. (2008). The Impact of South Africa's ICT Infrastructure on Higher Education. In Remenyi., *Proceedings of the 3rd International Conference of E-Learning*. Cape Town, South Africa. Academic Publishing Limited.

Bussu, B. (2004). The Open University of Tanzania: The African Virtual University (AVU). In UNESCO Institute for Information Technologies in Education (IITE), *Information and Communication Technology Usage in Higher Distance Education in Sub-Saharan Africa*. Moscow: UNESCO Institute.

Callon, M. (1991). Techno-Economic Networks and Irreversibility. In Law, J. (Ed.), *A Sociology of Monsters: Essays on Power, Technology and Domination (pp. ##-##)*. New York: Routledge.

Carlsson, L. (2000). Policy Networks as Collective Action. *Policy Studies Journal: the Journal of the Policy Studies Organization*, *28*(3), 502–520. doi:10.1111/j.1541-0072.2000.tb02045.x

Carnoy, M. (1999). *Globalization and Educational Reform: What Planners Need to Know*. Paris: UNESCO.

Carvin, A. (2000). E-Rate 101: How the Program Works. In Carvin, A. (Ed.), *The E-Rate in America: A Tale of Four Cities*. Washington, DC: The Benton Foundation.

Castells, M. (1994). The University System: Engine of Development in the New World Economy. In Salmi, J., & Verspoor, A. M. (Eds.), *Revitalizing Higher Education (pp. ##-##). Location?*IAU Press/Pergamon Press.

Central Intelligence Agency. (2008). *The World FactBook*. Retrieved January 12, 2009, from https://www.cia.gov/library/publications/the-world-factbook/geos/et.html

Collins, A., & Halverson, R. (2009). *Rethinking Education in the Age of Technology: The Digital Revolution and Schooling in America*. New York: Teachers College Press.

Cooper, D. (2001, Fall). The South African 'National Plan for Higher Education', 2001. *International Higher Education Newsletter.* Retrieved June 25, 2009, from http://www.bc.edu/bc_org/avp/soe/cihe/newsletter/News25/text004.htm

Council of Higher Education. South Africa. (2001). Developing African Higher Education. Retrieved June 8, 2009, from http://www.nepad.org/2005/files/documents/22.pdf

Cross, M., & Adam, F. (2007). ICT Policies and Strategies in Higher Education in South Africa: National and Institutional Pathways. *Higher Education Policy*, *20*(1), 73–95. doi:10.1057/palgrave.hep.8300144

Dede, C. (1998). Six Challenges for Education Technology. Retrieved June 13, 2009, from www.virtula.gmu.edu/pdf/ASCD.pdf

Department of Education. (1997). *Education White Paper 3: A Program for Higher Education Transformation.* Pretoria.

Department of Education. (2003). White Paper on e-Education: Transforming Learning and Teaching through Information and Communication Technologies (ICTs). GOVERNMENT GAZETTE, 26 AUGUST 2004

Dowding, K. (1995). Model or Metaphor? A critical review of the policy network approach. *Political Studies*, *43*(2), 135–158.

Evoh, C. J. (2007). ICTs, Secondary Education, and the Knowledge Economy: Exploring the Roles of the Private Sector in Post-Apartheid South Africa. *Journal of Education for International Development*, *1*(3).

Evoh, C. J. (2008). Collaborative Partnerships and the Transformation of Secondary Education through ICTs in South Africa. Unpublished dissertation. The New School University, Country.

Goddard, J., & Cornford, J. (2002). The University, ICTs and Development in the Information Society. In Mansell, R., Samarajiva, R., & Mahan, A. (Eds.), *Networking Knowledge for Information Societies: Institutions and Interventions. City, Country: Delft University Press.*

Haddad, W. (2007). ICTs for Education: A Reference Handbook. Retrieved October 22, 2007, from http://www.ictinedtoolkit.org/usere/pdfs/ICTs_for_Education_Analytical_Review.pdf

Hamdy, A. (2007). ICT in Education in Egypt. In G. Farrell and S. Isaac (Eds.), *Survey of ICT and Education in Africa (Vol. 2) 53 Country Reports*. Washington, DC: InfoDev.

Herselman, M. E., & Hay, H. R. (2003). (ICT) for South African Higher Education Institutions. In InSITE. In *Where Parallels Intersect*. Challenges Posed by Information and Communication Technologies.

Jaffer, S., Ng'ambi, D., & Czerniewicz, L. (2007). The Role of ICTs in Higher Education in South Africa: One Strategy for addressing Teaching and Learning Challenges. *International Journal of Education and Development using Information and Communication Technologies (IJEDICT), 3*(4), 131-142.

Jensen, M. (2006). Open Access: Lowering the cost of International Bandwidth in Africa. APC "Issue Papers" Series 2006 October 2006 http://rights.apc.org/documents/open_access_EN.pdf

Jenson, J. (2007). *Policy Unplugged: Dis/Connections between Technology Policy and Practices in Canadian School.* London: McGill-Queen's University Press.

Kozma, R. (n.d). Comparative Analysis of Policies for ICT in Education. *International Handbook on Information Technology in Education.* Retrieved October 23, 2007, from http://robertkozma.com/images/kozma_comparative_ict_policies_chapter.pdf

Latour, B. (1987). *Science in Action: How to Follow Scientists and Engineers through Society.* Cambridge, MA: Harvard University Press.

Latour, B. (1992). The Sociology of a Few Mundane Artifacts. In Bijker, W., & Law, J. (Eds.), *Shaping Technology / Building Society Studies in Sociotechnological Change.* Cambridge, MA: MIT Press.

Latour, B. (2004). On Using ANT for Studying Information Systems: A (Somewhat) Socratic Dialogue. In Chrisanthi, A. (Ed.), *The Social Study of Information and Communication Technology Innovation, Actors, and Contexts.* Oxford: Oxford University Press.

Magagulu, C. (2005). The Benefits and Challenges of Cross-Border Higher Education in Developing Countries. *Journal of Higher Education in Africa/RESA, 3*(1), 29–49.

Mbarika, V. W. A. (2002). Re-thinking Information and Communication Technology Policy focus on Internet versus Teledensity Diffusion for Africa's Least Developed Countries. *The Electronic Journal on Information Systems in Developing Countries, 9*(1), 1–13.

Min, W. (2001). Information and Communication Technology and Education: Potential for Partnerships. Executive Summary of Proceedings 23 – 27 April 2001, Hong Kong China. http://www.adbi.org/files/2001.04.ess41.information.communication.technology.education.pdf

Minishi-Majanja, M. (2007, August 9-23). Integration of ICTs in Library and Information Science Education in sub-Saharan Africa. Paper presented at the WORLD LIBRARY AND INFORMATION CONGRESS: 73RD IFLA GENERAL CONFERENCE AND COUNCIL, Durban, South Africa. Retrieved from http://www.ifla.org/IV/ifla73/papers/083-Minishi-Majanja-en.pdf

Moon, B. (2004). 'Open and Distance Learning for Teacher Education in Africa: Innovation and Change': A Toolkit for Education Policy Makers, Planners and Teacher Educators in Sub-Saharan Africa. *Region Human Development Working Paper Series,* 5. Washington, DC: The World Bank.

Ngugi, C. (2007). *ICTs and Higher Education in Africa: Status Reports on Information and Communication Technologies (ICTs) in Higher Education in eight African countries.* Cape Town, South Africa: The Centre of Educational Technology, University of Cape Town.

Pelgrum, W., & Law, N. (2003). *ICT in education around the world: trends problems and prospects,* Paris: UNESCO International Institute for Educational Planning educational assessment.". *Computers & Education, 37,* 163–178. doi:10.1016/S0360-1315(01)00045-8

Perraton, H., & Creed, C. (2000, April 26–28). Applying new technologies and cost-effective delivery systems in basic education. World Education Forum, Dakar, Senegal. UNESCO: Paris.

Pityana, N. B. (2004). Higher Education in South Africa: Future Perspectives. Keynote address at Bill Venter/Altron Literary Awards 2003; Wednesday 7 April 2004, Westcliff Hotel, Johannesburg. http://www.unisa.ac.za/contents/about/principle/docs/AltronAwardsspeech.doc

Privateer, P. M. (1999). Academic Technology and the Future of Higher Education. *The Journal of Higher Education*, *70*, 60–79. doi:10.2307/2649118

Sadat, S. (2007). Higher Education Transformation in South Africa Post 1994: Towards a Critical Assessment. *Solomon Mahlangu Education Lecture 2007*. Location: Centre for Education Policy Development. Retrieved June 22, 2009, from http://www.cepd.org.za/files/CEPD_SolomonMahlanguLecture1_Badat_2007.pdf

Trevor, C. (1991). *A Consultation on Higher Education in Africa: A Report to the Ford Foundation and Rockefeller Foundation, New York.* UNESCO Bangkok. (n.d). Technologies. Retrieved August 3, 2008, from http://www.unescobkk.org/index.php?id=663

William, M. (2008). *Broadband for Africa: Policy for Promoting the Development of Backbone Networks*. Washington, DC: InfoDev and the World Bank.

World Bank. (2002). *Constructing Knowledge Societies: New Challenges for Tertiary Education*. Washington, DC: The World Bank.

World Bank. (2009). *Accelerating Catch-up Tertiary Education for Growth in Sub-Saharan Africa*. Washington, DC: The International Bank for Reconstruction and Development / The World Bank.

KEY TERMS AND DEFINITIONS

Knowledge Economy: This is a system in which: the generation and the exploitation of knowledge plays a predominant part in the creation of wealth.

Actor-Network Theoretical Framework: This is based on the conception that social reality could not be forged to support successful policy implementation without strategic alliances and support from an encompassing network of technical and non-technical intermediaries.

Outcome-Based Education: This is an education system based on a student-focused model. It stresses the importance of setting clear standards for observable, measurable outcomes of students' education.

New Media Literacy: This system of literacy involves the integration of video, images and music, and animation comprehension that give rise to the new kinds of production.

Brain Drain: This is the loss of skilled intellectual and technical labor through the movement of such labor to more favorable geographic, economic, or professional environments.

Instructional Design: This is a theory that provides guidance on how to help people learn in different situations and under different conditions (page 10).

Government of National Unity: This is a term used in parliamentary system of government. The term is used to explain a case in which all the major political parties in a country are part of the governing coalition. This type of government occurs in parliamentary systems. Between April 27, 1994 and February 3, 1997 South Africa was ruled by.

Bandwidth: This is a term used to describe how much information can be transmitted over a connection.

ICT Maturity Tool: This is a guide produced by the Association of African Universities for studying the planning and integration of ICT resources in HE institutions in Africa.

E-Rate Policy: is a government-managed program that provides significant discounts on telecommunications technologies to schools and libraries.

ENDNOTES

1 For the purpose of this study, the term information and communication technologies (ICT), mean all "forms of technology that are used to transmit, store, create, display, share or exchange information by electronic means. This broad definition of ICT includes such technologies as radio, television, video, CD-ROMs, telephone (both fixed line and mobile phones), satellite systems, Intranet, Internet, computer and network hardware and software; as well as the equipment and services associated with these technologies, such as videoconferencing, e-mail and blogs" (UNESCO Bangkok, n.d; Association of African Universities, 2000)

2 The SAT-3/WASC cable connects Portugal to thc Capc in South Africa running through the following eight coastal countries: Senegal, Ivory Coast, Ghana, Benin, Nigeria, Cameroon, Gabon and Angola (Jensen, 2006, p. 1).

3 The "ICT maturity tool" is a guide produced by the Association of African Universities for studying the planning and integration of ICT resources in HE institutions in Africa.

4 The E-Rate policy was first introduced in the U.S.A. The E-Rate is a federally-managed program that provides significant discounts on telecommunications technologies to schools and libraries in the United States. Discounts range from 20 percent to 90 percent and are based on the percentage of students participating in the federal school lunch program who are served by the school or library. The E-Rate is administered by the Universal Service Administrative Company (USAC), a private, not-for-profit Corporation that is responsible for ensuring universal service to telecommunications services throughout the country." (Carvin, 2000, p. 3)

Chapter 3
Technological Infrastructure and Implementation Environments:
The Case of Laptops for New Zealand Teachers

Bronwen Cowie
University of Waikato, New Zealand

Alister Jones
University of Waikato, New Zealand

Ann Harlow
University of Waikato, New Zealand

ABSTRACT

The integration of ICT is the apparent goal of range of educational initiatives worldwide. To date, however, the impact of ICTs has lagged behind the rhetoric. Rather than technology transforming teaching and learning it appears that teachers often assimilate it into existing practices. This chapter uses Douglas Engelbart's (1992) notion of an improvement infrastructure to explore and explain the factors that have framed and shaped New Zealand teacher access to, adoption of, and resistance to the use of laptops. Engelbart posits that organizations should aspire to creating three levels of infrastructure for improvement: a core capability infrastructure, an infrastructure that enables the improvement of core work, and an infrastructure that enables the on-going improvement of the improvement processes. Improvement of improvement typically receives the least long-term strategic investment. For teachers with laptops improvement of improvement is what enables teachers to enhance their ability to use their laptop. In this chapter we show that this involves the system of teacher confidence and expertise, teacher professional development opportunities, teacher access to a reliable technological infrastructure, and the existence of a supportive school leadership and culture for ICT/laptop use.

DOI: 10.4018/978-1-61692-854-4.ch003

INTRODUCTION

The integration of ICT is the apparent goal of an extensive array of educational initiatives worldwide. One of the rationales appears to be to prepare children to take an active part in an increasingly complex and information rich world. Also evident is the view that ICT can enhance student learning within the current curriculum through a positive impact on student attitude to and approaches toward learning. To date however the impact of ICT technologies on education and schools has lagged behind the rhetoric. Rather than the technology transforming teaching and learning it appears that teachers often assimilate ICTs, including computer use, into existing classroom practices (Cuban, 2001). Selwyn (1999) argues that this is because computers have been 'inserted' into schools with very little consideration of teacher perspectives and the realities of classrooms. In this chapter we explore the personal and contextual factors that have framed and shaped New Zealand teacher access, adoption and resistance to the use of laptops provided for their personal use as part of a government initiative to foster teacher professional use of ICT. To do this we draw on Engelbart's (1992) notion of an improvement infrastructure and improvement community. Engelbart posits that organizations should aspire to creating three basic levels of infrastructure: a core capability infrastructure (this is what is needed to enable people to do the core work of the organization); an infrastructure that enables the improvement of core work, and an infrastructure that enables the on-going improvement of the improvement processes. He asserts that the third level is ultimately the most important to organizational effectiveness because it involves 'getting better at getting better'. He also notes that the improvement-of-improvement level typically receives the least long-term strategic investment.

FRAMING THE CONTEXT OF TEACHER ICT USE

It is now generally agreed that teacher computer use is shaped by a meld of personal and contextual factors (Owston, 2007). Teachers who are confident and competent in using ICT not only appreciate its usefulness but can also envisage possible benefits for their students (Jones, 2004). However, teacher response to innovation is never sequential, predictable or even able to be generalized (Windschilt & Sahl, 2002). ICT use is not just based on the individual being able to 'understand' the potential benefits of ICT use, but also on how well ICT-based activity 'fits' with the wider contexts within which they are operating (Selwyn & Facer, 2007). Thus, school-level factors influence teacher utilization of ICT. Zhao and colleagues (Zhao & Frank, 2003; Zhao, Pugh, Sheldon & Byers, 2002) provide evidence that, when the prevailing school culture is one of collaboration and mutual support for change, the diffusion of technology innovations is more likely. Strong school leadership, including a vision for change and planning for action to implement this vision, are crucial in any successful educational change initiative (Fullan, 2001), and all the more so in change that involves technology because this can lead to changes in school structures and systems and the teaching and learning process (Cuban, Kilpatrick & Peck, 2001). It is important that school principals work to share their goals and develop others as leaders within a school (Anderson & Dexter, 2000).

Teacher use of ICT, particularly any integrated classroom use, requires a reliable technological infrastructure that includes network systems, hardware and software (Cox, Preston & Cox, 1999). Teachers need easy access to a range of ICT resources if they are to make effective use of these in the classroom. Quality on-site technical support is important so that teachers can be confident that ICT equipment will be functional when they need it (Jones, 2004; Zhao *et al.*, 2002).

Teacher integration of ICT into teaching and learning in particular is challenging and takes time. Professional development needs to cater for varying levels of knowledge and expertise, and to balance teacher skill and pedagogical needs (Loveless, Devoogd & Bohlin, 2001)

Laptops provide a different context from computers for teacher professional and personal use of ICT. First and foremost laptops are portable. They can be carried from class to class, and they can easily be taken home. Portability coupled with exclusive use means that teachers can have the same set of tools and products of work available to them throughout the school day, and at home. Thus, laptops go a long way towards meeting Means, Roschelle, Penuel, Sabelli and Haertel (2003) proposal that, 'any given technology can support learning only to the degree that it is available for frequent, integral use within and outside school' (p. 165). Teachers in the United Kingdom and United States have reported increases in ICT confidence and competence with perceived positive impacts in the classroom consequent to their being provided with a laptop (Cunningham, Kerr, McEune, Smith & Harris, 2003; Falba, Grove, Anderson & Putney, 2001; Moses, Khambari & Luan, 2008). They appreciated the flexibility the laptop afforded in place and time of work. They also considered its use afforded greater access to resources for lesson preparation and provided for the streamlining of management and administrative tasks. There is also some evidence that laptops can support increased communication between teachers, students and parents and greater sharing of information between teachers (Rudd, 2001).

THE LAPTOPS FOR TEACHERS INITIATIVE AND EVALUATION

The *Laptops for teachers scheme* [TELA] (Ministry of Education, 2003) is one component of the New Zealand compulsory school sector ICT strategy. The laptops scheme reflected the government's commitment to increasing the use of ICT in schools to help improve student achievement and teaching practice. It was set up in recognition of the value of the laptop as a teaching tool. Initial advice sent to schools with Years 9 to 13 teachers in September 2002 was followed by implementation commencing in November 2002. The scheme was extended to Year 7 and 8 teachers in 2004, to Year 4 to 6 teachers in 2005, and to Year 1 to 3 teachers in 2006. To join the scheme teachers needed to be permanent full time or at least 0.8 full time equivalent. The stated goals of the laptops scheme were 'to develop teacher confidence and competence in the use of ICT for professional growth and collaboration, for teaching and learning, and for administration' (Ministry of Education, 2003, p. 4). Schools gained access to laptops for their teachers on the condition that they managed the integration of the laptops into the school environment, including providing and meeting the costs of additional ICT infrastructure, professional development and technical support.

The *Laptops for teachers* evaluation study was set up to monitor the impact of the laptops on teachers' professional lives. Another purpose was to generate information that might be used to adjust the scheme to optimize its impacts over the course of the implementation, rather than at the end of the four-year roll out. A mixed-methods approach incorporating three cycles of annual nationwide surveys and regional focus groups was used for each teacher cohort (Years 1-3, 4-6, 7-8, 9-13). For the Year 9 to 13 teachers the evaluation also included eight in-depth school case studies with data collected from the same individuals, where possible, for each of three years. Data from the focus groups informed the design and refinement of the surveys and vice versa with the bulk of the survey questions being retained over the six years they were used to allow for comparison of impacts. The evaluation targeted ten percent of the schools in the laptops scheme for each cohort. Care was taken to develop a stratified sample that spanned the dimensions of rural-urban, high to low socioeconomic status, large and small student population.

PATTERNS OF TEACHER LAPTOP USE

The laptops scheme was implemented with the intention of enhancing teacher collaboration and communication, administration and management, lesson planning and preparation, and supporting teacher use of ICT in the classroom. To a large extent it achieved these goals for each of the four cohorts of teachers. In each case, there was a consistent shift across the three years of data collection towards increased teacher confidence in their ability to use the laptop and in their self-reported use of their laptop for a range of tasks. For instance, by the third year of the survey cycles a majority of teachers in each cohort reported they were comfortable with word processing, sending emails and searching the Internet. The surveys indicated that laptops were used most frequently for student data management and administrative purposes including reporting to parents, in the latter case it is likely this was because schools generally required word-processed reports. By 2008, around three quarters of the Year 1 to 3 teachers who responded to the survey used their laptops to check notices and take notes at meetings. The second most common use was for the preparation of lesson materials. Teachers made active use of their laptops to conduct research related to their instructional goals and to customize / add visuals to lesson materials. The high specifications of the laptops played a role in supporting use for this purpose because they provided ease of access to the Internet. Teachers enjoyed being able to create and/or customize resources that were of a high quality for their students. It could be that the ease of sharing and modifying electronic resources contributed to teacher use of the laptops for lesson preparation. Certainly, teachers valuing collaboration of this sort has been reported by others (McGee *et al.*, 2002). The next most common use of the laptops was to exchange information. Email was said to have the advantage of providing a permanent record of a communication, which teachers and those they were seeking to contact could access at their convenience. Teachers were sharing ideas and organizing events with colleagues within and across schools. In some cases teacher professional organizations made extensive use of email to network. As more families had access to email teachers were moving to use this as a form of communication, with some primary teachers using it to update parents on their children's progress. For secondary teachers, it sometimes provided a more private means to communicate with shy students. This said, teachers did not want prompt regular email communication with parents to become the norm.

Teachers had found the laptop to be a motivational teaching tool that provided 'a different way of presenting information that grabs student attention'. Teachers at all levels made some use of their laptops in the classroom to display lesson materials and to access the Internet in order to answer student questions and/or illustrate ideas. Nevertheless, using their laptop for teaching and learning was the main goal for teachers and demand for professional learning opportunities to help teachers to make use of the laptop for teaching and learning grew over the course the evaluation. There was however some indication that teacher use of the laptops/ICTs might vary from subject area to subject area. As did teachers in England (Hennessy, Ruthven & Brindley, 2004), New Zealand secondary school English teachers emphasized the importance of face-to-face discussion. They were somewhat dubious of the role ICT could play in this. Mathematics teachers were ambivalent about the value of ICT/ the laptops; they used graphic calculators instead. In contrast, secondary science teachers saw ICT as being able to contribute everyday examples and illustrations of ideas. Science teachers from the case study schools reported extensive use of lesson materials that integrated text, simulations, interactives and real-world data (images and video clips) to stimulate student interest and engagement. Physical education teachers used the video capabilities of the laptops for analysis, teaching and assessment of student performance, both individual and team, curricular and extra-curricular (tennis, golf, netball). Social science teachers in one school considered their area of expertise 'lends itself nicely' to the use of *PowerPoint,* virtual field trips and websites such *Google Earth* and *Geographic Information Systems (GIS).* On the other hand, Year 1 to 3 teachers reported they used their laptops in all areas of the curriculum with most use reported for language, followed by mathematics and then science. It is difficult to be sure whether the predominance of use for these areas was due to the value accorded to these in national policy and hence classroom time or whether teachers found ICT particularly useful in these areas. Certainly, the teachers provided a range of instances for use in reading including using the digital photographs they took to prepare reading books for their children and their collating and presenting children's writing and artwork. As these examples show, teachers from Year 1 to 13 were able to make creative use of the laptops for teaching and learning.

ESTABLISHING THE FIRST LEVEL OF IMPROVEMENT INFRASTRUCTURE

Teachers appreciated the flexibility of workspace made possible by having a 'portable computer' so that they could work when and where they wanted (Phillips, Bailey, Fisher & Harrison, 1999). The laptop having the capacity to act as the sole repository for all their schoolwork added to this benefit. Teachers made regular use of the laptop at home and at school for the full spectrum of tasks detailed above. Teachers in rural communities along with those with young children, in particular, appreciated being able to work from home in the evenings or weekends rather drive considerable distances back to school to complete work. Focus group teachers described using their laptops in café sand when waiting during school drama rehearsals and sports events. Teachers found that laptops reduced their social isolation. At school they eased the challenges involved in sharing information – teachers often sat together teaching each other new techniques and/or sharing sites they had found and lessons that had gone well. At home, teachers could complete their school preparation whilst in the company of their families. This said, there was some concern that working at home might become an expectation; teachers were adamant this was not acceptable.

CONCEPTUALISING THE SECOND LEVEL OF IMPROVEMENT INFRASTRUCTURE

Engelbart (1992) defines the second level of an improvement infrastructure as providing for improvement, in this case the improvement of teacher use of the laptops. Teacher commentary in the study indicated that professional development, school technological infrastructure, and school leadership and organization shaped and constrained the opportunities and incentives teachers had to use their laptops. These factors influenced, in varying ways, all teacher uses of the laptops albeit they manifested in different ways for different teachers and for different uses of the laptop.

Professional Development

Policy-makers routinely use professional development as a tool to leverage change and in the laptops scheme, schools and teachers were obliged to undertake 40 hours of professional development over the three years of the laptop lease. Despite this, the secondary teachers surveyed in 2003 were largely unaware of this requirement. There was uncertainty as to what could count towards the 40 hours, this persisting throughout the study although this became less of an issue as time went on. Survey respondents reported they had had professional development on learning about the school network, using the administration programs, learning about specific software and beginner computer skills. Whole-staff professional development was recommended for institutionalized activities such as reporting, absences and data entry as a means of ensuring that consistency was maintained. It was also seen as having some value for skill development. Otherwise, generic professional development was said to lack immediacy and personal relevance.

As teachers sought to integrate the laptops into their work supported by limited formal and funded professional development, they were turning to colleagues for help and support. Teachers in each of the four cohorts identified peer mentoring and collegial support as the main mechanism for enhancing their use of the laptops for teaching and learning. Collegial help was described as the preferred and most prevalent form of professional development. Teachers acknowledged that certain individuals had particular expertise in ICT and emphasized the importance of opportunities to work in a sustained way with these colleagues as mentors. The professional development provided by same subject/level colleagues for ICT use in teaching and learning was seen to be especially valuable because it was 'in context'. Colleagues as mentors provided access to models of how a laptop could be used for teaching within the setting in which teachers found themselves. Those teachers in the focus groups who had the requisite expertise discussed the time commitment involved in providing mentoring. Young teachers who had always used ICT were a part of this group, particularly in primary schools. Colleagues indicated they were very aware of the demands placed on these teachers but neither group were able to suggest a solution to this problem - both groups acknowledged that schools may not necessarily have the funds to employ a designated ICT support specialist. Students and family members were also important sources of help and support. The general consensus was that without the collaborative culture that exists amongst New Zealand teachers, very little progress would have been made in the use of the laptops/ICT. One caution about informal collegial professional development was that it was dependent on teacher access to local expertise and thus could be haphazard. In addition, almost all of the focus group teachers spoke about professional learning as an individual process that involved exploration of and experimentation with their laptops and expressed a desire for more time to explore how to use their laptops.

ICT Infrastructure and Support

The provision of infrastructure, particularly computers, has tended to be the focus of ICT policy initiatives with an associated focus on student-computer ratios as an indicator of the success of these policies (Dale, Robertson & Shortis, 2004). Under the laptops scheme schools are required to manage the integration of the laptops into the school environment, including the provision of additional ICT infrastructure and technical support (Ministry of Education, 2003). School technological infrastructure including hardware, software and technical support were identified as a key constraint on teacher use of the laptops. The extent of the variation in infrastructure provision and access amongst teachers within the same department/syndicate and the same school, and between teachers in different schools was a key finding. Teacher focus group and case study commentary indicated that the nature of a school's technological infrastructure was the culmination of various antecedent decisions by school leadership under the Tomorrows' Schools (Lange, 1988) school self-management regime. Schools where ICT had long been a strategic focus tended to have well-developed ICT systems and resources including hardware, software and personnel with the expertise required to provide advice and guidance in the development of school ICT policy and facilities. Staff from these schools indicated that in-school personnel had been able to anticipate some of the demands of the laptops and had planned to address these. At the other end of the continuum, schools that had joined the laptops scheme to 'kick start' ICT developments in the school were working to connect all classrooms and to up skill teachers.

The introduction of laptops prompted further investment in ICT infrastructure in most of the focus group schools. However the focus of this investment was qualitatively different in different schools, consequent on the existing technological infrastructure. It would seem that school technological infrastructure plays a crucial but different role at different times in teacher and school ICT development. Generally, professional development needs were seen as less pressing in schools with a poorly developed infrastructure. In these schools the teacher focus was on the need for school-wide networking. In schools with a more established infrastructure the laptops prompted the purchase of additional ICT resources and, in some cases, ICT professional development. Increased teacher access to ICT/laptops and professional development led to increased demand for suites of computers for curriculum teaching in secondary schools, pods of laptops for sharing in primary schools and for data projectors to be permanently installed in classrooms.

Teachers in interviews made a distinction between easy access and ongoing access to a data projector. Teachers were not prepared to make a commitment to the use electronic resources unless they had reliable, and preferably ongoing, access to a data projector. The time and effort required to access and set up a data projector often exceeded any benefits that teachers anticipated, particularly since they envisaged as ideal the flexible use of the laptop as a tool to respond to student ideas and questions. They recounted how colleagues with reliable access used the laptop-plus-data projector as a 'natural thing'. Schools were slowly acquiring data projectors, albeit not at a rate teachers preferred. Teachers in interviews made a distinction between easy and ongoing access to a data projector. Easy access to other equipment in the classroom also made a difference to the use teachers made of their laptops during lessons. For example, those who had easy access to the Internet and to a scanner, printer, digital camera and/or video cameras were more likely to use their laptops to produce lesson materials and to use the laptop as a teaching tool with students. Laptops have offered teachers a 'portable office' but are more likely to be used routinely when there is reliable and convenient access to both school systems for administrative tasks, in particular, and to peripherals for use in the classroom as a teaching tool.

School Leadership and Support

Senior management leadership emerged as crucial to teacher use of laptops, irrespective of its form. In the initial stages, a leadership decision was required for a school to take part in the TELA scheme. A number of teachers reported their principals had encouraged them to join the scheme. Under the TELA scheme, teachers or their schools pay a portion of the lease for the laptops, the decision about who paid being one that was made by the Board of Trustees with the principal. Some teachers reported that their Board of Trustees saw the laptop as a personal item and were not prepared to fund the lease. Others explained that their Board and principal were actively pursuing a vision for ICT integration and were fully behind the scheme, to the extent of paying the lease costs. Teachers reported that the need to pay the lease cost had impacted on teacher participation in the scheme. Teachers were aware of the financial implications of a Board paying for teacher laptops and appreciated the Board paying some, or all, of the lease. They saw the need to pay as an equity issue for teachers and students. Where teachers within a school or department/syndicate did not have a laptop, or a computer, this limited their involvement in some administrative and management tasks and impeded the development and sharing of electronic lesson materials. Schools and teachers in interest/level groups could not move to fully electronic systems when only some had easy access to a computer/laptop. Teachers considered they should not have to pay for a tool that was increasingly being positioned as central to their work.

Subsequent to a school entering the scheme, school policies and practices determined the incentives and opportunities teachers had to use the laptops. School polices about acceptable use reflect a meld of the TELA scheme requirements and the benefits and opportunities the school envisions for teacher access to a laptop for their exclusive use. Some schools restricted teacher acceptable use of the laptops to school-related tasks; others allowed laptop use for all but inappropriate and objectionable tasks. Schools with a more flexible approach considered all teacher use could contribute to teacher use for professional purposes. In these schools the leadership focus was on reducing any barriers. School expectations for teacher laptop use ranged from the writing of reports, to in-school email communication and digital recording of the attendance register. In 2008, around half of the Year 1 to 3 survey teachers reported they were expected to use their laptop for planning and in classroom teaching. Teachers who were able to list schools expectations for laptop use were more likely to use their laptops more than once a day and for more hours per week. They were also more likely to have received formal professional development in the use of the laptop.

School leadership to develop policy and practice was exercised by different individuals in different schools. These individuals included the principal and/or member of the senior management (deputy principal); a small group whose membership consisted of senior management and teachers with expertise in ICT, and/or enthusiastic individuals. Where the integration of ICT was part of the school strategic plan and supported by senior management and/or the Board of Trustees the introduction of the laptops had been accompanied by careful planning for the integration of the laptops into school systems. Teachers were very appreciative of this and the implicit valuing and support for their efforts in using the laptops. In some schools a lack of ongoing leadership to bring about successful ongoing support for laptop use had led to integration problems. Where schools did not have active senior level leadership for ICT the resulting vacuum was filled, or not, at the department/syndicate level by the leader of these groups and/or by teachers with enthusiasm for and expertise in ICT. In these schools, ICT/laptop use was inconsistent and support for use was generally thought to be poor/inadequate by those interviewed. In sum, it would seem that leadership is important for initiating and sustaining the conditions that support teacher utilization of laptops and for helping teachers extend their use of the laptops. Without a clear vision and senior management level leadership, school-wide development may be haphazard and ad hoc, dependent upon individual capability and interest.

TOWARDS THE THIRD LEVEL OF IMPROVEMENT INFRASTRUCTURE FOR LAPTOP USE

Engelbart's (1992) argues that organizations not only need to focus on those factors that support improvement but also on the factors that enable the on-going improvement of improvement processes. This level of improvement infrastructure focuses on creating an environment in which innovation and improvement is ongoing. Over the last three years of the study we asked teachers to rate the importance of the factors we had identified as influencing their use of their laptop for classroom teaching and learning: leadership support, knowledge sharing and professional development, school technological infrastructure, time and teachers' own confidence. Teachers were then asked to identify the factor they found most important. The goal was to develop an understanding of how the factors operated as a system of influences. Each year, each of the factors was identified as very important by a substantial number of teachers in each of the three cohorts who were asked[1]. School networking and prompt technical assistance were considered to be 'very important' by between two thirds and three quarters of teachers. Confidence and time to experiment were considered to be 'very important' by around two thirds of teachers. Half of teachers considered leadership and professional development support to be 'very important' to their use of the laptop in the classroom. Easy access to equipment meant a lot to an increasing proportion of teachers.

When teachers were asked to identify the *most* important influence on them at the time of the survey[2] over a third rated school technological infrastructure as the most important influence on their laptop use. Likewise, just under a third of teachers gave priority to their opportunity to learn more about how to use their laptop. If those rating 'confidence and understanding' are added to this grouping then around half of the Year 1 to 6 teachers (all those asked) selected factors associated with personal knowledge and expertise as the most important influence on their laptop use in the classroom. A collaborative culture and leadership were rated as most important by only a small proportion of teachers.

Further analysis indicated that these factors were relevant to different teachers in different ways for different tasks. A majority of those who rated themselves as expert users identified technological infrastructure issues (school networking, access to equipment, and technical support) as the most important influence on their laptop use. On the other hand, over a half of intermediate users identified personal growth needs (confidence and understanding, time to experiment, and professional development) as being most important, suggesting that they viewed their own knowledge and expertise as a limit on their laptop use. Likewise, around two thirds of beginners identified professional learning needs as the most important influence on their laptop use. Similarly, focus group discussions across the school levels indicated that for beginners, help to use the laptop, including prompt technical support, is important when they are 'stuck'. With more experienced and knowledgeable users, attention often turns to the development of lesson materials, the knowledge of resources to support this and the skills to make use of these resources. Once teachers are able to prepare multi-sensory materials, it seems that the focus shifts to the need for ongoing access to a data projector and models of how to use ICT for teaching and learning. Competent teachers who have classroom access to a data projector and the Internet were eager for professional development to extend their knowledge and skills. They were interested in opportunities (and training on how to) to share their enthusiasm and expertise with colleagues.

Taken together this data suggests that laptop teachers bring their own experiences, abilities and knowledge to laptop ownership and contextual factors such as leadership, opportunities for professional learning, school technological infrastructure along with the affordances of the laptop itself enable and constrain teacher use. When school leadership values ICT use, and supports and encourages a collaborative culture within a school where teachers feel able, and are supported by an expectation, to share with others they benefit from wider opportunities to learn new ways of doing things. The hardware and software, including the school network and Internet access are readily available to the teacher and they are also supported by reliable technical help, and the school electronic administration practices are in place. This is the system that supports teachers to use their laptops both in and out of the classroom. It is these factors, as a system that support and sustain, and/or inhibit teacher use of laptops and ICTs. Individually, and as a system, they are manifest as enablers and constraints in different ways in different school settings and in different forms at different stages in teacher and school integration of the use of laptops and ICTs. With this support, the laptop teacher uses the laptop and gains confidence and ICT skills, and is thereby able to increase the use of the laptop for tasks that are part of the professional life of a teacher.

The Year 9 to 13 school case studies provided more nuanced evidence of the interplay of these factors, to emphasize that laptops in and of themselves do not catalyze change in school or teacher practices. The role of school technological infrastructure (hardware, software and technical support), teacher access to opportunities for professional learning, school and department leadership and culture for collaboration, along with teacher personal knowledge and expertise as interrelated aspects within an evolutionary process of change, was clearly illustrated by the changes in practice of one of the most ICT proficient secondary school users. Initially, this teacher was converting his lesson materials to electronic format and adding in interactives, images and video clips. He had monopolized one of the school's two data projectors and was using the materials he had developed in most lessons. By the next year, with the support of the school leadership, his classroom had been upgraded to include a ceiling mounted data projector, an interactive whiteboard and reliable access to the Internet. During the interview he demonstrated how he used these tools to project and interactively adapt lesson materials in response to student interests and needs. He had been given a semi-formal role in encouraging and supporting other teachers to use their laptops for teaching purposes. When interviewed in the final year of the secondary school evaluation, this teacher was keen to extend his knowledge of what was possible and was actively seeking out opportunities to do this. His colleagues acknowledged his contribution to the department and school-wide in modelling what was possible and supporting teacher ICT use. In another example of how enabling and inhibiting factors act as a system, the members of the technology department in one school all moved to use ICTs in their teaching and learning over the course of the study. In this case, only one of the three technology teachers accessed a laptop when the TELA scheme was introduced at the school. When his two colleagues saw his enthusiasm and his students' responses they joined the TELA scheme. As a group they lobbied the Board to upgrade the technology suite. The technology classrooms were wired, the staff workroom upgraded and a printer and scanner purchased for their use. The next year, when they were interviewed as a group, they described and demonstrated how they were using their laptops. This included preparation of student instructional materials, accessing resources, student data management and the use of photographs of student work as a tool for formative feedback. One of the teachers was still aiming for this breadth of use. The lead teacher was in the process of finding out how to access further professional development opportunities. The interplay of these factors school-wide was shown clearly by changes in another school. In 2004, only seven teachers at the school had laptops. These teachers tended to work alone. None was making much use of the laptops and they each begrudged having to pay the laptop lease. In 2005 a deputy principal with expertise in and a vision for ICT was appointed to the school. He provided the impetus for change. The Board of Trustees[3] asked him to investigate the introduction of an electronic student absence system. The deputy principal and two other teachers visited another school to see how that school managed this task. They returned and recommended that the school completely upgrade its infrastructure. They argued that the laptops scheme was the most cost effective way to provide teachers with access to a computer. The Board agreed and funded laptops for all the teachers in the school. Subsequently the school became eligible for a government funded

ICT infrastructure upgrade. Teacher, principal and Board attitude towards teacher laptops and ICT use had completely turned around. Those interviewed noted that the Board paying the laptop lease had had a 'huge impact on teacher morale'. Teachers 'were finding the laptops really, really useful' and teacher ICT literacy had improved. Laptops were also proving useful in other school-wide initiatives such as student data management and word-processed student reporting.

CONCLUSION

All institutions face challenges with the integration of information and communication technologies. For schools these challenges have been exacerbated by the tendency for policy initiatives to be hardware-driven without a complementary investment in time and resources to develop teaching and learning. The findings of this study lend support to the contention that any analysis of the impact of information technologies cannot afford to decontextualise it from the wider social and political variables that shape the larger context of schools; a systems analysis is required. Our synthesis of research on teacher laptop use resonates with studies on school improvement, change and teacher support for innovation with ICT (Owston, 2007). It indicates that it is not sufficient to consider professional development, available ICT infrastructure, resources and support, and teacher confidence and expertise in isolation. It is the convergence of teacher confidence and expertise, the professional development they receive, as well as access to reliable ICT resources that supports the integration of the laptops into teachers' professional lives. It is these factors in combination that support and sustain, and/or inhibit teacher use of ICT/laptops. Individually and in combination they are manifest as enablers and constraints in different ways in different school and department settings and in different forms at different stages in teacher, department and school integration of the use of ICT/laptops. Moreover, differences in school technological infrastructure highlight that government policies are not self-sufficient entities. The cultural, material and knowledge/expertise setting for school/teacher response to a particular policy is shaped in part by their response to preceding policies. School ICT infrastructures reflect the intersection over time of national and local school-based policies. The flow on from the differential value placed on ICT by different schools, in part explains current differences in school organizational, technological and personnel/expertise infrastructure. Schools with better-established ICT policies and practices not only had better-developed technological infrastructures, but also greater access to on-site expertise, and thus were better able to anticipate and provide for teacher needs. Enhanced teacher use of the laptops would seem to require access to facilities, professional development, technical support and organizational and administrative systems that support teachers to maximize the affordances of exclusive use of a laptop.

ACKNOWLEDGMENT

The authors wish to acknowledge support from the Ministry of Education for funding the study reported in this article.

REFERENCES

Anderson, R., & Dexter, S. (2000). *School technology leadership: Incidence and impact.* Center for Research on Information Technology and Organizations, University of California Irvine. Available from http://www.crito.uci.edu/tlc/findings/report_6

Cox, M., Preston, C., & Cox, K. (1999, September 2-5). *What factors support or prevent teachers from using ICT in their classrooms?* Paper presented at British Educational Research Association Annual Conference, University of Sussex, Brighton, UK.

Cuban, L. (2001). *Oversold & underused: Computers in the classroom.* Cambridge, MA: Harvard University Press.

Cuban, L., Kirkpatrick, H., & Peck, C. (2001). High access and low use of technology in high school classrooms: Explaining the apparent paradox. *American Educational Research Journal, 38*(4), 813–834. doi:10.3102/00028312038004813

Cunningham, M., Kerr, K., McEune, R., Smith, P., & Harris, S. (2003). *Laptops for teachers: An evaluation of the first year of the initiative (ICT in Schools Research and Evaluation Series No. 19).* Becta/DfES

Dale, R., Robertson, S., & Shortis, T. (2004). 'You can't not go with the technological flow, can you?': Constructing 'ICT' and 'teaching and learning.'. *Journal of Computer Assisted Learning, 20*, 456–470. doi:10.1111/j.1365-2729.2004.00103.x

Engelbart, D. (1992). *Toward High-Performance Organizations: A Strategic Role for Groupware.* The Bootstrap Institute. Retrieved from http://www.bootstrap.org

Falba, C., Grove, K., Anderson, D., & Putney, L. (2001). Benefits of laptop computers for elementary teachers. *Journal of Research on Technology in Education, 33*(5), 105–114.

Fullan, M. (2001). *Leading in a culture of change.* San Francisco: Jossey-Bass.

Hennessy, S., Ruthven, K., & Brindley, S. (2004). Teacher perspectives on integrating ICT into subject teaching: Commitment, constraints caution and change. *Journal of Curriculum Studies, 37*(2), 155–192. doi:10.1080/0022027032000276961

Jones, A. (2004). *A review of the research literatures on barriers to the uptake of ICT by teachers.* Retrieved from http://www.becta.org.uk/page_documents/research/barriers.pdf

Lange, D. (1988). *Tomorrow's Schools: The reform of education administration in New Zealand.* Wellington, New Zealand: The Government Printer.

Loveless, A., Devoogd, G., & Bohlin, R. (2001). Something old, something new….: is pedagogy affected by ICT? In Loveless, A., & Ellis, V. (Eds.), *ICT, pedagogy and the curriculum* (pp. 63–83). London: Routledge/Falmer.

McGee, C., Jones, A., Bishop, R., Cowie, B., Hill, M., Miller, T., et al. MacKenzie, K. (2002). *Teachers' Experiences in Implementing the New Zealand National Curriculum.* Wellington, New Zealand: Ministry of Education.

Means, B., Roschelle, J., Penuel, W., Sabelli, N., & Haertel, J. (2003). Technology's contribution to teaching and policy: Efficiency, standardisation, or transformation? *Review of Educational Research, 27*, 159–182. doi:10.3102/0091732X027001159

Ministry of Education. (2003). *The Digital Horizons. Laptops for Teachers Scheme.* Wellington, New Zealand: Learning Media.

Moses, P., Khambari, M., & Luan, W. (2008). Laptop use and its antecedents among educators: A review of the literature. *European Journal of Soil Science, 7*(1), 104–114.

Owston, R. (2007). Contextual factors that sustain innovative pedagogical practice using technology: An international study. *Journal of Educational Change, 8*, 61–77. doi:10.1007/s10833-006-9006-6

Phillips, R., Bailey, M., Fisher, T., & Harrison, C. (1999). Questioning teachers about their use of portable computers. *Journal of Computer Assisted Learning, 15*, 149–161. doi:10.1046/j.1365-2729.1999.152087.x

Rudd, P. (2001, September 20). *School Improvement through ICT: The Case of England.* Paper presented at the CIDREE Seminar: The Use of ICT in Supporting Effective Learning and Teaching. Scottish Education and Teaching Technology Show, SECC, Glasgow, Scotland.

Selwyn, N. (1999). Why the computer is not dominating schools: A failure of policy or a failure of practice? *Cambridge Journal of Education, 29*(1), 77–91. doi:10.1080/0305764990290106

Selwyn, N., & Facer, K. (2007). *Beyond the digital divide: Rethinking digital inclusion for the 21st century.* London, United Kingdom: Futurelab.

Windschitl, M., & Sahl, K. (2002). Tracing teachers' use of technology in a laptop computer school: The interplay of teacher beliefs, social dynamics, and institutional culture. *American Educational Research Journal, 39*(1), 165–205. doi:10.3102/00028312039001165

Zhao, Y., & Frank, K. (2003). Factors affecting technology uses in schools: An ecological perspective. *American Educational Research Journal, 40*(4), 807–840. doi:10.3102/00028312040004807

Zhao, Y., Pugh, K., Sheldon, S., & Byers, J. (2002). Conditions for classroom innovation. *Teachers College Record, 104*(3), 482–515. doi:10.1111/1467-9620.00170

KEY TERMS AND DEFINITIONS

Evaluation: Elucidating and understanding the internal dynamics and merit of how a program, organization, or relationship operates.

ICT Integration: Incorporation of ICT into classroom teaching and learning.

Improvement Infrastructure: A system that incorporates consideration of how to promote, sustain and accelerate improvement.

Laptop: A small personal computer that is light enough to be operated on the user's lap.

Professional Development: Knowledge and skill growth for both personal development and career advancement. Professional development encompasses all types of facilitated learning opportunities, ranging from college degrees to formal coursework, conferences and informal learning opportunities situated in practice.

School Leadership: The person or group of people who lead, rule and inspire others in a school e.g. principal, deputy principal, deans.

Systems Analysis: Examination of the separate elements and of the combination of these elements as a functioning entity.

Technological Infrastructure: ICT support that includes network systems, hardware, software, and technical support.

ENDNOTES

1 This question was asked in 2006, 2007 and 2008 and therefore only Years 7-8, Years 4-6 and Years 1-3 teachers responded to it

2 This question was asked in 2006, 2007 and 2008 and therefore only Years 7-8, Years 4-6 and Years 1-3 teachers responded to it

3 A Board of Trustees includes parent elected members, the principal and a staff and student representative. The Board is responsible for school governance which encompasses their appointing staff and managing all school budget matters with the exception of staff salaries.

Chapter 4
Perceptions of Students and Teachers about the Use of E-Learning / Sharing Portal in Educational Activities

Azad Isik
Cybersoft Information Technologies Ltd. Co., Turkey

Cengiz S. Askun
Middle East Technical University, Turkey

M. Yasar Ozden
Middle East Technical University, Turkey

ABSTRACT

This study examined the perceptions of the students and the teachers of METU Development Foundation Schools about the use of e-learning / sharing portal technology in their educational activities. Their perceptions were investigated in terms of three aspects: effects of the use of this technology on their perceived motivation, the perceived usefulness, and the perceived ease of use of this technology. A central server was installed for setting up an e-learning / sharing portal environment. Microsoft SharePoint, which is a Sharing Portal Software, was used to access to the central server. The study was conducted in the form of action research. The data were collected from 6th and 7th grade students by using a questionnaire. In addition to the questionnaire with students, interviews were conducted with the teachers. Descriptive statistics, frequency distributions, and descriptive analysis methods were used to analyze the results. The findings of the study indicated that the students and the teachers perceived that e-learning / sharing portal technology is a useful and easy to use technology. It was found out that the students and the teachers are satisfied with advantages of the use of this new technology in their learning environment. Furthermore, the teachers and the students stated that using the system affected students' perceived motivation towards the educational activities positively.

DOI: 10.4018/978-1-61692-854-4.ch004

INTRODUCTION

Computers have been integrated into every part of our daily routine and education is inevitably one of those areas. The powerful features of computers make them become an important instructional technology tool. Computers could not be used effectively before the Internet because they lacked interconnection. Computers' significance, for various educational purposes both face-to-face and distance, improved after the introduction of the Internet. The use of the Internet as an instructional tool forced educators to rethink their ways of teaching and administering courses (Longe, Ogege, et al., 2005).

The World Wide Web (WWW) made e-learning a reality by the use of various multimedia elements such as images, sounds, animations, interactions, and communication technologies such as e-mail and instant messaging tools. The worldwide e-learning industry is estimated to be worth over €38 billion according to conservative estimates; even though in the European Union only about 20% of e-learning products are produced within the common-market. In 2006 nearly 3.5 million students were participating in online learning at institutions ofhigher education in the United States (Allen & Seaman, 2008). A range of new terms such as e-learning, online learning and virtual learning are being used interchangeably. The terms virtual learning or online learning now describe a time-independent and place-independent educational activity in an online learning environment. Time and place independent means that teachers and students are separated by time or space, and course content is delivered through some kind of course management system. Course management systems support the delivery of various multimedia resources and textual materials whenever and wherever it is convenient for them.

Many research studies have demonstrated that a student's active involvement in the learning process enhances learning. This process is often referred to as active learning (Benek-Rivera & Mathews, 2004). Active learning can be defined as "instructional activities involving students in doing things and thinking about what they are doing" (Bonwell & Eisen, 1991). Interactive instruction or "learning by doing" has been found to result in positive learning outcomes (Picciano, 2002). Because many new technologies and Web-based activities are interactive, online coursework has a potential to create environments where students actively engage with materials, learn by doing, and refine their understanding as they build new knowledge (Johnston, Killion et al. 2005). When students actively participate in knowledge construction working with ideas becomes more important than covering the curriculum (Scardamalia 2002).

Computer systems provide a lot of advantages for their users, but they cannot improve performance if they are not used (Davis, Bagozzi et al. 1989). According to the Technology Acceptance Model (TAM), whether an information system is used or not is mostly determined by its perceived usefulness and the perceived ease of use (Gefen and Keil 1998). Davis (1989), states that "people tend to use or not to use an application to the extent they believe it will help them perform their job better." Davis (1989) also notes that the TAM, based on perceived usefulness, perceived ease of use, and attitude, has been widely used to predict user acceptance and use.

As a virtual learning environment (VLE), an e-learning / sharing portal (Weller 2007) is a software system designed to support teaching and learning. It facilitates the e-learning process over the Internet and typically provides tools such as those for assessment, communication, uploading of content, return of student's work, administration of student groups, questionnaires, tracking tools, wikis, blogs, chats, forums, etc. There are various names used to identify e-learning systems: learning management system (LMS), course management system (CMS), learning content management system (LCMS), managed learning environment (MLE), learning support system (LSS), learning platform (LP) or e-learning sharing portal (ELSP). Basically, it is a system that delivers education via computer-mediated communication (CMC) or online education (Weller 2007). Students and teachers would benefit from the advantages of virtual courses and virtual programs. Teachers and student can meet in an online learning environment where they are separated by time and/or space and using a carefully designed course management system they can interact at their own pace.

The purpose of the study was to investigate the effects of the integration of an e-learning system developed by the authors in an elementary school setting. Running on Internet Information Server (IIS), Microsoft's Web server application that comes with recent Windows server and workstation operating systems, the e-learning system was developed using Microsoft's SharePoint Portal Services and SharePoint Learning Kit that can be downloaded free from Microsoft's Web site. The study aims to investigate the perceptions of 6th and 7th grade students and their teachers about the use of this portal technology in educational activities. The portal application functions as an e-learning / sharing portal. Investigated were the effects of this portal on students' perceived motivation, students' perceptions and their teacher's perceptions about the ease of use and usefulness of the portal. The teachers were asked during the study about the advantages and disadvantages of this technology as well as their suggestions for its use. The specific research questions are

1. How do students perceive the use of the e-learning / sharing portal technology in terms of
   a. Its effects on their perceived motivation towards the educational activities?
   b. Its usefulness?
   c. Its ease of use?
2. How do teachers in a private elementary school perceive the use of the e-learning / sharing portal technology in terms of
   a. Its effects on students' perceived motivation towards the educational activities?
   b. Its usefulness?
   c. Its ease of use?
3. What do teachers think about the advantages and disadvantages of the use of the e-learning / sharing portal technology?

METHOD

The current study investigated the perceptions of students and teachers in a private elementary school about the use of e-learning / sharing portal technology in their educational activities. The study uses components of the case studies by action research (Erginel-Sanal 2006) and focuses on a single case: e-learning / sharing portal application in educational activities that was experienced by students and teachers of a private elementary school. Therefore, a deep understanding of the perceptions of the students and the teachers participated in the study can be achieved. The first author of this study teaches in the participating school. He is a participant in the study and added his reflections through his experiences.

This research study is implemented in a private elementary school that takes online learning serious. The school has carried out a lot of projects making use of e-learning methods. However, the teachers in the school had problems with sharing online resources even among themselves. Online communication is also a problematic area. While teachers can use e-mail as a communication tool, they cannot make use of e-mail when it comes to making announcements to students. Teachers could not give online assignments to students thus, they were faced with the arduous task of correcting the assignments using pen and paper technology. Knowing all these problems, the third author of the study offered the school administration the use of an e-learning / sharing portal as a remedy to these problems.

A case is a specific, unique, and integrated system which is bounded to contextual factors. Case study is described to be "the process of learning about the case and the product of our learning" (Stake 1994). The rich and detailed data obtained from case studies enable the researcher to understand the phenomenon in question in great depth (Patton 1987). Case study is regarded as a complex design strategy, and it investigates the phenomenon in its real life context (Robson 2002). It involves multiple methods of in-depth inquiry, such as interviews, observations, and document analysis, in which personal interactions take place between researcher and participants over an extended period of time (Patton 1987; Bogdan and Biklen 1998).

The most appropriate way to investigate in this study was the method of integrating case study by action research, allowing the researcher to work directly with the participants in the development of the indicators of engagement. Action research engages researchers, teachers and students "in a collaborative process of critical inquiry into problems of social practice in a learning context" (Argyris, Putnam et al. 1985).

The term "action research" was first employed by Lewin referring to it "as a way of learning about organizations through trying to change them" (cited in Robson 2002). Action research is conducted by employees such as school directors, teachers, educational specialists or employees of any kind of institution such as engineers, managers, planners or human resource specialists. Action research requires systematic data collection and analysis to understand and solve an existing problem or a problem that appeared during the implementation of research (Yildirim and Simsek 2006).

Martler (2008) describes action research as a practical tool for improvement where schools or classrooms are a laboratory and as a cyclical and iterative process, not a linear one, comprised of four stages: planning, acting, development, and reflection. Following the stages of action research approach, the study started with the planning stage where the problems were identified and a research plan was developed. During the acting stage, finding a solution to all identified problems, all features of the e-learning / sharing portal were implemented: Document sharing feature, communication tools, announcement system, and assignment and homework features were all used by the participants of the study. At this point, the data was collected and analyzed by quantitative and qualitative methods. Concurrent with the data collection process an action plan was prepared in the Development Stage. In the Reflection Stage the perceptions of the students and the teachers about the use of e-learning / sharing portal technology in educational activities was declared. All the stages of action research, listed in Figure 1 are followed up in this way by the researcher.

Data Collection

Quantitative methods were used to gather and analyze students' perceptions about the use of the e-learning / sharing portal in their educational activities. One of the main sources of data was the student perception questionnaire. The questionnaire was used to examine the perceptions of students about the use of E-Learning / Sharing Portal in terms of its effects on their perceived motivation, its usefulness, and its ease of use.

Qualitative methods were also used to gather teacher's perceptions. Informal structured interviews were conducted with the teachers to collect information about their perceptions on the use of E-Learning / Sharing Portal. Moreover, they were asked about its pros and cons as well as their suggestions.

Role of the First Author

As a participant of the study and as a teacher of the school, the first author assumed a dual role. Within this framework, he paid particular attention to helping the teachers and students at every level of the implementation. At the same time, he aimed

Figure 1. Stages of an action research

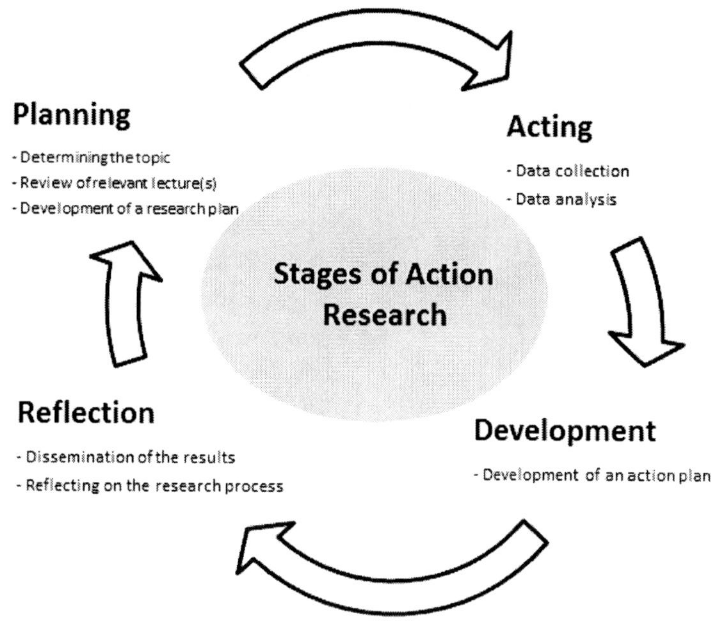

to collect data from multiple sources utilizing multiple methods of data collection. Being among the research participants enabled the first author to be a natural part of the research and to act as a source of data. This situation provides researchers with direct access to data sources and leads to obtaining insight into the phenomenon as well as understanding and interpreting it effectively (Yildirim and Simsek 2001).

As a researcher who was involved in participatory action research, he had an opportunity to experience the environment with the participants which enabled him to obtain an insider's view on the phenomenon (Patton 1987). He interacted with the participants for 6 months which allowed him to carry out systematic data collection and to become aware of the realities of the setting in which the study was conducted. The challenge of being an observer and participant provided him with an opportunity to understand the experience as an insider while describing the experience for outsiders (Patton 1987).

This close and collaborative relationship between the first author and the research participants, while being central to the study, bears potential threats to the reliability of the research and (Robson 2002), he took various actions in order to ensure and enhance the reliability.

Participants of the Study

The study was carried out in a private elementary school and it took about 6 months. The participants were 200, 6th and 7th grade students and 6 teachers. The participants used the applications during 2007-2008 school year. Initially there were 345 students involved in the activities but only 200 of them responded to the *Students' Perceptions about the E-Learning / Sharing Portal Questionnaire* (SPELSP-Q). As seen on Table 1, 115 (57.5%) of the participants were male and 85 (42.5%) of them were female.

Initially there were 26 teachers that participated in the study who used the e-learning / sharing portal applications, but only 6 of them were

Table 1. Participants of the study

	Gender			
	Male		Female	
	N	%	N	%
Participants	115	57.5	85	42.5

interviewed. This was due to the fact that only 6 of them worked on the development and experienced every feature of the e-learning / sharing portal. While the teachers on the development team were technology adopters and innovation developers and they worked on every detail of setting up the system, the other teachers worked only on the implementation of the ready-made materials. The development team was comprised of teachers from different subject areas, a mathematics teacher, two science teachers, a social sciences teacher, a Turkish teacher, and a computer teacher. Although one of the science teachers was not on the development team, but worked for the e-learning applications much more than the non-member teachers, she was included in the study. The first author was also on the development team and experienced personally every part of the action stages. He expressed his perceptions about the system as a teacher as well. Table 2 shows certain characteristics of the teachers participated in the study.

As seen in Table 2, the teachers have been working at METU Development Foundation Schools, a private K-12 school, for at least 3 years. Two of the teachers are male. 4 of them are female. All the teachers except the computer teacher have 6-month experience with e-learning / sharing portal systems did not have any experience with other e-learning systems.

The Study

Six computer literate teachers were selected to participate in the study and comprise the development team. One volunteering teacher from each of the following departments was selected: math, science, social studies, Turkish, and computer. The portal was designed with the help of the strategies developed by Ozden (2002). A screenshot of the e-learning/sharing portal is given in Figure 2.

Authors of the study were on the team as coordinating members. The team's first task was to learn how to use the portal, including how to prepare online activities. Then the next task was to teach other teachers in the school. Teachers were taught how to use the portal. Tasks taught included:

- Log into the system
- Manage user account information such as changing a password or adding a photo
- Create a new folder, upload and share documents
- Make use of tasks and calendar sections of the portal
- View, edit, or delete a discussion; manage permissions in the discussion
- Have access to other systems user's or student's information
- Handle announcements
- Manage a course syllabus
- Assign homework

Table 2. Characteristics of teachers

Questions	Math Teacher	Science Teacher (member of the team)	Science Teacher (worker of the system)	Social Sciences Teacher	Turkish Teacher	Computer Teacher (Researcher)
Number of years working as a teacher in the school	5 years	9 years	8 years	4 years	3 years	14 years

Figure 2. A screenshot of the default page, administrator's view

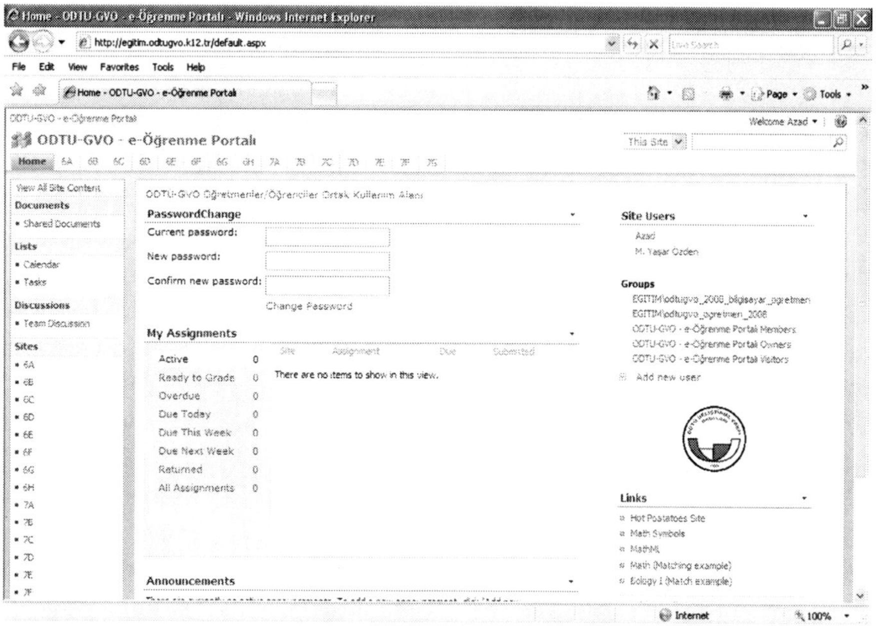

- Collect and grade assignments
- Give feedback

Teachers were trained how to prepare interactive Web-based teaching exercises; how to create interactive multiple choice, short answer, jumbled-sentence, crossword, matching/ordering, and gap fill exercises; and to integrate a Microsoft Office application to the activities.

Teachers of the development team began experiencing the portal in a real-life setting after the seminars on the use of the portal. They first started training other teachers and the students on the use of the portal starting with a short introduction. They later assign the other teachers and the students their user IDs and passwords. Students were given a trial quiz composed of multiple choice questions on computer hardware after receiving their login information. Several other quizzes were administered by other teachers on various topics such as math, science and social studies. After the successful experiences with the quizzes more complex activities were uploaded into the portal. Turkish teachers, for example, assigned essay writing and a PowerPoint presentation. As the students and the teachers got used to the applications delivered on the system, the demand and thus the usage statistics of the portal increased. The portal was used actively for 4 months by all teachers and students. The development team used it for 6 months.

At the end of the action stage of the study members of the development team were interviewed to get their perceptions about the usefulness, ease of use, advantages and disadvantages of the system. The perception questionnaire was also administered to reflect students' ideas.

Data Collection Instruments and Analysis

The study made use of two data collection instruments. To collect students' perceptions about the e-learning / sharing portal, *Students' Perceptions about the E-Learning / Sharing Portal Questionnaire (SPELSP Q)* was used while a structured interview protocol were employed to gather teachers' perceptions about the e-learning / sharing portal.

Students' Perceptions about the E-Learning / Sharing Portal Questionnaire (SPELSP-Q)

SPELSP-Q is the main instrument to collect students' perceptions about the use of E-Learning / Sharing Portal. Although originally it was developed (Tursak 2007) in English, a revised Turkish version was administered because of students' low English understanding levels. The questionnaire has five subsections namely *Self-Reported Computer Competency, Self-Reported E-learning Experience, Students' Perceived Motivation towards the Educational Activities, Perceived Usefulness, and Perceived Ease of* Use. The Turkish version of the questionnaire was first examined by one test and nine subject area experts from the elementary school's measurement and evaluation center for its accuracy, clarity and validity. There were several feedbacks on the number of questions, incompatibility of the directions and the questions, and repeating phrases in perception questions. After all these expert suggestions were satisfied by making necessary changes, the questionnaire was administered online via the portal and the collected data were entered into SPSS 10.0 for the analysis. Frequencies, percentages, means and standard deviations were calculated and once the data is collected and analyzed, the Cronbach's Alpha was found to be as 0.892. As Garson (2007) indicated, an alpha value of 0.892 is in a range that is widely accepted in social sciences. Number of questions and Cronbach's Alpha values for each construct are listed in Table 3.

Structured Interview Protocol

Another data collection instrument was a structured interview protocol to obtain teachers' perceptions about the use of E-Learning / Sharing Portal. Expert feedback and suggestions were also solicited for the questions in the protocol and they are revised accordingly. The protocol included some warm up questions before main questions before the main questions. Teachers were also asked for their permission to tape record the interview.

For the analysis of the interview data, descriptive analysis method was used (Yildirim and Simsek 2006). The method consists of four steps: Preparing a framework for descriptive analysis, processing data according to thematic framework, defining findings, and interpreting the findings. Accordingly, the data obtained was summarized and interpreted by using a pre-defined theme.

Preparing a Framework for Descriptive Analysis

Before preparing the framework of the interview, the research questions were examined deeply. The research questions were all related with the students' and the teachers' perceptions of the e-learning / sharing portal. Each part of the research questions was integrated into the framework one by one.

First, the framework was prepared to examine the perceptions of the teachers about the effects of students use of e-learning/sharing portal on their perceived motivation towards educational activities. Interest and enjoyment sub-factors were added to the first part of the framework. Perceived competence, willingness and participation sub-

Table 3. Students' perception questionnaire reliability statistics

	Number of Items	**Cronbach's Alpha**
Self-Reported Computer Competency	7	.804
Self-Reported E-learning Experience	4	.753
Students' Perceived Motivation towards the Educational Activities	9	.777
Perceived Usefulness	10	.787
Perceived Ease of Use	8	.689
Overall	**27**	**.892**

factors were later integrated into the structure of the framework.

Then, the perceived usefulness factor was integrated into the framework to get the teachers' perception on whether or not the use of the portal makes students work quicker, increase their performance and productivity or their job easier. A factor was added to the framework to examine how teachers perceive the portal as easily used by students or not and if they acquire skills. How teachers perceive the advantages and disadvantages of the portal is included in the framework next. Finally, a section requesting their suggestion about the use of the portal was added into the framework.

Processing Data According to Thematic Framework

Keeping the framework structure in mind, the applications were carried out by the teachers and students. The data was collected by the interview guide. All 6 teachers were interviewed according to the structured framework. The data was collected in the form of an audio recording.

Defining Findings

The records were converted to written material. Recorded written materials were defined according to the structured framework. Collected data were put into proper sub-factors one by one. The findings were added to the result part of this study.

Interpreting Findings

All the interviewees' perceptions analysis were put together under related sections, after that the sections were interpreted according to findings. General interpretations were made according to the subjects of the subsections of the framework. Common points were evaluated and added to the conclusion part of the study.

RESULTS

Students' Computer Competency Levels

Section 1 of the SPELSP-Q involves questions that ask students about their self-reported computer competencies. The responses are summarized in Table 4. As shown in the table, most of the students reported themselves as expert in the applications listed except online forums, blogs, and spreadsheet. 76% of the students described their competencies in e-learning as either expert or intermediate level.

Self-Reported E-Learning Background

In section 2 of the SPELSP-Q, students were asked about their experiences in online and Web-supported learning environments. According to the results shown in Table 5, 91.5% of the participants used the Internet in their courses, and 57% of them had taken at least one online or web-supported course before this study. Similarly 60.5% of the participants reported that they had used an e-learning / sharing portal in their courses before the study.

Students' Self Reported Usage

Table 6 shows students' frequency of use of the e-learning / sharing portal during the study. Only 11.5% of the participants reported that they never used it. About one-third of the participants reported that they used it more than three times a week while 56% reported just once a week.

Students' Perceptions

Students' perceptions about the use of e-learning / sharing portal were examined under three headings: Effects of the use of this technology and students' perceived motivation towards their

Table 4. Statistics of students' self-reported computer competencies

	Not Used		Beginner		Intermediate		Expert	
	N	%	N	%	N	%	N	%
Web browsers	10	5	14	7	67	33.5	109	54.5
Search Engines	3	1.5	9	4.5	40	20	148	74
E-mail	5	2.5	14	7	36	18	145	72.5
Online Forums & Blogs	43	21.5	34	17	68	34	55	27.5
Online Chat Applications	8	4	18	9	41	20.5	133	66.5
Word Processing Applications	4	2	2	1	33	16.5	161	80.5
Spreadsheet Applications	46	23	40	20	61	30.5	53	26.5
Presentation Applications	2	1	4	2	26	13	168	84
E-Learning Applications	21	10.5	27	13.5	72	36	80	40

educational activities, perceived usefulness and perceived ease of use. In this section there were 27 5-point Likert-type items ranging from strongly disagree to strongly agree.

Perceived Motivation towards their Educational Activities

Students' perceptions about the effects of their use of E-Learning/Sharing Portal on their motivation towards their educational activities were investigated by the use of 9 questions grouped in 4 indicator factors. Indicator factors were Interest / Enjoyment, Perceived Competence, Willingness and Participation.

Table 7 reports the results of the perceived motivation towards educational activities grouped under 4 indicator factors. In the Interest / Enjoyment group there were three statements: *e-learning / sharing portal applications increased my interest on education activities*, *e-learning / sharing portal applications made our educational activities enjoyable*, and *e-learning / sharing portal applications made our educational activities boring* (reverse coded). Responses to these statements indicated that 68.13% of participants indicated that they agree or strongly agree with the statements in this group while 19.75% of them indicated neutral and 12.13% reported negative perception. According to the results regarding the perceived competence, 64.0% of the participants responded positively, 12.5% negatively while 23.5% stated they were neutral. Similar responses were obtained for the willingness and participation factors as well as can be seen from the Table 7.

Students' Perceptions on Usefulness

Students' perceptions on the usefulness of the e-learning / sharing portal were investigated by six

Table 5. Statistics of students' self-reported experiences

	Yes		No	
	N	%	N	%
Have you ever taken any web-supported or online course before this semester?	114	57	86	43
Have you ever used the Internet for your course studies before this semester?	183	91.5	17	8.5
Have you ever used an e-learning/sharing portal applicationin your previous courses? *(Examples: Applications that provide sharing documents, forums, chats, on-line exams etc.)*	121	60.5	79	39.5

Table 6. "How frequently did you use E-Learning/ Sharing Portal in your educational activities?"

	N	%
Never	23	11.5
once in a week	112	56
three times in a week	48	24
Everyday	12	6
More than one in a day	5	2.5
Total	**200**	**100.0**

factors reported in Perceived Usefulness construct of Technology Acceptance Model developed by Davis (1989). These six factors were *work more quickly*, *job performance*, *increase productivity*, *effectiveness*, *makes job easier*, and *useful*. Statistics obtained from the statements within this group are summarized in Table 8.

The perceived usefulness subscale reports that overall two-thirds of the participants indicated positive responses while about 15% responded negatively and about 20% indicated that they are neutral (Table 8).

Students' Perceptions about Ease of Use

Students' perceptions on the ease of use of the e-learning / sharing portal were examined by four factors taken from perceived usefulness construct of Technology Acceptance Model (Davis 1989). These factors were *easy to learn, easy to use, easy to become skillful*, and *clear & understandable*.

Table 7. Descriptive statistics of perceived motivation

	SD		D		N		A		SA		Mean	Std. Dev.
	N	%	N	%	N	%	N	%	N	%		
Interest / Enjoyment	8.5	4.25	15.75	7.88	39.5	19.75	54	27	82.25	41.13	3.496	1.1321
Perceived Competence	11	5.5	14	7	47	23.5	70	35	58	29	3.75	1.1152
Willingness	15.7	7.8	16.7	8.3	48.0	24.0	53.3	26.7	66.3	33.2	3.213	1.231
Participation	16.0	8.0	21.0	10.5	50.0	25.0	66.0	33.0	47.0	23.5	3.535	1.142
Overall	**12.8**	**6.4**	**16.9**	**8.4**	**46.1**	**23.1**	**60.8**	**30.4**	**63.4**	**31.7**	**3.499**	**1.155**

Table 8. Descriptive statistics for sub-factors of perceived usefulness

	SD		D		N		A		SA		Mean	Std. Dev.
	N	%	N	%	N	%	N	%	N	%		
Work more quickly	14.0	7.0	17.5	8.8	41.5	20.8	67.0	33.5	60.0	30.0	3.208	1.178
Job performance	12	6	14.5	7.25	39	19.5	66.5	33.25	68	34	3.320	1.141
Increase productivity	8	4.0	15	7.5	56	28.0	66	33.0	55	27.5	3.725	1.070
Effectiveness	18	9	18	9	43	21.5	42	21	79	39.5	3.270	1.310
Makes job easier	13	6.5	16	8.0	27	13.5	65	32.5	79	39.5	3.905	1.197
Useful	14.0	7.0	11.7	5.8	42.0	21.0	66.0	33.0	66.3	33.2	3.800	1.161
Overall	**13.2**	**6.6**	**15.5**	**7.7**	**41.4**	**20.7**	**62.1**	**31.0**	**67.9**	**34.0**	**3.511**	**1.176**

Statistics obtained from the statements within this group are summarized in Table 9.

Similar to the results of perceived usefulness of the e-learning / sharing portal, more than two-thirds of the participants responded positively on all sub-factors of this construct. Overall 18.1% of the participants responded neutral and only about 10% responded negatively (Table 9).

Characteristics of the Teachers

Some descriptives about the teachers who participated in the study should be given before going into the details of their perceptions. As it is seen in Table 10, the least experienced teacher in the school was the Turkish teacher and she has worked for three years in the school. On the other hand, the science teacher has worked for 9 years and computer teacher has worked 14 years in the school. The computer teacher used many different e-learning / sharing portals during and after her Master of Science studies. None of the other teachers used an e-learning / sharing portal before. The computer teacher reported that she found the e-learning / sharing portal very beneficial.

The Teachers' Perceptions

The Teachers' perceptions about the use of e-learning / Sharing Portal were investigated by the use of interviews. Six interviews were conducted with the teachers from a private elementary school. Interview data were analyzed using the descriptive analysis approach described by Yildirim and Simsek (2006). A conceptual framework was created following the descriptive analysis approach (Table 11).

The Teachers' Perceptions about the Effects of the Use of E-Learning / Sharing Portal Technology on Students' Perceived Motivation towards Educational Activities

To investigate the effects of the use of this technology on students' perceived motivation towards educational activities, teachers were asked "How did the use of this technology effect the motivation of the students towards their educational activities? Positively, negatively or not effected?" Answers from all teachers were positive. To get detailed indicators of their observations, they were asked to explain the indicators which they observed to support their opinions. They added following observations as indicators;

- Mathematics Teacher: First of all, students use computers too much for that reason we have to use the tool in our educational activities too. This may create diversity and may increase our learning tools. When we use this technology in education I can say that the students are being motivated more than classical ways.

Table 9. Descriptive statistics for sub-factors of perceived ease of use

	SD		D		N		A		SA		Mean	Std. Dev.
	N	%	N	%	N	%	N	%	N	%		
Easy to Learn	8.5	4.25	14.5	7.25	30	15	47	23.5	100	50	3.578	1.147
Easy to Use	13	6.5	11	5.5	25	12.5	64	32.0	87	43.5	4.005	1.171
Easy to Become Skillful	13	6.5	5	2.5	42	21.0	49	24.5	91	45.5	4.000	1.165
Clear & Understand-able	11.5	5.8	9.5	4.8	48.0	24.0	65.0	32.5	66.0	33.0	3.823	1.109
Overall	**11.5**	**5.8**	**10.0**	**5.0**	**36.3**	**18.1**	**56.3**	**28.1**	**86.0**	**43.0**	**3.851**	**1.148**

Table 10. Characteristics of teachers

Questions	Math Teacher	Science Teacher	Social Sciences Teacher	Science Teacher	Turkish Teacher	Computer Teacher
How long have you been working as a teacher in METU Development Foundation Schools?	5 years	9 years	4 years	8 years	3 years	14 years
How long have you been working with E-Learning/Sharing Portal Applications?	0.5 years	0.5 years	0.5 years	0.5 years	0.5 years	8 years
Have you ever used any E-Learning/Sharing Portal before?	No	No	No	No	No	Yes
What was your purpose when using E-Learning/Sharing Portal?	-	-	-	-	-	I used an e-learning / sharing portal application in Distance Learning Courses of my Master Program; I used it for forums, on-line/homework and announcements.
Did you find it beneficial?	-	-	-	-	-	I found it very beneficial.

- Science Teacher 1: I think that, the system effected students perceived motivations positively, because I observed that the students who couldn't finish the application insisted on finishing the projects at their home. It is very difficult to make them do some in class activities at their home. Furthermore, I can say that they are concerned about the system as I inferred from their involved questions.
- Social studies Teacher: Students already have the ability to learn by the help of an electronic environment; I think that they did the activities pleasantly without facing with any negative challenges.
- Turkish Teacher: I think the share portal increased the working student's perceived motivations, but had no effect on non-working student's perceived motivations. No effects can motivate non-working students.
- Computer Teacher: Its affect was positive. The students are very interested in technology and we used their enthusiasm. Because they admire technology, this system increased their participation. Whatever you

Table 11. Conceptual framework for interview data analysis

1. Effects of the use of E-Learning/Sharing Portal Technology on Students' Perceived Motivation towards Educational Activities
a. Interest / Enjoyment
b. Perceived Competence
c. Willingness
d. Participation
2. Perceived Usefulness
a. Work more quickly
b. Job performance
c. Increase productivity
d. Effectiveness
e. Make job easier
f. Overall Usefulness
3. Perceived Ease of Use
a. Easy to Learn
b. Easy to become skillful
c. Clear & Understandable Interfaces
d. Overall Easy to Use
4. Advantages and Disadvantages
5. Suggestions

present on this system the students love it and they want to work.

- Science Teacher 2: I think it affected (the students) in a positive way. First of all the students are highly interested in such activities. They get excited when they hear that they are going to do computer based projects. They are very willing to come to computer laboratories. I observed the same with SharePoint applications. I've seen that some of the students worked more enthusiastically than usual when I gave homework on this system. Moreover, some of them asked me if I could send them more homework.

The first predefined indicator for perceived motivation was "Interest / Enjoyment." To investigate the teacher's perceptions about this factor, they were asked two questions: one for student's interests and one for enjoyment by the use of E-Learning / Sharing Portal. The first question was, "Have you observed that the use of the technology has increased students' interest to their educational activities?" The teachers stated that the use of this technology absolutely increased students' interest to the learning activities. Excerpts from some of the teacher's interviews are as follows:

- Science Teacher 1: The system increased the interest of the students; however using the system continuously in every lesson may decrease it.
- Social Sciences Teacher: They were interested in the applications we made, so I think that it increased the interest of the students.
- Science Teacher 2: Yes it increased. The students of this age are already very keen on working with computers. I've observed the same with SharePoint applications

On the enjoyment factor, the question "Have you observed that the use of the technology has increased students' enjoyment in their educational activities?" was asked. Teachers' responses were positive indicating that students enjoyed the activities.

The teachers also stated positive comments for the second predefined indicator for perceived motivation in the framework, *perceived competence* and they were asked if *they had observed that the use of the technology has increased students' satisfaction about their educational activities.*

The third indicator was *willingness* and to examine this indicator, teachers were asked if they have had observed that the use of the technology has increased students' willingness about their educational activities. Positive remarks followed the question. However Science Teacher 1 stated that she could not make observation about out of class activities. The teacher stated the following observations:

Final indicator for perceived motivation was the *participation* and teachers were asked two questions. One was about the change of students' participation and the other was about the change in their study time on educational activities. To the question on students' participation, teachers' comments were all affirmative:

- Science Teacher 1: It increased, but continuously doing this kind of activities may cause delay in catching up the curriculum. It can be effective in increasing student's motivation.
- Social studies Teacher: The students who think what is happening here are interesting activities, are the students who generally do not participate, so I can say that by the help of the students' curiosity to the new applications, there happened to be an increase in their participation in the educational activities.
- Science Teacher 2: Yes I mostly observed this at computer labs. But I think that the participation will increase if I give them opportunities to work by themselves. On

the other hand, it was not very easy to reach the students who did not have enough technology at home.

Although, Science Teacher 1 thinks that too much use of the system can cause students to get bored during the educational activities, the rest of the teachers think that the system would increase the overall participation of the students in the educational activities.

To the question on change in their study time on educational activities, Science Teacher 1 stated that she could not make enough observation to answer this question clearly, but rest of the teachers observed that the use of e-learning / sharing portal applications effected students' study time positively.

- Social Studies Teacher: The students are used to spending time in front of the computer, we can say that by using the e-learning activities, there happened to be an increase in their study time too.
- Turkish Teacher: When a student goes home he/she prefers doing his/her homework on computer to doing it on paper, which may mean that it increases the study time of students.
- Science Teacher 2: Some of the students, especially the ones who are very good at computers wouldn't have gotten interested if I had given the worksheet in written form. Probably the reason for why they worked so well is their access to computers.

The Teachers' Perceptions about Usefulness of this Technology

To investigate perceptions of the teachers about the usefulness of e-learning / sharing portal, teachers were asked what they thought about the usefulness of this technology in educational activities, was it useful or not. Confirming answers were reported and when asked to give detail responses, some of their responses are as follows:

- Mathematics Teacher: I think it was useful because as I mentioned before these applications help to increase the diversity in education. In our classrooms we put this into practice many times. We gave homework via this system. I think this system has a lot of advantages.
- Science Teacher 1: I find it helpful for students to do their work by using technology. They like to use computers; it does not matter whether it is for playing games or for studying lessons. They can observe their work better if it is in a visual environment. For many reasons I think that this system is very useful. The students not only take notes, they also do research, be in touch with their teachers on the same learning portal, take feedbacks in a very short amount of time, they can improve their work at home. When a teacher sees incomplete work or mistakes he/she can have her/his students to complete and save it at home. It is easier for teachers to follow the course of a project.
- Social Studies Teacher: The usefulness comes from the practical use of the system. The students of today's world like acting fast and this system allows them to do so. I think this system is just for them.

The Turkish teacher also reported negative observations about the usefulness of the system for lazy students. She added that the lazy ones are already being unsuccessful not only in this kind of activities but also in traditional learning environments. However, the overall comments of the teachers about usefulness were positive.

For the *work more quickly"* sub item under the perceived usefulness heading, while the science teacher 1 did not report any observation as she was not able to observe because of time restrictions, the rest of the teachers commented that student worked more quickly on the activities than they were in traditional setting.

The second indicator for perceived usefulness was *Job performance.* Although, the Mathematics Teacher stated that he could not observe a difference in students' job performance, the rest of the teachers commented on its positive effects.

When teachers were asked about their perception on whether there is an *increase in productivity*, the mathematics teacher reported that if appropriate materials were used it will increase students' productivities. Social studies teacher said that "I can say that it added some creativity to their creativity that they already have." While the computer teachers said "when they are on their own in front of a computer they gain self confidence and they don't hesitate to use their creative ideas during their work" an excerpt from the Turkish teacher states that "I think this system mostly depends on the creativity of the teacher. If the teacher prepares creative materials he/she can help students increase their creativity and productivity."

The teachers mostly stated that they had a chance to observe that the system forced the students to be productive in their educational activities, except for Mathematics Teacher and Science Teacher 2, because they had used multiple choice applications; however, they implied that creative applications would increase the students' productivities.

Another indicator was whether the portal *made their job easier*. Most of the teachers stated that the system was very helpful in students' access to the educational activities and made the students' work easier.

The final indicator was *overall usefulness*. For this indicator several questions were asked to the teachers. When asked if they observed that the use of the technology increased students' contribution in their educational activities, science teacher 1 stated that the students had access/login problems to the portal. She stated that if the problems were solved then their contribution would have been increased. The rest of the teachers' comments were all positive students' contributions.

Whether they have observed that the use of the technology improved students' opportunity to work on educational activities was another question. Here are some of the excerpts from teachers' comments:

- Science Teacher 1: Yes. Before e-learning applications we were giving all the educational activities in a written format but with e-learning portal the teacher can reach to the students on the Internet. The activities can reach to the students this way without using papers. I think that this situation increases the perceptions of students about subject materials.
- Computer Teacher: Not only at school but also at home it helps students to reach materials. It helps them to reach too many sources.

Finally, they were asked overall if they had observed the use of the technology useful. The Mathematics teachers' reported that "It can be improved; we can use this technology in such different good manners. A lot of different materials can be used here." The Turkish teacher, as well, commented that "I think it is very useful in bringing students to a higher level in education."

The Teachers' Perceptions about Ease of Use of this Technology

Within the framework there were four sub categories: easy to learn, easy to become skillful, clear and understandable interface, and overall ease of use. Overall, teachers' observations for the ease of use of the portal were quite positive and they classified the e-learning / sharing portal as an easy-to-use tool. However, the science teacher stated that it was not that easy to use if a student is not as computer literate as the other students. On the clear

& understandable item the mathematics teacher specifically commented, “I find it clear. I think it can be more visual with animations especially for 6th and 7th grade students.”

When they were asked if it was hard to understand the user interfaces of the e-learning / sharing portal for their students they responded positively.

- Mathematics Teacher: I have never come across such a situation. As I said before, the students are very keen on using computers and this system is no different than that.
- Science Teacher 1: After a few use it has become very easy to understand.
- Computer Teacher: We gave 10 minutes of instruction about this subject and after this 10 minute period the students begun using this interface. I think this means that it was not hard for them.

Some of the excerpts from the teachers on the overall ease of use of the portal are

- Social Sciences Teacher: They use the system efficiently, which shows that they found it easy to use.
- Turkish Teacher: When we first announced this e-learning portal to students they all got passwords. As far as I observed, at the beginning they had problems with these passwords, but now we don’t see these problems anymore.
- Computer Teacher: They found it very easy. They easily adapted.

Advantages and Disadvantages of the Portal

In the interviews, the teachers were also asked the advantages and disadvantages of this technology. They have reported several advantages and disadvantages, which are listed as follows;

Advantages

- It allows students and teachers to share documents easily between each other
- It provides easy to access developed materials
- It provides students observe their work better by its visual elements
- It allows teachers give immediate feedback to students
- It gives the chance for students to review the materials they need at home
- It is also advantageous for the students who are absent in the class
- It increases the student-student and student-teacher interactions
- The shy students get the opportunity to express themselves better
- It allows students to gain self-confidence when they are on their own in front of a computer and they don’t hesitate to use their creative ideas in their work
- It helps teachers to access school resources easily
- It allows teachers to easily distribute course materials to students
- It provides teachers the ability to easily assess students since all projects, quizzes, examinations, etc. are saved on the same computer
- It allows teachers to send course materials to the system so that students have a second chance to go over the materials at their home, free from time and place, and by this way teachers do not have to review the subject material in class over and over
- It increases the interaction not only with students but also between teachers and directors
- It allows teachers to draw out students’ attention more
- It allows teachers to record and broadcast a whole lesson for absent students or for

the ones who want to review the subject material

- It provides teachers with the ability to share audio-visual materials
- It allows teachers to announce all kinds of events
- Students do not need to deal with papers, it is also better for ecological purposes (the waste of paper decreases)
- It provides a time and place independent working environment
- It is provided on server usage so that teachers or students do not have to setup any software to their computers
- Students' and teacher' instant workings are protected in case of any technical problems occurred on the computers for example electricity outage, or the system breaking down
- It provides a convenient environment for regular backup service by centralizing the source codes. This protects students' project files against data lost
- It keeps the students' and the teachers' documents saved. This guarantees the safety of the documents in case of being deleted or saved mistakenly with a different name

Disadvantages

- Students' dealing with computers continuously for hours may decrease their concentration on educational activities
- In order to put this method into practice, all the teachers and students must have computers equipped with required technology and access to internet
- Students' using computer by themselves can make them antisocial
- Server can slow down when high numbers of online users keep the system busy simultaneously
- Students may misuse discussion boards (as they do it in their msn accounts), this may cause inconvenient situations for the school environment
- Keeping all the materials on a single server increases the risk of data loss
- Keeping all the materials on a single server increases the risk of accessing others' materials without permission

Teachers' Suggestions about the Use of the Portal

Finally, the teachers were asked to share their suggestions about the further use of this technology. These suggestions were listed as follows.

Suggestions Related with the Use of the E-Learning / Sharing Portal:

- The system can be used regularly in weekend homework, performance assignments, worksheets, and all in class activities
- The system can be used in all kinds of distance education or online education applications
- The system can be used in educational activities that need interaction between users who are distant from each other. For example, in an European Union project, teachers and students in different countries can make collective works. They can use the system for setting connections, sharing materials, etc.
- The system can be used to make online surveys
- The portal can be used for adult education also

Suggestions Related with the Improvement of the E-Learning / Sharing Portal:

- Some educational material development tools can be integrated to the system
- Instant messaging software can be included to the system

- The system accepts only a few kinds of file formats to transmit (like SCORM data), it can be improved to all types of files transmitted without examining file extension
- Survey construction steps can be clarified
- A back up unit can be integrated for keeping all users saved work more safe
- The system can be used for applying teleconferencing technologies such as setting up a live broadcast for educational purposes

DISCUSSION

In an era of rapid developing educational technologies, the Internet has become a powerful tool to provide learners with an alternative learning environment worldwide. The Internet and distance education have notably affected the ways in which we communicate and learn (Leh 1999). Distance education fosters learning and teaching in a variety of ways. One of the many advantages of distance education is that it offers instructors and students a flexible learning setting in terms of time and location. Learning does not require students to be physically present in the same place with the instructor (Walker 2005) nor to be at the same time. Distance education might be used for different purposes such as supported learning, blended learning, and entirely online learning. However, sometimes all those discovered opportunities are insufficient in solving the problems of some circumstances and in providing some facilities in online environments. One of these problem areas is teachers' and students' interacting in a professionally designed sharing platforms. Although, the Internet provides highly efficient, effective and widely used communication tool for users' interacting with each other, the number of special technology which provides effective sharing portal environments for educational activities are limited.

The technology used in this study was Microsoft SharePoint Server, a sharing portal server. This software used as an e-learning application that gets students and teachers together in a mutual virtual learning environment. Moreover, it provides a time and place independent, and a synchronous and asynchronous team working environment.

According to the Technology Acceptance Model (TAM), however, it is not enough just to integrate this new technology in their learning environment. The acceptance of this new technology should be checked. Information systems are created to be used. If the users do not accept them, they eventually fail (Davis 1989).

The object of this study is to investigate the effects of the integration of the e-learning / sharing portal as a new technology in a learning environment. To obtain information about the effects of the use of the portal and perceptions of students, the teachers were investigated in terms of its perceived effects on their perceived motivation towards educational activities, its usefulness and its ease of use. Also, to get a list of advantages, disadvantages and suggestions of the teachers were the secondary objective of this study.

As a result of this study including the interview, a wide variety of suggestions were acquired from the teachers. The teachers mostly made suggestions about the use of the system. Some suggestions were about improvement of the system used in this study. All suggestions were grouped into two categories and listed:

Suggestions Related with the Use of the E-Learning / Sharing Portal

- The system can be used regularly in weekend homework, performance assignments, worksheets, and in all class activities
- The system can be used in all kinds of distance education or online education applications
- The system can be used in educational activities that need interaction between users who are distant from each other. For example, in a European Union project, teachers and students in different countries can

make collective works. They can use the system for setting connections, sharing materials, etc.

- The system can be used to make online surveys
- The portal can also be used for adult education

Suggestions Related with the Improvement of the E-Learning / Sharing Portal

- Some educational material development tools can be integrated into the system
- Instant messaging software can be included to the system
- The system accepts only a few kinds of file formats to transmit (like SCORM data), it can be improved to accept all types of files transmitted without examining file extension
- Survey construction steps can be clarified
- A back up unit can be integrated for keeping all users saved work more safe
- The system can be used for applying teleconferencing technologies such as setting up a live broadcast for educational purposes

Suggestions for Practice

From the results of this study, the following suggestions are made for implementing e-learning / sharing portal technologies into educational activities.

- Prepare detailed, carefully designed activities for implementing them in e-learning / sharing portal environments. If an activity does not work properly in the system, users would get unmotivated, and eventually the activity would reduce students' learning performance.
- Find useful and easy to use educational material development software for using it in the e-learning / sharing portal. Microsoft Class Server or Hot Potatoes can be used for this purpose.
- Keep backups of the passwords for users in case they forget or lose their password. Give warnings about keeping passwords.
- Check the messages written in the class discussion part frequently. Delete the inconvenient content and give warnings to writers of that kind of messages.
- Use the announcement part regularly to encourage students use the system efficiently.
- Guide the students in using the calendar and agenda for improving their time management capabilities.
- Design creative educational activities so students' can increase their creativeness.
- Do the assessments as soon as possible to give the students immediate feedbacks. If the students do not see results of their performance timely, they will lose interest in the system.
- Do not prepare very lengthy activities, it may get students used to sitting in front of the computer for hours, and eventually it may result in antisocial individuals.
- Be sure that all the users of the system have computers with required equipment and an internet connection fast enough for using the system properly.
- Use precaution incase the servers slowing down. For example make backups of the account savings.
- Be sure that all the users have an active working ID and password. For example, even if a few students cannot enter to the system, it would result in confusion and losing control of classroom management, and consequently an ineffective working of the system.
- Plan at least a one-hour lecture to introduce the aim and the usage of the system at the beginning of the study. Also, give brief in-

formation about the advantages about the system.

Like most research studies, this study is also subject to certain limitations. One of these limitations would be that it is carried out in a private elementary school whose students are coming from relatively wealthy families and thus most of them have PCs at home. This way they have a chance of increased time to use the portal at home. The results would only be generalized to the 200 students and 6 teachers who have voluntarily participated in the study. The study is also limited by the quality of teacher prepared materials and activities for the portal. The findings would have been different if the materials were prepared by a professional team. Finally, the reliability of the study is limited to the extent that the subjects' responses to the instruments used were honest.

Further research can be carried out in different educational settings, using participants in varying grade levels and different private and public schools. The effectiveness of the use of the portal can also be tested using professionally prepared activities. Further, administrators' perceptions about the use of this kind of portal as well as its effect on schools' budget should also be investigated.

REFERENCES

Allen, E., & Seaman, J. (2008). *Staying the course: Online education in the United States*. Needham, MA: Sloan-C.

Argyris, C., & Putnam, R. (1985). *Action science: Concepts, methods, and skills for research and intervention*. San Francisco: Jossey - Bass.

Benek-Rivera, J., & Mathews, V. E. (2004). Active learning with Jeopardy: Students ask the questions. *Journal of Management Education*, *28*(1), 104–118. doi:10.1177/1052562903252637

Bogdan, R. C., & Biklen, S. K. (1998). *Qualitative research for education: An introduction to theory and methods*. Needham Heights, MA: Ally & Bacon.

Bonwell, C. C., & Eisen, J. A. (1991). Active learning: Creating excitement in the classroom (ASHE-ERIC Higher Education Report No. 1). Washington, DC: George Washington University.

Davis, F. D. (1989). Perceived usefulness, perceived ease of use, and user acceptance of information technology. *Management Information Systems Quarterly*, *13*(3), 319–340. doi:10.2307/249008

Davis, F. D., & Bagozzi, R. P. (1989). User acceptance of computer technology: A comparison of two theoretical models. *Management Science*, *35*(8), 982–1003. doi:10.1287/mnsc.35.8.982

Erginel-Sanal, S. (2006). *Developing reflective teachers: A study on perception and improvement of reflection in pre-service teacher education*. Ankara: Ankara, Middle East Tecnical University.

Garson, D. (2007). Scales and standard measures. Retrieved August 8, 2007, from http://www2.chass.ncsu.edu/garson/pa765/standard.htm

Gefen, D., & Keil, M. (1998). The impact of developer responsiveness on perceptions of usefulness and ease of use: An extension of the technology acceptance model. *SIGMIS Database*, *29*(2), 35–49. doi:10.1145/298752.298757

Johnston, J., & Killion, J., et al. (2005). Student satisfaction in the virtual classroom. *The Internet Journal of Allied Health Sciences and Practice, 3.*

Leh, A. (1999). Computer-mediated communication and foreign language learning via telecommunication technology. *Ed-Media: World Conference on Educational Multimedia, Hypermedia, and Telecommunications* Charlottesville, VA, Association for the Advancement of Computing in Education.

Longe, O. B., Ogege, F. J., et al. (2005). Students' perceptions of Web-based learning Tools: A case study of the Web course tool (Webct). *The African Symposium: An On Line Journal Of African Educational Research*, *5*(1): 20-27.

Martler, C. (2008). *Action research: Teachers as researchers in the classroom*. Thousand Oaks, ST: Sega Publications.

Patton, M. Q. (1987). *How to use qualitative methods in evaluation*. Newbury Park, CA: Sage.

Picciano, A. G. (2002). Beyond student perceptions: Issues interaction, presence, and performance in an online course. *Journal of Asynchronous Learning Networks*, *6*, 20–41.

Robson, C. (2002). *Real world research*. Malden, ST: Blackwell Publishing.

Scardamalia, M. (2002). Creative work with ideas: A luxury? *Annual meeting of the American Psychological Association*. New Orleans, LA.

Stake, R. E. (1994). Case studies . In Denzin, N. K., & Lincoln, Y. S. (Eds.), *Handbook of qualitative research* (pp. 236–247). Thousand Oaks, CA: Sage.

Tursak, M. (2007). *Perceptions of students and instructors about using remote access technology in programming language courses: a case study*. Ankara: Middle East Technical University.

Walker, S. L. (2005). Development of the Distance Education Learning Environments Survey (DELES) for higher education. *The Texas Journal of Distance Learning*, *2*(1), 1–16.

Weller, M. (2007). *Virtual learning environments: Using, choosing and developing your VLE*. London: Routledge.

Yildirim, A., & Simsek, H. (2001). *Nitel araştırma yöntemleri* [Qualitative research methods]. İstanbul: Seckin Yayincilik.

Yildirim, A., & Simsek, H. (2006). *Nitel araştırma yöntemleri* [Qualitative research methods]. İstanbul: Seckin Yayincilik.

KEYWORDS AND DEFINITIONS

Online Education: Teaching and learning activities delivered, for the most part, over the Internet in synchronous and/or asynchronous mode and it makes use of the Internet to interact with the instructor, fellow learners, and the content.

E-Learning / Sharing Portal: It is a special portal application that is used in educational activities, and it helps both teachers and students have a virtual space where they can share knowledge through different kinds of supervised activities, chats, and forums.

Technology Acceptance Model: As an adaptation of theory of reasoned action (TRA), using perceived usefulness, perceived ease of use, and attitudes as determinants, TAM explains an individual's acceptance or rejection of a computer-based technology (Davis, 1989).

Section 2
Enabling Students

Chapter 5
Student-Authored Textbooks:
Why They're Necessary and How They Can Be Done

Patrick M. O'Shea
Old Dominion University, USA

Jennifer K. Kidd
Old Dominion University, USA

Peter B. Baker
Old Dominion University, USA

Jamie A. Kaufman
Old Dominion University, USA

Dwight W. Allen
Old Dominion University, USA

ABSTRACT

This chapter describes a unique educational initiative requiring students to write their own, shared textbook using wiki technologies. This chapter attempts to address the strengths and weaknesses of this type of educational program. In addition, it explores the philosophical underpinnings of such a process, the implications of this process for educational systems in general, and several methods for incorporating this type of project into every level of education. Special emphasis is placed on exploring how student-authoring addresses skills including information literacy skills, that are underserved in more traditional educational settings.

INTRODUCTION

This chapter will describe and explore an initiative to develop student-authored textbooks at the university level using wiki software. Included in the chapter will be an explanation of the project itself, a discussion of the theoretical underpinnings of the project, an examination of research into the project's effectiveness, and an exploration of how the process can be implemented in other settings (e.g. K-12 or smaller classes). All of these elements will be discussed in order to

DOI: 10.4018/978-1-61692-854-4.ch005

demonstrate why this type of activity is necessary in 21st century educational settings and how it can be incorporated.

The project to be outlined in this chapter works as an exemplar of how to infuse 21st century skills throughout the curriculum rather than as one-off lessons (which have limited success in terms of student recall or skill level). As such, it demonstrates one desirable future for technology integration, not only in higher education, but also in the K-12 context.

It is, however, not enough to simply describe this project. This project must be placed within a larger context. As such, this chapter will have three missions:

1. Describe the project as it currently stands, including discussion of research results into the effectiveness of the process.
2. Explore the theoretical and philosophical underpinnings of the project, focusing primarily on how this type of project more effectively meets the needs of 21st century learners.
3. Discuss how this type of project can be implemented in different educational settings, such as K-12 classrooms.

BACKGROUND

New research is beginning to demonstrate the importance of setting up educational systems that facilitate the learning styles of Millennial learners. According to Sweeney (2006), these students are multi-taskers geared toward experiential learning and working collaboratively. In order to understand the educational process that this chapter will explore, it is necessary to provide background information on the nature of wiki software. Wikis are, first and foremost, "quick," as the original meaning of this Hawaiian word suggests (Lee, 2006). Leuf and Cunningham (2001) defined wiki as "a freely expandable collection of interlinked Web pages, a hypertext system for storing and modifying information–a database where each page is easily editable by any user with a forms-capable Web browser client" (p. 14). Franklin and Van Harmelen (2007) define a wiki as "a system that allows one or more people to build up a corpus of knowledge in a set of interlinked web pages, using a process of creating and editing pages" (p.5). Leuf and Cunningham pointed out that wiki technology has three major attributes in common: the participation of wiki community members in the editing of wiki pages (wikis), the opportunity for wiki members to build and develop "meaningful topic association" (p. 16) through numerous links between wiki and other webpages, and the supportiveness for wiki community members to collaborate in updating wiki content. Raman, Ryan, and Olfman (2005) share the same view with Leuf and Cunningham, defining wiki as a group collaboration software tool based on Web server technology that can be used to facilitate collaborative knowledge creation and sharing in an academic environment. Other researchers have confirmed this feature of wiki technology (Lamb, 2004; Wagner, 2004; Goodwin-Jones, 2005; Tokin, 2005).

Wikis are just one of the many new tools that collectively make up what has become known as Web 2.0. According to Knobel and Wilber (2009), Web 2.0 has at its center three main tenets—"participation, collaboration, and distribution" (p. 21). The Wikimedia Foundation (2009) states, "The term 'Web 2.0' refers to a perceived second generation of web development and design, that aims to facilitate communication, secure information sharing, interoperability, and collaboration on the World Wide Web."

As wiki technology also functions as an "open author system for a conjoined construction and maintenance of Websites" (Fuchs-Kittowsk & Köhler, 2002, p.10), it can be edited and repaired anytime, by potentially anyone, which makes people doubt the accuracy of its content. According to an empirical study conducted by *Nature*'s

Giles (2005), however, this is not necessarily true. Giles conducted a study on 42 articles in both Wikipedia and Encyclopedia Britannica Online related to various science topics and found that, while Britannica's articles had approximately three errors each, Wikipedia articles had only around four errors—not a statistically significant difference. Likewise, the *Nature* study categorized errors as small or large. They found that Britannica and Wikipedia had comparable numbers of major errors. This research has motivated responses from researchers who think that Wikipedia is superior to Britannica Online in many ways, such as the speed and collaboration associated with the former's editing process, the wealth and diversity of links within most articles, depth and detail of information, and the potential for students' involvement (Litterst, 2006; Shareski & Winkler, 2006). Wikipedia provides a good example for the application of wiki technology to the educational field because it demonstrates the possibility of groups of users creating content in meaningful ways. As Shareski and Winkler (2006) pointed out, it would be a mistake to reject the use of Wikipedia as a valuable resource and to turn a blind eye to the changing world in the 21st century.

USING WIKIS TO ALLOW STUDENTS TO WRITE THEIR OWN TEXTBOOKS

Student-Authored Textbook Project

In the fall of 2006, the instructors of the educational foundations course at Old Dominion University altered the structure of the course in order to incorporate the use of a student-written WikiText as the principal textbook.

Prior to the beginning of the course, instructors identified 75 topics, most of which were considered "key content" areas and featured prominently by typical educational foundations texts. These topics became the focus for student-written articles. Collectively, the student-authored articles became the principal textbook for the course. During the initial semester, the 200 or more students enrolled in the class were asked to select one topic on which to write a 1,000-word article, which would be posted on the Wikibooks platform. Up to three students were allowed to sign up for each topic, and each student who signed up would individually author an article on that topic. Student WikiText articles had to be based on five or more references, at least two from academic, peer reviewed sources, and at least two from popular sources. In addition, each student wrote five multiple-choice questions and included a sidebar (interesting, often supplemental material). By week four of the course, the majority of the textbook had been written.

During the next ten weeks the WikiText was read by peers. Through a system of reading groups about 70 students were assigned to read and rate each article. Eight to ten articles were assigned each week. Students were asked to rate the articles they read on a three point scale: 3–outstanding, many useful and professionally relevant ideas; 2–satisfactory, some learning; and 1–an unsatisfactory article from which little was learned. At the end of the week during which the articles were assigned, student ratings were tabulated and the highest rated article for each topic was selected to become a part of the official text from which quiz and exam contents were taken.

The process has remained fundamentally the same in each semester since the fall of 2006: students are responsible for writing the content of the textbook and rating the material that is created. However, details of the process have changed based on the results of formative evaluation and shifting requirements. For example, the course content has changed over time in response to changing state credentialing requirements, creating the need for different topics. This may appear to be a rather standard evolution of a teaching/learning format with dramatically differing premises and outcomes. It should be noted, however, that it highlights one of the most dramatic features of this new WikiText, that it can be easily modified as needed, almost in real time, a far cry from the several-year typical text revision process. Another of several changes was that the three-point rating scale was modified to add guidance to the rating process.

Theoretical Underpinnings

Aside from the feasibility of the project, as outlined in the discussions above concerning the wiki software itself and the project description, the instructional model that this chapter outlines is based upon constructivist learning theory. Windschitl (1999) describes constructivism as "premised on the belief that learners actively create, interpret, and recognize knowledge in individual ways" (p. 2). Further, Kinchin (2004) states that "there needs to be a complementary transition from a traditional view to a constructivist view" (p. 303).

However, what does a constructivist classroom look like? Windschitl (1999) states that they "should include problem-based learning, inquiry activities, dialogues with peers and teachers that encourage making sense of subject matter, exposure to multiple sources of information and opportunities for students to demonstrate their understanding in diverse ways" (p.2) and that the "teacher must not only be familiar with the principles underlying the topic of study but must also be prepared for the variety of ways these principles can be explored" (p.3). The wiki project, due to its student-centered nature, creates an environment much more naturally attuned to constructivism.

Issues, Controversies, Problems

As with any project of this complexity, magnitude, and nature, it would be expected that there would be questions concerning the impact of the process upon student learning. In addition to these questions, an additional set of questions was presented concerning the credibility of the process and product. The approach to answering these questions has changed over time, and although there remains work to be done on the precise nature of these interactions, the process is underway to answer them.

Initially, the approach was simply to ask students to indicate their perceptions and usage of the materials. The results from the initial cohort of students using the wiki were compared with the last cohort of students to use the traditional textbook, and the results were nothing short of shocking. Wiki students felt they were significantly more involved with the text, that they learned more from the text, used the text more often, gained a greater percentage of their learning from the text, believed the wiki product was better than other traditional textbooks, and had a greater impact on their grades (O'Shea, Curry-Corcoran, Baker, Allen, & Allen, 2007). When stated thusly, however, the true scope of the difference is not apparent. It is only through seeing how some of the actual percentages changed that one gets a true sense of the difference in opinion. For example, 41% of the last cohort to use the traditional text indicated they had "no involvement" with their text. That number dropped to less than 1% of the first cohort of wiki students. More than 27% of traditional textbook users stated that they learned "nothing" from reading their textbook. This percentage also dropped to less than 1% of wiki students. Nearly 38% of traditional textbook students stated that they never used the textbook to prepare for class, while only 5% of wiki students said the same. This type of turnaround was witnessed in question after question that was asked of these two cohorts of students.

Of course, it is impossible to generalize from this small sample, and self-reported data should not be viewed as conclusive. Understanding this, the instructional staff undertook a more rigorous research design that used a pre-test/post-test, control group model in order to answer questions dealing with the effect of the Wikibook process on student academic outcomes and other 21st century skills. The instrument used in this instance included teacher-made items for content knowledge, items adapted from the Epistemological Belief Sampler (EBS) for epistemological beliefs, and items adapted from the Standardized Assessment of Information Literacy Skills (SAILS) for information literacy. As there is no standardized core-competency exam, peers reviewed the teacher-made items in order to ensure content validity. In addition, effort was placed on looking at the quality of the material that students submitted, specifically the multiple-choice questions, as those are used in quizzes and exams.

It is important to understand that this analysis was done not only for the edification of the instructional staff and students, but also because it seemed the most direct means of evaluating the credibility of the process itself. As mentioned earlier, there was a certain amount of reticence involved with accepting this process (particularly on the part of other academics) due to the commonly held perception that "students can't write a credible textbook." The obvious response to this is to ask what qualities make a textbook "credible," as this information would allow the evaluation of the Wikibook on a set of known variables. As one might expect, there was no standard set of measures that would indicate credibility, and in fact, most research into this area indicates that one's sense of credibility is based generally on either trusting the material itself or trusting the source of the material (see work done by the Stanford's Web Credibility Project for more details). This left the instructional staff in a bit of a quandary, as it would be almost impossible to convince anyone that students can be authoritative figures in terms of content without concrete evidence that the material they were creating was credible in and of itself—a "catch 22."

The approach that the instructional staff decided upon was to compare students on learning outcomes. After all, that is the truest measure of whether a source is appropriate. In order to make this comparison, a pre-test/post-test, control group design was implemented where WikiText process served as the treatment and traditional textbook use as the control. All other variables concerning the class were held as similar as possible. The instructional staff designed a "core competencies" exam that covered that information that was essential to successful learning in the course. These core competencies were developed in collaboration with colleagues across institutions and based on instructors' years of experience teaching the course and others like it. Additionally, this exam included questions concerning information literacy, problem solving and critical thinking. Analysis of the data supports the assertion that the Wikibook is a credible learning source. Analysis of Variance (ANOVA) were run on these data that showed there was no statistically significant difference between wiki students and their traditional textbook-using peers in terms of academic performance on numerous measures (pre-test, mid-term, article rating, course grade, or information literacy). The only statistically significant difference identified in this analysis was in the wiki students' favor on the final exam.

Solutions and Recommendations/ Implementations in Other Settings

Having said all of that, the next logical step is to think about how this system could be administered in different settings. Among the reasons that the Wikibook process succeeded (to the extent that it has) are the facts that it was developed to leverage the unique characteristics of the course that uses it. In essence, the fact that the course enrolled 200+ university-level students each semester allowed the instructional staff to design a rather bold initiative. With fewer students, or students at a lower level, the initiative obviously would have to be modified. That, however, need not put off anyone who wishes to experiment with this type of process. For example, classes that enroll fewer students may wish to incorporate a wiki process that entails writing a chapter rather than a full textbook. If done effectively, and a new chapter were written each semester/year, a fully student-authored textbook could be built over time. Likewise, students at the middle or high school levels easily could be involved with writing a similarly appropriate text for their classes.

Another option would be to work collaboratively with other similar, concurrent classes in order to build the critical mass necessary to write a full textbook. If the communication methodologies were in place for students across a school, division, region, state or nation to work collaboratively, then the issue of small class sizes would not necessarily hinder the use of this process on a more far-reaching process.

In each of these cases, the intention is to facilitate the instructional dynamic that allows students to bring information into the classroom, not merely receive content passively from the class. There are innumerable methods and technologies available to teachers now that will allow them to design such learning experiences. What is needed is for teachers and administrators to think critically about what they ask of their students, decide on a direction to take, and find the technologies that will facilitate that direction. The process described within this chapter did not involve a huge financial cost. Nor did it involve a massive technological burden. What it did require, however, was a re-invention of the student role within the classroom and a commitment to the belief that students could fill that role effectively.

FUTURE RESEARCH DIRECTIONS

The focus of this chapter up to this point has been entirely on the practical applications of the wiki process within the educational domain. At this point, it is appropriate to move forward to explore a few of the emerging trends that this type of activity demonstrates. First, this type of learning activity centers upon the 21st century skills that are needed in order to fully educate global citizens (and workers). It is essential that students become adept at finding, analyzing, synthesizing, and reporting information as it becomes needed. This is the very nature of "Just In Time" learning. The wiki project is ideal for teaching this because it is founded on the principle of teaching these skills by asking students to perform them.

In addition, projects such as that recounted here represent a logical next step in the progression of technology integration at every level of instruction. The use of student-generated learning objects will help to facilitate the redefinition of the teacher/student partnership. No longer will the default educational paradigm consist of a one-way flow of information from the teacher to the student. Rather, the learning environment will be centered on a collaborative discovery of information, where the teacher is more focused on helping students make sense of the information that have found.

In practical terms, however, this will mean that there is a need for significant research into the efficacy of this type of instructional model. New, psychometrically sound instruments will need to be developed in order to measure changes in skills such as information literacy, critical thinking, motivation, engagement, and problem solving, more precisely. These new instruments, when used in conjunction with the types of student-centered learning environments that this chapter describes, will allow for research into the types of skills and knowledge acquisition that will be need for the 21st century and beyond.

CONCLUSION

It is now time to ask the most important question: Why is this type of activity needed? The answer to this question lies at the intersection of three very important phenomena. The first of these is the ubiquity of information that currently exists and will not likely lessen. Unless one has been living under a rock since the mid-90s, it should be absolutely apparent that we are figuratively "drowning" in information. In fact, since the mid 1990's, David Thornburg has been making calls for more educational focus on the context of information rather than simply on the content (Thornburg, 1996). In essence, he was among the earliest educators calling for the teacher to be the "guide on the side" rather than the "sage on the stage." Of course, this is simply a platitude unless concrete examples are provided to teachers. This chapter has provided one such example.

The second element of this intersection is the emerging understanding of the characteristics of Millennial learners. According to Sweeney (2006), these digital natives are proficient multi-taskers who are geared toward experiential learning and who desire to work collaboratively. If schools hope to reach these students fully, then it is imperative that educational institutions leverage the skills and knowledge that they bring with them into the setting. Traditional, teacher-centered educational experiences are no longer good enough.

The third element of this mixture is the rapid development of tools that allow users to generate content. These Web 2.0 tools have been introduced previously; however, their potential can only be realized when used by educators to leverage the strengths of Millennial learners (namely, their desire to be connected and to work collaboratively) and combine those characteristics with the free ability of plentiful information. There is much talk about wanting students to become informationally literate. The teacher can help students to learn how to find and digest information appropriately much more meaningfully at the epicenter of the confluence of these three elements.

Granted, there are issues that must be overcome. However, if there are questions about whether this type of project fits for a particular student population (e.g. elementary students) or a particular content area (e.g. geometry), then the starting point for the discussion should be to discuss why textbooks are used in education. If the intention of having textbooks is to (hopefully) have students master the content included within them by the end of the instructional period, then, given the nature of the information-rich time in which we live, it is reasonable to expect that individual students could master digestible "chunks" of that content in a much shorter period of time. If enough students master their individual "chunks" of content, then those can be combined for the benefit of their classmates. This being the case, then it is possible to conceive that there is no content area or grade level that should not be able to leverage this type of process, given enough forethought by the instructional leader. After all, the technology is already available, the information that is needed is already plentiful, and the students are capable. All that is needed now is the insight of the teachers and the institutional will to take advantage of these capabilities.

REFERENCES

Franklin, T., & Van Harmelen, M. (2007). Web 2.0 for content for Learning and Teaching in Higher Education. Bristol: JISC. Retrieved June 24, 2009, from http://www.jisc.ac.uk/publications/documents/web2andpolicyreport.aspx

Fuchs-Kittowsk, F., & Köhler, A. (2002). Knowledge creating communities in the context of work processes. *ACM SIGCSE Bulletin*, *23*(3), 8–13.

Giles, J. (2005). Internet encyclopedias go head to head. *Nature 438*(15), 900-901. Retrieved June 24, 2009, from http://www.nature.com/nature/journal/v438/n7070/full/438900a.html

Goodwin-Jones, R. (2003). Blogs and wikis: Environments for on-line collaboration. *Language Learning & Technology*, *7*, 12–16.

Kinchin, I. (2004). Investigating students' beliefs about their preferred role as learners. *Educational Research*, *46*(3), 301–312. doi:10.1080/0013188042000277359

Knobel, M., & Wilber, D. (2009). Let's talk 2.0. *Educational Leadership*, *66*(6), 20–24.

Lamb, B. (2004). Wide open spaces: Wikis, ready or not. *EDUCAUSE Review*, *39*(5).

Lee, A. (2006). The wonderful world of wikis. In A. Rolls (Ed.), *The reference shelf: Vol. 78 (2) New media* (pp.148-152). Bronx, NY: The H. W. Wilson Company.

Leuf, B., & Cunningham, W. (2001). *The wikiway: Quick collaboration of the web*. Boston, MA: Addison-Wesley Professional.

Litterst, G. F. (2005/2006). Your role in music history. *The American Music Teacher*, *55*(3), 50–51.

O'Shea, P., Curry-Corcoran, D., Baker, P., Allen, D. A., & Allen, D. W. (2007). New Levels of Student Participatory Learning: A WikiText for the Introductory Course in Education. *The Journal of Interactive Online Learning*, *6*(3).

Raman, M., Ryan, T., & Olfman, L. (2005). Designing knowledge management systems for teaching and learning with wild technology. *Journal of Information Systems Education*, *16*(3), 311–320.

Shareski, D., & Winkler, C. A. K. (2005/2006). Are wikis worth the time? *Learning and Leading with Technology*, *33*(4), 6–7.

Stanford Web Credibility Project. (2007). Web Credibility Research. Retrieved June 24, 2009, from http://credibility.stanford.edu/

Sweeney, R. (2006). Millennial Behaviors and Demographics. Retrieved June 25, 2009, from http://www.google.com/url?sa=t&source=web&ct=res&cd=1&url=http%3A%2F%2Flibrary1.njit.edu%2Fstaff-folders%2Fsweeney%2FMillennials%2FArticle-Millennial-Behaviors.doc&ei=5zVESvPABIOENKr-7JkB&usg=AFQjCNEaGFMJ_yjIIwMs7TCRtcAK3p8Y-Eg

Thornburg, D. D. (1996). *Campfires in Cyberspace*. USA: Starsong Publications.

Tokin, E. (2005). Making the case for a wild. *Ariadne, 42*. Retrieved June 24, 2009, from http://www.ariadne.ac.uk/issue42/tonkin/

Wagner, C. (2004). Wiki: A technology for conversational knowledge management and group collaboration. *Communications of the Association for Information Systems*, *13*, 265–289.

Wikimedia Foundation. (2009). Web 2.0. Retrieved June 24, 2009, from http://en.wikipedia.org/wiki/Web_2.0

Windschitl, M. (1999). The Challenges of Sustaining a Constructivist Classroom Culture. *Phi Delta Kappan*, *80*(10), 751.

ADDITIONAL READING

Allen, D. W., O'Shea, P. M., Curry-Corcoran, D. E., & Baker, P. B. (2007, April). New levels of student participatory learning: A WikiText for the introductory course in education. Paper presented at the meeting of the *American Education Research Association*, Chicago, IL.

Anson, C. M., & Miller-Cochran, S. K. (2009). Contrails of learning: Using new technologies for vertical knowledge-building. *Computers and Composition*, *26*, 38–48. doi:10.1016/j.compcom.2008.11.002

Baxter Magolda, M. B. (1992). *Knowing and reasoning in college: Gender-related patterns in students' intellectual development*. San Francisco: Jossey-Bass.

Bondy, E., Ross, D., Adams, A., Nowak, R., Brownell, M., & Hoppey, D. (2007). Personal epistemologies and learning to teach. *Teacher Education and Special Education*, *30*(2), 67–82. doi:10.1177/088840640703000202

Bråten, I., Strømsø, H. I., & Samuelstuen, M. S. (2005). The relationship between Internet-specific epistemological beliefs and learning within Internet technologies. *Journal of Educational Computing Research*, *33*(2), 141–171. doi:10.2190/E763-X0LN-6NMF-CB86

Brownlee, J. (2004). Teacher education students' epistemological beliefs. *Research in Education*, *72*(2), 1–17.

Chai, C. S., Khine, M. S., & Teo, T. (2006). Epistemological beliefs on teaching and learning: A survey among pre-service teachers in Singapore. *Educational Media International*, *43*(4), 285–298. doi:10.1080/09523980600926242

DeBacker, T. K., Crowson, H. M., Beesley, A. D., Thoma, S. J., & Hestevold, N. L. (2008). The challenge of measuring epistemic beliefs: An analysis of three self-report instruments. *Journal of Experimental Education*, *76*(3), 281–312. doi:10.3200/JEXE.76.3.281-314

Hashweh, M. Z. (1996). Effects of science teachers' epistemological beliefs in teaching. *Journal of Research in Science Teaching*, *33*(1), 47–63. doi:10.1002/(SICI)1098-2736(199601)33:1<47::AID-TEA3>3.0.CO;2-P

Hofer, B. K. (2001). Personal epistemology research: Implications for learning and teaching. *Journal of Educational Psychology Review*, *13*(4), 354–383.

Hofer, B. K. (2004). Epistemological understanding as a metacognitive process: Thinking aloud during online searching. *Educational Psychologist*, *39*(1), 43–55. doi:10.1207/s15326985ep3901_5

Howard, B. G., McGee, S., Schwartz, N., & Purcell, S. (2000, April). *Constructivism and teacher epistemology: Training teachers in classroom computer use.* Paper presented at the annual meeting of the American Educational Research Association, New Orleans, LA.

Interstate New Teacher Assessment and Support Consortium. (2001). *Model standards for licensing general and special education teachers of students with disabilities: A resource for state dialogue.* Washington, DC: Council of Chief State School Officers.

Nist, S. L., & Holschuh, J. P. (2005). Practical applications of the research on epistemological beliefs. *Journal of College Reading and Learning*, *35*(2), 84–92.

Nussbaum, E. M., & Bendixen, L. D. (2002, April). *The effect of personality, ability, and epistemological beliefs on students' argumentation behavior*. Paper presented at the annual meeting of the American Educational Research Association, New Orleans, LA.

Nussbaum, E. M., & Bendixen, L. D. (2003). Approaching and avoiding arguments: The role of epistemological beliefs, need for cognition, and extraverted personality traits. *Contemporary Educational Psychology*, *28*, 573–595. doi:10.1016/S0361-476X(02)00062-0

Orcnowski, P. (2004). Congress questions sky-high costs of college textbooks. *Black Issues in Higher Education*, *21*(14), 6–7.

Ostorga, A. N. (2006). Developing teachers who are reflective practitioners: A complex process. *Issues in Teacher Education*, *15*(2), 5–20.

Paulsen, M. B., & Feldman, K. A. (2005). The conditional and interaction effects of epistemological beliefs on the self-regulated learning of college students: Motivational strategies. *Research in Higher Education*, *46*(7), 731–768. doi:10.1007/s11162-004-6224-8

Peng, H., & Fitzgerald, G. E. (2006). Relationships between teacher education students' epistemological beliefs and their learning outcomes in a case-based hypermedia learning environment. *Journal of Technology and Teacher Education*, *14*(2), 255–285.

Perry, W. G. (1970). *Forms of intellectual and ethical development in the college years: A scheme*. New York: Holt, Rinehart & Winston.

Pintrich, P. R. (2002). The role of metacognitive knowledge in learning, teaching, and assessing. *Theory into Practice*, *41*(4), 219–225. doi:10.1207/s15430421tip4104_3

Pintrich, P. R., Smith, D. A. F., Garcia, T., & McKeachie, W. J. (1991). *A Manual for the Use of the Motivated Strategies for Learning Questionnaire (MSLQ)*. Ann Arbor, MI: National Center for Research to Improve Postsecondary Teaching and Learning.

Pizzolato, J. E. (2006). Meaning making inside and outside the academic arena: Investigating the contextuality of epistemological development in college students. *The Journal of General Education*, *55*(2), 228–251.

Rodríguez, L., & Cano, F. (2006). The epistemological beliefs, learning approaches and study orchestrations of university students. *Studies in Higher Education*, *31*(5), 617–636. doi:10.1080/03075070600923442

Schommer, M. (1998). The influence of age and education on epistemological beliefs. *The British Journal of Educational Psychology*, *68*, 551–562.

Schommer, M., & Dunnell, P. A. (1994). A comparison of epistemological beliefs between gifted and non-gifted high school students. *Roeper Review*, *16*, 207–210. doi:10.1080/02783199409553575

Schommer, M., & Walker, K. (1995). Are epistemological beliefs similar across domains? *Journal of Educational Psychology*, *87*(2), 424–432. doi:10.1037/0022-0663.87.3.424

Schommer-Aikins, M., Duell, O. K., & Barker, S. (2002). Epistemological beliefs across domains using Biglan's classification of academic disciplines. *Research in Higher Education*, *44*, 347–366. doi:10.1023/A:1023081800014

Schommer-Aikins, M., Mau, W., Brookhart, S., & Hutter, R. (2000). Understanding middle students' beliefs about knowledge and learning using a multidimensional paradigm. *The Journal of Educational Research*, *94*, 120–127. doi:10.1080/00220670009598750

Schraw, G., Bendixen, L. D., & Dunkle, M. E. (2002). Development and validation of the Epistemic Belief Inventory. In Hofer, B. K., & Pintrich, P. R. (Eds.), *Personal epistemology: The psychology of beliefs about knowledge and knowing* (pp. 103–118). Mahwah, NJ: Erlbaum.

Stahl, E., Pieschl, S., & Bromme, R. (2006). Task complexity, epistemological beliefs and metacognitive calibration: An exploratory study. *Journal of Educational Computing Research*, *35*(4), 319–338. doi:10.2190/1266-0413-387K-7J51

Staley, D. J. (2009). Managing the platform: Higher education and the logic of wikinomics. *EDUCAUSE Review*, *44*(1), 37–46.

Tsai, C. (2004). Beyond cognitive and metacognitive tools: The use of the Internet as an 'epistemological' tool for instruction. *British Journal of Educational Technology*, *35*(5), 525–536. doi:10.1111/j.0007-1013.2004.00411.x

Wood, P., & Kardash, C. (2002). Critical elements in the design and analysis of studies of epistemology. In Hofer, B. K., & Pintrich, P. R. (Eds.), *Personal epistemology: The psychology of beliefs about knowledge and knowing* (pp. 231–260). Mahwah, NJ: Erlbaum.

KEY TERMS AND DEFINITIONS

Constructivism: The learning theory founded upon the idea that students are best served when they are allowed to construct their own knowledge.

Credibility: An individual phenomenon that dictates how much trust a person has in a source of information. This is usually founded upon either trusting the source of that information or trusting the content itself.

Information Literacy: The ability to be critical about information in a meaningful way. This includes the ability to find resources and evaluate their accuracy.

Millennial Learner: Students who have been raised in technology-rich societies. These individuals are considered "digital natives" and generally are characterized by greater technological proficiency and a desire for collaboration and communication.

Web 2.0: Internet-based technologies such as blogs, podcasts, wikis, grassroots video, and social networking. These technologies shared characteristic includes the allowance of active participation by the audience.

Wiki: A piece of educational software that allows multiple users to edit shared information sources.

Chapter 6
Say it Down!
Scaffolding English Language Learners' Academic Writing with Speech Recognition Technology

Karen P. Kaun
Knowledge iTrust, USA

ABSTRACT

English Language Learners (ELLs) are in urgent need of instruction and tools to support their academic writing in English, which is essential to achievement in every academic subject and to overall school success (August & Shanahan, 2006). This chapter assesses the potential of speech recognition (SR) software, which through advances in research and development fueled by myriad commercial applications, now holds promise for new application in the classroom. SR has been studied for use in general education and by students with learning disabilities for academic writing. However, few studies to date have analyzed the impact of SR on ELLs' writing. This study shows that SR software supported student pronunciation skills, which in turn may impact word fluency and text production. In addition, students used the software along with other semiotic tools (language, document-based questions, and other curricular material) to enhance their writing during the New York State Education Department Examination in Social Studies, which scores students' essays for how they utilize higher level thinking skills and the extent to which they support their ideas with facts, examples, and details. Finally, this chapter explores how the constraints and affordances of the SR technology as a scaffold transformed with the students' mastery of spoken language and literacy.

INTRODUCTION

Statement of the Problem

The "No Child Left Behind" (NCLB) Act of Congress (2001) mandates that states use annual assessments aligned to their current academic standards in subject matter content including math, English language arts, and science to track achievement and progress over students' K-12 careers. All students including English Language Learners (ELLs), also referred to as Limited English Proficient (LEP) by NCLB, who have been enrolled in an English Language School

DOI: 10.4018/978-1-61692-854-4.ch006

System one year or more must take the state English Language Arts exam–which involves not only reading and answering multiple choice questions, but also requires writing essays in their non-native language. This policy is not in accord with research findings on ELLs who, depending on their individual learning needs and programs of instruction, can take three to five years to develop oral proficiency and four to seven years to develop academic English proficiency (Hakuta, Goto, Butler, & Witt, 2000).[1]

ELLs are in urgent need of instruction and tools to support their academic writing, which is a predictor of school success (Nagin, 2006) and young people's overall life chances. Literacy in English is essential to achievement in every academic subject and to overall school success (August & Shanahan, 2006). The facts illustrate the need. Whereas 10% of students who spoke English at home failed to complete high school, the percentage was three times as high (31%) for language-minority students who spoke English and five times as high (51%) for language-minority students who spoke English with difficulty (National Center for Education Statistics, 2004). According to the National Center of Educational Statistics (2009), the median income of persons ages 18 through 65 who had not completed high school was approximately $24,000 in 2007 versus approximately $40,000 for those with a high school credential, including a General Educational Development (GED) certificate. Among adults in the labor force, a higher percentage of dropouts are unemployed compared with adults who earned a high school credential (U.S. Department of Labor, 2007). Dropouts also make up higher percentages of the nation's prison and death row inmates.

In summary, literacy is a powerful instrument, at times defining our very lives with its facility. And writing ability, particularly in the academic settings of the United States, can open or close doors for a child.

Theoretical Framework and Context of the Study

Vygotskian sociocultural theory served as the foundation for research that was conducted from January to June 2008. The research was inspired by findings from a previously conducted pilot project[2] to help Latino middle school students who are English Language Learners (ELLs) to improve their academic writing. During the pilot, students in a New York City middle school were given access to a Web-based writing environment that provided online social studies materials with background information on the civil rights movement of the late 1950s and 1960s and on the immigration rights protests of early summer 2006. They were also introduced to a curricular scaffold that showed them how to analyze the materials from social, technological, economic, political, scientific and geographic perspectives and use these perspectives to build a cohesive essay. Classroom discussions were often quite lively; yet, many students who were active participants in the oral discussions had difficulty getting their ideas on paper. This finding became the inspiration for the subsequent research study that will be elaborated in this chapter. The central question: How can oral language and other "mediating tools" (Vygotsky, 1981) including speech recognition technology (SR) be harnessed to enhance ELLs' academic writing? To explore this question, an enhanced instructional approach was developed that utilized Dragon NaturallySpeaking speech recognition software and a planning tool[3] to help students transcribe their oral language to written text. Finally, five Latino ELL eighth-graders from the same New York City public middle-school,[4] who had varying degrees of oral and literacy competence in English, participated in case study research that was conducted over fifteen sessions, from January to June, 2008. These students received whole group and one-on-one instruction for writing that was scaffolded with the mediating tools. Following is a review of Vygotskian theory that underscores the importance of semiotic mediation in supporting students' learning within their zones of proximal development.

REVIEW OF THE RESEARCH

Vygotskian Theories of Language and Learning

In Vygotsky's view, speech and thinking develop independently of each other, but at a certain point in development they converge where "thinking becomes verbal and speech becomes intellectual" (Vygotsky, 1987, p. 112). In other words, language serves as a vehicle of thought (Vygotsky, 1987, p. 112).

All human activity is mediated by cultural tools (Cole, 1993) which arise from social interaction. For Vygotsky, semiotic mediation, which is the connection between the individual and the social, the internal and the external, is the key to all aspects of knowledge co-construction (John-Steiner, 1996). Semiotic resources (Vygotsky, 1981) include:

language; various systems for counting; mnemonic techniques; algebraic symbol systems; works of art; writing; schemes, diagrams, maps, and technical drawings; all sorts of conventional signs, and so on. (p.137)

Learning is not equivalent to development, but creates the possibility of development (John-Steiner, et al, 1994) "through culturally organized, specifically human, psychological functions" (Vygotsky, 1987, p. 90). Vygotsky's notion of the zone of proximal development was motivated by his claim that intrapsychological (personal) functioning grows out of interpsychological (between or among individuals) functioning (Wertsch & Stone, 1985).

A major contribution by Vygotsky to educational research is the concept of the Zone of Proximal Development (ZPD), which is the distance between the actual developmental level and what can be achieved through collaboration with more capable peers (Vygotsky, 1978). Vygotsky (1987) stated that the ZPD does not exist outside of learning, but is created during learning when a variety of developmental processes are activated through the children's interaction with people in their environment including their peers (Vygotsky, 1987). Children internalize the processes that occur during these interactions. The internalized knowledge is transformed on the basis of their own experiences, orientations and existing knowledge. These higher mental functions which develop through social interaction are meditated by semiotic resources (Vygotsky, 1981) which include language, writing and mnemonic techniques.

The Notion of Scaffolding

Wood, Bruner and Ross (1976) were influenced by Vygotskian (1987) views on the Zone of Proximal Development when they conceptualized scaffolding as a process that enables a child to carry out a task or achieve a goal beyond his unassisted efforts. The term scaffolding was and still is used interchangeably as a noun and a verb. It is a "structure, guided in a specific form by tacit assessment of a child's independent capabilities" (Pea, 2004, p. 425). It is also a process carried out and adjusted over time until a child is able to successfully complete the task him/herself. While scaffolding, as originally conceived by Wood et al. (1976), described child development as a series of informal social interactions, at-home, between mother and child, the notion of scaffolding was in time embraced in formal education settings. It is now more broadly applied to curricular structures and materials and technology. Pea notes that the "seeds for diffusion" (p. 429) for the definition of scaffolding are inherent in Vygotsky's writings. For the purpose of this discussion, a scaffold refers to instructional processes mediated by semiotic resources such as certain technological and curricular tools designed to help learners navigate their ZPD.

Pea (2004), who has been researching how information technologies can support learning, has developed a framework for the description of scaffolding. The framework includes an explanation of how scaffolding functions for a learner. "Channeling" (p. 432) places constraints around the task, thereby increasing the potential for its completion. "Focusing" (p. 432) points the learner's attention to relevant steps of a task, again increasing the potential for its completion. "Modeling" (p. 432) provided by an expert, can demonstrate a more advanced solution to the task. The scaffolds do not make the task easier, but make it possible for a learner to complete the task with support (Bruner, 1976) which is gradually "faded" (Pea, 2004, p. 438) as the learner becomes more of an expert.

Orality and Literacy

Vygotsky (1987) believed that "written speech" (p. 202) or writing was difficult for children because it involved a double abstraction process (Cole, 2006). The first abstraction involves the conversion of sounds, intonations, and expressions of oral speech to text on paper. He wrote:

Written speech is an entirely unique speech function. Its structure and mode of functioning are as different from those of oral speech as those of inner speech are from external speech. Even the most minimal level of development of written speech requires a high degree of abstraction. Written speech lacks intonation and expression. Its lacks all the aspects of speech that are reflected in sound. (Vygotsky, 1987, p. 202)

The second abstraction involves, as Vygotsky put it, "a conversation with a white piece of paper" (Vygotsky, 1987, p. 202) or the lack of "an interlocutor" (Vygotsky, 1987, p. 203). He added, "still like oral speech, it is a conversational situation" (p. 203). Vygotsky also wrote:

Written speech is the algebra of speech. The process of learning algebra does not repeat that of arithmetic. It is a new and higher plane in the development of abstract mathematical thought.... In the same way, the algebra of speech (i.e. written speech) introduces the child to an abstract plane of speech. (p. 203)

He further stated that written communication is "maximally expanded and formal" (p. 204) and requires the situation to be established in full detail so it can be understood. Everything must be made more explicit in writing.

A great deal of early research that was generated on literacy pointed to "the great divide" (Street 1984, 2005) between orality and literacy, or the notion that literacy endows those who are able to write and read with increased cognitive abilities such as thinking that is more rational, logical, abstract, detached, decontextualized and critical. Researchers whose work has shaped the cognitive divide theory include Eric Havelock (1963), Marshall McLuhan (1962, 1964, 1977), Jack Goody (1968, 1977, 1986, 1987) and Ian Watt (1963) and Walter Ong (1982). Their publications were highly influential in their time yet highly contested later on by scholars who include: Scribner and Cole (1981), Heath (1983) Tannen (1982, 1989) and Sulzby (1989, 1994, 1996).

Tannen (1989) has written about the myth of the orality-literacy dichotomy and demonstrates how the line between them is blurred through an analysis of the spoken and written narrative. To show that communicators will often mix modes depending on their perceived communication needs, Tannen demonstrates through discourse analysis how a short story "cut across spoken and written modes" (Tannen, 1989, p.18) when its author felt that she needed to inject emotion and immediacy into the tale to provoke action. Conversely, Sulzby (1996) observes that, when talking in formal monologues, some children engage in "book-talking" (e.g. oral language with few breaks or irregularities in the utterances, a neutral tone and a formal structure that resembles organized text) and cites this as evidence that children acquire emergent literacy skills through the combined influence of oral and written media. She concludes that literacy occurs along a spoken-written continuum as young children often speak written language and write oral language.

As it relates to English Language Learners, August and Shanahan (2006) report that ELLs need extensive oral English development incorporated into their literacy instruction if they are to become as successful, in text-level skills, as their native English speaking peers. In addition, ELLs who interact with English-speaking natives have additional opportunities to use English and a wider repertoire of language skills, including those associated with academic or school discourse (Genesee, Lindholm-Leary, Christian, 2006). Listening, speaking, reading and writing occur naturally in classroom events and mutually support each other in the overall development of a second language (Peregoy & Boyle, 2005). Frequent opportunities to engage in talk in meaningful and collaborative and interactive discussions to "test ideas for writing, including brainstorming… can build multiple literacy skills" (pp. 31-32) including the ability to expand upon ideas and articulate connections between prior knowledge and the topic at hand (Meltzer & Hamman, 2005b). In addition, speaking and listening can support student motivation to write (Meltzer & Hamman, 2005b).

If as the research suggests, there is a relationship between the oral and written, what are some of the ways and means that oral language can be harnessed for writing, particularly for ELLs who find writing in their non native language to be more cognitively demanding (Cummins, 2000) than speaking? One semiotic tool that shows promise is speech recognition software (SR).

Speech Recognition Studies, Working Memory, and Writing

A speech recognition system consists of: a microphone, for the person to speak into, speech recognition software and a computer to process and interpret the speech. By talking to the computer via a headset with a microphone, users see their text appear on the screen and in documents. Every action that can be done by keyboard and mouse can be done with speech input; such as, dictate text, navigate through programs or texts, apply functions like making words bold, and opening or closing files. The user trains the software to how she or he speaks. Then the software adapts dynamically to the particular speech patterns of the user. When a person first begins to use the speech software, the recognition and performance can be poor. The performance of the speech recognition software improves as usage and training time increases.

Until the late 1990's, commercial speech recognition systems were "discrete" in nature. This required the user to speak in an unnatural, command-like manner, with a pause between each word (to allow time for the computer to process the input, and to delineate to the computer when individual words ended). The increase in desktop computer processing power and better algorithms led to the development of "continuous" systems which match whole chunks of speech with statistical models of sentences and phrases. These allow the user to speak at near-normal speed and still obtain a high accuracy rate. Currently, continuous systems can give an accuracy of 90%-95%, depending on training.

Speech recognition (SR) software enables a computer to recognize spoken words and convert them to digital text in, for example, a Microsoft Word document. It proves to be a potentially powerful scaffolding tool because it harnesses English Language Learners' speaking skills, which develop prior to their writing skills. It may also reduce some memory demands thus freeing the ELLs to attend to higher level writing processes.

To date most studies which examine the effects of speech recognition on outcomes in K-12 writing have focused on students with learning disabilities and/or native English speakers, not English Language Learners. Until a few years ago, speech recognition software was not perfected to the point where it could with a high percentage of accuracy accommodate young voices, let alone young voices speaking English with accents. It was not until 2008 that Nuance (makers of Dragon) released their Dragon NaturallySpeaking version 10, which included a new option for English speakers with regional Spanish accents. Nonetheless, studies that have examined the effects of SR shed light on its affordance[5] as a writing tool to augment text generation and to increase writing fluency and quality.

As a general finding across all dictation studies, children generally wrote longer texts when dictating, relative to handwriting (Graham, 1990; Hidi & Hildyard, 1983; McCutchen, 1987; de la Paz, 1999; Reece & Cumming, 1996; Scardamalia, Bereiter, & Goleman, 1982). For students with learning disabilities, simply the physical act of writing often interfered with content generation.[6] For both LD and general education students, attention to lower-level skills interfered with higher-order planning (Scardamalia et al, 1982). Difficulty with writing may also effect student motivation and persistence during writing (de la Paz, 1999; Meltzer & Hamman, 2005b) and students may restrict what they put on paper to avoid spelling difficult words or composing complex sentences (de la Paz, 1999).

MacArthur and Cavalier (2004) examined the composing of two groups of students those with learning disabilities (LD) and those without, in three writing modes: handwriting, dictating to a human scribe, and SR. For students with LD, essays dictated to a human scribe were significantly better in quality than SR essays, which were superior to handwritten essays. These results suggest that both dictating to a scribe and SR impose less transcription load for students with LD than does handwriting. Yet Quinlan (2004) observed SR offers both benefits and challenges to a writer.

SR provides the writer with a visible representation of the developing text. Thus, SR affords the opportunity for rereading and dynamic planning, as do handwriting and word processing. Composing with SR requires contending with recognition errors. The methods available for correcting SR errors somewhat resemble those used to correct spelling errors in word processing. Thus, frequent errors may induce intensive monitoring and editing. (p. 338)

Wilson-Meddeb (2004) studied the effects of speech recognition technology on college-level writing tasks. Three students adopted a strategy of correcting the compositions as much as possible during the speech sessions. To perfect the compositions, it was necessary to make changes in the surface features of their talk (e.g. lexical choice, utterance length and pronunciation) to accommodate the software. Wilson-Meddeb (2004) concluded, "with the advent of a technology that automatically maps an acoustic speech signal to text, one can't help but wonder to what extent our notions of print literacy are likely to be affected" (p. 5).

Indeed, SR technology has made significant leaps in recent years due to intensive acoustic modeling research and development and the technology is now used with myriad devices to support writing, including to dictate text messages over the new generation of smart phones. Because multi-billion dollar commercial applications have driven significant improvements in speech recognition capabilities in recent years, this technology, that is revolutionizing how people (and people and machines) communicate across the globe, has matured and now holds much promise as an innovative writing intervention tool for English Language Learners.

Summary

Sociocultural theory, which originated with Vygotsky, posits that human mental functioning is a mediated process, which employs semiotics resources. These resources powerfully connect the external to the internal. As Lantolf (2000) succinctly says:

Vygotsky's proposal for unifying psychology was that while biological factors formed the basis of human thinking, in and of themselves, they were insufficient to account for our ability to voluntarily and intentionally regulate our mental activity. We achieve this ability as the result of the internalization of culturally mediated artifacts, including, above all, language. (p. 206)

As it concerns the ZPD, Vygotsky's research shows that learning collaboratively with others through social and institutional practices of schools shapes development.

Writing is a communicative act that is both social and cognitive. It involves the mediation of numerous resources by and between people. Talk, is a semiotic resource that can support writing in a number of ways, including: idea generation, building connections between prior and new knowledge, reducing working-memory demands to free up resources for higher level writing skills, and increasing students' motivation to write.

METHODOLOGY

Rationale

How can oral language and other "mediating tools" (Vygotsky, 1981) including speech recognition technology (SR) be harnessed to enhance ELLs' academic writing? To answer the research questions posed, case-study was chosen as the method, as it provides a holistic understanding of cultural systems of action (Feagin, Orum & Sjoberg, 1990) such as those that would occur in a classroom setting. A case relies on multiple sources of data that may converge in a triangulated fashion for validation. For example, statements made in an exit interview (e.g. "It was easy") may be compared against transcripts of recorded events (e.g. a student dictating into SR effortlessly). Case studies also benefit from the "development of prior theoretical propositions to guide data collection and analysis" (p. 14). For example, the proposition, *ELLs' oral proficiency may be harnessed to scaffold their academic (reading and writing) proficiency*, prompts the researcher to look for evidence of this in students' writing.

Building on a Pilot Study

Students in 8th grade in New York State are required to take an examination in Social Studies from the New York State Education Department (NYSED) each year in June. The test consists of two parts. Part one contains multiple choice questions on topics that are covered in the eighth grade social studies curriculum. Part two contains short answer questions based on photographs, drawings, maps, charts and graphs and documents from historical periods in time. For example, the June 8, 2006 test included a 1913 photograph of protesting garment workers in New York City. The prompt asked students to identify a goal of the protesters, which required them to synthesize contextual cues from the image with the English caption and the words printed on the signs. These are known as document-based questions (DBQ).

Document-based questions relate topically to the essay question that students also answer in part two and provide students with informational prompts that can be transferred to the essay. On June 8, 2006, the two-part essay question was: "Discuss reasons immigrants came to the United States" and "Discuss hardships faced by immigrants after they arrived in the United States." Students are expected to write a well-organized essay that is both descriptive and analytical and supports their thesis with relevant facts, examples, and details (NYSED, 2008, p. 11). These expectations are very high for all students, especially for ELLs who may be working at the surface-feature level of composition.

In the continuation of this study, a semiotic tool that provides sustained guidance in the writing process was created to help students plan their essay. This tool was inspired by the "STOP and DARE" planning intervention for writing developed by Susan De La Paz (2001) and reminds students to **D**evelop their topic sentence, **A**dd supporting ideas, **E**nd with a conclusion.[7] In addition, Dragon NaturallySpeaking, a speech recognition technology, was introduced to the students to harness their oral capabilities as a bridge to writing. This chapter will focus on how the speech recognition software impacted student writing.

Background on the students, the sessions and how the tools were introduced and used follow.

Setting and Participants

The research was conducted at the same middle school as the pilot, during the school's Saturday academic enrichment academy from January through June 2008.

More than a dozen ELL[8] students attending the school's academy were identified by the school staff as possible participants in the research. The students were primarily from Mexico, Dominican Republic, and Puerto Rico. All students were welcomed to the sessions. Of those students who were in and out of the sessions in the beginning weeks, five consistently came, trained the SR software to their voices, and stayed throughout the duration of the study. These became the focal students for the case study. Four students were Mexican, three girls (Maria, Esperanza and Selma) and one boy (Juan), and one girl (Katrina) was of mixed race (African and Puerto Rican) descent. All of the students were 13 years of age when they began the program. All of the students were in English-language only classes (math, social studies, science, ELA), that employed ESL-techniques at the time of the research.

Juan was born in the United States to a Mexican immigrant (mother) and Mexican American (father). Although Juan had been learning English since kindergarten, his main language at home with his parents continued to be Spanish. In addition, while Juan had strong oral English proficiency, he often interchanged Spanish for English (code switched) to perform word comprehension checks or as the social situation and group interaction dictated. During our time together he reported that he "already knows a lot of English" and he also liked engaging in the discussions about the social studies topics. When we began our sessions, he said he enjoyed writing, but I noticed that he often had difficulty generating his ideas on paper. The results section will focus on data from certain aspects of Juan's experiences with the SR technology that are generally reflective of experiences and perceptions of the other four students and relate to two significant findings of this research.

Data Collection Procedures

The five ELL students received small group instruction and one-on-one instruction from 11:30am to 1:00 pm during the school's Saturday academy over 15 sessions. In the first session, the students were introduced to the NYSED document-based question (DBQ) format, on the topic of the Great Depression. In the second and third sessions, students learned how they could use the planning tool to structure an essay. In the 4th through 10th sessions, students trained the SR software to their speech. Each student had his/her own laptop with SR software. The laptops were labeled with the individual student names and students took their own laptops each time they used them for a SR session, an essential action once SR was trained to their individual voices. Students dictated into microphones. These training sessions were taped to analyze the patterns students adopted in using the speech recognition software.

Over the next six sessions, students continued to train the SR software with the help of an instructor while, at the same time, they delved deeper into the topic of immigration and reviewed writing techniques. By the eleventh session, the students were using the SR software to take notes and compose responses to an essay question. Students were taped dictating to the SR in order to compare what they said to what was actually transcribed. All this data was compared to help determine how the mediating tools and the social interaction during instruction were impacting students' writing.

Data Sources

The data collected from these sessions include: Handwritten samples of students' writing; digital audio recordings of the discussions and interactions during the sessions; digital audio recordings of students' oral input into the SR software; output of SR in Microsoft Word; students' SR-assisted writing; and digital audio recordings of post-session interviews. The handwritten samples provide a benchmark of student writing prior to and during scaffolding. The digital audio recordings demonstrate how the instructional scaffolds were implemented in the sessions and how the tools were mediated by instructor and students within the zone of proximal development to reach the desired effect of improved academic writing.[9] Students' SR-assisted writing offers insight into how students' oral ability can be harnessed to scaffold their academic writing.

Data Analysis

Pea (2004), who has been researching how information technologies can support learning, has developed a framework for the description of scaffolding. The framework includes an explanation of how scaffolding functions for a learner, as follows:

1. Channeling, which "reduces the degrees of freedom for the task at hand by providing constraints that increase the likelihood of the learner's effective action" and completion of a task (Pea, 2004, p. 234);
2. "Focusing attention of the learner by marking relevant task features" (Pea, 2004, p. 432);
3. "Maintaining directedness of the learner's activity toward task achievement" (Pea, 2004, p. 432); and
4. "Modeling more advanced solutions to the task" (Pea, 2004, p. 432).

A data analysis tool[10] was developed that utilizes Pea's (2004) framework and expands it by applying these factors to the analysis of the impact that participant interaction and talk, semiotic mediation and the functionality of the SR technology had on a user experience. For example, visual input from Dragon "focuses" and "maintains" the user on task completion by providing instantaneous feedback on the progress of the initial voice training session. Modeling from an instructor can further support user success with the voice training and subsequent successful usage of the product.

The term affordance, coined by Gibson (1997) describes how objects (e.g. SR technology) are perceived in the environment (i.e. the interrelated conditions in which something exists or occurs) in terms of their possibilities for action (e.g. dictating with SR to write words on paper). The next section takes a deeper dive into the affordances and constraints of SR technology and its impact on student writing. I was surprised when Juan informed me about a particular affordance he found in one of the constraints of the technology. This affordance warrants further research.

Figure 1.

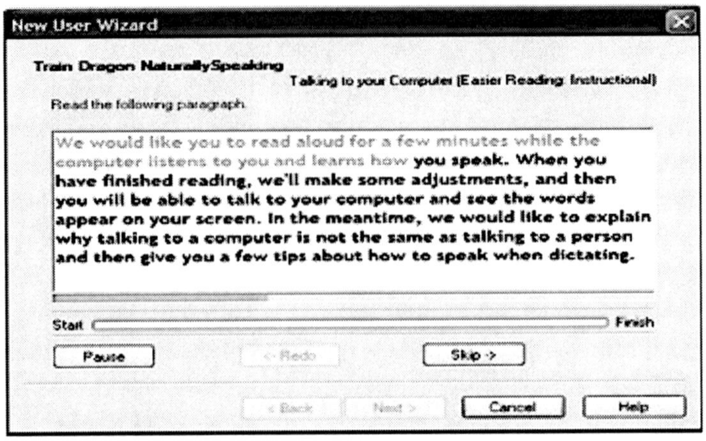

RESULTS

On January 26th, the class participated in a group Dragon training session[11] with all students microphoned to their laptops, sitting approximately three feet apart from each other, reading their training scripts. The training was unsuccessful for many students who needed more individual support. On January 26th, while other students were working in groups discussing and revising essays, I sat with Juan and helped him train the software. The SR software generated a script on Juan's computer screen (see Figure 1). It highlighted the words and sentences as Juan read along. When the software didn't recognize a word or sentence Juan said, it re-highlighted the word or sentence as a prompt for Juan to repeat it. Juan had some difficulty pronouncing words and had to repeat text, but in the end he was able to successfully complete the script and the training, and later was able to produce transcriptions with up to 80% accuracy.

In Table 1, Pea's framework is utilized to analyze what impact the participant interaction, the mediation of the semiotic resources (the software, the talk), and the software's functionality had upon Juan's experience.

Juan had a moderately difficult SR training session of 13 minutes[12] as he was forced to repeat words and sentence many times. When he was stuck, he was able to continue with support and modeling. In previous student training sessions, I noticed that pauses often interrupted the flow of the voice training. When I suggested that Juan "just read right along," Juan followed the instruction and was successful completing the sentence. Also, when I modeled word flow and annunciation this also helped Juan to complete a sentence and ultimately the training. While Dragon is designed to help users to be successful with the product; in this session, it was very important that Juan had the support of an instructor to help him to get through the training. Otherwise, the constraint of word pronunciation on successful completion may have been too frustrating.

We discussed Juan's perception of the training afterward, and he remarked that the first session–when the students trained Dragon together as a group–was "very hard" and the second session–when he received direct attention–was "kind of hard." When asked why he thought there was a difference between the first and second session, he answered, "My word pronunciation got better? I don't know." This notion stayed with Juan as we will later see.

Following the training, Juan began dictation. While Juan spoke, he could see accurate transcription or transcription errors in the software's toolbar

Table 1. Juan training SR software

Juan Training SR 1_26_08	Dialogue	Result
50:47 Juan	A week later a crowd gathered together in Carnegie Hall. The crowd became silent as the orchestra came up. There was a long silence as the crowd leaned forward. (c)	The SR software provides a script that users read to voice train the software. This channeling constraint enables the SR algorithm to match Juan's digital phonemes to words in its word dictionary.
50:47 Juan	That's leaned right? (f)	
	[Juan checks his pronunciation in order to complete the sentence.]	Juan is becoming more aware of his word pronunciation.
50:58 Karen	Yes. Leaned. (ma)	I agree and help Juan to maintain his activity toward task completion.
51:01 Juan	There was a long silence as the crowd leaned forward in their chairs and listened to the announcer. Carnegie hall is proud to present Susie. (c, f)	When the SR cannot match a user's phonemes to words in its dictionary, the software directs the user to re-read the sentence and focus on the task at hand until the word is understood. This has both a channeling and focusing effect.
51:05 Karen	Ok. There was a long silence as the crowd leaned forward in their chairs and listened to the announcer. Carnegie hall is proud to present Susie. (mo)	I do not want Juan to become frustrated and again maintain the directedness of his activity toward task achievement by modeling a steady unbroken word flow with clear annunciation of the words.
51:15 Juan	There was a long silence as the crowd leaned forward in their chairs and listened to the announcer. Carnegie hall is proud to present Susie. (c,f)	Juan follows my lead, but Dragon prompts him to re-read the sentence. He pauses.
51:20 Karen	Just read right along. (ma)	Pauses can disrupt the SR, because the software depends on cadence and rhythm of the user's voice to translate sounds into text, so I provide a suggestion to maintain Juan's activity.
	[Juan repeats the sentence three more times. A message pops up that announces he has successfully completed training.]	

Key: Channeling (c) Focusing (f) Modeling (m) Maintaining (ma)

and in the Word document, almost as quickly as he said the words (Figure 2).

In early April, Juan produces the following text. The words in brackets indicate transcription errors.

Juan

4/05/08

(Dragon Dictation)

BARACK OBAMA ON IMMIGRATION

This to see that they were the security is only one side of the equation. He voted for final passage of a bill in September 2006 that called for 700 miles of fencing along the US Mexican border. I **[I]** *supported its lesson and a comprehensive bill to establish a guest worker program provided a patch* **[path to]** *citizenship for most of the estimated 12 million illegal immigrants in the US and emphasize what your* **[worker]** *skills or Visa set off* **[instead of]** *a really nice and beef up border security.*

We must encourage them to come out of hiding get right with the law. He said in **[paying]** *a fine* **[,]** *learning English* **[,]** *not committing any crime and then going to the back of the line to apply for citizenship., also has advocated and produce me*

Figure 2.

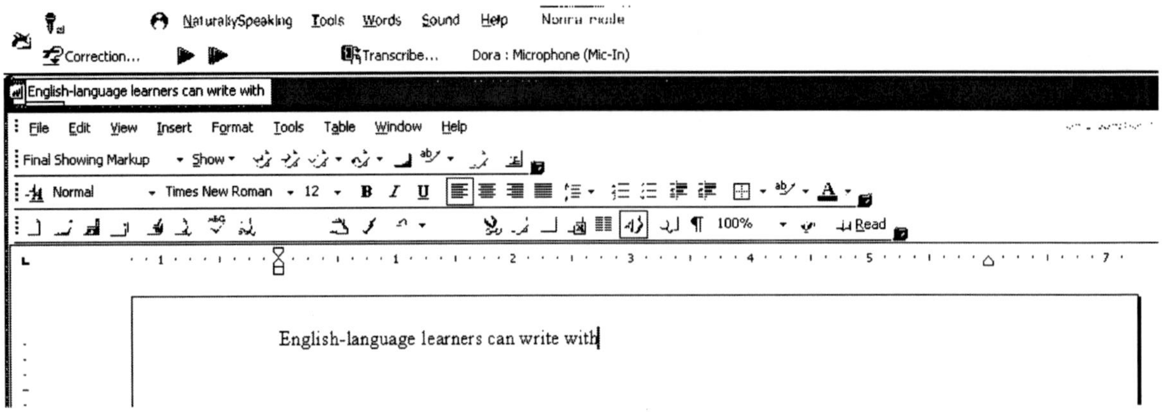

to **[that employers need to]** *do more to check the* **[legal status of their workers]** *new is that that.*

When Juan was asked about his experience with Dragon that day, he mentioned that Dragon didn't correctly transcribe all his words; however he concluded that this was beneficial to him because it would help him improve his word pronunciation. Herein lay an affordance of the software, that was unanticipated by me. It is possible that SR software can be used to strengthen ELLs' word pronunciation and fluency, which will in turn strengthen their writing.

Chenoweth and Hayes (2001) found that increased language use and better pronunciation related to greater fluency and resulted in a higher rate of text production and a lower frequency of revisions. In addition, MacArthur, Graham & Fitzgerald (2006) stated that fluent text production is important because during complex tasks, such as writing, cognitive processes compete for limited resources within working memory. "Inefficient processes can consume resources that might otherwise be devoted to higher level processes such as planning and revising" (p. 122).

Students can read from texts and compare the output of the SR transcription to the texts. They can mark the transcription errors and review them with instructors for pronunciation. Students can reread the words in the same or different sentences into the SR software. They, with their instructors, can then determine if there is an increase in transcription accuracy. Users are recorded by Dragon while they are dictating; therefore, students can go back and listen to these recordings, mark their transcription errors and review the recordings with their instructors for pronunciation, syntactic and other errors. Interestingly students who go through this process of being mediated by SR may also read more by default.

As to SR's potential to help students to write essays that are more aligned with expectations on state tests, the amount of text generated by Juan increased with his use of the SR software. This finding correlates with the observations by McCutchen (1987) and Reece & Cumming (1996) in studies with native English language speakers. In addition, with the increase in text came an increase in details to support his thesis. Below is Juan's handwritten response to an essay prompt.

Juan

1/26/08

(handwritten)

Was life in the 1900s more difficult for immigrants than it is today?

I think that life back then was a little easy because since the Italians fighted for their rights they're not immigrants now. For the mexicane now ins hard crossing the frontier because the migration is watching for the Mexican not to cross if they catch them they get reported and send back or probably they send them to jail now.

Juan had 15 minutes to write the response to the question following a lengthy review of DBQ documents and a discussion on immigration. He wrote that life was "a little easy," provides explanation, but adds very little detail to support his claim. Note that his comment that the "Italians fighted for their rights" was a fact he incorporated from the DBQ visual (see Figure 3).

Over the course of the Saturday sessions, Juan became very interested in child labor issues and immigration and he orally composed notes from two articles with the SR software. The first paragraph (below) includes notes from an article on early child labor and protective laws. The bold brackets indicate the correct words or phrases where the transcription was incorrect.

Juan

6/10/08

(Dragon without typed edits)

Child labor was a serious issue in New York well **[while]** *exact figures are not known experts believe that around 18 A.D.* **[1884]** *there were probably 60,000 200,000 chosen* **[children]** *between the ages of eight and 16 working in New York City only about 34% of the states chosen between five and 21 attend public school to compulsory education laws eight to 74* **[1874]** *car* **[required]** *children between the ages of eight and 14 to 10* **[attend]**

Figure 3.

Photograph of New York City Garment Workers, 1913

Source: *Historical Atlas of the United States*, National Geographic Society, 1988

6 Based on this photograph, identify one goal of this protest by immigrant workers. [1]

Score

school for 14 weeks a year in 1996 **[1896]** *a new educational pass ever cartoon* **[law passed that required children]** *ages eight to talk* **[go]** *to a school for time* **[full time]** *children between ages tone of what you* **[12 and 14]** *were required to a school at least eight***[y]** *days each year.*

In the second paragraph, Juan edited and paraphrased as he read a 1973 article from *Time* magazine entitled "Sweatshops in the Sun." The article is about child labor in the 20th century. Below are the last few sentences of the paragraph he composed.

I **[It]** *is not uncommon among foreign* **[farm]** *children in the US as many as 300,000 agricultural workers understand* **[under 17]** *to spend more time in the field than in school about 95% of its neighboring* **[laboring]** *children are cheap cheap community, some Mexicans many receive hardly an education often on June degrees as he frequently near danger is far missionary* **[farm machinery]** *and toxic pesticide*

The New York State Education Department social studies essay scoring rubric directs scorers to identify the degree to which students richly support the theme with many relevant facts, examples, and details. While there are numerous transcription errors, the SR software correctly transcribed enough of Juan's spoken words for him to be able to highlight key words, ideas and phrases for him to further edit his notes and/or create an outline. These notes could help him to compose an essay that is rich with supporting examples or "good information," as Juan mentioned in the discussion of his usage and perceptions of SR in Table 2.

Juan read an essay question, formulated a thesis and orally composed an essay by reading articles, highlighting important supporting information, and dictating verbatim or paraphrasing what he was reading. In the 6/11/08 interview, when asked what corrections he would make in his essay, Juan said "spelling." While his comment indirectly indicated that his focus was on spelling mechanics rather than form, his previous comment about searching for "good information" and "im-

Table 2. Juan's note taking techniques

6/11/08	Dialogue
Karen	When you were writing the essay about immigration did you approach it?
Juan	I was reading the story and getting the good information. I highlighted. Whatever I highlighted, I wrote.
Karen	Did you highlight the information in your book?
Juan	No it was already highlighted (from previous sessions). I read some parts and took the most important parts from what I highlighted. I spoke it and I wrote it down.
Karen	You wrote it down or you spoke it down?
Juan	(Laughs) I spoke it down.
Karen	So the question was "Was life more difficult in the 1900s than it is today?" What were you looking for in the book? What were your arguments?
Juan	Everybody had to work in order to eat. It was harder than it is today because now you don't have to work, only the father and mother. The mother and the kids had to work to get money to eat.
Karen	So that part of your argument was that the whole family had to work. So you were looking for evidence of that in the articles you were going through and you dictated that with Dragon. (He agrees.) If you had time to correct your Dragon essay, what would you have done?
Juan	I would have corrected my mistakes.
Karen	What mistakes were in the essay?
Juan	Spelling.

portant parts" demonstrated that Juan was also supporting his essay with an analytical argument, yet not thinking about the steps involved in this process. Here was an opportunity for us to delve into a refresher discussion about the purpose of writing and for me to model my own thinking processes in the art of composing an argumentative essay. This would help Juan to continue to develop an essay that would be more in line with the NYSED expectation.

As mentioned previously, a fundamental aspect of the scaffolding process is "fading"–which is gradually removing the supports (Pea, 2004). On June 10, Juan and I had a discussion about his experiences with the SR technology that day. Table 3 is a transcript of the discussion.

Though Juan says above that "now most of my words come out" so that pronunciation correction is no longer the major benefit (affordance) he still mentions "show my mistakes" at the end of the conversation, demonstrating that the scaffold for pronunciation hasn't competed faded but is in transition. It is interesting to observe how the constraints and affordances of the technology itself fade and redirect the support of the scaffolding tool for the user. When error-free transcription is constrained by Dragon's "understanding" of Juan's words–Dragon is a scaffolding tool for better word pronunciation. When Dragon is able to more accurately transcribe Juan's words (and its potential as a word pronunciation scaffold fades), then Dragon's potential as a writing scaffold increases for Juan.

Limitations of the Research

The accuracy of speech recognition technology has improved greatly since it was first introduced to the consumer marketplace over a decade ago. Indeed today, a native speaker might expect the transcription accuracy of the software to reach 95% with some adjustments made for error in the process of using the software. While the software developers of Dragon NaturallySpeaking have

Table 3. Juan's impressions of SR

6/10/08	Dialogue	Observation
Karen	The last time we spoke, you said it helped because you could see where you were getting words wrong. Do you still think that?	The constraint of the software was a benefit to Juan (an affordance).
Juan	Now, most of my words come out.	The affordance is fading with the constraint.
Karen:	So now you think differently about it.	
Juan	I say some words and the words come out.	There is a shift in perception.
Karen	So you think it would be useful to help you write now?	
Juan	Yeah.	Now the SR is becoming more of a tool for writing.
Karen	Do you like writing?	
Juan	No.	
Karen	Do you think you'd like writing more if you had this in the home or in the classroom?	
Juan	Yes.	
Karen	Why?	
Juan	Whatever I sawit will write it down for me. It will show my mistakes.	"Saw" is read. Whatever he reads will be transcribed. If, he reads out loud and mispronounces a word, he will see the mistake.

incorporated new acoustic models for better coverage of non-native and regional accents, non-native English speakers and children still may not expect to achieve such high transcription levels.

The research was limited by the time the students had spent with the software, which was eight sessions after the initial training was completed. Also as with all technology in the classroom, it is an art to intertwine content instruction with technology use, especially when the technology is new. It was important to find a balance of time spent teaching content so students had something to write about; time for learning how to use the planning mnemonic, and time spent exploring the features and benefits of SR. With more time, the students could have improved the accuracy of the voice transcriptions. Together, the students and I might also have devised additional ways to use the SR software to support their writing needs. In addition, because the classes weren't mandatory and took place on weekends, there were times when students didn't attend. This necessitated often repeating material that was missed so students could receive the full benefit of this pedagogic intervention. Finally, the number of students participating in the study was small and their oral and literacy skills were average to above average compared to other ELLs in their school. Therefore, the results of this study are not readily generalized. This said the, data provide me and perhaps other researchers with promising directions for future research.

In conclusion, speech recognition technology is a promising scaffold for ELL students' academic writing. Juan's data shows how SR software in combination with other semiotic tools can help to support ELLs' writing in tests that rate students' compositions on analysis and supporting details. Finally, the constraints and affordances of the SR technology as a scaffold transform with students' mastery of spoken language.

REFERENCES

August, D., & Shanahan, T. (Eds.). (2006). *Developing literacy in second-language learners: Report of the National Literacy Panel on language-minority children and youth. The Center for Applied Linguistics*. Mahwah, NJ: Erlbaum.

Bereiter, C., & Scardamalia, M. (1987). *The psychology of written composition*. Hillsdale, NJ: Lawrence Erlbaum Associates.

Bruner, J. (1978). The role of dialogue in language acquisition. In Sinclair, A., Jarvelle, R. J., & Levelt, W. J. M. (Eds.), *The child's concept of language*. New York: Springer Verlag.

Chenoweth, N. A., & Hayes, J. R. (2001). Fluency in writing: Generating text in L1 and L2. *Written Communication*, *18*, 80–98. doi:10.1177/0741088301018001004

Cole, M. (1993, April). *Vygotsky and writing: Reflections from a distant discipline*. Paper presented at the Annual Conference on College Composition and Communication, San Diego, CA.

Cummins, J. (2000). *Language, power, and pedagogy: Bilingual children in the crossfire*. Buffalo, NY: Multilingual Matters Ltd.

De la Paz, S. (1999). Composing via dictation and speech recognition systems: Compensatory technology for students with learning disabilities. *Learning Disability Quarterly*, *22*, 173–182. doi:10.2307/1511284

Feagin, J., Orum, A., & Sjoberg, G. (Eds.). (1991). *A case for case study*. Chapel Hill, NC: University of North Carolina Press.

Garcia, O., Kleifgen, J., & Falchi, L. (2008). *Equity in the education of Emergent Bilinguals: The case of English language learners*. Research Review Series Monograph, Campaign for Educational Equity, Teachers College, Columbia University.

Genesee, F., Lindholm-Leary, K., & Christian, D. (2006). *Educating English language learners: A synthesis of research evidence*. Santa Cruz, CA: Center for Diversity in Education. doi:10.1017/CBO9780511499913

Gibbons, P. (2002). *Scaffolding language, scaffolding learning*. Portsmouth, NH: Heinemann.

Goody, J., & Watt, I. (1963). The consequences of literacy. [reprinted in Goody 1968: 27-68]. *Comparative Studies in Society and History*, *5*(3), 304–345. doi:10.1017/S0010417500001730

Goody, J. R. (1977): *The domestication of the savage mind*. Cambridge, UK: Cambridge University Press Goody, J.R. (Ed.). (1968). *Literacy in traditional societies*. Cambridge, UK: Cambridge University Press.

Goody, J. R. (1986). *The logic of writing and the organization of society*. Cambridge, UK: Cambridge University Press.

Goody, J. R. (1987). *The interface between the written and the oral*. Cambridge, UK: Cambridge University Press.

2007Grade 8 intermediate level test social studies. Rating Guide. Book 2: Document-based question. June 6, 2007.

2006Grade 8 intermediate level test social studies. Rating Guide. Book 2: Document-based question. June 8, 2006.

Graham, S. (1990). The role of production factors in learning disabled students' compositions. *Journal of Educational Psychology*, *82*, 781–791. doi:10.1037/0022-0663.82.4.781

Graham, S., & Harris, K. R. (2006). Explicitly teaching struggling writers and their classmates strategies for mastering the writing process. *Intervention in School and Clinic*, *41*, 290–294. doi:10.1177/10534512060410050601

Greene, J. (2002). Civic report: High school graduation rates in the United States. Manhattan Institute for Policy Research. Manhattan Institute. Retrieved September 28, 2008, from http://www.manhattan-institute.org/html/cr_baeo.htm

Hakuta, K., Goto Butler, Y., & Witt, D. (2000). How long does it take English learners to attain proficiency? *University of California Linguistic Minority Research Institute Policy Report* 2000-1.

Havelock, E. (1963). *Preface to Plato*. Cambridge, MA: Harvard University Press.

Hidi, S. E., & Hildyard, A. (1983). The comparison of oral and written productions in two discourse types. *Discourse Processes*, *6*, 91–105. doi:10.1080/01638538309544557

John-Steiner, V. (1996, February). Creativity and collaboration in knowledge construction. Paper presented at National Council of Teachers of English Assembly on Research. Vygotsky Centennial: Vygotskian Perspectives on Literacy and Research. Chicago, IL.

John-Steiner, V., Panofsky, C., & Smith, L. (Eds.). (1994). *Sociocultural approaches to language & literacy: An Interactionist perspective*. New York, NY: Cambridge University Press.

Kaun, K., Arora, P., & Bucuvalas, A. (2007, April). Designing an enhanced web-based civil rights curriculum for Latino English Language Learners. Paper presentation at the American Educational Research Association (AERA) Annual Conference, Chicago, IL.

Kellogg, R. T. (1988). Attentional overload and writing performance: effects of rough draft and outline strategies. *Journal of Experimental Psychology. Learning, Memory, and Cognition*, *14*(2), 355–365. doi:10.1037/0278-7393.14.2.355

Kellogg, R. T. (1990). Effectiveness of prewriting strategies as a function of task demands. *The American Journal of Psychology, 103*(3), 327–342. doi:10.2307/1423213

Kindler, A. (2002). *Survey of the states' limited English proficient students and available education programs and services: 2000-2001 summary report*. Washington, DC: National Clearinghouse for English Language Acquisition.

Lantolf, J. P. (2000). *Sociocultural theory and second language learning*. Oxford: Oxford University Press.

Lantolf, J. P. (2006). Sociocultural theory and Second Language Learning: State of the art. *Studies in Second Language Acquisition, 28*, 67–109.

Lantolf, J. P., & Pavlenko, A. (1995). Sociocultural theory and second language acquisition. *Annual Review of Applied Linguistics, 15*, 38–53. doi:10.1017/S0267190500002646

MacArthur, C., & Cavalier, A. (2004). Dictation and speech recognition technology as test accommodations. *Exceptional Children*, 71.

MacArthur, C. A., & Graham, S. (1987). Learning disabled students composing under three methods of text production: Handwriting, word processing, and dictation. *The Journal of Special Education, 21*, 22–42. doi:10.1177/002246698702100304

McCutchen, D. (1987). Children's discourse skill: Form and modality requirements of schooled writing. *Discourse Processes, 10*, 267–286. doi:10.1080/01638538709544676

McCutchen, D. (2006). Cognitive factors in the development of children's writing. In MacArthur, C. A., Graham, S., & Fitzgerald, J. (Eds.), *Handbook of writing research* (pp. 115–130). New York: The Guilford Press.

McLuhan, M. (1962). *The Gutenberg Galaxy: The Making of Typographic Man*. London: Routledge & Kegan Paul.

McLuhan, M. (1964). *Understanding Media: The Extensions of Man*. New York: McGraw Hill.

McLuhan, M., & Logan, R. K. (1977). Alphabet, mother of invention. *Et Cetera, 34*, 373–383.

Meltzer, J., & Hamann, E. T. (2005). *Focus on classroom teaching and learning strategies*. Providence, RI: Education Alliance Northeast and Islands Regional Education Lab, Brown University.

Nagin, C.National Writing Project. (2006). *Because Writing Matters: Improving Student Writing in Our Schools*. San Francisco: Jossey-Bass.

National Center for Education Statistics. (2004). *The condition of education*. Retrieved February 22, 2009, from http://nces.ed.gov/programs/coe

National Center for Education Statistics. (2009). *High school dropout and completion rates in the United States, 2007*. Retrieved October 8, 2009, from http://nces.ed.gov/pubsearch/pubsinfo.asp?pubid=2009064

New York City Department of Education, Office of English Language Learners. (2009). The performance of New York City's English language learners. Retrieved February 22, 2009, from http://schools.nyc.gov/NR/rdonlyres/3B377E6B-5E22-4E63-A4DA-2B7FD14E5D62/57000/ELLPerformanceReport2009.pdf

Ong, W. (1982). *Orality and literacy: The technologizing of the word*. London, New York: Metheun. doi:10.4324/9780203328064

Pea, R. D. (2004). The social and technological dimensions of "scaffolding" and related theoretical concepts for learning, education and human activity. *Journal of the Learning Sciences, 13*(3), 423–451. doi:10.1207/s15327809jls1303_6

Peregoy, S. F., & Boyle, O. F. (2005). *Reading, writing and learning in ESL: A resource book for K-12 teachers*. Boston: Pearson Education.

Quinlan, T. (2004). Speech recognition technology and students with writing difficulties: Improving fluency. *Journal of Educational Psychology, 96*(2), 337–346. doi:10.1037/0022-0663.96.2.337

Reece, J. E., & Cummings, G. (1996). Evaluating speech-based composition methods: Planning, dictation, and the listening word processor. In Levy, C. M., & Ransdell, S. (Eds.), *The science of writing: Theories, methods, individual differences, and applications* (pp. 361–380). Mahwah, NJ: Erlbaum.

2004Revised generic scoring Rubric for Document-Based Questions (DBQs) on the Grade 8 Intermediate-Level Social Studies Test.

Scardamalia, M., Bereiter, C., & Goleman, H. (1982). The role of production factors in writing ability. In Nystrand, M. (Ed.), *What writers know: The language, process, and structure of written discourse* (pp. 175–210). San Diego, CA: Academic Press.

Scribner, S., & Cole, M. (1981). *The Psychology of Literacy*. Cambridge, MA: Harvard University Press.

State University of New York and New York State Education Department. (2008). Grade 8 intermediate level test social studies. Book 2: Document-based question. June, 4, 2008.

Street, B. (1984). *Literacy in theory and practice*. Cambridge, UK: Cambridge University Press.

Street, B. (2005). *Social Literacies: Critical approaches to literacy in development ethnography and education*. London, New York: Longman.

Sulzby, E. (1985). Children's emergent reading of favorite storybooks: A developmental study. *Reading Research Quarterly, 20*, 458–481. doi:10.1598/RRQ.20.4.4

Sulzby, E. (1994). Children's emergent reading of favorite storybooks: A developmental study. In Ruddell, R. B., Ruddell, M. R., & Singer, H. (Eds.), *Theoretical models and processes of reading* (pp. 244–280). Newark, DE: International Reading Association.

Sulzby, E. (1996). Roles of oral and written language as children approach conventional literacy. In Pontecorvo, C. (Eds.), *Children's early text construction*. Mahwah, NJ: Erlbaum.

Tannen, D. (1982). The oral/literate continuum in discourse. In Tannen, D. (Ed.), *Spoken and written language: Exploring orality and literacy* (pp. 1–16). Norwood, NJ: Ablex.

Tannen, D. (1989). *Talking voices: Repetition, dialogue, and imagery in conversational discourse*. Cambridge, UK: Cambridge University Press.

Time (1973, July 30). Sweatshops in the sun. *Time*. Retrieved from http://www.time.com/time/magazine/article/0,9171,907638,00.html

Torrance, M., & Jeffery, G. (1999). *The cognitive demands of writing: Processing capacity and working memory in text production*. Amsterdam: Amsterdam University Press.

Vygotsky, L. S. (1978). *Mind in society*. Boston: Harvard University Press.

Vygotsky, L. S. (1981). The instrumental method in psychology. In Wertsch, J. (Ed.), *The concept of activity in Soviet psychology*. Armonk, NY: Sharpe.

Vygotsky, L. S. (1987). Thinking and speech. In L. S. Vygotsky, R. W.Rieber (Series Eds.), & A. S. Carton (Vol. Ed.), *The collected works of L. S. Vygotsky*. Vol. 1: *Problems in general psychology* (N. Minick,Trans.). New York: Plenum.

Vygotsky, L. S., & Luria, A. (1994). Tool and symbol in child development. In van der Veer, R., & Valsiner, J. (Eds.), *The Vygotsky reader*. Oxford, UK: Blackwell.

Wertsch, J., & Stone, C. A. (1985). The concept of internalization in Vygotskys account of the genesis of higher mental functions. In Wertsch, J. (Ed.), *Culture, communication, and cognition* (pp. 162–179). New York: Cambridge University Press.

Wilson-Meddeb, E. J. (2004). *The interaction between speech recognition dictation technology and language use: A sociolinguistic study.* Unpublished doctoral dissertation.Columbia University, New York.

Wood, D., Bruner, J., & Ross, G. (1976). The role of tutoring in problem solving. *Journal of Child Psychology and Psychiatry, and Allied Disciplines, 17*, 89–100. doi:10.1111/j.1469-7610.1976.tb00381.x

Zehr, M. A. (2009, January 8). English-learners pose policy problem. *Edweek.* Retrieved January 15, 2009, from http://www.edweek.org/login.html?source=http://www.edweek.org/ew/articles/2009/01/08/17ell.h28.html&destination=http://www.edweek.org/ew/articles/2009/01/08/17ell.h28.html&levelId=100

KEY TERMS AND DEFINITIONS

English Language Learners: English Language Learners or Limited English Proficient (LEP) are NCLB terms that refers to individuals whose native language is not English and who are in the process of acquiring it. Bilingual scholars (Garcia et al, 2008) argue that emergent bilingual is a more appropriate term for students whose language abilities should be viewed as a national resource rather than a deficit.

Speech Recognition: Technology that converts spoken words into machine readable input that enables productivity, for example, computer users to dictate text directly into word documents, navigate through programs or browse the internet or handheld users to dial a mobile number by voice command.

Scaffolding: Instructional processes mediated by semiotic resources such as certain technological and curricular tools designed to help learners navigate their Zones of Proximal Development (ZPD).

ENDNOTES

1. In 2000, Hakuta et al collected and analyzed data on ELL students to determine how long it takes them to develop oral and academic language proficiency in English, or what Cummins (1981) terms Basic Interpersonal Communicative Skills (BICS) and Cognitive Academic Language Proficiency (CALP). Oral proficiency was tested using the Idea Oral Language Proficiency Tests, which assess vocabulary, comprehension, syntax and comprehension. Academic literacy proficiency was tested through instruments that included the *Woodcock Language Proficiency Battery,* which assesses not only students' academic oral skills, but also reading and writing.
2. The STEPS to Literacy pilot (Kaun, 2007) was conducted by a group of researchers from Teachers College, Columbia University and the author of this chapter was a team member. The pilot was conducted in a New York City school and focused on Latino ELLs who make up approximately 68% of the total New York City Department of Education (NYCDOE) ELL school population (NYCDOE, 2009) and 70% of the nation's ELL population (Edweek, 2009).
3. For this research study, the author independently developed and implemented two new scaffolds: a mnemonic device for the planning of an argumentative essay and speech recognition software to harness students' oral capabilities for writing. This chapter focuses on the affordances and constraints of speech recognition technology.

4 The first pilot group of students had graduated to high school.

5 The term *affordance* is defined as "a potential for action, the capacity of an environment or object to enable the intentions of the student within a particular problem situation" (Tanner & Jones, 2002, p. 78).

6 De la Paz (1995) has observed that students forget ideas because they can't write their thoughts down fast enough.

7 Note the **R** in Dare, for "reject arguments for the other side," was not included in this study.

8 The New York City Department of Education defines English Language Learners as students who speak a language other than English at home and score below proficient on English assessments when they enter the school system.

9 These scaffolds support NYSED Learning Standards for English Language Arts: Standard 1: Students will read, write, listen, and speak for information and understanding. Standard 2: Students will read, write, listen, and speak for literary response and expression. Standard 3: Students will read, write, listen, and speak for critical analysis and evaluation. Standard 4: Students will read, write, listen, and speak for social interaction.

10 Three data analysis tools were developed in total: one for the analysis of student writing against the NYSED rubric for DBQ essays; another for analysis of the instructor-student interaction; and a third for the analysis of the impact of the SR technology on student writing.

11 Product managers for Dragon advise that while it is best to train the software in a natural setting (e.g. students together in a classroom versus a student in isolation) it is also beneficial for students to have the support of an adult while they are training the software. The software comes with a noise cancellation microphone and the software adjusts for its surroundings; however, often students are distracted by their peers reading the same training scripts and find it difficult to stay on task without hesitating or making reading errors that will impede the training.

12 In comparison, his sister Selma has a short SR training session of 5 minutes and 29 seconds.

Chapter 7
Design and Development of Personalized Learning Environments

Raja Maznah Raja Hussain
University of Malaya, Malaysia

ABSTRACT

This chapter describes a pedagogical approach to engage students in online learning environments, using XNAMEX Becta's model for personalized learning and student engagement (PLEaSE). PLEaSE maximizes learning out comes by supporting students at times and in places that are appropriate to their needs and in ways that suit their personal dispositions In this study, students are encouraged to explore, develop, reflect and construct their own knowledge and create their own learning content, while the instructor plays the role of coach and facilitator. This study is part of an ongoing action research project on the Scholarship of Teaching and Learning (SoTL) in Higher Education, whose purpose is to design and develop the Pedagogy of Engagement Integrating Technology (PoEIT) model. PoEIT engages learners in the use of online tools such as forums and blogs while developing their soft skills using Moodle platform. This study shows that with the right integration of pedagogy and technology students can be transformed to become independent learners.

INTRODUCTION

Preparation of students for the 21st century requires changes in curriculum and pedagogy. Preparation is to ensure that students are ready and able to meet the Malaysian Qualification Standard (MQS) and similar standards as set by the National Educational Technology Standards for Students. The categories of skills (ISTE, 2007) required by the students in this preparation are listed as follows: (1) creativity and innovation; (2) communication and collaboration; (3) research and information retrieval; (4) critical thinking, problem solving, and decision making; (5) digital citizenship; and (6) technology operations and concepts.

The onus is on teachers and instructors to interest students in researching for creative strategies. More collaborative techniques and innovative

DOI: 10.4018/978-1-61692-854-4.ch007

technologies are required to engage students with 21st century skills. Students can only be trained through a total immersion in a technology-based learning environment, while solving real problems, using new tools to reflect, to develop content and to engage in social interactions. The emphasis is on the skills and knowledge required by students to learn and live productively in a digital society, and on creativity and innovation in technology.

Technology allows students to personalize their learning. Personalized learning has the purpose of encouraging students to become more involved in making decisions about what and how they want to learn (Campbell, et al., 2007). According to Leadbeater (cited in Campbell, et al. 2007) personalization is a socially oriented idea which could operate at five deeply structured levels:

1. Providing more customer friendly services
2. Giving people more say in navigating their way through services
3. Giving users more say over how money is spent
4. Users becoming co-designers and co-producers of services
5. Self-organization by individuals working with the support and advisory systems provided by professionals

Leadbeater (2003) believes that personalized learning is the promotion of self-realization, with students construed as active and responsible co-authors of their educational scripts. This will result in deep learning whereby students set their own learning targets, adopt continuous self-assessment for learning and develop the flexibility in learning beyond the classrooms. In this environment the technology tools such as Moodle allow for continual support by the professionals (instructors and tutors) and an advisory system to take place anytime and anyplace. Moodle as a learning management system (LMS) enables the students to navigate the learning journey while developing various skills in self-organization and life-long learning.

TRANSFORMING TO PLEaSE

Personalized learning requires redesigning of courses to allow for active and reflective learning to take place. In this chapter the author shares her experience in transforming her teaching in an undergraduate course for teacher trainees. It involves a reexamination of her beliefs and approach to teaching and learning in a technology-based learning environment. She believes that to learn about ICT, students should be immersed in ICT where learning is face to face and further supported online. The objectives of the Personalized Learning and Student Engagement (PLEaSE) are to: (1) engage learners in active learning; (2) encourage learners in collaborative and critical learning; (3) reinforce the development of soft skills; (4) facilitate construction of learners' own knowledge; and (5) explore projects based on the real-world environment.

Personalized learning can develop independence in students. Students learn to be co-producers and managers of their learning. Managing learning involves managing the given tasks related to course projects, managing the content of what they are learning, and managing the peers who are co-producers and co-learners in the team. In PLEaSE, students can co-author their educational scripts, thus allowing for individual interpretations of goals and values of education. As an innovation, personalized learning environment is a change that has to be managed. Transforming the traditional learning environment to a personalized learning environment requires scaffolding from the instructors who can provide guidance through mature thinking, patience and intentional support.

BACKGROUND

The course under examination is the Technology for Primary Education course. This course is an introduction to technology based learning for the teacher trainees. It is compulsory for third year bachelor of education students to pass the course. In the last cohort there were 73 students ranging between 21 to 22 years old. A survey of students' prior ICT skills was conducted on the first day of class to ascertain their readiness to learn in a technology-based learning environment. These students were found to be familiar with the latest ICT tools, and the majority owned a mobile phone (some with 3G capability), mobile broadband and some owned laptops which they carried to class. Most students were familiar with social networking tools and were subscribers to Friendsters, MySpace, Facebook and Blogs.

ENGAGING STUDENTS

The course was designed to introduce the students to ICT tools, ICT pedagogy and how to create learning environments where technology facilitates the student learning. Students were also introduced to the concept of personalized learning and student engagement (PLEaSE) (see Figure 1). This requires modeling of pedagogical change by the instructor and tutors. According to Bowen (2005) engaging students involves "getting students to engage and actively participate in their learning process; to engage with the object of study (ICT in primary education); to engage with the context of the study (primary education); and to engage with the human condition (learning how to interact in a social environment)."

David Merrills' First Principles (2002) guided the author in the design of strategies to engage students through project-oriented problem based learning (PoPBL) activities which require team-

Figure 1. Elements of personalized learning and students' engagement (PLEaSE)

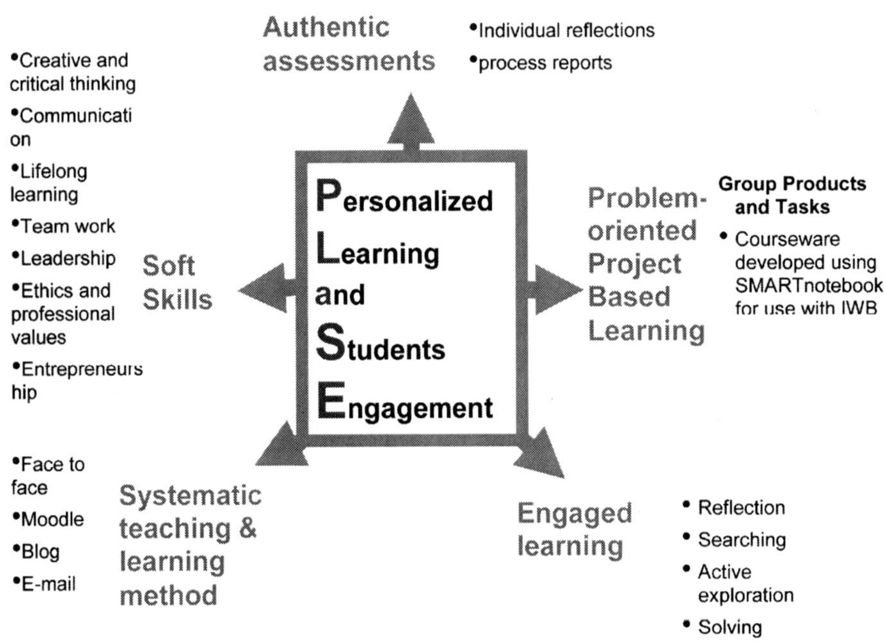

work, collaborative learning, problem solving, creative thinking and research. According to Merrill, learning is facilitated when learners are engaged in solving real world problems; when existing knowledge is activated; and when new knowledge is demonstrated as well as applied by the learners and finally integrated into the learner's world.

The process of inquiry and inductive learning built into the PoPBL activities was based on the principles of engagement theory, a framework for technology-based learning and teaching as proposed by Kearsley & Schneiderman (1999). Engagement theory is based upon the idea of creating successful collaborative teams that work on ambitious projects that are meaningful to people outside the classroom. In this case the project was for the teams to develop learning resources using SMART notebook software for primary school teachers to use with Interactive White Boards (IWB). The three components of engagement theory (which is summarized in the Relate-Create-Donate strategy) imply that learning activities occur in a group context, are project-based and have an outside focus (Kearsley & Schneiderman, 1999):

- **Relate:** students work in teams or collaboratively
- **Create:** students work on authentic projects that are meaningful to them
- **Donate:** students share their finished projects with a larger audience outside the classroom

Technology was used in all the individual and group activities pertaining to relate-create-donate strategy which allowed the teacher trainees to experience technology as a professional tool and as a culture. The ICT pedagogy allowed them to examine the roles of the teacher and students. They were able to see and experience how ICT could be used by a teacher to assess learners' prior knowledge, to provide mastery learning through coaching, mentoring and scaffolding processes and to assess individual and group learning.

The class met face-to-face once a week for three hours for 14 weeks. A virtual learning environment was created on a learning management system to support student learning outside of the classroom hours, to engage them with the technology-based learning environment and to provide them with a personalized learning environment. The learning environment provided students with the content and resources, activities and opportunities for reflection and articulation and the necessary learner support to guide learners as well as give them assistance and feedback during learning (Oliver, 1999). As part of the course orientation, students were introduced to the virtual learning environment and the learning management system (LMS) so that they would become familiar with the new learning environment, the tools and the available resources.

The Learning Management System (LMS)

The virtual classroom was managed using the learning management system, Moodle. The technology enhanced the support provided by the lecturer and the tutors outside of the class time. Moodle, an open source LMS was relatively easy to use and the students, because of their past experience with social networking software had minimum problems navigating through Moodle. The virtual classroom concept was adopted where access to the course was made available 24/7, and support from the instructor and tutors were made available and not limited to face to face meeting. For the students, this course was their first experience in online learning. The transformation, from face to face classroom which they were familiar with to a blended classroom, went quite smoothly. Most students embraced the change quickly. A few needed much prodding and convincing from the instructor, tutors and their peers to be more motivated to move onboard. The first couple of weeks saw peer mentoring and coaching happening face-to-face and online.

During the three-hour weekly class meetings, the first hour was often used for activation of prior learning followed by lecture and demonstration. The subsequent two hours were used to involve students through group discussions and practice sessions. Two computer labs were utilized to ensure that each student had access to a computer for at least two hours a week during the class time. The students used the computers and some used their own laptops to conduct research and to complete the tasks related to the course during the two hours.

Relating: Working in Teams or Collaboratively

Project oriented problem based learning (PoPBL) was used in the completion of the class's final project. PoPBL enables students to collaborate, to learn and to stretch their thinking (Bean, 2001). The final assignment required students to work in groups of 4 individuals to develop instructional materials for use with the Interactive White Boards (IWB). Each group had to develop materials for English, Math and Science lessons. The final project helped the students to learn about Interactive White Board as a tool to engage learners in whole classroom interaction and at the same time developed instructional design competencies. The instructional design employed the objectivist-constructivist blended design approach (Chen, 2007) whereby constructivist design has the strength to promote meaningful learning whereas objectivist design has the advantage to produce efficient learning. Thus the technology supported PoPBL project approach allowed for the development of meaningful and efficient learning.

It was a challenge for the students to learn to use the IWB tool and the software to develop the content in just five weeks. The software was downloaded by the students into their own personal computers or laptops, which they used outside the class time, mostly at home. The project development was monitored closely by the instructor and tutors. The group reported weekly for four weeks on their progress during the face-to-face class meetings. The final products were showcased to the whole class. The IWB products were uploaded to Airset.com, a tool for collaboration which was taught to the students during the class. By uploading their final projects to Airset.com, students **donated** their products for use by other teachers.

Creating and Donating: Authentic Meaningful Projects

Students experienced knowledge construction activities where sharing and generating ideas became a habit. Their forum space in Moodle became a teaching and learning classroom, where students posted questions and ideas that were of concern to them. The forum topics were mostly triggered by issues discussed in the class, or stories told by the instructor, questions to ponder and readings and links posted online by both the instructor and the students. The interactions created a learning community. Twenty-eight new forum titles were created by the students in fourteen weeks. One forum was created by a student after the semester was over to discuss a topic from another class in the subsequent semester. The forum space was a reflection of what the teacher trainees were concerned about. Such topics as ICT use in primary schools and the roles of teachers were popular (Figure 2).

Issues such as lack of infrastructure and ICT facilities in schools reflected the concern that the teacher trainees had in relation to their future posting as teachers. Higher order thinking was observed to have been employed in the forum where students created contents from knowledge that they researched on the Internet and from their personal experiences. On many occasions peer-teaching and mentoring took place in the online classroom as evidenced in the discussion in Figure 3. The learning environment had contributed

Figure 2. Discussion topics started by students

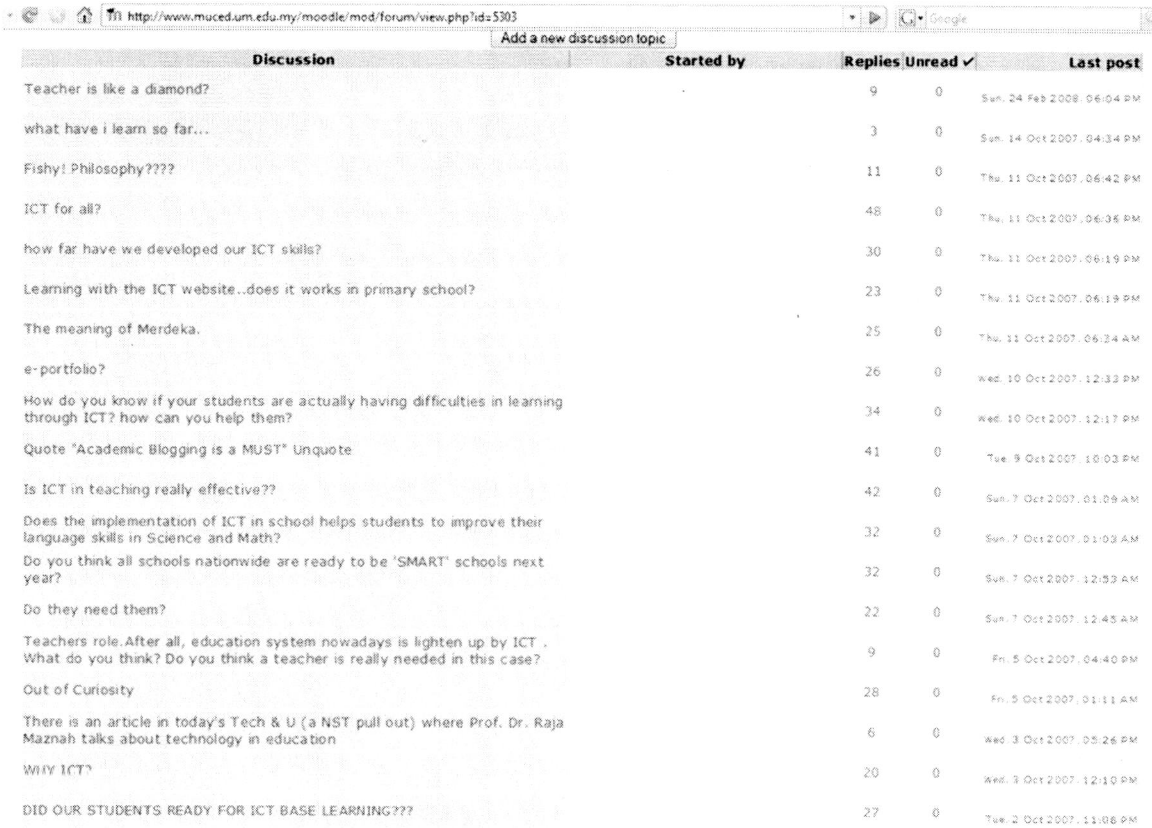

http://www.muced.um.edu.my/moodle/mod/forum/view.php?id=5303

Add a new discussion topic

Discussion	Started by	Replies	Unread ✓	Last post
Teacher is like a diamond?		9	0	Sun, 24 Feb 2008, 06:04 PM
what have i learn so far...		3	0	Sun, 14 Oct 2007, 04:34 PM
Fishy! Philosophy????		11	0	Thu, 11 Oct 2007, 06:42 PM
ICT for all?		48	0	Thu, 11 Oct 2007, 06:36 PM
how far have we developed our ICT skills?		30	0	Thu, 11 Oct 2007, 06:19 PM
Learning with the ICT website..does it works in primary school?		23	0	Thu, 11 Oct 2007, 06:19 PM
The meaning of Merdeka.		25	0	Thu, 11 Oct 2007, 06:24 AM
e-portfolio?		26	0	Wed, 10 Oct 2007, 12:33 PM
How do you know if your students are actually having difficulties in learning through ICT? how can you help them?		34	0	Wed, 10 Oct 2007, 12:17 PM
Quote "Academic Blogging is a MUST" Unquote		41	0	Tue, 9 Oct 2007, 10:03 PM
Is ICT in teaching really effective??		42	0	Sun, 7 Oct 2007, 01:09 AM
Does the implementation of ICT in school helps students to improve their language skills in Science and Math?		32	0	Sun, 7 Oct 2007, 01:03 AM
Do you think all schools nationwide are ready to be 'SMART' schools next year?		32	0	Sun, 7 Oct 2007, 12:53 AM
Do they need them?		22	0	Sun, 7 Oct 2007, 12:45 AM
Teachers role.After all, education system nowadays is lighten up by ICT . What do you think? Do you think a teacher is really needed in this case?		9	0	Fri, 5 Oct 2007, 04:40 PM
Out of Curiosity		28	0	Fri, 5 Oct 2007, 01:11 AM
There is an article in today's Tech & U (a NST pull out) where Prof. Dr. Raja Maznah talks about technology in education		6	0	Wed, 3 Oct 2007, 05:26 PM
WHY ICT?		20	0	Wed, 3 Oct 2007, 12:10 PM
DID OUR STUDENTS READY FOR ICT BASE LEARNING???		27	0	Tue, 2 Oct 2007, 11:08 PM

to the creation of self-directed learners (Hartley & Bendixen, 2001) who were able to regulate, guide and direct their learning. Self-directed learning was also evident in the weblogging activity that each student had to conduct as a course requirement.

Weblogging and Reflective Learning

Learning by reflection was utilized in the course to allow students to engage in knowledge creation and to explore the connections between course materials and their individual life or psyche (Bean, 2001). Reflection was enabled via weblogging. Weblogging on Blogspot was a graded course requirement. Criteria for grading the blogs were agreed with the students at the beginning of the course. It was a common understanding that the blog was an academic exercise and students were to use good English to write and present their ideas. Each student created a blog on the first day of class. A minimum of 10 postings were required over a period of 14 weeks. Students were required to blog and reflect on their lessons and readings, at least once a week. They were instructed to start reflecting by thinking about "Today I learn, today I question." Their blogs were closely monitored by the teaching team. New blog entries were fed to the teaching team through bloglines.

Students posted their blog links as their personal website in their profile on the class Moodle. Students were also encouraged to visit their friends' blogs and leave comments. Blogging helped the students to personalize their content

Figure 3. A threaded discussion started by a student

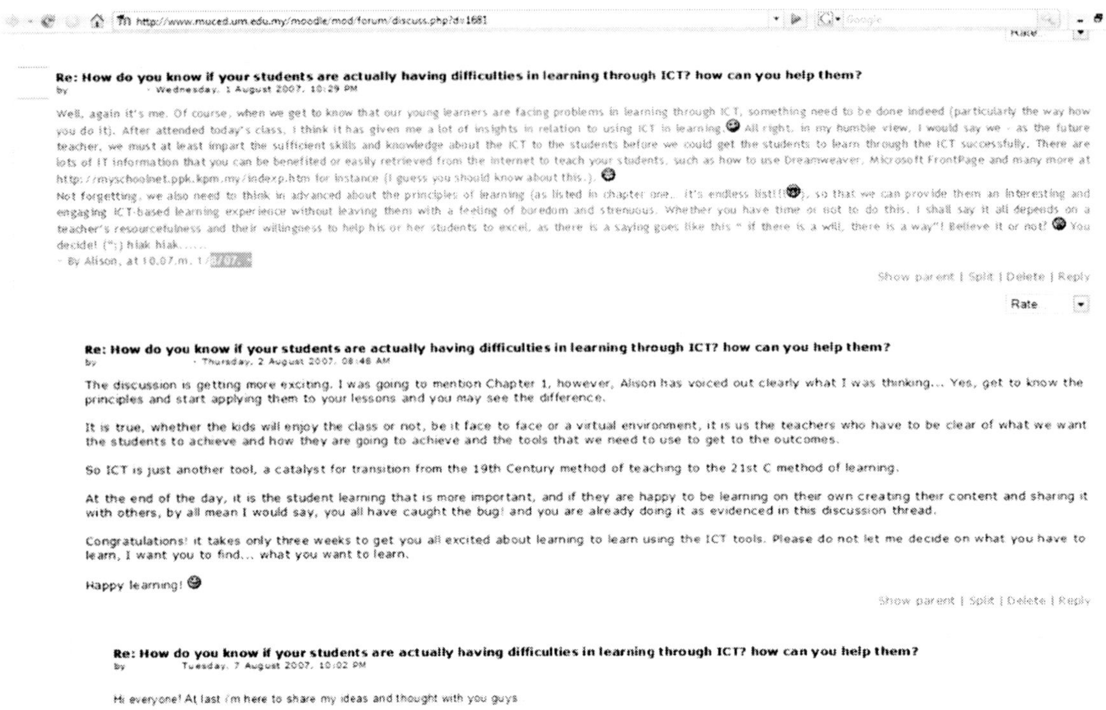

knowledge, based on what they had learned and understood. Some students used the opportunity to read and search for more information which they were certain could benefit their friends by enriching their blogs with links and ideas. Some even provided tutorials on specific skills and knowledge to benefit the peers. For most students this was the first time that they blogged for academic purposes. It took a while to convince everyone to share their thoughts with and communicate what they have learnt to others. Good blogs were shared with the class thus encouraging others to benchmark their work. Benchmarking helped the students to keep track of their learning and to improve their work by accessing their peers' reflections.

Soft Skills Acquisition

Besides preparing student teachers with the pedagogy to engage learners in technology-based learning environments, lecturers and tutors were also responsible for making sure that future teachers would be adequately equipped with the necessary soft skills which are:

1. Creative and critical thinking;
2. Communication;
3. Life long learning;
4. Team work;
5. Leadership;
6. Ethics and professional values; and
7. Entrepreneurship

Such skills are also known as generic skills. Year 2007 was the first time that the public universities in Malaysia had to assess their students' acquisition of soft skills during their third year of study. Soft skills were embedded into the teaching and learning activities and were assessed formally. In this course students were given orientation on the need to assess their soft skills as one of the learning outcomes, on the first day of class.

Self-assessment of soft skills was encouraged. To find out if students were able to assess their soft skills a message was posted by the instructor that told students to assess their soft skills and to give evidence to show that their soft skills had improved. Thirty-nine (53%) students responded to the message. The responses were mostly positive and lengthy. Students indicated that they had developed the soft skills and were able to give evidence to show that they were able to assess their learning and the course had helped them to achieve learning outcomes related to soft skills. Here is an example of the response:

Re: MY Soft Skills acquisition

by Student #1 - Wednesday, 3 October 2007, 11:38 AM

As far as I'm concerned, I've developed most of my soft skills since entering this course. For instance

1. ***Communication:*** *Before this I've always worked with the same group members but luckily for this course I've a chance to work with new group member (INA) who is from the same course (B.Ed TESL). I had the opportunity to communicate and work with her. Besides that, blogging also developed my communication skills as I'm able to communicate my ideas and also tighten our friendship.*
2. ***Creative and critical thinking:*** *Undeniably, this course requires me to work on a few projects and activities such as web-based learning, IWB assignment, designing posters, etc. So, I've to utilize creative and critical thinking skills in order to produce high-quality products. Moreover, blogging and forum also developed my reasoning skill in discussing and responding to the topics or issues raised. (Thanks for providing wide intellectual exploration!!!)*
3. ***Team work:*** *most of the work assigned need to be accomplished in group. As a result, I find that I've also developed skills of working in a clique of friends as I believe that more heads are better than one and also create synergy. It also teaches me how to cooperate with others when doing particular work esprit de corp!*
4. ***Leadership:*** *in my group, we never appointed a group leader as I believe that everyone is a leader. Each of us has responsibility to lead and guide ourselves. But, in completing certain tasks, I volunteered myself to plan and divide the work among us. I feel quite proud as my leadership skills can be developed and I do hope to further hone this skill in the future.*
5. ***Ethics and professional values:*** *of course as teachers-to-be, we should equip and practice the ethics and professional values. Some of the values which I think I've developed are we should give serious commitment when completing particular tasks, never practice procrastination and be open-minded.*
6. ***Entrepreneurship:*** *I think this is one of the soft skills which I still lack. So, I need to be more active and seek for opportunities.*
7. ***Lifelong learning:*** *this course has made me aware of the importance of life-long learning specifically in the educational field. In this 21st century, there is a rapid and tremendous development of technology and it also enormously influenced the use of ICT tools in classroom. Thus, as teachers in the technology explosion era, we need to learn, learn and learn so as to equip ourselves with sound knowledge especially about the educational technology.*

Transformation

From the blogs and the discussions in the forums, students were observed to have transformed from novice users of technology to practitioners who were engaged and immersed in the use of technology and at the same time they learned to sharpen their soft skills. The learning outcomes for the projects were achieved whereby students were able to develop the products, in the form of IWB courseware, which necessitated learning of new tools, message design, instructional design, project management, social networking tools and the learning management systems. Besides achieving the planned learning outcomes the students also displayed outcomes related to peer mentoring, coaching and benchmarking that were not planned for in the course syllabus. From the forums and personal testimony, it is evidenced that these future teachers have been empowered with their newly acquired technology skills and soft skills giving them the confidence to engage their future students in technology.

CONCLUSION

As a world of "one size fits" all gives way to a world of personalisation, education would need to make adjustments to survive (Heppell, 2008). This chapter is an attempt to share the author's experience of training undergraduate teacher trainees to embrace technology in teaching and learning and to prepare them for such a world of personalization through the practice of personalized learning and student engagement (PLEaSE). By modelling the pedagogy for use of ICT in teaching and learning, teacher trainees were immersed in the technology-based learning environment. Through PoPBL they were empowered with tools and techniques to solve real world problems. Teacher trainees were provided with opportunities to personalize learning, to reflect on their journey individually and in groups, to learn face-to-face and online. They used Web 2.0 tools to communicate, collaborate, socialize and manage their learning. Learning transformation was observed from the quality of interactions in the course forums, weblogs and the products submitted at the end of the semester.

This experience is also an attempt to explore the scholarship of teaching and learning (SoTL) in a scholarly teaching practice to develop the Pedagogy of Engagement Integrating Technology (PoEIT) model (Raja Hussain, 2006) where technology is integrated into the teaching and learning, making the pedagogy more interesting and challenging. The sharing of the scholarly practice is also meant to be a form of reflection on the teaching and learning practiced in the technology enhanced learning environments. Thus making the teaching public, open to critique and evaluation from others so that the community can build on this work (Hutchings and Shulman, 1999).

In the personalized learning environment students could learn through reflection, knowledge construction and social interaction which are lifelong learning skills. In order to train teachers who are ready for the 21st century the instructor has to be able to: 1) please students, have faith in them and support their learning through coaching and mentoring; 2) model the philosophy, the use of the strategies and the use of the supporting technology; 3) engage students in learning through careful instructional design and development, taking into consideration students readiness, prior ICT skills, time management and appropriate reward system; and 4) support online learning through scaffolding, regular feedback and monitoring of student learning.

REFERENCES

Bean, J. C. (2001). *Engaging ideas: The professors guide to integrating writing, critical thinking, and active learning in the classroom*. San Francisco: Jossey-Bass.

Campbell, R. J., Robinson, W., Neelands, J., Hewston, R., & Mazzoli, L. (2007). Personalized learning: Ambiguities in theory and practice. *British Journal of Educational Studies*, *55*(2), 135–154. doi:10.1111/j.1467-8527.2007.00370.x

Chen, S. J. (2007). Instructional design strategies for intensive online courses: An Objectivist- Constructivist blended approach. *Journal of Interactive Online Learning*, *6*(1), 72–86.

Hartley, K., & Bendixen, L. D. (2001). Educational research in the Internet age: Examining the role of individual characteristics. *Educational Researcher*, *30*(9), 22–26. doi:10.3102/0013189X030009022

Heppell, S. (2008). Education 2020. *ESCalate-News, 10*(Spring), 29-31. Retrieved April 27, 2008, from http://www.escalate.ac.uk/4439

Hutchings, P., & Shulman, L. S. (1999). The scholarship of teaching: New elaborations, new developments. *Change*, *31*(5), 10–15. doi:10.1080/00091389909604218

ISTE. (2007). The National Educational Technology Standards for Students: The Next Generation. Retrieved January 10, 2008, from http://www.iste.org/net

Kearsley, G., & Shneiderman, B. (1999). Engagement Theory: A framework for technology based teaching and learning. Retrieved January 10, 2008, from http://home.sprynet.com/~gkearsley/engage.htm

Merrill, M. D. (2002). First principles of instruction. *Educational Technology Research and Development*, *50*(3), 43–59. doi:10.1007/BF02505024

Oliver, R. (1999). Exploring strategies for online teaching and learning. *Distance Education*, *20*(2), 240–254. doi:10.1080/0158791990200205

Raja Hussain, R. M. (2006, September, 9-11). Pedagogy of Engagement Integrating Technology (PoEIT). Paper presented at the Malaysian Educational Technology Association Convention, Johor, Malaysia.

Chapter 8
Peer Assistance and Interaction in an Online Forum

Ugur Kale
West Virginia University, USA

ABSTRACT

This study examines peer interaction and peer assistance observed in on an online forum, part of a graduate level instructional design course during the 2008 spring academic term. It incorporates both content analysis and social network analysis techniques. The content analysis results showed that the four types of peer assistance adopted from an existing framework were adequate to categorize the peer assistance that the students received during the study. Students tended to receive more Reflective assistance from their peers if their reading reflections provided high relevance to the course projects. Social network analysis results revealed that while 70% of the students provided peer assistance to one another, they were less likely to go beyond the course requirement of posting toward to end of the semester. Also, a further analysis demonstrated how SNA approach may help examine the influences of actor attributes on their observed communication.

INTRODUCTION

Collaboration allows learners to share knowledge with one another in an effort to enhance their own knowledge base. By providing knowledge that benefits others' learning and acquiring information from those who have more knowledge, learners are able to acquire skills and experiences that may not be achieved easily otherwise through their individual efforts. Online asynchronous forums have been popular in educational settings as they provide students with the opportunities to collaborate on an "anytime and in anyplace" basis. Students are believed to provide better reflection and responses in such settings as they have the extended time to read one another's messages and provide a more articulated responses (Dede, 2004; Leach, 2002).

Despite the potentials, there are issues with the use of online forums. Research studies observed participation level in asynchronous forums to be low (Hewitt, 2005; Romiszowski & Mason, 2004;

DOI: 10.4018/978-1-61692-854-4.ch008

Winiecki, 2003) and the information exchange in the posted messages not to be necessarily elaborative and thoroughly detailed (Gunawardena, Lowe, & Anderson, 1997). Existing research also indicates that assisting participants' dialogue is one of the major factors that affect their participation level and message content. Prompting issues (Carboni, 1999), encouraging response (Caggiano, Audet, & Abegg, 1995; Kale, Brush, & Saye, in press), providing structured guidance and clarification on expectations (Dennen, 2005; Yang & Liu, 2004) lead to high participation level and more reflective message content. Most research efforts, however, focused on instructors' role, ignoring possible peer assistance and peer interaction that may also account for students' observed online participation (Hew & Cheung, 2008).

The current study attempts to address this gap by applying necessary theoretical and methodological perspectives, namely content analysis and social network analysis approaches in examining asynchronous communication of students in an online forum. The forum focused in the current study was part of a graduate level instructional design course in a Mid-Atlantic university in 2008. The course provided students with experiences to employ prototyping concepts for developing computer-based instructional products. Students used the online forum to post their reflections on readings and to discuss their course projects. The study analyzed students' postings to examine the observed peer assistance and the patterns of peer interaction.

THEORETICAL FRAMEWORK

Peer Assistance

According to the cognitive apprenticeship, learners observe the "performance" of others and start to perform with gradually decreased assistance from more capable others (Collins, Brown, & Holum, 1991). In this view, the more "capable of others" are not only instructors but also students who possess the necessary knowledge to be able to assist other students who lack the knowledge. In online forums, the messages exchanged between students may be in the form of assistance such as feedback, suggestions, or encouragement. Students' participation level may be different if they receive such assistance and information exchange from their peers as opposed to from their instructors (Poole, 2000), who may actually dominate the discussion. As Mazzolini and Maddison (2003) found, frequent postings from instructors can lead to shorter discussions. Students may tend to rely on instructors' expertise and thus may feel hesitant to contribute to the discussion if it reflects too much instructors' point of view.

Even though information exchange among students may be important to their online participation, research examining various types of assistance they provide to and receive from each other is limited. Majority of research focusing on assisting online dialogues examines strategies employed by instructors (Hew & Cheung, 2008) and various types of assistance that peers provide to each other in online settings have not been clearly defined. Thus, the first research question in the current study is:

RQ1. What types of peer assistance did students receive from each other in an online forum?

A Model for Examining Peers Assistance

Hew and Cheung (2008) identified various peer facilitation techniques based on a group of student teachers' participation in an online forum. The students in their study were observed to facilitate each others' dialogues through these strategies, namely introduction, engagement, and monitoring. Although these techniques may be useful, employing them as an initial framework in the current study may be problematic. First, the data came from a structured online discussion of a graduate level course where students were assigned to the roles of facilitators and participants, preventing a natural online communication. Second, the single case examined in the study makes the findings applicable mainly to similar setting-teacher education programs. On the other hand, a model we synthesized in our recent work (Kale et al., in press) incorporating both a cognitive apprenticeship view (Bonk & King, 1998; Collins et al., 1991; Tharp, 1993) and online moderators' roles (Anderson, Rourke, Garrison, & Archer, 2001) may be a better choice to examine online peer assistance.

Based on a cognitive apprenticeship perspective, Bonk and King (1998) consolidated a set of strategies to assist development of expertise and understanding, which was derived from the existing models developed by Collins et al. (1991) and Tharp (1993). Coaching and scaffolding, modeling, feedback and reinforcement, encouraging articulation, and questioning are some of the main strategies. Even though these techniques may be promising, they focus mainly on the cognitive aspect of assistance. The framework formulated by Anderson and his colleagues (2001), on the other hand, emphasizes facilitation of online discourse through different roles of online moderation. These roles, namely direct instruction, facilitating discourse, and instructional design and organization, highlight the different aspects of assistance such as affective and organizational strategies, which may also be observed in online peer interaction.

We used these models in our recent work to examine types of assistance provided on an online forum used by K-12 teachers as part of their professional development (Kale et. al, in press). The constant-comparative content analysis (Lincoln & Guba, 1985) employing these models as an initial framework revealed various types of assistance that were classified under five main categories: Informative, Directive, Reflective, Affective, and Administrative For the context of the current study, the description of the these categories were adapted as the following:

- **Informative:** Students share information such as explanation, feedback, resources, and clarification for their initial posting in the discussion.
- **Directive:** The emphasis is to switch students' focus to different or potential issues with their course project implementation.
- **Reflective:** Reflective assistance requests or encourages students to respond to questions, reflect on their projects, or simply provide their input to the discussion.
- **Affective:** Affective assistance reveals one's positive feelings about their peers' course projects and its process. It may be in the form of sharing excitement to see each others' project completion.
- **Administrative:** In Administrative assistance, students share information regarding scheduling, planning, or technical supports related to conducting their course projects.

Table 1. Comparison of frameworks for assistance types online

Kale et al.	Hew & Cheung	Anderson et al.	Bonk & Kim, Collins et al., Tharp
Informative Directive	Monitoring	Direct Instruction	Cognitive/Pedagogical
Reflective Affective	Engagement	Facilitating Discourse	
Administrative	Introduction	Inst. Des./Organization	

See Table 1 for the adapted synthesized framework (Kale et al. in press) with the aforementioned models.

Because of their relevant theoretical basis and the tested high inter-reliability (Cohen kappa (N=91) =.90), the categories synthesized are suitable to adopt in the current study as an initial framework to examine peer assistance.

Peer Interaction

Preliminary efforts to examine participation in online forums have tended to focus solely on message metrics (e.g., number of messages) or the message content only (e.g., content analysis) (Caggiano et al., 1995; Carboni, 1999; Hawkes & Good, 2000; Leach, 2002; Meehan & Burns, 1997; Pomeroy, 1997; Selwyn, 2000; Stephens & Hartmann, 2002). Such data collection and analyses do not address the relationship among messages. Failure to examine the message flow and relations of messages may be problematic. For example, a high number of messages (metrics based analysis) a student posts might not be an accurate indication of her high level participation if her messages are not directed to other students (relation based analysis). Similarly, students' high number of postings may not reflect their active participation in the overall communication if they communicate with only a small number of students. As such, examining message relations may offer key insights into the function of an online forum by interpreting the student postings not as individual message units, but as a representation of their interaction (Russo & Koesten, 2005).

Monge and Contractor (2003) suggest using multilevel theoretical frameworks for analyzing relations in social networks. There are various communication network theories that may provide possible explanations regarding the observed communication patterns in a social network. For the purpose of the current study, two theories are of interests: Theory of homophily and theory of electronic proximity (see Monge & Contractor, 2003 for other communication network theories). The theory of homophily posits that communication between actors is positively influenced by high level of similarity among their attributes. For example, it may be possible to observe a more frequent message exchange among same gendered students or students who belong to the same project groups. The theory of proximity from an electronic communication perspective hypothesizes that additional communication channels may influence the amount of communication in the existing channel. For example, students may interact less in an online forum if they meet their needs through different communication channels such as face to face meetings. The second research question in the current study is:

RQ2. What interaction patterns did students have in an online forum as observed in the relations of their messages and how were these patterns explained by the theories of homophily and electronic proximity?

A Model for Examining Peer Interaction

Social network analysis (SNA) provides us with an analytic framework for studying relations among social entities in a social network (Wasserman & Faust, 1994). Online messages among students can be considered relational ties and messages represent directional relationships (e.g., a student sends messages to others). SNA may help better explain online participation and information exchange. For the purpose of the current study, two social network constructs are of interest; Density and Centrality.

Density is indexed as the ratio of observed links to all possible links in a network (Wasserman & Faust, 1994). While the value of 0 indicates no link between any social entities in the network, the value of 1 indicates a network in which each social entity is connected to every other one. Measuring density in an online forum may show the amount of communication among its participants overtime. *Centrality* refers to the degree to which a social entity is a key entity within a network (Monge & Contractor, 2003). One commonly used measures of centrality is degree centrality. One entity is said to be high in its out-degree if it has a majority of links directed toward others. It also has high in-degree if it receives many links from the other entities.

METHOD

An exploratory case study design that incorporates both content and social network analysis was used in the current study. Case study approach helps the researcher understand a particular phenomenon of interest with rich details (Merriam, 1998).

Context

The online forum examined in the current study was part of a graduate level instructional design course in a Mid-Atlantic university in 2008. The course provided students with experiences to employ prototyping concepts for developing computer-based instructional products. Based on students' initial interest in the course, they were assigned to work in groups. Students (Female N= 3, Male N=6) worked on group projects for which they developed prototypes of computer based instruction. They used an online forum to post their reflections on readings at various weeks during the semester. In the forum, students were asked to focus on issues that they think are important or interesting to discuss and were also required to reply a peer.

Data

The data included all the messages that the students posted in the forum (N=292), including students' reflections on given weekly readings and responses to their peer.

Analysis

Content analysis (Herring, 2004) approach was used to examine peer assistance. An adapted version of a framework that we synthesized in our recent work (Kale, et al., in press) guided the categorization of the observed assistance types. The unit of analysis was a posted message. In addition, a further analysis focused on messages that students posted for their reading reflections. A message content rubric that the instructor formulated was an initial framework. These included: (1) *Recall*-providing summary of readings only. (2) *React*-providing reactions to the themes discussed in the readings. (3) *Relate*-explaining how themes from readings are relevant to students' projects. The unit of analysis was the individual reflection message.

SNA approach guided the analysis of peer interaction. In order to measure density and centrality concepts, the UCINET 6 (Borgatti, Everett, & Freeman, 1999), a comprehensive SNA software program was used. UCINET runs based on a sociomatrix that represents predetermined relations in a network. Figure 1 shows an example. There is a label for each social entity put on the column and on the row in the matrix. Whether there is a directional tie between two entities (e.g., a posted message sent from x to y) can be represented by the value of 1 entered in the cell where the x on the row and y in the column intersect in the matrix.

Figure 1. An example of a sociomatrix with three social entities

.	A	x	Y
A	0	0	0
X	0	0	1
y	0	0	0

Figure 2. Types of peer assistance observed in the forum

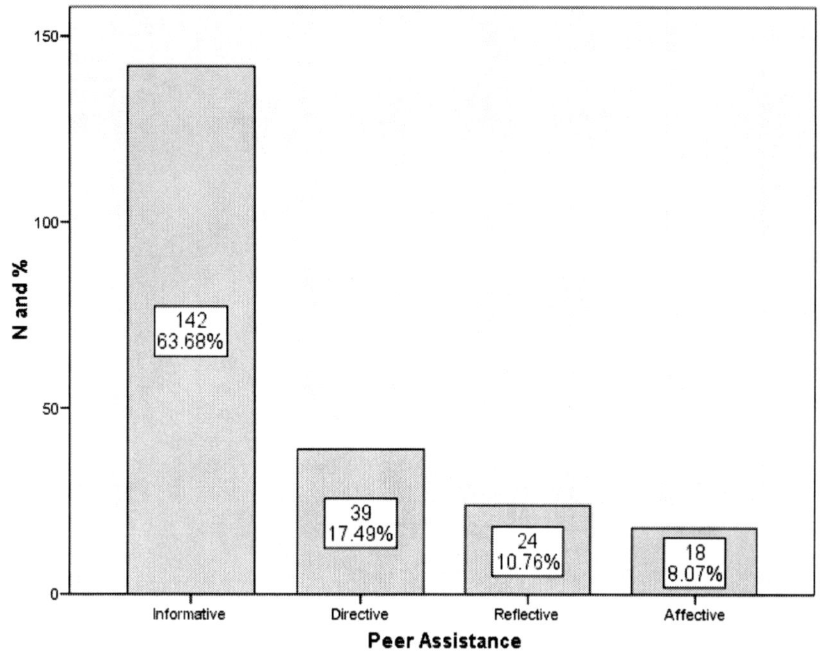

RESULTS & DISCUSSION

RQ1. Peer Assistance?

Out of five initial categories from our earlier work, (Kale et al., in press), only four peer assistance types were apparent in the current study (Figure 2).

Table 2 shows brief definitions and examples for each category.

In more than half of the messages, students provided *Informative* peer assistance to each other. None of the messages included *Administrative* assistance, indicating the minimal technical support that students may have needed. (See Figure 3 for peer assistance over time).

Peer assistance decreased toward the end of the semester. The sudden increase in the *Reflective* assistance in Week 12 may be an analysis of interest, however. Examined overtime, 82% (N=9) of the individual reading reflections in the same week exemplified a direct relevance to students' projects (Figure 4).

Table 2. Peer assistance, definition, and examples

Peer Assistance	Definition	Examples from the data
Informative	Explaining, feedbacking, resourcing, or clarifying	- I agree. My thoughts on this also.... - This is a great point because.....
Directive	Directing focus or pushing exploration	-But what we want to do is.... -Think about the reasons to understand...
Reflective	Requesting, questioning, or encouraging for response and input	- Is there a level of confusion you are averting through eliminating the color? - It will be fun reading what others have to say...
Affective	Showing positive feelings, excitement, or appreciation	-I still enjoyed your team project... - I look forward to seeing your input in class...

Figure 3. Peer assistance overtime

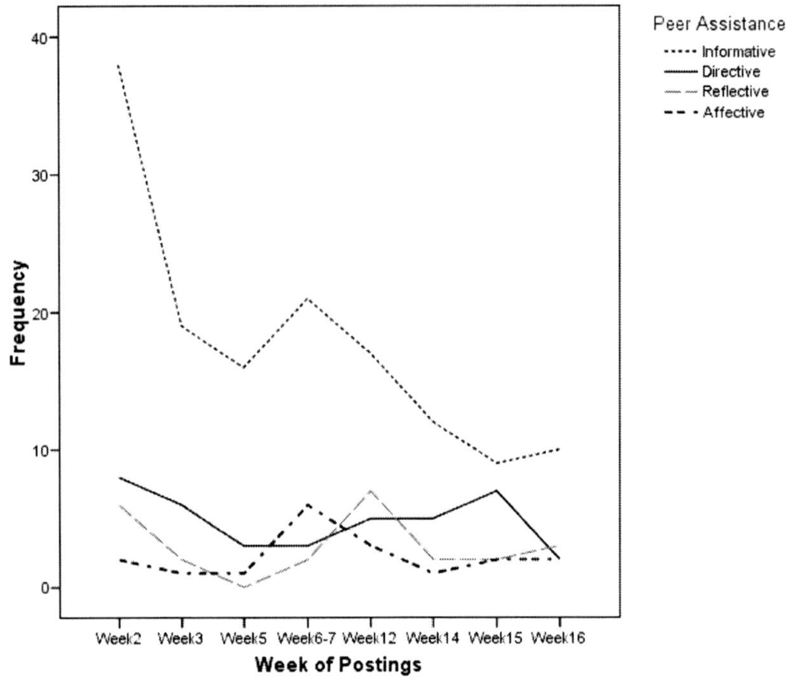

Figure 4. Level of individual reading reflection overtime

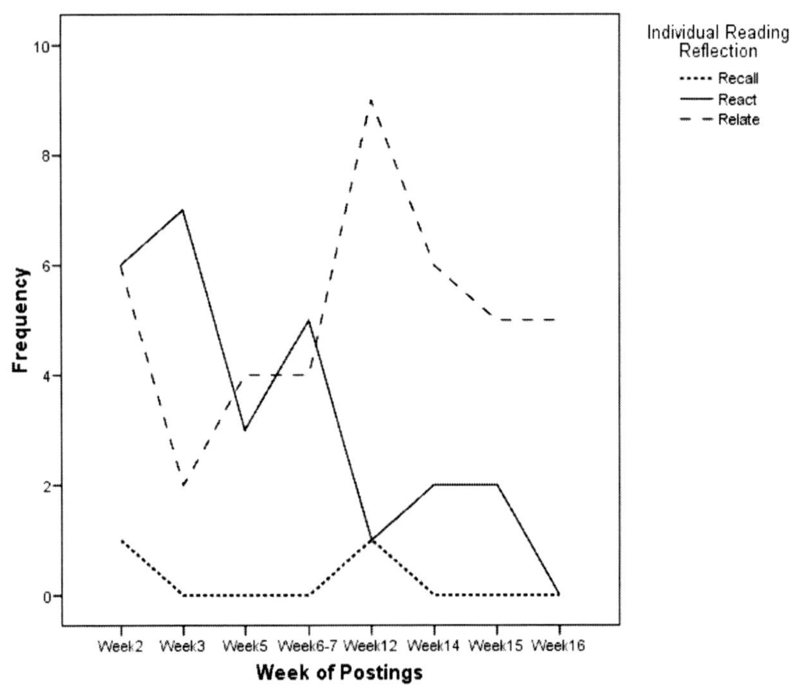

Table 3. Density Scores Overtime

	Week2	Week3	Week5	Week6-7	Week12	Week14	Week15	Week16	Overall
Δ (Dens.)	0.60	0.53	0.32	0.43	0.43	0.27	0.26	0.21	0.70

This may be due to the fact that students completed the usability testing of their prototypes by the same week and thus had more issues to talk about. Students, when seeing each others' usability findings, could be interested in hearing more about the projects, and thus may have posted messages that requested each others' response.

RQ2.Peer Interaction Patterns?

Density scores indicated that 70% of the students provided peer assistance to each other during the semester (Table 3). The decrease toward the end of the semester shows that students less frequently responded to each others as the time progressed. Students were less likely to go beyond the requirement of posting a reflection and one peer response toward to end.

Table 4 shows the in degree and out degree scores of each student.

While each of the students M and F provided more than 50 peer assistances, they received relatively less number of responses from other students (less than 25). On the other hand, students H and V reached the highest in-degree centrality (29 and 40 respectively) indicating a high number of messages they received from other students. Figure 5 shows the network graph of such interactions more clearly.

A message directed from a student to another student is shown as an arrow with a direction from that user to the second user. Arrows toward RE indicate students' individual reflection on readings. Different colors and shapes classify the student groups working on different projects. Thickness of the lines is indexed to the frequency of messages exchanged between students.

A further analysis, called *Clique,* focused of identifying emerging groups in relation to the observed communications. A clique is defined as a subset of a network in which the members are more strongly tied to one another than they are to other members of the network (Hanneman & Riddle, 2005). The UCINET program found the following two cliques in the observed interaction of students:

1. H, V, F, Y, T, M, **D, L**
2. H, V, F, Y, T, M, **A**

While most of the students were the members of these two cliques (H, V, F, Y, T, M), students D and L appeared to be in only one clique that the student A is not part of. The observed interaction as also seen in Figure 5 corroborates with this finding; there's no interaction between student A and student D and L (See Figure 5). Given that Student A and D were in the same group complet-

Table 4. Degree Centrality Scores

Group No	Student ID	Out Degree	In Degree
5	M	**56**	23
2	F	**52**	22
1	H	30	**29**
3	T	17	26
1	V	9	**40**
4	A	14	13
5	L	11	22
4	D	11	16
2	Y	6	15

Figure 5. Network graphic of the students' online interaction

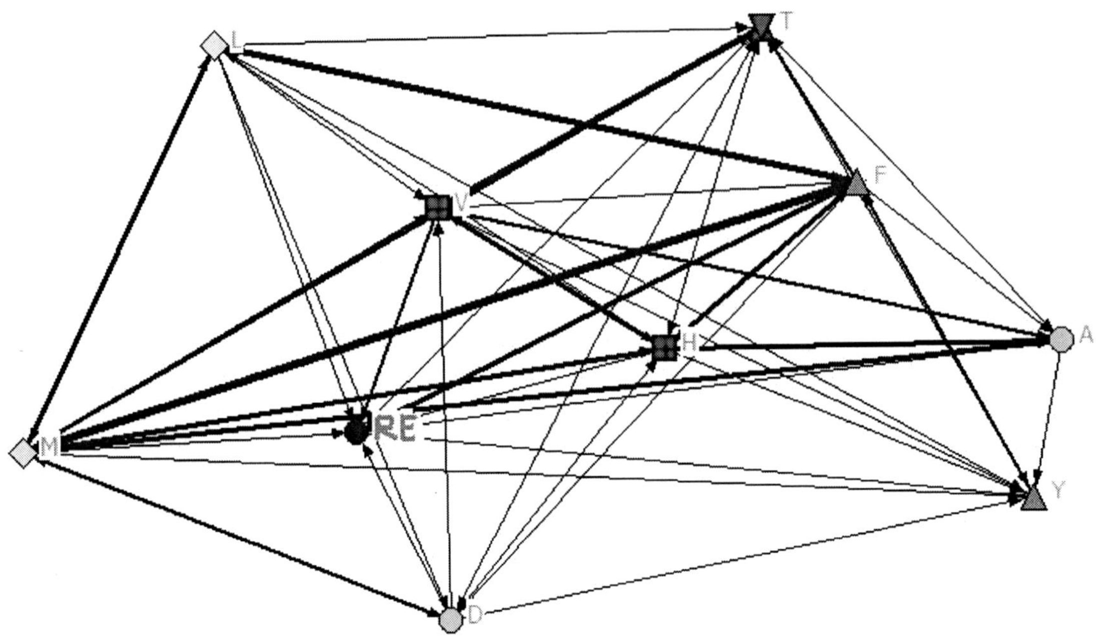

ing their projects, their lack of interaction in the online forum look peculiar.

The theory of proximity from an electronic communication perspective may explain this finding, however. According to the theory, additional communication channels may influence the amount of communication in the existing channel (Monge & Contractor, 2003). For example, students may interact less in an online forum if they meet their needs through different communication channels. Students A and D may have not felt the necessity of using the online forum to communicate with each other as they may have already had frequent face to face meetings to complete their projects. Though this is a possible explanation, it requires further analysis of student groups' meetings, which is beyond the scope of the current paper.

According to the theory, the level of similarity among actors' attributes influences their communication with one another. That is, students are likely to interact with others students if they have the same attributes (e.g., gender, group membership). Hence, a further analysis examined how the theory of homophily might explain the observed peer interaction. The purpose was to demonstrate how SNA approach may help examine the influences of actor attributes on their communication. As such, the analysis focused on only two major attributes-gender and project group membership to observe how they might influence students' communication. This required the generation of two matricies. First one presents students' gender and group membership as an independent data set (Figure 6) and the second one presents students' degree centralities as a dependent data set (Figure 7).

Then, the Node Level Regression function in the UCINET program using these two matricies produced a regression statistics regarding the degree to which each of the attributes predicted the observed interaction among students. Table 5 shows the output of the regression statistics for both InDegree and Outdegree centrality scores.

As seen in the table, none of the attributes significantly predicted the amount of communica-

Figure 6. Matrix for attributes as an independent data set

	gender	group
H	2	1
V	2	1
F	1	2
Y	1	2
T	1	3
D	1	4
A	2	4
M	1	5
L	1	5

Figure 7. Matrix for centrality scores as an independent data set

	Out-Degree	In-Degree
H	30	29
V	9	40
F	52	22
Y	6	15
T	17	26
D	11	16
A	14	13
M	56	23
L	11	22

tion among peers. That is, being the same gender or being in the same project group did not increase the amount of messages that the students received from and sent to one other. While theory of homophily did not provide meaningful explanations for these findings, no further elaboration will be made given the limited number of participants in the study.

EDUCATIONAL IMPORTANCE

The current study incorporated various analysis techniques to examine messages in an online forum. By employing content analysis, this study not only tested an existing framework to examine peer assistance but also attempted to reveal the relation between students' individual postings and

Table 5. Regression analysis summary in UCINET

InDegree	**MODEL FIT**				
		R-square	Adjusted R-square	F Value	Sig.
		0.314	0.020	1.375	0.352
	REGRESSION COEFFICIENTS				
		Independent	Un-stdized Coefficient	St'dized Coefficient	Sig.
		Intercept gender group	25.612904 3.182796 -2.322581	0.000000 0.192124 -0.443347	1.000 0.337 0.845
Outdegree	**MODEL FIT**				
		R-square	Adjusted R-square	F Value	Sig.
		0.043	-0.367	0.134	0.856
	REGRESSION COEFFICIENTS				
		Independent	Un-stdized Coefficient	St'dized Coefficient	Sig.
		Intercept gender group	33.494625 -7.881721 -0.032258	0.000000 -0.208103 -0.002693	1.000 0.657 0.521

their peer response patterns. The results indicated that if students' reading reflections provided high relevance to their course projects, they tended to receive more *Reflective* assistance from their peers.

By employing SNA techniques, this study demonstrated the use of novel indices for the observed interaction patterns. Also, the further analysis of SNA focusing on actor attributes exemplified how to examine their effects on the observed communication patterns. By interpreting and redefining key social network concepts in education terms, this study has the potential to provide a model for future education research that may need to employ the same analysis approach in asynchronous computer mediated communication settings.

REFERENCES

Anderson, T., Rourke, L., Garrison, D. R., & Archer, W. (2001). Assessing teaching presence in a computer conferencing context. *Journal of Asynchronous Learning Networks, 5*(2). Retrieved July 7, 2007, from http://www.sloan c.org/publications/JALN/v5n2/v5n2_anderson.asp.

Bonk, C. J., & King, K., S. (1998). *Electronic collaborators.* Mahwah, NJ: Erlbaum.

Borgatti, S. P., Everett, M. G., & Freeman, L. (1999). *UCINET V. Software for social network analysis*. Harvard, MA: Analytical Technologies.

Caggiano, M. E., Audet, R., & Abegg, G. (1995, April). *A Pilot study of an electronic community of interdisciplinary secondary science teachers.* Paper presented at the Annual Meeting of the National Association for Research in Science Teaching, San Francisco, CA.

Carboni, L. W. (1999). *How might an online discussion forum support teachers' professional development in mathematics? A first look.* Paper presented at the Annual Meeting of the Association of Mathematics Teacher Educators, Chicago, IL.

Collins, A., Brown, J. S., & Holum, A. (1991). Cognitive apprenticeship: Making thinking visible. *American Educator, 15*(3), 6–12, 38–46.

Dede, C. (2004). Enabling distributed learning communities via emerging technologies-part one. *T.H.E. Journal, 32*(2), 12–22.

Dennen, V. P. (2005). From message posting to learning dialogues: Factors affecting learner participation in asynchronous discussion. *Distance Education, 26*(1), 127–148. doi:10.1080/01587910500081376

Gunawardena, C. N., Lowe, C. A., & Anderson, T. (1997). Analysis of a global online debate and the development of an interaction analysis model for examining social construction of knowledge in computer conferencing. *Journal of Educational Computing Research, 17*(4), 397–431. doi:10.2190/7MQV-X9UJ-C7Q3-NRAG

Hanneman, R. A., & Riddle, M. (2005). *Introduction to social network methods. Riverside.* CA: University of California, Riverside.

Hawkes, M., & Good, K. (2000). Evaluating professional development outcomes of a telecollaborative technology curriculum. *Rural Educator, 21*(3), 5–11.

Herring, S. C. (2004). Content analysis for new media: Rethinking the paradigm. In *New research for new media: Innovative research methodologies symposium working papers and readings* (pp. 47–66). Minneapolis, MN: University of Minnesota School of Journalism and Mass Communication.

Hew, K. F., & Cheung, W. S. (2008). Attracting student participation in asynchronous online discussions: A case study of peer facilitation. *Computers & Education, 51*(3), 1111–1124. doi:10.1016/j.compedu.2007.11.002

Hewitt, J. (2005). Toward an understanding of how threads die in asynchronous computer conferences. *Journal of the Learning Sciences, 14*(4), 567–589. doi:10.1207/s15327809jls1404_4

Kale, U., Brush, T., & Saye, J. (forthcoming). Assisting teachers' thinking and participation online. *Journal of Educational Computing Research, 41*(3).

Leach, J. (2002). The curriculum knowledge of teachers: A review of the potential of large-scale, electronic conference environments for professional development. *Curriculum Knowledge, 13*(1), 87–120. doi:10.1080/09585170110115303

Lincoln, Y., & Guba, E. (1985). *Naturalistic inquiry*. Newbury Park, CA: Sage Publications.

Mazzolini, M., & Maddison, S. (2003). Sage, guide or ghost? The effect of instructor intervention on student participation in online discussion forums. *Computers & Education, 40*, 237–253. doi:10.1016/S0360-1315(02)00129-X

Meehan, M. L., & Burns, R. C. (1997, March). *E-mail survey of a listserv discussion group: Lessons learned from surveying an electronic network of learners*. Paper presented at the Annual Meeting of the American Educational Research Association, Chicago, IL.

Merriam, S. B. (1998). *Qualitative research and case study applications in education*. San Francisco: Jossey-Bass Publishers.

Monge, P. R., & Contractor, N. S. (2003). *Theories of communication networks*. New York: Oxford University Press.

Pomeroy, J. R. (1997). *The rural learning network: A teaching and learning collaborative*. Paper presented at the Annual NREA Convention, Tucson, AZ.

Poole, D. M. (2000). Student participation in a discussion-oriented online course: A case study. *Journal of Research on Computing in Education, 33*(2), 162–177.

Romiszowski, A. J., & Mason, R. (2004). Computer mediated communication. In Jonassen, D. H. (Ed.), *Handbook of research on educational communications and technology* (2nd ed., pp. 397–426). Mahwah, NJ: Erlbaum.

Russo, T. C., & Koesten, J. (2005). Prestige, centrality, and learning: A social network analysis of an online class. *Communication Education, 54*(3), 254–261. doi:10.1080/03634520500356394

Selwyn, N. (2000). Creating a connected community? Teachers' use of an electronic discussion group. *Teachers College Record, 102*(4), 750–778. doi:10.1111/0161-4681.00076

Stephens, A., & Hartmann, C. E. (2002). *Using an online discussion forum to engage secondary mathematics teachers in teaching with technology*. Paper presented at the Annual Meeting of American Educational Research Association, New Orleans, LA.

Tharp, R. (1993). Institutional and social context of educational practice and reform. In Forman, E. A., Minick, N., & Stone, C. A. (Eds.), *Context for learning* (pp. 269–282). New York: Oxford University Press.

Wasserman, S., & Faust, K. (1994). *Social network analysis: Methods and applications*. Cambridge, UK: Press Syndicate of the University of Cambridge.

Winiecki, D. J. (2003). Instructional discussions in online education: Practical and research-oriented perspectives. In Moore, M. G., & Anderson, W. G. (Eds.), *Handbook of Distance Education* (pp. 193–211). Mahwah, NJ: Erlbaum.

Yang, S. C., & Liu, S. F. (2004). Case study of online workshop for the professional development of teachers. *Computers in Human Behavior, 20*(6), 733–761. doi:10.1016/j.chb.2004.02.005

Section 3
Enabling Communities

Chapter 9
Harnessing the Potential of Cooperative Interaction:
Building Social & Physical Presence during Online Learning

Caroline L. Hilk
University of Minnesota, Twin Cities, USA

Michael C. Mensink
University of Minnesota, Twin Cities, USA

ABSTRACT

As educators make greater use of online learning environments and virtual communities, increased attention is being paid to the aspects of computer-mediated communication which facilitate constructive interaction between learners. The benefits of face-to-face cooperative learning are being pursued in the evolving computer-supported collaborative learning (CSCL) environment. The success of computer-supported collaborative learning is influenced by the amount and quality of social and physical presence available in the online environment. This chapter offers several best practices for enhancing learners' perceptions of social and physical presence within the digital realm, and it suggests future avenues of research which may lead to further improvements in the instructional potential of online learning environments.

INTRODUCTION

The recent influx of online distance learning courses has lead to the increased use of chat rooms, e-mail, and instant messaging, replacing the means for academic discussions previously accomplished only through physical proximity. Annetta and Holmes (2006) note that many classroom activities previously construed as 'face-to-face' have shifted into the online environment, and educators face increasing pressure to turn traditional, face-to-face courses into Internet-based courses.

As online courses become more commonplace for schools, instructors are beginning to encounter the difficulties inherent in substituting face-to-face discussion activities with computer-mediated equivalents. These online activities become even more challenging when instructors attempt to implement cooperative learning within their Internet-delivered courses. Instructional designers, familiar with learning theory and pedagogical methods, are often employed by educational

DOI: 10.4018/978-1-61692-854-4.ch009

institutions to facilitate this transition to CSCL (Smith, Passmore, Faught, 2009; Gros, 2001).

In this chapter, we review relevant research and theory on cooperative learning as it relates to online instruction, and discuss the obstacles educators must overcome for the effective use of student collaboration in the digital classroom. In addition, we identify and review the relevant research on two important psychological concepts deeply involved in online instruction: social and physical presence. Finally, we offer several evidence-based best practices for enhancing learners' perceptions of social and physical presence within the online learning environment and conclude with suggestions for future avenues of research which may lead to further improvements in the instructional potential of CSCL.

BACKGROUND

Cooperative learning has been thoroughly researched by psychologists and educators during the last half century, and during the last two decades this research has begun to examine the use of computers and virtual environments to support learners' interaction. *Cooperative learning* is defined as the use of small groups during instruction with the explicit purpose that students work together to maximize their own and others' learning (Johnson, Johnson, & Holubec, 2003). Based on the theory of social interdependence, this structured learning environment is only as successful as students' sense of interdependence with one another and their individual accountability to make contributions to the collective learning goal (Johnson & Johnson, 1999). Positive interdependence is the most crucial element for establishing a meaningful cooperative relationship within a face-to-face or virtual learning environment. Positive *social interdependence* exists when group members perceive their success as dependent on the success of the whole group: each individual's efforts affect the outcomes of everyone else in the group.

Research has shown that cooperative learning is a highly successful instructional technique in traditional classrooms for students of all ages (Gillies, 2007; Johnson, Johnson & Smith, 2006; Sharan, 1990). Building productive cooperative relationships within a learning environment requires attention to the type of goals, interactions, and expectations shared by students. Online collaborative learning is assumed to have benefits similar to face-to-face cooperative learning (Harasim, 1990; Kreijns, Kirschner, & Jochems, 2003) and may also have some advantages over traditional settings (e.g. Lapadat, 2002; Jorczak, 2008).

Computer-Supported Collaborative Learning

A rapidly expanding field of educational research investigates the use of *computer-supported collaborative learning* (CSCL) as a method of engaging and retaining students in the online environment. In this chapter, we refer to CSCL as any educational experience in which networked computers and/or the Internet are used to facilitate structured interactions among students in groups or pairs. Peer collaboration has a significant influence on students' reported levels of engagement, motivation, and satisfaction during online learning (Jones & Issroff, 2005). This sense of collaborative community is essential to overcoming some of the potential hindrances in synchronous and asynchronous distance learning, including social isolation and de-personalization (Hiltz, 1997; Rovai, 2002).

Collaborative learning also has several cognitive benefits within a computer-mediated course structure. Research has shown that collaborative learning groups can foster critical thinking, shared understanding, retention of learned material and deeper level processing when compared with individualistic learning methods (Garrison, Anderson, & Archer, 2000; Gokhale, 1995; Johnson

& Johnson, 1999; 2003). From the theoretical perspective of social constructivism, the learning group is only as valuable as the interactions that foster thoughtful discussion. Instructors must be deliberate when establishing group norms and structuring learning tasks to promote increased interdependence within groups; otherwise, the result may be a series of student monologues with minimal interaction and few cognitive gains (Garrison, 2007).

Presence Defined

In the context of computer-supported collaborative learning, *presence* is the degree to which online students believe that other participants are physically real and paying attention during their course interactions (Kirschner, Strijbos, Kreijns, and Beers, 2005). A prerequisite for effective collaborative interaction online is the development of a sense of presence, both physical and social. Relationship-building can be a challenge in a digital environment such as an online classroom, where students usually have limited physical representation of themselves when interacting with other students. In many online courses, for example, students see only the names and email addresses of group members when they chat or interact in a text-based discussion thread.

Although many other interpretations of presence have been offered (e.g., Lombard & Ditton, 1997), this chapter utilizes a definition of presence in which the physical reality of a student participating in a traditional, face-to-face classroom represents the general baseline experience of perceived presence, to which we compare other computer-mediated experiences. Typically, we do not consciously consider our presence within physical reality unless explicitly prompted to do so (Ijsselsteijn, Freeman, & De Ridder, 2001). It is only when attempting to simulate or replicate reality through technological means that an individual may consciously consider how much or how little presence they perceive within a virtual environment. By establishing that a face-to-face classroom environment represents the typical baseline of both physical and social presence, we will consider the ways that students' sense of presence during online learning may fluctuate in response to the affordances and limitations provided by instructional technology.

Physical Presence

Physical presence refers to the sense individuals have of themselves or an object being physically real and located within a physical space, either real or simulated (Ijsselsteijn & Riva, 2003; Lombard & Ditton, 1997). Although researchers debate how individuals determine what is real and what is simulated within a computer-mediated physical space (Mantovani & Riva, 1999): we again return to our baseline representation of students in a physical classroom, perceiving themselves as fully physically present within the environment. It is important to note that although students in physical classrooms can be described as fully physically-present, mere physical presence does not guarantee attention. As many educators can attest, students may be mentally elsewhere even when physically present in the classroom.

Physical presence has also been defined as one's sense of 'being there' during a computer-mediated interaction (Ijsselsteijn, Freeman, & De Ridder, 2001; Lombard & Ditton, 1997) or the inability to recognize a virtual environment, experience, or stimuli as simulated (Lee, 2004). To give an example of a situation where an individual might experience full physical presence within a virtual environment, consider this example from the motion picture *The Matrix*, in which the main character Neo finds that he has spent his entire life trapped in a computer simulation. Morpheus and Neo reenter the Matrix, where Neo immediately notices that he has a completely realistic illusion of 'being there'.

Morpheus: This is the construct. It is our loading program. We can load anything from clothing, to equipment, weapons, training simulations, anything we need.

Neo is having a hard time getting a grasp of this.

Neo: Right now....we're inside a computer program?

Morpheus: Is it really so hard to believe? Your clothes are different. The plugs in your arms and head are gone. Your hair has changed.

Neo puts a hand to his head and touches his hair.

Morpheus: Your appearance now is what we call residual self image. It is the mental projection...of your digital self (Wachowski & Wachowski, 1999).

Convincing simulations, such as virtual reality, may certainly influence individuals to believe they are physically present within a virtual environment (much like Neo in *The Matrix*). However, for situations involving education, students' sense of physical presence in online learning environments follows a more innocuous reality: seated in a chair, at home, in the library, or a coffee shop physically interacting with classmates and instructors via their computer monitor, keyboard, and mouse.

Physical Presence and Learning

The influence of physical presence on learning outcomes in online coursework has generally been less studied than other forms of presence, such as social and cognitive. This gap may be due in part to the limitations instructors have in establishing physical presence for students in virtual environments. It may also be due to the fact that within online learning environments, social presence can be established through various types of communication between students, while establishing physical presence necessitates the use of other technological means. Ijsselsteijn and Riva (2003) note that one's sense of physical presence is established through a feedback loop involving emotional, cognitive, and perceptual factors. Due to this complex process, research on technology-influenced physical presence has typically involved virtual reality simulations and other technologies that strive to fool perceptual systems into a belief that one is more physically present within a simulated environment than in actuality (Mania & Chalmers, 2001). As online courses typically do not utilize virtual reality technologies, social presence has been more accessible and widely explored in educational settings and application.

Although it has been overlooked in much of the research, physical presence has been shown to have a direct influence on how students and teachers interact in online and physical classrooms. Specifically, both instructors and students within an online classroom must find alternatives to nonverbal communication (i.e., body language, facial expressions) due to the lack of shared physical proximity (Murphy & Manzanares, 2008; Tu & Yen, 2006). While a lack of proximity may enable some students to voice a minority viewpoint, research also suggests that group opinions and decisions are less influenced by minority views within a virtual space, compared with face-to-face communication (McLeod, Baron, Marti, & Yoon, 1997). One potential explanation offered for this finding was that politeness norms were more salient during face-to-face communications, compared to more distant computer-based discussions.

In addition to the benefits for communication, physical presence also has an effect on social and motivational outcomes. For example, prejudiced attitudes appear to be reduced when individuals are within physical proximity of a group, rather than isolated (Castelli & Tomelleri, 2008). Some researchers have also suggested that a lack of physical presence can in turn decrease student's perceptions of social presence within online courses (Kirschner et al., 2005). Motivational gains due to physical presence have also been observed: individuals demonstrated increased performance on a given task when an evaluator was physically present compared to when the evaluator was virtually present through a mediated interface (Lount, Park, Kerr, Messe, & Seok, 2008).

A secondary element of physical presence is the users' perception of and ability to physically interact with objects within a learning environment. This ability has been shown to have a direct and beneficial effect on learning. For example, Martin and Schwartz (2005) found that nine- and ten-year-old students who had difficulty mentally completing fraction problems demonstrated measurable benefits to their abilities after being allowed to manipulate physical representations of fractions (i.e., pies and tiles). It should be noted that students may demonstrate similar benefits from computer simulations, especially if concepts are abstract and not readily manipulated except via computer representations (Sarama, Clements, Swaminathan, McMillen, & Gómez, 2003). However, physical manipulation of objects appears to provide benefits to learning, especially when directly related to the instructional content (Chao, Stigler, & Woodward, 2000; Martin & Schwartz, 2005).

To summarize, students' sense of physical presence appears to have a positive effect on both learning processes and outcomes. Intergroup communication and notions of social presence also appear to be enhanced by perceptions of physical presence. In addition, physical presence influences cognitive and motivational outcomes, and may also influence emotional states associated with the learning experience, including students' sense of 'flow' (Takatalo, Nyman, & Laaksonen, 2008). In essence, recognition of students' sense of physical presence within online learning environments appears to be of vital importance for positive learning outcomes.

Social Presence

Short, Williams, and Christie (1976) originally defined *social presence* as the ability to communicate socio-emotional cues that establish the perception of the existence of a 'self' during interactions. In other words, social presence is a measure of the degree to which an individual feels socially connected to the other members of his or her group. While the early social presence research focused on face-to-face interactions, this concept has been adopted by the field of instructional technologies to represent the interpersonal elements within a virtual space (Lobry de Bruyn, 2004; Rourke, Anderson, Garrison, & Archer, 2001). It is important to note that in this chapter, we refer to social presence as an internal, cognitive-emotional-perceptual artifact (Ijsselsteijn & Riva, 2003). The communication of socio-emotional cues, personalized greetings, and the use of emoticons are a few of the ways social presence is established during computer-mediated communication.

Social presence has also been defined in a similar manner for the Community of Inquiry model of learning. Within this model, social presence consists of affective, interactive and cohesive elements (Garrison, 2007; Garrison, Anderson, & Archer, 2000). Affective indicators include the expression of emotion, self-disclosure, and use of humor. Interactive indicators generally refer to those intentional actions which link one member's contribution to a new statement such as complimenting another's ideas or referring explicitly to the content of another's message. Cohesive elements are statements and words that acknowledge being part of a collective group or team. It is yet unknown how each of these different social presence indicators may uniquely influence student learning outcomes.

Social Presence and Learning

Theoretical analysis suggests that social presence is affected by user's perceptions of the learning environment, medium, and social space (Kreijns, Kirschner, & Jochems, 2004). In other words, the ways in which an instructor organizes learning objectives and structures tasks within the online environment have an effect on the amount of social presence perceived by students (Rourke, Anderson, Garrison, & Archer, 1999). An experimental study conducted by Stacey (2001) found maintaining a cohesive group was essential for accomplishing the required collaborative tasks within a virtual learning environment. In order for students to engage in meaningful collaborative activities they must achieve a sense of warmth, belonging, and trust within their educational community. A valued learning experience is a function of pedagogy, content and community (Gilroy, 2001).

Generally when students perceive social presence and group cohesion as high, they function as a productive, collaborative group who transition successfully through academic tasks. The model offered by Kreijns, Kirschner, and Jochems (2004) separates three components within the affective structure of group work that reinforces social interaction: affiliation, impression formation, and attractiveness. These three factors influence group cohesion, desire, and willingness to contribute to the collective understanding. Positive dynamics are necessary for students to build a community in which they are willing to offer their perspective and engage in meaningful knowledge construction. Affiliation, similar to interdependence, requires a form of contact (or presence) with one another that fosters a sense of belonging. The second component is the social cognitive process during which an individual forms impressions of other group members through their interactions and content of communications. This impression formation is a critical factor that will determine whether a student desires to be part of the group. The third social factor necessary for group development is a perception of attractiveness and competence of other group members. Feelings of presence, trust, support and goal interdependence (in the form of learning) are critical dimensions of establishing a productive online learning community (Rovai, 2002).

Co-Presence

Despite the growing interest in both social and physical presence there has been a noticeable lack of integration of both aspects simultaneously within educational research and application. For example, although the Community of Inquiry model defines and utilizes social presence in a similar manner to the research reviewed here, physical presence is noticeably absent (Garrison, 2007; Garrison, et al., 2000). Within the psychological literature on presence, it is noted that the combination of both social and physical presence creates an internal perception of *co-presence* (Ijsselsteijn, et al., 2001; Zhao, 2003), the sense that an individual is physically with others in a shared space. Although some researchers have combined their conceptual definitions, it is important to note that we view co-presence as a slightly different psychological concept from social presence. For example, it is possible to establish social presence without physical presence via technologies that enable communication and socialization. However co-presence, as defined here, can only be achieved when students perceive both physical and social presence within an environment.

Depending on the content and goals of the course, establishing co-presence for students in an online course may be of great value, especially to researchers and educators interested in computer-supported collaborative learning. While the primary responsibility for structuring opportunities to build social presence is given to course instructors (Aragon, 2003), affordances to enhance physical presence are typically facilitated by instructional designers and/or programmers.

However, educators do have options in selecting course elements that may ultimately benefit both physical and social presence, creating a sense of co-presence for students within a virtual space.

Technologies for Increasing Social and Physical Presence

We advocate that instructors use a structured decision-making process when deciding which tools to use in online collaborative learning environments. The learning objectives, intended outcomes, and characteristics of the students should provide rationale for the chosen collaborative activities and environmental structure. Communicative interaction is necessary for online collaborative learning, but it is not sufficient to facilitate meaningful relationship-building between students and instructor. The elements of immediacy and intimacy should also not be overlooked when trying to foster collaborative learning (Burgoon & Hale, 1987; Tu & McIsaac, 2002). In order to develop a sense of social presence, students should be allowed time to introduce themselves and become comfortable with the necessary tools in the learning environment. Instructors can facilitate appropriate involvement and emotional communication that increase the human representation of other learners. There are varying degrees of face-to-face and real time social cues provided by instructional technology; designers and course developers should not assume that social presence will occur unassisted in the computer-mediated environment. Students require guidance and modeling to become effective online collaborators (Kirschner, Sweller, & Clark, 2006; Rovai, 2002).

Even within commonly-used course management systems, such as WebVISTA and Moodle, options exist for increasing students' sense of co-presence. In addition, educators may choose to utilize other available technologies in their courses to increase social and physical presence. Some technologies that have been investigated in previous research include multi-user virtual environments, digital representations, presence awareness systems, scripting and other audio-video technologies.

Multi-User Virtual Environments

Three dimensional, multi-user virtual environments (MUVEs) are simulated worlds in which multiple users interact with each other and the environment via personal representations, or *avatars*. The most popular MUVE is currently *Second Life* (www.secondlife.com), which currently attracts much attention from educators, researchers, and Internet enthusiasts. Multi-user virtual environments enable users to interact with individuals and objects that may not otherwise be possible, due to physical location or proximity. In their research, Edirisingha, Nie, Pluciennik, and Young (2009) provide an example of this contact in creating a *Second Life* simulation of a Saami village for an upper-level archaeology course. Students are able to explore a virtual representation of the environment as well as socialize with one another, thus enabling both physical and social presence. Baker, Wentz, and Woods (2009) offer excellent advice for the utilization of *Second Life* as an educational tool; although as with many of the recommendations in this chapter, there are potential benefits as well as costs to using such a learning environment.

Digital Representations

Another method that may prove useful in increasing students' sense of presence is through the use of digital representations, or avatars. Avatars are typically defined as a digital representation controlled by a human user in a virtual environment that often resembles the user in appearance and/or behavior (Bente, Ruggenberg, Kramer, & Eschenburg, 2008). This representation could be a computerized animation that strongly resembles the user, as found in *Second Life*, or a student's digital photo attached to email posts and chats. Many online course management systems allow users to attach a digital image to their student profile. If used properly, avatars can potentially increase students' sense of social and physical presence in an online environment (Bailenson, Yee, Merget, & Schroeder, 2006). It is important to note that in order to increase users' sense of physical and social presence avatars should resemble users as much as possible. Digital images such as simple face portraits are effective. As discussed later in this chapter, digital representations that are not accurate or too salacious can potentially cause distractions to students during the learning experience.

Presence Awareness Systems

Although less practical then some other technologies, systems are now being developed and researched that simultaneously increase both social and physical presence of users. Awareness systems enable users to maintain an awareness of others' movements, efforts, availability, or location at a distance (Gross, Stary, & Totter, 2005). For example, Romero, et al. (2007) investigated the effects of a presence awareness system on family communications. They found that presence awareness systems increased users' perceptions of connectedness, especially when the system allowed personal communication, effective timing in the message, and concrete information provided by the users. Some developers have also pursued initial attempts to create technologies that impart physical information about other users, such as a bench that creates a warming sensation for the user when another individual is seated nearby on a virtual bench (Gaver, 2002). Presence awareness systems may become more commonplace in the future and may enable an enhanced sense of both physical and social presence for users in online environments.

Conferencing Technology

Educators can also use conferencing technologies such as video and audio to increase students' sense of presence. In one study the experimenter created a learning environment that provided students with one of four communication types: video and audio (videoconferencing), audio only (audioconferencing), text chat with image, or text chat only. Students' generally perceived video and audio together as providing more naturalistic communication, as well as an increase in their communication output compared to the other communication forms (Yamada, 2009). However, depending on the needs and aims of the online course, video and audio may not be realistic options. Still, when possible, various forms of video and/or audio should be considered as options for increasing students' perceptions of physical and social presence.

A Balanced Model of Social and Physical Presence

Emerging technologies enable educators to establish moderate levels of physical and social presence within virtual learning environments, although some may be more effective than others. It is important to stress that physical and social presence should be viewed as conceptual continua. Most of this chapter has focused on the consequences of an absence of presence: when physical presence is low, users may feel remote and detached from the learning environment, and when social presence is low, users may feel socially isolated and disconnected from the learning community. In worst case scenarios, low levels of social and physical presence may cause students to abuse others within their online course or terminate involvement altogether (Eve & Brabazon, 2008).

Alternatively, physical and social presence can also become too high for students to the point they may become distracted from the intended learning outcomes. A virtual environment that becomes too 'real' for users may create a sense of unease, confusion, or fear. Similarly, within environments where users perceive too much social presence, group members may engage in excessive self-disclosure or irrelevant chatter, ultimately neglecting the intended educational goals. Due to these possible outcomes, instructors should be mindful that the affordances they make to increase physical or social presence are meaningful and useful. Research suggests that highly interesting, but irrelevant elements may function as seductive augmentations (Park & Kim, 2008), intriguing or engaging additions to multimedia instruction that are unrelated to the learning goals. Such augmentations can potentially cause a seductive details effect (Harp & Mayer, 1998), during which overall learning decreases as students' attention is drawn to distracting details or seductive add-ons.

Seductive augmentations can result from the potential affordances made within virtual environments that enable behaviors or visualizations that are not possible within a realistic face-to-face classroom. For example, within *Second Life*, users are able to fly around the environment a highly interesting and entertaining ability for many students. However, for most instructional uses of *Second Life*, students' acrobatics while attempting to engage in a structured learning activity may be detrimental to the intended educational outcomes. A second example involves an anecdote from one of authors who spent several class sessions in *Second Life*. Although avatars can be useful in increasing users' sense of physical presence, *Second Life* also allows users to select avatars which do not resemble people in either behavior or appearance. In the author's case, one of the other students had selected a human-sized raccoon in a sports coat as his avatar, which other students found highly distracting and impersonal. As the author noted, it was very difficult for other students to take this individual seriously during discussions due to the unrealistic nature of his avatar.

We strongly advocate for instructors to consider the optimal balance of social and physical presence required for their instructional goals. We refer to this equilibrium as the *balanced model of social and physical presence* (as shown in Figure 1). Students should feel both socially and physically connected with fellow learners within a virtual environment without becoming too extreme on either dimension.

FUTURE RESEARCH DIRECTIONS

The current literature strongly suggests that instructional designers and educators consider the influence of both social and physical presence when designing online learning environments. In this chapter, we have offered some evidence to suggest that *both* social and physical presence have an influence on learning outcomes; however this claim needs to be investigated further. Within educational research, the positive effect of increasing students' sense of social presence is well documented. Put simply, groups function

Figure 1. Balanced model of physical and social presence during online collaborative learning

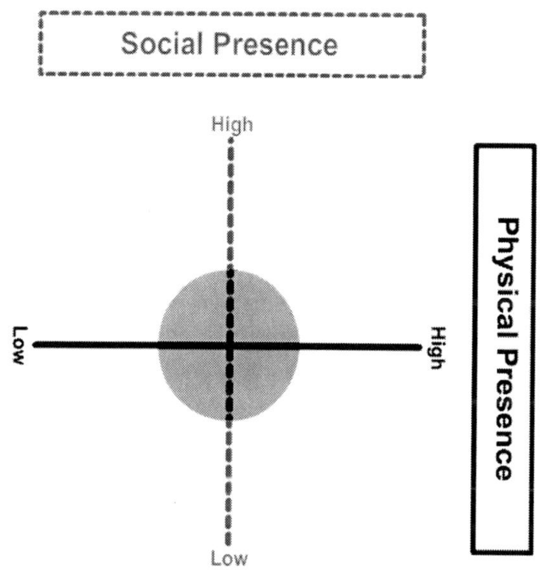

better when individual members perceive other members as socially connected and cohesive. This requirement appears to hold true whether learning occurs within a face-to-face classroom or virtual learning environment.

However, students' perception of their own physical presence and the physical presence of other group members during computer-supported collaborative learning should not be ignored by educational research. This consideration becomes even more important when we examine the role physical presence potentially plays in establishing students' sense of co-presence within a virtual learning environment. It is our opinion that students who perceive they are connected to group members in both a social and physical sense will demonstrate greater educational outcomes compared to students that do not share this perception.

Although social presence has been well studied within educational research, future investigations should continue to address how increases in social presence may influence cooperative behaviors in virtual learning environments. While various methods currently exist to increase social presence, future work in this area should also investigate options that may not be currently available or realistically implementable at this time. Additionally, better measures of social presence should be pursued and standardized in order to fully understand the concept of social presence and its impact on student learning.

As noted throughout this chapter, physical presence has not been examined to the extent social presence has by educational research. While many explanations for the lack of research exist, one simple view is that social presence, compared to physical presence, is easier to study and manipulate within virtual learning environments. Recognizing that physical presence may play an important role in educational outcomes is somewhat contrary to the aims and beliefs of many instructional technology researchers. However, it is necessary for educational researchers and instructors to recognize that moving traditional face-to-face instruction to a virtual environment has benefits as well as costs to instructional goals. Although the educational opportunities available in virtual learning environments are many, aspects of physical classrooms that are not replicable in such environments may have unforeseen consequences on learning outcomes.

Future research into physical presence should investigate precisely how different types of learning environments may influence students' sense of physical presence. While it may be the case that students flourish regardless of how physically 'present' they feel in virtual learning environments, previous research would suggest this outcome unlikely. Rather, a complex interaction may occur between social presence and physical presence, the result of which is a sense of co-presence the students perceive within a virtual learning environment. In this chapter, we have offered some evidence to suggest that *both* social and physical presence have an influence on learning outcomes; however this claim needs to be investigated through the development of accurate measures and technology which can more thoroughly address the importance of presence within virtual learning environments.

CONCLUSION

In this chapter, we have reviewed research that suggests that social and physical presence must be considered when designing and implementing virtual learning environments. Based on this evidence, it is our opinion that social and physical presence play vital roles in establishing and maintaining cooperative behaviors during computer-supported collaborative learning. While social presence has been studied by educational researchers, few experiments have examined the singular contribution of physical presence, or potential interactions between social and physical presence within virtual learning environments. These questions will likely increase in importance as the physical spaces of traditional classrooms continue to be supplemented or replaced by online learning environments.

Although virtual learning environments provide numerous opportunities for improved course delivery, the rapid development of instructional technology has also created a temporary period in which educators are utilizing new tools before research has fully investigated the potential consequences on learning. While online learning environments do provide increased opportunities to collaborate without the constraints of location and/or time, additional research should be conducted on the potential influence of students' physical and social presence on educational outcomes within virtual learning environments.

Ultimately, as technologies continue to evolve and improve, it remains imperative that educators mindfully consider the ways in which student factors may interact with new forms of learning environments. Technology offers many new and exciting ways of creating learning environments, but consideration should be given to both intended and unintended consequences they may have on the learning process.

REFERENCES

Annetta, L. A., & Holmes, S. (2006). Creating presence and community in a synchronous virtual learning environment using avatars. *International Journal of Instructional Technology & Distance Learning, 3*(8), 31 – 47. Retrieved February 7, 2007, from http://www.itdl.org/Journal/Aug_06/article03.htm

Aragon, S. R. (2003). Creating social presence in online environments. *New Directions for Adult and Continuing Education, 100*, 57–68. doi:10.1002/ace.119

Bailenson, J. N., Yee, N., Merget, D., & Schroeder, R. (2006). The effect of behavioral realism and form realism of real-time avatar faces on verbal disclosure, nonverbal disclosure, emotion recognition, and copresence in dyadic interaction. *Presence (Cambridge, Mass.), 15*(4), 359–372. doi:10.1162/pres.15.4.359

Baker, S. C., Wentz, R. K., & Woods, M. M. (2009). Using virtual worlds in education: Second Life® as an educational tool. *Teaching of Psychology, 36*(1), 59–64. doi:10.1080/00986280802529079

Bente, G., Ruggenberg, S., Kramer, N. C., & Eschenburg, F. (2008). Avatar-mediated networking: Increasing social presence and interpersonal trust in net-based collaborations. *Human Communication Research, 34*(2), 287–318. doi:10.1111/j.1468-2958.2008.00322.x

Burgoon, J. K., & Hale, J. L. (1987). Validation and measurement of the fundamental themes of relational communication. *Communication Monographs, 54*, 19–41. doi:10.1080/03637758709390214

Castelli, L., & Tomelleri, S. (2008). Contextual effects on prejudiced attitudes: When the presence of others leads to more egalitarian responses. *Journal of Experimental Social Psychology, 44*(3), 679–686. doi:10.1016/j.jesp.2007.04.006

Chao, S. J., Stigler, J. W., & Woodward, J. A. (2000). The effects of physical materials on kindergartners' learning of number concepts. *Cognition and Instruction, 18*(3), 285–316. doi:10.1207/S1532690XCI1803_1

Edirisingha, P., Nie, M., Pluciennik, M., & Young, R. (2009). Socialisation for learning at a distance in a 3-D multi-user virtual environment. *British Journal of Educational Technology, 40*(3), 458–479. doi:10.1111/j.1467-8535.2009.00962.x

Eve, J., & Brabazon, T. (2008). Learning to leisure? Failure, flame, blame, shame, homophobia and other everyday practices in online education. *Journal of Literacy and Technology, 9*(1), 36–61.

Garrison, D. R. (2007). Online community of inquiry review: Social, cognitive, and teaching presence issues. *Journal of Asynchronous Learning Networks*, *11*(1), 61–72.

Garrison, D. R., Anderson, T., & Archer, W. (2000). Critical inquiry in a text-based environment: Computer conferencing in higher education. *The Internet and Higher Education*, *2*(2-3), 87–105. doi:10.1016/S1096-7516(00)00016-6

Garrison, D. R., Anderson, T., & Archer, W. (2001). Critical thinking, cognitive presences, and computer conferencing in distance education. *American Journal of Distance Education*, *15*, 7–23. doi:10.1080/08923640109527071

Gaver, B. (2002). Provocative awareness. [CSCW]. *Computer Supported Cooperative Work*, *11*(3), 475–493. doi:10.1023/A:1021277326673

Gillies, R. M. (2007). *Cooperative Learning: Integrating Theory & Practice*. Thousand Oaks, CA: SAGE Publications.

Gilroy, K. (2001). Collaborative e-learning: The right approach. *DestinatioKM.com White Paper*. Retrieved October 15, 2005, from http://www.destinationcrm.com/articles/default.asp?articleid=1767

Gokhale, A. A. (1995). Collaborative learning enhanced crtical thinking. *Journal of Technology Education, 7*(1). Retrieved November 27, 2006, from http://scholar.lib.vt.edu/ejournals/JTE/v7n1/gokhale.jte-v7n1.html

Gros, B. (2001). Instructional design for computer-supported collaborative learning in primary and secondary school. *Computers in Human Behavior*, *17*(5-6), 439–451. doi:10.1016/S0747-5632(01)00016-4

Gross, T., Stary, C., & Totter, A. (2005). User-centered awareness in computer-supported cooperative work-systems: Structured embedding of findings from social sciences. *International Journal of Human-Computer Interaction*, *18*(3), 323–360. doi:10.1207/s15327590ijhc1803_5

Harasim, L. (1990). *On-line education: Perspectives on a new environment.* New York: Praeger Publishers.

Harp, S. F., & Mayer, R. E. (1998). How seductive details do their damage: A theory of cognitive interest in science learning. *Journal of Educational Psychology*, *90*(3), 414–434. doi:10.1037/0022-0663.90.3.414

Hiltz, S. R. (1997). Impacts of college-level courses via asynchronous learning networks: Some preliminary results. *Journal of Asynchronous Learning Networks*, *1*(2), 1–19.

Ijsselsteijn, W., Freeman, J., & De Ridder, H. (2001). Presence: Where are we? *Cyberpsychology & Behavior*, *4*(2), 179–182. doi:10.1089/109493101300117875

Ijsselsteijn, W., & Riva, G. (2003). Being there: The experience of presence in mediated environments. In Riva, G., Davide, F., & Ijsselsteijn, W. A. (Eds.), *Being there: Concepts, effects and measurements of user presence in synthetic environments* (pp. 3–16). Amsterdam, Netherlands: IOS Press.

Johnson, D. W., & Johnson, R. T. (1999). Making cooperative learning work. *Theory into Practice*, *38*(2), 67–73. doi:10.1080/00405849909543834

Johnson, D. W., Johnson, R. T., & Holubec, E. J. (2003). *Cooperation in the classroom.* Edina, MN: Interaction Book Company.

Johnson, D. W., Johnson, R. T., & Smith, K. A. (2006). *Active Learning: Cooperation in the College Classroom.* Edina, MN: Interaction Book Company.

Jones, A., & Issroff, K. (2005). Learning technologies: Affective and social issues in computer-supported collaborative learning. *Computers & Education*, *44*, 395–408. doi:10.1016/j.compedu.2004.04.004

Jorczak, R. L. (2008). *The effects of task characteristics on higher-order learning in online collaborative learning*. Unpublished doctoral dissertation, University of Minnesota, Minneapolis, MN.

Kirschner, P., Strijbos, J., Kreijns, K., & Beers, P. J. (2005). Designing electronic collaborative learning environments. *Educational Technology Research and Development*, *52*(3), 47–66. doi:10.1007/BF02504675

Kirschner, P. A., Sweller, J., & Clark, R. E. (2006). Why minimal guidance during instruction does not work: An analysis of the failure of constructivist discovery, problem-based, experiential, and inquiry-based teaching. *Educational Psychologist*, *41*(2), 75–86. doi:10.1207/s15326985ep4102_1

Kreijns, K., Kirschner, P. A., & Jochems, W. (2003). Identifying the pitfalls for social interaction in computer-supported collaborative learning environments: A review of the research. *Computers in Human Behavior*, *19*, 335–353. doi:10.1016/S0747-5632(02)00057-2

Kreijns, K., Kirschner, P. A., & Jochems, W. (2004). Determining sociability, social space, and social presence in (a)synchronous collaborative groups. *Cyberpsychology & Behavior*, *7*(2), 155–172. doi:10.1089/109493104323024429

Lapadat, J. C. (2002). Written interaction: A key component in online learning. *Journal of Computer-Mediated Communication*, *7*, 4.

Lee, K. M. (2004). Presence, explicated. *Communication Theory*, *14*(1), 27–50. doi:10.1111/j.1468-2885.2004.tb00302.x

Lobry de Bruyn, L. (2004). Monitoring online communication: Can the development of convergence and social presence indicate an interactive learning environment? *Distance Education*, *25*(1), 67–81. doi:10.1080/0158791042000212468

Lombard, M., & Ditton, T. (1997). At the heart of it all: The concept of presence. *Journal of Computer-Mediated Communication*, *3*(2), 20.

Lount, R. B. Jr, Park, E. S., Kerr, N. L., Messe, L. A., & Seok, D. H. (2008). Evaluation concerns and the Kohler effect: The impact of physical presence on motivation gains. *Small Group Research*, *39*(6), 795–812. doi:10.1177/1046496408323215

Mania, K., & Chalmers, A. (2001). The effects of levels of immersion on memory and presence in virtual environments: A reality centered approach. *Cyberpsychology & Behavior*, *4*(2), 247–264. doi:10.1089/109493101300117938

Mantovani, G., & Riva, G. (1999). "Real" presence: How different ontologies generate different criteria for presence, telepresence, and virtual presence. *Presence (Cambridge, Mass.)*, *8*(5), 540–550. doi:10.1162/105474699566459

Martin, T., & Schwartz, D. L. (2005). Physically distributed learning: Adapting and reinterpreting physical environments in the development of fraction concepts. *Cognitive Science: A Multidisciplinary Journal*, *29*(4), 587-625.

McLeod, P. L., Baron, R. S., Marti, M. W., & Yoon, K. (1997). The eyes have it: Minority influence in face-to-face and computer-mediated group discussion. *The Journal of Applied Psychology*, *82*(5), 706–718. doi:10.1037/0021-9010.82.5.706

Murphy, E., & Manzanares, M. A. R. (2008). Contradictions between the virtual and physical high school classroom: A third-generation Activity Theory perspective. *British Journal of Educational Technology*, *39*(6), 1061–1072. doi:10.1111/j.1467-8535.2007.00776.x

Park, S., & Kim, K. (2008). The use of pedagogical agent as a tool to improve learning interest: Based on the distinction between individual interest and situational interest. In K. McFerrin et al. (Eds.), *Proceedings of Society for Information Technology and Teacher Education International Conference 2008* (pp. 2777-2781). Chesapeake, VA: AACE.

Romero, N., Markopoulos, P., van Baren, J., de Ruyter, B., Ijsselsteijn, W., & Farshchian, B. (2007). Connecting the family with awareness systems. *Personal and Ubiquitous Computing*, *11*(4), 299–312. doi:10.1007/s00779-006-0089-0

Rourke, L., Anderson, T., Garrison, D. R., & Archer, W. (1999). Assessing social presence in asynchronous text-based computer conferencing. *Journal of Distance Education*, *14*(3), 51–70.

Rourke, L., Anderson, T., Garrison, D. R., & Archer, W. (2001). Methodological issues in the content analysis of computer conference transcripts. *International Journal of Artificial Intelligence in Education*, *12*, 8–22.

Rovai, A. P. (2002). Building sense of community at a distance. *International Review of Research in Open and Distance Learning*, *3*(1).

Sarama, J., Clements, D. H., Swaminathan, S., McMillen, S., & Gómez, R. M. G. (2003). Development of mathematical concepts of two-dimensional space in grid environments: An exploratory study. *Cognition and Instruction*, *21*(3), 285–324. doi:10.1207/S1532690XCI2103_03

Sharan, S. (Ed.). (1990). *Cooperative Learning: Theory and Research*. New York: Praeger Publishers.

Short, J., Williams, E., & Christie, B. (1976). *The social psychology of telecommunications*. London: John Wiley & Sons.

Smith, G. G., Passmore, D., & Faught, T. (2009). The challenges of online nursing education. *The Internet and Higher Education*, *12*(2), 98–103. doi:10.1016/j.iheduc.2009.06.007

Stacey, E. (2001). Quality online participation: Establishing social presence. *Research in Distance Learning*, 138-153. Retrieved October 25, 2005, from www.deakin.edu.au/education/ripvet/conferneces/2000/RIDE/Ch13_Stacey.pdf

Takatalo, J., Nyman, G., & Laaksonen, L. (2008). Components of human experience in virtual environments. *Computers in Human Behavior*, *24*(1), 1–15. doi:10.1016/j.chb.2006.11.003

Tu, C. H., & McIsaac, M. (2002). The relationship of social presence and interaction in online classes. *American Journal of Distance Education*, *16*, 131–150. doi:10.1207/S15389286AJDE1603_2

Tu, C. H., & Yen, C. J. (2006). A study of multidimensional online social presence. In L. W. Cooke (Ed.), *Frontiers in Higher Education* (pp. 77-102). New York: Nova Science Publishers. Wachowski, A., Wachowski, L. (Writer), & J. Silver (Producer). (1999). *The Matrix* [Motion picture]. United States: Warner Brothers.

Yamada, M. (2009). The role of social presence in learner-centered communicative language learning using synchronous computer-mediated communication: Experimental study. *Computers & Education*, *52*(4), 820–833. doi:10.1016/j.compedu.2008.12.007

Zhao, S. (2003). Toward a taxonomy of copresence. *Presence (Cambridge, Mass.)*, *12*(5), 445–455. doi:10.1162/105474603322761261

ADDITIONAL READING

Andriessen, J. (2006). Collaboration in computer conferencing. In O'Donnell, A. M., Hmelo-Silver, C. E., & Erkens, G. (Eds.), *Collaborative learning, reasoning, and technology* (pp. 197–232). Mahwah, NJ: Erlbaum.

Biocca, F., Harms, C., & Burgoon, J. K. (2003). Toward a more robust theory and measure of social presence: Review and suggested criteria. *Presence (Cambridge, Mass.)*, *12*(5), 456–480. doi:10.1162/105474603322761270

Brady, J. V., Hienz, R. D., Hursh, S. R., Ragusa, L. C., Rouse, C. O., & Gasior, E. D. (2004). Distributed interactive communication in simulated space-dwelling groups. *Computers in Human Behavior*, *20*(2), 311–340. doi:10.1016/j.chb.2003.10.022

Conceicao, S. C. O. (2006). Faculty Lived Experiences in the Online Environment. *Adult Education Quarterly: A Journal of Research and Theory*, *57*(1), 26-45.

De Greef, P., & Ijsselsteijn, W. A. (2001). Social presence in a home tele-application. *Cyberpsychology & Behavior*, *4*(2), 307–315. doi:10.1089/109493101300117974

De Wever, B., Schellens, T., Valcke, M., & Van Keer, H. (2006). Content analysis schemes to analyze transcripts of online asynchronous discussion groups: A review. *Computers & Education*, *46*, 6–28. doi:10.1016/j.compedu.2005.04.005

Fahy, P., Crawford, G., & Ally, M. (2001). Patterns of Interaction in a Computer Conference Transcript. *International Review of Research in Open and Distance Learning*, *2*(1).

Hammond, M. (2005). A review of recent papers on online discussion in teaching and learning in higher education. *Journal of Asynchronous Learning Networks*, *9*(3).

Hewitt, J. (2005). Toward an understanding of why threads die in asynchronous computer conferences. *Journal of the Learning Sciences*, *14*(4), 567–589. doi:10.1207/s15327809jls1404_4

Hiltz, S. R., & Goldman, R. (2005). *Learning Together Online: Research on Asynchronous Learning Networks*. Mahwah, NJ: Erlbaum.

Ijsselsteijn, W. (2005). Towards a neuropsychological basis of presence. *Annual Review of Cybertherapy and Telemedicine*, *3*, 25–30.

Ijsselsteijn, W., de Ridder, H., Hamberg, R., Bouwhuis, D., & Freeman, J. (1998). Perceived depth and the feeling of presence in 3DTV. *Displays*, *18*(4), 207–214. doi:10.1016/S0141-9382(98)00022-5

Ijsselsteijn, W., Lombard, M., & Freeman, J. (2001). Toward a core bibliography of presence. *Cyberpsychology & Behavior*, *4*(2), 317–321. doi:10.1089/109493101300117983

Jorczak, R. L., & Bart, W. (in press). The effect of task characteristics on conceptual conflict and information processing in online discussion. *Computers in Human Behavior*.

Olson, G. M., & Olson, J. S. (2000). Distance matters. *Human-Computer Interaction*, *15*(2), 139–178. doi:10.1207/S15327051HCI1523_4

Palloff, R. M., & Pratt, K. (2005). *Collaborating online: Learning together in community*. San Francisco: John Wiley & Sons.

Pena-Shaff, J. B., & Nicholls, C. (2004). Analyzing student interactions and meaning construction in computer bulletin board discussions. *Computers & Education*, *42*, 243–265. doi:10.1016/j.compedu.2003.08.003

Picciano, A. G. (2002). Beyond student perceptions: Issues of interaction, presence, and performance in an online course. *Journal of Asynchronous Learning Networks*, *6*(1), 21–40.

Rourke, L. (2000). Operationalizing social interaction in computer conferencing. *Proceedings of the 16th Annual Conference of the Canadian Association for Distance Education*. Retrieved November 19, 2005, from http://www.ulaval.ca/aced2000cade/francais/Actes/Rourke-Liam.html

Schellens, T., & Valcke, M. (2005). Collaborative learning in asynchronous discussion groups: What about the impact on cognitive processing? *Computers in Human Behavior*, *21*, 957–975. doi:10.1016/j.chb.2004.02.025

Schellens, T., & Valcke, M. (2006). Fostering knowledge construction in university students through asnychronous discussion groups. *Computers & Education*, *46*, 349–370. doi:10.1016/j.compedu.2004.07.010

Schroeder, R. (2002). *The social life of avatars: Presence and interaction in shared virtual environments*. New York: Springer.

Smith, A. (2003). Authenticity and Affect: When Is a Watch Not a Watch? *Library Trends*, *52*(1), 172–182.

Stahl, G. (2006). Group Cognition: Computer Support for Building Collaborative Knowledge. Retrieved June 20, 2006, from http://www.cis.drexel.edu/faculty/gerry/mit/

Swan, K. (2003). Developing social presence in online discussions. In Naidu, S. (Ed.), *Learning and teaching with technology: Principles and practices* (pp. 147–164). City.

Veldhuis-Diermanse, A. E. (2002). CSCLearning? Participation, learning activities and knowledge construction in computer-supported collaborative learning in higher education. Unpublished doctoral dissertation. Wageningen Universiteit, Nederland. Retrieved August 15, 2004, from http://www.gcw.nl/dissertations/3187/dis3187.pdf

Weinberger, A., Stegmann, K., Fischer, F., & Mandl, H. (2007). Scripting argumentative knowledge construction in computer-supported learning environments. In Fischer, F., Kollar, I., Mandl, H., & Haake, J. M. (Eds.), *Scripting Computer-Supported Collaborative Learning* (pp. 13–38). New York: Springer. doi:10.1007/978-0-387-36949-5_12

KEY TERMS AND DEFINITIONS

Avatar: Digital representation, controlled by a human user in a virtual environment, which resembles the user in appearance and/or behavior.

Balanced Model of Social and Physical Presence: A model of physical and social presence that advocates for appropriate levels of each in virtual learning environments to create an optimal learning environment.

Computer-Supported Collaborative Learning (CSCL): The use of networked computers to facilitate groups of students working together toward a mutual goal or outcome.

Co-Presence: Sense an individual has of being both physically with and socially connected to others within a shared space.

Cooperative Learning: Instructional method in which students work together for the mutual benefit of one another.

Physical Presence: Perception an individual has of his or herself or an object being physically located within a physical space.

Social Interdependence: A shared understanding that the success or failure of a group is dependent on the success of failure of each individual in that group.

Social Presence: Feeling an individual has of being connected socially to others in a shared space.

Chapter 10
Empowering Faculty Communities for Fostering and Assessing Student Performance in Virtual Landscapes

Holly Lynn Baumgartner
Lourdes College, USA

Garrick Ducat
Mercy College of Northwest Ohio, USA

ABSTRACT

This chapter presents a case study and a narrative of an experimental course, an undergraduate allied health interdisciplinary seminar, and its corresponding faculty learning community exploring how collaborative learning may be fostered in a virtual world. The objectives of the course included enhancing student technology literacy, engendering reflective practice, and creating a student-focused faculty learning community; additionally, the faculty learning community both inspired and was inspired by students, fueling innovative teaching practices which, as a result, have infused the college curriculum. Receiving mentoring from learning community members, students were responsible for the design, development, and implementation of a virtual solution to a student defined, healthcare-based, needs analysis. The last part of this case study provides explication of the RIME model of student and learning community assessment for use in teaching with a multi-user virtual environment (MUVE) which may, by extension, be applied to other emergent technologies and social media. This instrument assesses student learning outcomes in the areas of retention, immersion, motivation, and engagement.

INTRODUCTION

From *CSI* to *Law and Order*, Second Life and other virtual worlds are permeating popular culture; however, the effective use of these worlds in educational settings is still in its infancy. In fact, the first major meta-analysis analyzing 46 studies comparing face-to-face to online learning was completed only recently by the U.S. Department of Education. The results of the study concluded that "blended learning," that is courses or programs that include both face-to-face and online elements,

DOI: 10.4018/978-1-61692-854-4.ch010

"has been more effective" (Means et al., 2009, p. xvii). Arne Duncan, the U.S. Secretary of Education, commented in a press release on the study that "this new report reinforces that effective teachers need to incorporate digital content into everyday classes and consider open-source learning management systems, which have proven cost effective in school districts and colleges nationwide" (U.S Department of Education, 2009). The possibilities offered by immersive environments for college curricula cannot be ignored. Although Mercy College already offers online and face-to-face courses, the college was receptive to exploring new hybrid learning forms, specifically a blended experimental course. As assessment was a critical question for both faculty and administrators, we created and implemented a tool, referred to as the RIME model, to gauge four crucial achievement factors including retention, immersion, motivation, and engagement. Additionally, the formation of a faculty learning community undergirded several of these factors with mixed results.

The professors chose Second Life (SL) as the multi-user virtual environment (MUVE) for the course. Second Life is "A 3-D online digital world imagined and created by its residents" (Linden, "What Is," 2008). Not only is Second Life a popular choice for Ohio Colleges, but it has more than 200 other US college presences who are deciphering its educational potential (Villano, 2008). "Second Life is ideally suited for (at least) two kinds of learning activities – empathy based learning and encounter learning" (LaChapelle, 2007, para. 5). The foundation of Second Life is to offer a space that can be manipulated and constructed through the creativity and self-expression of the user. Being the industry standard environment, Second Life has gained international recognition for its successes in building large scale communities of diverse populations. When Second Life was first created, it wasn't much more than a playground; however, today, Second Life is a fully functional society with a very real economy.

Contributing to that economy, a growing number of corporations and academic institutions have established mirror identities within Second Life. Some of the important statistics to consider are that as of October 2007, Second Life had more than 10 million registered users with the U.S. cornering 34.56% of the demographic. The largest age group is composed of 25-34 year olds, paralleling our college's demographic. In September 2007 alone, \$6,685,585 in U.S. dollars was exchanged in Second Life with nearly six billion Linden dollars currently in circulation (Linden, "Economic," 2008; 2009). Although SL is, therefore, an intriguing MUVE from purely a culture studies perspective, it was selected for its ease of use, accessibility to students, and, most importantly, for its global adoption.

First, we provide a context for the creation of the course and its corresponding faculty learning community (FLC). Secondly, we describe our student cohort, along with the actual interdisciplinary course, and student semester projects within Second Life. Then we examine the faculty learning community and its connections to the student cohort. The avatars, (that is, the virtual representation of students), faculty learning community members, and professors all interacted in-world. In addition, we explicate our RIME model of student assessment. Finally, we discuss our conclusions and directions for future study. The evolution of our pedagogical process taught us the benefits of re-envisioning our fields and the importance of Gwendolyn Pough's Conference on College Composition and Communication address to be "forward thinking enough to imagine new combinations and collaborations" (2009) between disciplines as well as various college constituencies.

BACKGROUND

Multi-user virtual environments (MUVEs) have generated an explosion of interest among educators, but a systematic pedagogical approach has not been undertaken. As Cohen and Castner ask, is the classroom "designed to be a showcase for technology at the expense of good instructional design?" (p. 3). The possibilities for the college curriculum offered by MUVEs can propel insightful and effective pedagogy. These immersive virtual environments by the nature of their communal engagement shape, augment, and challenge student learning. Rather than a simple "presentation of content," as Rick Nigol of eLearn Campus points out, MUVEs aid in "the creation of context wherein learners can apply and reflect upon the new knowledge they encounter. It is a matter of moving beyond 'knowing' something to being able to do something with this new knowledge" (quoted in Keesey, 2009).

The collaborative possibilities of digital environments extend beyond the virtual world to engage multiple college constituents. In our learning community, the inclusion of not just faculty, but students, academic support specialists, and administrators ensured the course became what Christopher Keesey describes as an "engine for creating an experience" (2009) transcending the course confines to embrace the program level resulting in an impact on the entire institution. Furthermore, the layering of various computer technologies, especially when coinciding with assignments significant to student life and culture, is an important contribution to the college curriculum. The "horizontal knowledge assemblage" (Fountain, 2007) of social media may also figure in the preparation of student-citizens who, in the words of Charles Bazerman, "can responsibly represent, reflect on, and act in the worlds they inhabit and rebuild" (2008).

Virtual worlds may become ekphrastic spaces, that is, they are able to "interpret, inhabit, confront, and speak to their subjects" in much the same manner as an ekphrastic poem responds to and narrates a work of art (American Academy, 2007-2009). A virtual world as an ekphrastic space opens up what Robert Miltner calls "collaboration as conversation" (2001, para. 1ff). In this conversation, our students flowed between responder and respondent, producer and consumer, the dynamic movement fueling learning processes.

Mission

Mercy College is a small, urban, undergraduate, healthcare institution serving the Northwest Ohio and Southeast Michigan regions. Although the college does offer general education degrees, its specialized niche tends to overshadow the liberal arts curriculum. At the same time, most newer or emergent technologies do not yet have a toehold. With these strictures, it is increasingly vital to inspire faculty, as well as students, to enhance their own collaborative learning, especially when best practices from the liberal arts could prove adaptable and beneficial to the nursing and allied health programs. Conversely, importing allied health concepts into general education could stimulate greater participation and interest among students.

Undertaking the mission to tie these disparate halves together, we applied for and received an Ohio Learning Network Innovation Grant. Throughout the following year, we researched the pedagogical significance of immersive learning environments, especially in a college setting where resistance does not stem from lack of interest, but from lack of knowledge. Therefore, in order to do this, we developed an interdisciplinary course integrating *Second Life,* humanities, and health care education. Our objectives for the course included:

- Enhancing student technology literacy
- Engendering reflective practice
- Creating a student-centered learning community, and, most importantly,
- Devising a comprehensive assessment model.

The last objective took on greater significance as our programs underwent accreditation from their respective governing bodies, such as the State Medical Board, the Commission of Collegiate Nursing Education, and the Joint Review Committee on Education in Radiologic Technology, all of which are placing heavier emphasis on student outcomes and the challenges of closing the assessment gap. Moreover, the course needed to incorporate the ideals of a senior level, interdisciplinary seminar requiring project-based and cooperative learning. Our goals for students, which were shared with them on the syllabus, involved a series of salient questions and themes as evolutionary guides:

- **Foundational Questions:** How are Second Life and "real" life correlated? In what ways does Second Life and its virtual landscape shape or contribute to "real" life?
- **Problematic Questions:** How might the virtual world misuse, misconceive, and/or misunderstand the aims of education: traditional, hybrid and online?
- **Subversions and Interrogations:** How would this world challenge the participant in such a way as to function as a site of change?
- **Culture Studies:** How does our "island" mirror and/or contribute to socio-cultural attitudes?
- **Subtexts:** What ethical implications are raised in the in-world conversion, creation, and contact processes?

We conducted a brief overview with students of the above questions during the first session and then used them as a skeleton map throughout the first month. The questions served as discussion points in class while readings from prominent researchers and critical responses from students also coalesced around these thematic prompts with responses posted on the class blog as homework.

THE COHORT

Mercy College offers a series of Interdisciplinary Seminars (IDS) which are 300 level courses. At least one IDS course is required for bachelor degree students. Other students may take IDS courses as humanities substitutes. Jarmon, Traphagan, Mayrath, and Trivedi have shown that SL in conjunction with an IDS focus has "effectively fostered experiential development of interdisciplinary communication awareness and strategies" (2009, p. 180). Our course is called Mercy in a Virtual World: Your Professional Second Life (4 credit hours) and directly targeted students in the bachelor of science in nursing program for its first run. Still, the students had diverse educational backgrounds, including one student with a bachelor's degree in psychology, two transfer students, and one with an associate's degree in another allied health program. In spite of the senior level course number, the cohort included predominantly sophomores and juniors. Both traditional and non-traditional students were represented. None of the students had ever been in a virtual world, and only one had heard of Second Life. On a practical level, other than word-processing, none of the students had computer experience, so the pitfalls of online collaboration and its accompanying technologies were a lesson on their own (for all of us). Our students also came to recognize, as Alison E. Regan and John D. Zuern discuss, the "asymmetrical distribution of technology resources" and the necessity for interrogation of these disparities (2000, p. 186).

THE COURSE

Each class was divided into two parts: a theoretical, discussion based portion and a practical portion. The first two weeks of the semester focused on defining virtual worlds, examining the psychology of them, performing culture study work on the Second Life inhabitants through interviews, reading current studies, and conducting research on the academic work that has already been performed on MUVEs. On the practical side, students worked on creating an avatar, touring Second Life through a virtual treasure hunt, and learning the basics of building and/or scripting. For both parts of each session, exploration was a crucial motivating factor. As de Freitas and Neumann point out in a recent edition of *Computers and Education*, "Exploration of virtual and physical environments aids the learner to find new boundaries, to push back on what they know and to help them to engage socially and conceptually with others" (2009, p. 346). To assist them in their explorations, the professors appointed two student group leaders. Leaders chose their own groups and established Wordpress© blogs to archive their project efforts and to communicate with their groups. Critical readings continued throughout the semester along with student critical response journals which were submitted weekly through the class blog. Tutorials and other resources were posted on the class blog, and students kept their own resource lists on their individual group blogs.

As the semester continued, students launched into their major semester work. The semester long assignment responded to Linda Nelson et al.'s suggestions for a carefully structured problem or "trigger" for a productive assignment. "Triggers need to be broad and complex enough to allow the students to explore the wider determinants of health and social care. If the focus is too narrow, it restricts the exploration and creativity of the students and has the potential to limit their learning" (2004, p.104). In our case, the assignment was to design and build a learning space in-world that met two criteria: 1) identified a need in the medical field and 2) served an educational purpose. As the first step, student groups performed a needs analysis in their health care professions to locate a partially or totally unmet need as well as design a means of communicating it within a MUVE. Within their needs analyses, groups were also expected to determine their audience demographic. These student-designed projects received mentoring both in and outside of class from faculty learning community members including an instructional designer, a humanities professor, a sociologist, a psychiatric counselor, and a nurse practitioner. The bound proposals (one 65 pp. in length) contained photos of the images and objects they planned on using as well as the written materials (notecards, slide shows, and posters) to be incorporated in SL. Students also researched and wrote annotated bibliographies (12 and 17 pp. respectively) on their topics to establish a firm knowledge base. As one group outlined in their annotated bibliography "We have gathered detailed information on each culture and then compiled this information as a group… journal articles, websites, and books were used. Extensive research was done to ensure credibility of the sources. Also, to increase the validity of our information, we utilized a professor from Mercy College who specializes in culture."

In conjunction with their research, the groups were responsible for the design, development and implementation of a virtual solution to their defined needs analysis. Projects ranged from a cultural awareness training space for healthcare practitioners to a three-tiered educational center focusing on the primary, secondary, and tertiary means of prevention targeting high school students. In the first part of the creation process, the walls of a conference room were lined with large white sheets of paper. The groups storyboarded their projects around the room, garnering feedback from each other and from professors as they rendered their concepts into graphical representations. Groups were also responsible for an accurate accounting of their expenditures on purchases in-world. Each group was allotted $500 Linden dollars; however, for the scale of the projects desired, the initial funds were quickly depleted. Therefore, students worked in-world to gather objects from freebie sites and from residents who gifted them materials.

The last month of the semester was a blitz-build with class sessions both in the lab as well as off-campus in-world. Students found this section of the course the most satisfactory because they saw their plans come to fruition. David Bell argues that "This is, in fact, a recurring motif in discussions of 3-D MUVEs like Second Life." He further clarifies "that new forms of creative expression are enabled by these virtual worlds, and that this creativity is both a manifestation of some inherent desire to create (stifled in the alienated labouring of the capitalist workforce) and at once the source of and expression of particular regimes of value" (2009, p. 520). According to faculty learning community members, these projects certainly differed from any other projects assigned in the curriculum, and, as students discovered, were unlike any others they found in SL. Students cited creativity as the aspect of the course with the most meaning to them. At the same time, their projects drew on the established teachings of their field yet expressed them in a novel form that exposed nuances the students might not have otherwise conceived. These student insights were apparent during their capstone event, a public presentation and unveiling before the president of the college and various other members of the academic community. The course sequence was designed so that subsequent courses will continue to build on the established research of the pilot student cohort.

The Projects

Group One: Prevention Project

The set of four buildings on the top in Figure 1 is the Prevention Project. The signpost introducing the facility states, "The intention of our project is to educate the public on popular American medical issues. We are using prevention as our means of education. As these medical issues are so prevalent, prevention of each has become a necessity."

The four issues under exploration are cancer, eating disorders, addiction, and sexual health. The group based choices on survey research conducted at the beginning of the project, deciding to target 15-25 year olds and topics relevant to this age group as a result. Each of the four buildings was then further broken into three floors with

Figure 1. (Top) Exterior of two Second Life student projects. (Left) Interior of sexual health room of prevention project. (Right) Muslim floor of the Cultural Training Center.

each floor devoted to a level of medical prevention. The group explains:

Primary prevention includes facts and figures as well as other educational materials concerning the topic. Secondary prevention encompasses testing, screening, and early detection of illness. With this, we have included examples in each topic of prevention and early detection tools. Tertiary prevention is the coping mechanisms one may use once diagnosed and treated with an illness. This may include counseling or alternative medicines.

The group also posed pre and post tests to gauge the effectiveness of their campaign.

During final presentations, prevention students also distributed audience handouts which included a "Proposed Outcome Statement," the "Final Outcome of the Project Statement," a "Cost Analysis," and a "Summary of Each Structure." Portions of those handouts are presented below:

- Proposed Outcome Statement

Ideally, Second Life may be implemented in health classes in high schools to allow students the opportunity to experience these events without having the aftereffects that would occur in a real life experience. We also hope that these simulations can be used to educate medical providers on the experiences that their patients will go through.

- Final Outcome of Project

The current state of the Prevention Project has left its creators very proud. Our original intentions…were achieved. We …provide information …which is user friendly, easy to understand, and most importantly pertinent to our target age group. Our group did an excellent job of finding visual aids, videos, images and facts that will help our audience learn about prevention.

For the following summaries, each participant wrote her own description of her building and the purpose of her prevention topic:

- Summary of Each Structure:
  - Addiction Prevention

My first floor includes information on the signs and symptoms concerning addiction to alcohol, prescription drugs, narcotics, and smoking. Pictures will catch the eye of the avatar when they first arrive at the first floor of prevention. The building is dark as the topics that are covered are dark and gloomy. For the second floor, there are videos that I hope will make an impact on someone's life. This floor includes information and images of what can happen to an individual if they decide or continue to practice poor life habits. Some of these images may be gruesome but are intended to have a powerful impact on the user's life. The third provides information that will lead an individual to recovery. It shows recovery centers that will be helpful to someone experiencing one of these specific diseases.

- Eating Disorders Prevention

The first floor of the eating disorder building consists of various pictures associated with each of the four disorders. Also provided is general educational information such as definitions, complications, statistics, and signs and symptoms. The second floor includes more pictures, tests or screening that can be done, and other preventative measures associated with the four disorders. The eating disorder building's third floor consists of resources that one can utilize if they have experienced any of the four disorders. A picture is provided and can be clicked on to take them to the link.

- Teen Pregnancy and STD Prevention

The outside of the sexual health tower has the themes that are inside the building, such as AIDs, teen pregnancy, STDs and testing. Each wall on the inside of the tower gives details about each subject displayed on the outside of the tower. Each wall is designed to inform the SL seeker of the facts concerning sexual health. One wall, designated to teens and young adults, displays the reality of unsafe sex. The first, second and third floor are primary, secondary, and tertiary prevention. The third floor includes sites that one may visit to seek more information on the subjects as well as any help they might need. The floor of each level has the unique texture of contraceptives and condoms used to prevent pregnancies and STDs.

- Cancer Prevention

The cancer prevention building is brightly colored on each wall to signify the color of that cancer's awareness ribbon. Large ribbons were placed for each cancer type on the front outside of the building. When you teleport into the first floor, each corner covers a different type of cancer. The breast cancer corner shows images of facts and figures on prevalence of breast cancer, as well as images of unhealthy breast examples. The colon cancer corner shows examples of the anatomy of the colon, where colon cancer is typically found, and also provides facts on colon cancer. Lung and oral cancer round out the other two corners, and they respectively cover the signs and symptoms as well as facts behind the illnesses. On the second and third floor of the cancer prevention building, you will find links to videos of screening tests used to detect and prevent each illness as well as coping mechanisms and support groups for each illness.

Group Two: Cultural Training Center

On the bottom right in Figure 1 is the Cultural Training Center in which each floor considers a different culture and their medical practices. In the Guiding Statement of their Annotated Bibliography, the Cultural group wrote:

The educational focus for this project is to increase the knowledge of healthcare workers and students who are interacting with other cultures. We have included information on each culture and the special practices that they use, along with the rationale for these practices and/or beliefs. We also included an area on what culture is, cultural competence, and how culture can be a factor in health care. We hope to achieve increased understanding of cultures for those who interact with cultures different from their own.

Likewise, on its audience handout, the culture group provided an honest commentary for the professors' prompt on their "Expectations" and "Accomplishments" excerpted below:

- **Expectations**

Our original plan when first given this endeavor was to create a culture center where healthcare professionals and students can go to get a quick overview on cultural competence. Each member of our group chose a culture... The information we gathered was on family, health practices, religion, birthing practices, preventative measures, and communication.

We then decided to make a round building. We planned for the building to be two stories with the top floor being devoted to culture and the bottom floor to individual cultures. The bottom floor would then be divided into quarters. Each quarter would be decorated according to culture and have objects from each culture that would present a notecard with information to the avatar when touched. Within each room were planning to have multiple simulations for the avatar to experience cultural events or changes.

For both groups, the original proposals and storyboards were deeply ambitious. The FLC agreed not to make any suggestions to students about trimming the scope of their projects or to state any cautions regarding the workload in text or speech but instead chose to approve the projects. The plan was when students came to the professors with concerns about finishing, they would then help groups modify and adjust the storyboards to a more reasonable and manageable level. The irony is that students never did come to us. They persisted in their original goals with only slight modifications and seemed determined to build and polish until the very last moment before final presentations. As an example, the culture group accounted the changes made to its original blueprint at the same time affirming its pleasure with the final product.

- **Accomplishments**

Although our finished project differs from the original, we are extremely proud to present our five story cultural center. Each floor provides information on a different culture with one floor designated to defining culture. Notecards are present in all of the rooms for avatars and guests to take information with them. Also, each floor is decorated with objects relevant to each culture. Only a few simulations are present throughout the center because they proved to be hard to create because of the time constraints of the project.

Post presentation, after the audience dispersed, all students not only did homegrown summative course assessments, but they also revisited one of the preliminary questions given on the first day, examining how the projects in Second Life and Second Life itself could and did function as a site of change for them. The combination of the practical usages for their projects outside of class, the affirmation of a real world audience, and the ownership both of their topics and their own project parameters all contributed to immediate meaning accessibility.

FACULTY LEARNING COMMUNITY

The sequential nature of the course is also reflected in the sequential development of the faculty learning community. As Milton Cox describes, the development of a "faculty learning community program is one approach that engages community in the cause of student and faculty learning and of transforming our institutions of higher education into learning organizations" (Cox, 2004, p. 5). Each member of the learning community had ample opportunity to interact with colleagues. We wanted to stretch our definition of community outside of the classroom and to engage in dialogue with other college constituents. The pedagogical framework of learning communities and steep learning curve associated with MUVEs were new experiences for most members. Acclimating members to a virtual environment was a necessity as most had never experienced a virtual world that defied the norms of their reality; therefore, training in the technological skills necessary to work within MUVEs as well as training in assessment were offered to members of the faculty learning community. As W. Michele Simmons and Jeffrey T. Grabill point out in an issue of *College Composition and Communication*, "the issues that most communities face as they imagine who they are and what they might be require what rhetoricians have always understood to be acts of invention" (2007, p. 423). The open ended possibilities of the learning community provide the continued opportunity for administration, faculty, and staff to discover their own capacities for innovation.

Fostering a faculty learning community had direct results on the student portion of the learning community. The faculty learning community provided the students with many benefits. Student projects, for example, were enhanced through mentoring by members of the FLC. The nursing full professor talked to students in one group about the most serious issues facing health care practitioners today. The college counselor talked to a group about issues of concern to young people, especially high school and entry level undergraduates. The sociology professor brought in food samples from his home country of Korea (including bean paste cookies which were not a big hit) and discussed medical practices in Asia for another group. These interactions with faculty fostered a sense of accountability in students as well as legitimizing their project topics. Having faculty present in a consultant role made students feel less like students and more like younger colleagues performing noteworthy work.

Conversely, interactions with students produced ripples in the FLC. Faculty were intrigued by the student projects and began thinking of ways to utilize similar assignments in their own classes. Other faculty members who were inspired by the class projects have expressed interest in petitioning students to help build learning objects to facilitate faculty teaching. Students performed another important function in the faculty learning community; at the end of the semester, students were asked to join the FLC for future iterations of the course. As Cox points out, the students "play an important role in faculty development," and their involvement can lead to "gains in personal, social, and professional development" (2004, p.7). Likewise, he adds, "sensitivity to and respect for other points of view, other cultures, and other people are enhanced for both students and faculty" (p.7).

Finally, the FLC provided a real world audience for group final presentations. College assembly discussions and word-of-mouth outside of the FLC generated curiosity about SL throughout the college so that other members of the college attended as well. Knowing they would have an external audience prompted students, on their own, to arrive at class dressed formally and professionally, which was neither required nor expected. They also had made additions to their original presentations, such as handouts, structured "lectures", and a building demo for the audience. Professors also asked team leaders to make their group blogs public so that attendees would have an opportunity to comment. Clearly, student investment skyrocketed knowing the FLC was to be in residence for their project unveilings. FLC members in attendance were provided an opportunity to critique each group as part of the class assessment process.

A semester after the course in student focus groups, group leaders offered input on ways to better integrate the FLC into the classroom. The consensus was that having discussions with subject matter experts proved beneficial to the group projects. Furthermore, as team leader Sarah Hooper states, it was helpful to have a "more experienced perspective to just bounce things off of and who understood what we were talking about and coming from and could just give us some insight" (personal communication, June 4, 2009). On the other hand, she suggests that the FLCs function in the class as a whole was unclear (2009). Team leader Sara Knoblauch adds that "it would have been better to have some people with more experience in Second Life to help with building and constructing rather than just looking at the projects" (personal communication, June 4, 2009), indicating again that technological disparities remained the most difficult of the challenges to overcome.

RIME ASSESSMENT MODEL

Another constituency of the FLC was the course professors themselves. Establishing an FLC provided a cushion of support to the professors for the experimental nature of the course. By including administrators in learning community membership, the administration as a whole became invested in the project. At FLC meetings, informal discussions about the pathway the assessment practices was following insured that information was disseminated to the rest of the administration who then had both a better understanding of the course and a greater willingness to grant us autonomy. With typical first time course constraints removed, the FLC had fewer qualms about suggesting and supporting alternative assessment practices. With the addition of material from FLC discussions and from our grant consultant Anthony Fontana assigned by the Ohio Learning Network, we conceptualized the RIME model for assessment weaving together a tapestry of both qualitative and quantitative research.

The archeology of virtual worlds provided a landscape rich in student learning outcomes. The RIME instrument assessed student learning outcomes in the areas of Retention, Immersion, Motivation, and Engagement. The strategy of the instrument involves bundling multiple technologies and embedding questions that speak to each component of the model. A balance of technologies that encourage self assessment along with more objective analyses contributes to the validity of the model. Some parts of the RIME model involved online surveys, class and group blogs that served dual purposes of reflecting on and archiving of course content, homegrown versions of Angelo and Cross's Classroom Assessment Techniques, filmed video interviews, and focus groups. Multiple methods of assessment make the RIME model a comprehensive tool. Its hybrid permissiveness makes the RIME model adaptable to multiple courses. The Fall 2008 version of the RIME student performance instrument is explicated below:

Class and Group Blogs

Class Blog

To maintain communication outside of the course, the professors developed a class blog using the blogging engine Wordpress that acted as the course website. The purpose of the site was to serve not only as a communication tool, but also as a means in which to post and submit class assignments including the weekly critical reflections. As mentioned previously, the students enrolled in the course were unfamiliar with virtual worlds and were apprehensive. To overcome this obstacle, professors gathered articles and other texts, and based on these, developed questions that corresponded to the salient "skeleton" questions listed within the course syllabus. Provided below are examples of the type of questions that were asked of the students.

- Because it is a "highly social medium," what does Second Life's allure indicate about American culture? About humanity in general?
- Before you read the article, please discuss the following:
    - How important of a role is the visual in your perception of someone the first time you meet? Why?
    - How important is it to recognize someone's gender? Why?
    - What things make a person seem credible to you on first sight?

The blog also served another purpose in that it provided the professors with insight into the possibility of offering the course in a blended/hybrid mode of delivery. With Second Life as the medium, the professors allowed students an opportunity to leave the class early with the understanding that they would complete the weekly assignments listed in the blog. Students were permitted some class sessions outside of lab time once their groups had been determined and their semester projects had been designed. The understanding was that instead of meeting in the classroom, each group was expected to be active in Second Life for the duration of the face-to-face course and to record their individual efforts within the required group blogs.

Figure 2. Survey responses

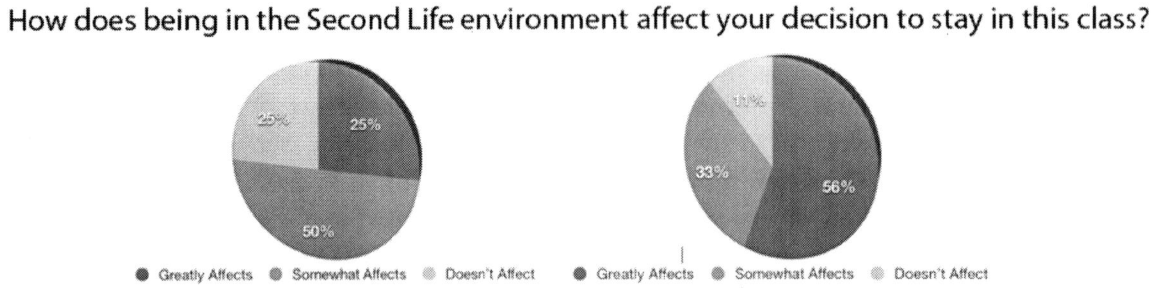

Group Blogs

The group blogs provided a means by which students could document their progress as they developed their spaces in-world and by which they could communicate with group members more efficiently than email, although texting via cell phone proved to be the primary method of communication when peers were absent. The criteria provided by the professors relative to the group blogs were quite minimal, and the end result showed a sharp contrast between how each group perceived the word "documentation". One group chose to have the group leader serve as the blog manager which meant summarizing their project status on a weekly basis. The other group used their blog more as a repository for conversations between group members. Groups' blogs are also discussed below.

Surveys

During the semester, the professors conducted five online surveys, one every three weeks. The surveys consisted of a mix of multiple choice and multiple answer questions each pertaining to a component of the RIME model. The results generated from the multiple choice and multiple answer questions were summarized and transposed graphically to display change over time. To gauge retention, students were asked whether utilizing Second Life affected their decision to stay in the class. When the survey was originally deployed, only 25% of the eight respondents felt that the use of Second Life "greatly affected their decision to stay in the course. The results of the last survey, conducted at the end of the term, showed that of the nine respondents, the percentage had risen to 56% (Figure 2).

The surveys also included two Likert-based questions and two corresponding open-ended questions that were developed to measure the students' change in attitude regarding the use of MUVEs. Results from the open-ended questions were analyzed for recurring themes and comments and also used as a means to gather feedback prior to the next class meeting. One of the most provocative open-ended questions asked students, "What is the one thing that you least understand?" Once the group project description and criteria were presented, students began responding that building, locating objects, and scripting were difficult tasks they did not fully understand. As a result, proceeding sessions were structured to include a practical component that focused on a particular feature or function within Second Life specific to their major projects. Results from the first survey showed that when asked whether the knowledge of virtual worlds would help them in their chosen career, out of the 8 students responding, the replies were evenly split between agree and disagree. When asked the same question at

Figure 3. Survey responses

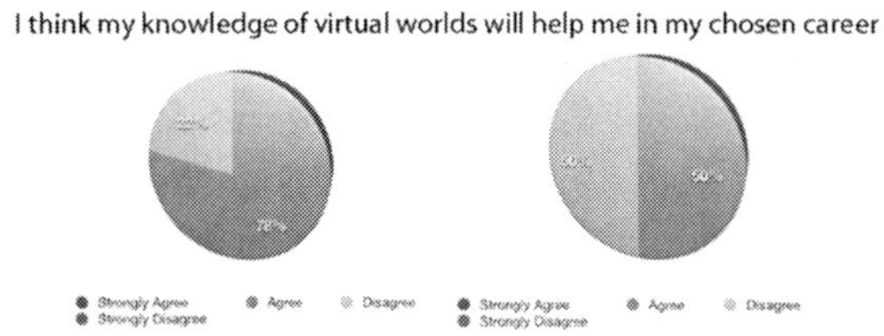

end of the term, students still only replied agree or disagree, even though strongly agree/disagree were also options, but the variance had changed to 78% agree and 22% disagree (Figure 3).

Focus Group

Semi-structured focus groups with the two group leaders were conducted one semester after completion of the course to have them reflect on the course experience and offer suggestions for improvement to aid in the redesign of the next iteration. The focus group interview protocol included a series of questions that focused specifically on the RIME model with others that served as manipulation checks to confirm that the responses received were truthful. Questions were coded with either an "R," "I," "M," "E" to correspond with that category with some deliberate overlap.

Guided Reflections

At the midpoint of the term, students were asked to take part in a guided reflection either individually or in pairs that had them respond honestly to a series of questions discussing preconceived notions, group projects, course value, and future considerations. Each student, or pair of students, was asked the same seven reflection questions and several flexible, additional questions derived from conversational prompts. The overwhelming consensus from the interviews indicated that students either misinterpreted the course description or were provided inaccurate information prior to registering for the course. A fair number of students professed that they thought the course was meant to be an independent study and were confused when they realized that "IDS" stood for interdisciplinary study. The video also serves as a glaring contrast with the final presentation video in terms of student articulation of their knowledge base, confidence in their abilities, and pride in their combined efforts.

End of Term Evaluations

A requirement for the institution is that each student is expected to complete an end of term evaluation for each course in which they are enrolled to provide feedback to the instructor(s) about their experiences and practical suggestions for improvement. Professors also distributed a second set of questions post presentations. As part of the Likert-based portion of the evaluation, 86% of the seven students who responded felt that the instructor engaged them in active learning. This correlates very closely with the responses received during the guided reflection taping (above) when students were asked whether they valued the experience gained in the course. Additional comments received from the open-ended responses (listed below) prove that the students valued the experience though were not shy to admit the amount of work was overwhelming. Some comments included:

"I think lightening the course load would help the future students, because with the project and its parts, I felt like sometimes I was just rushing through the critical thinking and not really thinking about them."

"Start building earlier, kind of crammed at the end. Warn students that it is very time consuming."

"Tell the students the project day one! Allow more full class building days, earlier."

"Less written homework, Second Life in itself is a lot of work."

On the other hand, students also recognized the value of the course content:

"Helped me learn how to use a virtual world in a useful manner"

"I think the critical thinking helped me to learn in this class, because it taught me a lot about Second Life."

Likewise, 87.5% would also recommend the course to a friend in spite of the work load and the challenges they faced.

RESEARCH AND METHODOLOGY

The Innovation Grant acted as a catalyst for scratching below the surface of virtual technologies. Most tools are not the main focus of a pedagogically-sound course, but should, instead, be a vehicle for teaching content. As Matt Villano mentions in *Campus Technology*, "Once you've got a space in a virtual learning environment, the next step is to look at your existing curriculum and figure out how you can use the technology to supplement it" (2008). Second Life, as the vehicle, gave shape to this course experience and provided the immersive environment for collaboration while, at the same time, offering a professional stage for workforce development. James Rhem (1995, "Close Up," p. 4) suggests that creating a deeper learning experience involves four important areas: "Motivational context," "Learner activity," "Interaction with others," and "A well-structured knowledge base." Rhem asserts that "some level of choice and control" are necessary for motivational context (p. 4).

In this course, students had ownership of both their semester-long group projects as well as having a stake in the course itself. In focus group discussions, team leader Sara Knoblauch affirms, "The flexibility of the course helped because it allowed us the freedom to learn" (2009). Her comment suggests that many courses with more rigid classroom and assignment boundaries actually constrain student learning. Team leader Sarah Hooper adds that "Having the freedom to choose what we wanted was nice…because then you're more passionate about what you're doing, and you want to be there. You want to be creating something and trying to educate others with it" (2009). The desire to create something of value also figured into learner activity. Course assignments entailed a balanced mix of outside critical studies, research and writing, and in-world scripting, imagination, and design. This mix fostered active rather than passive learning, connecting the theoretical to the practical, and thus achieving praxis.

The collaborative learning demanded a certain level of interaction with others since interaction was the basis for the semester-long major projects, for communication with the faculty learning community, and for in-world interaction with other SL visitors and residents. Salmon points out that "visiting and immersing oneself in learning locations and cultures can involve doing so in those no longer in existence or accessible in RL [real life]" (2009, p. 529). As an example, in the beginning of the semester, we took students to an alternative healing center in SL. The owners of the island, one a practicing physician the other an alternative medicine practitioner, were based in London, England. Interacting with people from a different country, in an already developed in-world environment, and experiencing an alternative healing session that was completely outside the traditional medical boundaries of their nursing programs facilitated multiple levels of interaction and debate among the students. More importantly, the sessions modeled behaviors for the class, for the groups, and for the in-world settings the professors actually giving a lecture or providing more specific guidelines or rules.

On the first day, the professors of the course spent almost an hour explaining the experimental nature of the course and the fluid and open-ended nature of the major project. The syllabus also contained a caveat to that effect. This discussion generated many questions and concerns, some fear, some puzzlement, and some suspicion. The nature of the course also meant rethinking our instructional design and adjusting our pedagogies to better fit this educational chimera. Of the positives, "Exploration implies greater opportunities for learning, more social interactive learning and increased learner control over content production and sharing and practice of skills" (2009, p. 347), as de Freitas and Neumann discovered. On the downside, technology skills were uneven as were critical thinking and conceptual thinking skills in our students. This unevenness left some students feeling overwhelmed or even resentful at times. Social interactive learning can produce exponentially greater academic results than solely individualized learning. However, with any social interaction, miscommunication will occur. Tensions developed in the groups over who was and was not "pulling their weight." Some of these flare ups appeared in their blog postings. Other than a brief talk with the group leaders to ensure that no bullying was taking place, we left students alone to sort out their interactions themselves, which they eventually did.

Finally, for Rhem, a well structured knowledge base implies "engaging and reshaping the concepts students bring with them" (1995, p. 4). He explains that "the more fully new concepts can be connected with students' prior experience and existing knowledge, the more likely it is they will be impatient with inert facts and eager to achieve their own syntheses" (p. 4). Our challenge was to connect the disparate pieces of a general education base to the highly didactic content of an allied health curriculum. As Sara Knoblauch asserts, this course allowed "us to take what we have learned in nursing and apply it to something else. Normally we take what we learn in nursing and memorize it and then apply it to patient care. This [course] involves everything we have learned, all our nursing skills, all our techniques, how to research. This is a good class to test your knowledge, test your skills and bring everything together" (2009). By prompting students to draw on these experiences in conjunction, they would begin to understand the importance of both parts of their college experience to their professional careers.

RIME OUTCOMES

Retention

Retention was chosen as a facet of the RIME assessment model because faculty carry an important responsibility at our college in monitoring the retention figures associated with their individual courses. This debate is not confined to Mercy College.

Over the past 20 years, few topics in American higher education have commanded as much attention from as many college and university administrators as student retention. In fact, only a handful of the most elite liberal arts colleges and research universities have escaped what, for many US campuses, has become an overriding obsession to stem a "tidal wave" of student drop out, which is at its highest level between the first and second year. A parallel concern relates to the less than 50% national five-year rate of baccalaureate degree completion, a rate that has declined over the past 10 years. (Astin & Oseguera as cited in Barefoot, 2004, p. 9)

Likewise, Bahr points out that "estimates suggest that as many as 2 out of 5 first-time postsecondary students (40%) attend 2 or more institutions within 4 years of initial enrollment" (2009, pp. 272-273). The retention objective for the course was to first retain students in a rigorous and highly experimental course. The sequential nature of the course encourages the accrual of a campus presence in SL. A campus presence also opens doors for students outside the classroom. Second Life, therefore, is becoming more fully incorporated into the college to aid in retention at the institutional level.

Retention was self-assessed by students through questions that had them consider whether their decision to remain in the course could be attributed to the use of Second Life or if Mercy College should continue the course. With a beginning population of 10 students, the term ended with nine students having completed the course which brought the retention rate to 90%. Mercy College of Northwest Ohio reported to the U.S. Department of Education's Integrated Postsecondary Education Data System (IPEDS) a persistence rate (completion rate) college wide of 61% based on the 2001 incoming cohort (2009). IDS courses in general usually have a much higher attrition rate due to the level of difficulty of the courses themselves (399 level) and where they fall within the programs.

Immersion

Since education in a MUVE has come to be called immersive learning and since Second Life has only existed for approximately seven years, it was therefore deemed necessary to incorporate immersion into the RIME model. "SL is experiential, collaborative and immersive in ways that no virtual learning environment (VLE) or remote synchronous classroom ever could be" (Salmon, 2009, p. 529). We also discovered, at least for our student population, a strong qualitative correlation between immersion and motivation. As Sarah Hooper explains, "I think if it were something different where I just had to write a paper about an idea and create a proposal it wouldn't be fun. Putting it on paper and even making storyboards wasn't as fun as being in-world and creating it and seeing it come to life and being able to actually play with it. I think definitely being in a virtual world made it more interesting" (2009). Even in the lab, "'the avatar's interactivity within the environment and with other avatars aids it's [sic] 'feeling' of presence and immersion, dialogue and encounter" (Salmon, 2009, p. 527).

One of the best ways to gauge immersion was to monitor student group blogs which revealed very different leadership styles. One group involved more of a reporting approach in which the group leader would provide a weekly report emphasizing what tasks had been completed and those that needed to be completed prior to the next class meeting. The second group involved a community approach where generic posts were created, and each team member would provide a comment listing their accomplishments and the project completion status.

Within the group blogs students profiled their avatars, chronicled important lecture materials, communicated on development strategies, posted images and notes depicting the evolution of the building process. For the professors the posting of links to subsequent research materials within the group blogs that consolidated their research efforts for external visitors proved surprising since it was never listed as an expectation.

Each week critical readings were assigned that demanded of students ever deeper immersion levels in SL or in MUVE's in general. "Immersion in virtual environments and augmented realities shapes participants' learning styles, strengths, and preferences in new ways beyond what using sophisticated computers and telecommunications has generated thus far" (Dunleavy, Dede, Mitchell, 2008, p. 8). Students were required to post on the class blog their critical responses to the guided heuristic accompanying each reading set. The responses indicated the immersion levels of students in the breadth and depth of their answers. 209 entries were posted for 9 students over 12 of 16 weeks. Readings included studies on virtual worlds, SL research specifically, health care's studies in MUVEs, and research on identity and investment in SL.

Motivation

The challenge of any course, no matter the modality, is to develop a pedagogy that keeps students motivated and engaged in the curriculum. From day one both instructors realized that motivating students who possessed little to no experience with virtual worlds or 3D environments was going to be a challenge. Several studies have examined both the virtual worlds and their accompanying challenges. "Overall findings of these inquiries report that learners feel motivated as a result of the graphical interface of 3D MUVES since they are visually appealing, animated, and interactive" (Omale et. al, 2009, p.481). Indeed, after just a couple weeks the instructors' fears and preconceived notions were lessened as the students began to quickly grasp and conceptualize all of the concepts presented. These observations confirm de Frietas and Neumann's (2009) conclusions that "The main advantages with more immersive media-rich learning experiences for the learner include the potential to provide better simulations of real-life contexts for training or to enhance deeper conceptual thinking for learning" (p. 344).

In focus group discussions, team leader Sarah Hooper explained how motivation directly stemmed from a sense of ownership of, and therefore investment in, the course: "Definitely having our own stake in it and our own choice …motivated us to do well in it. Made us a little bit more passionate" (2009).

Engagement

One of the qualitative outcomes in this project was the teaching / learning connection. "A student's engagement and identity as a learner is shaped by his or her collaborative participation in communities and groups, as well as the practices and beliefs of these communities" (Dunleavy, Dede, Mitchell, 2008, p. 9). The contours of collaboration took on interesting forms as students flowed between the role of both student and educator, inspired by and inspiring others, which greatly added to their understanding and absorption of the material, and, in turn, made them more engaged in their learning activities. Because they had joint ownership of the course, they had the opportunity to share what they discovered. Not only did students help to tutor each other both in class and on group blogs, but they took great pleasure in sharing their findings with us. They also "taught" the FLC and gave a mini lecture on building to their audience, including the college president, as part of the final presentations. "The role of the learner in innovating practice has become more of a driving factor in development" (de Freitas & Neumann, 2009, p. 346).

Interaction does not have to always be positive. One team had personality and work ethic conflicts that played out in the classroom as well as in the blog archives. Professors talked to the team leader about the nature of the conflicts with the goal of stepping in if any bullying or other negative behaviors were present. When none were apparent, the team was left to resolve the issues on their own, which they did. Bill Anderson suggests: that "the context in which students engage in interaction impacts the nature and extent of that interaction" (2006, p. 108). We co-created a "contribution-based pedagogy" in which the dynamic context fosters meaning, empathy, and, conceivably, agency.

FUTURE RESEARCH DIRECTIONS

Although the course is scheduled to run in the upcoming academic year, this case study included only one iteration of the course at the time of this writing and a relatively homogenous group of students. The students shared similar backgrounds with their varying technical aptitudes working to the advantage of the study as a method of control. However, the limitation requiring the most intention for improvement involves the professors themselves. We discovered that we conflated our roles by serving as both professors to the course and leaders to the faculty learning community. By not delineating our roles, we did not balance the time requirements of either one. Precedence was always given to the students, but, especially in the beginning, the time requirement was greater than anticipated for the course development.

In the future, we will need to allocate more time for the faculty learning curve in the semester prior to the course. From both a research and mentoring standpoint, the faculty learning community needs better definition of their roles and responsibilities as members of a learning community. The symbiotic nature of the student cohort and the faculty learning community may be tightly interwoven as the graduates of the course become contributing members of the faculty learning community.

Being a small college, Mercy cannot afford to purchase an island in Second Life for use by one course, even if that island may eventually be used by the whole college. Therefore, the Dean of Students, who is a member of the faculty learning community, sought out alternative funding sources. Donations were solicited from the Mercy College alumni board to purchase an island. Both students and faculty learning community members presented to the alumni so that they could understand both the virtual environment and the type of work performed by students. Innovative education involves both continuous internal and external constituent support. Continuing this endeavor demands administrative and institutional support which in practice indicates that, in addition to their other responsibilities, FLC members need to contribute to an ongoing marketing campaign. While a business model approach makes some faculty uneasy, repeated publicity began to counter any residual institutional fear or hostility directed towards new technology. When that campaign was successful, SL research was validated by the institution through college assembly and board of trustee presentations.

Institutional validation encourages FLC members to utilize their various knowledges for their own MUVE based research projects. The campus counselor has introduced the idea of a suicide prevention project involving the Northwest Ohio College Counselors Association, an association she initiated, for a suicide hotline within SL. The Dean of Science and a biology professor are exploring the intricacies of creating interactive learning objects within a MUVE. These objects will allow students to explore the biological sciences in novel ways while also lessening the constraints on the lab. Enabling students to tour the internal structures of a kidney or heart with their avatars is one of the goals of the science department. The Chair of the Health Care Administration program has explored partnerships with other colleges. His interest has led to new articulation agreements with local colleges and the first steps in forging connections together within SL. The Vice President of Student Affairs hopes to use the island for open houses in the student recruitment process thereby involving his entire staff. A small faculty learning community with its attendant virtual course has initiated a ripple effect garnering attention and participation throughout the college.

CONCLUSION

Despite some of the limitations of the project, by awakening to the plethora of communication technologies available to us, both professors and students recognized our potential for agency through the assembly of texts capable of material action. The course coupled with the faculty learning community indicated that collaborative efforts and immersive technologies may cultivate some of the most important skills our students need to be involved, rhetorically-capable members of our local, national, global, and college communities.

It is increasingly important that colleges, and by extension, high schools allow space and allocate resources for pedagogical exploration. Too often "experimental" connotes being structureless or superficial while the real work involved in pursuing such a project is not recognized. Faculty and sympathetic administrators both need to advocate for the legitimacy of professional development in education technologies. The cooperative practices involved in learning communities, with their complex relationships, along with project based learning make this endeavor advantageous on multiple levels for the college curriculum but in the future should also be considered for the often more standardized high school curriculum. Regardless of the educational level, a faculty learning community coupled with a specific course yields improved student-to-faculty relations and refined technological skills necessary for both faculty and students in today's world, as well as encouraging higher order thinking leading to enterprising teaching practices, such as new assessment tools.

The RIME model as an assessment tool is in a formative stage just as the technologies are. Yet, it may be implemented across multiple learning modalities. By addressing some of the most important areas effecting student achievement such as motivation and engagement, the RIME model attempts to close the loop on assessment. It asks professors to not just collect data but respond to it. Future iterations of the course will continue to use social media technologies while at the same time incorporating new ones that will speak to each facet of the RIME model. The model does not just assess, it forces students to reflect on and archive their learning experiences drawn from course content. Future research might continue to analyze and refine this assessment tool.

REFERENCES

Academy of American Poets. (1997-2009). Ekphrasis: Poetry confronting Art. Retrieved March 15, 2009, from http://www.poets.org/viewmedia.php/prmMID/5918

Anderson, B. (2006). Writing power into online discussion. *Computers and Composition*, *23*, 108–124. doi:10.1016/j.compcom.2005.12.007

Bahr, P. R. (2009). College hopping: Exploring the occurrence, frequency, and consequences of lateral transfer. *Community College Review*, *36*(4), 271–298. doi:10.1177/0091552108330903

Barefoot, B. O. (2004). Higher education's revolving door: Confronting the problem of student drop out in US colleges and universities. *Open Learning: The Journal of Open and Distance Learning*, *19*(1), 9–18.

Bazerman, C. (2008). *Writing realities, changing realities. CCCC Call for Program Proposals*. Urbana, IL: NCTE.

Bell, D. (2009). Learning from Second Life. *British Journal of Educational Technology*, *40*(3), 515–525. doi:10.1111/j.1467-8535.2009.00943.x

Cohen, J. A., & Castner, M. H. (2000). Technology in classroom design: A faculty perspective. In Lloyd, L. (Ed.), *Teaching with Technology: Rethinking Tradition* (pp. 1–20). Medford, NJ: Information Today.

Cox, M. D. (2004, Spring). Introduction to faculty learning communities. *New Directions for Teaching and Learning*, *97*, 5–23. doi:10.1002/tl.129

de Frietas, S., & Newmann, T. (2009). The use of 'exploratory learning' for supporting immersive learning virtual environments. *Computers & Education*, *52*, 343–352. doi:10.1016/j.compedu.2008.09.010

Dunleavy, M., Dede, C., & Mitchell, R. (2008). Affordances and limitations of immersive participatory augmented reality simultaneous for teaching and learning. *Journal of Science Education and Technology, 18*, 7–22. doi:10.1007/s10956-008-9119-1

Fountain, R. (2007). Wiki Pedagogy. *Dossiers Technopedagogigues*. Retrieved April 4, 2007, from: http://www.profetic.org/dossiers/dossier_imprimer.php3?id_rubrique=110

Integrated Postsecondary Education Data System (IPEDS). (2009). Data Center. National Center for Educational Statistics at US Department of Education Institute of Educational Sciences. Retrieved June 1, 2009, from: http://nces.ed.gov/ipeds/datacenter

Jarmon, L., Traphagan, T., Mayrath, M., & Trivedi, A. (2009). Virtual world teaching, experimental learning and assessment: An interdisciplinary communication course in Second Life. *Computers & Education, 53*, 169–182. doi:10.1016/j.compedu.2009.01.010

Keesey, C. (2009, April 6). From tourists to residents: An exploration of virtual world use in education. *Using Second Life for Teaching and Learning in Higher Education* [Webinar]. Ohio University, City, OH.

LaChapelle, N. (2007). Some foundation for Second Life pedagogy. *Educause* Blog. Retrieved April 7, 2009, from http://www.educause.edu/blog/hireded/somefoundationsforsecondlifepe/167081

Linden Research, Inc. (2008). What is Second Life? Retrieved January 15, 2008, from http://secondluife.com/whatis/

Linden Research, Inc. (2009). Second Life. Retrieved January 15, 2008 and July 9, 2009, from http://secondlife.com/statistics/economy-data.php

Means, B., Toyama, Y., Murphy, R., Bakia, M., & Jones, K. (2009). Evaluation of evidence based practices in online learning: A meta-analysis and review of online learning studies. U.S. Department of Education Office of Planning, Evaluation and Policy Development, Center for Technology and Learning. (ED-04-CO-0040 Task 0006).

Miltner, R. (2001, Fall). Where the visual meets the verbal: Collaboration as conversation. *Enculturation* 3(2).

Nelson, L., Sadler, L., & Surtees, G. (2005). Bringing problem based learning to life using virtual reality. *Nurse Education in Practice, 5*, 103–108. doi:10.1016/j.nepr.2004.05.001

Omale, N., Hung, W. C., Luetkehans, L., & Cooke-Plagwitz, J. (2009). Learning in 3-D multiuser virtual environments: Exploring the use of unique 3-D attributes for online problem-based learning. *British Journal of Educational Technology, 40*(3), 480–495. doi:10.1111/j.1467-8535.2009.00941.x

Pough, G. (2009). The remix: Revisit, rethink, revise, renew. *Conference on College Composition and Communication Call for Program Proposals*. Urbana, IL: NCTE.

Regan, A. E., & Zuern, J. D. (2000). Community-service learning and computer-mediated advanced composition: The going to class, getting online, and giving back project. *Computers and Composition, 17*, 177–195. doi:10.1016/S8755-4615(00)00028-1

Rhem, J. (1995). Close up: Going deep. *The National Teaching and Learning Forum, 5*(1), 4.

Salmon, G. (2009). The future from (second) life and learning. *British Journal of Educational Technology, 40*(3), 526–538. doi:10.1111/j.1467-8535.2009.00967.x

Simmons, W. M., & Grabill, J. T. (2007, February). Toward a civic rhetoric for technologically and scientifically complex places: Invention, performance, and participation. *College Composition and Communication*, *58*(3), 419–448.

U.S. Department of Education. (2009). U.S. Department of Education study finds that good teaching can be enhanced with new technology [Press Release]. Retrieved June 30, 2009 from http://www.ed.gov/news/pressreleases/2009/06/06262009.html

Villano, M. (2008). Immersive learning: World teaching. *Campus Technology*. Retrieved January 17, 2008, from: http://www.campustechnology.com/printarticle.aspx?id=57065

KEY TERMS AND DEFINITIONS

MUVE (Multi-User Virtual Environment): A specific type of virtual reality that involves more than one user interacting with the virtual space.

Virtual Reality: Although the term is not used in this paper, readers may be more familiar with it as a search term than MUVE. Therefore, virtual reality is an umbrella term for an immersive environment, developed on a computer that responds to the behaviors of the end user.

Learning Communities: A group of like minded individuals who embrace the idea of learning from one another.

Learning Community: This usage refers specifically to the Mercy College faculty learning community

Assessment: (specifically student assessment) The evaluation of student learning that occurs at the course, program, and institutional level.

Second Life: A MUVE in which the function, appearance, and governance of the space are dictated entirely by the virtual inhabitants.

RIME Model: An assessment instrument gauging, students learning outcomes in the areas of retention, immersion, motivation, and engagement.

Active Learning: Model of instruction that encourages higher order thinking by placing the responsibility of learning on students.

Retention: The rate of maintaining students in a course or institution. In the RIME model retention also refers to the activities used to retain those students.

Immersion: Continuous and progressive interactivity within a MUVE.

Motivation: The student response to a pedagogy that keeps students interested and active in the curriculum.

Engagement: The level of investment that students have with course material.

Interdisciplinary: Course(s) that involve the integration of two or more disciplines, one drawn from the Liberal Arts.

Blended Learning: Educational mode of delivery that combines face-to-face and online pedagogical approaches and technology.

Chapter 11
Collaboration and the Use of Three Dimensional Interface within a Virtual Learning Environment

Brian G. Burton
Abilene Christian University, USA

Barbara Martin
University of Central Missouri, USA

Doug Thomas
University of Central Missouri, USA

ABSTRACT

This chapter's goal is to examine the experiences and perceptions of undergraduate students using a 3D Virtual Learning Environment. After creating a 3D didactic constructivist virtual environment, student conversations were observed for collaborative elements. Findings revealed that five forms of collaboration amplified the learning process and indeed occured within the virtual learning environments. Results further suggested that the 3D VLE project, though limited in time and scope, successfully created a community of learners.

INTRODUCTION

Virtual learning environments have allowed students and teachers to interact without regard to location or time (Hobbs, 2004). According to Dalgarno (2002, p. 3), the primary characteristics of a 3D environment include: (1) the use of 3D vector geometry to describe objects shape and coordinates in the environment; (2) the user's view is dynamically rendered according to their location and direction that they face; (3) the user is able to interact with some objects in the environment; (4) the environment may include 3D audio. Dillenbourg (2000) further argued "the difference between other constructivist environments and what virtual environments potentially offer can be described as making students not only active, but also actors" (p. 8). However use of the 3D VLE

DOI: 10.4018/978-1-61692-854-4.ch011

as an educational tool, without good pedagogy, can hamper student learning rather than enhance it. Since collaboration is an important part of the educational process of any learning community (Bruffee, 1999) and, given that communication is necessary within a 3D VLE, collaboration has been chosen as the theoretical lens to view learning within this 3D VLE. The questions guiding this inquiry are: How does the collaboration process contribute to learning within a 3DVLE? And what are the perceptions of the students regarding the effectiveness of the collaborative process within the 3D VLE?

CONCEPTUAL UNDERPINNINGS

Collaboration

Why is the occurrence of collaboration within 3D Virtual Learning Environments important? According to Bruffee (1999), conversation must exist for re-acculturation to occur. Without re-acculturation, the student will not gain the essential vocabulary that is critical to the educational process. By examining conversations within the 3D VLE, it is possible to check for the existence of collaboration. Consequently, as Bransford et al. (1999) noted, "It is easy to forget that student achievement in school also depends on what happens outside of school" (pp. 16-17). By recognizing the communities and the acculturation of the learner Bruffee (1999) argued it is possible to create a new community and new conversation that is necessary when creating new knowledge.

Moreover, Bruffee (1999) expanded this concept of learning as a collaborative process by casting the process of learning as the re-acculturation of the learner. Meaning that in order to fully participate in a community of learners, a student or learner must gain new vocabulary, knowledge and language skills as one continues to participate within the culture of learning. This learning process is, by its very nature, a collaborative process (Bruffee). Furthermore, in this re-acculturation process, Bruffee argued that the learner must gain a new vocabulary to participate within the collaborative community. Without the proper vocabulary to express ourselves effectively, he postulated that often we are unable to participate, let alone understand the communities with which we have find ourselves because "our worlds were closed by walls of words" (Bruffee, 1999, p. 6). Thus by distributing knowledge and authority amongst themselves, a group becomes a collaborative community.

Consequently, in defining what collaboration includes, Crook (1996) listed three basic cognitive benefits of peer collaboration: articulation, conflict, and co-construction. Crook noted that peer collaboration causes students to be more explicit in the public declaration of their ideas. When a student states his or her concept, he or she must be clear and concise in opinion and interpretation. A student will inevitably be faced with conflicting interpretations causing conflict to arise. In the resolution of this conflict, students must defend their interpretation and reflect on their stance. Borrowing from Vygotsky (1978), Crook's co-construction is the process of students constructing shared knowledge by sharing and building upon each others' ideas.

Collaboration within a Constructivist Approach

Wulff, Hanor, and Bulik (2000), noted that the instructor can aid the development of collaboration within a constructivist approach by "redistribut[ing] learning control and power by supporting and/or developing interaction-exchange formats, such as synchronous and asynchronous chat sites and display rooms to cultivate social and individual presence" (p. 150). This non-foundational view allows students to learn in a collaborative fashion, rather than with the traditional foundational view in which knowledge is dispensed from the teacher (Bruffee,

1999). By creating constructivist environments, educators can provide a structured situation for the learner to gain competency over a complex concept (Barab, et al., 2005; Dede, 2005). Barab, Dodge, and Thomas (2007) argues designing curriculum that transforms classroom practices from didactic lectures to inquiry-based and from individual to shared knowledge is critical for student learning. Their project Quest Atlantis (Gee, 2004; Koster, 2000; Squire, 2006) included but was not limited to the elements of role playing and learning. This ultimately allows the participants to virtually travel to three-dimensional worlds where they select developmentally appropriate tasks and discussions with other students (Barab, Dodge, & Thomas). Dede (2009) further argues that the more a virtual environment is immersed in effective design strategies the greater the participants' involvement in the environment. Dede (1995) also noted that the surrogate persona in the virtual world for students is the "Avatar." According to Jensen (1999) these 3D virtual worlds are socially dynamic, occupied space for the student. Thus the more engaged the student is in a 3D virtual environment the more the learning will come from a non-foundational approach such as collaboration (Bruffee).

The 3D desktop based interface allows students and faculty to interact either synchronously or asynchronously within a virtual universe. According to Dede (2005), initial uses of this technology incorporated online gaming in immersive environments. Samples of these immersive environments can be seen in River City (Dede, Nelson, Ketelhut, Clarke, & Bowman 2004) Quest Atlantis (Barab, Thomas, Dodge, Carteaux, & Tuzun, 2005), Runescape (Jagex, 2004), There (Forterra Systems, 2004), SecondLife (Linden Labs, 2007) as well as many other online games and environments. Specifically, the QuestAtlantis Project (Barab, Kling, & Gray, 2004) was developed from the supposition that consequential learning does not occur with abstract content but within context. The 3D virtual environment examined in this inquiry was created with the elements of learning by doing rather than learning by reading or listening in the forefront of its design.

While an abundance of research is available on collaboration and constructivist education models, there is only a limited amount of research in these constructs in their use within 3D virtual learning environments (VLE) (Barab et al. 2005; Dede et al., 2004). Since such research is limited, it was decided by these researchers to contribute additional research to this new method of educating students. In this case study, a 3D virtual learning environment utilizing a dialectic constructivist approach was constructed. Next, learners were given a project which provided the organized scaffolding for learning and the opportunity for the learner to collaborate with other learners to further develop opportunities for learning.

METHOLOGY

Population and Sample

The sample was drawn from a population of 1600 students attending an open-admissions two-year public campus in the Midwest and 4800 students attending a private, religiously-oriented campus in the South. These sites were selected due to the broad cross section that these college students represent. Merriam (1998) noted that such sampling is used to reflect the average person or situation.

Within the population of the public campus comprising 1660 students, 47 percent are full-time, 65 percent are female, and 55 percent are traditional-age college students. The population of the private campus comprised 4800 students, 86 percent are full-time, 55 percent are female, and 89 percent are traditional-age college students. While students at the public college typically considered minority are few in number (4%), the students attending this university are economically and educationally disadvantaged (89% receive financial aid, 74% require one or more developmental education course). The private college had a higher diverse enrollment with 21% being classified as minority.

Specifically, the sample for this research was 28 students (15 from the public institution and 13 from the private university) enrolled in similar computer programming courses. After completion of the research project within the 3D VLE, students completed a survey. Based upon the student's progress within the 3D VLE and the answers received on the survey, the researcher utilized purposeful sampling to select students to participate in an interview. Purposeful sampling is the process of selecting subjects to provide additional insight and direction in the development of a theory (Bogdan & Biklen, 1998).

Data Collection

Four instruments of data collection were used. First, it was necessary to create a dialectic constructivist 3D Virtual Learning Environment to see if collaboration and knowledge spiral occur within such an environment. Developed by the researchers, the 3D VLE utilized the Torque Game Engine produced by Garage Games (2006). The Torque Game Engine was modified to create an environment that enabled learners to interact in a dialectical constructivist environment that facilitates collaboration (Dalgarno, 2002).

The 3D VLE was modified to incorporate the ability of the avatar to interface with a database and to enable the tracking of the learner through the project. The 3D VLE was further adapted by the researcher to allow the development of the dialectic constructivist system, and the logging of collaboration evidence.

A complete record of all electronic conversations was kept while the learners participated in the learning project. Data captured included the individual user, the date and time of the text, and the conversation itself. Also collected during this phase of the research was the second set of data which comprised the success of the student in the identifying and resolving the programming challenge.

The third set of data was a survey created by the researchers. This survey was distributed after the completion of the project. The survey provided Likert type scale and open-ended questions. The survey's reliability was examined through a test-retest format with a.91 alpha coefficient. Once the reliability was established and the survey instrument was modified according to suggestions provided by the representative group, the survey was administered to participants whose responses were then used to decide which students would be interviewed to gather additional information during the fourth phase.

The fourth set of data was open-ended interviews with selected participants. The goal of these interviews was to provide rich, thick, descriptions of the participants' experience. Based upon the student's progress within the 3D VLE and the answers received on the survey, the researchers utilized purposeful sampling to select students to participate in an interview. Purposeful sampling is the process of selecting subjects because it is believed that they will provide additional insight and direction in the development of a theory (Bogdan & Biklen, 1998). The criteria for selection of the students were based on the degree of participation within the virtual learning environment and gender to assure that both males and females were included in the interviews.

Virtual Learning Environment

A key component of this research project was the creation of a Virtual Learning Environment. This 3D VLE utilized the Torque Game Engine provided by Garage Games and a content pack purchased from BraveTree Productions, LLC. This commercial engine was modified to allow the gathering of collaborative data. Once the modifications to the Torque Game Engine were completed, the 3D environment was created and textured using Autodesk 3DS Max and Adobe

Figure 1. Participant–server interaction

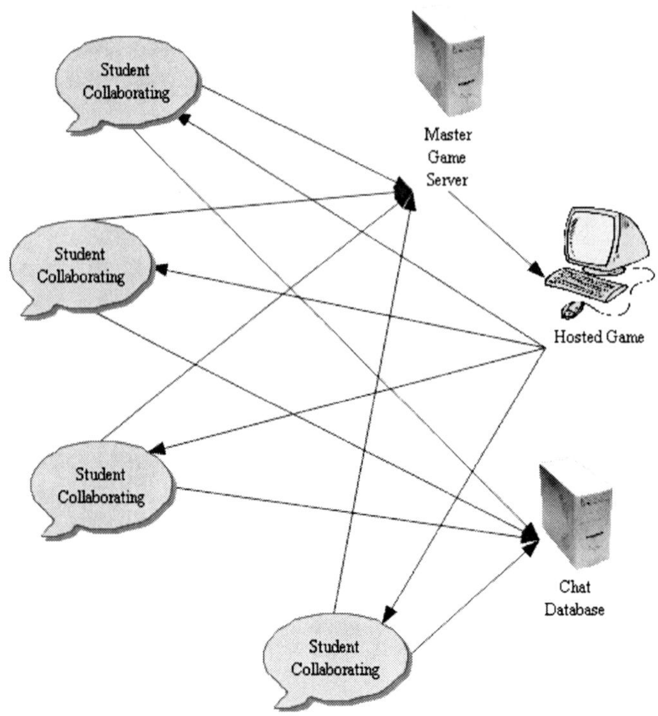

Photoshop. The 3D environment contained the virtual landscape, male and female avatars for the students to select from, virtual objects to simplify interaction, as well as the virtual environment for the avatars to collaborate.

The process of collaboration within the 3D VLE was a three-step process (see Figure 1). Participants created their own account which enabled them to connect to the chat database. After login, the 3D VLE enabled the participant to then connect to a Master Game Server, which provided a link to the hosted game. All chat messages were saved to the Chat Database hosted on a remote server and forwarded to all active participants through the hosted game.

The VLE had seven (7) documented problems and three (3) undocumented problems. Students were challenge to collaboratively solve the problems. When functional the game is designed to allow students to create a bot that simulated artificial intelligence to compete with pre-created bots or other participants' bots. Students were encouraged through the availability of helps, chat, and initial directions to collaborate with fellow participants to find and resolve the problems.

Survey

At the end of the VLE time, participants were asked to complete a survey that contained both Likert type and open-ended questions. The survey contained seven (7) Likert style questions and three (3) open-ended questions. Each of the Likert-type questions consisted of a five-point scale ranging from (1) Never or No to (5) Daily or A Great Deal. The survey was designed to measure the frequency the participants utilized technology to collaborate and communicate and the amount of outside communication concerning the project.

Interview Protocol

After reviewing the surveys, 10% of the participants were purposefully selected (based on degree of participation and gender) and interviewed by the researcher. Semi-structure questions were used during the interview (Gay, 1996). The questions were designed to further probe the research questions into the student's experience in the 3D VLE and his or her responses to the survey. The interviews conducted by the researcher utilized semi-structured, open-ended questions to allow for rich, detailed data. Research in the areas of collaboration (Bruffee, 1999; Crook 1996) and organizational learning guided the development of the interview protocol. The interview process allowed for triangulation of the data gathered from the VLE and the survey and was conducted as a strategy to gather further descriptive data. Interviews were conducted by email with participants being given the opportunity to verify and modify the drafts of the interview (member check) and revise to improve the authenticity of the collected data.

Data Analysis

Bogdan and Biklen (1998) noted that data analysis must involve working with, organizing, and breaking data into manageable units. The process of coding, or identifying categories, classifications, and themes derived from the participants of the study was useful in the organizing of the data. Utilizing the framework proposed by Hara, Bonk, and Angeli (2000), student interaction was categorized into five classifications: (1) Elementary clarification: observation and identification of a problem and its elements. This includes identification of linkages to gain a basic understanding of the problem. (2) In-depth clarification: gaining an understanding of the problem so that it "sheds light on the values, beliefs, and assumptions which underlie the statement of the problem." (3) Inferencing: Use of induction and deduction in the analysis of the problem. (4) Judgment: Making a decision. (5) Application of strategies: "proposing coordinated actions for the application of a solution" (p. 125).

For the purpose of this study, the classification categories of (6) off-topic conversation, (7) salutations and (8) flaming (a hostile or demeaning statement directed at another student) were added to provide greater clarity within the data analysis.

The second step was axial coding to aid in making comparisons and connections between and among the identified themes. The final step was summarizing (Thomas & Brubaker, 2000). The summarizing process is designed to promote synthesis of the data, identification of patterns, and aid in the discovery of what was important, could be learned, and what could be shared.

Quantitative data was analyzed using SPSS 13.0 using descriptive statistics. Mean, frequencies, and standard deviation were provided. These descriptive statistics provided a comparison of means between the students as well as the participating institutions. The analysis of the data in this manner helped the researchers in gaining a better understanding and insight of the success rate of the participants and their conversations during the study. Given the short time of data gathering, students were considered successful in solving the programming challenges if one (1) of the seven (7) documented or three (3) undocumented problems is solved. Thus after analyzing the data, a table quantifying the types and topics of conversation was created, enabling a greater understanding of the participants' collaboration.

DISCUSSION OF FINDINGS

During the two (2) weeks of data gathering, the students were able to solve four (4) of the programming challenges, and fully implement two (2) of the fixes. During the time of data collection, it was noted that the students were initially much more concerned about the undocumented problems which impacted the appearance of the environment than the documented problems which affected the actual usability of the environment. For the participants to successfully diagnose four

Table 1. Number of chat conversations by classification

Classification	Conversations
Elementary Clarification	201
In-Depth Clarification	92
Inferencing	35
Judgment	37
Application	62
Off-topic	174
Salutations	67
Flaming	14

Note: N=682 examined conversations

(4) of the ten (10) problems and successfully fix two (2) of the problems, it is concluded that the students were successful in this programming challenge, likely due to the emphasis on collaborative processes.

The chats captured from the 3D VLE provided a rich picture of collaboration. Of the 682 conversations that occurred during the two weeks of data gathering, a vast majority (62.6%) were found to be collaborative in nature (see Table 1).

While participants were able to easily move and communicate within the 3D VLE (see Figure 2) the majority of conversations was initially off-topic or focused on learning the environment. After approximately two and a half (2.5) hours of working inside the 3D VLE, there was a dramatic drop in off-topic conversation. At this same point, there was a noticeable change toward conversations that were seeking in-depth clarification and application. From the surveys, several comments were made concerning the initial general collaboration. As one student noted, "Most of it was us helping each other understand the mechanisms of the environment, figuring out what was tied to what." Another student suggested that the collaboration allowed for the "clarification of goals, discussion of problems, fun banter, answered questions that others raised, and some arguments when misunderstandings arose."

From one participant interviewed it was confirmed that participants used a variety of means

Figure 2. Communication within the 3D VLE

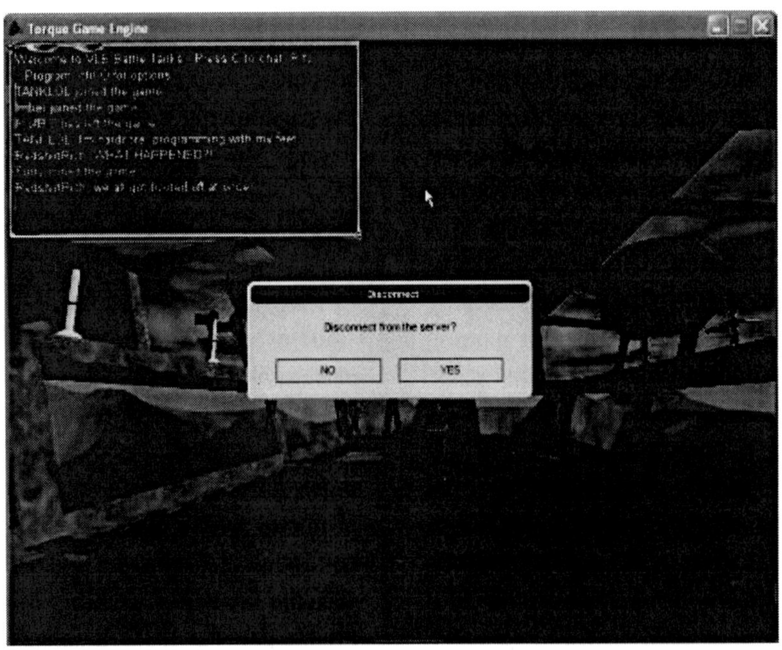

to collaborate on the project: "Online, there were many different types of discussions, from productive collaboration to general silliness. Outside of the VLE, more productive communication occurred via text messaging and e-mail chat programs". Unfortunately, not all communication was not of a positive nature. While the amount of flaming (a hostile or demeaning statement directed at another student) was relatively low (14 total occurrences, or 2% of the total conversations), it was mentioned by some respondents on the survey. Some considered it "fun banter" while other students mentioned the flaming stating that "I was flamed. And was given advise on the hot keys and how to crash the game" and "well when I was on with other people there was a lot of joking, some flaming…".

The collaboration on a project such as what the participants where tasked with in this case study generally takes the form of the students sharing what they had tried and learned in attempting to solve the problems. One student remarked that when they were able to collaborate with other participants "it helped to hear what others had already tried and to hear suggestions", enabling him to more quickly understand the nature of the tasks.

The survey results demonstrated that the majority of participants received help from and provided help to other participants. Thirteen (13) of the fourteen (14) survey respondents stated that they received at least some help from other participants (see Table 2). Twelve (12) of the fourteen (14) participants stated that they provided help to others (see Table 3). When asked what type of help they received, participants stated that: "Yes, I received help learning to toggle the resolutions in the game so that I was able to see more per command window." and "I sometimes help from other users in the VLE. Often this was simply communication about where certain pertinent lines of code existed within the scripts of the program."

Thus according to the data presented in Tables 2 and 3, many participants felt like they provided more help than received help. As summed up in the following participants' statements:

"I was able to answer a LOT of questions regarding the general nature and purpose of the VLE program and clarify upon limitations within the game world. Tentative solutions posed by other members of the VLE were presented to me and I was able to comment upon them and offer advi[c]e on how to implement them."

"Well, once [I] noticed that everyone was standing around the terminal and [I] let them know they didn't have to in order to program so then they spread out."

Table 2. Help received from participants (N=14)

	No	Sometimes	Regularly	Often	A Great Deal
Did you receive help from others?	1	10	1	2	0
Mean = 2.29, Std. Dev. =.83					

Table 3. Help provided to other participants (N=14)

	No	Sometimes	Regularly	Often	A Great Deal
Did you provide help to others?	2	5	4	2	1
Mean = 2.64, Std. Dev. = 1.15					

Student perceptions of virtual environments are a key to their success. If a student does not enjoy the environment or does not interact and communicate with others in the environment, the opportunities for learning through collaboration are obviously greatly reduced. In this data set, sixty-two (62.4) percent of survey respondents found that they at least regularly, if not more frequently, communicate with others in the 3D VLE (see Table 4). One student remarked that "it helped to hear what others had already tried and to hear suggestions", enabling him to more quickly understand the nature of the tasks. Other students, after an initial time of learning the environment and participating in off-topic conversation, cajoled his fellow participants to work on the tasks presented with: "Hey kids... it s time to go to work".

While communication about the project outside of the 3D VLE was discouraged, 78.6% of survey respondents admitted to communicating with others either face to face, through chat or text messaging. As one participant responded during his interview,

Outside of the VLE, more productive communication occurred via text messaging and e-mail chat programs. Often, this was due to me not being logged in to the VLE while others were online and had questions about the general VLE program or wanted to get a second opinion on ideas they had had for solving some of the problems in the VLE. I received a number of text messages during dinner!

From this acknowledgement, it is clear that the 3D VLE project, though limited in time and scope, successfully created a community of participants. Many participants noted that they found collaboration and 3D VLE fun: "The VLE experience was fun, although it was MORE so when other users online were also in the same room physically". A key to the success of any multi-user environment is having enough participants so that collaboration can occur. During low usage periods of the 3D VLE environment, comments such as: "I suppose I'll stop talking to myself" and "Why should I chat? Why should anyone chat?" making it clear that multi-user environments are not as enjoyable when there is no one else is available to communicate or collaborate.

SUMMARY OF FINDINGS

In summing up of the actual chats and the examination of students' perceptions of the effectiveness of collaboration within a 3D VLE, the data suggests several key points. First the data suggests that when a designer of a 3D virtual environment considers and utilized effective design strategies such as collaborative problem solving the student will be engaged to a greater degree. This finding supports what Dede and Barab (2009) noted as important in designing virtual environments, engagement of the student. Also revealed in the data set is the notion students do in fact take on a socially construct persona through their "Avatar" (Dede, 1995). Also suggested by the data set is the concept that while 3D VLEs do encourage collaboration, alternative means of communication beyond in-system chat must be provided or allowed for to encourage an even greater degree of collaboration. So recognizing that students will use both in school and out school tacit and explicit knowledge (Bransford et al., 1999; Nonaka & Takeuchi, 1995) a designer

Table 4. Frequency of communication with others

	None	Occasionally	Regularly	Often	A Great Deal
Inside 3D VLE	1	3	7	2	1
Outside 3D VLE	3	6	3	2	0

of a 3D virtual learning environment can use both to enhance the collaboration within the learning setting. Furthermore, the findings revealed that the five (5) forms of collaboration: Elementary Clarification, In-Depth Clarification, Inference, Judgment, and Application indeed occur with virtual learning environments. Thus again borrowing from Vygotsky (1978), these students constructed shared knowledge by using and building upon each other's ideas.

So as Dillenbourg (2000) noted "the difference between other constructivist environments and what virtual environments offer can be described as making students not active, but also actors" (p. 1). By showing that all forms of collaboration can occur within persistent 3D virtual learning environments, this research provides further evidence that we can enable our students to move beyond merely being active, but to be actors in their own educational environments.

IMPLICATIONS

With the prediction that within the next ten (10) years, students will be spending at least a portion of their school day in virtual classrooms (Fox, Anderson, & Rainic, 2005), it is crucial that such environments be pedagogically sound and one in which collaboration and learning are fostered. Since according to Dede (2005), "In the future students will participate in far-flung, loosely bounded virtual communities (independent of cohabitation, common course schedules, or enrollment at a particular campus)" (p. 10). We as educators must provide students with pedagogically sound 3D virtual education settings. Such an education, according to this inquiry, must include learning in a collaborative environment. By creating learning situations with the 3D virtual environments which allows all five (5) forms of collaboration to occur, the door is opened to allowing students to learn in virtual environments which are more engaging that those in traditional settings.

Dalgrano (2002) has proposed that 3D environments have potential to encourage learner to learner collaboration. This research has confirmed that potential. By allowing students to build upon each other's ideas synergy of knowledge is created and the possibilities of solutions to problems enhanced. Further, the findings of this research directly impact the traditional educational model of today and can help to remove reservations regarding alternative learning structures for the future. Distance learning and traditional education now have new tools within the 3D virtual learning environment that can be used as supplements, and in some cases replacements, for other resources such as expensive equipment or texts. Perhaps students with learning needs or gifted students, as well as those who are physically challenged, or even those requiring greater attention due to behavioral problems can achieve an enhanced learning setting in such a controlled environment.

FUTURE DIRECTIONS FOR RESEARCH

With collaboration now being effectively established within VLE, many areas remain to be researched regarding impact upon student learning outcomes. What impact does being able to select and design the *avatar* have upon learning outcomes? If a student is given an avatar and told that the avatar is very good in a subject that the student struggles with, is learning impacted? Is cheating more or less prevalent in a virtual learning environment? An additional field of research could even deal with the development of virtual real estate. With online environments such as Second Life (Linden Research Inc, 2007) now available, the examination of how such environments will impact learning is essential to examine. Of course more research into the area of collaboration and its utilization within 3D VLE is needed.

CONCLUSION

Through the use a case study model, a 3D virtual learning environment utilizing a dialectic constructivist approach was constructed and examined in this chapter. While there has been much written on collaboration and constructivist educational models little research has examined the use of both of these constructs in a 3D virtual environment which necessitated the need for such a study. This inquiry established the potential of using an effectively design virtual environment to enhance collaboration among the students and ultimately creating a community of learners.

Education systems are increasing faced with a continuous challenge to provide more services and better inclusive educational opportunities to those whom it serves. As technology continues to advance, it can serve as a catalyst to contribute sound educational experiences in a myriad of settings. Within this chapter, the focus has been to examine one aspect of the learning process, collaboration, within a virtual learning environment. Bruffee (1999) has made such a compelling argument that it is through conversation and collaboration that all learning takes place, it is essential that the 3D Virtual Learning Environments be designed to support collaboration effectively.

REFERENCES

Barab, S., Dodge, T., & Thomas, M. (2007). Our designs and the social agendas they carry. *Journal of the Learning Sciences*, *16*(2), 263–305.

Barab, S., Kling, R., & Gray, J. H. (Eds.). (2004). *Designing for virtual communities in the service of learning*. Cambridge, UK: Press Syndicate of the University of Cambridge.

Barab, S., Thomas, M., Dodge, T., Carteaux, R., & Tuzun, H. (2005). Making learning fun: Quest Atlantis, a game without guns. [from http://inkido.indiana.edu/research/onlinemanu/papers/QA_ETRD.pdf]. *Educational Technology Research and Development*, *53*(1), 86–107. Retrieved July 3, 2005. doi:10.1007/BF02504859

Bogdan, R. C., & Biklen, S. K. (Eds.). (1998). *Qualitative research for education: An introduction to theory and methods* (3rd ed.). Needham Heights, MA: Allyn & Bacon.

Bransford, J. D., Brown, A. L., & Cocking, R. R. (Eds.). (1999). *How people learn: Brain, mind, experience, and school*. Washington, DC: National Academy Press.

BraveTree Productions LLC. n.d, [Computer Software]. Eugene, OR.

Bruffee, K. A. (1999). *Collaborative learning: higher education, interdependence, and the authority of knowledge* (2nd ed.). Baltimore: Johns Hopkins University Press.

Crook, C. (1996). *Computers and the collaborative experiences of learning*. London: Routledge.

Dalgarno, B. (2002). The potential of 3D virtual learning environments: a constructivist analysis. *E-Journal of Instructional Science and Technology, 5*(2). Retrieved November 24, 2004, from http://www.usq.edu.au/ electpub/e-jist/docs/Vol5_No2/dalgarno_frame.html

Dede, C. (2005). Planning for neomillinnial learning styles. *EDUCAUSE Quarterly*, *1*, 7–12.

Dede, C., & Barab, S. (2009) Emerging technologies for learning sciences: A Time of rapid advances. *Journal of Science Education and Technology*. Retrieved September 2, 2009 from http://resources.metapress.com/pdf-preview.axd?code=061561872p271487&size=largest

Dede, C., Nelson, B., Ketelhut, D. J., Clarke, J., & Bowman, C. (2004). Design-based research strategies for studying situated learning in a multi-user virtual environment. In *Proceedings of the Sixth International Conference on the Learning Sciences* (pp. 158-165). Mahweh, NJ: Erlbaum. Retrieved May 20, 2005, from http://muve.gse.harvard.edu/muvees2003/documents/dedeICLS04.pdf

Dillenbourg, P. (2000). Virtual Learning Environments. EUN Conference 2000: Learning in the New Millennium: Building New Education Strategies for Schools. Retrieved November 24, 2004, from http://tecfa.unige.ch/tecfa/publicat/dil-papers-2/Dil.7.5.18.pdf

Dillenbourg, P., Baker, M., Blaye, A., & O'Malley, C. (1996). The evolution of research on collaborative learning. In E. Spada & P. Reiman (Eds.), *Learning in humans and machine: Towards an interdisciplinary learning science* (pp. 189-211). Oxford: Elsevier. Retrieved November 1, 2004, from http://tecfa.unige.ch/tecfa/publicat/dil-papers-2/Dil_7_1_10.pdf

Fox, S., Anderson, J. Q., & Rainie, L. (2005). *The future of the Internet*. Washington, DC: Pew Internet & American Life Project. Retrieved March 1, 2005, from http://www2.scedu.unibo.it/roversi/SocioNet/Future_of_Internet.pdf

Garage Games. n.d. (Computer Software) Retrieved January 5, 2006, from http://www.garagegames.com

Gay, L. R. (1996). *Educational research: Competencies for analysis and application* (5th ed.). Englewood Cliffs, NJ: Prentice-Hall.

Gee, J. P. (2004, May). *Video games: Embodied empathy for complex systems*. Paper presented at Electronic Entertainment Exposition, Los Angeles, CA.

Hara, N., Bonk, C. J., & Angeli, C. (2000). Content analysis of online discussion in an applied educational psychology course. *Instructional Science*, *28*, 115–152. doi:10.1023/A:1003764722829

Hobbs, V. (2004). *The promise and the power of distance learning in rural education*. Arlington, VA: Rural School and Community Trust.

Jensen, J. F. (1999). From "flatland" to "spaceland": Spatial representation, enunciation and interaction in 3D-virtual worlds. *Webnet Journal*, *1*(1), 44–57.

Koster, R. (2000). *The laws of online world design.* Retrieved October 12, 2009 from Raph Koster'sWebsite: http://www.raphkoster.com/gaming/laws.shtml

Linden Research, Inc. (2007) www.secondlife.com

Merriam, S. B. (1998). *Qualitative research and case study applications in education*. San Francisco: Jossey-Bass Publishers.

Nonaka, I., & Takeuchi, H. (1995). *The knowledge-creating company: how Japanese companies create the dynamics of innovation*. New York: Oxford University Press.

Squire, K. (2006). From content to context: Videogames as designed experiences. *Educational Researcher*, *35*(8), 19–29. doi:10.3102/0013189X035008019

Vygotsky, L. S. (1978). *Mind in society: the development of higher psychological processes* (Cole, M., John-Steiner, V., Scribner, S., & Souberman, E., Eds.). Cambridge, MA: Harvard UP.

Wulff, S., Hanor, J., & Bulik, R. J. (2000). The roles and interrelationships of presence, reflection, and self-directed learning in effective world wide web-based pedagogy. In Cole, R. (Ed.), *Issues in web-based pedagogy* (pp. 143–160). Westport, CT: Greenwood Press.

ADDITIONAL READING

Allen, I. E., & Seaman, J. (2004). *Entering the mainstream: The quality and extent of online education in the United States, 2003 and 2004*. Needham, MA: Sloan-C.

Barab, S. A., Makinster, J. G., Moore, J. A., & Cunningham, D. J. (2001). Designing and Building an on-line community: the struggle to support sociability in the inquiry learning forum. *Educational Technology Research and Development, 49*(4), 71–96. doi:10.1007/BF02504948

Champion, M., & Freeman, D. (1998). Globalization and distance education mega-institutions. In Currie, J., & Newson, J. (Eds.), *Universities and globalization* (pp. 241–256). Thousand Oaks, CA: Sage Publications.

Dalgarno, B., & Heberg, J. (2001). *3D learning environments in tertiary education*. Retrieved October 11, 2009, from http://www.ascilite.org.au/conferences/melbourne01/pdf/papers/dalgarnob.pdf

Dede, C., L'Bahy, T. B., & Whitehouse, P. (2002). *Designing and studying learning experiences that use multiple interactive media to bridge distance and time*. Retrieved October 11, 2009, from http://www.lesley.edu/faculty/tbrownlb/T502/index.htm

DiPaola, S., & Collins, D. (2003). A social metaphor-based 3D virtual environment. *Educators Program from the 30th Annual Conference on Computer Graphics and Interactive Techniques, Quicktakes,* 1-2.

Fox, S., Anderson, J. Q., & Rainie, L. (2005). *The future of the Internet*. Washington, DC: Pew Internet & American Life Project. Retrieved March 11, 2008 from http://www2.scedu.unibo.it/roversi/SocioNet/Future_of_Internet.pdf

Ge, X., & Land, S. M. (2003). Scaffolding students' problem-solving processes in an ill-structured task using question prompts and peer interactions. *Educational Technology Research and Development, 51*(1), 21–38. doi:10.1007/BF02504515

Kozma, R. B. (2003). Technology and classroom practices: an international study. *Journal of Research on Technology in Education, 36*(1), 1–14.

Michael, D., & Chen, S. (2006). *Serious games: games that educate, train and inform*. Boston: Thomson Course Technology.

Uribe, D., Klein, J. D., & Sullivan, H. (2003). The effect of computer-mediated collaborative learning on solving ill-defined problems. *Educational Technology Research and Development, 51*(1), 5–19. doi:10.1007/BF02504514

Young, M. F., Barab, S., & Garrett, S. (2002). Agent as detector: an ecological psychology perspective on learning by perceiving-acting systems. In Jonassen, D. H., & Land, S. M. (Eds.), *Theoretical Foundations of Learning Environments* (pp. 147–169). Mahwah, NJ: Erlbaum.

KEY TERMS AND DEFINITIONS

Bot: A three-dimensional avatar that is controlled by in-game artificial intelligence.

Collaboration: Where two or more people work together to achieve a goal. Peer collaboration will include articulation, conflict, and co-construction (Crook, 1996).

Flaming: The act of posting a hostile message.

Foundational View of Learning: According to this traditional view, knowledge is transferred from teacher to student (Bruffee, 1999).

Nonfoundational View of Learning: According to this view, knowledge is socially constructed by the community through social interactions (Bruffee, 1999).

Three Dimensional Virtual Learning Environment (3D VLE): A virtual learning environment that utilizes a three dimensional interface (Dalgarno, 2002). For the purposes of this research it will be limited to desktop computer based interfaces.

Chapter 12
Field Notes from the Wild: Adults Learning in a Virtual World

Suzanne Aurilio
San Diego State University, USA

ABSTRACT

This chapter takes a novel orientation to understanding adults as learners by arguing that the context rather than age of the learner is more indicative of their approaches to learning to use technologies. Drawing on data from a study of everyday avatars learning to build the online virtual world Second Life®, this chapter argues that learning through recreational activities such as these adults do in Second Life® is adult learning and a kind of 21st century learning that takes place in the wild of virtual worlds. In order to imagine ourselves, students and colleagues or corporate employees engaged by and in world-building, educators must view online technologies as rich social contexts rather than simply educational technologies. The roles of teachers, trainers or support personnel are as designers for learning. They create contexts where the learning objectives they have set can be achieved.

INTRODUCTION

This chapter takes a novel orientation to understanding adults as learners by arguing that the context rather than age of the learner is more indicative of their approaches to learning technologies. While assumptions about adult learners have also been formulated for and within contexts, such as the work-place, and higher or continuing education (Merriam, Caffarella & Baumgartner, 2007), they provide little guidance for understanding how adults learn *in the wild* of a virtual world, such as the online 3D world Second Life®.

In this chapter I draw data from a study of everyday avatars[1] (Lave, 1988) learning to create the 3D virtual world, Second Life®. Taken from a virtual ethnography (Mason, 1999) of Second Life® Residents, these data consist of participant-observer field notes, individual and group interviews with approximately 20 avatars over 6 months. The purpose of this chapter is to provide evidence of how adults learn naturally

DOI: 10.4018/978-1-61692-854-4.ch012

in a technological environment and to consider implications of these findings on teaching and learning in conventional settings.

BACKGROUND

Over the last 20 years, new learning theories have begun to emerge that take into account how the activities made possible by computers lead to new assumptions about how people learn. Proponents of constructionism (Papert, 1991) view learning as a psychological process of constructing knowledge (Piaget, 1970) that happens particularly well when learners create something personally meaningful. The things they create derive their meaning from the social relations, context and culture surrounding them (Brown, Collins & Duguid, 1989; Lave, 1988; Lave & Wenger, 2001). Computers and now the Internet provide unprecedented opportunities for learning because they are creative, social contexts.

A more recent body of research extends these same ideas to the study of users of virtual worlds. Virtual worlds include on and offline computer games and worlds (e.g. Whyville.net) where users engage in elaborate social contexts and activities. These activities can include trading goods, creating one's avatar (a digital representation of oneself) or achieving goals to win points. In his work with videogame players, Gee (2003) identified thirty-six learning principles built into good video games. His work is supported by others (Black, 2006; Kafai, in press, Kafai, Fields & Cook, under review; Steinkuehler 2005, 2007) who have also demonstrated that "what [people] are doing when they are playing good [computer] games is often good learning" (Gee, 2003 p. 198). Problem-solving, decoding and using the vernacular of the world, and developing an identity through group affiliations and communities of practice are some of the ways learning occurs in these environments.

Only within the last few years has research along this same trajectory included adults in massively multiplayer online worlds such as World of Warcraft and Second Life®. These studies show that *play*, whether structured gaming (Yee, 2006) or unstructured creative endeavors (Kozlov & Rheingold, 2007; Ortiz de Gortari, 2007) is part and parcel of these worlds. They also show that seasoned, middle-aged users find the social aspects of the game most rewarding even when their peers question the age appropriateness of their interest (Quandt, Grueninger & Wimmer, 2009). These studies suggest that adults engage in these virtual worlds to accomplish and enjoy the same things youths do: problem-solving, decoding and using the vernacular of the world, and developing an identity and group affiliations (Boellstorff, 2008; Steinkuehler, 2005; Yee, 2006). Both adults and youths learn how to effectively be in these worlds, and in the process, develop a constellation of skills and knowledge (Steinkuehler, 2007). These are the same 21st century skills and knowledge, educators and employers argue are necessary for success in the future (Partnership for 21st Century Skills, 2004).

Even with the foundation provided by the above-mentioned research, conceptualizing adults learning in these contexts is problematic. First, the mainstream press has helped construct an image of virtual-world users as primarily asocial, male adolescents; adult users are additionally perceived as engaging in age-inappropriate activities (Quandt, Grueninger & Wimmer, 2009). Overall, virtual worlds are seen more negatively than not, making it difficult to perceive the diversity of virtual-world users, and the legitimacy of their activities not only in themselves, but also as contexts for learning (Steinkuehler, 2007). Second, research of virtual worlds and their users is relatively new and it takes time for findings to reach larger audiences and change public opinion. Current research suggests that virtual world users include a growing number of diverse men and women who are college-educated professionals, married, with and without children, or single (Quandt, Grueninger & Wimmer, 2009, Yee, 2006). Third, educators and trainers of adults draw on adult learning theories and the so-called digital native-immigrant divide to inform their practice. These constructs create barriers rather than openings to understanding adult learners because they are based on narrow assumptions of where, how and why they learn. Both also assume a falsehood that adults, by nature of being an adult, learn differently than their younger counterparts (Tennant, 1998). While many adults do come to learning in order to upgrade professional skills and knowledge, and many do go back to college to do so, these situations do not characterize adults, but the contexts in which they have traditionally learned. On close inspection, adult learning theories are not learning theories at all but sets of principles and practices formulated by practitioners to solve real world problems (Merriam, Caffarella & Baumgartner, 2007; Parsons & Johnson, 1978; Tennant, 1998).

THE STUDY

The Context: In the Wild

The wild, in this case, was the 3D online virtual world, Second Life® (SL™) and refers to learning that happens naturally in the environment and which is *about* Second Life®. Launched in 2003 by Linden Labs, it is the most popular virtual environment of its kind for persons 18 years old or older. In it, individuals imagine and create worlds of their own. They use the platform's 3D modeling tools to create objects based on geometric shapes, called prims (primitives) and the Linden Scripting Language to add functionality to them. They also use external software to create animations and gestures (movements), and more complex 3D sculpted prims (sculpties), which are complex textures for objects. Over 90% of Second Life® has been created by users (Residents) (Boellstorff, 2008). It has a real economy where objects and services are bought, sold, and traded, and hundreds of communities, organizations, and businesses existing solely in Second Life® (Boellstorff, 2008). In addition, over 70 accredited colleges and universities (Lang, 2007), and many more institutions, nonprofit and for-profit educational organizations, libraries, and museums have a presence in the environment (Second Life® Educators Wiki, 2008).

Learning in Second Life® means learning how to create it with its 3D modeling tools, external programs and Linden Scripting Language. Residents also must learn *how to learn*. This involves finding the people, places and things that facilitate one's learning. For someone with no gaming experience, it takes approximately 30 hours to master the basics of using an avatar, (e.g., moving and dressing it) and the software interface (e.g., searching, using inventory and taking snapshots) (C. Arreguin, personal communication, June 9, 2009). As in online game spaces, such as World of Warcraft and EverQuest, it is not uncommon for the most engaged (and competent) users to spend the most time in-world, 20-40 hours per week or more (Ortiz de Gortari, 2007; Steinkuehler, 2007; Yee, 2006).

Methodology

The objectives of the study were to discover and describe the ways Residents talked about and experienced creating and learning to create in this virtual world. The data presented are drawn from an ethnographic study I conducted between October 2008 and May 2009 of Residents engaged in creating Second Life®. Using my professional avatar, Aurili Oh, I conducted semi and unstructured interviews, and observations with everyday Residents focusing on learning practices related to their creative endeavors. I used a systematic, iterative approach of collecting and analyzing everyday language, and an observational heuristic to analyze the research site (Spradley, 1979, 1980).

This interpretive analysis is grounded on the following assumptions. First, I studied avatars as compared with studying the people *sitting at the keyboard* controlling the avatar. This marks the project as a virtual ethnography (Mason, 1999). I took as a given the empirical legitimacy and psychological authenticity of what was happening on my computer screen as happening in the virtual space (Geertz, 1973) and as real. As Markham (1998) noted, "Online experiences are real, how could experience be otherwise" (p. 5).

Second, ethnography as a research tool is always a partial account, and thus a contestable "inscription of a social discourse" (Geertz, p. 9). Virtual ethnography adds a layer of complexity because as online researchers (Hein, 2006; Markham, 1998, Mason, 1999, Taylor, 1999) have argued, study participants and researchers are always occupying two locations, the virtual and the physical. This methodological challenge is important to mention because as users of virtual worlds, educators and learners must also deal with these same conditions.

Although I focused on avatars, at the end of data collection I also surveyed the seven main study participants for real life demographic information. Six of the seven were female. Their ages ranged from 33 to mid-50s, with five of the seven participants in their 40s. Two were married and three were single. One was separated and one was going through a divorce. Five of the seven spent on average 40 hours per week in Second Life®. The remaining two spent on average 30 hours per week in-world. As to highest educational level attained, one participant was just shy of a master's degree and two had bachelor's degrees. Two had some college credit, one had special training and one had less than high school diploma. They all rated themselves as just as skillful as, or more skillful with technology than their peers.

Findings

The findings to follow are presented thematically. The first section, Creating My Special World, provides examples of some of the reasons these Residents learn. Their reasons can also be understood in terms of specific contexts that engage Residents creatively and thus with learning. The second section, Second Life Learning®, illustrates some of the ways these Residents learned and include learning-by-doing, asking for help, belonging to groups, and affiliation through classes and contests.

Creating My Special World

Learning in SL™ means learning how to create one's special world. Whether Residents were creating a world (Figure 4) or an object[2], such as a piece of furniture, each had created an avatar, and with that an identity. The avatar is then the first creative canvas users encounter. Upon entering Second Life® for the first time, users create an avatar name, gender, and look. The avatar gender and look can be changed at will and as users become more familiar with the platform's tools, they are able modify their avatar appearance. The seven Residents I focused on all kept a consistency to their avatars even though several changed hair color and style, skin tone and clothing regularly.

Three of them, Arieaa, Celia and Star identified themselves with fairies. Taken from European folklore, fairies are human looking, feminine creatures, associated broadly with mythologies, magic and playfulness. One common trait of fairies is to wear wings. Star had hundreds of pairs of wings, changing them to suit her clothing and mood. Arieea[3] expressed her fairy self elaborately in her profile (Figure 1). The following passage is the text she provided in the *About* section of her profile which is pictured in Figure 1.

~★Fae-Arieaa★~美仙女 is often seen dancing in the moonlight, tending to her flowers and fishing. She loves gardens, waterfalls, nature, music, art poetry and tiny creatures. As an ethereal nature spirit, she has evolved into a playful pansexual being and hermaphodite [sic] (having the characteristics of both genders)♥(although sometimes she still enjoys being a regular girl) ;)♥Two-

Figure 1. Arieea's Second Life® Profile (©2010 Suzanne Aurilio. Used with permission.)

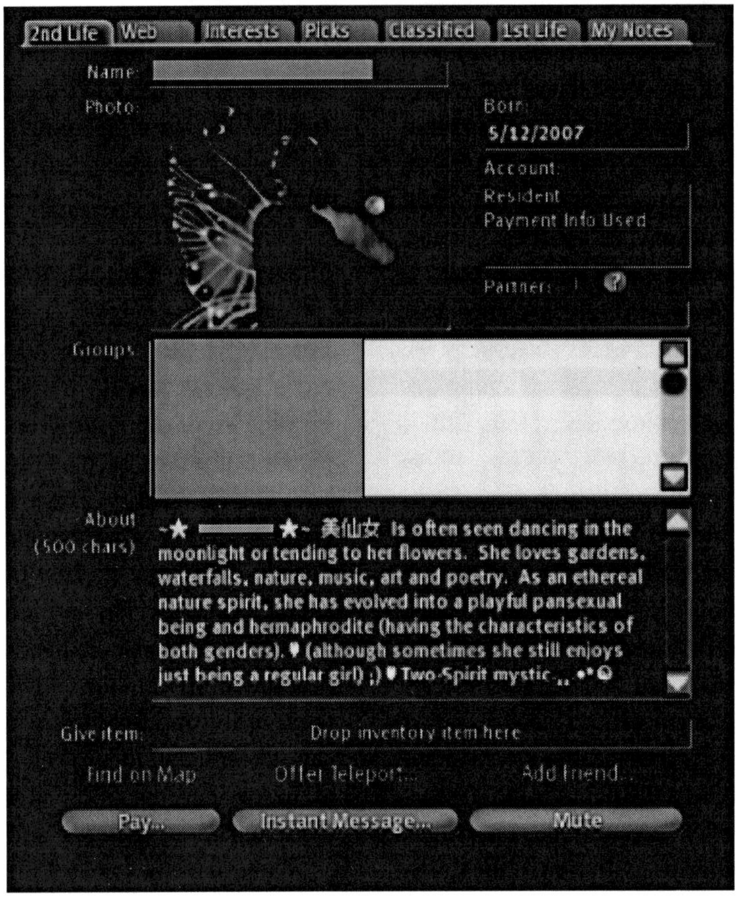

spirited mystic. (Arieaa, personal communication, October, 2008)

In this example, the Latin term *Fae* is a shortened form of *faerie*, another spelling for fairy that Arieaa had chosen. She uses almost the entire 500 characters in the About section, (middle of Figure 1) to poetically depict herself using text and ornate symbols. Celia wrote this in her About section, "like a butterfly, this sprite has a bit of curiosity and a tendency to flit about exploring. Sometimes quiet and sometimes exuberant." (Celia, personal communication, December 31, 2008). Star identified as a fae too, and said that her wings also symbolized the birdlike quality of personal freedom she felt in SL™, a freedom from the pain and stress of her real life (Star, personal communication, December 21, 2008).

Fairies are a kind of fantasy character and are common in Second Life®. Some Residents however represented themselves in terms of an idealized self. Jules said she saw herself as a representation of her real life self. To make this point she compared herself to Arieaa who was in real life a man (Michael) in his mid 40s. To Jules, Arieaa was a character different from her real life, whereas Jules saw her second life® as an extension of her real life. In SL™, she had a wide social network, with some of her friendships extended into real life. For example, she was friends with Michael and they had talked on the phone a few times. She had other friends who she came to know through

Figure 2.

~*~.:*:.~*~Suzie~*~.:*:.~*~

Partnered 02/11/08 to Kathy

(¯`v´¯)

`*.¸.*´ Kathy

¸.•´¸.•*¨) ¸.•*¨)

(¸.•´ (¸.•´ .•´ ¸¸.•¨¯` & Suzie

Love You Babe ! *Inseparable*

*(`'·.¸(`'·.¸ * ¸.·'´)¸.·'´)*

*(¸.·'´(¸.·'´ * `'·.¸)`'·.¸)*

"A kiss is a lovely trick designed by nature to stop speech when words become superfluous." Ingrid Bergman (Suzie, personal communication, October 12, 2008)

SL™ but had established relationships with in real life, never having met them face-to-face. In real life she danced in clubs in a dance troop; in SL™, she had become the creator and owner of a well-known nightclub. For Jules, being a club owner was an idealized not a fantasy experience (Jules, personal communication, November 16, 2009). Suzie and Kathy identified themselves strongly through their partnership and many of their creative works were expressions of their relationship. They were officially partnered[4] in Second Life® which meant that on each of their profiles, the other was identified in the Partner textbox (See Figure 1, middle right column). Suzie and Kathy created a world together on their island and in their shop, *Inseparable Things*. The shop's logo consisted of two lilac colored hearts drawn and knotted together by a thick, black velvet tie. In each of their profiles they used ornate graphical characters describing their relationship to one another. Figure 2 shows Suzie's profile text.

Avatars are fully customizable and to change one's appearance, users drag and drop a folder of clothing, body parts and animated attachments onto their avatars. Celia said Second Life® was like playing with 3D paper dolls (Celia, personal communication, December 29, 2008). Robots, furies (upright walking animals) and vampires made up the Resident population in Second Life®, as did humanoid female and male avatars with hyper-idealized bodies. Some males have Hulk-like muscular bodies and some females have Barbie-like bodies. Creating one's avatar, and thus identity, involves learning how to create or find clothing, jewelry, body parts, such as hair and skin, and animations such as walking and dancing styles, and standing poses. For example, Arieaa made her own tattoos. She learned how to use Gimp, a free graphics editing software to create tattoos, which are transparent textures designed from clothing templates. Clothing templates are readily available in-world and on the web. Celia had learned how to create skins in another virtual environment, and had brought these skills into her Second Life®, creating skins for her Second Life® avatar. Jules, Suzie and Kathy on the other hand, purchased most of their clothing, skins and hair. For Jules being creative did not necessarily mean making something from scratch. It meant creating a look with the resources at hand. Suzie and Kathy were uncomfortable playing around with their avatars for fear of messing them up. Like Jules, they preferred to customize themselves with the things other residents had already designed.

To conclude, creating one's special world involves at its base, a desire create an avatar, and with that an identity. But because avatars in Second Life® are fully customizable, they become creative canvases. If users are tall in real life they can be short in Second Life®. Residents can create avatar parts from scratch or purchase them pre-made from other Residents. In both cases they must learn how to use the tools and resources available. Creating parts, such as tattoos requires external programs, while finding stylized clothing requires Residents knowing where shops are, how to purchase and attach body parts, clothing, accessories and animations (e.g., walks and dances). Embedded in these tasks and activities are subsets of skills and knowledge Residents must learn. In the next section, I address several of the ways Residents learn these skills.

Second Life® Learning

Learning-by-Doing

By doing certain things, he makes perceptible certain connections which had been previously ignored. Thus his acts in relation to these things get more meaning; he knows better what he is doing or 'is about' when he has to do with them; he can intend consequences instead of just letting them happen. (Dewey, 1916)

Second Life®, like all virtual worlds requires a great degree of user (and learner) agency. It is fundamentally a learning-by-doing environment, where learning-by-doing has many forms. Several Residents described one form as trial and error, calling it tinkering, messing around and experimenting. As Kathy explained, "trial and error means doing a task a particularly way, seeing if that works, then trying another way if it does not" (Kathy, personal communication, November 8, 2008).

Here Kathy described her trial and error process of creating a particle effect,[5] a scripted object. "You set values in there and observe the output.

Figure 3. Example of Part of a Particle Effect Script (©2010 Suzanne Aurilio. Used with permission.)

```
forever
  ,PSYS_PART_MAX_AGE,          4.0          //Lifetime, in seconds, that a particle lasts
  ,PSYS_SRC_BURST_RATE,        0.5          //How long, in seconds, between each emission
  ,PSYS_SRC_BURST_PART_COUNT, 6             //Number of particles per emission
  ,PSYS_SRC_BURST_RADIUS,      10.0         //Radius of emission
  ,PSYS_SRC_BURST_SPEED_MIN,  .4            //Minimum speed of an emitted particle
  ,PSYS_SRC_BURST_SPEED_MAX,  .5            //Maximum speed of an emitted particle
  ,PSYS_SRC_ACCEL,            <0,0,1>   //Acceleration of particles each second
  ,PSYS_PART_START_COLOR,     <1,0,0> //Starting RGB color
  ,PSYS_PART_END_COLOR,       <1,0,0> //Ending RGB color, if INTERP_COLOR_MASK is
on
  ,PSYS_PART_START_ALPHA,     1.0          //Starting transparency, 1 is opaque, 0 is
transparent.
  ,PSYS_PART_END_ALPHA,       1.0          //Ending transparency
  ,PSYS_PART_START_SCALE,     <.25,.25,.25> //Starting particle size
  ,PSYS_PART_END_SCALE,       <1.5,1.5,1.5> //Ending particle size, if
INTERP_SCALE_MASK is on
  ,PSYS_SRC_ANGLE_BEGIN,      300 * DEG_TO_RAD //Inner angle for ANGLE patterns
  ,PSYS_SRC_ANGLE_END,        60 * DEG_TO_RAD//Outer angle for ANGLE patterns
  ,PSYS_SRC_OMEGA,            <0.0,0.0,0.0> //Rotation of ANGLE patterns, similar to
llTargetOmega()
        ]);
```

If it isn't what your [sic] after you try different values. After a period you learn what changing the values does. So you have learnt [sic] from it." (Kathy, personal communication, November 11, 2008). The "values" she refers to are in the script (Figure 3), a computer programming language. Values are combinations of digits in the syntax of the script enabling it to carry out sequences of commands, such as changing the color of an object upon impact with the ground. Figure 3 is an example of part of the script controlling a basic particle effect. In the left column of Figure 3 are the script parameters, in the center column are their values, and in the last column are explanations of each parameter. Kathy, Suzie, Mica and Arieaa all learned how to use scripts by experimenting with them, reading the explanations, changing values and seeing what happened. Of the four of them, only Mica had had training in computer programming in real life some 20 years earlier.

Seeking and finding strategies are also a kind of trial and error and critical to successful Second Life® learning. All the Residents I interviewed talked about their importance. For example, while Jules was terraforming[6] her island (Figures 4 and 5), a project that took several days, she had tried five different ways of getting her terraforming done, (1) video tutorials, (2) in-world tutorial boards, (3) using another tool, (4) asking friends and (5) asking more experienced builders. Suzie described this form of trial and error as *common sense*, that is, knowing how to find the answers you need, when you need them. Celia also emphasized the importance of seeking and finding strategies. She said,

I have more respect for people who try to find the answers themselves before asking. I get annoyed with people who ask questions over and over again for trivial stuff that is say in the FAQ, when the information is blatently [sic] out there and all you have to do is look but want everyone else to do the work for you. I tend to scour and scour for the answer until I cant [sic] stand it anymore before I speak up and ask. (Celia, personal communication, January 12, 2009)

While these Residents said that trial and error was a main learning strategy, most of them emphasized that they also needed to get the basics down first beforehand. However, realizing they needed to get the basics down usually came in the process of learning. For example, they would decide to make something and realize they did not know where to start. Several said they preferred getting started with instructional manuals, in-world tutorial boards, and web-based resources (video and text-based tutorials, the SL™ Wiki, and discussion boards). Several combined these approaches with taking classes and engaging actively with the communities around classes.

Classes often took place at SL™ building schools and teaching and learning sandboxes, parcels set aside for Residents to practice building. Suzie and Kathy, however, described themselves as self-taught (e.g., using tutorials). Arieaa and Jules had never taken classes they said. For Arieaa, classes did not fit with her learning style; for Jules the time commitment and timing of classes did not fit her schedule (Jules, personal communication, November 11, 2008).

Learning is Social

The socialness of learning in Second Life® takes shape synchronously and asynchronously. Text and text-based communication seem to dominate many learning exchanges. Synchronous and asynchronous exchanges intersect each other because as Residents learn together "face-to-face" they also access the instructions and tutorials built into objects, the platform and the surrounding play space on the web (i.e., in the form of wikis, blogs, discussion forums). These resources are, at their base, social because they have been created by Residents for other Residents. In the following section I illustrate three forms of the socialness

Figure 4. Jules' 8192 square meter parcel before terraforming (©2010 Suzanne Aurilio. Used with permission.)

of learning: Asking for help, belonging to groups and affiliation through classes and contests.

Asking for Help

Asking other Residents for help was a common learning strategy. These Residents emphasized the importance of having someone more experienced to rely on. Celia noted that although she would typically seek out answers on her own, she found that she was more inclined to ask others at Serenity, the teaching and learning sandbox she belonged to, because it was easier to ask, and the people she had come to know there were "all very warm and welcoming" (Celia, personal communication, January 12, 2009). Star shared the same feeling and both she and Celia felt a commitment to Serenity because of its community orientation, the friendships they built, and the resources those connections provided. At Serenity it was not uncommon for a builder to pose a question in the local chat to everyone who was in range to hear. Arieaa and Jules felt more comfortable asking friends than strangers. Suzie saw Kathy as more knowledgeable than her and thus relied on her for help. Suzie said that instant messaging the creator of an object she had purchased was also very helpful and that most of time she got the help she needed. Suzie and Kathy, Arieaa and Jules each had their own land on which they did their creative work. Spending more time on their private land, they tended to rely on smaller circles of close friends. Star, Celia and Mica built primarily in public sandboxes where they had friends to rely on but where it was common to ask whoever was around.

Belonging to Groups

Star and Aurora[7] said that belonging to building groups helped them stay connected and informed about the group's events and resources. Tips and announcements were distributed asynchronously via notecards (in-world documents) as well as in

Figure 5. Jules' 8192 square meter parcel after terraforming and addition of landscaping and buildings (©2010 Suzanne Aurilio. Used with permission.)

real-time through group instant messaging (IM). Members could also pose questions in the group IM for all members who were in-world to see. In this way Residents belonging to such active groups had a ready-made live help channel. Celia often lurked in her building groups, offering help if she thought she could. Aurora moderated a group and left the IM window open all the time; if no one responded to a question she would respond with a tip on where to find the answer. Star and Aurora talked about the importance of belonging to teaching groups in Second Life®. Here Aurora talks about what she got from belonging to them.

Teachers [Group]–also TLL–were the people at my original mock class they were the original judges. I passed that class and they have always been supportive to me. TLL is loose support–they don't hold your hand, but if you need help–they can help or know who can. From textures to a free sandbox–to teachers who have been there. Asking where I can get soundfiles that can be downloaded without breaking any Copyright laws. (Aurora, personal communication, January 25, 2009)

Affiliation through Classes and Contests

Star, Celia, Mica/Aurora were members of teaching and learning sandboxes that offered classes and contests. Star was a sandbox helper and teacher at Serenity, where Celia and Mica also frequented. Sandboxes are themselves social spaces; teaching and learning sandboxes are destinations for builders (novice and experienced) to connect informally with each other and practice building. Star, Celia and Mica/Aurora enjoyed taking classes because they connected with other builders, formed new friendships and connected with building and teaching groups. Star and Mica/Aurora took classes to learn how to teach too. "I often created in order to teach a technique. [I ask myself] what's the easiest way to do this? How do I explain this to people who can't build or rez [make it appear] a prim?" (Star, personal communication, January 3, 2009). Here Mica explains how the desire to teach others how to build a particular object motivated him to learn how to build it himself.

When I started SL - I saw a product I wanted. It was beautiful and magnificent and it was way way way out of my price range. I have tried to make it in the past, but didn't understand how things went. Last night I decided to try making it [a snow globe] for a class build. I got up the courage and built it- not perfect, but i saw my mistakes and worked on that- easy fixes. Because i want iothers [sic] to have the magnificent snow globe- or in my case, a Moondust Globe, I made it and worked to get it done, so others can build it as well. (Mica, personal communication, October 28, 2008)

Aurora taught classes at CookieCutter, another teaching and learning sandbox. Like Star and Celia, feeling like she belonged to a supportive community was why she spent time there and contributed as a teacher. Celia said of Serenity,

[It was] just the right chemestry [sic] of activities [classes and contests] and people.... When I arrived they were all very warm and welcoming. I have taken classes a few other places, several at CookieCutter and as nice as Sienna [the owner] is..I am not sucked in there. And there is nothing 'putting me off' at CookieCutter but I am not hanging out there all the time. I do feel a commitment at Serenity. I often return (not always) my prize lindens and I would like to teach a couple classes at Serenity. (Celia, personal communication, January 12, 2009)

Serenity also provided regular contests as a way to learn through practice. Contest participants were given a particular project (e.g., texturing an object) or theme to build to (e.g., making a Halloween scene) with rules and a time frame for completing it. At the end of contests, the best builds would be rewarded with feedback from the contest participants, the contest coordinators, and small cash prizes. The atmosphere at contests was jovial and playfully competitive with participants who were regulars and friends teasing one another. Celia and Star participated regularly in Serenity contests and like other contest participants learned not just from the building but also from interacting and comparing themselves with other builders. Celia participated in a themed contest at another sandbox at one point and said, "I am curious to see..how I might do amongst another group of people...curious to see how other groups do their competitions (Celia, personal communication, January 25, 2009). Contests and classes at Serenity emphasized creativity with a fun, community spirit. They provided structured learning-by-doing activities, focused on completing small projects with clear goals and rewards.

SUMMARY

The first section, Creating My Special World, highlighted the avatar as one creative canvas of this virtual world, providing evidence of the meaning Residents draw from their creative activities. The second section, Second Life Learning®, highlighted some of the ways learning happens. These include knowing how to seek and find answers, tinkering and figuring things out, getting the basics down first and utilizing classes and contests are some of the ways learning occurs. The socialness of Second Life® learning is both "face to face" and in the form of Resident created wikis, tutorials, blogs and discussion board.

Solutions and Recommendations

Learning through recreational activities such as these adults do in Second Life® *is* adult learning. It is a kind of 21st century learning that takes place in the wild of virtual worlds and on the Internet. The first question to ask is whether these strategies fit with the real world contexts in which our virtual contexts are always embedded. In other words, can we imagine ourselves, our students and colleagues or corporate employees engaged by and in world-building? If so, then we must take steps to become socially involved Residents of the virtual world we plan to inhabit. This requires a shift in mindset for those of us who see online technologies primarily as tools rather than as rich social contexts. One way to shift our orientation is to think of our work as educational designers who *design for learning*. As teachers, trainers or support personnel our role is to create contexts where learning objectives we have set out can be achieved.

Another and perhaps more interesting direction would be to include learners in the learning-design process. In technologically complex, dynamic environments, knowledge and skills are necessarily distributed among users and resources. Learning then becomes the sine qua non of participation, thereby displacing the notion of teacher as the final authority and expert. This creates another opportunity for teachers and trainers to adopt new roles as facilitators of learning. It also redistributes authority and expertise among all learners in ways that students rarely experience in school-settings. The potential for empowering individual learners to excel and mentor other learners is great within such a context.

Finally, at the heart of these findings is the observation that learners must be personally invested in the virtual world to make the most of it. It is not enough to simply apply a virtual world as an educational technology in a time-constrained context in which the instructor builds an instructional world for learners to interact with. World-building should be the crux of what learners do and what they learn, and they should be deeply engaged with it over time, technically, emotionally and socially.

FUTURE RESEARCH DIRECTIONS

Along the trajectory of this study and those sited, there is much to understand about the activities in which virtual world users engage. They do acquire 21st century skills, however we are only just beginning to describe and define them as such. In addition, learning will increasingly be situated solely in shared virtual environments, and as a result, new orientations to educational research are needed that can account for the complexities. These include the social implications of users occupying two locations at the same time and the technological affordances and constraints of an environment.

CONCLUSION

Adults learning in a recreational virtual world present educators new and challenging ideas about why and how adults learn. At the same time, this study provides some evidence that adults do not learn differently than youths but that the context drives learning for both. A virtual world, such as Second Life®, is a platform in which users world-build, and learn to do so socially, as well as through forms of learning-by-doing.

REFERENCES

Belenky, M. F., Clinchy, B. M., Goldberger, N. R., & Tarule, J. M. (1997). *Women's ways of knowing: The development of self, voice, and mind (10th Anniversary Edition)*. New York: Basic Books.

Black, R. W. (2006). Language, culture, and identity in online fanfiction. *E-learning, 3* (2), 170-184. Retrieved May 10, 2008, from http://dx.doi.org/10.2304/elea.2007.4.4.384

Boellstorff, T. (2008). *Coming of age in Second Life®. An anthropologist explores the virtually human*. Princeton, NJ: Princeton University Press.

Brown, J. S. (2000, March/April). Growing up digital: how the web changes work, education, and the ways people learn. *Change, 32*(2), 11–20. doi:10.1080/00091380009601719

Brown, J. S., Collins, A., & Duguid, S. (1989). Situated cognition and the culture of learning. *Educational Researcher, 18*(1), 32–42.

Cross, K. P. (1981). *Adults as Learners*. San Francisco: Jossey-Bass.

Csikszentmihalyi, M. (1996). *Creativity flow and the psychology of discovery and invention*. New York: HarperCollins Publishers.

Cskiszentmihalyi, M. (1978). Intrinsic Rewards and emergent motivation. In Lepper, M. R., & Greene, D. (Eds.), *The hidden costs of rewards: New perspectives on the psychology of human motivation* (pp. 205–216). Hillsdale, NJ: Erlbaum.

Dewey, J. (1916). *Democracy and education*. Retrieved on July 14, 2009, from http://www.ilt.columbia.edu/publications/Projects/digitexts/dewey/d_e/chapter06.html

Estabrook, L., Witt, E., & Rainie, L. (2007). *Information searches that solve problems: How people use the internet, libraries and government agencies when they need help*. Location: Pew Internet & American Life Project. Retrieved February 13, 2008, from http://www.pewinternet.org/pdfs/Pew_UI_LibrariesReport.pdf

Gee, J. P. (2003). *What video games have to teach us about learning and literacy*. New York: Palgrave Macmillan.

Geertz, C. (1973). *The interpretation of cultures*. New York: Basic Books.

Glot, R., Meiszner, A., & Sowe, S. K. (2007). *FLOSSCom – Using the principles of informal learning environments of FLOSS communities to improve ict supported formal education. Phase 1: Analysis of the informal learning environment of floss communities*. FLOSSCom. Retrieved January 31, 2008, from http://opensource.mit.edu/papers/FLOSSCom_WP2_Phase_1_Report_v070709_1.pdf

Halpern, D. F., & Hakel, M. D. (2003). Applying the science of learning to the university and beyond: Teaching for long-term retention and transfer. *Change, 35*(4), 36–41. doi:10.1080/00091380309604109

Harel, I. (1990). Children as software designers: a constructionist approach for learning mathematics. *The Journal of Mathematical Behavior, 9*(1).

Horrigan, J. (2006). *The internet as a resource for news and information about science*. Location: Pew Internet & American Life Project. Retrieved February 13, 2008, from http://www.pewinternet.org/pdfs/PIP_Exploratorium_Science.pdf

Horrigan, J., & Rainie, L. (2006). *The internet's growing role in life's major moments*. Location: Pew Internet & American Life Project. Retrieved February 13, 2008, from http://www.pewinternet.org/pdfs/PIP_Major%20Moments_2006.pdf

Jenkins, H. (2006). *Confronting the challenges of participatory culture: Media education for the 21st century*. Retrieved April 23, 2009, from http://www.henryjenkins.org/2006/10/confronting_the_challenges_of.html

Kafai, Y. B. (In press). Synthetic play: Teens gaming together and apart in virtual worlds. In Y. Kafai, C. Heeter, J. Denner, & J. Sun (Eds.), *Beyond Barbie and mortal kombat: New perspectives on gender and computer games*. Cambridge, MA: MIT Press. Retrieved May 10, 2008, from http://www.gseis.ucla.edu/faculty/kafai/paper/whyville_pdfs/PAP_kafai_bbmk.pdf

Kafai, Y. B., Fields, D. A., & Cook, M. (forthcoming). *Your second selves: Avatar design and identity play in a teen virtual world.* Paper submitted to DiGRA07. Retreived May 10, 2008, from http://www.gseis.ucla.edu/faculty/kafai/paper/whyville_pdfs/DIGRA07_avatar.pdf

Knowles, M. (1984). *The adult learner: A neglected Species* (3rd ed.). Houston, TX: Gulf Publishing.

Lang, G. (2007, July 25). Current list of universities in Second Life®. Message posted to http://secondliferesearch.blogspot.com/2007/07/current-list-of-universities-in-second.html

Lave, J. (1988). *Cognition in practice: Mind, mathematics, and culture in everyday life.* Cambridge, UK: Cambridge University Press. doi:10.1017/CBO9780511609268

Lave, J., & Wenger, E. (1991). *Situated learning legitimate peripheral participation.* Cambridge, UK: Cambridge University Press.

Lenhart, A., Simon, M., & Graziano, M. (2001). *The internet and education.* Location: Pew Internet & American Life Project. Retrieved February 13, 2008, from http://www.pewinternet.org/pdfs/PIP_Schools_Report.pdf

Markham, A. N. (1998). *Life online researching real experience in virtual space.* Walnut Creek, CA: AltaMira Press.

Mason, B. (1999, January). Issues in virtual ethnography: Ethnographic studies in real and virtual environments: Inhabited information spaces and connected communities. In K. Buckner (Ed.), Proceedings of esprit i3 workshop on ethnographic studies (pp. 61–69). Edinburgh: Queen Margaret College.

Meadows, M. S. (2008). *I avatar the culture and consequences of having a second life.* Berkeley, CA: New Riders.

Merriam, S. B., Caffarella, R. S., & Baumgartner, L. M. (2007). *Learning in adulthood. A comprehensive guide* (3rd ed.). San Francisco, CA: Jossey-Bass.

Mitham, N. (2007, July 11). Age ranges and gender analysis. Message posted to: http://www.kzero.co.uk/blog/?p=887

Ortiz de Gortari, A. (2007, September). *Second Life® survey: User profile for psychological engagement and gambling.* Paper presented at The Virtual 2007 Conference: Interaction, Stockholm, Sweden.

Papert, S. (1991). Situated constructionism. In Harel, I., & Papert, S. (Eds.), *Constructionism: Research reports and essays, 1985-1990* (pp. 1–10). Norwood, NJ: Ablex.

Parsons, J., & Johnson, T. (1978). *Adults learn differently than children. An examination of an old basic assumption.* Washington, DC: National Inst. of Education. (ERIC Document Reproduction Service No. ED166372)

Partnership for 21st Century Skills. (2004). *The road to 21st century learning: Policymakers' guide to 21st century skills.* Retrieved April 22, 2005, from http://www.21stcenturyskills.org/images/stories/otherdocs/P21_Policy_Paper.pdf

Piaget, J. (1970). *Genetic epistemology.* New York: Columbia University Press.

Prensky, M. (December 2005/January 2006). Listen to the natives. *Educational Leadership, 63*(4), 8-13. Retrieved August 19, 2006, from http://www.ascd.org/cms/objectlib/ascdframeset/index.cfm?publication=http://www.ascd.org/authors/ed_lead/el200512_prensky.html

Robbins, S. (2008). *Chapter 3 method: Developing the faceted classification.* Retrieved March 8, 2009, from http://www.sarahrobbins.com/RobbinsChapter3Method.pdf

Second Life® Education Wiki. (2007). Retrieved from http://www.simteach.com/wiki/index.php?title=Second_Life_Education_Wiki

Smith, M. K. (1999). Andragogy: The encyclopaedia of informal education. Retrieved June 15, 2009, from http://www.infed.org/lifelonglearning/b-andra.htm

Spradley, J. P. (1979). *The ethnographic interview*. Fort Worth, TX: Hartcourt Brace Jovanovich.

Spradley, J. P. (1980). *Participant observation*. New York: Holt, Rinehart and Winston.

Steinkuehler, C. (2005). *Cognition & learning in massively multiplayer online games: A critical approach* (Doctoral Dissertation, University of Wisconsin-Madison, 2005). Retrieved on February 19, 2008, from http://website.education.wisc.edu/steinkuehler/thesis.html

Steinkuehler, C. (2007, November). Massively multiplayer online gaming as a constellation of literacy practices. *E-learning*, *4*(3), 297–318. doi:10.2304/elea.2007.4.3.297

Steinkuehler, C. (2008). Massively multiplayer online games as an educational technology: An outline for research. *Educational Technology*, *48*(1), 10–21.

Taylor, T. L. (1999, November/December). Life in virtual worlds: Plural existence, multimodalities, and other online research challenges. *The American Behavioral Scientist*, *43*(2), 436–449. doi:10.1177/00027649921955362

Tennant, M. (1988). *Psychology and adult learning*. London: Routledge. doi:10.4324/9780203441619

Turkle, S. (1995). *Life on the screen: Identity in the age of the internet*. New York: Touchstone.

Wenger, E. (1998). *Communities of practice: Learning, meaning, and identity*. Cambridge, UK: Cambridge University Press.

Yee, N. (2006, June). The demographics, motivations, and derived experiences of users of massively multi-user online graphical environments. *Presence (Cambridge, Mass.)*, *15*(3), 309–329. doi:10.1162/pres.15.3.309

ADDITIONAL READING

Bransford, J. D. (2006). *Virtual environments as ways to reorganize thinking about reasearch and education.* Presentation given in Second Life®, Oct 2, 2006. Retrieved March 15, 2008, from http://www.simteach.com/wiki/index.php?title=John_Bransford_Transcript_2_October_2006

Brown, J. S. (2006, September/October). Environments for the 21st century: Exploring the edge. *Change, 38*(5), 18-25. Retrieved November 15, 2007, from http://www.educause.edu/ir/library/pdf/ff0604S.pdf

Clark, C. (2008, January). *Do i need a Second Life®? The opportunities and challenges of virtual worlds.* Poster session presented at the Educause Learning Initiative 2008 Annual Meeting, City, St/Country.

Dickey, M. D. (2005). Three dimensional virtual worlds and distance learning: Two case studies of active-worlds as a medium for distance education. *British Journal of Educational Technology*, *36*(3). doi:10.1111/j.1467-8535.2005.00477.x

Franceschi, K. G., Lee, R. M., & Hinds, D. (2008, January 7-10). *Engaging e-Learning in virtual worlds: Supporting group collaboration.* Proceedings of 41st Hawaii International International Conference on Systems Science (HICSS-41 2008), Waikoloa, Big Island, HI, USA. IEEE Computer Society 2008.

Gee, J. P. (2008). Good video games, the human mind and good learning. In Willoughby, T., & Wood, E. (Eds.), *Children's Learning in a Digital World* (pp. 40–63). Malden, MA: Blackwell Publishing.

Hein, C. (Ed.). (2006). *Virtual Methods, issues in social research on the internet*. New York: Berg.

Jakobsson, M. (2006). Questing for knowledge—virtual worlds as dynamic processes of social interaction. In Schroeder, R., & Axelsson, A. (Eds.), *Avatars at work and play: Collaboration and interaction in shared virtual environments* (pp. 209–225). London: Springer.

Kendall, L. (2002). *Hanging out in the virtual pub: Masculinities and relationships online*. Berkeley, CA: University of California Press.

Nardi, B. A., & Harris, J. (2006, November). *Strangers and friends: Collaborative play in world of warcraft*. Proceedings of the 2006 20th anniversary conference on computer supported cooperative work. Retrieved May 26, 2008, from http://darrouzet-nardi.net/bonnie/pdf/fp199-Nardi.pdf

New Media Consortium. (2007). The Horizon Project: Call to scholarship 2007-8. Retrieved November 11, 2007, from http://www.nmc.org/pdf/Horizon-Project-Call-to-Scholarship.pdf

Partnership for 21st Century Skills. (2004). *The road to 21st century learning: Policymakers' guide to 21st century skills*. Retrieved April 22, 2005, from http://www.21stcenturyskills.org/images/stories/otherdocs/P21_Policy_Paper.pdf

Pearce, C. (2008, April). The truth about baby boomer gamers a study of over-forty computer game players. *Games and Culture*, *3*(2), 142–174. doi:10.1177/1555412008314132

Rheingold, H. (1993). *Virtual communities*. Accessed on May 13, 2008, from http://www.rheingold.com/vc/book/intro.html

Second Life ® (2008). http://secondlife.com

Smith, R. B., Hixon, R., & Horan, B. (2001). Supporting flexible roles in a shared space. In Churchill, E. F., Snowdon, D. N., & Munro, A. J. (Eds.), *Collaborative virtual environments digital places and spaces for interaction* (pp. 160–176). London: Springer-Verlag.

Snowdon, D. N., & Munro, A. J. (Eds.). (2001). *Collaborative virtual environments digital places and spaces for interaction* (pp. 202–224). London: Springer-Verlag.

Steinkuehler, C. (2008). Massively multiplayer online games as an educational technology: An outline for research. *Educational Technology*, *48*(1), 10–21.

Taylor, T. L. (2002). Living Digitally: Embodiment in virtual worlds. In Schroeder, R. (Ed.), *The social life of avatars: Presence and interaction in shared virtual environments* (pp. 40–61). London: Springer.

Taylor, T. L. (2006). *Play between worlds: Exploring online game culture*. Cambridge, MA: MIT Press.

KEY TERMS AND DEFINITIONS

Avatar: A 3D representation of a user in a virtual world.

Constructionism: A learning theory positing that knowledge is constructed and that this process most effective when learners create an artifact.

Learning-By-Doing: In Second Life®, an array of learning strategies situated in the environment and Residents' creative endeavors.

Massively Online Multiplayer Game: Able to support hundreds of thousands of players simultaneously.

Second Life®: An online 3D virtual world imagined and built by its users.

Virtual World: An online 3D environment open to users who sign up for accounts.

ENDNOTES

1 An avatar is the 3D graphical representation of the user. I use this term because this study was conducted entirely in Second Life® as

a virtual ethnographer (1999) in which my avatar interacted with other avatars

2 Some Residents build out land parcels, creating elaborate worlds they spent time in. Others created objects (e.g. furniture, clothing)

3 All proper nouns, (e.g. Resident names, names of places) and identifying descriptors of places (e.g. the logo of Inseparable Beings) are pseudonyms.

4 Official Partners: Users can designate a partner on their profiles in-world. The purpose os to make the relationship visible to the community. A Residents sends a proposal to another Resident using a web-based from provided by Linden Labs. To create a partnership will cost each partner L$10. Divorce costs the person requesting it L$25.

5 Particle Effects: Two-dimensional graphic images created by adding a script to a prim. Examples of particle effects are the flames of burning fires, the glistening bling of a piece of jewelry, or floating hearts that pop out of a greeting card upon opening it.

6 Terraform: The SL® editing tools that allow Residents to shape a land mass to create mountains, rivers and underwater seascapes.

7 Aurora is the 2nd avatar of the person controlling the avatar Mica.

Chapter 13
Using the 3V Model to Explore Virtuality, Veracity and Values in Liminal Spaces

Simon Atkinson
Massey University, New Zealand

Kevin Burden
University of Hull, UK

ABSTRACT

Adaptation and adoption of immature emergent technologies for instruction fails to account for the challenge to, and creation of, new concepts of self, identity and community both in real and virtual spaces. New insight is necessary to develop social policy responses, including those of educational systems and institutions, to the consequences of these new conceptualisations. This chapter presents an original theoretical model which aims to assist in the interpretation of existing theory, exploring the interrelated dimensions of values, virtuality and veracity disturbed by the adaptation of emergent technologies. It invites an exploration of existing theoretical and methodological instruments available within the broader Social Sciences to examine emerging notions of identity. The emergent theoretical model visualizes a set of complex assumptions within the concepts of the "real-virtual" interface created by emergent technologies; the 3V model represents one means of explore internal structure to this liminal space and invites further empirical study.

INTRODUCTION

The fear of change that appears to pervade our education systems is perhaps rooted in a fundamental lack of comprehension. What is technology? How do we recognize it, measure it, evaluate it? Even within the nation state there are huge variations across educational sectors, and within sectors, across differing social geographies, in the adaptation and adoption of technology. There is a need to provide policy makers and practitioners with explanations, and methods of comprehension, although these are undoubtedly problematic. Technology adoption patterns in all societies, developed and developing, are complex and difficult to represent. Socio-economic, gender, ethnic and

DOI: 10.4018/978-1-61692-854-4.ch013

educational differences suggest digital citizenship is a multi-faceted and complex phenomenon.

In this chapter, we draw on our own academic development and pedagogical practice with emerging technologies and associated practices. We propose a new model for describing and researching cyber behaviour. This model may even, we venture to suggest, provide the basis for new insights at an institutional level into how technologies affect change.

Web 2.0 emergent technologies offer students and staff new opportunities to explore new concepts of self and identity. These tools and services are creating, recreating and evolving new communities both in real and virtual spaces. Existing social theory is struggling to accommodate these changes and social policy responses, including those of educational systems and institutions, and we need new models to account for these new conceptualizations. An original theoretical model, the 3V model (Atkinson & Burden, 2007) described here, aims to facilitate interpretation of existing theory, provide a context for the evaluation of learner and staff conceptions of identity in new liminal spaces between the 'real' and 'virtual' worlds. There are a range of well developed and well tested theoretical and methodological instruments within Social Science research and many of these can be applied to, and integrated into, the 3V model. What the 3V model aims to do is provide a framework for a set of complex assumptions concerning the concept of the 'real-virtual' interface; it seeks to provide a visualization of these liminal spaces and offers a framework for further empirical study.

Despite anecdotal evidence, there is little substantive evidence to indicate how cyber behaviour, specifically that relating to Web 2.0 community applications such as Myspace, Bebo, Facebook, Flickr, YouTube and Voicethread, changes the social practices, personal behaviour and socio-cultural expectations between individuals. As educators in tertiary institutions in two English speaking countries at opposite ends of the globe (New Zealand and the United Kingdom), we are interested in understanding this behaviour. Our institutions advocate 'lifelong learning' and provide tertiary level programmes for Early Years (Kindergarten) practitioners through to professional development programmes for established practitioners in Higher Education. In our work, the concept of 'digital literacy' is a contentious point of professional discourse. That the real impact of technology adoption on learner performance, expectations and behaviour is poorly understood is evidenced by the lack of appropriate policy responses across the educational sectors within a single national state's education system. As the commercial sector laments Universities' inability to provide graduates with appropriate skills, Universities themselves are struggling to provide flexible and effective access to digital support for learning. There is a pressing need for education at all levels to understand the fundamental shifts in the norms of inter-personal communication and patterns of user engagement, and what the consequences of this change might be.

These shifts are fundamental and ill-defined. There is a requirement to define what we mean by '*emerging technology*'. It is, at times, difficult to distinguish between the emergence of a new technology, and the fusion of various disparate technologies into single devices. An example of this is the convergence of previously disparate devices, telephone, video player, music player into a single portable unit. Researchers must also be clear about the socio-cultural and socio-economic contexts in which claims about technology are being made. There is a real danger that we talk of emerging technologies and societal impact from a 'Developed World' perspective. This Occidental bias in much of the published literature needs to be accounted for in our theorizing. Finding models that apply to all societies, at whatever stage of technological sophistication, will be a challenge.

A RICH HERITAGE OF RESEARCH PERSPECTIVES

Researchers risk ignoring much that predates the Internet at our peril. Earlier theoretical constructs that underlie our collective efforts are extremely diverse and have much to offer. Political Science's interest in power and representation, Elitism and Pluralism, through to Computer Science's interest in Actor-Network Theory all shed light on behaviour in unique ways. So does anthropological and sociological study from Georg Simmel's notion of 'stranger' (Simmel, 1949) and Alfred Schütz's exposition of 'intersubjectivity' in the field of phenomenology, the notion that shared cognition is essential in the formulation of ideas, notably in the process of meaning-making (Schütz, 1967). Cultural-Historical Activity Theory and, more latterly, the concept of 'knotworking' developed in the work of the Scandinavian Activity Theory movement, specifically the development of a hypothesis on co-configuration expansive learning (Engestrom *et al.*, 1999) also provide useful starting points for acknowledging the familiar in the apparently novel. In this chapter, we will situate our reflections in the work of Communications and Media Studies from Innis' space-time considerations (Innis, 1951) to Michael Cole and Jan Derry's assertion that we are the technology we apply (Cole & Derry, 2005).

LIMINAL SPACES

There is a point at which a technology becomes established, moves from being emergent to new, and from new to 'matter of fact'. These stages vary depending on context, but each might be said to have moments at which they stand as neither being in one state or the other, neither emergent not established. As this is true of the technology itself, it is also true of human's adoption of that technology, and of its deployment. Our usage moves from novice to expert, from self-conscious activity to unquestioned behaviour. As usage evolves so do we, as the technology can be said to be in a 'liminal state', so can we be described in these terms.

Liminality (from the Latin līmen, meaning 'a threshold') denotes a state of being between two different existential planes, on the 'threshold'. The 'liminal' is a concept much explored in anthropological theories concerning ritual when societies develop mechanisms for the passage of the individual from one social status to another as in many rites of passage (Gennap, 1960). The liminal state is one in which uncertainty and indeterminacy defines the position of an individual; the identity of the individual is acknowledged as being in transition from one recognised state to another anticipated state. Where the individual fails to complete the transition and is held in between these states, people might be said to be permanently liminal.

Differences in individuals' status and in social hierarchies are often suspended during these ritual transitions, such as during religious pilgrimages where the status of 'pilgrim' obfuscates all other differentiations. A new social structure, however temporary, is created, that of 'communitas', in which a shared endeavour sustains relationships through the liminal state. Liminality in anthropology might also be said to occur when one is exposed to the unfamiliar as well as the new. Unfamiliarity in a given social situation creates a sense of ambiguity, uncertainty as to how to act, how to represent oneself and what manifestations of oneself others will see or expect to see. There is something inherently 'liminal' about our use of emerging technologies.

Examples of this liminal state in Western societies might be considered the 'space' between being a single person and being married, so that 'engagement' could be termed a liminal state, or the period between finishing one's University exams and graduation, or perhaps more complex a notion such as the period between the end of childhood and recognised adulthood, perhaps 'adolescence is a liminal state'. Societies introduce alternative rules for these liminal spaces in which individuals are recognized as operating outside the usual social constraints. The acceptance of behaviours in Carnival that would be unacceptable the day before or the day after, the kiss under the ritual space defined by hanging mistletoe provides 'ritual cover' for an act that may be prohibited at other times, in other spaces.

Beyond the social realm there are other liminal spaces. Dusk and dawn, twilight, represents a liminal 'zone' between night and day. These are observable liminal zones, but others might be considered the threshold of midnight, between one day and the next, or 31st December in the western calendar as a threshold for a year. Increasingly, dispersed families live this liminal festival annually as relatives in New Zealand move into the New Year while geographically distant families celebrate the end of the previous year. The Scottish tradition of 'First-Footing' in which good luck is brought to the house if the 'first foot' across the threshold in the New Year is a dark haired male bringing symbolic coal, shortbread, salt, black bun and whisky is a ceremonial acknowledgment of this liminality.

Physical space also has its liminalities, 'no man's land' and other disputed territories, as well as places where one is simply going from somewhere to somewhere else such as airport terminals, train stations and hotels. Spaces in myth that are transitional such as purgatory represent spaces that are 'in-between' and are useful metaphorical depictors of liminality. An exclamation that the long wait for a decision is 'like being in purgatory' is more common place than 'I am in a liminal state', but amounts to the same thing. Physical spaces in our natural landscape can also represent thresholds and suggest liminal spaces. In our built environment these liminal features are doors, windows, crossroads, junctions and bridges. In the natural environment they might be identified as springs, caves, shorelines, rivers (as boundaries), volcanic features, river fords and mountain passes. These natural features become mythic portals to esoteric knowledge and ideas of passage to some 'other space'. Liminality is often sacred and frequently dangerous.

The individual's context, prior experience and expectation define the liminal space. The airport worker and the airplane passenger experience the space of the airport departure lounge very differently, as does the hotel guest and the chambermaid. This notion of the liminal space is important in considering how emerging technologies are seen as shaping and forming new relationships, new identities and new conceptions of self. The degree to which an emerging technology creates or mitigates against liminality, whether an emerging technology creates a divide or a bridge, is important in our ability to respond as policy makers and educators.

NETWORKING AND CONNECTIVISM

Manuel Castells' social theories regarding the 'networked society' and George Siemens' development of these, and related, ideas in the realm of education in the form of 'connectivism' both merit further elaboration.

Manuel Castells' academic lineage, in the fields of urban sociology, organisation studies, social movements, the sociology of culture, political economics and the Internet suggest a strong association with notions of space. His seminal works in developing the concept of the 'network society' began before the exponential growth of the Internet in the 1990s with the advent of the World Wide Web. Castells' observation of changing forms of complex commercial networks and his recognition of evolving social structures in response, namely 'The Fourth World', denoting that sub-population of the socially excluded in a global society, have been frequently cited.

From a background in French academia, within the discipline of urban sociology, Castells began in the 1980s to explore the role of new technologies in reshaping economic patterns of organisation. He recognised the need to acknowledge the immaterial, as well as material, elements that underpinned the economic activity on global information networks. This gave rise to the term 'space of flows', the 'space' in which real-time, long-distance communication shaped economic activity. Castells' The Rise of the Network Society (1996), The Power of Identity (1997), and End of Millennium (1998); published as a trilogy and subsequently revived have had significant influence (Castells, 2000; Castells, 2004a; Castells, 2004b).

Castells recognises the interdependence of three social dynamics; *production, power*, and *experience*. The means by which societies organize their economy, the organs of state and their institutions, and the ways in which individuals create personal meaning through collective action, are the irreducible sources of these social dynamics. These elements must be understood, both as discrete and inter-related entities. This ability to see the inter-relationships and co-dependences of geographically dispersed networks led to his examination of the development of the Internet as a complex confluence of the roles of the state (manifest in military and academic forms), social movements (notably computer 'hackers'), and commercial enterprise. The conflicting interests of these disparate groups identified the economic structures that allowed the Internet to flourish.

In The Information Age, his seminal trilogy, Castells states:

People increasingly organize their meaning not around what they do but on the basis of what they are, or believe they are. Meanwhile, on the other hand, global networks of instrumental exchanges selectively switch on and off individuals, groups, regions, and even countries, according to their relentless flow of strategic decisions. There follows a fundamental split between abstract, universal instrumentalism, and historically rooted, particularistic identities. Our societies are increasingly structured around a bipolar opposition between the Net and the self. (Castells, 2000)

Castells' thesis of organisational networks, contrasted to the self as defined against a background of social flux, has been a powerful interpretive concept for exploring the impact of the Internet. If a network can be simplified as denoting to connected entities, be they individuals or organisations, then the multitude of bipolar relationships afforded by the Internet is clearly a network. A network creates opportunities for information to flow, but it also creates dependencies, and disruptions to the network have an impact beyond any two points. A point within a network, a node, may be privileged or relatively insignificant depending on the degree to which failure at that node disrupts the effectiveness of the network. Successful nodes, those to which other parts of the network 'seek' a connection, become more successful, more privileged. One simple illustration would be the network of citations in journal articles and written book chapters. Each author, in creating a journal article (the node), cites the work of others (other nodes) and in doing so might be said to create a network of citations. The more a specific node is cited, the more successful it becomes. If a very privileged node (frequently cited work) were to fail (be uncovered as plagiarism, for example) the impact on the network would be more significant that if it were a very minor (less cited) node.

Nodes could be tangible products such as the example just given or something less physical like a concept or idea, or a community or belief system. The resulting networks can be flexible or fairly rigid but less established networks, where new nodes are formed more easily, provide opportunities for spontaneity and originality, creativity and innovation.

These ideas have been explored by George Siemens in his notion of 'connectivism'. Siemens suggests that learning, "defined as actionable knowledge", exists outside the individual, within a network or nodes within a network. Being part of, or indeed 'being', a network that connects these significant nodes is what allows the individual to learn.

Connectivism is driven by the understanding that decisions are based on rapidly altering foundations. New information is continually being acquired. The ability to draw distinctions between important and unimportant information is vital. The ability to recognize when new information alters the landscape based on decisions made yesterday is also critical. (Siemens, 2004)

The skills required to function in this shifting, continually evolving, knowledge landscape include, according to connectivism, the need to embrace diversity, remain open to new 'connections', nurture existing connections, recognise disparate ideas as potential nodes, value currency in ideas and being prepared to revise one's decisions based on new knowledge.

Siemens places the individual at the centre of the connectivist model of learning. The individual has personal knowledge made up of a personal network (the individual node), which belongs to a larger network (nodes comprising a learning set or social group), which in turn belongs to an extended network (an academic discipline). Knowledge flows through and back across this network ensuring that the individual has access to current, live and relevant, constantly updated knowledge. Blogging and tweeting represent contemporary manifestations of these Mandelbrot style networks of nodes.

Our ability to learn what we need for tomorrow is more important than what we know today. [...] As knowledge continues to grow and evolve, access to what is needed is more important than what the learner currently possesses. (Siemens, 2004)

Castells identified early in the information age the radical shifts of information exchange, hermeneutics and power with the imbalances in society that would result, suggesting a fluid and dynamic network of knowledge creation and exchange. Siemens extends this notion into the realm of learning to suggest learning is no longer an individualistic activity but one which takes place within these dynamic networks. The tools one uses to engage with these networks impact on the user and the network, and indeed act to modify the tool itself.

The tools, or technology, used to maintain our learning networks might most easily be conceptualised as hardware in communications and information technology, electronics and digital computers and communications devices. Technology might also be seen in all manufactured materialism, in packaging, cars, planes and physical constructions of all kinds. This conceptualisation of technology is highly limited and Cole and Derry argue this it is inadequate, suggesting that technology and intelligence are indivisible. They propose a broadening of our definition of 'technology' beyond the 'tools' to incorporate the social context of deployment (Cole & Derry, 2005). To build on the analogies promulgated by Castells and Siemens, one can see how the tools as nodes are indivisible from network that is the social context, the collective intelligence. There is no node without a network, and no network without nodes.

Moving beyond the 'social construction of technology' after Latour and others, who suggested that technology is not so much a determinate of human action, but that rather, human actions serve to shape technology, the Cultural-Historical Activity Theorists have advocated that technology is social milieu. Cole & Derry propose that technology can be conceptualised as forms of 'tool-mediated social practice'. The degree to which the node and network create each other warrants further research. An examination into the use of the abacus in mathematical reasoning has shown different brain processes being developed between those who are expert users and those who are non-expert, suggesting the possibility that nurture becomes nature through the use of specific tools (Hanakawa *et al*, 2003). This raises the interesting question as to whether engagement in the plethora of online social networking tools will change the way people think.

How then does one identify these nodes and networks, these 'tools as social-milieu' and recognise these liminal spaces where technology emerges and new user identities are forming? How does one plan for educational activity in spaces where the conventions of communication are evolving? Are actors in the virtual spaces of Facebook (www.facebook.com) or Second Life (www.secondlife.com) entering liminal spaces where cultural values differ from those in the real world? Do the technologies and tools act as socially mediated practice, through which new 'generations' (irrespective of age) are learning to deal with changing value constructions?

A RESPONSE: 3V MODEL

The '3V' model seeks to illuminate these complex assumptions concerning 'real-virtual' interfaces as mediated through our experience of technology. The model visualizes internal structures to this realm, these liminal spaces, and provides a framework for further empirical study. We aim to share with colleagues from all social science disciplines a conceptual framework that allows them to invest their specialist traditions, investigative models and theoretical approaches.

The intention of the 3V model is to facilitate enquiry which is flexible enough to cope with a range of new emerging technologies as they originate and those that are evolving into different convergences. It aims to be a model of enquiry suitable to all social contexts. It is possible within the model described to select one emerging tool and study it with reference to a number of different cultural contexts, just as it would be possible to take a single cultural perspective and concentrate on the comparison of a dozen specified tools. The 3V model aims to identify the nature, position and impact trajectory of technologies on three axes, the first V is *Virtuality*, the second V is *Veracity* and the third V is *Values*.

Virtuality

Liminality offers a utopian moment in which the weight of limiting social regulations is lifted. Liminality is crucial to the adaptive powers of a culture. Liminal zones are virtual environments or spaces. (Sheilds, 2003)

The concept of virtual or liminal spaces, the in-between, where social and interpersonal communication has different potentialities is one crucial element in the 3V model, which we define in terms of *virtuality*. The degree to which one is 'present' in the spaces one occupies form key elements of an individual's identity.

The relationship between spaces and personal behaviour was explored by Georg Simmel (1858–1918), a pioneer of 'social structure', who suggested that there were significant differences between life patterns of urban and rural people, that the pedestrian pace and long-term physical association with 'place' in rural contexts allowed the development of deeper connections than was possible in urban settings, but encouraged a narrow and conformist tendency in social thought which stifled originality and personal expression. Urban life, in contrast, was one of the indifferent stranger, oblivious to each other's patterns of behaviour, allowing individual expression but encouraging a dispassionate attitude to the overwhelming amount of activity that surrounds one, sometimes leading to isolation. Simmel idealises the nature of Man's sociability as natural and free of constraint, as creating social realities through the accumulation of individual interactions. This has particular contemporary relevance to our understanding of how Web 2.0 tools suggest an ability to create effective peer networks (Simmel, 1949).

This has interesting relationships with the work of the political economist H.A. Innes on the 'centre' and 'periphery' in communications theory and the idea that space and time are directly related to the patterns of communications within specific traditions. Innes sought to develop a grand theory of history that examined culture's relationships to space and time. His thesis was that less technological, non broadcast means of communication, typified by oral cultures, placed their emphasis on the relationship with time, the preservation of knowledge and the perpetuation of close traditional relationships. More technologically sophisticated, broadcast based forms of communication encouraged an emphasis on spatial reach, and considerably less on time related concepts (Innis, 1951).

Taken together, Simmel and Innes, in different fields, languages and contexts, describe a pattern of cultural development in which stable physical, peripheral and 'narrowband' communication amongst the familiar, contrasts with the urbanised, technologically sophisticated 'broader-casting' to 'strangers'. However, within the environment of social networking tools such as MySpace or Facebook, there is precisely a blend of these two domains. Innes's question that the relative stability of a culture is dependent upon the balance and proportion of their media is one with obvious implications for the study of the Internet.

Veracity

The concept of *veracity* develops from the work of cyberculture theorists such as Nakamura that explores an individual's sense of personal identity development (Nakamura, 2002). In the 3V model, we are concerned with the concept of veracity in so far as it supports the development, both individual and collective, of identity. Whilst the printed text has established conventions, of recognisable fonts denoting 'gravitas', of processes of authority and peer-review, and the industrial complexity of publishing houses, the value of the world-wide web as a source of information remains highly contested, not least amongst academics. The 3V model is not directly concerned with the factual accuracy of individual elements of information placed on the web, although this is indeed of significance as new patterns of interpretation, assignment of authority and new concepts of credibility and authorship emerge. Rather the model seeks to illuminate the ability of the individual to suspend their externally imposed boundaries of space, time, gender, ethnicity, age and social status and to express themselves independently of the real-world.

Marshall McLuhan proffered the notion of the 'global village' (McLuhan, 1965) before the advent of the personal computer. This concept captures succinctly the contradictions of a spatially diverse 'territory' without boundaries suggesting visions of 'idle gossip over the white picket fence'. Levinson provided a fuller expansion of McLuhan's concepts updated for the advent of the Internet and suggested that not only was McLuhan correct in his assertion that the communications technologies of his time had become extensions of the human sense, but that new emerging technologies have developed into a virtual nervous system for humankind (Levinson, 1999). Mass communications research into shifting perceptions of truthfulness and reality, as experienced by the individual, is vital to a proper understanding of the Internet as well as to what it now means to be an individual.

Values

The concept of *values*, perhaps the most contested, is the third element in the 3V model. There has been considerable interest in the development of instruments to measure cultural values, notably with a view to establishing commonalities across geographically dispersed peoples as well as subgroups within single political states. Tools such as the Kluckhohn-Strodtbeck Value Orientation Preference Model (VOM) (Kluckhohn & Strodtbeck,

1961) attempt to identify common value references across otherwise disparate groups. The VOM identifies responses to questions concerning basic human nature (good-mixed-bad), the relationship to nature (dominate-harmonious-subordinate), the sense of time (past-present-future), activity orientation (being-becoming-doing) and social relations (hierarchical-collateral-individual). Responses to these orientations produce a values profile in which homogenous groups display high degrees of correlation. Social Psychologist Milton Rokeach, also in the 1960s, developed a more projective model, focussing on the 'desired' rather than the notion of 'orientation'. Rokeach designed a 36 point instrument requiring respondents to prioritise statements in order of importance as life's "guiding principles", 18 elements defined as terminal values and 18 as instrumental (Rokeach, 1973). Terminal values are those where desirable "end-states of existence" are envisaged and instrumental values are those which denote "desirable modes of conduct" (ibid, p7).

Whilst we use the term 'values' in much the same way as Kluckhorn and Rokeach, we have some reservations about both of these instruments that have been focussed on *apriori* cases of defined 'cultures' or established notions of individualism. We are interested in newly emerging cultures and personal identities and are seeking to measure changes in cultural value systems which are often poorly understood, or where the very existence of a 'culture' is disputed. We use 'values' applied to the broader concept of 'cultural values', and in doing so must acknowledge that there is disagreement as to both the definition and usefulness of the term and concept of culture. In the English language, the term 'culture' and 'cultivation' were, until the 19th Century, largely coterminous and the development of the well cultivated individual as a 'well-cultured' one naturally gave rise to the notion of the well-cultured group, the civilised as opposed to the barbarian, the cultured and the uncultured. As the term developed to capture the inter-generational shared practices of all social groupings, it acknowledged that all societies, even, and perhaps particularly, the colonised, had a culture of sorts defined by differences. The values thus associated with these cultures were also consequently defined by differences. The Internet era presents an interesting challenge to the assumptions, and vocabulary, of 'differences' in cultural values. Heterogeneity and homogeneity are no longer easily assessed with reference to spatial boundaries and the range of formative experiences to which individuals are experienced, and which informs their sense of self and other, is growing at a phenomenal rate.

AN OPERATIONAL MODEL

Existing models applied to the learning context directly, such as the 4-E model cited by Collis (Collis & Moonen, 2001), suggest how one may measure the effectiveness and likelihood of adoption of a given technology. It does not assist in the understanding of what impact the adoption of any given technology may have on users. Existing models acknowledge the importance of the range of environmental factors, but do not illustrate how the environment itself might be directly affected.

The ability of the 3V model to represent the relative position of technologies in a longitudinal form is also seen as valuable. It would be possible, for instance, to plot the emergence of say, 'Instant Messaging' (typified by, for example, MSN messenger), both in terms of its different impacts in different contexts, and its evolving impact in one context over an extended period of time. Whilst it may not appear significant that one can plot a single technology, the ability to plot a multitude of technologies offers the prospect of being able to look at similar patterns of societal adoption for previously emerged technologies, and therefore suggests an ability to forecast what may happen to as yet unimagined technologies. The model itself is visualised as a cube with the virtuality and veracity dimensions plotted on the X and Y axes and values on the Z axis.

The model, illustrated in Figure 1, creates a three dimensional space for theorising the impact of existing and emerging tools. Tools can usefully be evaluated in terms of these three dimensions, virtuality, veracity and values, along a continuum of 'virtual-real', 'trustworthy-uncertain', 'stable-disrupted', respectively. The emergence of new forms of social mediation is the result of 'rupture', or 'disruption', and we should therefore look to assess the degree to which a tool defies, contradicts or alters existing patterns of interaction.

Data might be gathered on one or more of the dimensions of the matrix. Early practical workshop experiments suggest that respondents understood the concept of virtuality and veracity with considerable ease, but struggled with the concept of values as represented. This is unsurprising, since values are regarded somewhat differently across a range of social sciences and the terminology is inexact. However, the model does seek to identify the degree to which the value assumptions, however defined within a given culture, are potentially disruptive or threatened by a particular emerging technology. Value disruption will be relative within any given culture. The significance of this relative disruption, and how the 3V model can help to illustrate it, might be illustrated with reference to the mobile phone, or portable telephony. There is significant anecdotal evidence that mobile telephony is changing the way that people relate to each other, shifting people's concepts of time, personal space and privacy. In plotting in the 3V model, the different responses of various socio-economic or socio-cultural groupings recording their perceptions of mobile telephony, one can begin to see how technologies impact differently across society.

We have already indicated that even within one language, namely English, the terminology varies between academic disciplines when describing similar or equivalent concepts. The continuums described here, are therefore mutable, and this is likely to be an area of further refinement should specific academic fields of enquiry wish to adapt the model.

Illustrated in Figure 2 are two tools from a given socio-cultural context. 'A', is an avatar engagement in Second Life, where it is suggested the

Figure 1. The 3V model as a three dimensional space

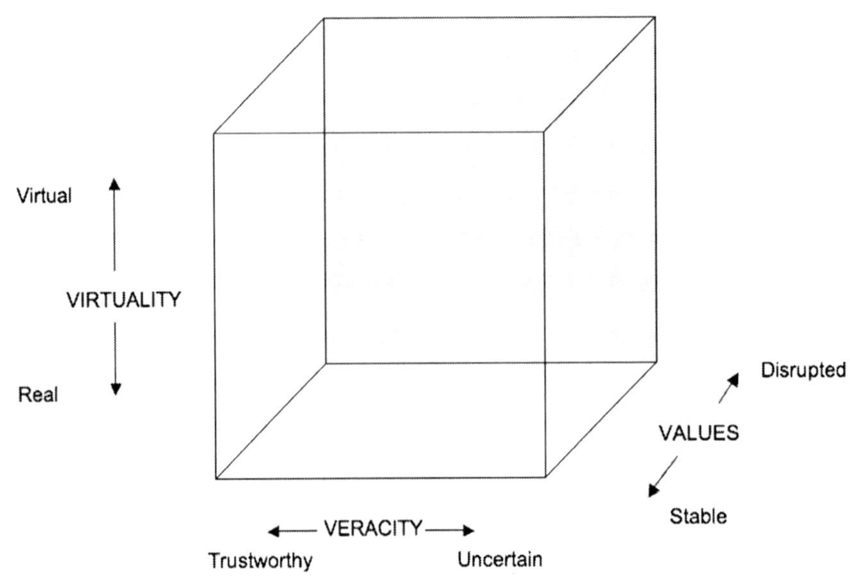

degree of virtuality is nearly total (although less so arguably than text based fantasy), where the veracity of representations cannot be guaranteed as there is little or no opportunity to verify the truthfulness of representations made, and where the value systems are too new, given the recency of the technology, to be known. By contrast, 'B' might be used to suggest the position of a face-to-face encounter in the classroom, where the sense of the real is determined by presence, where the truthfulness of the messages transmitted are measurable and familiar and where the established conventions render the value disruption minimal.

Each dimension of the matrix allows data to be plotted against it, independently of others. One does not need necessarily to collect and plot data in a single study against all three dimensions. Building a single, dual or three dimensional model will depend on the data collection methodology adopted. We believe that many existing instruments and theoretical approaches will prove compatible with this research model and we are eager to develop and adapt a range of data gathering means to populate and refine the 3V model. One might, for example, make use of an existing and well-established anthropological instrument for identifying generalised value differences within contemporary cultural settings, namely the Kluckhohn-Strodtbeck Value Orientation Preference Model (Kluckhohn & Strodtbeck, 1961). Using this instrument to identify differing cultural perspectives between a 'real-life' cohort and that same group of individuals as a 'Second Life' cohort would provide useful data for the value dimension of the 3V model.

CASE STUDY

By way of illustration, a case study of a professional workshop response to the 3V model and its application is provided. The data was collected purely for the purpose of explaining the model and exploring its potential for visualising emerging technologies relative to one another.

At a presentation to 40 educational technologists, and learning technology related academic staff during a related conference in December

Figure 2. Situating two tools in a given socio-cultural context (hypothetical)

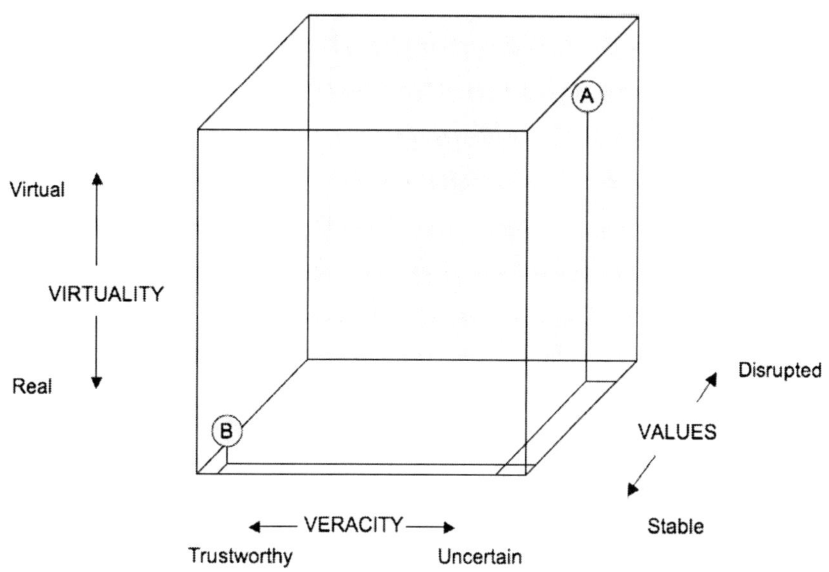

Table 1. Scale values for 3V model axis

Tool	Virtuality Real: Virtual	Veracity Trustworthy: Uncertain	Values Stable: Disrupted
#	1 2 3 4 5 6 7 8 9 10	1 2 3 4 5 6 7 8 9 10	1 2 3 4 5 6 7 8 9 10

2007, 20 A4 sheets detailing eight 'tools' were distributed to the audience. Working in pairs, respondents were asked to identify, on the three scales of the 3V model, each represented by a scale of one to ten, where they would opt to position each 'tool'.

Each tool, listed in the left hand column of Table 1, had alongside it three columns representing the three axes of the model and in each cell of the resulting table the numbers one to ten. Not all respondents completed all fields in this proof of concept exercise, but 18 out of the 20 responses were returned. Face-to-face was included as an indicator of comprehension, given that the low value expectations for this mode of communication were predictable. One might reasonably expect the 'virtuality' response for face-to-face to be near to 'one' for real. Where a return gave a high value (in one case, ten) it was concluded that the data collection instrument had been poorly understood, rendering the results unreliable. Four responses were excluded from the aggregated results on this basis. The mean average for each reliable return (n=14) are in Table 2.

Simple as this small proof of concept pilot exercise is, it identifies a number of interesting issues related to technologies. There is, within this 'community of practice' a reasonable consensus regarding tools, which are highly 'virtual', and those that are not. Other observations include the suggestion that whilst World of Warcraft and Second Life were both seen as highly virtual experiences, the degree of veracity and value disruption diverge. This suggests that whilst superficially similar as technologies the perceived 'purpose' of them produces significantly different responses.

These results, tabulated above in Table 2 and selectively plotted within the 3V model provide an immediate visualisation of the relative placement of tools. In Figure 3, this is illustrated for three tools with A in the position of Skype, B of face-to-face and C of an Avatar in Second Life without voice.

Understanding the relative position of emerging technologies, and the shifting position of established technologies relative to emerging ones, is a useful insight for policy makers and planners.

Table 2. Results of 'proof of concept' exercise

Tool		Virtuality	Veracity	Values
Skype		3.0	2.8	3.8
Face-to-face		1.4	1.9	3.3
Mobile Phone		2.9	3.4	3.9
MSN messenger		5.6	5.2	5.3
Synchronous Chat		6.2	5.9	6.0
'World of Warcraft'		9.0	7.2	6.7
Second Life (without voice)		9.2	7.7	7.4
Blogging		5.3	5.5	4.4

The 3V model offers one means by which a series of tools can be visualised within a three dimensional space which illustrates a variety of societal responses and impacts. The model itself is very flexible. Data might for instance usefully illustrate how two different cohorts, such as school-age children and senior-citizens, rate a number of tools in a similar socio-cultural context, so providing quantifiable data for different sub-cultures' responsiveness to emerging technologies. The model might also be used longitudinally to plot how cohorts over a period of time might 'reposition' technologies.

Further research along these lines is ongoing and the visualisations promise to be rich and useful in understanding the relationship between virtuality and veracity and the degree of values disruption. Extending the principle of reusing existing research methodologies from across the Social Sciences, it is suggested that the interpretive and evaluative power of the 3V model would benefit from an anthropological instrument for identifying generalised value differences within contemporary cultural settings, specifically the Kluckhohn-Strodtbeck Value Orientation Preference Model (Kluckhohn & Strodtbeck, 1961).

The origins of the Value Orientation Preference Model (VOM) are in the work of the Harvard Values Project in the United States in the 1940s and 1950s, in which a team of anthropologists believed there was predictive potential in an instrument which could distinguish cultures based on their responses to five common human concerns. The five elements have been challenged and refined, however the original model still has merit. The VOM suggested there were three possible responses to each of the five contexts presented and that the ranking of these fifteen elements could define the 'character' of a given culture. These responses were described as 'value orientations'.

The essential methodological instrument of the VOM is a survey, consisting of approximately 16 situations based around the basic five dimensions, sometimes more, with associated questions. Originally designed in a story/response format to aid those with differing levels of written comprehension, the instrument can be read, or listened to, and has therefore proved effective with both non-literate and literate respondents. The tool can

Figure 3. Visualisation of responses for 3 'tools'

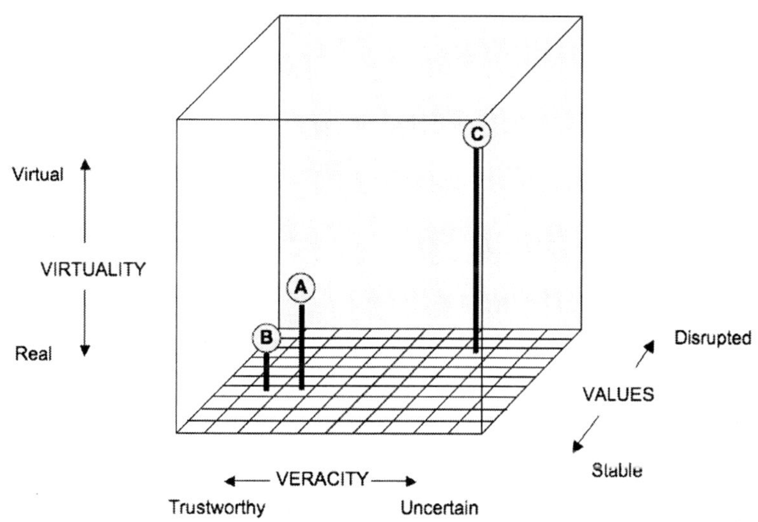

be applied to provide a research-focussed analysis of cultural differences, or as a developmental awareness-building tool to formulate social policy. For a fuller exposition of the original VOM see Kohls (1981) and Russo (2000). Whilst there is recognition that each culture will express all three possible responses at some time, a pattern of intra-cultural stability is theorised. Diversity within any given culture is acknowledged and acculturation is also anticipated. The VOM has been applied, and found to be useful in a wide range of disciplines where an interest in 'value orientation' persists, including in higher education with language students (Ortuno, 1991) and those in dentistry (Marino & Stuart, 2005).

Kluckhohn and Strodtbeck themselves were clear that they did not see the model as complete and that further requirements were encouraged. In reviewing the VOM in the light of the 3V model, it has been concluded that applying the spatial dimension as suggested by Michael Hills (2002) and others, has obvious applications in considering the values disruption of online communication tools. The concept of spatial responsibility as being an individual or collective endeavour is likely to have important consequences for cyber behaviours. Hills also suggests dimensions relating to work, gender and state-individual relationships. In subsequent iterations of the 3V models, use of the VOM will explore further dimensions to extend responses to the axes of veracity and virtuality.

CONCLUSION

We have introduced a new conceptual model for the evaluation of emerging technologies. This is in response to the apparent fear of change that appears to pervade our education systems. We suggest this fear is rooted in a fundamental lack of comprehension. Educators and policy makers have yet to develop effective language and mechanisms for identifying emerging and converging technologies, for measuring them and evaluating their potential impact. The 3V model suggests one means by which researchers might seek to clarify, problematise and comprehend new technologies using any number of data collection tools from existing social science methodology and visualise the results.

It is acknowledged that technology adoption patterns in all societies, developed and developing, are complex and difficult to represent. The socio-cultural context of adoption, its multifaceted aspects of socio-economic, gender, ethnic and educational differences suggest that 'digital citizenship' and cyber behaviour are highly complex phenomena. It is vital, however, that we work across the social sciences to build on research methodologies and pedagogical practice to develop new models for describing and researching cyber behaviour.

REFERENCES

Atkinson, S., & Burden, K. (2007). *Virtuality, veracity and values: Exploring between virtual and real worlds using the 3V model. ICT: Providing choices for learners and learning: ASCILITE 2007*. Singapore: Ascilite.

Burnett, R., & Marshall, P. D. (2003). *Web theory: An introduction*. London: Routledge.

Castells, M. (2000). *The Rise of the Network Society*. Oxford: Blackwell Publishers.

Castells, M. (2004a). *End of Millennium*. Oxford: Blackwell Publishers.

Castells, M. (2004b). *The Power of Identity*. Oxford: Blackwell Publishers.

Cole, M., & Derry, J. (2005). We Have Met Technology and It Is Us. In Sternberg, R. J., & Preiss, D. (Eds.), *Intelligence and Technology: The Impact of Tools on the Nature and Development of Human Abilities*. Mahwah, NJ: Erlbaum.

Collis, B., & Moonen, J. (2001). *Flexible learning in a digital world*. London: Kogan Page.

Engestrom, Y. E., Engestrom, R., & Vahaaho, T. (1999). When the centre does not hold: The importance of knotworking. In Chaiklin, S., Hedegaard, M., & Jensen, U. J. (Eds.), *Activity theory and social practice (pp. ##-##)*. Aarhus: Aarhus University Press.

Gennap, A. V. (1960). *The Rites of Passage*. London: Routledge and Kegan Paul.

Hills, M. (2002). Kluckhohn and Strodtbeck's values orientation theory. In Online Readings in Psychology and Culture (Unit 6, Chapter 3). Retrieved 10 July, 2007, from http://www.wwu.edu/~culture

Innis, H. A. (1951). *The bias of communications*. Toronto: University of Toronto Press.

Kluckhohn, F. R., & Strodtbeck, F. L. (1961). *Variations in value orientations*. Evanston, IL: Row, Peterson and Company.

Kohls, L. R. (1981). *Developing intercultural awareness*. Washington, DC: Sietar Press.

Levinson, P. (1999). *Digital McLuhan: a guide to the information millennium*. New York: Routledge.

Marino, R., & Stuart, G. W. (2005). The validity and reliability of the tertiary student values scale (tsvs). *Medical Education*, *39*, 895–903. doi:10.1111/j.1365-2929.2005.02244.x

McLuhan, M. (1965). *Understanding media: The extensions of man*. New York: McGraw Hill.

Nakamura, L. (2002). *Cybertypes: Race, ethnicity, and identity on the Internet*. London: Routledge.

Ortuno, M. M. (1991). Cross-cultural awareness in the foreign language class: The Kluckhohn model. *Modern Language Journal*, *75*, 449–459. doi:10.2307/329494

Rokeach, M. (1973). *The Nature of Human Values*. New York: The Free Press.

Russo, K. W. (Ed.). (2000). *Finding the middle ground: Insights and applications of the value orientations method*. Yarmouth, ME: Intercultural Press.

Schütz, A. (1967). *The phenomenology of the social world*. Evanston, IL: Northwestern University Press.

Sheilds, R. (2003). *The Virtual*. London: Routledge.

Siemens, G. (2004). Connectivism: A Learning Theory for the Digital Age. Retrieved 24th August, 2009, from http://www.elearnspace.org/Articles/connectivism.htm

Simmel, G. (1949). The sociology of sociability. *American Journal of Sociology*, *55*(3), 254–261. doi:10.1086/220534

KEY TERMS AND DEFINITIONS

3V model: The 3V model is a three dimensional representation of a given technology's relationship to virtuality, veracity and values for the purpose of facilitating the visualisation of emergent technolo gies. Such visual representations are intended to provide an insight into the impact and trajectory of technologies.

Virtuality: Defines the extent to which a personal experience is deemed to engage one as a 'presence', the degree to which one is present or represented in a given space as one intends.

Veracity: Deals ostensibly with the notion of personal truth. The degree to which ones experiences might be said to be trustworthy and dependable within a personal frame of reference rather than any externally imposed set of criteria

Values: Values as used in the 3V Model explores the disruption to collective culturally references notions of belonging, shared space and shared time. Values here suggests those attributes which might determined a sense of membership within one given culture for the purpose of differentiating itself from another.

Liminal: Defines the space between any two defined and pre-determined states of being. To be between these states is to be in a liminal state or space.

Section 4
Enabling Teachers

Chapter 14
Social Networks:
Implications for Education

Mary Hricko
Kent State University, USA

ABSTRACT

Online social networks (SNs) are dynamic Web 2.0 applications that can be used for teaching, learning, and research activities. These SNs offer a myriad of collaborative features for generating content and fostering interactive communication. Although many K-16 administrators tend to focus on the negative consequences of using such applications, online social networks, if managed effectively as instructional tools, can provide opportunities for educators to help students develop 21st century skills. This discussion provides an overview how online social networks can be used in education and offers guidelines for implementation.

UNDERSTANDING SOCIAL NETWORK SITES

The ever-increasing mainstream use of social networks no doubt has had an impact on our information culture. Social network sites have nearly replaced email as the primary mode of communication exchange on the Internet because they offer a rich array of free multimodal features that enable users to share music, photos, videos, and files in a seamless manner. As a result, it is no wonder why our students spend more time on social network sites than on any other web sites on the Internet. Yet despite this reality, many administrators and educators are still reluctant to transition these technologies into the classroom.

Since most social network users are under the age of 35, these platforms are seen as cyberspace "hang outs" for young people (NSBA par 3). As a result, it is often difficult to consider social networks as platforms for education. In turn, administrators and educators have raised many questions on how and if social networks can support learning. Eberhardt (2007) summarizes some of the primary concerns:

DOI: 10.4018/978-1-61692-854-4.ch014

1. How significantly do social networks affect student learning?
2. How do social networks create challenges for students' intellectual development?
3. How does or can this behavior help students develop the identify they need to effectively address complex questions, take a stand based on their beliefs, and negotiate meaning with others?

The lack of research on this subject often reaffirms the negative assessment that social network sites should be left out of the classroom. Critics, who believe that the medium cannot substitute for environments that foster structured formal learning, argue that the knowledge attained through social networks is superficial at best. Yet, research shows us that informal learning is often just as beneficial to our students. If given the opportunity to interact with teachers and other experts in an open environment, students are more likely to participate in the learning. Students gain what is often referred to as a "collective intelligence" or "wisdom of crowds" which results from the learning community that develops in an educational social network environment. In fact, the 2007 Horizon Report suggests "the features that make these tools so compelling are features that we need to understand and incorporate into higher education (for) to harness the power of social networking (is) to build rich, interactive, (and) robust learning communities." (45)

BACKGROUND OF SOCIAL NETWORKS

Social network sites that emerged in the late 1990's are online communities that enable individuals to communicate, collaborate, and share content. Unlike newsgroup and listserv platforms, social network applications are much more dynamic because they offer a wide range of "read-write" features to allow users to generate and interact with the content. When an individual obtains an account through a social networking application, he or she is asked to create an online profile. A profile may consist of a simple format page or a series of pages that can contain a wide range of information related to the individual's educational background, work experience, and interest areas. Depending upon the social networking application, the individual can then modify and customize the profile and build additional pages within the application to create a personalized web space that includes photos, videos, and even music. The user can also enhance the page by adding a wide range of interactive applications such as RSS news feeds or micro-applications such as widgets.

Once the profile is established, the individual can seek out other users in the larger network of the application to create an inner circle of contacts or "friends." Individuals build their network by inviting or "friending" others to link to their page. As an individual links to other profiles, a social network emerges. This inner circle of individuals will then have access to each other's profile spaces to share information and communicate with each other directly. Although individuals usually link to people they know from a specific social network (education, work or shared cause), there are many instances in which people establish connections with individuals they have never met. Boyd & Ellison (2007) note that "participants are not necessarily "networking" or looking to meet new people; instead they are primarily communicating with people who are already a part of their extended social network". As a result, it is very easy for people to have a network of "friends" they will never meet face to face.

There are many different types of social networking applications, but all share the same basic structures. The profile page is usually built upon an existing template that enables the user to modify the profile design by changing the layout or features of the main page. All social network applications provide the ability to set up privacy parameters that determine how access to information will be distributed. If an individual does not want certain "friends" to have access to photos or certain postings, he or she can limit access. Some networks also allow users to moderate the content that is posted on a public communication space. However, many individuals often disregard the use of these features and readily give access to their pages.

Some of the more common communication tools found within a social network include blogs, discussion tools, instant messaging chat, and email. Most social networking sites offer the ability to send online messages privately as email or publicly on what is referred to as a "comment wall." The comment wall can be seen by all of the individual's contacts unless restrictions have been established. Social networks also provide easy tools for creating multimedia products and enable users to share photos, audio, and video. Widgets, RSS feeds and other external tools to gather information can also be integrated within the network to further synchronize communication between other social networking applications. For example, if someone is using Facebook and Twitter to post blog comments, both tools can be integrated so the individual needs to post in only one of the platforms. Individuals can also send documents, music, links and other materials to individuals in their network through shared platforms. It is this dynamic interconnectivity that appeals to many people.

Popular press coverage of these tools tends to focus on the negative outcomes of social networks and their abuse. Numerous articles in educational journals warn parents and teachers about the dangers of social networking sites. Recent crimes linked to some social networking sites have even led to the development of social media watch groups. In response, many school districts restrict the use of social networks in classroom instruction and set up filters to block access to these sites. In some cases, as a result of public outcry, some public libraries have also limited access to these sites. Yet, despite such action, everyday another 60,000 students create a social networking profile (NSBA par 3). Millions more manage multiple social networking sites already. Whether or not instructors are willing to admit it, the mainstream dominance of this Web 2.0 technology has enough indirect force to inevitably forge its way into the classroom

HOW SOCIAL NETWORKS SITES ARE EMERGING IN EDUCATION

According to the 2008 Pew Internet & American Life Project Survey Report, social networks are the fastest growing web sites on the Internet. Just consider the following:

- In 2007, 1 in 4 Americans had a MySpace account.
- 86.6 million adults in the USA are using social networking sites on a weekly basis.
- 98% of college students surveyed use a social networking tool DAILY.
- 51% of students have two or more different social network accounts
- 94% of those students stated that they preferred using their SN tool more than email.

In the last five years, social networking sites have emerged as the primary web spaces for individuals to connect, collaborate, and communicate. Even though students create these accounts initially for social use, they also use these sites for learning. In turn, it is the students, and not the educators, serving as the driving force to integrate social networks into the classroom.

In the 2007 Horizon Report, social networking sites were considered among the most popular emerging technologies in education. Similar research reports from the National School Boards Association (NSBA) and the Pew Internet & American Life Project identified that over 55% of teens had created a social networking profile on MySpace or Facebook for educational purposes.

Since MySpace continues to be popular among teenagers, many colleges and universities have begun creating institutional MySpace sites to provide information about their programs to recruit potential students. As these students move on to college campuses, many of them continue to maintain their MySpace accounts, but also create Facebook accounts.

Facebook still dominates the social networking market for college campuses with over 35 million accounts. Ellison et al (2008) noted in their study that 94% undergraduates at Michigan State University were Facebook users. Such figures are fairly consistent across college campuses. However, Facebook's open enrollment to expand accounts to other users has increased its market share considerably. At this writing, Facebook is the leading social networking application in the global market with more than half of its users off campus.

Although these two social networking sites have the greatest market share, other social networking sites are gaining popularity. LinkedIn, a business oriented social networking tool used to establish professional contacts, has now become the leading social networking site for business and industry. Ning, which lets users customize their social networks and allots much greater control over the design of the space, has gained popularity among open source developers and bloggers. Sites focusing on K-12 education such as ChitChat (http://chitch.at/) and ePals (http://www.epals.com) are popular among administrators, since teachers have more control to secure the environment. Elgg, which appeals to open source users has made a greater impact on colleges and universities that want to host their network on a local server. At present, there are over 200 active social network applications, all of which meet the needs of specific user groups.

In many cases, users have access to multiple social networks. As mentioned before, students with MySpace accounts will often add Facebook accounts when they go to college to maintain their old connections while transitioning into the new environment. As students develop connections in the new social network, they often invite friends from the old network to join as well. This activity then bridges the two networks together. The fact that students can continue their associations with friends from different networks is one of the reasons that the use of social networks is more appealing than email. With institutional email accounts, access is limited to those only affiliated with the institution. In social networks, affiliations are determined by the users. In similar fashion, when Facebook users graduate, they seek out connections through LinkedIn. It is interesting to note that despite the efforts it takes to manage several networks, many users are often reluctant to leave them when they begin new accounts elsewhere.

Another reason for the increased use of social networking applications in education may be due to online instruction, itself. John Sener (2007) suggests that "the growth of enrollment in online education indicates a preference for life online." Discipio (2008) suggests "21st Century learning comes from the combination of innovative pedagogy and a global community with the networking tools that students are using outside the classroom" (11). Students seem to understand that using such tools increases their academic productivity. For this reason alone, educators must begin to reexamine their assessment of social network sites and find ways to integrate these tools into instruction.

EDUCATIONAL USES OF SOCIAL NETWORKS

There are many possibilities for educational applications of social network sites both in and out of the classroom. Some instructors are simply using social networking tools to engage in research where others have begun to integrate social networking applications for blended and fully integrated online instruction. To understand the various educational uses of social networks, the following overview offers discussion and examples of each application.

Research

One of the most common reasons that educators and students are using social network sites in education is for research. Educators and students join social networking sites that enable them to obtain resources, training, and professional development on subjects that interest them. Steve Hargdon's social network site, Classroom 2.0 in Ning has over 9000 members that share information on emerging technologies for teaching and learning. Within the Classroom 2.0 network, there are several sub-groups that focus on specific technologies and educational activities. Individuals participating in these sub-topic groups support one another's research interests through collaboration, resource sharing, and information building. Facebook, MySpace and all of the other social networks have groups on nearly every academic discipline. A social network can conceivably bring together the leading researchers in a given field which can generate important and meaningful discussions that novice participants can benefit from by just observing.

Since many educators are using these tools for research, students also see the value in using social networks for the same reason. Students share notes, help one another with homework, and answer one another's research queries. Research has shown that "one of the most common topics of conversation on the social networking scene is education. The NSBC Report found that "60 percent of students who use social networking talk about education topics online and surprisingly, more than 50 percent talk specifically about schools work." CARMUN (http://www.carmun.com), a social networking application created by Jonathan Edson, offers both undergraduate and graduate students the ability to create research communities to facilitate projects with other students and create global connections. For graduate students, such connections help build future scholarly relationships that are often needed in academe. CARMUN's inclusion of research oriented applications such as citation generators, reference texts, and other bibliographic tools creates an open lab environment for students to work on projects.

Since social networks encourage collaborative writing activities through their communication tools, it is easy to understand why researchers at a distance use these tools to work on writing projects such as grants or white papers. Researchers working on a project together could post it as a draft in a blog and then facilitate discussion of the elements of the proposal or document in various forums to help organize the final writing of the paper or proposal. Meetings regarding the project can easily be conducted through the chat features or in conjunction with another tool such as Skype. The date stamp that is posted along with the documents also makes a record for the documents that are produced. Archiving features and database capabilities also make it easy to retrieve various drafts of a given document. In the end, there is no wait to make copies of the document; everyone has immediate access to it as it is being revised and written.

The Virtual Nuclear Magnetic Resonance Facility (VNMRF) Virtual Science Lab is a social network that enables researchers to use their skills and expertise to analyze data, share results from experiments, and problem solve scientific queries without having to leave their physical labs and institutions. The individual research communities established by the VNMRF social network enable scientists from all over the world to develop subject-specific global research groups which help identify field experts and potential consultants for specialized research projects. The network also provides participants information about ongoing experiments that might have been conducted in isolation. As a result, researchers are able to gain access to results of experiments immediately and build upon the information they receive through the network to conduct additional lab work. In similar fashion, the Social Computing Lab at Rochester Institute of Technology (social.it.rit.edu) is designed to study social media projects. By connecting various researchers through the use of social networks, universities and colleges could save money on travel and other expenses.

In addition to lab facilities, many libraries are also involved with using social networking for research activities. In some cases, chat reference, research services, and other training can be offered to patrons at a distance through the use of social networks. For example, many public libraries are creating social networking sites for their youth services programs to teach children social media literacy and online safety in the use of read-write tools. Social networks can also help expand outreach to patrons who have difficulty coming to the library, but want to participate in library programs. Video of the program can be uploaded or streamed through the site for patrons to review in real-time or at a later date. Patrons can also form reading circles within the social network to discuss books and in the process offer other patrons commentary of various books to read. Librarians can also blog about new materials available to patrons, reference resources, and upcoming events that may be of interest to certain patron groups. Posted research on various queries can also help patrons who may be working on the same projects. By linking these individuals through the social network, librarians can help people find research partners who are doing the same type of work.

Project Management

School districts, academic departments, and various college units use social network sites to work on curricular projects, and link faculty and staff for meetings, professional development training, and other important activities. Instead of having educators sit in face-to-face in meetings, posting materials and documents online through the network enables individuals to work on documents, post information, and respond to inquiries from multiple sites. The time efficiency in using such tools to complete projects can make departments more productive. Social networks can be set up to provide information about events and activities and other important information that educators may need to share with each other. For example, if several educators in a unit need to revise curricular standards, setting up a social network to work on the revisions might be useful especially if unit members cannot meet due to schedule conflicts. The World Association for Online Educators (WAOE) has set up a social network in Ning to work on various group initiatives. The network enables WAOE members from all over the world to connect and engage in various activities that promote the development of international online education projects. For example, members of the group used the site to plan a conference in Second Life. In similar fashion, social networks can be used to develop learning communities for professional development training. Staff who cannot attend the face to face meeting times to participate in the training may be able to access training materials from the social network.

Conferences and pre-conference workshops are also being set up in SNs to archive materials and extend continuous dialogue about sessions, presentations. Kent State University's Learning Community Writing Matters set up a social networking site in Ning to facilitate the Northeast Ohio Writing Center Association Conference. Conference planners initially used the site for organizing the conference, but later invited participants who attended the conference to join the network and continue the conversations that were held at the various conference events. In the end, a networked community developed and now conference participants are still able to interact with one another to share resources and more conference planning. Given the numerous multimedia tools available to stream video and share content, more and more academic institutions may begin to consider the possibilities of using social networks to set up an actual online conference. After setting up accounts in the social network, attendees can interact with each other before, during, and after the conferences. Even if the conference is a face-to-face venue, the inclusion of a social network to continue the conversations offers participants the opportunity to gain many more resources and opportunities for discussion, particularly on the sessions they couldn't attend. Having access to the resources of all the sessions is invaluable to conference attendees on many levels.

Academic Support Services

Academic support services, which include library, computer, and tutoring programs have begun to make use of social network sites to expand outreach and services to students who are not able to take advantage of traditionally based services. For nonresidential students, social networks can be beneficial for establishing a campus connection with students and faculty in their program area. Colleges and universities can establish cohort groups based upon degree programs so students can meet and interact with other individuals (other students, faculty and staff) in the same curricular area.

Social networks can be used to improve retention and recruitment. Ellison et al (2008) found in their study on MSU students that there existed "a positive relationship between certain kinds of Facebook use and...social capital" (23). Social capital which refers to the resources one gains through relationship building has been proven to be a valuable determinant in retaining students. Students that feel "connected" are less likely to drop out of school. Social capital also provides assistance and support, knowledge sharing, and information students may not be able to obtain in the classroom. Students in cohort groups can form study groups and tutor each other on difficult subjects. For students unable to take advantage of traditional on-campus academic support services, online tutoring programs through the use of social networks are an invaluable resource.

In similar fashion, both libraries and computer help desks are offering students academic support through the use of social networking. At the college level, academic libraries can easily build instructional programs through the use of social networks, The University of Kentucky – Open Library Project serves to assist remote access students with resources and library support for research by connecting students to discipline area librarians. Hence, education majors needing assistance with ERIC documents can interact with the Education librarian through the social network in an online chat reference scenario. For computer lab helpdesks, IT departments can blog about network issues and inform students about workshops on emerging technology tools.

Social networks can also be used as portals for academic departments. At the Kent State University Geauga Campus, Mitch Myers is using the social network Ning to set up a science portal for students and faculty involved in science curriculum at the campus. The portal is designed to help students in different science content areas build cohorts in their majors and connect with faculty from the campus's two sites. Hence, a student majoring in Chemistry can connect to a student majoring in Microbiology to work on a collaborative project with a Nursing student. Such internetworking simulates the type of real world exchange that students need to experience to learn how to share and build information products, obtain information from a variety of contacts, and seek assistance from individuals outside their area.

Academic coordinators and faculty in specific departments can post information about course scheduling, upcoming events, department meetings for adjunct faculty, and research opportunities for students. In the portal, students share notes, sell books, and connect to department staff and faculty whereas faculty collaborate in team teaching, peer review of assignments, and research between the two sites. In turn, the science portal helps establish a comprehensive learning community that fosters development of students, staff, and faculty associated with the various science disciplines at the campus.

Student Services

In addition to using social network sites for academic support, many higher education institutions are using social networking technologies as extensions of their student services. Berg, Berquam & Christoph (2007) examined ways in which campus student service units could transform traditional campus activities through the use of social networking tools and outline the following suggestions:

1. **Registration:** Academic program guidelines, course requirements, and faculty information can be posted to offer students details that may assist in schedule planning. Students can connect with advisors, faculty, and other students to ask questions about specific courses.
2. **Advising:** Advisors can post information regarding student services programs, workshops for student support, and information related to academic program deadlines. Information about scholarships, internships, and graduation requirements can be shared.
3. **Counseling:** Administrators can use the social networking site to outline policy and procedures for student conduct. For example, a forum on research ethics can be offered to students and faculty to review university guidelines. Students can ask questions regarding policies regarding grade changes, make-up exams, and other academic issues.
4. **Study Groups and Tutoring:** Social network sites can be used to develop cohort groups in high attrition courses to help with retention. An advisor or faculty can monitor the group to provide support and assistance.
5. **Cohort Groups:** First year students, nontraditional students, and other student groups can establish support groups within the site. Information about student group activities and events could be posted through the site.
6. **Marketing:** In some instances, social networking sites could be used to recruit new students and provide information to parents seeking information about the campus.

Several institutions also build in-house networks to connect teachers, students, and parents. At the University of Pennsylvania, Pennster is a social network created for first year students to meet one another before they begin the semester. At Kent State, the learning community Writing Matters set up a social network to connect writing center student tutors initially from the eight KSU campuses to support one another and share ideas about writing pedagogy. After coordinating an academic conference through the network, the group expanded to inclusion of writing center directors, tutors, and other interested individuals from fifteen institutions in Northeast Ohio. Hence, what began as a network for undergraduate tutors has now grown into a consortium of writing center directors, staff, researchers, and students interested in the field of writing center instruction. Connections such as these benefit individuals engaged in similar university work and serves to foster support and assistance for developing better programs.

Instruction

Educators looking for new teaching tools find the many features of social networks appealing for creating activities that foster collaborative learning. In most cases, educators are using social networks to supplement traditional instruction or to develop new modes of blended learning in the classroom. In fact, since many social networking applications are open source, these tools are not only easy to use, but easy to modify. Educators looking to create unique learning environments for their online teaching style are not hampered by the limitations that some course management systems often present. As fully integrated online learning environments, social networks make it easy to embed multimedia elements to engage students in multimodal activities. One does not need to worry about whether or not the course management tool can manage the upload of a file that is media rich or make all types of modifications in the layout to accommodate the tool's requirements.

In addition, there are many K-12 friendly social network sites specifically geared for classroom instruction. Among them, Imbee (http://www.imbee.com), TIGed (http://www.tiged.org), Think.com (http://www.think.com), Haiku Learning Management system (http://www.haiku.com), and ePals (http://www.ePals.com). These sites are not only free to educator, but offer specific built-in features that enable instructors the ability to control, monitor, and manage all activity that occurs in the use of the network. These sites can be set up as closed networks –made accessible only to those individuals associated with the specific class. In addition, all of these sites have corresponding teacher networks for educators to share lessons or to work on global group projects.

Furthermore, and most importantly, social networks make it easy to teach students digital literacy skills. Liebowitz (2007), who asserts that "knowledge transfer and assimilation foster innovation" believes that social networking sites "increase a student's knowledge by learning from the network members. The outreach to learning not only increases the potential for learning, but for expanding the diversity of learning." Likewise, Discipio (2007) notes that social networks "incorporate innovative pedagogy...that empower students" (10). Students can take their learning beyond the classroom and expand their cross-cultural understanding to develop the skills they will need for the digital marketplace. Through the use of social networks as learning communities, students can work with larger audiences to improve their communication skills, writing abilities, and most importantly, critical thinking through diverse peer to peer learning. Daniel (2008) explains that "in virtual learning communities (such as social networks), learners bring to the discussion, experiences and personal beliefs and values. This implies that related experiences have an impact on how learners contribute to the process of knowledge negotiation and construction." As a result, students become more responsible for their own learning, which is crucial in the development of sustaining lifelong knowledge building.

Since there is little research available on educators using social network sites exclusively for online instruction, it is difficult yet to determine how social networks influence the quality of learning. As more educators begin to teach in these tools, it will be useful to measure the learning outcomes through social network analysis. Until more work is done in this area, research on other collaborative technologies such as wikis and blogs can serve as the foundation for understanding the instructional merits of social network environments. The outreach to learning not only increases the potential for learning, but for expanding the diversity of learning." Using Ning for instruction at Kent State University, educators note greater levels of student-to-student interaction and the development of much more user-generated content. Students in these classes are willing to use different types of communication tools to seek and create information, build learning relationships with each other, and establish a greater sense of community. In several instances, students begin to facilitate discussions on their own by creating forum topics that are related to course content, but are important for them to discuss further. In turn, students are actively involved in their learning.

CONCERNS ABOUT SOLUTIONS FOR USING SOCIAL NETWORKS IN EDUCATION

Despite the fact that social networks have proven to be useful for teaching, learning, research and other educational services, many administrators are still reluctant to make use of such tools at their institution. Many K-12 districts not only block the use of social networking tools, but in some cases have even gone so far as to prevent teachers from connecting with students through social networks. Many school districts have set up filters that block any access to social networks for any purpose. In several states, there is even legislation to consider regulating student-teacher contact on social networking sites external to the school environment. In Missouri, for example a bill is being sponsored to prohibit educators from using social networking accounts that are open to students, but restrict access to parents and administrators. There is a concern that "teachers" should not be "friends" with their students. In similar fashion, many colleges and universities caution faculty of their use of social networks to connect with students outside the classroom environment.

For this reason, it is important to examine each area of concern and discuss possible solutions for educators and administrators to consider.

Site Management

The most common concern that administrators have regarding the use of social network applications for instruction involves site management and control. Since many social network sites are free, controlling content posted on the sites, ensuring that the site adheres to acceptable use policies, and monitoring site activity can be difficult. Free social networking sites also present exposure to advertising messages that may be inconsistent with the institution's mission. Several university administrators also question the social network applications archiving features in terms of privacy and FERPA. Another problem lies in the application's terms of service. In November 2006, Facebook administrators removed Ursuline College's site that was being used for the office of counseling and career services because the college had violated the social network's "terms of service." According to Meegan Cox, Facebook charged that the college had violated "a policy that forbids organizations from creating Web pages on the site" and for "using the site for commercial marketing purposes." The Ohio college had been using the site to provide information about academic programs and events being held at the college. For this reason, it is important that individuals planning on using social network sites for educational projects take the time to review the applications "terms of use" to see what limitations may pose potential problems.

Even though administrators cannot monitor the content on some social networking applications like Facebook and MySpace because they cannot access individual pages, some social network sites such as Ning and ePals provide omniscient control to the site creator. Hence, if a teacher creates a site for class, it is possible to moderate all content posted on the site. Furthermore, most social network developers have begun to create network applications that offer greater levels of security to attract K-12 markets. Elgg's (http://www.elgg.com) educational social networks have safeguards in place to eliminate the dangers found in more open social networks. For example, educators can set up a social network within a social network to monitor all student activity. Educators also have the ability to establish levels of privacy for group and individual work. Yan (2008) cites that "these types of networks give schools the ability to control the level of openness, define permission settings and disallow outsiders who do not have passwords. Elgg offers schools the ability to run and host their own network locally on their own server. Staff can download the software free of charge and have complete control of the code which helps schools customize the tool."

Site management is also problematic because it also takes a great deal of time in terms of the design, development, and delivery. Unlike a course management system that is usually integrated into the university or districts' student information system, a social network is independent. As a result, an educator may have difficulty migrating content from one semester to the next as well as other data such as various student information. Such work can be time consuming and generate problems when students withdraw from the class during the semester. Managing course enrollment may be problematic for instructors with larger classes.

Educators using social networks to teach their classes may also have to obtain special approval for FERPA guidelines to ensure that the tool they are using will secure student information. If a student files a grievance against an instructor as a result of the tool, there may be no support for that instructor because the instructor did not use the college's approved course management system. Hence, an educator may need to monitor all aspects of the site in great detail to avoid any potential problems that may occur. Moderating all activity on the site can be incredibly time consuming, especially if the class size for the course is large or the instructor is teaching several sections of an online course.

Educators who decide to teach with social networks also need to realize that they may be the tech support for their course. IT administrators in the district or at the university may not support technology that is open source or not approved as the primary tool for distributed learning activities. Educators may have to address technical issues on their own when students have problems with the technology.

Criminal Activity

As with every new technology that is popular with young people, social networks are now being blamed for a wide range of negative youth behavior, including serious criminal activities. Recent media cases such as the Megan Meier MySpace incident have prompted many school districts to block access to these sites. When Meier committed suicide after being humiliated by a group of individuals, including adults, on Myspace, there was such a public outcry that several states responded by enacting severe penalties for cyberbullying. (See http://www.cyberbullyalert.com/blog/category/cyber-bullying-law/).

News articles that suggest social network sites are making students violent have prompted K-12 administrators to develop severe punishments for both students and teachers engaged in questionable uses of social network sites. Teachers have been fired for content placed on social network sites, students have been expelled, and state education departments have begun to support strict regulations regarding the use of social networks. The Ohio Teachers' Association sent out a public memo to all members warning them about the use of social networking after several teachers had been accused of inappropriate behavior by an investigation spearheaded by the *Columbus Dispatch* newspaper. In similar fashion other teaching professional groups across the United States have prepared documents advising members about the use of social network sites.

Although there are several cases that support individual rights in the classroom environment, such as Tinker vs. Des Moines, (1969) in which the Supreme Court ruled that teachers do not "shed their constitutional rights...at the schoolhouse gates," recent Court decisions have placed limitations on this precedent as it relates to student rights. In Morse v. Frederick (2007), the Court held that "schools may restrict student speech at school sponsored events, even those events occurring off school grounds." In fact, many school administrators and law enforcement agencies are using the content found on social networks such as Facebook and MySpace as a source of evidence against students engaged in policy violations. At North Carolina State University, citations of alcohol and drug abuse were given to students whose

Facebook pages revealed photos of underage drinking in dormitory rooms. Pennsylvania State University police used Facebook to track down students who rushed the football field after the Penn-Ohio State game. In response, a recent case (December 2008) in Florida has generated a lawsuit by the ACLU suggesting that a student's free speech is protected. According to the ACLU, "students cannot be punished for posting comments online from their home computers criticizing their teachers. The fact that academic institutions are willing to use these tools to punish students, but not to teach them is a great hypocrisy."

Both administrators and educators need to understand that restricting students from using social network sites at schools will not solve the problem of inappropriate behavior such as cyber-bullying or the posting of inappropriate content. The only way we can help our students understand why such activity is problematic is if we show them how to use social media properly. Educators can instruct students on the ethical use of social networking sites and teach students about standards of communication. Discussions can focus on cyberbullying and other inappropriate online behavior to help students learn what to do when they see such activity occur. Students need to develop their social media literacy skills because the workplace of the future demands it. Students will learn about the ethics of electronic communication by participating in activities that demonstrate why it is necessary. Preventing students from using social networks will not teach them how to use these tools appropriately.

For school districts that do allow students to access social networks on-site, there is a concern that students are using these tools to engage in academic misconduct. Since the NSBA Report found that more than 50% of teens are using social networking sites to focus on schoolwork, some educators have become concerned that social networks have become the latest tools for cheating. Students can easily connect to one another to discuss test questions, complete course assignments, and enlist their friends to responses to essay questions. In short, study groups become cheating teams. In March 2008, a student faced 147 academic charges for running an online chemistry study group where classmates could exchange questions and homework tips. Administrators at Ryerson University charged that Chris Avenir's Facebook group was contributing to cheating and other academic misconduct. Other educators have noted that social networks have become new term paper mills, where students find other students to help write research papers and other assignments. Although it may be easier for students to engage in academic misconduct in an online environment, it is incumbent upon educators to develop assignments and projects that limits a student's ability to cheats.

Privacy Issues

Another issue regarding the use of social networking sites involves concerns about securing the privacy of students. In December 2008, Brad Ward, a coordinator for electronic communications at Butler University noted that an unauthorized Facebook group for the Butler Class of 2013 had been created for his university. Trying to find out who created the group, Ward realized that numerous phony Class of 2013 groups were created by the same company, College Prowler. Ward expressed great concern on his blog that the students who had joined these groups shared their contact information with a company and not the actual university or college whose name was associated with the site. Hence, discussion of this incident across blogs and eventually, in the Chronicle of Higher Education raised more questions regarding the privacy issues of social networks on campuses, in turn reaffirming the need to be wary of these tools.

Even though most social networks have improved their privacy features, there is great concern from administrators and educators that the open source nature of these tools does not secure information. Students who do not want their contact information shared across a network may be unwilling to participate in a social network application that requests personal information to establish a profile. Even though Facebook modifications have improved the ability to create privacy features and allows users unprecedented control to determine who can see what information, many educators are still reluctant to use this tool for teaching. After several complaints about Facebook privacy features, Levy (2007) notes that in response to the roll out of a News Feed, Facebook responded "quickly to install privacy controls to let people opt out of the information flow" (46) In fact, Chris Kelly, Facebook's Chief privacy operator has noted that "Facebook is about replicating the social restrictions of the offline world" (46).

For the most part, issues regarding privacy need to be addressed by the institution using the tool. The Communications Decency Act ("CDA") (47 U.S.C. Sec. 230) protects social networking websites from liability with respect to negligence claims based on third-party content published on the website and the consequences stemming from such content. In *Doe v. MySpace, Inc.*, No. 07-50345, 2008 WL 2068064 (5th Cir. May 16, 2008), the plaintiff argued that MySpace negligently failed to implement appropriate technological safeguards to prevent the plaintiff, a 13-year-old, from registering on MySpace. The so-called "Good Samaritan" provision of the CDA sets out, at 47 U.S.C. Sec. 230(c)(1), that "[n]o provider or user of an interactive computer service shall be treated as the publisher or speaker of any information provided by another information content provider." Hence, rather than restricting the use of social networks on site, institutions need to make sense of how they can develop measures to secure the privacy of participants using these tools. The problem is that many administrators simply do not want to take the time to figure out how to ensure student privacy in tools they cannot manage on their own servers. For this reason, educators using social networks for teaching must be very selective of the tools they use. Newer social networks geared specifically toward K-12 use include many more levels of privacy controls. In some cases, there are controls specifically for every individual feature in the tool.

Accessibility Problem

In a review of social networking technologies, AbilityNet, a nonprofit organization, found that most social networking applications were not accessible for people with disabilities. In the findings, none of the sites reviewed would allow login without the identification of a CAPTCHA image. A CAPTCHA image is usually a random display of distorted words or letters which can only be deciphered by people and not by software. "Those unable to interpret the graphic due to vision impairment, dyslexia or learning difficulties are therefore blocked from proceeding any further."

Likewise, the American Federation for the Blind (AFB) fond that "the most serious accessibility issue was the inability to create user accounts on MySpace, Friendster, or Facebook without sighted assistance." As with the study done by AbilityNet, AFB found that "none of the social networking sites offer an audio version—like Google's Blogger now does—or an alternate means of registering for people who are blind. LinkedIn is the only site in the evaluation that did not use a CAPTCHA as part of its registration process."

Cluttered web pages with many links can also complicate use for a person who is blind. The layouts of many social networks include frames and structures that cannot be accessed through the use of a screen reader. While sighted users might quickly scan web pages for the most important information, screen reader users generally have to listen to web pages from start to finish, top to bottom, left to right. Because these sites are free, most of them contain several online ads. Ads make it more cumbersome for screen reader users because they have to scroll down the page, and go through the scattered ads, before they can find what they're looking for. This is especially difficult on Friendster because ads are scattered throughout the pages.

In addition to this problem, most links and photos are not labeled on social network sites. According to the AFB, "unlabeled links cause problems for people using a screen reader because although the screen reader will read the link, it sounds like gibberish." Despite these problems with accessibility, the AFB found that the main features—messaging, adding friends, browsing, editing, and commenting—are accessible. In addition, some social networks enable developers to manipulate the code to adhere to accessible web design guidelines.

DEVELOPING STRATEGIES TO USE SOCIAL NETWORKS

Educators and administrators need to understand that institutional social networking can be managed effectively. Implementation of a tool needs to be conducted in a process that adheres to the institution's acceptable use guidelines. For individual educators using social networks to teach, it is important to find out how other educators have incorporated the tool into their instruction. Doing so first will provide information about classroom management strategies, strengths and weaknesses of using the tool to teach, and additional features that educators can use to make the tool more applicable for the educational environment. Facebook, for example, not only offers specific applications for course set up, but has several groups for educators teaching with the social network. These groups offer useful information and tips on course design and delivery. MySpace offers a network link for institutions to quickly locate each other so that administrators and educators can easily find models for how to set up a site for their institution. Both Elgg and Ning developers are willing to work with academic institutions to help customize the social network for educational use. The very nature of social networking as communities of support makes it easy to find assistance in development of the tools for educational purposes.

For administrators and educators considering the use of social networks in the academic environment, here is a list of guidelines to consider:

1. Know the laws

The Federal Children's Online Privacy Protection Act ("COPPA") which protects the collection of personal information online from children 12 and under has developed new requirements for social network sites that allow individuals 18 and under to create accounts. Among these requirements are the following:

- Continuing to dedicate resources to educate parents and educators on child safety online;
- Using "best efforts" to acknowledge consumer complaints within 24 hours of receipt with a follow-up of the steps taken within 72 hours;
- Implementing a series of operational changes including:
    - "Age locking" to reduce the number of times a user can change their age above or below the 18 year old threshold;
    - Age restrictions on certain website functions that make it harder for adults to contact children such as limiting the ability of users over 18 to search in school sections
    - An image monitoring policy with technology to hash inappropriate images;
    - Limitations on tobacco and alcohol advertisements to those under 18 and 21 respectively;
    - Expanded age specific classifications for events;

- Expanded reporting functionality for violations including a drop down for categories such as pornography, cyberbullying and unauthorized use;
- Enhancing safety tools for members such as the ability to set profiles to private, the ability to block others and requiring those under 18 to affirmatively consent to having reviewed posted safety tips before registration; and
- Enhanced tools for parents such as the ability to remove a child's profile.

It is also important for educators to find out if their state has any specific regulations regarding the use of social network sites. Understanding state legislation for communication technologies is important because it helps administrators develop policies for the use of these tools.

2. Establish a policy for use

After review of the existing laws regarding social network sites or communication technologies, it is important for administrators to review their institution's existing acceptable use policies. All too often, many college and university acceptable use policies have not been updated to include discussion of collaborative and social media communication technologies. Most policies simply list guidelines for email use.

If the tools are used for institutional purposes such as marketing or information sharing, then it is incumbent upon administrators to determine detailed policy guidelines for the use of these tools for these purposes. These guidelines should determine and define what type of activities can be conducted on the sites, who will monitor site activity, and what disciplinary actions will be taken should users of the site violate policies. Failure to detail every aspect leaves room for interpretation that can lead to serious problems should an incident of abuse occur. It is also important to determine authority control and protocols regarding the management of such sites. Who will be responsible for removing individuals from the network? Can a student be dismissed for engaging in illegal activity on the network? Who will monitor teacher and faculty use of these tools? These questions and more should be discussed to develop a strategic policy regarding the use of social networks at the school or campus.

Interestingly, many social networks already have such policies written out which could serve as models for administrators. Several social networks related to education also have groups that discuss such issues on a regular basis. In many cases, one can use the network to find assistance in developing the policy.

3. Evaluate tools carefully (before, during, and after)

Administrators and educators should establish criteria for review to ensure the social network application that they choose best fits the purpose for which it will be used. Educators groups in the various social networks can offer first hand information regarding the use of the tool in their practice. By comparing the comments and testing the tools, educators can determine which tool will work best for them. The fact that several tools are specifically geared toward K-12 makes it easier to work with developers on modifying the tools to meet the needs of the district.

It is recommended that educators actually use the tools to determine their strengths and weaknesses for the purpose for which they will be needed. For example, if someone is just using a social network for academic research, they may not be as concerned about securing privacy in the network as someone who is planning to teach with a social network application. Knowing and understanding the terms of use agreements in various social network applications is also essential. Some social network applications do not allow business ventures to take place on their tool. For example, certain social network applications prohibit the selling of merchandise through the tool. Universities trying to sell sweatshirts and other school merchandise may lose their accounts because they are using the tool for business purposes.

4. Teach students how to use social networking tools properly

Whether or not administrators or educators decide to use social networks in the classroom as teaching tools, it is important that we develop strategies to educate students how to use these tools effectively. Carter et. al. (2007) believes that "it is incumbent upon those in the teaching profession who are informed to share recent thinking about the conscientious use of technology, about the negative consequences of using technology, and about personal freedoms and choices" during their discussions with students (685). Educators involved in every discipline can make time to discuss these topics when they discuss ethical standards in using technology for research. Reinforcing proper use of social networks is a school wide (campus wide) endeavor.

Eberhardt (2007) outlines the following strategies to help students use social networks:

a. Educate incoming students about the advantages and disadvantages of online social networking through printed materials, online resources, and orientation programs, first year experiences courses, and other relevant means.
b. Train student leaders to promote diverse learning and developmental benefits of online social networks.
c. Host campus programs that engage students in discussions about the roles that online networking plays in their life, offering concrete examples of how they can facilitate their virtual connections.
d. Distribute materials to warn students about the potential dangers of displaying some information online.
e. Discuss with students the negative images that their profiles and groups can generate, and inform them of the consequences that these portrayals could have ontheir campus involvement or future professional life.
f. Initiate conversations with colleagues about how departments can integrate the use of social networks to connect with students.
g. As educators, create profiles that serve as models for appropriate online behavior.
h. Research student use of online social networks to address issues before they become problems.

5. Conduct assessments

Educators using social networks should take the time to conduct assessments of the tool on several levels. First of all, a general technical assessment should be done to determine if the tool is effective in terms of its function. Secondly, for educators using the tool to teach, it is important to develop assessments of the tool in terms of learning. Both administrators and educators should evaluate the tool for its features and technical support. Since many tools are not supported by local IT staff, it is important that the tool developers be accessible. Although most social network tools have help FAQs and other resource guides to assist in the development of the tool, as with any technology application, some help desks are better than others. Technical support for social networks should always be evaluated.

FUTURE DIRECTIONS REGARDING SOCIAL NETWORKING APPLCIATIONS IN EDUCATION

As the use of social networking sites continues to dominate the Internet in terms of applications, it is apparent that such sites are not a passing trend as many critics would like to suggest. Some of the areas that will need further development include:

- Improved accessible design for users with special needs
- Better archiving and database features to improve search strategies and information organization within the tool
- Layouts for mobile devices to improve access and use.
- Improved features to enhance more seamless interconnectivity among other social media tools
- Additional features that incorporate Web 3.0 applications

It is likely that as educators begin to use social network tools in the classroom to supplement instruction and for blended learning, social network developers will begin to develop more course management features to integrate into the tool to create better classroom environments. For example, some social network tools do not offer features to build grade books within their system. Although some networks such as LinkedIn may not desire to include such elements in their tool design, developers wanting to improve their market share in the educational arena will begin to develop more course related elements. Facebook has begun to do this with various applications specifically for courses. In addition, Blakey (2007) reports that at Stanford University, there is a course on Facebook in which students are working on such applications. "The ten-week course meets once a week for three hours and requires students to build two Facebook applications in three-person teams"

Social networks must address their accessibility issues if these tools are to be used in education. Developers must provide features that enable users with special needs to generate content and create profiles through the use of assistive technologies. Tools that enable users to modify the content so that a screen reader can decipher it must be easily integrated into the design. For example, just the simple modification of giving users the ability to resize the default text size on the site would be useful to individuals with visual impairments. Likewise, users should be able to add content in a number of ways. The social network that develops a system in which speech-to-text content creation can occur will no doubt increase its users.

Other trends will be determined by the inclusion of other social media and Web 3.0 tools. Individuals overburdened with too many accounts want to maintain "one-stop" type of systems in which all of their accounts are integrated into one feed. Social networks unable to build inter-connectivity to other social networking applications will be replaced by the systems that do. For example, Ning has begun development to include a wiki feature within the tool for users that do not want to use blogs. Additional tools to enhance video delivery and improve the use of audio will also be improved.

In addition to improved development, it is possible that social network research will increase with specific focus on education applications. Social network analysis will begin to examine how social capital occurs in an online social network as opposed t a face to face social network. Results of these studies will no doubt impact the use of social networks for teaching and learning.

CONCLUSION

George Lukacs argues "our knowledge is not only personal; it is also participant." If we accept this idea, then we need to reexamine our attitudes about using social media to teach our students. According to ISTE's National Educational Standards for Students: the Next Generation, students need to develop skills in the following areas:

1. Creativity and Innovation
2. Communication and Collaboration
3. Research and Information Fluency

4. Critical Thinking, Problem-Solving & Decision-Making
5. Digital Citizenship
6. Technology Operations and Concepts

Given the existing research on collaborative media tools, there is little doubt that social network applications offer the types of digital environments that foster development of all these skills. With guidance from teachers, students can learn how to engage in participant web technologies to collaborate and create digital products. Students can develop their social media literacy skills in a safe environment that is carefully managed and monitored. They can learn about the ethics of generating content and find ways to be creative in their expression through the presentation of multi-modal artifacts. They can learn to become digital global citizens which is crucial for tomorrow's global marketplace.

One of the best practices in education involves connecting learning to real world situations. Preventing students from accessing social networks for learning and collaborative work will not help them learn how to use these tools properly in different contexts. Engagement through the use of such tools prompts innovative inquiry that leads to the development of critical thinking, resource building, and user-generated content which are needed skills in today's knowledge driven economies. Educators have a unique opportunity to bridge gaps in their instructional practice by using tools that are valued by their students. One of the most important elements in teaching involves making students feel secure in their learning environment. Since many of our students are comfortable in the use of social networks, it makes great sense to meet them where they feel most at ease. Educators need to reexamine their criticism of social networks and instead explore ways in which they can leverage these tools to impact student learning. If the ultimate goal is to help our students understand how to interact in our emerging online culture, then it is pertinent that we provide them environments in which they can learn how to communicate, collaborate, and generate knowledge through a social network.

REFERENCES

AbilityNet. (2008, January 18). Social networking sites lock out disabled users. Retrieved January 31, 2009, from http://www.abilitynet.org.uk/enation85

American Federation for the Blind. (2008). Are social networking sites accessible to people with vision loss? Retrieved from January 31, 2009, from http://www.afb.org/Section.asp?SectionID=57&TopicID=167&DocumentID=3153

Benson, H. C. (2000). *Socratic Wisdom.* New York: Oxford University Press.

Berg, J., Berquam, L., & Christoph, K. (2007, March/April). Social networking technologies: A poke for campus service. *EDUCAUSE Review*, 32–42.

Blakely, L. (2008). I'm majoring in facebook, how about you? Retrieved Janurary 31, 2009, from http://money.cnn.com/2007/10/08/magazines/fortune/blakely_facebook.fortune/index.htm

Boyd, D. M., & Ellison, N. (2007). Social network sites: Definition, history, and scholarship. *Journal of Computer-Mediated Communication, 13*(1), article 11. Retrieved January 31, 2009, from http://jcmc.indiana.edu/vol13/issue1/boyd.ellison.html

Brown, L. (2008, March 6). Student faces facebook consequences. *The Toronto Star.* Retrieved January 31, 2009, from http://www.thestar.com/News/GTA/article/309855

Carnevale, D. (2006). College tries to be cool but runs afoul of facebook. *The Chronicle of Higher Education, 54*(4), 67.

Carpenter, S. (2008). CDA protects Myspace from underage user's negligence claim. Retrieved January 31, 2009, from http://privacylaw.proskauer.com/tags/social-networking/

Carter, H., Fougler, T., & Ewbank, A. D. (2008, May). Have you googled your teacher lately: Teachers' use of social network sites. *Phi Delta Kappan*, 681–685.

Chin, G., Myers, J., & Hoyt, D. (2002). Social networks in the virtual science laboratory. *Communications of the ACM, 45*(8), 87–92. doi:10.1145/545151.545156

Discipio, T. (2008, September/October). Adapting social networking to address 21st century skills. *Multimedia & Internet @Schools. 15*(5), 10-11.

Eberhardt, D. (2007, September/October). Facing up to Facebook. *About Campus*, 18–26. doi:10.1002/abc.219

Ellison, N., Steinfeld, C., & Lampe, C. (2008). The benefits of Facebook friends: Social capital and college students' use of online social network sites. *Journal of Computer Mediated Communication, 12*(4). Retrieved January 31, 2009, from http://jcmc.indiana.edu/vol12/issue4/ellison.html

Felix, K. (2008, September/October). AASL study shows schools accept social networking. *Multimedia & Internet @Schools, 15*(5), 8.

Hensler, B. (2008). ACLU sues to protect Broward student's free speech in a Web 2.0 world. ACLU. Retrieved January 31, 2009, from http://www.aclufl.org/

International Society for Technology in Education. (2008). National Educational Technology Standards for Students: The Next Generation.

Karrar, T. (2007). Facebook as a learning platform. Retrieved from http://elearni200715ngtech.blogspot.com/2007/10/facebook-as-learning-platform.html

Levy, S. (2007, August 27). The Facebook effect. *Newsweek*. 8/9, 40-46.

Liebowitz, J. (2007). *Social networking: The essence of innovation*. Lanham, MD: The Scarecrow Press.

Morse v Frederick 127 S. Ct 2818 (2007)

National School Boards Association. (2007). Creating and connecting: Research and guidelines on online social and educational networking. Retrieved January 31, 2009, from http://www.nsba.org/site/docs/41400/41340.pdf

Salaway, G., & Caruso, J. B. (2007). The ECAR Study of undergraduate students and information technology. Boulder, CO: Educause Center for Applied research.

Sener, J. (2007). In search of student generated content in online education. e-mentor, *4*(21). Retrieved from http://E-mentor.edu.pl/org

Use of social network websites in investigations. Wikipedia Retrieved January 31, 2009 from http://en.wikipedia.org/wiki/Use_of_social.netwrok_websites_in_investigations

Ward, B. (2008). Blog post title? *Squaredpeg.com* Blog. Retrieved January 31, 2009, from http://squaredpeg.com/index.php/2008/12/18/facebook-pay-attention/

Yan, J. (2008). Social technology as a new medium in the classroom. *The New England Journal of Higher Education,* Winter 27-30 22:4.

Chapter 15
The Integration of Social Networking in Creating Collaborative Partnerships in Education

Larry S. Tinnerman
Indiana State University, USA

James Johnson
Indiana State University, USA

ABSTRACT

Technological communication advancements in recent years, including, but not limited to, the Internet, cell phones, PDAs and texting, have changed communication, accessing information, and doing business. Unfortunately, education has often lagged behind in the effective implementation of these technological advances. This chapter examines one technological development that has the potential to change the higher educational landscape. The use of online social networking tools can be used to help establish connections student to student, student to faculty, faculty to student and faculty to faculty. These tools can be used to encourage scholarly collaboration in a constructivist manner that builds upon the social learning theories of Albert Bandura and Lev Vygotski.

INTRODUCTION

'There will be no social networking during school hours' are words that may be heard echoing down the halls of too many public schools across this nation. Each year new teachers leave the hallowed halls of higher education with a fresh optimism about the future and a backpack filled with new technology-based teaching pedagogy. Within weeks, their attempts to implement these skills will often be met with the limiting attitudes that began this section. The fact that public education is one of the most conservative entities on the planet makes change slow at best and impossible at worst. The fact is the world is changing. The way that people, particularly young people, communicate, collaborate and learn is evolving at an increasingly rapid pace while monolithic educational systems are falling further behind day by day.

DOI: 10.4018/978-1-61692-854-4.ch015

In the genesis of social, economic, educational, or technological change … there are often two major forces at play, limiters and drivers. Limiter forces are often those elements that tend to slow or restrict the progress of change, while driver forces have the general effect of accelerating change. One unique aspect of both limiters and drivers is that they have the ability to reverse roles over time. As we look at the various technical innovations emerging in classroom pedagogy, we will consider the impact of both drivers and limiters and their versatile nature.

By federal regulation, all public schools in this nation employ filters on their networks. The motivation behind these filters is quite sound. Network administrators and school administration take the role of network security very seriously. However, these security precautions usually reach beyond the realm of data and information in an attempt to assure the safety of student users. The school interprets this responsibility as the power to limit student access to potentially dubious entities and materials. However, in the quest to filter out the "undesirable", most network administrators have limited access to virtually all-possible avenues of social collaboration. Blocked areas include social networking sites, even those whose prime focus is that of education, blog sites, discussion forums, external email sites, and even some basic internet sites that contain streaming media. This action is often reactionary in nature and the secondary consequences are rarely considered.

Research is hinting at a change in the manner in which people process information. The older generation (40 plus) has been referred by Prensky (2001) as digital immigrants. This designation indicated that the older generation lacked the technology emergence that members of the younger generation seemed to enjoy from birth. It was thought that the ease with which people could access technology would have a profound effect on their willingness to adopt new uses of said technology. However, as the tech bubble has continued to expand, all Americans are touched one way or another by this revolution. One example is the use of cell phones and texting. The American Psychological Association may be well advised to consider the inclusion of a new diagnosis in the DSM desk reference. The may be classified as "Technology Withdrawal Anxiety Syndrome". What science is finding is that people, particularly the younger generation, are somehow tied to their technology in a very real manner. The situation alludes to the fact that people have become dependent upon technology for communication, scheduling and information retrieval. Where once an individual had to make a trip to the library or consult the all knowing encyclopedia for their source of information, today's citizen is just a few clicks away from a source of information, news, stocks, blogs, podcasts, live feeds, recipes... the list just goes on and on. In addition, rather than waiting until one gets home to make a phone call, people make multiple calls to individuals, often in the same day or even the same hour. Parents appear to be in constant contact with their college students and vice versa. All this instant technology has caused people to expect instant gratification in regards to any situation that may arise in life. What is interesting is that there even appears to be a change in how individuals process and distribute information. Due to limited resources, individuals of the older generation gathered information using the "Expert" model, which employed a broadcast system. School classrooms were generally lecture format where the expert broadcast information to the students. Entertainment was largely movies and limited TV choices where entertainment was broadcast to the audience. It was not uncommon for a family spending "quality time" together as meaning watching a TV program or movie. The dynamic change that has occurred in today's culture is more akin to a "collective" mentality. Today, individuals gather information from a wide variety of sources and individuals. The role of the expert has been diminished in many ways being often replaced by YouTube and other media outlets. Cable news is available 24 hours a day and even channels like ESPN provide simultaneous feeds of information around the clock. Today's adolescent would laugh at the idea of quality time with family being spent watching a television set. Even if the individual is watching the TV, they are often simultaneously texting, chatting or blogging in a greater network of communication and information exchange. The impact of this change upon education is profound! Students are asked to leave their collective social network behind for seven hours each day and subject themselves to a largely broadcast environment dominated by "experts". They feel cut off from what they view as the real source of new information and therefore often interpret school as out of touch or irrelevant. The challenge for educators is to understand this social change and to develop pedagogy that best integrates this new form of learning into the classroom. Alas, however, the dynamics of today's school environments are often restrictive and force new teachers to comply with what are often outdated practices.

While many educators acknowledge the rapid change that is happening in a global society, few steps are taken to address these dynamics. With such significant changes come shifts in the roles of schools and teachers and their redefinition of the primary responsibility to educate students. In this chapter, an examination will be conducted of how some of these changes are manifesting themselves each day in the nation's schools. We will particularly examine the major shift in the communication and learning styles of today's student population. Finally, using series of case studies we will see how an increasing number of resilient classroom teachers are pushing educational boundaries by introducing a new set of pedagogical tools into the modern classroom. Some of these tools include Web 2.0, Blogs, Digital Back Channeling, Twitter and Chat, WIKI's, Social networking sites such as FaceBook, Ning, and MySpace and a more complete integration of technology in a meaningful way into the classroom. Some of the obstacles and potential risks these tools may present and how various teachers confront these issues will be discussed.

BACKGROUND

Taking Advantage of Changes in the Way Students Communicate: Using Social Networking to Create Collaborative Partnerships

A definite change is taking place on campuses around this country. The change is happening even if educational institutions choose to ignore it. Research is hinting at a change in which people process information. This change is referenced in the book titled Millennials Rising: The Next Great Generation by Neil Howe. The older generation (X'ers) was referred to by Prensky (2001) as digital immigrants. This designation indicated that the older generation lacked the technology emergence that members of the younger generation (Millenials) seemed to enjoy from birth. It was thought that the ease with which people could access technology would have a profound effect on their willingness to adopt new uses of said technology.

In recent news events, the words Twitter, Blog, and Social Networking are becoming household terms as people in repressive countries try to tell their stories to the rest of the world. One also becomes aware of the great propaganda danger as various elements try to control the flow of this information. Verification becomes increasingly critical, yet at the same time, more difficult to accomplish. The control of information becomes an important tool in shaping opinion and policy. Students are often the key recipients of this information overflow and therefore are in the greatest need of the skills to analyze the quality of the message. This becomes a critical skill that must be taught, but is sadly often overlooked. Using social networking tools, educators have a unique ability to facilitate an open discussion surrounding these issues.

Students in the current generation, the Net Generation, are characterized as multi-askers who favor graphics over text, who communicate with equal ease in person and online, who expect instantaneous responses, and who prefer Google to the library. But though they may never need to consult an instruction manual for an electronic gadget, their comfort with technology may not be synonymous with competency (Oblinger & Hawkins, 2005).

Social Learning Theory posits that people learn from one another, via observation, imitation, and modeling. The theory has often been called a bridge between behaviorist and cognitive learning theories because it encompasses attention, memory, and motivation (Bandura, 1986, 1997; Vygotsky, 1978).

The following sections will present a series of case studies that highlight how social networking is being used to facilitate communication, collaboration and cooperation between university faculty, students, emeriti faculty and university graduates. Some of these cases encountered various obstacles, which will be discussed and analyzed. As the cases are presented, the reader is asked to keep in mind those elements that present themselves as limiters and those can be categorized as drivers.

Technology and Communication: From Cave Drawings to Books and Beyond

Available technology has always dictated the manner in which individuals and societies have shared information and knowledge. In the early days of mankind, the technology was limited and the use of storytelling while sitting around a tribal campfire was the main source of communication. Information was passed on by word of mouth from one individual to another. While the population was small and extremely local, this form of communication met most of the societies needs. As the hunters and gatherers became more diffused in their location, inventive methods of communication at greater distances were developed. Sticks with notches or carvings that conveyed an agreed upon meaning were used to increase communication. The use of drums also was used in communication. As the society grew, so did the need for more refined means of communication. Iconic drawings on cave walls and finally rolls of bark started to tell the stories that were often told around the tribal fires. Now the stories began to take on a life and consistency that exceeded the life of the story teller. These early graphic representations were the precursor to the written language. At a later point in history, a formal alphabet began to evolve from the iconic pictographs and eventually a kind of syntax. New technology emerged in the form of papyrus scrolls inscribed with inked text. The role of 'scribe' became an important position in the culture. The job of the scribe was to record the important stories and information of the culture so that it may be preserved for future generations. It was during this time that this new method of communication began to accelerate technological advancement. Discoveries could now be passed on from one individual to another. This permitted early scholars to build upon the work of their predecessors without having to start from the very beginning each time. Information and knowledge began to flourish. The written word spawned a technological revolution. Control of the information recorded by scribes, first on scrolls and later in books were held in high regard, but also protected by the elite members of society. The vast majority of society still relied on the spoken word and storytelling to pass on the important aspects of the society. This was all about to change with the invention of the printing press. It is not coincidental that the first item to be printed was something that was considered of great value to the society, The Bible. As books and the written word became more accessible to the common man and woman, the importance of education also became valued. Literacy education was recognized to be the key to increased intellectual freedom and a social status. Governments and social elite began to recognize the power of this medium and struggled to control the flow of information, granting access to some and denying it to others.

In all these historical examples we can find both drivers and limiters. The need to communicate and share information from the location of a new hunting ground to the religious printing of the Gutenberg Bible are all driven by a desire to share and consume information. Where the stories around the campfire started to prove to be ineffective, adaptations and innovation in communication methods were explored and perfected. One of the limiters at each stage of development involved technology. And yet, this very limiter of technology became the stimulus to develop new technologies. In so doing, the limiter became the driver. When examining the history of communication one of the most profound observations has to do with the pace of communication evolution. From 3500 BC until 1455 AD, there was moderate change in the manner and pace of information communication. An explosion relative to the previous period occurred following the invention of the printing press in 1455. Then in 1835, advancements began to accelerate with the harnessing of electricity as a mode of communication. Between 1835 and 1925, less than 100 years in length, mankind had advanced more than the previous 3000 years and now was able to transmit information through the airwaves. This rapid evolution continued with the invention of the microprocessor and the development of communication networks like the Internet and cell phones. What may have been unrecognized at this time was that with technological advancement, there might also have been changes in the fundamental manner in which humans gather and process information. Between 1985 to the present day, more information has been stored and transmitted than the previous 3500 years. This pace is continuing to accelerate at an incredible rate (Oslin, 1992).

SOCIAL NETWORKING: A DEFINITION

(Boyd & Ellison, 2007) defines a social networking site as "web-based services that allow individuals to (1) construct a public or semi-public profile within a bounded system, (2) articulate a list of other users with whom they share a connection, and (3) view and transverse their list of connections and those made by others within the system. The nature and nomenclature of these connections may vary from site to site".

To better understand the properties of a social network, one must understand recent evolutions in the Internet itself. Prior to 2003, the Internet was referred to as Web 1.0. Since 2005, the Internet has been using technology known as Web 2.0. There has been a fundamental shift in how the Internet is accessed and utilized.

One of the biggest changes that can be observed has to do with the flow of information. In the early days of the World Wide Web, experts using highly trained technicians and web programmers who knew the secret language of the Internet prepared content. The primary mode of access was to read a web page. The primary unit of content was, in fact, the web page, which was prepared by web designers. There was very little interaction outside of email, so the web was classified as static. As mentioned before, web designers who posted content onto the various web pages through a standardized web browser who knew how to translate the code generated the main vehicle of access. Everything was hosted and client based as all the WebPages were stored and offered through a centralized web server. Content was created by, posted by, and updated by a small group of web coders who spoke the cryptic language of the Internet. These Internet content 'gate keepers' were lovingly know as "geeks" (Heer & Boyd, 2005).

In 2003, a subtle change started to take place in the manner in which individuals gathered and processed information. Where, before, in what is now called the Web 1.0 era of the internet, information was provided by a few to the many, a new protocol began to develop referred to as Web 2.0. This new system was based on the concept of the many to the many. The idea was to have the users of the Internet take a more active role in its development and evolution. Users were encouraged, by a host of new Internet tools, to write and contribute. Everyone had something to say, and the sheer numbers served as a kind of quality control mechanism. A perfect example of this is Wikipedia. Individuals post information regarding various topics. They in fact become the experts. The site becomes self-regulating in so subsequent posters correct much as inaccurate information that is posted very quickly. In the academic world, Wikipedia may certainly not be considered an authoritative source, but increasingly it is becoming a place to start to find authoritative sources. Increasingly, posters are beginning to cite the sources of information contributed. What Wikipedia represents in Web 2.0 is fundamental changes in the way people use the web. It is now more dynamic and able to adjust to meet the needs of the users (Heer & Boyd, 2005). Everyone is now able to contribute. Blogs, Twitter tweets, and wikis are all examples of these social networking and collaboration tools.

Now society is poised on the edge of another evolution in Internet technology. While academic research is striving to keep up with current trends, many of the trade magazines can give us insight into what is on the horizon. There is now discussion of the emergence of Web 3.0.

*Some Internet experts believe the next generation of the Web–***Web 3.0***–will make tasks like your search for movies and food faster and easier. Instead of multiple searches, you might type a complex sentence or two in your Web 3.0 browser, and the Web will do the rest. In our example, you could type, "I want to see a funny movie and then eat at a good Mexican restaurant. What are my options?" The Web 3.0 browser will analyze your response, search the Internet for all possible answers, and then organize the results for you. (Strickland, 2008)*

Where are we Going with Technology?

In 1957, Marshall McLuhan, a noted educational futurist stated the following:

It's natural today to speak of "audio and visual aids" to teaching, for we still think of the book as the norm, of other media as incidental. We also think of the new media–press, radio, movies, TV–as MASS MEDIA & think of the book as an individualistic form. Individualistic because it isolated the reader in silence & helped create the Western "I." Yet it was the first product of mass production.

A great deal has happened since 1957, and yet the question remains the same. Is the educational establishment still trying to hold on to the old paradigm, which is centered on the factory model of mass production? Mass production's premise is that manufacturers create a product where one size fits all and everything is interchangeable. Much educational technology of today is just layered onto the old skeleton of educational ideology, and brings to fore the question, "Is this the best use of this technology". Education, for centuries, has been based on a largely oral tradition. Books are simply a visual aide to that oral tradition (McLuhan, 1957). McLuhan, (1957) states that: "Today in our cities, most learning occurs outside the classroom. The sheer quantity of information conveyed by press-mags-film-TV-radio far exceeds the quantity of information conveyed by school instruction & texts". Can this idea be any truer today than it was in 1957?

A relevant aspect of this discussion comes from the videotape titled Paradigm Pioneers (Barker, 1993), which stated that when there is a paradigm shift, it is necessary to abandon everything from the previous paradigm. As we look around our global culture in business and industry, we find that companies that are integrating technology are doing just that. Before the.com boom of the 1990's, business being conducted online was a pipe dream. The revolutionaries that founded eBay, Amazon and the like were so successful because they chose to create their own paradigm. Education, however, which is mired in tradition and tenure, is very slow to change, let alone abandon anything that is perceived to be working. Much of technology in the classroom is just doing the same old, same old with new tools.

Educators propound reforms, but schools remain the same. Without material agency, new methods fail. A scheme captures the educational imagination–spokes-people think it out, the daring to try it, researchers document its effects and the committed demand its adoption. Thus, the idea diffuses from various centers–but then, sporadically, resistance builds, enthusiasm falters, influence weakens; ineluctably, distinctive practices gravitate back to the norm. Pedagogical weathering soon makes the new shingles indistinguishable from the old (McClintock, 1992).

If educators expand their vision, technology offers forward thinking constructivist teachers a means to achieve truly new and exciting ways to implement learning in and out of the classroom. Several myths that are widely accepted by many educators limit the implementation of new technological thinking.

First, the school building, in traditional thought, is simply a space where teaching takes place. It is the location of learning. Often times there are a mixing of the ideas of schooling and learning. Even field trips are linked to a time and a place making formal learning bound to these constraints. Social networking belies this notion. Recent events on the world stage show the power of information and images emerging from repressive countries. Before governments sent troops, now they send cameras. Secondly, the school often promotes the idea, if not intentionally, that real learning occurs on a schedule from about 7:30 AM to 3:30 PM for nine and a half months out of the year. This unspoken idea binds both teachers and students to the fallacious concept that anything that is learned outside of the curriculum is irrelevant. The No Child Left Behind Act only tends to reinforce this notion. This unspoken idea tends to isolate the community and the home environment from the school. Thirdly, all relevant teaching is performed only by certified, highly qualified teachers, making many classrooms resistant to the infusion of community resources and input.

Technology, particularly technology utilizing social networking tools, can shatter all these myths. The scope of learning that can be accomplished using this new form of communication can be mind shattering. Communication and information is present 24 hours a day, 7 days a week. It comes in the forms of television, media, computers, the Internet, applications, books on tape, E-Books, CD's ... the list continues. The important fact is that none of these things are the sole possession of the classroom or the teacher. They are present in the community, in most homes, in public libraries and can even be found in public areas such as bookstores and cyber cafes. Society, and particularly our students, is, at all levels immersed in technology. If we only limit our discussion to the use and availability of computers in the classroom, we fall victim to the old paradigm of thought discussed at the beginning of this section. While one cannot argue the availability of computers in the classrooms has a profound impact upon learning, there is a larger question that needs to be answered, that being, with current technology, are traditional classrooms having a negative impact on learning?

For a true paradigm shift to occur, the schools of the future must embrace, coordinate and utilize all the forms of technology available from computers to video records to books on tapes and beyond. Innovative thinking requires that we take the basic theories of learning and think of them in terms of technologies implementation. There is, however, a broader problem that is often overlooked. Most educational planners are digital immigrants having not grown up with computers (Prensky, 2001). This has created a huge gap between educators and their students who are digital natives having always had the Internet and computers (Prensky, 2001). Our students, regardless of race, socioeconomic status or class are immersed in technology. They have at their hands a limitless quantity of information. As educators, we must utilize this strength within all of our students and not merely limit it to what can be found in the school building or inflexible curriculum. One attribute of the current generation is their ability and, in some cases, need to communicate at will. This quality can both be a strength and a weakness. If educators choose to cultivate this evolving quality, they are presented a unique opportunity to refine an educationally productive tool. The technology/communication paradigm shift forces us to rethink how we teach and embrace the full capacity of what these changes bring. We must educate our students to be the future pioneers in business, industry and education, not just the caretakers of the old. Future educators must design a plan to educate future students using technology as the vehicle for teaching, not just an add-on component. Future curricula must integrate not only computers, which are available either in the students' homes, the public libraries or various educational cyber cafes around the area, but must also include the utilization of all resources in the community. These resources can include families, business and industry, public and private institutions, media of all types and all available technology including cell phones, CD's, DVD's, PDA's, Computers and Software. Future educational planners must be prepared to let go of many of the traditional preconceptions of how schools should be run. Based on the premise of basic learning theory they must strive to create new paradigms for educating students. Schools must begin to shift from their roles as merely dispensers of knowledge to centers aimed at the coordination and integration of information in a spirit of scholarly collaboration.

WEB 2.0 SOCIAL NETWORKING TOOLS EXPLORED

Social Networking Sites

Social networking sites have been one of the fastest growing phenomena on the Internet (Table 1). Some such sites, such as facebook.com and myspace.com boast international membership numbers approaching that of small countries. The tools associated with these sites are used by individuals to find jobs, collaborate on various projects, combine common interests and provide a forum of both creative and non-creative endeavors. They are moving us form an I/me social consciousness to a more we/us perspective. In following paragraphs, we will examine some of the various tools found in these social networking sites.

A Case Study: Scholars Collaborative Partnership

Entry into positions of higher education is becoming an increasing competitive undertaking. Students finishing their doctoral work should also have taken the opportunity to begin their professional portfolio in scholarly publication. Employers often determine the potential for scholarly activity on the part of the applicant through the use of portfolios. It has been observed that many students leave their program of study with only their dissertation in hand. During the graduate

Table 1. Top 12 social networks re-rank (ranked by monthly visits, Jan 2009)

Rank	Site	Unique Visits	Monthly Visits	Previous Rank
1	facebook.com	68,557,534	1,191,373,339	2
2	myspace.com	58,555,800	810,153,536	1
3	twitter.com	5,979,052	54,218,731	22
4	flixster.com	7,645,423	53,389,974	16
5	linkedin.com	11,274,160	42,744,438	9
6	tagges.com	4,448,915	39,630,927	10
7	classmates.com	17,296,524	35,219,210	3
8	myyearbook.com	3,312,898	33,121,821	4
9	livejournal.com	4,720,720	24,221,354	6
10	Imeem.com	9,047,491	22,993,608	13
11	reunion.com	13,704,990	20,278,100	11
12	ning.com	5,673,549	19,511,682	23

Source: complete.com (2009)

years exists an excellent opportunity to present at conferences, publish; collaborate with faculty in publication and research. Many graduate students do not take advantage of this opportunity nor do they realize the necessity of a research agenda when they apply for higher education jobs. One of the main issues revolves around a kind of detachment from the university community experienced by many graduate students. As most graduate students are already employed and have family responsibilities, there is often little opportunity to explore scholarly possibilities that exist at the university. In many cases, these graduate students are only familiar with those faculty members who actually teach their particular classes. This isolation is often compounded when the graduate student is also an international student.

In the spring semester of 2009 at Indiana State University, a social networking site titled *The Collaborative Scholars Partnership* was established using Ning: www.ning.com. This social network strove to connect both graduate students and university faculty. Here, students could establish collaborative connections with each other and with faculty members at the university, many of whom were unknown to these students. In addition, the members were enrolled as members of a list serve which broadcasts information to their email address as to upcoming conference opportunities; grant funding opportunities, calls for manuscripts and calls for journal articles. The space also established a location for Blogging where individuals discussed issues and topics leading to future research and publication opportunities. Each member, both student and faculty member alike, were asked to post a research interest profile. In so doing, members were able to search for individuals with similar research interests. This site, while still in the beginning stages, has already spawned an increase in scholarly productivity among the university community.

Discussion Forums

Online Educators, from their beginnings have used discussion boards or forums. The first boards were bulletin board groups followed by NewsNet groups. When online course management sites such as Blackboard and WebCT were created, discussion boards were a central feature. Over the years discussion boards have matured and added features such as rating systems, RSS feeds, and polls. The ability to offer discussions boards used to be a for-pay only feature but many free and open source options have been created and put in service. Some include PHPbb, Moodle, Google Groups and Windows Live Groups. Some discussion boards are hosted by a provider while others like PHPbb are setup on a server by the owner and need to be programmed but are more customizable.

Many instructors utilize the discussion board feature in Blackboard and students benefit from its use especially in distance education classes. Courses that are online and even face-to-face classes need a tool to allow students to expand upon projects and encourage further discussion and research. The instructor facilitates the research needed to submit a good post. A rubric, which lays out the grading and behavior of the board, sets the proper tone for successful learning. A common pattern in discussion boards is the instructor will post a question to begin the thread (a focused discussion) and have the students post 8-10 sentences each to express their thoughts, opinions and research. Then a few days after the initial posts are due students pick 3-4 other student posts to reply to. Instructors should encourage students to post as much as they wish to add to the discussion.

Other educational uses for discussion boards include posting resources for other instructors to talk about teaching practices and successes and challenges in teaching. In the College of Education at Indiana State University discussion boards through Ning social networks are used to share meeting dates, web sites, grants to apply for, conferences to attend or present at and more.

Wiki

The Wiki is the potentially central element for collaboration. Individuals and even strangers can work together on a project, each contributing their small part. This tool combines the information of many people to be developed and shared by many. This tool can also be used in the university classroom in face to face/ hybrid classes as well as distance learning classes.

A Case Study: Exploring Wiki Use in the Classroom

Individuals in a graduate class were asked to create a list of 25 annotated bibliographic entries surrounding a particular topic. In classes before the advent of a wiki, students were often given this assignment, but working alone, would often replicate the sources of other students. As such, a combined bibliography might only have a fraction of the sources it may otherwise have. Using a wiki, students are asked once again to contribute 25 sources each. However, when they post their entries, if another student already posts one of their sources, they must find another source to replace it. The advantage of this exercise is to encourage early posting and in the end, in a class of 20 students, the finished list is one of 500 citations. Then the students are asked to collaboratively edit the list and find errors. Finally, using only sources from this bibliography, students are each asked to compose a scholarly paper. Students then use a second wiki to post their papers where fellow students perform a peer evaluation assist aid in the editing. The project moves from the realm of the individual to the world of the entire class. The resulting work, when evaluated by the professor, is much more polished and professional.

A Case Study: How a Public School Teacher Used Wiki Spaces to Collaborate with a Retired University Professor (*Contribution by Virgil Wenturine and John W. Larner, Ph.D.)*

In this case study, we can see the effect of collaboration between two individuals from widely diverse technological, sociological and generational points of reference. Dr. Jack Larner, senior member of the pair, shared the case with me. His use of colorful language has been preserved so as to help the reader get a true measure of the man. This case clearly illustrates how social networking tools can bridge both generational and technological gaps to produce a rich academic environment for students. The experiment was not without problems and obstacles, which are also discussed, but lay the groundwork for increasingly effective future collaborative efforts.

When integrating technology into the classroom, there are a number of hurdles to clear. Therefore, it becomes imperative to start small, in order not to be overwhelmed by the technology itself. One way to be able to do so is through building a class Wiki. A Wiki, if not familiar, is a software application that permits a teacher to create an online site to post events, display assignments and homework, hold discussions, post pictures, and link to virtually any site or resource desired. Once the ease of manipulating the software is apparent, it takes classroom discussion to another level. Consider the following example.

Virgil Wenturine, teaching sociology at Richland High School near Johnstown, PA contacted his social studies methods professor, John W. (Jack) Larner, Ph.D., to take part in a Wikispaces unit about gangs. Larner, retired for nine years, had taught high school in Texas across the 1970's. Even though he had a history doctorate in hand, Jack wanted to teach high school, something he thoroughly enjoyed. Virgil was a non-traditional student at Indiana University of Pennsylvania (IUP) where he met Larner in the early 1990's; a long-term friendship was born.

Virg, from his IUP student days onward has been not only comfortably computer literate; but, is ever on the prowl, seeking more advanced skills related to teaching. However, with characteristic modesty, Virg claims: "I'm not that computer literate, just trying to get over the intimidation of technology and resolved to stay with the curve." Currently, he is enrolled in an online Ed Tech MA program. In this context and via a school district committed to technology, Virg constantly learns and applies new tech-techniques. One of his latest is the application of workspaces to his sociology class and, courageously, inviting Larner's co-teaching participation. But, Larner, well, he's another story!

Jack, reluctantly convinced by his computer-talented students, made a few awkward attempts to learn electro-skills with them at IUP's labs; but nothing worked. He persisted in using his father's 1909 Underwood typewriter; and, in characteristic Larner ways, termed computers "electro-static douche bags"! A latter-day Luddite, that Jack Larner. Wow, does it ever get more unreconstructed than that!

Things would change. After retirement, Larner began an inventory of inmate art and writing on the cell walls of the recently closed West Virginia Penitentiary with a small book as the intended product. Even someone as compu-resisting as Jack almost instantly recognized that a digital camera and laptop for frequent downloads of high pixel images would be required. A former IUP student, highly computer-accomplished, became Jack's sidekick, trainer, and co-author. Later, when asked where he learned computer skills, Larner would say: "In prison." Others invariably concluded: "About time!"

None of this is reported to celebrate either Virg or Jack; but, rather to provide rich context for what comes next. Virg, when working with Jack at IUP, liked his Texas approach: "Git the kids mud wrestling!" Involvement was, of course, Larner's point. However, Virg was meanwhile seeing bold, effective new ways to "git em mud wrestling" online. Further, he also realized that a teacher can reach out to the professionals in their network, inviting them to express their professional opinion on any social, political, or other issue.

Rather bravely, Virg asked Larner to co-teach with him a unit on gangs. Larner was fed Virg's open-ended start-up questions, responded to them in ways designed to provoke student mud wrestling; then the site was opened to students. And, did they ever mud wrestle!

There they are in Richland High School outside Johnstown, PA; and, there is Larner 1,300 miles removed in Richards, Texas, a tiny, depleted village amidst the wilds of east-central Texas. Larner would pose Virg's open questions about gangs, gather insights, and share them with the Richland students. The real beauty of the project is how it provides for exponential growth with each participant. From that, possibilities for wider ranges of participants opened to Virg and Jack. It was decided that some "outlanders" with expertise would be invited to help initiate and sustain mud wrestling in the upcoming unit, crime, punishment, and justice.

Larner, in addition to publishing West Virginia Penitentiary Cell Wall Markings, also did a short history of the joint, gathering a relatively vast volume of information directly bearing on the crime-punishment-justice unit. Virg asked him to come up with the plan. Now, armed and dangerous with the interactive teaching technology, Larner worked with Virg to lead the kids to mud wrestle topics such as: questionable incarceration practices, misdemeanor, felony, appeals, time, good behavior, early parole, clemency, release, and recidivism. Following all this, 87 cell wall images were posted for the kids to create Animotos using appropriate selections of images and music to state their views re topics such as: release vs. recidivism; contrition vs. vengeance; rehabilitation vs. intransigence.

Three experts in law enforcement-related matters were invited to take part. An Arizona woman active on behalf of Native Americans and Hispanics was included owing to her public opposition to treatment of Maricopa County Jail inmates by the celebrated Sheriff Joe Arpaia. An Ohio First Deputy Sheriff, formerly a guard at West Virginia Penitentiary, as well as an Emergency Medical trainer in Texas who also serves as a part-time Deputy Sheriff also were invited. The latter, in the emergency med work, often deals with crime scenes. Each person presented unique perspectives; and, each presented unique philosophy ranging from strong to moderate conservatism to liberalism.

But, laws of two perverse Irish mathematicians governed: Finnagle's law of infinite variables and, of course, Murphy's Law: if it can go wrong, it will. Finding technology is not immune to these laws, this is where gaps between theory and application appeared. Poor Virg, Jack, and their students became enveloped in issues, not always of their making. Yes, the tech aspects worked beautifully; and, students were quick and handy with all aspects of them. Even Larner rose to the tech, learning how to deploy it rather well, despite his curmudgeonly views of yore! Virg, in the midst of an excellent tech-teaching course, applied the visual-sound Animoto dimension. However, this plan was the final one to be completed prior to the end of the school year. Many unforeseen events partially, even fully, derailed plans.

We knew that Virg would take his track team to state finals, costing him three days with the class. But, instructions for the sub boldly stated that the kids were to be kept focused online. Larner would oversee that aspect with daily rejoinders, prompts, and twists. However, for reasons the sub could not be expected to control, vital time was lost. Also, often with virtually no notice, students were pulled from class. Sometimes one or a few, other times significant groups of them; all in due course of wrapping up the year. Seniors, making roughly half the class, often were called to special assemblies and the like. On and on, all too many days where we utterly lacked a critical quorum for business.

Larner insists on taking blame for yet another issue under-cutting the plan: the guest experts. Virg counters by saying we are merely facing a learning curve issue; next time will be a charm, new concerns will arise, they will in turn be resolved, and so on. Larner wishes that he had provided more specifics instructions to the guests so Virgil could have posted them right on the site. They seemed to have the impression that one appearance was sufficient; and, Larner feels he failed to encourage sufficiently their continued interaction with the class. Next time, we will improve that aspect.

Alas, all of this rather seriously truncated the unit. Our wrap-up never was done. Only one or two Animoto slide shows were completed. For all the excitement at its high tide, suddenly the waters receded into silent calm–it was over.

Next time, we resolve–are truly determined–that a highly interactive use of tech such as Wikispaces will be used when we are certain the time is available and, sparing dire emergencies, is likely not to be interrupted. Also, we shall provide guests at the outset with all information and instructions students receive regarding participation. We will direct and inspire the kids to interact much more with our guests. During the unit, we shall make more frequent contact with the guests. We shall not linger unduly on any one component of the plan, tempting though it might be, as we did with the felony case in this one. We shall more completely police the kids when they use crypto-jargon rather than generally understood English. And the list continues.

Virg and Jack urge all teachers who may be digital immigrants in the land of the computer-savvy digital natives to do as we try to do; get in there and mud wrestle the tech applications, just as those, in turn, will get the kids mud wrestling the highest, most complex concepts of the content. Yes, they learn facts; but the process of learning via the technology of our time must be channeled and developed for them by us, the brave and bold computer immigrants.

First attempts to design and deploy networking can teach unplanned, but useful, lessons. One useful tid-bit is that the project provided Virg and Jack with ways to go beyond impatience with student progress, abbreviated schedules, attendance difficulties, and the occasional network snafus. Once the students learn the concept, and begin to follow the rules, we can move faster, reinforce English skills, promote authentic evaluations, and not just rely on discussions to promote content. The project also taught them how flexible the Wikispace can be by implementing it as a springboard activity, or act as the focus of the objective for the lesson, perhaps even to evaluate, and/or conclude the unit to provide reflection. The possibilities are endless, as per most technology.

Look forward to some totally unexpected wonderful things that can emerge in the course of Wikispaces networking. Virg, once Larner's student, had become his prof's teacher, richly enhancing Jack's repertoire of teaching strategies. Larner, in the process, became a born-again Texas high school teacher; but, ever-more effective thanks to the unique blessings of online inter-facing given him by his "student". His students, no doubt, see Virg, not only as teacher; but, as facilitator, coach, and referee. Both Virg and Jack look forward to being recidivists, repeat offenders, by deploying these highly engaging, enriching online tactics.

LinkedIn

In a fast-paced job market the right connections are hard to find. Once a job is secured some people might feel isolated while they are settling into the new position and need to find people who work in a similar position. What about when a supervisor or colleague asks about ideas for a new project or grant? A professional "social" network may be a good resource. A top site that offers services to help professionals network with each other is LinkedIn.com.

LinkedIn provides a profile for each member to post their experiences, present and past jobs they have served in, education background and recommendations by other LinkedIn members. The site even has discussion and announcement boards for professionals to discuss current events, projects and other interests to members. To become linked to another member people must have a real connection through past experience with the person or be invited to link together. There are also add-on features to link WordPress blogs, Google documents and collaboration sites like Huddle. The discussion groups give professionals another avenue to research and discuss topics and projects they are interested in with others having similar interests. This site also provides a way for someone to get listed in search engines through their public profile.

Finally LinkedIn provides a job searching and posting resource area. Companies can post jobs and job seekers can search for LinkedIn exclusive jobs as well as jobs posted to the web at SimplyHired.com. Once a user finds a job in which they are interested, LinkedIn finds connections they might know at that company or link to other professional contacts in their network that may know someone at that company. This gives people a better chance at a personal connection to a job search and hopefully help land that new job. Just as sites like Facebook are helping old classmates and friends find each other and reconnect, LinkedIn is helping professionals build their network of friends and keeping linked to each other.

Microblogging (Twitter and EdModo)

A small, compact social networking tool called microblogging has gained in popularity due to software such as Twitter. A microblogging program allows users to send short bursts of information, which are called tweets in Twitter, telling people what they are doing or thinking at any given moment. These tools make great simple communication tools for keeping people connected together who may not see each other on a regular basis or who never meet. Celebrities, companies and friends use this tool to send en mass news that "followers", people who subscribe to their updates or tweets, can read to stay informed of current happenings. A microblogging tool designed for use in education is EdModo which allows students, parents and others to receive news, assignments, events, and even files from a teacher. Twitter is the most popular microblogging tool, which had many add-ons to collect the data streamed through the site. Some top tools for delivering tweets are TweetDeck, Tweetie Seesmic, and TwitterFeed.

In K-12 education many school and technology administrators see the need for using new Web 2.0 or social networking tools but are blocked by filters or are afraid to open tools such as Twitter, blogs and other social sites because of the chance of inappropriate content becoming accessible. An answer to the filtered, safer content comes with microblogging using a tool called Edmodo. Edmodo is a free microblogging tool that can help bridge communication between teacher and student and teacher and parent(s) and be more user-friendly than email. Users are not required to have an email account to join and use the site. This is a web-based tool that allows teachers to create groups (or classes) that have access codes to join making a secure site they can control. Once students and/or parents join the group, teachers can send a variety of postings out such as assignments; web site links, notes (simple text message style,) upcoming calendar events, and even files to open at the user's local computer. Each group is color-coded and has a summary of posts on it plus each post can be tagged for quick searching and finding. The posts are even broadcast in an RSS feed that can be subscribed to. Students and parents who are members of the group can submit any posting to the group to share with others and the teacher can delete any posting not appropriate for school. The creators and owners of the site are also helpful in removing inappropriate postings should a teacher need help. The site was launched in September 2008 and plans for new services as well as premium services are in the works.

Students and faculty in higher education do not have the limitations of web site and online tool filtering, as does K-12 education. Filtering of Internet access is not required so that available tools should be readily available for use in teaching and interacting with students. The popular and much talked about microblogging tool used throughout the world is Twitter. Twitter allows users to type in information or updates in short bursts of 140 characters or less. These messages are similar to the Short Message Service (SMS) sent through cell phones. Tweets can include web site URLs and links to other Twitter users.

Instructors can use Twitter as an instant feedback mechanism. A question could be posed in class through Twitter and students post replies or answers and the entire conversation will be recorded for later review. To manage Twitter feeds TweetDeck is a good tool to view tweets and social network updates like on Facebook. An instructor can choose many different ways to deliver information and can embed Twitter feeds into many popular social networks. There are also several sites that offer application add-ons such as Twitttown.com and other software sites.

Twitter is not designed nor recommended for use in K-12 education, as it is prone to adult-oriented postings and people who become followers just to blast advertising and non-educational materials.

A Case Study: Using Blogging as a Feedback Tool in Higher Education

I am a professor of education where I teach classes at both the graduate and undergraduate level in education. One of the major obstacles with students involves opening lines of communication beyond the basic assignments. One way that I attempt to do this is the creation of a private blog area using the blogging tool in the Blackboard course management system. I use the system for both my face-to-face hybrid classes and distance learning classes. The method is quite simple. I create a private blog area viewable only by the particular student and myself. Students are asked to post once a week in this area. They can post questions, comments, reflections, recommendations, course related items that cause them personal stress or any other elements that the student feels as significant. In return, each week, I read each of their entries and post private responses. This I consider to be vital. If the students are going to take the time to post, they must be assured that you are listening. I have been doing this for the past two years and the outcomes are fairly remarkable. I have taught the same undergraduate pedagogy class four different times. It has evolved each semester into a more student-centered course. In large part, student feedback and comments have helped shape this transformation. Establishing this one on one networking with the students has helped them feel empowered in the class. In addition, the dialogue helps me, as the instructor, appreciate and know my students better. If I receive numerous comments regarding an assignment, including confusion concerning the instructions, I know that I must immediately address the issue with the class, either by email or at the next class meeting. This additional tool has proven to be invaluable in my instruction.

Another usage of the blog tools involves private journaling. During the field placement portion of the pedagogy course, students are required to keep journals of their observations and to provide reflection each day on their experiences. The first time I taught the class, I asked the students to record their reflections in a notebook. As might be expected, a number of students lost their notebooks half way through the experience. Others, one could tell, would wait until the journal was actually due and try to catch up with all the daily entries covering several weeks. By asking them to record their entries each day using the blog tool, I had the opportunity to review the journals more frequently. I was also able to offer support, feedback and comments in an ongoing manner. This provided a rich dialogue between student and instructor. In addition, if I saw that a student made an interesting observation that could be useful to the class, I could instruct the student to post it to a discussion forum accessible to the entire class.

What reflective journaling accomplished is to open lines of communication between the student and the instructor, provide a forum for active feedback and assessment, help identify topics of interest for the entire class, encourage student activity, help keep students on task with daily reflective responsibilities and empower the student to take an active role in the improvement of future classes. In so doing, this simple act has moved the course activity from teacher centered to student centered with students taking a more active role in their educational experience.

Digital Back Channeling

Back channeling is the process of both formally and informally gathering information from a particular audience. In days past, many of these messages came in the form of questions asked by students in class. With the advent of new communication software, back channeling has moved into the digital age. Researchers use these tools often to get instantaneous feedback. In commercial markets, individuals are asked to respond via "clickers" or other feedback tools as to their instantaneous reactions to a marketing technique. In the classroom, instant polls of the students can take place. The tools do not have to be elaborate. In one instance, students were given simple laser pointers. The right side of the room indicated a "yes" response while the left side indicated a "no". When asked polling questions, students just pointed the laser beam to the appropriate location. The responses were anonymous, yet students felt involved.

A Case Study: Using Twitter for Digital Back Channeling

Students in a large lecture class are given the opportunity to post questions and comments concerning the lecture of class presentation to a large screen in the front of the classroom. On the screen is a Twitter interface. Students can access this interface either with their cell phones by text messaging or via laptop computers at their desks. As the class progresses, these conversations add a layer of student interaction to the class proceedings. For example, the professor is discussing Bloom's Taxonomy. He mentions that synthesis is one of the stages. A student in class does not recognize the term and tweets his confusion. Another student responds to the query with a response. If a question arises that is of common interest, the professor can delve more deeply into the issue. In addition, the professor may assign a small group to investigate the issue and then report via the twitter board their findings. This process works in both small and large gatherings, although may be best suited for larger audiences. It provides for more active student involvement in discussion, Q&A, and inquiry.

An Analysis of Common Issues, Controversies, Problems and Possible Solutions

In this section, we can address some of the common limiter issues that confront the use of social networking tools in the classroom. We will attempt to limit discussion to the university setting.

Administrative Resistance Due to Security Issues

As mentioned previously in this chapter, many educators are resistant to the use of social networking tools in the classroom. This attitude may be, in part, justified due to the many potential risks from unsavory elements found on the Internet. It must be pointed out, however, that these same elements are present on the Internet outside of social networking sites as well. If proper safeguards are employed, including the setting up of privacy filers, this risk can be minimized.

Sites that are left open to the general public, unfortunately, become havens for Internet predators that often prey upon members of the younger generation. Security and privacy becomes a major issue. Another confounding issue that exists often lies in the student user. Poor judgment and Internet user choices often place students in difficult situations. Schools need to deploy and teach Internet safety programs. Students as both Internet and social network consumers must be implicitly trained in avoiding potential dangers and pitfalls that may result from social networking. Schools also need to have well developed acceptable user policies (AUP) outlining the proper behavior expected on school networks and computers. The AUP can help to address concerns about Internet safety and consequences for breaking the rules in the policy. Federal funding and discounts in K-12 schools require an AUP and Internet Safety program such as i.Safe and that schools are in compliance with the Children's Internet Protection Act.

A recent case was in the news concerning a small Pennsylvania University and an undergraduate education major. The student was found to have a picture showing her at a campus party drinking a beer. At the time, the student was underage and the university reacted by attempting to withhold her teaching certificate, citing dispositional concerns. In the resulting court case, the student prevailed and was awarded her certificate. Subsequently, the student was unable to find employment due to the negative publicity that the court case produced. While this was a private social networking site, the problem clearly existed.

Fears of Cheating

Many educators fear that collaboration eventually equals cheating. In the previous Generation X period, it was often viewed necessary that individuals do their own work. Group activities were carefully orchestrated and controlled by the classroom teacher or instructor. In the new social paradigm during an age of open source publication, Wikipedia and collaboration, the net-generation is quite comfortable to "share the load". In many graduate classes, students often have some difficulty in the acceptance of academic integrity regulations in regards to plagiarism. The Internet has produced the illusion of open access to all forms of information that appear free to be used. This issue is producing a great deal of stress in academic circles and may be indicative of a paradigm shift taking place in how we share and utilize information. Once again, setting and explaining clear expectations to the students in this regard can solve a multitude of potential problems. It is interesting to note that with all the intricate tools for communication, one of the major problems that constantly exist in university is a lack of communication.

Access to the Technology

Many times, the excuse is made that the technology is too expensive or unavailable. Unlike K-12 schools that are mandated to employ filters to block access to social networking tools, higher education institutions are under no such restriction. Therefore the technology is readily accessible. The other more positive aspect of social networking is the fact that most of the tools are open source (easily adaptable to meet individual needs) and are free. The issue that often causes university Information Technology administrators concern is the fact that nearly all of these services are hosted off-site. There is a mindset among many IT professionals to maintain absolute control over anything that enters or exits "their" network. To have university instruction and communication taking place through these other sites is unnerving to these administrators. Due to laws protecting student privacy, they are constantly in fear of the legal ramifications that may occur. Their fears are not without merit. Once again, the answer involves the taking of a clear proactive approach where difficulties are anticipated and a clear plan is established and communicated to all stakeholders.

FUTURE RESEARCH DIRECTIONS

The fact that social networking is a tool that students use in their daily lives cannot be disputed. It offers a great potential in the defining of how classrooms of the future will appear. It could well be that the concept of a physical classroom itself will become obsolete. In regards to the implementation of cutting edge technology into the classroom, the matter has often been the situation of second adoption. Education sees a technology that is working in business and then adopts it for the classroom. This is often despite the fact that the transition is neither logical nor appropriate. Researchers must begin to take a more proactive role in this process. Rather than responding to a situation that is already occurring, universities should be looking at what appear to be profound changes in the manner in which this generation chooses to gather its information and communicate that information. Higher educators need to be aware of and be ready to respond to the constant social changes that continue to take place. If education can become proactive in this evolution, it can become the pilot of this change rather than just a passenger.

CONCLUSION

In this chapter, we examined the concept of social networking, and from an educational perspective, some of the particular tools found in the Web 2.0 iteration of the World Wide Web. What has become clear is that there is a change happening in our society, especially among the 30 year old and younger generations. We have seen how Internet users have moved from a purely receptive point of reference to one where each person becomes an architect in the future design and direction of these amazing communication tools. Each day the number of conversations increases worldwide. Because of the increases of communication, walls of separation begin to crack and crumble. A new age of information collaboration is blooming right before our eyes. In regards to social problems, where before 100 individuals would be actively seeking a solution, now millions are joining in the conversation. Do we invite them to the table?

As we examined the history of communication, the key to social and technological evolution has been linked to the transfer and integration of new ideas and information. Writing, the printing press, broadcast radio and subsequently television, the 24-hour news cycle and the Internet have all been tools that have transformed and continue to transform our world. Students not only study distant cultures from a book, they can experience them through online media. Now, through social networking, it is possible for students to actually interact with the members of distant cultures. The Google Earth project is in the process of mapping the entire world. Soon, you will be able to walk down a street in a distant city. This is already possible in many of the larger locations and will only improve with time. University educators must set the bar to which education must rise. Educators cannot ignore the usage of social networking tools as they will not go away. The business world has embraced these tools and they have become a way of life. Failure to address and utilize these tools will certainly result in an educational system that is out of touch with and irrelevant to the vast majority of students.

REFERENCES

Bandura, A. (1986). *Social Foundations of Thought and Action*. Englewood Cliffs, NJ: Prentice-Hall.

Bandura, A. (1997). *Self-efficacy: The exercise of control*. New York: W.H. Freeman.

Barker, J. (Writer). (1993). Discovering the future series: Paradigm pioneers.

Carr, P. (2001). Changing the culture. *For a Change*. Retrieved from http://findarticles.com/p/articles/mi_m0KZH/is_3_14/ai_30122398

Heer, J., & Boyd, D. (2005). Vizster: Visualizing online social networks. In *Proceedings of Symposium on Information Visualization* (pp. 33-40). Minneapolis, MN: IEEE Press.

Howe, N., & Strauss, W. (1993). *Millennials rising: The next greatest generation*. New York: Vintage Books.

McClintock, R. (1992). *Power and pedagogy: Transforming education through information technology*. New York: Teachers College, Columbia University.

McLuhan, M. (1957, May). Classrooms without walls. *Explorations*. Retrieved October 10, 2005, from http://www.tcpd.org/Thornburg/Handouts/McLuhan.pdf

Oblinger, D., & Hawkins, B. (2005). The myth about students. *EDUCAUSE Review*, *40*(5), 12–13.

Oreilly, T. (2007). What is Web 2.0?: Design patterns and business models for the next generation of software. *Communications & Strategies*, *1*, 17.

Oslin, G.P. (1992). *The story of communications*. Location: Mercer University Press.

Prensky, M. (2001). Digital natives, digital immigrants. *Horizon*, *9*(5).

Strickland, J. (2008). How Web 3.0 will work. *HowStuffWorks.com* (March 2008). Retrieved from http://computer.howstuffworks.com/web-30.htm

Vygotsky, L. S. (1978). *Mind and society: The development of higher mental processes*. Cambridge, MA: Harvard University Press.

ADDITIONAL READING

Association of College and Research Libraries. National Conference (13th: 2007: Baltimore Md.), & Thompson, H. A. (2007). *Sailing into the future: charting our destiny: proceedings of the Thirteenth National Conference of the Association of College and Research Libraries, March 29-April 1, 2007, Baltimore, Maryland*. Chicago: Association of College and Research Libraries.

Association of College and Research Libraries. National Conference (14th: 2009: Seattle Wash.), & Mueller, D. M. (2009). *Pushing the edge: explore, extend, engage: proceedings of the Fourteenth National Conference of the Association of College and Research Libraries, March 12-15, 2009, Seattle, Washington*. Chicago: Association of College and Research Libraries.

Bast, D. S. (2007). *Teens and computers what's a parent to do?: A basic guide to social networking, instant messaging, chat, email, computer set-up, and more*. Charleston, SC: Book Surge.

Boddie, J., & Boston Patent Research. (2004). *FirstSearch technology report: Social networking platforms & technologies*. Somerville, MA: Boston Patent Research.

Burke, J. (2009). *Neal-Schuman library technology companion: A basic guide for library staff* (3rd ed.). New York: Neal-Schuman Publishers.

Carr, P. (2001). Changing the culture. *For a Change*. Retrieved from http://findarticles.com/p/articles/mi_m0KZH/is_3_14/ai_30122398

Coates, J. (2007). *Generational learning styles* (1st ed.). River Falls, WI: LERN Books.

Computer-mediated social networking: First international conference, ICCMSM 2008, Dunedin, New Zealand, June 11-13, 2008, revised selected papers (2009). (1st ed.). New York: Springer.

Courtney, N. (2007). *Library 2.0 and beyond: Innovative technologies and tomorrow's user*. Westport, CT: Libraries Unlimited.

Courtney, V. (2007). *Logged on and tuned out: A nontechie's guide to parenting a tech-savvy generation*. Nashville, TN: B&H.

Daniels, P. (2007). *Policing the Internet*. Detroit, MI: Greenhaven Press.

Engdahl, S. (2007). *Online social networking*. Farmington Hills, MI: Greenhaven Press.

Espejo, R. (2007). *User-generated content*. Farmington Hills, MI: Greenhaven Press/Thomson Gale.

Espejo, R. (2008). *Should social networking web sites be banned?* Detroit, MI: Greenhaven Press.

Espejo, R. (2009). *Has technology increased learning?* Detroit, MI: Greenhaven Press.

Farkas, M. G. (2007). *Social software in libraries: Building collaboration, communication, and community Online*. Medford, NJ: Information Today.

Fields, A. M., & Díaz, K. R. (2008). *Fostering community through digital storytelling: A guide for academic libraries*. Westport, CT: Libraries Unlimited.

Goetchius, A. (2008). *Career building through social networking*. New York: Rosen Pub.

Hartl, M., & Prochazka, A. (2008). *RailsSpace: Building a social networking Website with Ruby on Rails*. Upper Saddle River, NJ: Addison-Wesley.

Himmel, M. A. (2009). *The social factor: Innovate, ignite, and win through mass collaboration and social networking*. Upper Saddle River, NJ: IBM Press.

Howe, N., & Strauss, W. (1993). *Millennials rising: The next greatest generation*. New York: Vintage Books.

International journal of virtual communities and social networking. Hershey, PA: IGI.

Jakubiak, D. J. (nd). *A smart kid's guide to social networking online*. New York: PowerKids Press.

Kroski, E. (2008). *Web 2.0 for librarians and information professionals*. New York: Neal-Schuman Publishers.

Lademo, S. (2003). *The magic and the miracle of social networking: How to be successful using the power of networking*. Landover Hills, MD: Abet Pub.

Liberman, D. (Artist). (2002). The millennial learner: Challenges and opportunities. To improve the academy: Resources for faculty, instructional and organizational development.

Liebowitz, J. (2007). *Social networking: The essence of innovation*. Lanham, MD: Scarecrow Press.

Lupa, R. M. (2009). *More than MySpace: Teens, librarians, and social networking*. Santa Barbara, CA: Libraries Unlimited.

Lytras, M. D., & Naeve, A. (2007). *Ubiquitous and pervasive knowledge and learning management: Semantics, social networking and new media to their full potential*. Hershey, PA: Idea Group.

Magid, L. J., & Collier, A. (2007). *MySpace unraveled: A parent's guide to teen social networking from the directors of BlogSafety.com*. Berkeley, CA: Peachpit Press.

Martínez Alemán, A. M., & Wartman, K. L. (2009). *Online social networking on campus: Understanding what matters in student culture* (1st ed.). New York: Routledge.

Mason, R., & Rennie, F. (2008). *The e-learning and social networking handbook: Resources for higher education*. New York: Routledge.

Mooney, C. (2009). *Online social networking*. Detroit, MI: Lucent Books.

Morris, T. (nd). *All a twitter: A personal and professional guide to social networking with Twitter*. Indianapolis, IN: Que.

Oblinger, D., & Hawkins, B. (2005). The myth about students. *EDUCAUSE Review*, *40*(5), 12–13.

Parthasarathy, S., Prasad, K. N., Raghavan, K. S., & Sarada Ranganathan Endowment for Library Science. (2009). *Library and information systems from Alexandrian heritage to social networking: Essays in honour of Prof. S. Parthasarathy*. New Delhi: Ess Ess Publications for Sarada Ranganathan Edowment for Library Science.

Yuen, S. C., Yuen, P. K., & Duan, X. (2008). A guide to publication in educational technology. *Journal of Educational Technology Development and Exchange*, *1*(1), 105–114.

KEY TERMS AND DEFINITIONS

Back Channeling: Method of communication used by participants to converse with each other and presenters or instructors during class instruction or conferences using social networking tools.

Blogging: Shorthand for weblog, is a communication tool that can be used as a journaling tool or writing platform to allow people to express opinions, share news, share research or post multimedia to the World Wide Web.

Microblogging: A communication form that allows short bursts of information in the form of text, web site addresses, audio or video.

Web 2.0: The set of next generation Internet or web-based tools designed to allow users to interact and contribute to the content of the World Wide Web.

Wiki: An online web site designed to allow multiple users to contribute content, and edit previously posted information to create a community of experts or collaboration on projects.

Chapter 16
A Dinosaur Hatches its Eggs:
Using Technology as a Pedagogical Tool

Linda B. Pincham
Roosevelt University, USA

ABSTRACT

Oksika, Johnson, and Buteau (2009) state that incorporating new pedagogy into teaching is attributed to the instructor's feelings about themselves and what they have previously learned. In other words, if one has a positive attitude towards technology, one will be more inclined to incorporate it into one's teaching. This chapter discusses changed attitudes and mindsets toward technology, particularly in the mindsets of the secondary education faculty in the author's college. Because technology has been integrated in the college's secondary education courses, the faculty, including the author of this chapter, had to learn about new technologies to teach as well as model to their students. This chapter also discusses the author's personal journey into using technology as a pedagogical tool. Various technology methods taught to secondary education students will be highlighted, with a concluding sampling of students' ideas to illustrate the creative thinking that technology integration can produce.

INTRODUCTION

There is a cartoon that is reminiscent of my personal journey into technology. The cartoon is a picture of a caveman proudly presenting a freshly-chiseled wheel to a group of other cavemen. Instead of being applauded for this insightful invention by his peers, the caveman is confronted with protest signs that say "No wheels here", "No new technology", and simply "No." Regardless of the protests, the wheel symbolized the beginning stages of technology. I wish I could say that I started out as the caveman with the chiseled wheel when it came to using technology in my instruction, but I was once, unfortunately, one of the sign holders. As an instructor, I survived by knowing the basics of using a computer and was quite comfortable with Microsoft Word© and to some extent, Microsoft Excel©. I used email to communicate with my students and colleagues.

DOI: 10.4018/978-1-61692-854-4.ch016

Instructionally, however, I used overhead transparencies for my lectures, and I shied away from multimedia presentations and eLearning platforms like Blackboard©. I discovered I was not alone. Many of my colleagues in secondary education (SEED) were just like me. We were all quite comfortable with our technology level. However, the more I ventured into schools to observe our students working in actual classrooms, the more I saw advance technology usage by both middle and high school students and their teachers. Instead of writing the typical book report, middle school students were creating digital stories to showcase their readings. I observed high school students presenting individual and group reports with the use of the Internet and power point. Teachers were using Smart Boards, or interactive white boards, as an instructional tool. Class attendance and maintaining grades were no longer kept in spiral notebooks but were done electronically. In my observations, I also noted how some teachers were even using blogs and various forms of online discussions as part of their instruction. The plagiarism software program, Turnitin.com©, was common in many high school English classes. Finally, as a parent of a high school student, I could track his weekly assignments and grades by simply connecting to EdLine©. These are all technology tools that are commonplace in our nation's middle and secondary schools.

My colleagues and I realized that we had to do more in our instruction in preparing future secondary teachers to be not just good teachers but teachers who knew how to use technology to enhance their lessons as well as manage their classroom. The 21st century train had quickly caught up with us, and we had to jump onboard, like it or not. We had to embrace technology or be quickly out of date with our instruction. We did not want our pre-service teachers to be at a major disadvantage entering the world of teaching. According to the National Center for Education Statistics (2000), 85 percent of teachers claim they feel somewhat prepared to used technology in their teaching. As a program, we wanted all of our teacher candidates to feel very prepared in this area, not just somewhat prepared. Furthermore, one of the conditions for teacher certification in the state of Illinois is successfully passing the Illinois Assessment of Professional Teaching (APT) exam, which includes questions based on technology standards set by the Illinois State Board of Education. Therefore, we had to critically evaluate how technology was being taught and integrated into the SEED teacher preparation program. Instead of relying on and hoping that our students would get the technology exposure and practice they needed in their field placements, we knew that in order to prepare our students fully, we as a faculty had to use and model various forms of technology ourselves and facilitate its use by our students by integrating it into our instructional program in meaningful and practical ways.

Using the metaphor of the dinosaur as "old technology," this chapter will focus on two areas: (1) technology growth in our college and the secondary education program area ("The Incubation Period" and "Laying the Eggs"), and (2) my personal growth as an older faculty member using technology as a pedagogical tool to enhance instruction ("Hatching the Eggs").

THE INCUBATION PERIOD: KEEPING TECHNOLOGY AT A "SAFE AND COMFORTABLE" LEVEL

Technology in the Classroom Course

In our College of Education, graduate students were once required to take one a 3-hour course in technology (Technology in the Classroom) as of one of the requirements to complete the Master of Arts in Secondary Education. The M.A. program was a 36 hour program which included 24 hours of teacher preparation courses for Illinois state certification in secondary education and 12 hours of courses that would lead toward the

M.A. degree. After completing Technology in the Classroom, students were to be literate in the following outcomes:

- Use computer applications to manage educational tasks
- Integrate technology into lessons (instructional planning)
- Retrieve, analyze and present information gathered from the Internet
- Use e-mail to send and receive messages and attachments documents
- Articulate the issues involved in integrating technology into teaching and learning
- Use technology to enhance students' problem-solving skills
- Explain, analyze and demonstrate classroom uses of technology
- Use web-based tools to develop home pages and electronic portfolios

Technology in the Classroom is a hands-on course, taught by instructors with technology and/computer backgrounds. Classes are heterogeneously mixed with students, graduates as well as undergraduates, across other teacher preparation programs: secondary education, early childhood, elementary, special education, and language and literacy. The main objective of the course is to get students engaged in using technology to enhance classroom instruction at their grade level of interest. Listed below include some of the projects that students are responsible for creating:

- Desktop Publishing: Newsletter
    - Students create a two-page newsletter for parents using *Microsoft Word* for both graphics and special text effects.
- Spreadsheet Grade-book and Budget
    - Using Microsoft Excel, students design a spreadsheet grade-book for 15 students and 10 appropriate grade level assignments. The grade books include a legend for assigning 10-week grades and have to demonstrate use of a minimal number of Excel functions. The second part of this assignment involves students producing a budget for use of discretionary funds to support technology for their future classroom.
- Power Point Presentation
    - Students, in pairs, produce a power point presentation based upon a reading assignment for the class.
- Teaching/Learning Video using Windows Movie Maker
    - Student, in pairs, create a four-minute teaching video with an instructional plan. Each video's minimal requirements include a title, introduction, teaching component, summary and concluding segment.
- Applying IBM's Learning Village
    - Students design a home page suitable for use in their future teaching. Minimum requirements for the web page include the incorporation of a 10 second video clip introducing the student as teacher.
        - Web Quest
    - Students design a Web Quest to accompany a unit plan. Both a student web quest page and teacher web quest page have to be included.
- Electronic Portfolio
    - Each student creates an electronic portfolio using the web-based tool, TaskStream.com©. All work is submitted electronically and maintained in the electronic portfolio.
    - Students are also required to use discussion boards in Blackboard, map educational journeys with the software program Inspiration©, use digital cameras and scanners, create PDF files, demonstrate knowledge of

Photoshop elements, and create digital stories.

A colleague quoted a student in the Introduction of her book, *10 Easy Ways to Use Technology in the English Classroom,* who said, "Can't you just teach me something I can use in my classroom tomorrow?" (Firek, 2003, p. xiii). Firek, a former instructor of the Technology in the Classroom course, stated that although the students appreciated the projects learned in the course, this particular question was something she heard repeatedly in her class. Gillingham et al. (1999) discussed three problems with colleges of education having a single course in technology to prepare students. First of all, the technology course is often a survey-type course that places too much emphasis on topics such as computer operating systems, software types, and applications instead of how technology might lead to instructional strategies or classroom management and assessment. Secondly, there is the issue of students' knowledge base of technology. Many students are required to take such a course but may already have the basic skills and/or experiences that are being taught in a survey-type course. Finally, Gillingham described how the timing placement of the course could lead to problems. For example, if students take the course too soon, they may not see any connections to other education courses; if they take the course too late in their program, the classroom and instructional strategies they learned in other courses may not include technology at all or what was learned in the technology course might be easily forgotten.

Some of these problems cited by Gillingham became evident in our single technology course, though there were also positive outcomes as well, especially the projects student designed specifically for their content area. However, the instructors of the Technology in the Classroom course learned rather quickly each semester that this course was beginning to become less and less a needed requirement for the majority of our secondary education students, who were already equipped with technology experiences and skills. Many of the students felt that what they were learning in this course was often segmented, and they were curious as to how to make the pieces of technology fit into their particular discipline. They wanted to learn how to use technology as a pedagogical tool to make their personal instruction rich and exciting for their future students.

Paper Portfolios

A major assignment for the secondary education student teachers is the completion of the final portfolio. The portfolio is a culmination of artifacts from each course in the student's program of study in secondary education. Some of the artifacts include a philosophy of education; classroom management plan; and a unit plan from the student's first secondary course, the content methods course, the pre-student/field placement, and from student teaching. Students may also include their resume, transcripts, letters of recommendations, samples of projects, and student samples/photos from their student teaching placement in their portfolio. The portfolio began with an introduction, an essay relating the College of Education's Conceptual Framework to what was learned in the student's program of study, the creating of the artifacts, and the student's experiences in student teaching. The portfolio was then read and evaluated by the student teacher's university supervisor and another full-time secondary education faculty member.

Students submitted their portfolios in three-ring binders or bound copies. The portfolios were stored in the SEED office. Many of them were beautiful creations and masterfully put together. However, as each semester concluded, the portfolios began to take up more and more space in the SEED office. We either had to find more space to shelve the portfolios, or there had to be another plan.

LAYING THE EGGS: INTEGRATION OF TECHNOLOGY IN THE SEED PROGRAM

Like it or not, being comfortable or not, we are living a highly technical age, and we are literally forced to embrace it. Coppola (2004) asserted that "educators and policymakers widely agree that new technologies should be employed in ways that will mimic real-world uses in order to prepare students for the workplace…." (p. 15). In the year 2000, the Illinois State Board of Education published its "Content Area Standards for All Teachers." For the first time in Illinois, standards for teachers were not just set for mathematics, social studies, language arts, and science but also for technology. "The technology standards for all teachers will ensure that teachers are prepared to take full advantage of the learning potential of technology and telecommunications. The Illinois Professional Teaching Standards and the content-area standards when adopted will guide the continuing professional development of teachers for certificate renewal." (Illinois Technology Standards for All Teachers. http://web54.sd54.k12.il.us/district54/lts/dmoore/techstandards/illtech.htm). Revised in 2001, the Illinois Technology Standards for All Teachers include the following eight standards:

1. Basic Computer/Technology Operations and Concepts
2. Personal and Professional Use of Technology
3. Application of Technology in Instruction
4. Social, Ethical, and Human Issues
5. Productivity Tools
6. Telecommunications and Information Access
7. Research, Problem Solving, and Product Development
8. Information Literacy Skills

Furthermore, to build in more accountability in meeting these core technology standards, a new state certification test, the Assessment of Professional Teaching (APT), with a technology assessment component, was implemented. Graham and Semich (2006 affirmed that "effective use of technology is being elevated to the highest level of importance on the education continuum" (p. 2). The Illinois APT confirmed our college's realization that we had to do more as a college to prepare our students to meet these technology standards. We recognized that a single course in technology would not necessarily help our students meet that goal.

Recognizing the need to support technology in the college's teacher preparation program, the Technology and Learning Library (T.A.L.L.) was created in our college in 2003. All of a sudden, faculty had access to various forms of technological tools and multimedia, such as digital cameras with video, digital video cameras, digital voice recorders, microphones, and a classroom set of laptops kept in a laptop cart that came with a network wireless printer. The challenge was how to get faculty to use these new technologies to "update" their teaching practices. Literature does reveal that technology that is not systematically integrated into teacher preparation programs and the lack of training and time often limits opportunities for both faculty and students to use technology to enhance instruction. Graham and Semich (2006) support specialized training as well as faculty commitment as important factors for effective integration of technology throughout the instructional and learning process. Therefore, training and encouragement of using these new tools in the College of Education were critical.

Each program area created a technology plan (See Table 1 for Technology Plan for Secondary Education, 2006-2007) based on the four technology goals of the college: effectively using multimedia in teaching, using technology tools for assessment, establishing professional development activities regarding use of technology, and integrating discipline-specific technology into the SEED methods courses. As a program area, the secondary faculty brainstormed the action steps, needs/new resources, and assessment(s) for each goal.

Changes in the Secondary Education Curriculum

According to NCES (2006), colleges of education are finding it more academically appropriate to infuse technology in courses: 93 percent within methods courses and 71 percent in content courses.

Using the technology plan as a starting point, the SEED program decided to offer *Technology in the Classroom* as a 3-hour elective for any secondary education students who felt they needed it; however, the course itself was eliminated as a requirement for the Master of Arts degree in Secondary Education in the fall of 2005. Instead, various aspects of the course have been integrated in four required secondary education courses: SEED 301/40, Seminar in Secondary Education; in each content methods course; SEED 350/450, Field Experiences in Secondary Education; and

Table 1. Technology plan secondary education, 2006–2007

GOAL #1: Effectively using multimedia in teaching			
OBJECTIVES	ACTION STEPS	NEEDS/NEW RESOURCES	ASSESSMENT
Increase the number of full and part-time faculty integrating digital multimedia into assignments in syllabi	Brainstorming session at Department meeting to decide which digital multimedia might be infused into existing syllabi; Department chair and COE Technology Coordinator (Fall 2006)	Use current syllabi	Survey to reassess faculty members' comfort level using digital tools in general. Archive revised syllabi and sample student artifacts.
	Co-teaching opportunities with faculty who comfortably integrate digital multimedia in assignments (Spring 2007)	Software installed on all full-time faculty members' computers, for both home and office.	Informal assessment of individual members' experience and comfort level with using digital multimedia software.
Enhance and improve full and part-time faculty members' use of hardware and software for presentations.	Provide in-service training as needed; encourage all faculty to teach in Smart Classrooms and provide the necessary training; Department Chair and COE Technology Coordinator (Spring 2007)	Availability of Smart Classrooms	Survey to assess full and part-time faculty members' needs

GOAL #2: Use technology tools for assessment			
OBJECTIVES	ACTION STEPS	NEEDS/NEW RESOURCES	ASSESSMENT
Develop a plan which uses technology to assess SEED students' electronic portfolios and artifacts (DRF)	Department Chair and COE Technology Coordinator; Planning retreats to review progress of DRFs (Spring 2007)	Availability of Taskstream, computer and projector Availability of Taskstream for all faculty members Planning time for possible retreats	Monthly discussion in department meetings

continued on following page

Table 1. continued

GOAL #3: Establish professional development activities regarding use of technology			
OBJECTIVES	ACTION STEPS	NEEDS/NEW RESOURCES	ASSESSMENT
Improve and enhance full and part-time faculty members' knowledge of the various instructional and assessment components of Taskstream and Blackboard	Workshops on Taskstream and Blackboard; SEED faculty, Department Chair and COE Technology Coordinator (Spring 2007)	Part-time faculty access to Taskstream and Blackboard Workshops for any faculty member as needed/ requested	Informal assessment of individual experience and comfort level with using Taskstream and Blackboard
Competency of all SEED faculty in use of all Office components, including Access, Excel, PowerPoint and full features of Outlook.	Workshops as needed; COE Technology Coordinator (Fall 2007)	Availability of home and office computers with Office installed	Informal assessment/demonstration of Office components
Understanding the differences between search engines, capabilities, and legal issues related to technology use	Workshops as needed; COE Technology Coordinator (Fall 2007)	Availability of home and office computers with Office installed	Informal discussions at department meetings
Full-time faculty publish multimedia online products, such as home pages, web sites	Workshops as needed; COE Technology Coordinator (Spring 2007)	Microsoft Front Page installed on all faculty office and home computers	Posting of faculty members' home pages and website

GOAL #4: Integrate discipline-specific technology into the SEED methods courses			
OBJECTIVES	ACTION STEPS	NEEDS/NEW RESOURCES	ASSESSMENT
Stay current in the field by researching current uses of technology as tools of instruction in middle and high school settings	Share sessions of latest technology tools of instruction at department meetings (for example, technology instructional journals; software); workshops on use of latest software that teachers and students are using in real classroom setting (Fall 2007)	Educational technology journals Software upgrade (for example, Inspiration) Hardware upgrade	Monthly discussion in department meetings
Use of technology in unit/ lesson planning to address multiple intelligences and learning styles	Workshops on how to integrate video, audio and digital images in varying formats for use in instruction and classroom activities for Methods instructors and instructors for SEED 301/401, SEED 350/450, and SEED 360/460 (Fall 2007)	Availability of hardware and software for instructors' personal use (take home to practice, for example)	Technology artifacts in electronic portfolio

SEED 360/460, Student Teaching and Seminar in Secondary Education (see Table 1, Goal 4: Integrating Discipline-Specific Technology into the SEED Methods courses).

Both Seminar in Secondary Education and Field Experiences in Secondary Education have been changed from three hours to four hours in order to meet the needs of technology integration. In the graduate level of Seminar in Secondary Education), five technology workshops that provide students with instruction and coaching in order for the students to produce support materials relevant to student led sessions in providing direct instruction and leading discussion are incorporated. These sessions are 2.5 hours in length and are held in the same week of instruction at five different points in the course. Each student has to download an examination copy of Inspiration© for use in producing or mapping their educational autobiographies. They also have to subscribe to the on-line teacher planning and organization tool, Taskstream© as well. Using Microsoft Movie Maker and Power Point with audio and graphic inserts, students create a digital video to accompany their unit plan and other student-led projects. In the content-area methods courses, students incorporate some form of interactive multimedia in their unit plan, such as a web quest or virtual field trip. In Field Experiences in Secondary Education, the final course before student teaching, students create a digital video of their field experiences. In both the Field Experience course and student teaching, students are required to create some form of interactive multimedia in their unit plan, such as a web quest or virtual field trip. In creating these extra multimedia projects for their unit plan, students often have to think constructively and "think like a teacher" to create projects that are engaging and interactive for potential middle or high school students.

Gillingham (1999) discussed one of the major drawbacks of in integrating technology in courses as "invisibility of technology" on students' transcripts. Hiring agents like principals and superintendents may not understand students' expertise or experience in technology because there is no course with a grade to illustrate that this competency has been met. Therefore, Gillingham stresses the use of student portfolios that incorporate or demonstrate technology applications in teaching. The next discussion will demonstrate how electronic portfolios are used with our secondary students to assess their learning for the program area and how students use the portfolio to demonstrate their knowledge of technology.

A Move from Paper to Electronic Portfolios

Students in secondary education are required to maintain an electronic portfolio for two purposes: (1) program assessment of student work (see Table 1, GOAL #2: Use Technology Tools for Assessment and (2) a storehouse of students' personal work. Using the online teacher planning and organizational tool, Taskstream©, students maintain a Direct Response Folio (DRF) from the beginning of their program to their exit. For each course evaluation, students post required artifacts and write a reflective statement, outlining what they learned from the course and how their learning connects to the college's conceptual framework. The artifacts each have a built-in rubric for scoring, so instructors have the ability to review students' work and give feedback or post a final evaluation. Assessments for accreditation requirements using Taskstream© take the form of online data collection and reporting for each content area in the SEED (as well as other program areas) program.

There is no longer of an issue of space in the SEED office to store students' portfolios, since all of the portfolios are digitized. Furthermore, students have a portfolio of all of their work in their secondary program that they can show to future employers. They can either use their DRF or wcreate a more professional portfolio that contains their resume, various artifacts, etc.

Integrating technology in the secondary education courses and moving from paper to electronic portfolios literately forced faculty to learn how to use technology as an instructional tool. We had all heavily relied on the instructors of Technology in the Classroom to teach our students everything they needed to know about technology. With the onset of technology integration, however, I felt I could no longer hold up that "No to Technology" sign like the cavemen in the cartoon. I had to come of age for the good of my professional growth and personal development as well as for my students. I consider myself to be a constructivist, and I attempt to model that concept to my students. Constructivist teaching can be characterized by various activities in the classroom that promote active engagement in students by having them mimic real-world situations in order to enhance conceptual thinking over rote learning (Coppola, 2004). This concept of constructivism is what I "preach" to my students. So, in reality, how could I possibly incorporate technology without modeling or demonstrating it? I really wanted to embrace the idea of using technology to change my teaching methods and at the same time, teach my future teachers how to "think outside the box" by incorporating technology in their projects and presentations. The technology plan actually became my inspiration. I saw it as more than a plan on a piece of paper. I saw it as a beacon into the 21st century for our program area. I incorporated the plan as one of my professional goals: to use and model more technology in my instruction. So, this is where the story of my journey into the world of technology begins. The following describes how I began to "hatch the eggs."

HATCHING THE EGG: MY PERSONAL JOURNEY

I vividly recall a lecture I was giving to students in a summer course some years back. I had several overheads to use as part of my lecture. To my dismay, the overheads slipped out of my hands, fell onto the floor, and got completely out of order. One of my students responded: "You really should think about Power Point. It's really easy to do. Much easier than overheads. It's easier than you think!" Other students immediately concurred. Power Point to me at that time was such an enigma. I knew some faculty used it, but I shied away from it. I had no desire to try it because it seemed too difficult. I didn't want to take the time to learn how to use it.. However, trying to organize my overhead sheets as quickly as I could, I was slightly embarrassed at my antiquated method, thinking about how each overhead was made—typing out the material, copying pictures, putting overhead sheets in the copier, making copies. That did take a lot of personal time. I realized at that moment that life with overheads had to come to an end.

Smart Classroom Signups

Roosevelt University has various classrooms called "Smart Classrooms" or presentation classrooms for faculty use. These classrooms are equipped with a ceiling-mounted LCD projector with a large pull-down screen and built-in computer. Other built-in devices are the DVD player, VCR, and document camera. To ensure that I get one of the Smart classrooms, I always request one as my regular classroom for instructional purposes prior to the beginning of each semester. In my mind, if I were assigned a Smart classroom (because they get assigned quickly throughout the university), then I would be obligated to use the built-in tools in my instruction. When I first used the Smart Classroom, I was intimidated with the built-in technology and afraid that I would embarrass myself in front of my students for the lack of knowledge of operating the equipment. Now, I feel I can't teach without this type of arrangement. The Smart Classroom helps my lessons to be interactive and constructive through power point lectures, technology demonstrations, and ease of using video/movie clips. When my students have presentations, the tools they need for effective presentations are there. They don't have to worry about ordering a projector or DVD player, for example.

Teaching with Taskstream© and Blackboard

Currently, all students in the teacher preparation program are required to purchase Taskstream©, an online teaching and planning tool, at the beginning of their academic program. As previously cited, our students now use Taskstream© to create and maintain electronic portfolios that contain program artifacts for evaluation instead of creating bulky paper portfolios in three-ring binders.

In its beginning stages, everyone in the college did not "get on board" with Taskstream©. This caused many inconsistencies within the college;

and faculty training, including adjunct faculty training, became crucial. However, from the onset, I fell in love with the capabilities of Taskstream©. Through self teaching and experimentation, I learned how to create resource pages for each of my courses. Students find it especially useful to have access to all of the power points, rubrics, handouts, web resources, and student exemplars through my resource pages. I also used Task stream's Discussion Board and message center for emails. With Taskstream©, I teach students how to create lesson and unit plans and rubrics. Students have direct access to state and national standards and could automatically link the appropriate standards in their unit plans. On the administrative side of Taskstream©, I designed the portfolio templates that contained artifact topics for each course and created most of the scoring rubrics for the artifacts in the SEED program using Taskstream©. This enabled students to easily create their portfolio and for faculty to evaluate artifacts through Taskstream©. I often visited other faculty classes to help their students create their individual portfolio. Suddenly, I was branded "Taskstream Queen" in the college by my colleagues.

I once shied away from Blackboard, until I discovered its usefulness during the summer sessions. I do not make Taskstream© a requirement for students taking my classes over the summer, as I may have students from other majors and students-at-large from outside the university. Blackboard is available to all enrolled students for no fee. Because I want my summer students to have the same types of access to resources as my semester students who used Taskstream, with the use of Blackboard they also have access to all of my Power Point lectures, class assignments, scoring rubrics for projects, and the opportunity for threaded discussions and email. An adjunct professor convinced me of the usefulness and "easiness" of Blackboard's grade book, which I now use all year.

Use of Laptops

Duhaney (2001) strongly suggested that faculty within teacher education institutions model appropriate uses of technology. In order to accomplish modeling of appropriate uses of technology, I teach with a class set of laptops. For the first eight weeks of the semester in the course Seminar in Secondary Education (undergraduate level), my instruction heavily relies on student use of laptops. Instead of interrupting class time to move students to one of the computer labs, I have the laptop cart with a network wireless printer in my classroom. Since this is the first course in secondary education course for undergraduates, they create their personal digital portfolio using Taskstream. I do a "show and tell –like demonstration of the stages of creating a portfolio via the large screen and LCD projector in the Smart classroom as students, each with a laptop, actually set up their portfolio. Throughout the semester, I also demonstrate all of the tools in Taskstream© and then have students practice them. For example, when teaching students how to create a lesson plan, I have students, either individually or with a partner in their same content area, create a lesson plan in class using Taskstream©. They can either send the lesson to me for feedback or they can print it out in class. When introducing forms of assessments, I introduce the Rubric Wizard on Taskstream©, then have the students create a performance assessment with an accompanying rubric. By the time students create their own unit plan, they are comfortable with the tools that Taskstream© has to offer because they have practiced in class with the use of laptops. As part of their unit plan, students also have to create an original digital video to introduce their unit plan, use the video as part of instruction or to conclude their unit plan, or use it as a culminating project. I demonstrate to students how to use Microsoft Movie Maker and allow some class time for them to practice. Finally, students are required to micro teach one of their lessons from their unit plan. On several occasions, students will "teach" using Power Point as part of their instruction and have their peers (as students) perform a task using the laptops.

Tech Focus in Field Experiences Course

The field experience course (Field Experience in Secondary Education) was changed from three hours to four hours so that technology could be integrated. Each week after the first two and half hours of instruction, the third hour is spent on a focus in technology. The areas of technology focus include the following: overview of tools in Taskstream©, such as the Lesson and Unit Builders and Rubric Wizard; updating and personalizing all portfolio artifacts; creating a professional portfolio; web quests, virtual field trips, power points, digital videos, and digital stories (with an emphasis on use of digital camera and/or digital video cameras to import pictures or video). In the last hour of class, we meet in to the computer lab as a class for the tech focus where students can work individually or with a partner. I lead the demonstration for the particular tech focus and then allow the remaining class time for student work.

Teaching a Hybrid Course

A major but personally rewarding challenge was teaching a six-week hybrid summer course that met twice a week. The focus of the course was on structured classroom inquiry approaches. My students consisted of teachers new to the field or students who just completed student teaching. In this course, the students examined their own problems in teaching and learning, learned and used methods of research that applied to a classroom-based project, and gained experience reading and using relevant published research studies. Every third class was online and Blackboard-based, so I had to figure out how to create various groups for threaded discussions and how to use digital drop boxes. The students enjoyed the online version because it allowed them more time outside the class to do their research projects. The six weeks during the summer quickly came to an end. I reached the conclusion that a hybrid course is the "best of both worlds" for the faculty member who is not quite comfortable with full online instruction but is willing to try some online component. The combination of face-to-face and online interaction and instruction build two very distinct learning communities.

Student Projects

Graham and Semich (2006) believed that in order to truly transform pedagogy, faculty should do more than just integrate technology in their teaching. They should also have the students themselves involved in activities with technology in the classroom. Three favorite projects that my students produce are web quests, the digital video, and the digital story. With the exception of the digital story, the web quest and digital video are creations to accompany the students' unit plans. For both the web quest and digital video, I show former student examples of each and review the main components of each project. I like to use the analogy of "leading a horse to the water" because I show the students the tools for creating both projects, but they essentially teach themselves how to create them. They have to "drink the water." This is the case for constructivist teaching. Coppola (2004), in referring to the constructivist model, affirms that "students must actively work on their own learning and help one another" (p. 20) and that teachers become more "facilitators and coaches, less dispensers of knowledge" (p. 20).

To illustrate my point on constructivism, there was an undergraduate student in my Seminar in Secondary Education course who said she just could not create a digital video for her plan. In a private meeting after class one evening, she cried, and out of frustration, she complained rather harshly about my methodology of the digital video project. She felt that I was being an unfair instructor and that I should use class time to have students work on their digital video under my explicit directions. I was disturbed by her complaint, but I did not give in. Somehow, after that emotional meeting, the student figured out how to create a digital video. She did submit one for that course in a timely manner, and it met the requirements. A semester later, I observed this same student in the Field Experiences in Secondary Education course teaching a group of tenth-grade students. Part of her lesson included a video introducing World War I that she created! It was a wonderful lesson to observe, and she and I both were very proud. She thanked me for making her figure out how to create a digital video on her own and came to the conclusion that creating digital videos was "easy." She said she saw the benefits of the digital video as an instructional tool and that she would create more for her lessons to her students as needed.

As mentioned previously, the web quest and digital video are created to accompany the students' unit plans by introducing the unit, concluding the unit, be a part of the instruction in the unit, or be a culminating project for the unit. I am always impressed each semester by the creativity produced by my students. The following highlights a few student examples:

Examples of Web Quests

- A graduate history major created a web quest around the Salem Witch Hunt as a culminating project to her unit on the Salem Witch Trials. The 5-day web quest had students assuming roles of the accused and the accusers. Students conducted research on various aspects of the Salem witch trials. The end project was a mock jury with roles of the defendants, the jury, the defense team, and the prosecution.
- A graduate physics teacher created a web quest titled "The Physicist: The Ultimate Roller Coaster Ride" as an introduction to her unit on the laws of physics. Through research teams, students discovered how roller coasters work and then used that information to build a simple model of a virtual roller coaster. In their design, students were expected to change variables such as height of hills, length of track, mass of the coaster, and speed of the coaster. In the process of completing this Web Quest, students learned about the different types of roller coasters and the different materials used to build them, and the history of roller coasters. They also learned about the basic laws of physics that affect roller coaster design.
- A graduate English major created an interdisciplinary web quest titled "Biographers of Everyday Americans," designed for middle school students. Individually, students wrote biographies of an everyday American who lived through one of the following important eras or events in our nation's history—the American Revolution, the Civil War, or the Great Depression. For example, a student could choose to research and write about an African-American man who lived in the South during the American Revolution or a Hispanic woman who lived in California during the Great Depression, or a white man who lived in New England during the Civil War. Each biography had to include the following elements:

1. Descriptions of the subject's childhood, career, family life, historical context (what was going on in the world around him/her and how did it affect his/her life)
2. Photographs or drawings from the era
3. A variety of primary and secondary sources including newspaper articles from the era
4. A bibliography

Examples of *Digital Videos*

- An undergraduate math student used her digital video to introduce her unit and to raise interest and curiosity on the topic of probability. The video opens with a live weather report, which cuts to a thunderstorm and lightening with upbeat music and her voice as a voiceover in the background. As she describes what probability is and the numerous places where it can be found, colorful images transition in and out.
- An undergraduate social studies major used her digital video to summarize her unit on the Mughal Empire in India. As powerful and colorful images of emperors of this time period in India are shown, the student describes fascinating tidbits about each emperor. Moving music from the film *Jodhaa Akbar,* a sixteenth century love story about a marriage of alliance between a great Mughal emperor, Akbar, and a Rajput princess, Jodhaa, is heard throughout the video.
- Another impressive digital video was created by an undergraduate math major whose video served as a review on shapes and using formulas to find the area of the shapes. The video began with "What We Already Know" and showed images of real-world shapes along with the geometric shapes. The video ended with "What We Can Now Do With What We Know" and showed how using this knowledge can be applied to real-world situations. The student narrates throughout the video and reviews each formula by giving concrete examples.

The digital story in the Field Experiences in Secondary Education course is more of a reflective tool than an instructional one. The digital story, unlike the digital video, is a constructive project designed for students to reflect on their experiences in their field placement, by examining their personal assumptions about schools and their role as a future teacher, especially in terms of democratic ideals and respect for diversity. The overall goals of the digital story focus on the following:

- Establishing a theme and purpose.
- Providing specific events and/or experiences to support the theme or purpose.
- Demonstrating a transformation of self-understanding, i.e., initial views/experiences in the field placement vs. final views/experiences.

Much time is spent on the initial stages of the digital story—how to basically tell a story instead of the technical aspects of creating the story electronically. As I show examples of digital stories created by former secondary education students, I use the questions and points below as a guide for discussion. As students become more comfortable with the goals of the digital story, I move toward the technical aspects of creating the digital story.

Creating a Digital Story

Telling the Story

- What is the meaning of your field experiences?
- What have I learned?
- Tell your own story.
- Don't list events.
- What is the theme?
- What is my central message?
- Use a Story Arch to shape your script.

Creating the Story

- Use images for symbolism.
- Use music to set a mood.
- Use voice.

Pacing

- Zooming
- Fading in and out
- Music or sound effects

Emotional Content

- Tell a story that you care about.
- Voice tone is important.

Remember!

- Your point of view.
- Emotional content to help shape your script.
- Story Arch.

The following highlights some examples of digital stories created by my students:

- A female graduate math major talks about her personal experiences of being educated at premier Chicago parochial, college-prep high school and the differences she found in working in a Chicago inner-city college-prep high school.
- A female graduate theater arts major talks about the importance of compassion and letting "one's walls down" and her realization that "Teachers need to be more than just educators. They need to be there for their students."
- A male graduate business major tells a light and witty story based on a quote: "Kids don't care how much you know until they know how much you care." As he tells his story, Eric Clapton's "Change the World" plays in the background.

Many students choose to publish their web quests, digital videos, and digital stories on the Internet via YouTube, Facebook, or MySpace pages, as long as they are not in copyright violations. There were many times when students had technical questions about the use of Microsoft Movie Maker and importing voice, music, and/or video for which I did not always have an answer. However, answers were always found, either by a faculty resource in the college or by other students. The important thing is that I was modeling the use of this technology to my students, and I was constantly learning what I did not know. I then use this new learning for the next group of students. In their model for integrating technology to transform pedagogy, Graham and Semich (2006) concluded: "When faculty model technologies themselves, this motivates students to learn and use technologies and provides opportunities for both faculty and students to share new ideas relative technology application in the learning process" (p. 6).

CONCLUSION

There are three stages that faculty move through relative to making change: confidence, competency, and creativity. (Earle, 2000). In my personal journey of "hatching the eggs" of technology, I have developed confidence and competency through basic trial and error. Most of the technology I now use for instruction was self-taught or I learned from fellow colleagues and students. It took many worthwhile hours of practice and experimentation. By consistently using technology in my instruction, I am becoming more competent, and my lessons are more creative, constructive, and interactive.

The U.S. Department of Education (2003) claims that "technology is now considered by more educators and parents to be an integral part of providing a high-quality education." For example, one of my students and her husband and family of two little boys moved from one district in Illinois to a more affluent district because of the generous technology in the affluent school district. Her oldest son, a third grader, will be attending an elementary school where every class has a Smart Board or interactive white board. This is a sign and reality of the times. Students in teacher-preparation programs are facing a world of high technology in the schools. They need to be fully prepared for by understanding how to use technology as an instructional tool as well as how to use it to manage and assess their own future students. Becker (2000) claimed that in secondary schools, it is the teacher's own limited skill and expertise in computers that prevent them from using technology with their students. Not only do my colleagues and I have to be ready for all the advantages that technology have to offer in the college classroom but we also need to seriously prepare our future secondary teachers to be ready for the 21st century classroom.

REFERENCES

Becker, H. J. (2000). Findings from the teaching, learning, and computing survey: Is Larry Cuban right? *Education Policy Analysis Archives, 8*(51). Retrieved June 19, 2009, from http://epaa.asu.edu/epaa/v8n51

Coppola, E. M. (2004). *Powering up: Learning to teach well with technology*. New York: Teachers College Press.

Cuban, L. (2001). *Oversold and underused: Computers in the classroom*. Cambridge, MA: Harvard University Press.

Duhaney, D. C. (2001). Teacher education: Preparing teachers to integrate technology. *International Journal of Instructional Media, 28*(1), 23–30.

Earle, R. S. (2002). The integration of instructional technology in public education: Promises and challenges. *Educational Technology, 42*(1), 5–13.

Firek, H. (2003). *10 easy ways to use technology in the English classroom.* Portsmouth, HH: Heinemann.

Gillingham, M. G. (1999). Technology in teacher preparation: Preparing teachers for the future. *Journal of Technology and Teacher Education, 7*(4), 303–321.

Graham, J., & Semich, G. (2006). A model for effectively integrating technology across the curriculum: A three step staff development program for transforming practice. *International Journal of Information and Communication Technology Education, 2*(1), 1–10.

Graham, J., & Semich, G. (2006). Integrating technology to transform pedagogy: Revisiting the progress of the three phase TUI model for faculty development. Retrieved May 21, 2009, from www.igi.global.com/downloads/excerpts/Reference/IGR4510_F17OA3gb35.pdf

Illinois Technology Standards for All Teachers. (nd). Retrieved June 15, 2009, from http://web54.sd54.k12.il.us/district54/lts/dmoore/techstandards/illtech.htm

Illinois Technology Standards for All Teachers. (nd). Retrieved June 15, 2009, from http://www.isbe.net/profprep/PDFs/techstandards.pdf

National Center for Education Statistics. (2000). *Teachers' tools for the 21st century: A report on teachers' use of technology. (Report No. NCES 2000-102)*. Washington, DC: U.S. Department of Education.

National Center for Education Statistics. (2007). Educational technology in teacher education programs for initial licensure: A statistical analysis report. Washington, DC: U.S. Department of Education. Retrieved June 25, 2009, from http://nces.ed.gov/pubs2008/2008040

Osika, E. R., Johnson, R. Y., & Buteau, R. (2009, Spring). Factors influencing faculty use of technology in online instruction: A case study. *Online Journal of Distance Learning Administration, 12*(1). Retrieved June 11, 2009.

Protesting against new technology – The early days. Cartoon retrieved June 8, 2009. www.inkcinet.com.au/Web/CARTOONS/2007/2007~34

U.S. Department of Education. (2003). Federal funding for educational technology and how it is used in the classroom: A summary of findings from the Integrated Studies of Educational Technology. Washington, DC: Office of the Under Secretary, Policy and Program Studies Service. Retrieved June 25, 2009, from www.ed.gov/about/offices/list/os/technology/evaluation.html

ADDITIONAL READING

Bai, H., & Ertmer, P. A. (nd). Teacher educators' beliefs and technology uses as predictors of preservice teachers' beliefs and technology attitudes. *Journal of Technology and Teacher Education*, *16*(1), 93–112.

Baldwin, R. G. (1998). Technology's impact on faculty life and work. In Gillespie, K. H. (Ed.), *New directions for teaching and learning: The impact of technology on faculty development, life, and work* (pp. 7–14). San Francisco: Jossey-Bass.

Bates, A. W., & Poole, G. (2003). *Effective teaching with technology in higher education: Foundations for success*. San Francisco: Jossey-Bass.

Bauer, J., & Kenton, J. (nd). Toward technology integration in the schools: Why it isn't happening. *Journal of Technology and Teacher Education*, *13*(4), 519–546.

Brzycki, D., & Dudt, K. (nd). Overcoming barriers to technology use in teacher preparation programs. *Journal of Technology and Teacher Education*, *13*(4), 619–641.

Donlevy, J. (2005, March). Envisioning the future: The U.S. Department of Education's national technology plan (Teachers, technology, and training). Washington, DC: U.S. Department of Education. Retrieved June 29, 2009, from http://www.findarticles.com/p/articles/mi_hb3096/is_200503/ai_17415530/

Duderstadt, J. J. (2002). *Higher education in the digital age: Technology issues and strategies for American colleges and universities*. Westport, CT: Praeger.

Ertmer, P. A., & Quinn, J. (2007). *The ID casebook: Case studies in instructional design*. Upper Saddle River, NJ: Pearson/Merrill Prentice Hall.

Fournier, J., & Lane, C. L. (2006). Transitioning from paper to electronic portfolios in beginning composition. *Catalyst*. Office of Learning Technologies. Retrieved June 26, 2009, from http://catalyst.washington.edu

Judson, E. (nd). How teachers integrate technology and their beliefs about learning: Is there a connection? *Journal of Technology and Teacher Education*, *14*(3), 581–597.

Junco, R., & Mastrodicasa, J. (2007). *Connecting to the net generation: What higher education professionals need to know about today's students*. Washington, DC: NASPA, Student Affairs Administrators in Higher Education.

King, K. P., & Griggs, J. K. (Eds.). (2006). *Harnessing innovative technology in higher education*. Madison, WI: Atwood Publishers.

McCrory, R., Putnam, R., & Jansen, A. (nd). Interaction in online courses for teacher education: Subject matter and pedagogy. *Journal of Technology and Teacher Education*, *16*(2), 155–180.

Mishra, P., Koehler, M. J., & Zhao, Y. (2007). *Faculty development by design: Integrating technology in higher education*. Charlotte, NC: Information Age Publishers.

National Technology Standards for Teachers. (2008). Retrieved June 29, 2009, from http://www.iste.org/AM/Template.cfm?Section=NETS.

Neiderhauser, D. S., Linstrom, D. L., & Strobel, J. (nd). Evidence of the NETS*S in K-12 classrooms: Implications for teacher education. *Journal of Technology and Teacher Education, 15*(4), 483–512.

Rowley, J., Dysard, G., & Arnold, J. (nd). (). Developing a new technology infusion program for preparing tomorrow's teachers. *Journal of Technology and Teacher Education, 13*(1), 105–123.

Schrum, L., & Dehoney, J. (1998). Meeting the future: A teacher education program joins the information age. *Journal of Technology and Teacher Education, 6*(1), 23–27.

Seldin, C., & Seldin, P. (1998). Bringing senior faculty on board the technological revolution: One model. *Journal of Educational Media and Library Service, 35*(3), 209–217.

Sharp, V. (2008). *Computer education for teachers: Integrating technology into classroom teaching*. Boston: McGraw Hill.

Shelly, G. B. (2006). *Teachers discovering computers: Integrating technology in the classroom*. Boston, MA: Thomason Course Technology.

Shelly, G. B. (2008). *Teachers discovering computers: Integrating technology and digital media in the classroom*. Boston, MA: Thomason Course Technology.

Snoeyink, R., & Ertmer, P. A. (2002). Thrust into technology: How veteran teachers respond. *Journal of Educational Technology Systems, 30*(1), 85–111.

Soloman, G., Allen, N., & Resta, P. (Eds.). (2003). *Toward digital equity: Bridging the divide in education*. Boston: Allyn and Bacon.

Thorburn, D. (2004, February). Technology integration and educational change: Is it possible? *Educational Communications and Technology*. Retrieved from www.usask.ca/education/coursework/802pages/thorburn/ind

Weigel, V. B. (2002). *Deep learning for a digital age:Technology's untapped potential to enrich higher education*. San Francisco: Jossey-Bass.

Chapter 17
The Trend of Commitment: Pedagogical Quality and Adoption

Patricia Baia
Albany College of Pharmacy and Health Sciences, USA

ABSTRACT

Through the lens of Technological Pedagogical Content Knowledge (TPCK), this chapter's goal is to understand how commitments affect readiness to innovate and how readiness to innovate affects commitments. Even further, it initiates the conversation on what engages faculty to change and improve their own teaching. Can faculty's commitment to pedagogical quality (CPQ) predict instructional technology adoption? Current Instructional Technology Adoption Models (ITAMs) ignore issues of pedagogy and are mostly developed for an alternative audience and environment, outside the realities and characteristics of higher education. A literature review explores exiting models for factors motivating full-time faculty to incorporate technology. Three audience categories naturally emerge (non-educational, K-12, and higher education), which highlight how each community treats teaching and learning differently. In addition, a study was conducted to analyze relationships between CPQ and adoption. Results indicated CPQ is related to instructional technology adoption through beliefs, academic title, years taught, tenure status, intrinsic and extrinsic motives, and curriculum.

INTRODUCTION

The education system is being challenged to change as innovative technology changes the ways we think about interactions with information and knowledge, and as new generations of students pass through with new expectations and new needs.

DOI: 10.4018/978-1-61692-854-4.ch017

As technological innovation continues, levels of readiness and expertise for faculty, schools, students, parents, and educational technologists become increasingly important; it is clear that "different technologies are deployed at different rates in different ways at different settings" (Molenda and Sullivan, 2002 p 3). What elements would constitute effective professional development programs for faculty? Researchers need to investigate effective ways to help each population successfully work with new instructional technologies. Effective professional development may require an understanding of the kinds of motivations and psychological resistances that determine how faculty will decide to use new technologies. To what degree, for example, is the adoption of instructional technology related to a faculty's disciplinary affiliation or commitment to high quality instruction? As information technologies become increasingly woven into social expectations, the pressure to adopt them in education can only increase. Informing educational leaders and decision makers on the full range of issues concerning development and deployment of technology and innovation is increasingly a critical priority. It is vital to examine the role of faculty's commitment to pedagogical quality (CPQ) when adopting instructional technology in higher education. CPQ is defined in this work as the faculty's value of teaching and student learning.

Research Rationale

In higher education, there are many reasons why an instructor would or would not adopt technology. These might include intrinsic and extrinsic motivations, "withitness" (Kounin, 1970), obstacles, beliefs, environment, commitments to pedagogical quality, specialization/ discipline, and efficiency. This study seeks to tease apart some of these issues in an attempt to bring the field a useful model, showcasing components that predict instructional technology adoption. Employing Mishra and Koehler's (2006) concept of Technological Pedagogical Content Knowledge (TPCK), this chapter first will examine characteristics of faculty in higher education and the nature of faculty's commitment to pedagogy, plus critically reflect on the state of Instructional Technology Adoption Models (ITAMs). TPCK offers a new way of looking at instructional technology and its adoption in higher education. Shulman's (1987) original model distinguished and linked content and pedagogy. As an "emergent form of knowledge that goes beyond content, pedagogy, and technology" (p1028), Technological Pedagogical Content Knowledge highlights what faculty members need to know to teach in an information age (See Figure 1).

The TPCK model shows these 3 components as cohesive. It presumes that Technology, Content, and Pedagogy should not be isolated from each other, or good teaching and successful technology implementation will be compromised. It also suggests the restructuring of professional development experiences to foster their interconnections. Specifically, as there continues to be a push for instructional technology adoption and for faculty to change the way they teach, their lack of knowledge in educational theory and practice becomes clearer. Faculty are primarily hired because they are subject matter experts in their field, but do not necessarily have pedagogical knowledge. When considering the adoption of instructional technology, both content and pedagogy should be considered as a unit. If one component is changed,

Figure 1. Technological pedagogical content knowledge: reconstructed diagram (T= Technology, C = Content, P = Pedagogy) (Mishra and Koehler, 2006)

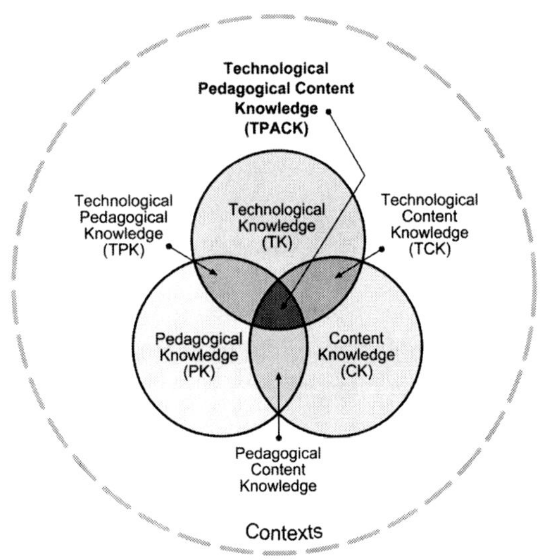

the others should move with it. "Viewing any of these components in isolation from the others represents a real disservice to good teaching" (Mishra and Koehler's, 2006, p1030). The quality of teaching is determined by knowledge in all three elements.

The concept of commitment to pedagogical quality (CPQ) should revolve around these TPCK's notion of teaching. CPQ is defined as a faculty member's value of teaching and student learning. It exposes various questions: Are faculty members aware of the unity needed between these three elements? Are they committed to acquiring, maintaining, and changing this knowledge as they continue to teach and as new instructional technologies surface? TPCK is a presumed template for the design and development of a higher education ITAM, as this value of teaching becomes a part of CPQ.

As faculty members are subject matter experts in their field, it may be that some are instructionally neutral, meaning they are not educational experts and do not have specialized knowledge of educational theory or practice (Major and Palmer, 2006). For example, law or pharmacy professors are content experts in their respective disciplines, but their only introduction to teaching methods, practices, beliefs, learning styles, student concerns, or instructional technologies may be inherited from their own student experiences. A lack of commitment to pedagogy by subject matter experts may contribute significantly to faculty members' lack of willingness to adopt instructional technology to further their own teaching and their students' learning. Mishra and Koehler (2006) claim TPCK knowledge "...would not be typically be held by technologically proficient subject matter experts, by technologists who know little of the subject or pedagogy, or by teachers who know little of that subject or about technology"(1029)

If support staff were more aware of the faculty's knowledge of and commitment to pedagogy, they could engage faculty further into the benefits, best practices, and implementations of instructional innovations. If faculty were more aware of their own TPCK knowledge, they would be able to adopt instructional technologies successfully and correctly, plus further equipped to understand their own knowledge gaps when seeking support and assistance. The concept of commitment to pedagogical quality (CPQ) should revolve around these TPCK's notion of teaching.

Theoretical Framework

Constructivism is a theoretical framework focusing on both social and psychological ways of knowing (Philips, 2000; Philips 1997, Laurillard, 2002). It suggests that individuals construct knowledge for themselves using previous experience, knowledge, and understanding as building blocks (Spigner-Littles and Anderson, 1999). There has been much written and debated on the underpinning constructs that comprise constructivism (Vygotsky, 1978; Wertsch, 1991; Dewey, 1997; Gros, 2002; Sewell, 2002). Philips (2000) defines social constructivism as knowledge that is influenced by social forces, tools, and ideologies. Through psychological constructivism, learners make their own knowledge by internalizing and processing meaning. Both assume meaning or knowledge is actively constructed in the human mind, but Richardson (2003, p.1625) identifies the significant difference in focus:

"Social constructivism focuses on how the development of that formal knowledge has been created or determined within power, economic, social, and political forces....Psychological approach focuses on the ways in which meaning is created within the individuals mind and more recently, how shared meaning is developed within a group process."

This chapter assumes the value of Constructivist Pedagogy, grounded within the psychological approach to constructivism (Richardson, 2003, Laurillard, 2002). Constructivist Pedagogy is defined as the "creation of classroom environments, activities, and methods that are grounded in a constructivist theory of learning, with goals that focus on the individual learner, who develop deep understanding in the subject matter of interest and habits of mind, that aid future learning" (Richardson, 2003 p. 1627). There are five principles of a constructivist pedagogical classroom (Lunenberg, 1998 p. 78):

1. "Posing problems of emerging relevance to learner"
2. "Structuring learning around big ideas or primary concepts"
3. "Seeking and valuing learners' points of view"
4. "Adapting curriculum to address learners' suppositions"
5. "Assessing learning in the context of teaching"

As this framework focuses mainly on student development, Richardson (2003) suggests a need for professional development in higher education to foster constructivist pedagogy. It is important for instructors to understand how learners interact with their world (Laurillard, 2002). This valuable consideration is crucial during professional development design and gives a workable approach when creating affective interactions to optimize learning. Furthermore, Laurillard states, "There is no professional training requirements for university academics in terms of their teaching competence, as there is for school teaching" (p12). This is an important point as we look at pedagogical commitment to teaching and learning in higher education.

Objectives

There are many ITAMs used in higher education settings, but no one has attempted to organize, categorize, and critically evaluate the appropriateness of the ITAMs. The simple act of finding these models in the literature is a scavenger hunt, across multiple disciplines with creative search methods. The organization of each to tease out a pedagogical focus is crucial. We know that education has specific goals and qualities that are unique to develop successful teaching and learning initiatives (Grosso de Leon, 2001). An adoption model which incorporates elements of content, technology, and pedagogy is worth investigating. Particularly, it is the faculty member's commitment to the quality of instruction which may play a larger role in adoption. Such a model could show the relationship between each factor to adopt and give insight to professional development design and approaches. Engaging faculty in these initiatives and supporting them through their adoption process could be a useful aim of such a model. This chapter describes the professorate, characterizes current instructional technology adoption models (ITAMs), explores each model's focus on commitment to pedagogical quality (CPQ), and analyzes possible relationships through a study of higher education faculty.

BACKGROUND

The role of commitment to pedagogical quality in the adoption of instructional technology is an important factor to investigate. TPCK highlights what faculty members need to know to teach in an information age. CPQ describes faculty commitments to acquire, maintain, and change this knowledge as they continue to teach and as new instructional technologies surface. An adoption model which focuses on content, technology, and pedagogy is worth investigating and may be central to facilitation of instructional technology adoption in higher education. Existing ITAMs should be built upon elements that comprise higher education, faculty characteristics, and their commitment to excellence. In academia, these components become necessary for faculty to obtain TPCK in a college or university setting (Mishra and Koehler, 2006). This literature review informs the following questions: How are faculty in higher education described? Can current instructional technology adoption models (ITAMs) be categorized or grouped based on certain primary features? What are these primary features? Within existing ITAMs, is there a model that focuses on faculty commitment to pedagogical quality (CPQ)? If so, how is it constructed?

Faculty Characteristics

Public and private institutions of higher education employ faculty for the primary roles of teaching, scholarship (research and publishing), and service (Wergin, 1994; Boyer, 1990). These three themes obscure a complex collection of sometimes contradictory tasks that are required of professors; faculty are expected to participate in committees, advise students, develop curriculum, organize scholastic activities, attend events, adopt technology, act as a liaison, continually self-educate in their respective fields, attend and present at workshops and conferences, and play an active role in the community (Lucas and Murray, 2002). Technological innovation has altered traditional habits of functioning and knowing within the profession. Distance education, computer-mediated communication and electronic publishing are examples of innovations that have transformed the faculty role (Wolcott, 1998; Morris, 2004).It is clear faculty juggle their time to engage in instructional technologies initiatives with more highly valued scholarly activities, such as research and publications (Wolcott, 1997 and 1998; Camblin, and Steger, 2000). But the truth is administrators also push for faculty to get on board with instructional technology activities. In addition, each institution's mission gives differential weight to teaching, research, and service (Boyer, 1990). So how does a faculty member decide what, when, and how they should commit their time? Bradshaw (2002), Boyer (1990), Diamond (2002), and Pryor and Pryor (2005) suggest academic title, teaching experience, and tenure status as motivators that affect faculty's involvement in change.

In addition, The Model of Reasoned Action (MORA) (Pryor and Pryor, 2005) identifies personal and social factors that affect the decision processes and is a useful tool for analyzing factors that contribute to behavior changes in educators. The personal factors focus on attitudes and feelings about the behavior, whereas social factors focus on perceptions of social pressure. MORA is important because "it is based on the assumptions that most people are usually rational, and that they use the information they have in making decisions" (p. ix). This model helps explain how attitudes form and how they can be influenced. Faculty and administration could gain insight from understanding this key model when implementing change. Perhaps even more important, how to understand the decisions people make to adopt or not adopt instructional technology, plus how to influence those decisions in the desired direction.

Allowing organizational structures to be flexible and fluid can facilitate successful and beneficial change (Ajzen, 1985). Boyer's Scholarship of Teaching (1990) defines four levels of scholarship: discovery, integration, application and teaching. Boyer states, "Theory surely leads to practice. But practice also leads to theory. Teaching, at its best, shapes both research and practice" (p. 16). Alternatively, Diamond (2002) believes "any attempt to define scholarship within a particular context of faculty work is doomed to failure" (p. 76) because it is difficult to list specific activities that would apply throughout the disciplines and research interests of each faculty member and department. He suggests less focus on the specific activity and more on the qualities that make an activity scholarly. Seen in this light, one could ask how any task of a faculty member could be made "more scholarly"? Presumably, the "more scholarly" an activity is, the more likely it is to be valued in an academic environment. Can teaching be made "more scholarly"? Can a faculty member's approach to teaching and learning be valued as a scholarly commitment? And what about instructional technology? Is there an adoption model that incorporates attitudes toward pedagogy as a way to engage faculty toward adoption? What are the qualities of scholarly activity which could be developed within disciplines and research that explore instructional technologies and development? Currently, these technologies are expected to be adopted by faculty in and outside the classroom, but are not necessarily valued in the definitions of scholarship, teaching, and service during evaluation procedures. Faculty characteristics are connected to this review as it showcases responsibilities, expectations, and personal factors that may affect TCPK and adoption.

Instructional Technology Adoption Models (ITAM)

At this point, it may be beneficial to define terms that will be used frequently. Adoption is generally defined as the stage in which technology is selected for use by a faculty or organization. Instructional Technology or innovation is the new tool being adopted for teaching and learning purposes (in or outside the classroom). Both of these definitions are developed from Sahin's (2004) qualitative work on understanding faculty adoption. Furthermore, Luppicini (2005, pg 104) would describe technology as "the organization of knowledge for the achievement of practical purposes, as well as any tool or technique of doing or making". Finally, the term model will be used to identify a pattern, plan, representation, or description designed to show the structure or workings of instructional technology adoption. Currently, it is difficult to find a piece of work that collectively identifies ITAMs or categorizes them. This gap in research disconnects theoretical and practical aspects of research on instructional technology. The process of tracking down each adoption model is a tedious and tiring task. As practitioners and theoreticians, we cannot understand each ITAM if we cannot compare or identify their components, relationships, or differences. It is important to be able to locate, understand, and compare models to unfold the properties and characteristics of each and how they may fit together. In this review, notable models are identified. Notable models are those which have been cited by others or have been applied in broad contexts. Particularly, these models substantially contribute to or transform the way faculty adopt technology in education. Under-developed or less defined models were not included.

Few ITAMs were specifically developed for the higher education context. There are many non-educational and K-12 models used to analyze the way higher education faculty work with technology (i.e. Diffusion of Innovation, Model of Diffusion, Learner/Adoption Trajectory Model, etc.). Non-educational models do not address pedagogical issues. K-12 models will have pedagogical elements, but their focus is disconnected from the characteristics and cultural practices of faculty members in higher education. In short and described below, many ITAMs used today in higher education were not originally designed for this setting.

The non-educational and K-12 ITAMs are frequently used out of context and may be inappropriate to foster the use of instructional technology by faculty in higher education. Some researchers (e.g., Rogers, 1995; Dooley, Metcalf, and Martinez, 1999) use these models as a template to build or adapt new models for higher education. For example, Rogers applied his own Diffusion of Innovation (Rogers, 1962), targeted for "agriculture, family planning, public health and nutrition" (Rogers, 1995, p. xvi) in developing countries, to a higher education audience. This general theory of innovation adoption grew as faculty in higher education and teachers in K-12 were analyzed as innovators. The emphasis became more commonplace as new editions of his books were published (Rogers, 1995) and more researchers expanded on his work. Dooley, Metcalf, and Martinez (1999) used the Model of

Diffusion (Dooley, 1999), Diffusion of Innovation (Rogers, 1995), and Hall and Hord's (1987) Stages of Concern to examine a rural school district. They suggested diffusion and change studies can be "translated into a variety of different contexts and to a vast array of innovations" (pg 114). The constructivist view of learning (Philips, 2000; Philips 1997, Laurillard, 2002), sensitive to critical issues of context, would disagree with Dooley et al.; from the constructivist point of view, learning models need to be constructed for a specific population (in this case, higher education faculty), taking into consideration the characteristics that make higher education institutions different (i.e. pedagogy, faculty rewards, institutional structures, professional development, faculty scholarship and service roles, etc). Transferring theories from one domain to another can yield new insights, but for instructional technology, these IT adoption models (Diffusion of Innovation, Model of Diffusion, Learner/Adoption Trajectory Model, etc.) neglect pedagogy and constructivist analyses of learners. As these models were developed for K-12 or non-educational environments, how can pedagogical notions and higher educational characteristics be placed more centrally in an ITAM specifically meant for higher education? Details of each model will be addressed further within the non-education category below.

Though current ITAMs have suggested some strategies that might help faculty adopt new technologies, there is yet only weak technology adoption by their faculty (Hagenson and Castle, 2003; Camblin and Steger, 2000). Perhaps better ITAMs are needed to continue efforts to engage faculty in instructional technology adoption. Responding to and encouraging pedagogical commitments may be the answer. Professional development opportunities can be designed to approach this commitment and engage faculty into using the tools necessary to accomplish sound pedagogical teaching and learning practices.

Non-Educational Models

A cluster of non-educational models of innovation adoption examined societal, business, or corporate audiences (Rogers, 1995; Zhao and Cziko, 2001; Fichman, 1992; Sid and Malcolm, 1985; Weinberg, 2004; Fishbein and Ajzen, 1975; Durrington, Repman, and Valente, 2000; Beaudry, and Pinsonneault, 2005; Geroski, 2000). These adoption models have been applied to or used as the foundation to address faculty adoption of instructional technology in higher education, but do not address the pedagogical mission that typifies the higher education environment. Diffusion and vocational models emerged as two primary non-educational types frequently applied to higher education today (see Table 1). These particular cases are examined because they are frequently used in higher education as models of adoption. Let's look closely at some examples of each, as we unpack this audience category.

Diffusion Models

The most commonly discussed and frequently used non-educational model is Roger's (1995) Diffusion of Innovation. Based on a linear form of communication, this model was developed for "agriculture, family planning, public health

Table 1. Non-educational ITAMs

	Primary Feature	Adoption Models	Pedagogical Focus
A	Diffusions	Rogers, 1962 and 1995; Zayim, Yildrim, and Saka, 2006; Jacobsen, 1997 and 1998; Fishman, 1981-1991, 1992; Geroski, 2000	None
B	Vocational	Weinberg, 2004; Beaudry and Pinsonneault, 2005	None

and nutrition" (p. xvi) in developing countries. Essentially, it is the how, why, and at what rate new thoughts and innovations are spread through cultures and society until it is common (first through early adaptors then by the majority). The categories of innovation adoption and the notion of a "change agent" grabbed the attention of educational researchers. Innovators, early adaptors, early majority, late majority and laggards are categories seen in higher education to identify "ideal types" of faculty, as they adopt technology in or outside the classroom (Zayim, Yildirim, and Saka, 2006; Jacobsen, 1997 and 1998;) Rogers (1962) himself is guilty of making a leap to education, as he created new book editions of Diffusion of Innovation. As these new editions (2nd ed. 1971, 3rd ed. 1983 and 4th ed. 1995) materialized, more behavioral science research began to refer to education, faculty, and their structures as new applicable audiences for this model.

Rogers (1995) spoke of change agents as leaders who influence new ideas in higher education. In terms of instructional technology, these change agents might be workers in instructional technology positions, centers, and departments, which have become common entities in education (http://chronicle.com/jobs/) (i.e. instructional technologists, designers, distance learning programs, Centers for teaching and excellence, etc.). However, recognition of the fundamental mission of education, teaching and learning, is missing in this model. This model does not show concern for the distinct features of the professorate and their needs to learn more about pedagogical ideas. It is good at describing adoption of innovation in ways that conform to data observed in many different settings. It lacks a specific focus on teaching and learning.

Similarly, Fichman (1992) and Geroski (2000) use diffusion theory, but focus on an analysis of characteristics within business, corporate, economic and policy environments which affect user adoption. Fichman's review of eighteen empirical studies (between 1981-1991) highlight the difficulties in the use of non-educational diffusion models in an educational context. His research suggests that adoption is much more successful when an individual adopts an independent-technology (an innovation that imposes a small knowledge burden on the adopter). This suggests questionable results for organizations that have comprehensive multi-user technologies (i.e. higher education) versus independent-technology environments (i.e. business). Because higher educational institutions are complex, multi-user, and multi-technology environments, Fichman might hold little confidence for technology adoption, as the burden on the adopter is larger. Psychological constructivists might argue, on the other hand, that a more contextual adoption model of instructional technology is needed, which focuses on audience, pedagogy, faculty roles, and commitment.

Geroski (2000) does not connect education and diffusion theory, but rather elaborates on the nature of technology use over time, focusing on the epidemic (diffusion happens slowly) and probit (diffusion happens at different rates for different types of organizations) aspects of technology diffusion within policy structures. Geroski business focus would not work in an educational environment where time constraints and utilization standard are present. Fichman (1992) and Geroski (2000) imply educational environments are different from non-educational environment in number and type of technologies that are adopted.

Vocational Models

The vocational category of ITAMs contains models which focus on the characteristics, qualities, and experiences of working adults, plus conditions that surround them. Work environments and human behaviors are continually referenced in vocational instructional technology adoption initiatives. For example, Weinberg (2004) developed the Human Capital Accumulation Model (HCAM), based on the Vintage Human Capital Model that emerged from economics. The vintage model assumes young workers as the primary adopters and beneficiaries of new technologies. However, Weinberg broadens HCAM to include the effects of technology change and an individual's level of experience. His work reveals experienced workers can be among the first to adopt new technologies and seem to benefit and accomplish much more work than their younger inexperienced employees. This may depend on the alignment of the innovation, cultural priority, and institutional reward structure. For example, it could be that younger faculty members at research universities are warned against technology adoption to the extent that it impedes them from engagement in more culturally valuable activities (research and publication), whereas younger faculty at a community college are rewarded for adopting technology, such as distance learning, because it enhances the institutional mission of the community college (Lucus and Murray, 2002).

Similarly, Beaudry and Pinsonneault (2005) analyze cognitive and behavioral efforts in adoption practices in work environments (i.e. banks, hospitals, etc., particularly management positions) through a Coping Model of User Adoption (CMUA). This model uses primary appraisals (a user's assessment of the expected consequence of a situation) and secondary appraisals (a user's assessment of his/her control over the situation) as measures to explore technology adoption patterns of employees. This level of assessment is creeping into higher education as more institutions promote instructional technology adoption. Administration and standard abiding agencies are looking for this data and push faculty and instructional technology support to develop models of assessment by using CMUA to reveal adoption effectiveness. However, this model does not take into account higher education characteristics; such as student learning, teaching effectiveness, support structures, and instructional design.

Vocational models, typically developed and applied in non-educational environments, are on the rise in higher education. As components and characteristics of humans are the main focus of these models, it naturally leads us to look in its direction as a way to understand and influence adoption. However, environmental factors and qualities that comprise higher education were not taken into consideration as factors that may affect adoption and change in the vocational models. These qualities in higher education are extremely different from those in business. Pedagogical components, content, and technology (Mishra and Koehler, 2006) form a triad of essential features in education.

Each model in this category legitimately describes technology adoption and innovation, but was developed for non-educational environments. Diffusion and vocational models are missing pedagogical components and frameworks that define academia as a systematic and intellectual community. Higher education and their faculty are a unique audience, one that transforms and develops knowledge across generations through teaching and learning initiatives. Non-educational models, used out of context within higher education, are missing these considerations and do not suggest education-specific ways to engage faculty in instructional technology adoption. The goals of education may play a unique role in higher education identity. Educational goals are not shaped directly by market forces. Instead it is the subject matter discipline, concerns for student learning, and decisions of semi-independent faculty that motivates this group (Grosso de Leon, 2001).

K-12 Models

Though they share an educational mission, higher education and K-12 facilities are very different in most aspects of their operation including: policies, standards, administration, goals, environment, budget, staffing, curriculum, student population, reward systems, faculty scholarship and service roles, etc. (New York State Education Department, http://www.nysed.gov/). This category includes adoption models that specifically

Table 2. K-12 ITAMs

	Primary Feature	Adoption Models	Pedagogical Focus
	Operation characteristics	Bradshaw, 2002; Dooley, Metcalf and Martinez, 1999; Sherry and Gibson, 2002; Sherry, Billig, Tavalin and Gibson, 2000; Sugar, Crawley and Fine, 2004; Zhao and Cziko, 2001; Toledo, 2005; Ajzen, 1985; Hagenson and Castle, 2003; Sahin and Thompson, 2007; Rogers, 1995; Gladhart, 2001; Russell, 1996	Medium

examine or target a K-12 audience (see Table 2) (Bradshaw, 2002; Dooley, Metcalf, and Martinez, 1999; Sherry, and Gibson, 2002; Sherry, Billig, Tavalin, and Gibson, 2000; Sugar, Crawley and Fine, 2004, Zhao and Cziko, 2001; Toledo, 2005). Unlike the non-educational category (who do not discuss pedagogy at all), these models approach pedagogical components of adoption as either secondary or as implicit. For example, Sugar, Crawley, and Fine (2004) studied teacher decisions to use technology in the classroom, from four southeastern school districts in the United States. Using Ajzen's (1985) Theory of Planned Behavior, the study sought to identify teacher's beliefs about adoption. The results indicated that the primary reason teachers adopted instructional technology was their students. Teacher beliefs valued instructional technology for various reasons: student preparation for careers, learning new skills, technology exposure, engagement, and society's dependency on technology. In addition, Zhao and Cziko (2001) used Perceptual Control Theory to examine teacher's goals and beliefs when implementing technology in the classroom. This goal-oriented model of behavior, assumes humans (in this case, teachers) as purposeful agents of internal objectives who interact within a given environment (classroom or K-12 environment). Their findings are similar to Sugar, Crawley, and Fine (2004), as the motivation for technology adoption revolved around it effectiveness on student learning.

The Learning/Adoption Trajectory Model is a technology integration and diffusion model for K-12 teachers, administrators, and staff (Sherry, and Gibson, 2002; Sherry, Billig, Tavalin, and Gibson, 2000), although it sometimes has been applied to the analysis of faculty adoption of instructional technology in higher education contexts (Hagenson, and Castle, 2003; Sahin and Thompson, 2007). According to this model, teachers pass through five stages as they become increasingly informed adopters of technology: learners, adopters, co-learners, re-affirmer or rejecter, and leaders. This model merges teaching and learning in technology adoption as faculty build a community of interdependence. Similarly, Toledo (2005) developed a five-stage model (pre-integration, transition, development, expansion, system-wide integration) of adoption and integration. By examining Rogers's (1995) Diffusion of Innovation's decision stages, Gladhart's (2001) levels of adoption, and Russell's (1996) six stages of learning to use email technology, Toledo's categories articulate K-12 themes of leadership, support, resources, teacher and student use. Each researcher's work, some central to K-12 and others migrating to higher education, lacks the necessary components to toggle between environments. As discussed above, it is clear higher education environments, goals, and faculty responsibilities are very different from the precollege environment.

Many emerging and frequently used models in higher education developed from K-12 models. In addition, many K-12 models start from or build upon non-educational models. Since K-12 models are structured within an educational environment, they more typically address the role of teaching and learning in technology adoption, but still lack unique traits of higher education. And,

Table 3. Higher education ITAMs and features

	Primary Feature	Adoption Models	Pedagogical Focus
A	Beliefs	Ferguson, 2004; Sugar, Crawley and Fine, 2004; Zayim, Yildirim, and Saka, 2006; Davis, Bagozzi, and Warshaw, 1989; Wolski and Jackson, 1999; Hall and Hord, 1987; Dooley, 1999; Langer, 2005; Kotter, 1996; Dwyer, Ringstaff and Sandholtz, 1990	Low
B	Motives	Mitchell, 1999; Ertmer, 1999; Rockwell, Schauer, Fritz, and Marx, 1999; Schoepp, 2005; Roberts, Kelley and Medlin, 2007; Jacobsen, 1998; Kotter, 1996; Shea, 2007; Kezar and Eckel, 2000; Dooley, 1999; Langer, 2005; Bai and Lehman, 2003; Chism, 2004; Spotts, 1999; King and Lawler, 2003; Cranton and King, 2003; McKenzie, 2002; Galbo, 1998; Dolezalek, 2004	Low
C	Adequacy of Resources	Barone and Hagner, 2001; Jacobsen, 1997 and 1998; Hagner, 2001; Kearsley and Shneiderman, 1998; Mars and Ginter, 2007; Buckley, 2002; Garrison, Anderson, and Archer, 2000	Medium

even in these models, pedagogical components are secondary or implicit. A disconnect may be occurring because the faculty characteristics in higher education are much different then K-12 teachers. It is essential to recognize technology adoption models in higher education that grew from K-12 environments. Their failures, described by Earle (2002), may be due to the model being used out of context.

Higher Education Models

Instructional technology adoption models, created specifically for higher education, showcase factors that affect the way faculty adopt instructional technology in or outside the classroom. Table 3 shows examples of such models grouped by a primary feature (beliefs, motives, or adequacy of recourses), with particular attention to the degree the model concerns itself with issues of pedagogy. These categories are not meant to be exclusive; indeed, some models may fit within multiple areas (i.e. Hall and Hord, 1987 or Kotter, 1996, Zhao and Cziko, 2001). Also, there is likely other ways of categorizing these models. Regardless of categorization, three issues became apparent: the value of comparing ITAMs to examine their assumptions and appropriateness for higher education, lack of attention to issues of teaching and learning in existing models, and the potential need for a new adoption model that comprises the primary features of existing models and includes a pedagogical focus.

Because teaching and student success are such an important part of the missions of colleges and universities, one might expect issues about pedagogy to be included in higher education ITAMs. Pedagogy can be defined as a deep knowledge of the processes and practices of teaching and learning. Deep knowledge refers to "knowing what teaching approach fits the content, and likewise… knowing how elements of the content can be arranged for better teaching" (Mishra and Koehler's, 2006, p1027). It includes the instructor's own philosophical beliefs about teaching, experiences, environments, and learning goals and ultimately of the value of teaching and the value of student learning. Let's take a closer look, as we dig deeper into higher education models and their primary features.

A. Beliefs of Faculty

The Concerns Based Adoption Model consisted of seven stages of concern: awareness, informational, personal, management, consequence, collaboration, and refocusing (Hall and Hord, 1987). This model reveals that faculty concerns change over time in an expected and progressive manner. Faculty beliefs (Sugar, Crawley and Fine, 2004; Zayim, Yildirim, and Saka, 2006; Davis, Bagozzi, and Warshaw, 1989; Wolski and Jackson, 1999; Ferguson, 2004; Dwyer, Ringstaff and Sandholtz, 1990) about teaching with technology are identified as a critical component of adoption. These beliefs include technology's usefulness in education, its effects on student learning, and the value it brings to the course content. What is missing from the Concerns Based Model and the research on faculty beliefs is the process and practice of teaching. It is obtained only if the faculty member participates in reflection practices.

The Theory of Reasoned Action (TRA) and the Technology Acceptance Model (TAM) are expectancy models which investigate intentions, behaviors, perceived usefulness, and perceived ease of use that predict technology usage (Davis, Bagozzi, and Warshaw, 1989; Wolski and Jackson, 1999). Particularly, these models address faculty attitude about the "usefulness" of the technology to aid teaching and learning. However, research indicates (Wolski and Jackson, 1999) TAM fails to capture relevant components (i.e. faculty workload, external influences/pressures of others) of adoption in context of the educational organization.

Ferguson (2004) examined the relationship between faculty beliefs about teaching with technology and teaching strategies. Over a period of four years, Ferguson investigated five faculty members at a small liberal arts college in southern United States. Data collected from this case study revealed that faculty who practiced constructivist teaching methods or were considered self-starters embraced the use of technology as a tool to engage students into active learning. Although through a narrow lens, this research does consider the professoriate and modes of teaching during its investigation. Dwyer, Ringstaff and Sandholtz (1990) would add an instructor's resistance to change as a factor that also influences technology adoption. Dwyer et al. (1990) identified 5 stages of evolution: Entry, Adoption, Adaptation, Appropriation, and Invention. These stages showcase the progression of faculty to change and adopt instructional technology, but do not focus on the commitments to pedagogical quality in relation to that change, only attitudes. The difference is commitment is a pledge, promise, or obligation to be engaged and involved in teaching, whereas an attitude is a state of mind or a feeling one may have toward teaching.

B. Motives

A large group of higher education adoption models identify and distinguish between motivation, incentives, obstacles, and barriers. Examples included in this group signify prototypical models which demonstrate these primary qualities. For example, faculty motivation to adopt instructional technologies can be affected by career status, perceptions of reward structures, and intrinsic/extrinsic factors to teach with technology (Mitchell, 1999; Ertmer, 1999; Rockwell, Schauer, Fritz, and Marx, 1999; Schoepp, 2005; Shea, 2007).

Ertmer (1999) elaborates further between external (first-order) and internal (second-order) barriers. First-order barriers would include lack of access to technology, support, time constraints, and tenure and promotion guidelines which do not promote innovation. Second-order barriers would include beliefs about instructional technology, teaching methodologies, and attitude toward change. Similarly Rockwell, Schauer, Fritz, and Marx (1999) reveal specific factors: time requirements, cost, instructional design, instructor-student relationships, reward structure, degree programs, policy, and training. In addition, their study (a survey of 207 faculty and 30 administrators) revealed faculty do indeed have pedagogical concerns, such as "providing innovative instruction and applying new teaching techniques" (p. 5). However, their work falls short on how to address this intrinsic concern.

A new study of 44 accounting faculty by Roberts, Kelley, and Medlin (2007) revealed three personal factors as the highest motivators to adopt instructional technology. These included personal interest in: instructional technology, improvement in their teaching, and enhancing student learning. This new research considers the value of teaching and learning as high motives for adopting technology in the classroom.

Shea (2007) studied experienced online faculty to examine motivational factors that both encourage and discourage teaching in an online environment. Through an analysis of 386 faculty teaching in 36 colleges, Shea unfolded six motivators: gender, age, employee status (full-time/traditional v. part-time/non-traditional), voluntariness (choosing to teaching online v. being required), computer skill level and institution type. Six barriers also emerged with four sharing the stage with motivation: age, academic status/tenure, online teaching experience, voluntariness, institutional differences and computer skills. Shea recognizes that a pedagogical concern does not surface for faculty as a motivator or barrier to adoption. In fact, through a factor analysis, flexibility unfolds as a leading factor toward online adoption and inadequate compensation the leading barrier. It would be interesting to see future studies explore these findings further and look particularly at pedagogy as a factor.

Jacobsen (1998) expands on Rogers's Diffusion of Innovation (non-educational model) by looking specifically at higher education. The attention in her work is on incentives (personal gratification, student learning and engagement in course content, student's future careers, collaborative learning initiatives) and faculty barriers (lack of time, lack of equipment/support/money, and a reward structure which does not recognize instructional technology use during evaluation). She uses Roger's Innovation Adoption Curve (innovators, early adaptors, early majority, late majority, and laggards) to suggest factors which shape how faculty adopt instructional technology, thus distinguishing early adopters from other categories of adoption. Furthermore, Kotter's (1996) Barriers to Empowerment would add faculty's lack of skills or knowledge and organizational/support structures, as barriers to integrate technology. Both authors highlight the need for campus-wide planning and investment in training and support for adopting instructional technology, but neither identifies faculty's commitment to pedagogical quality or available opportunities to engage faculty.

Kezar and Eckel (2000) conducted a study of "transformation" in six higher educational institutions over a period of four years. Kotter's (1996) conceptualization of the transformation process champions "vision" as the key to change. "Vision refers to a picture of the future with some implicit or explicit commentary on why people should strive to create that future…motivates people to take action…[and] helps coordinate the actions of different people" (p 68). Kotter describes traits of vision as imaginable, desirable, feasible, focused, flexible, and communicable. Kezar and Eckel (2000) identified five core strategies for transformation and highlighted the need for balance among change strategies. It is this vision which is critical to transformation as meaning construction or sense-making among campus members is favored. In this model, the change facilitator and change implementation process moves to the foreground when adopting technology. This can mean shifting the way faculty and administrators think about innovation and attending to issues such as: attitudes, readiness, culture, beliefs, values, environment, procedures, policies, and the change process in general (Dooley, 1999; Rogers, 1995; Kezar and Eckel, 2000; Langer, 2005). What appears to be left out of this model is the way individuals think about pedagogical knowledge. Mishra and Koehler (2006) would argue the significance of pedagogical knowledge in relation to content and technology.

King and Lawler (2003) remind us that professional development is a form of adult education, one that is learner-centered and transformative.

Their model of professional development addresses both motivational and technology needs. Professional development generates an opportunity to nurture transformative learning on faculty's goals, their practice, and how they think about work (Cranton and King, 2003). This promotes continued lifelong learning. However, McKenzie (2002) distinguishes between adult learning and training. She identifies adult learning as involving activities that match a person's preference, interests, need, style, and developments. Training is primarily concerned with creating conditions to transfer new tools and skills into daily practice (McKenzie, 2002). The old passive form of training, the "sit and get" model, left adult learners without the ability to apply new skills or gain new knowledge (Galbo, 1998). This is the training setting where an audience (participant or student) absorbs new information from an expert. This instructional method is still used frequently today in the work place (Dolezalek, 2004, Bai, and Lehman, 2003; Chism, 2004; Cranton, and King, 2003; Dolezalek, 2004; Galbo, 1998; King, and Lawler, 2003; McKenzie, 2002; Spotts, 1999). It is these professional development opportunities, which contribute to faculty motives to adopt instructional technology in or outside the classroom. Specifically, the design of each workshop or training would need to appeal to adult audiences in higher education and the faculty profession.

Bai and Lehman (2003) introduce four assertions to address reluctant faculty members by developing training that attends to their content and teaching needs with enhanced support strategies and a continuous communication network. Chism (2004) and Spotts (1999) would agree with these assertions, as they describe the faculty learning cycle when designing a course as Plan, Act, Observe, and Reflect. They discovered faculty decisions to adopt instructional technology are based on personal growth, organizational influence, and classroom environment (i.e. flexible or active learning).

C. Adequacy of Resources

Geographical location, enrollments, traditional and alternative course delivery, curriculum, organizational and social structures, faculty rewards and roles, instructional technology, and administration are examples of constraints and resources (Barone and Hagner, 2001; Jacobsen, 1997 and 1998; Mars and Ginter, 2007) that contribute to faculty adoption. Through my analysis, two subcategories of ITAMs that emphasize adequacy of resources naturally emerged:

1. **Institutional Structures**: Based on the notion that educational organizations are "loosely coupled systems" (p341), Mars and Ginter (2007) explored the "connections between the patterns of faculty to adopt instructional technology and clarity of institutional policies regarding such practices" (p328). Results indicate that loosely coupled organizations are not effective in producing consistent and thorough adoption practices, where as tightly coupled environments have clearly defined policies and directives with structured initiatives. Findings indicate faculty adopt in response to a push they receive from administration, disciplinary interest, collegial and department support, student demands, opportunities to advance their career, incentives, or to improve their instructional skills.
2. **Instructional Structures**: Classroom structure or lack of structure plays a key role as faculty move toward student engagement in learning through technology integration (Hagner, 2001; Barone and Hagner, 2001; Kearsley and Shneiderman, 1998; Jacobsen, 1997 and 1998; Buckley, 2002). The focus of this subcategory is on the importance of student engagement in learning activities and interactions (Kearsley and Shneiderman, 1998). Models of engagement emphasize individualized instruction and interactiv-

ity when promoting the use of technology and integration. Learning-centered environments (Buckley, 2002) emphasize the special engaging features of technology that can be capitalized on through technology integration: interactivity, varied information formats, electronic communication, formative and open-ended assessments, authoring tools and simulations. In addition, Garrison, Anderson, and Archer's (2000) Community of Inquiry Model was developed from computer-mediated communication and computer conferencing technology. Social, cognitive, and teaching presence are three key elements used to frame important communication media to support instructors and students. The Community of Inquiry Model does not really speak to adoption, but focuses specifically on effective teaching for online learning and structure. Adoption is assumed in the model and the concern is more about effectiveness and experiences after adoption. This model has taken the lead in distance learning initiatives, particularly in online courses and discussion boards. In addition, the element of teaching presence is taking over higher education technology adoption initiatives. Faculty are involved in developing the structure of the classroom and work to develop, facilitate, guide and evaluate learning activities in and outside of it. Faculty and student experiences when online and offline have showcased the need to establish such a concept. A pedagogical focus is present within this model, but its focus is solely concentrated on the communication component of teaching.

Clearly, there are many instructional technology adoption models that can help explain and guide the development and usage of innovation. Adoption model utility was predetermined, to some extent, by whether the model is used outside the context it was originally designed for. However, little effort has been made to organize these models by their primary features. Three audience categories naturally emerge (non-educational, K-12, and higher education) as an initial way to group these models. Making these groupings highlights how they differently treat teaching and learning. A pedagogical focus is not found in non-educational models because their goals and qualities are much different than those of academia. K-12 models address some pedagogical qualities, but their focus is disconnected from the characteristics and cultural practices of a faculty member situated in higher education. Higher education models take the necessary considerations of faculty characteristics, environmental qualities, and technology, but neglect the focus on pedagogy. Two subcategories, Motives and Adequacy of Resources, surfaced and looked narrowly at teaching. It is evident that faculty are motivated to improve their teaching and enhancing student learning. In addition, through the lens of communication, the Community of Inquiry Model touches on issues of pedagogical quality. A new adoption model may be needed that integrates the primary features of existing higher education models (beliefs, motives, and adequacy of resources) and includes a pedagogical focus on commitment to quality of teaching, commitment to pedagogical quality being the valuing of teaching and student learning.

Summary

If they are to be applied to a higher education context, existing instructional technology adoption models (ITAMs) should be built upon elements that comprise a higher education institution, faculty characteristics, and faculty commitment to instructional excellence. Plus, what is the unity that exists between content, pedagogy and technology knowledge? In academia, these components become necessary for faculty to obtain Technological Pedagogical Content Knowledge (TPCK) in a college or university setting (Mishra and Koehler, 2006). Higher education characteristics and the faculty profession are two unique entities which have very different goals and features from other environments (Lucas and Murray, 2002; http://www.nysed.gov/; Wolcott, 1997 and 1998; Camblin, and Steger, 2000). Instructional Technology Adoption Models (ITAMs) can be categorized when looking at audience and their primary features (see Tables 1, 2, and 3). Currently, instructional technology adoption models are used out of context and with an audience they were not originally designed for. Content, technology and pedagogy knowledge is an important grouping and their components cannot be separated. K-12 and higher education models showcased a low pedagogical focus. However, the focus on pedagogy is completely missing in non-educational ITAMs. Currently, there are no ITAMs designed for a higher education audience, which covers all primary features (attitudes, motives, and adequacy of resources) plus looks specifically at faculty's commitment to pedagogical quality. As shown above, attitudes, motives, and adequacy of resources have been studied independently from each other and play a large role in adoption. But where does a deep knowledge of the processes and practices of teaching and learning come in? What is the role of faculty's commitment to pedagogical quality when adopting instructional technology? It seems we are left with many unanswered questions as we look for a successful ITAM in higher education.

METHOD

The purpose of this study is to identify what motivates full-time faculty in higher educational institutions to incorporate instructional technology in or outside the classroom, with emphasis on faculty commitment to the quality of teaching. It will test the hypothesis that each faculty's commitment to pedagogical quality is a strong predictor of instructional technology adoption. This work challenges future research to explore higher education and faculty characteristics, specifically the quality of faculty's commitment to pedagogy, as a way to develop instructional technology adoption models. Practically, this information will aid administrators and instructional technology staff when supporting and assisting faculty in incorporating technology in instruction. It will also inform faculty on how to identify their own commitments to the profession [education] and how those commitments are related to their acceptance of change or innovation, plus mediators that affect adoption. Essentially, its goal is to understand what engages faculty to change and improve their own teaching with technology; even further how these commitments affect readiness to innovate and pedagogical quality. The research questions are:

Question 1: What is the relationship between commitment to pedagogical quality (CPQ) and instructional technology adoption?

Question 2: To what degree do beliefs, motives, adequacy of resources, and categorical variables (mediator variables) predict instructional technology adoption?

Question 3: What is the relationship between CPQ and the mediator variables?

These questions focus on the ways in which meaning was shaped within each faculty and how a common meaning may have developed within the professorate. The value of teaching and student learning is central to foster a constructivist pedagogy. It is this psychological approach to constructivism which frames this work.

Participants

This study investigates full-time faculty in higher education, who teach in Albany, New York, and are employed at an institution that is a member of the University Heights Association (UHA).

Faculty members are experts in various disciplines and subjects, each teaching a variety of courses.

Sites and Setting

The University Heights Association (UHA) established in 1995 a partnership among four institutions of higher education within the Capital Region around Albany, NY. The four private institution members include: Albany College of Pharmacy, Albany Law School, Albany Medical College, and The Sage Colleges. Not only does each institution share in a geographical community, each believes in "a unique combination of quality education, premium health care, public discourse of important issues, cutting edge research and technology, vibrant neighborhoods and progressive public and private partnerships" (http://www.universityheights.org/).

Albany College of Pharmacy. A private, not-for-profit, professional pharmaceutical and health school located in New York State's capital, Albany, New York, the Albany College of Pharmacy was founded in 1881 and is one of the only independent schools of pharmacy in the United States. It is accredited by Middle States Association of Colleges and Schools, Commission on Higher Education, and the New York State Board of Regents. It employs 86 full-time faculty (http://www.acphs.edu/). Participation in this study will be offered to each full-time faculty member.

Albany Law School. Established in 1851, Albany Law School is the oldest independent law school in North America. Located in Albany, New York, it a member of the American Bar Association (ABA) and employees 50 full-time faculty (http://www.albanylaw.edu). Participation in this study will be offered to each full-time faculty member.

Albany Medical College. Founded in 1837, Albany Medical College is one of the oldest private not-for-profit medical schools and maintains a large full-time faculty population (50). Its curriculum emphasizes "wellness, prevention and patient education" (http://www.amc.edu/Academic/) and offers only graduate (advanced) degrees. Participation in this study will be offered to each full-time faculty member.

Sage College of Albany "The Sage Colleges is an independent private institution of higher education comprised of three colleges: Russell Sage College, a comprehensive, undergraduate college for women in Troy, NY; Sage College of Albany, a co-educational undergraduate college of applied studies in Albany, NY; and Sage Graduate School offering applied master's and doctoral degrees" (http://www.sage.edu/aboutsage/index.php). Participation in this study will be offered to each full-time faculty member (100) who is employed at the Sage College of Albany Campus. This college shares the Albany neighborhood with the other three private institutions mentioned above and a student centered bookstore located in the Albany College of Pharmacy.

Instruments

This study adapted a survey originally developed at Middle Tennessee State University (http://www.mtsu.edu/~itsurvey) in 1998 and then revised in 2000 to assess the effectiveness of instructional technology, by measuring the depth and breadth of content covered, student performance, and good teaching practices. Permission was obtained to use the survey and alter it. In addition, one question (question 20) was used from the University of Alaska, Anchorage's Faculty Technology Survey (Chapman, 2004) regarding faculty perspectives on instructional technology. Permission was provided September 24th 2007, and the question was altered to reflect the needs of this study. The edited survey was piloted to obtain feedback on the adequacy of questions, terms, and format. A panel of faculty, subject matter experts, and technology professionals was consulted from the

Capital District Educational Technology Group (CDETG), a professional group of faculty (at varying levels of technical expertise, some with none) and instructional technology specialists who work in higher education institutions in and around the Albany, NY area, (http://www.cdetg.org). Fifteen CDETG members were randomly selected from a members list and emailed a link to the electronic survey during the summer of 2007 (using SurveyMonkey, http://www.surveymonkey.com). The randomization occurred by putting each members name in a hat and drawing 15 participants. Participants were asked to read and complete the survey, then reply to the email with feedback on understanding. Follow up questions included:

- Did you find particular questions difficult to understand?
- Was any part of the survey confusing?
- Did you want to indicate something but couldn't, given the format/limitations of the survey?
- Did you think it was too long? Too short?
- Were there related questions you thought should have been asked? Removed?

Changes were implemented based on responses. In addition, the survey went through a second round of revision at the hands of three educational researchers with experience in survey design. The goals of this revision were to make the format of items consistent, shorten the survey as much as possible, and ensure that the variables in the proposed instructional technology adoption model were represented. Table 4 shows the final questions, categorized by measurement.

Mann and Stewart (2000) report the advantages of using an electronic survey including; access to unique populations, time, cost, collection methods, ease of use, and accessibility. Internet communication and research has advanced much and is considered a widely available technology. Accessibility to the internet for each of the four colleges was established by their IT departments, through informal conversation within the CDETG group. All (n=286) full-time faculty at Albany College of Pharmacy (n=86), Albany Law School (n=50), Albany Medical College (n=50), and The Sage College of Albany (n=100) received an email with, a consent form, instructions to complete the consent form, and directions on how to access and complete the survey (Appendix B) electronically on SurveyMonkey.com. Additional correspondence through email continued only for further clarification on how to access the survey or complete questions on the consent form. Data collection took place over a 1-month period during the Spring 2008 semester. Email reminders were sent out, as needed, to each faculty member to encourage participation. After a month, the survey responses, including quantitative and qualitative data, were collected and analyzed. Response rate yielded 104 responses.

Data

This research explored the relationship between CPQ (independent variable) and instructional technology adoption (dependent variable). Specifically, it investigates how beliefs, motives, adequacy of resources, and the categorical variables mediate this relationship. The survey data was collected electronically, and results were quantitative in nature with some qualitative data on comments, concerns and feedback. Overall, survey comments (q27) were recorded and coded by connections (similarities) and gaps. Categorical variables (q22-q26) describe years of higher education experience, academic rank, tenure status, and specialization of participants. Both descriptive and inferential statistics will be calculated, and a relationship measure (backwards stepwise regression) employed for analysis of remaining questions. Table 4 showcases each survey question in relationship to the study's variables.

Table 4. Survey question[s] associated with variables

Dependent Variable: Faculty's adoption of instructional technology
Q1 In the 2 most recent semesters you have taught, rate the degree to which you used the following instructional technology tools: a.Presentation software, b.Spreadsheets, c.Internet content, d.Word Processing, e.Audio, f.Video, g.Animation, h.Email, i.Discussion Boards, j.Chats, k.Course Management System, l.Blogs, m.Podcasts, n.Wikis
Q20. Which of the following five statements represents your perspective? I am personally committed to incorporating technologies into my teaching as much as possible, I occasionally select and use technologies that I feel are particularly suited to my course content and students, I use little or no technologies in my course now, but may wish to do so in the future, I use technologies in my teaching, but prefer not to, I do NOT use technologies in my teaching.
Independent Variables: Commitment to Pedagogical Quality
Q3. Teaching is the most important part of my job.
Q5. I am eager to find new ways to help students learn.
Q7. The content of my course is more important than the way I teach the course
Q11. I feel my teaching is successful when I thoroughly cover the course content.
Q14. I enjoy teaching.
Q16. I feel my teaching is successful when my students demonstrate their learning.
Q18. I change my teaching plans and strategies to foster student learning.
Categorical Variables
Q22 Enter the number of years you have taught in higher education
Q23. Check your academic title: professor, associate professor, assistant professor, instructor, other.
Q24. Your institution is considered a: Teaching College, Research College, Both, I don't know, other.
Q25. Are you tenured? Yes or no
Q26. What is your specialization/discipline?
Q27. Please share any survey comments, concerns, or feedback.
Mediator Variables: Beliefs, Motives, and Adequacy of Resources
Beliefs about Instructional Technology
Q2. I believe that the use of technology in education can enhance student learning in my discipline.
Q4 I believe the use of instructional technology is counterproductive to student learning.
Q6. I believe the use of instructional technology can enhance my teaching.
Q17. I believe instructional technology is important in higher education.
Motives
Q19. Rate the degree to which the following are available to you at your institution for the use of instructional technology: Monetary incentives or rewards, Administrative recognition, Peer recognition, Advantage for tenure or promotion, Release time, May lead to a research publication, Professional development opportunities.
Q21. To what degree is using instructional technology personally satisfying to you.
Adequacy of Resources
Q8. The administration in my institution supports my use of technology in education.
Q9. I have adequate training opportunities at my institution to develop the technical skills required for instructional technology use
Q10. My office computer or laptop is adequate for supporting my use of technology in education
Q12. I have access to instructional technology technical support
Q13. I have sufficient time to incorporate instructional technology into my courses.
Q15. The classrooms at my institution are sufficient and support my use of technology in education.

Analyses

Descriptive statistics, graphic representations, and correlations were used to detect preliminary patterns, relationships, and participant characteristics across data. Data were analyzed in various ways by the researcher for summaries, themes, gaps, emerging categories, relationships that may explain teaching with instructional technology. A backwards stepwise regression analysis was used to see the degree to which commitment to pedagogical quality (independent variable) explains or predicts instructional technology adoption (dependent variable). In addition, mediator variables and categorical variables exist as intermediaries to investigating the relationships between the dependent and independent variables (see Figure 2).

A regression was used to examine relations among the study's primary constructs. This approach was chosen since it indicates the contribution of each variable in the prediction of technology adoption and it compares the degree of influence from each included variable (direct or indirect effects). Considering the number of variables that exist in this study, this method was chosen as the best mode to predict a relationship. These linear methods provide a clue about how two or more variables may fit in relationship to other variables (Brase and Brase, 2003). It is important to reiterate that this study is looking for linear correlational (not necessarily causal) relationships. Furthermore, this study does not attempt to distinguish between a thoughtful and unreflective adoption of instructional technology. The study implicitly assumes that technological adoption is a conscious and positive choice of individual faculty members.

FINDINGS

The response rate of 37% yielded 104 usable surveys. Fifty-six percent of respondents indicated that their institutions were teaching colleges, 32% described their institution as both teaching and research, none considered their institution to be solely a research college, 12% fell into an "other" category and identified either a law school, medical college, or they did not know. The respondents ranged in disciplines. The disciplines reported were in health (33.7%), pharmacy (15.4%), liberal arts (12.5%), science (11.5%), law (8.7%), business and communication (4.8% respectively), and education (1.8%). The other 11.6% skipped this question.

Figure 2. Possible variable relationships

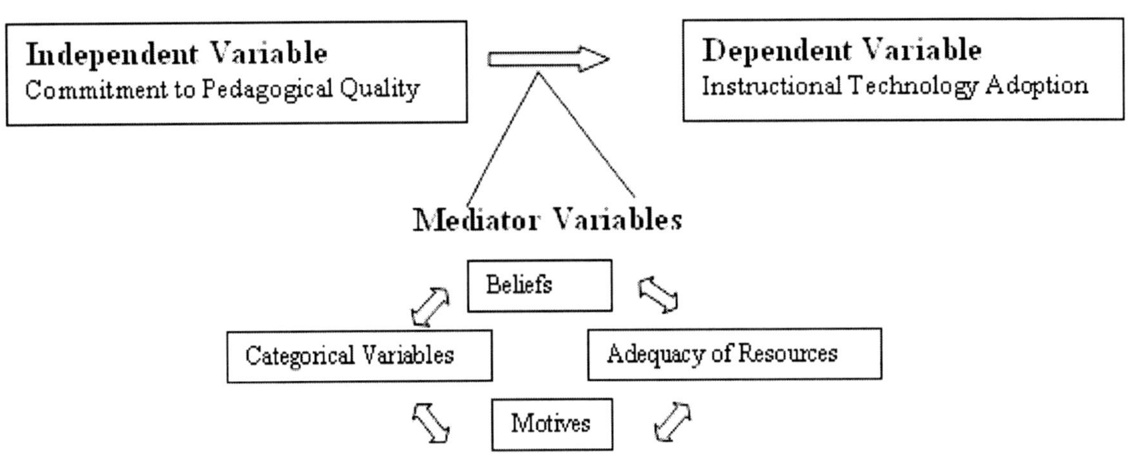

Respondents were predominately non-tenured (60.4%). Adjunct faculty were not surveyed; full-time faculty were the only participants in the study. Faculty who participated held varying academic titles: Professor (19.2%), Associate Professor (40.4%), Assistant Professor (31.3%), or Instructor (9.1%). Respondents identified the number of years they have taught in higher education. Years of experience ranged between 1 to 40 years with a mean score of 15.12. Information about non-respondents could not be collected directly or systematically, but, by comparing respondent characteristics with the general characteristics of the faculty of the University Heights Association, one can infer that non-respondents were mostly (60%) assistant and associate professors with 2% holding tenure status. It seems non-respondents tend to be instructors as well as untenured assistant and associate professors.

Every participant (n=104) who responded to the survey used some level of technology in education. This may be because faculty who are already using technology in education are more attracted to completing an electronic survey or are looking for an outlet to showcase their accomplishments. Instructional technology adoption was measured in terms of "intensity," "extensity," and "intention." Intensity is the frequency of use. From the list of 14 technologies (Table 5), intensity was high for presentations, word processing, email, internet content, and content management systems (CMS); each ranking in the "frequently used" and "extensively" category. Spreadsheets, animation, blogs, podcasts, and wiki's were used the least with a ranking of "never" and "rarely". The other technologies (audio, video, discussion boards and chats) fell into a low/middle range with use combination at "never," "rarely," or "occasionally."

Survey respondents (faculty) were questioned regarding their commitments to pedagogical quality (independent variable), their use and perception of instructional technology adoption (dependent variable), and mediator variables (beliefs about instructional technology, motives, adequacy of resources and categorical data. Descriptive statistics can be seen in Table 6.

Table 5. Intensity: frequency of use

Answer Options	0 never	1 rarely	2 occasionally	3 frequently	4 extensively	% Response
a.Presentation	8.7	7.7	15.4	27.9	40.4	100%
b.Spreadsheets	34.6	21.2	17.3	18.3	5.8	97.10%
c.Internet content	1.0	4.8	29.8	44.2	18.3	98.10%
d.Word Proc	3.8	3.8	10.6	30.8	48.1	97.10%
e.Audio	22.1	21.2	29.8	16.3	5.8	95.20%
f.Video	12.5	14.4	45.2	19.2	6.7	98.10%
g.Animation	51.9	17.3	16.3	7.7	1.9	95.20%
h.Email	5.8	1.9	2.9	21.2	66.3	98.10%
i.Dis. Boards	35.6	16.3	24.0	12.5	8.7	97.10%
j.Chats	70.2	10.6	11.5	1.9	0	94.20%
k.CMS	9.6	8.7	12.5	18.3	50.0	99.00%
l.Blogs	86.5	4.8	4.8	1.9	1.0	99.00%
m.Podcasts	80.0	5.8	8.7	1.9	1.9	99.00%
n.Wikis	84.6	7.7	3.8	1.9	1.0	99.00%

Faculty's adoption of instructional technology was measured three ways: Intensity (question 1), Extensity (question 1), and Intention (question 20). Intensity is the frequency of use of each technology (Table 5), Extensity is the average use of all the fourteen technologies for each respondent, and Intention is the faculty's intent to use technology. Table 6 shows the descriptive statistics for both Extensity and Intention. In the Extensity inquiry, faculty's' range of scores was 9-42 with a mean score of 23.4, and Intention ranged from 1-4 with a mean score of 3.29. As the mean describes the central location of the data and the standard deviation describes the spread; results indicate these respondent have a strong intention to use instructional technology and a mid to low use rate of each of the fourteen technologies (instructional technology adoption).

Commitment to pedagogical quality (CPQ) is comprised of questions 3, 5, 7, 11, 14, 16, and 18. This variable takes a closer look at the participants' value of teaching and student learning. Faculty's CPQ ranged between 14-26, with a mean score of 21.57, indicating that, in general, these respondents had strong commitments to the quality of their teaching. Each range was calculated through SPSS's descriptive statistics tool, which revealed the collective min and max of respondent's answers. Beliefs about instructional technology (beliefs) were measured through questions (2, 4, 6, and 17). Beliefs ranged between a 7-16 with a mean score of 13.50. Generally, respondents' beliefs about instructional technology were positive. Motives to use instructional technology (motives) examined respondent's perceptions of the presence of both intrinsic and extrinsic incentives through questions 19 and 21. Motives ranged

Table 6. Descriptive statistics for variables

Variables	N	Min	Max	Possible	Mean	SD
Extensity	89	9	42	0-56	23.40	6.89
Intention	104	1	4	0-4	3.29	0.64
CPQ	101	14	26	0-28	21.57	2.49
Beliefs	103	7	16	0-16	13.50	2.09
Motives	95	2	25	0-32	10.19	4.05
AoR	101	2	23	0-15	13.86	4.78
Years Taught in HE	99	1	40	open	15.12	10.27
Academic Title	99	1	4	0-5	2.30	0.89
Institution Type	100	0	4	0-5	1.68	1.13
Tenure Status	101	1	2	0-2	1.60	0.49
Specialization	N	Min	Max	Possible	Mean	SD
Health	104	0	1	0	0.34	0.47
Business	104	0	1	0	0.05	0.21
Communication	104	0	1	0	0.05	0.21
Education	104	0	1	0	0.02	0.14
Law	104	0	1	0	0.09	0.28
Liberal Arts	104	0	1	0	0.13	0.33
Pharmacy	104	0	1	0	0.15	0.36
Science	104	0	1	0	0.12	0.32

between 2-25 with a total mean score of 10.19. Broken down further, extrinsic motives (question 19) ranged from 7-25 with a mean score of 7, and intrinsic motives (question 21) ranged from 2-4 with a mean score of 3. In short, these respondents indicated a very low degree of extrinsic incentives for adopting technology (the shape of the curve is skewed to the right), but relatively high intrinsic motivation (the shape of the curve is skewed to the left). Adequacy of resources (AoR) was measured through questions 8, 9, 10, 12, 13, and 15. AoR ranged between 2-23 with a mean score of 13.86.

Respondents' mean score indicates a strong commitment to pedagogical quality, a positive set of beliefs about instructional technology, and high intrinsic motivation to use it in education. A middling mean score for AoR indicates faculty occasional/frequent level of satisfaction with their institution's adequacy of resources. A low mean score on extrinsic motivation indicates that faculty perceived a lack of institutional incentives to use instructional technology. In addition, it is important to note CPQ and belief scores are at or near the maximum possible level, a ceiling effect (Table 6). In general, a high mean score creates a problem of generalization; it may be that any patterns found may not extend beyond this population. Plus CPQ's scores have a lack of variability, a restriction of range. Restricted range correlations may be greater in a more varied population or it may be this study's sample was different from the population originally hypothesized about. These distributions are important to note and may signify a reduced size in correlation in subsequent analyses.

A Cronbach alpha was conducted for each variable. This test was conducted to measure the reliability of each variable. All variables (except CPQ = .422) statistically demonstrated inter-item consistency, greater then .60 (Table 7). The low Cronbach alpha for CPQ was an anticipated finding, because the hypothesized operations it measured were two-fold; the value of teaching and the value of student learning. As these operations define this variable, their presence and depth may be difficult for respondents to express.

Both a Bartlett's test of sphericity and Kaiser-Meyer-Olkin's (KMO) measure of sampling adequacy revealed a factor analysis is an appropriate analysis for the CPQ variable, yielding a highly significant value ($p < .001$) and an accepted value of .529 respectively (Table 8). A factor analysis (using a principal component extraction) revealed CPQ's commonalities among its items (Table 8). An eigenvalue of 1.0 or greater was required to retain a factor. Each of the seven question extractions accounted for the shared variance among CPQ with a range between 43.3%-76.5%. The factor analysis yielded three factors that met the criteria. The 'value of student learning' (questions 5 and 18) was the first factor extracted and accounted for 26.6% of the variance. The second factor was the 'value of teaching success' (questions 7, 11, 16) and accounted for 19.9% of the variance after rotation. Finally, the 'value of teaching' factor (questions 3 and 14) accounted for 15.9%. The 'value of teaching success' was not a planned factor in this measure of CPQ and the questions that comprise this factor were conceived to measure the valuing of student learning and teaching. Future research may need to include interviews to clarify this construct and re-design questions. In addition, there are other issues that need to be taken into account when interpreting CPQ scores: number of survey responses; the wording of survey questions 3, 5, 7, 11, 14, 16, and 18; the limitations of a survey as a research instrument; and the faculty sample. These issues

Table 7. Cronbach alpha of variables

Variable	Cronbach Alpha
CPQ	0.422
Instructional Technology Adoption	0.725
Beliefs	0.770
Motives	0.767
AoR	0.816

Table 8. CPQ factor analysis

Item	Extraction		
Q3	.646	KMO	. 529
Q5	.650	Bartlett	Approx. Chi-Square = 74.381
Q7	.542		df = 21.000
Q11	.649		Sig = .000
Q14	.691		
Q16	.433		
Q18	.765		

Table 9. Intensity correlations with CPQ

Technology	Pearson Correlation	Sig. (1-tailed)
Presentation	-.013	.45
Spreadsheet	.157	.06
Internet Content	.178*	.038
Word Processing	.207*	.02
Audio	.281**	.003
Video	.187*	.031
Animation	.005	.48
Email	.192*	.028
Discussion Board	.221*	.014
Chats	.191*	.031
CMS	.194*	.026
Blog	.042	.337
Podcast	-.054	.296
Wiki	-.045	.329

will be discussed in detail later in this chapter. Additionally, CPQ will be discussed as both a summed variable and then by each question to find relationships and predictors at the item level.

A correlation was conducted between intensity (frequency of use) and commitment to pedagogical quality (CPQ). Eight tools showed a positive low correlation with (CPQ): Internet content, word processing, audio, video, email, discussion boards, chats and content management systems (Table 9). Asterisk items highlight areas which represent a significant correlation. The indicated use of these instructional technology tools points to a relationship with respondent's commitment to pedagogical quality.

CPQ as a Summed Variable

Correlations were used to determine the strength and direction of relationships between each variable (Table 10). Asterisk items highlight areas which represent a significant correlation. Six variables produced significant associations: extensity, intention, CPQ, beliefs, motives, and AoR. The two measures of instructional technology adoption (extensity and intention) are positively correlated ($r = .340, p<.01$). That is, the more positively a respondent felt about the use of instructional technologies the more likely they were to use different types. A positive correlation between CPQ and extensity can be seen ($r = .348, p = .00$) and no relationship exists between CPQ and intention ($r = -.040, p>.1$). Of interest, motives ($r = .207, p<.05$) and beliefs ($r = .516, p=.00$) are correlated with intention. Beliefs had a low correlation with extensity ($r = .182, p=<.05$). Plus, motives were found to be correlated with AoR ($r = .266, p<.01$). In addition, categorical variables showed relationships among variables. Tenure status ($r = .205, P<.05$) and academic title ($r = .214, P<.05$) showed a low correlation with CPQ. A low and negative correlation is present for the number of years faculty taught in higher education with CPQ ($r = -0.238, p = 01$) and beliefs ($r = -0.209, p<.05$). Specialization/discipline also played a significant role with intention and beliefs. A low correlation exists between health and intention ($r = .220, p<.05$) and law and AoR ($r = .214, p<.05$). A negative low correlation can be seen between liberal arts and AoR ($r = -0.206, p< 0.05$). In addition, a low and negative correlation exists for faculty with a specialization in business and their intention to use instructional technology adoption ($r = -.247, p<.01$). Lastly, communication and extensity showed a small correlation at r = .201, p<.05. These correlations are laid out in Table 10 for reference.

Two separate backward stepwise regressions were conducted; one with Intention (q20) as the dependent variable and the other with Extensity as the dependent variable (Table 11). A backwards stepwise regression was the best way to determine which variable had the greater predictive power for adopting instructional technology, specifically CPQ predictive qualities. All variables, but motives were normally distributed. As motives measures questions 19 and 21 (intrinsic and extrinsic incentives), results showed a slightly skewed curve following a few large outliers. In some cases, extreme values in data provide useful information about values of some of the coefficients and a realistic guide to the scale of errors (Brase and Brase, 2003). This study will proceed with the regression analysis with the motive variable assumptions in mind. One way to protect against type 1 error is to take a more exploratory approach to data analysis, and a backwards stepwise regression is well-suited to exploratory analysis. Exploratory analysis looks for reasonable statistically detectable relations and counts on replication to confirm them (Williams, 2003). Patterns are suggestive and need confirmation through replication. The analysis begins with an examination of the combined effect of all of the variables on the dependent variable. One by one, variables (usually starting with the weakest predictor) are removed, and a new analysis emerges.

Table 10. Pearson correlation among variables

Continuous variables						
	Intention	Extensity	CPQ	Beliefs	Motives	AoR
Intention		0.34**	0.04	0.52**	0.217*	-0.04
Extensity	0.34**		0.35**	0.18	0.12	0.05
CPQ	0.04	0.35**		0.18	-0.01	0.08
Beliefs	0.52**	0.18	0.18		0.14	0.07
Motives	0.21*	0.12	-0.01	0.14		0.27*
AoR	-0.04	0.05	0.08	0.07	0.27*	
Continuous variables with categorical variables						
	Intention	Extensity	CPQ	Beliefs	Motives	AoR
Years Taught in HE	-0.11	-0.01	-0.24**	-0.21*	0.13	-0.07
Academic Title	0.12	-0.02	0.21*	0.14	-0.15	0.08
Institution Type	0.01	-0.17	-0.12	0.05	-0.11	0.01
Tenure Status	0.05	-0.19	0.21*	0.15	-0.10	0.06
Health	0.22**	0.02	0.07	0.19	-0.01	-0.14
Business	-0.25**	0.07	-0.02	-0.14	-0.07	-0.05
Communication	0.11	0.20*	0.13	0.18	-0.06	0.05
Education	0.16	0.01	0.10	0.17	-0.02	-0.01
Law	-0.14	-0.18	0.17	-0.09	-0.11	0.21*
Liberal Arts	0.01	0.01	-0.11	-0.11	0.01	-0.21*
Pharmacy	-0.07	-0.03	-0.06	-0.01	0.12	0.20
Science	-0.07	0.04	-0.10	-0.05	0.02	0.11

* Correlation is significant at the .05 level (1-tailed) ** Correlation is significant at the .01 level (1-tailed) Correlation sample size ranged from 83-103

The results provide coefficients for each variable, telling the degree to which each (when combined with the others) contributes to predicting the dependent variable (Williams, 2003).

Findings revealed beliefs about instructional technology (beliefs) ($R2 = .160$, $p < .05$) as a significant predictor of intention to use instructional technology, accounting for 16% of the variance. Motives and faculty in Health disciplines were almost significant at p=.055 and p=.058), respectively: together accounting for 7% of the variance. These coefficient scores might suggest a trend; it implies further study may be needed to warrant how motives and the field of health contribute to intention. Remarkably, CPQ (R2=.160, p<01) and institutional type (R2 = .160, p<05) were statistically significant predictors of extensity, accounting for 32% of the variance. The other variables have no impact on extensity. Of note, the number of years taught in higher education was the only mediator variable found to be statistically significant to CPQ (R2=.077 p<.01), accounting for 7% of the variance.

CPQ Analyzed by Item

Stepwise regression analysis was used to explore further the relationships between items that constituted the, CPQ variable and both intention and extensity (Table 12). Results showed question 7 (the way I teach is more important than course content) accounted for 9% of the variance in extensity ($R2 = .096$, $p < .05$). This finding shows that respondents' use of instructional technology might predict their greater concern for teaching processes rather than course content. In addition, question 5 (eager to find new ways to help students learn) is statistically significant ($p < .05$) and

Table 11. Backwards stepwise regressions

Intention						
		Unstandardized Coefficients		Standardized Coefficients		
Model		B	Std. Error	Beta	t	Sig.
14	(Constant)	1.656	.409		4.045	.000
	Beliefs	.096	.030	.327	3.191	.002
	Motives	.026	.013	.195	1.945	.055
	Health discipline	.218	.113	.195	1.927	.058
Extensity						
		Unstandardized Coefficients		Standardized Coefficients		
Model		B	Std. Error	Beta	t	Sig.
15	(Constant)	7.355	7.167		1.026	.308
	CPQ	.885	.316	.312	2.800	.007
	Institution Type	-1.410	.684	-.230	-2.060	.043
Commitment to Pedagogical Quality (CPQ)						
		Unstandardized Coefficients		Standardized Coefficients		
Model		B	Std. Error	Beta	t	Sig.
12	(Constant)	22.611	.447		50.627	.000
	Years taught in HE	-.067	.024	-.277	-2.723	.008

question 16 (my teaching is successful when my students demonstrate their learning) is marginally significant (p = .052); together they account for 7% of the variance for intention (R2 = .079). This finding revealed two factors: 1. Faculty's intention to use technology in education is related to those who are eager to use new ways to help students learn, and; 2. Faculty who feel their teaching is successful when their students demonstrate their learning co-varies with their intention to use instructional technology.

Potential limitations of a self-reporting survey involve honesty and accuracy of responses. This inquiry acknowledges these potential limitations, but assumes participants have been truthful and accurate in their responses because there would be no special advantage for dishonest or exaggerated responses. In addition, the anonymity of the survey supported the likelihood of candid responses, and question format (reverse responses, placement/order of questions, and language use) assisted in triangulation (Mann and Stewart, 2000). However, the reader should keep in mind that this survey about technology adoption was administered through technological means. It is possible that non-responders differed systematically from responders and that this difference was due in part to the means of survey administration. That is, technology users might be more likely than non-users to complete an Internet–based survey. In addition, non-respondents were mostly assistant and associate professors with a small population holding tenure status. The profile of non-respondents does not seem to match the profile of respondents. It would be worthwhile to produce a future study with a sample size yielding alternative faculty demographics.

DISCUSSION

This research assumes that Technology, Content, and Pedagogical Knowledge (TPCK) should not be isolated from each other; good teaching and successful technology implementation require their integration (Mishra and Koehler, 2006). TPCK highlights what faculty members need to know to teach in an information age. This value of teaching is part of the commitment to pedagogical quality (CPQ) variable. Commitment to pedagogical quality describes faculty's commitment to acquiring, maintaining, and changing this

Table 12. CPQ analyzed by question (Q3, Q5, Q7, Q11, Q14, Q16, Q18)

Extensity						
Model		Unstandardized Coefficients		Standardized Coefficients	t	Sig.
		B	Std. Error	Beta		
6	(Constant)	8.213	6.361		1.291	.200
	Q7	1.604	.767	.219	2.091	.040
	Q14	3.042	1.660	.192	1.833	.070
Intention						
Model		Unstandardized Coefficients		Standardized Coefficients	t	Sig.
		B	Std. Error	Beta		
6	(Constant)	2.978	.578		5.152	.000
	Q5	.267	.126	.206	2.126	.036
	Q16	-.190	.097	-.191	-1.965	.052

knowledge as they continue to teach and as new instructional technologies surface. An adoption model which focuses on content, technology, and pedagogy was deemed worth investigating and may be central to facilitation of instructional technology adoption in higher education. As this work suggests, there is a need for professional development in higher education to foster constructivist pedagogy. It is this constructivist's lens which is valuable during professional development design and gives a workable approach when creating affective interactions to optimize learning. This work challenges future research to explore higher education, faculty characteristics and their commitment to pedagogical quality, as a way to develop instructional technology adoption models. This study's purpose is to identify what motivates full-time faculty in higher educational institutions to incorporate instructional technology in their instructional practice. It is clear faculty's commitment to pedagogical quality occurs or exists with instructional technology adoption.

Current instructional technology adoption models (ITAMs) show a lack of focus on pedagogy and are mostly developed for an alternative audience and environment, outside the realities and characteristics of higher education. Three audience categories naturally emerge (non-educational, K-12, and higher education) as an initial way to group these models. Essentially, an ITAM should be written to be audience-specific for the purpose of implementation. Thus, models should be tailored to non-educational communities, K-12 educational settings, and higher educational institutions. By creating these groupings, ITAMs will be better able to meet the needs of each community, highlighting how they treat teaching and learning differently. Since this study is interested in higher educational institutions, we have learned that higher education has specific goals and qualities that are unique to developing successful teaching and learning initiatives (Grosso de Leon, 2001). Thus, higher education ITAMs should be developed within its context. Preliminary research outlined in the literature review suggest beliefs about instructional technology (beliefs), motives, and adequacy of resources (AoR) affect instructional technology adoption (Table 3), but little was found to describe the importance of an instructor's commitment to pedagogical quality in technology adoption.

Practically, this information will aid administrators and instructional technology staff when supporting and assisting faculty in incorporating technology in instruction. Most importantly, it will inform faculty on how to identify their own commitments to education and how those commitments are related to their acceptance of change or innovation. Essentially, its goal is to understand what engages faculty to change and improve their own teaching through the use of technologies, what affects their readiness to innovate and improve their pedagogical quality.

In subsequent sections, I will first discuss the relationship between commitment to pedagogical quality and instructional technology adoption, second the degree to which beliefs, motives, adequacy of resources, and categorical variables (mediator variables) predict instructional technology adoption, then finally the relationship between commitment to pedagogical quality and the mediator variables.

Commitment to Pedagogical Quality and Instructional Technology Adoption

A central question in this study is whether an instructor's commitment to pedagogical quality would explain the instructor's willingness to adopt technology in education. Instructional technology adoption was measured in three ways: 'intensity' (the frequency a particular tool is used), 'extensity' (the average use of fourteen identified technologies), and 'intention' (faculty's intent to use technology). It is important to reiterate that this study is looking for linear correlational (not necessarily causal) relationships. Furthermore, this study does not attempt to distinguish between a thoughtful and unreflective adoption of instructional technology. The study implicitly assumes that technological adoption is a conscious and positive choice of individual faculty members.

A Commitment to Pedagogical Quality (CPQ) score was the sum of responses to seven questions (questions 3, 5, 7, 11, 14, 16, and 18) that measure the respondents' valuing of teaching and student learning. Due to CPQ's low Cronbach alpha measure (.422) and the factor analysis indicating three measures rather than two, the CPQ variable was measured as a summed variable and then by each question to find relationships and predictors at the item level. In this study, CPQ's scores were clustered at or near the maximum possible level (ceiling effect) and thus restricted in range. As a new construct, this study is the first attempt to measure CPQ and define it as the value of teaching and student learning. In future research, the questions that comprise this variable may need to be redesigned to allow more range of responses and look closer at a new measure of CPQ, the 'value of teaching success'..

CPQ as a Summed Variable

Respondents indicated their use of fourteen instructional technology tools during the last two semesters they have taught (intensity). These tools fell into either a rank of high use (Internet Content, Word Processing, Email, and CMS), middle use (Spreadsheets, Audio, Video, Discussion Boards), or low use (Animation, Chats, Blogs, Podcats, and Wiki's). CPQ was found to be positively correlated with intensity for specific tools including Internet Content, Word Processing, Audio, Video, Email, Discussion Board, Chats, and CMS. When paired with CPQ, this finding indicates faculty's use of particular tools is related to faculty's value of teaching and/or their value of student learning. For example, it may be faculty use internet content (which was given a high use rank) because they value this tool as an important teaching and learning resources. On the opposite end, faculty may not value "Chats" as a teaching and learning resource. Future research should include participant interviews to sort through high, middle and low use relationships (intensity) between CPQ.

Technological Pedagogical Content Knowledge (TPCK) highlights what faculty members need to know to teach in an information age. It presumes that Technology, Content, and Pedagogy must not be isolated from each other for good teaching and successful technology implementation. This value of teaching is part of the CPQ construct. This study suggests Faculty are committed to acquiring, maintaining, and changing their knowledge as they continue to teach and as new instructional technologies surface. We see this through the results of the CPQ construct as a summed variable and then by each question. A backwards stepwise regression showed CPQ predicted extensity (range of technology use). This indicates a possibility that those with a strong commitment are willing to try a variety of approaches. In addition, it is also possible that faculty who like to experiment with technologies coincidentally have a strong commitment. These two possibilities are important to note because this study did not gather data to investigate the nature of the relationship. Just that a relationship exists. Further research is needed to forecast the nature of the relationship between CPQ and extensity.

CPQ Analyzed by Item

Because the CPQ items showed low consistency, correlations were explored between extensity and individual CPQ items. Respondents to this survey were more likely to use a variety of software (extensity) when they indicated they valued the processes of teaching over the content they taught (question 7). This finding hints at the possibility that TPCK is not a unified construct, but that pedagogical knowledge has primacy over technological and content knowledge when it comes to successful technology integration in teaching. Taking this notion a step further, pedagogical knowledge is a fundamental necessity for successful teaching, learning, and technology adoption to occur. The questions used in this survey looked more at attitudes and motives, but it is practical to think that pedagogical knowledge, knowledge of good teaching practices, provide a framework into which knowledge of technology and content are woven to enhance student learning. Future research should investigate faculty's level of content and teaching knowledge in relationship to their value of teaching over the content they taught. This empirical investigation could contribute much to the field of educational theory and practice.

Two CPQ items were significantly correlated with intention to use instructional technology. Respondents that were "eager to find new ways to help students learn" (question 5) and "regarded student learning as a chief evaluative criteria for success in teaching" (question 16), reported more likelihood to use technology. Commitment to student learning may be an important motivating variable in faculty adoption of technology. These results provide clear evidence that commitment to pedagogical quality should be considered a valuable part of technology adoption models in higher education.

Mediator Variables and Instructional Technology Adoption

Instructional technology adoption is a strong initiative in higher educational institutions pushing faculty to change and innovate. There are factors (mediator variables) that affect the adoption process. Mediator variables investigated in this study consisted of beliefs about instructional technology (beliefs), motives, adequacy of resources (AoR), and categorical variables (academic title, institution type, tenure status, and specialization). Various research in the literature review described the complex and expected role of each faculty member in higher education, including and going beyond teaching, scholarship, and service (Wergin, 1994; Boyer, 1990; Lucas and Murray, 2002; Wolcott, 1998; Morris, 2004; Camblin, and Steger, 2000). In addition, academic title, teaching experience, and tenure status are factors that predict faculty's involvement in change (Bradshaw, 2002; Boyer, 1990; Diamond, 2002; and Pryor and Pryor, 2005).

Results of a backwards stepwise regression revealed that 16% of the variance in faculty's intent to use technology is predicted by their beliefs about instructional technology. It is easy to imagine that a faculty member who believes instructional technology can enhance student learning in their discipline would be more likely to use technology to enhance teaching and learning. Not surprisingly, faculty members who reported more frequent extrinsic and intrinsic motives for technology use reported a stronger intent to use technology. However, it is not clear why results revealed faculty who teach health related courses intend to use technology more than other disciplines. It is possible that the health professions may promote the use of technology more in practice and educators are transferring its importance in the classroom. Also, it could be an institutional factor, considering out of the four colleges, one was a medical school and another a pharmacy school. It maybe that faculty at Albany Medical College and Albany College of Pharmacy are more likely to use technology. Future research may need to use a larger and more diverse sample of respondents to study how these two variables contribute to 'intention'.

Faculty beliefs about instructional technology were found to be related to the range of technology use and intention to use technology. These findings reinforce current research in the field pertaining to beliefs as an influence on instructional technology adoption (Ferguson, 2004; Sugar, Crawley and Fine, 2004; Zayim, Yildirim, and Saka, 2006; Davis, Bagozzi, and Warshaw, 1989; Wolski and Jackson, 1999; Hall and Hord, 1987; Dooley, 1999; Langer, 2005; Kotter, 1996; Dwyer, Ringstaff and Sandholtz, 1990, Pryor and Pryor, 2005). Specifically, this study examined faculty's beliefs about instructional technology's ability to enhance student learning in a discipline, be productive to learning, enhance their own teaching, and serve as an important aspect in higher education. The Model of Reasoned Action (MORA) (Pryor and Pryor, 2005) describes how personal and social factors affect the decision process. The personal factors focus on attitudes and feelings about the behavior, whereas social factors focus on perceptions of social pressure. This model helps explain how beliefs form and how they can be influenced.

Institutional type was found to be related to the range of technology use (extensity). Institutional type was comprised of four choices; teaching college, research college, both, or other (Figure 3, pg 45). The majority of respondents (56%) considered their college to be a teaching college, 32% were both, none answered research college, and 12% chose other. The extent to which a respondent used technology was predicted by the perceived mission of the respondent's institution. For our respondents, the way an institution defines its mission (or the way they interpret the mission) is important, and it does affect the extent to which technology is used. This may be due to the specific types of institutions that were used in this study, who may highlight these factors as more important than the standard teaching/research dichotomy. An instructional technology adoption model which takes institutional type into consideration for predicting extensity could investigate the way faculty, administration, and support staff, think about and implement technology in higher education. Clearly, the institutional type variable sets higher education apart from other entities (Barone and Hagner, 2001; Jacobsen, 1997 and 1998; Hagner, 2001; Kearsley and Shneiderman, 1998; Mars and Ginter, 2007; Buckley, 2002; Garrison, Anderson, and Archer, 2000). It is this distinction, which highlights the need for higher education ITAMs to be developed for its audience, based on the unique qualities these institutions comprise.

Commitment to Pedagogical Quality and the Mediator Variables

Most respondents in this study were non-tenured (60.4%). Non-tenured faculty were more committed to the quality of teaching and student learning than tenured faculty. Similarly, assistant and associate professors were more committed to pedagogical quality. There are various possible explanations for these correlations. Non-tenured and lower ranked faculty may, in general, be newer to their faculty roles and approach teaching with greater "freshness" and enthusiasm. It is possible too that "newer" untenured faculty may differ from their older colleagues in their sensitivity to student activity in the learning process. It is also possible that the criteria for achieving tenure and promotions have a negative influence on a faculty's commitment to pedagogical quality. In addition, it may be beneficial to investigate the properties of each academic title to determine a set of qualities that comprises each. Future research could examine these possible relations in more detail.

The number of years a respondent taught in higher education (question 22) accounted for 7% of the variance in CPQ. Data revealed 67 respondents fell into the 1-20 years teaching range and 32 respondents taught 21-40 years (n=99), with a mean score of 15 years of teaching. Clearly, faculty members who taught 20 or fewer years tend to be more committed to pedagogical quality. Why are professors who have taught more than 20 years less committed to teaching? What characteristics of these two populations influence this distinction between levels of commitment? With this said, I do not think that all faculty who have been teaching for awhile will fall in this category, since the distinction is very small (7%). But it is important to note as administrators and technology staff work to enhance the instructional technology adoption efforts among each faculty member. Thus, a comprehensive analysis would need to be conducted to look particularly at years of teaching experience in higher education as a lead variable in commitment. In addition, the CPQ variable could be altered to include alternative questions that expand beyond the faculty's value of teaching and student learning. The faculty's value of scholarship, service, and teaching could operationalize CPQ or maybe it is the institution's value of teaching and student learning. Either way, there is much opportunity in the educational field to further investigate the concept of CPQ and evaluate its role in education. This research is an initial investigation and begins the conversation about CPQ.

As a possible explanation for the correlation of these three variables (academic title, tenure status, and number of years teaching) with CPQ, these variables could be considered connected. In fact, it is usually part of the promotion and tenure (PandT) policies at each institution to link each of these demographics together (Boyer, 1990). However, even though they are linked and common, each higher educational institution has its own PandT policies which redefine how they are applied and achieved. Future research should investigate relationships between these variables and promotion and tenure guidelines at each institution. This study did not collect promotion and tenure data from its participants or sample colleges. However, a scattered pattern did emerge regarding respondents results. For example, individuals who taught for 7 years (N=8) were both professors with tenure (N=3) and assistant professors without tenure (N=5). Institutional characteristics (such as promotion and tenure guidelines, hiring strategies, institution type, etc.) will be different (Bradshaw, 2002, Boyer, 1990, Diamond, 2002, and Pryor and Pryor, 2005) and may alter the relationships between these three variables. This data would be interesting to gather and analyze against academic title, tenure status, and number of years teaching. Further research is needed to investigate inter-variable relationships among institutions that have these different characteristics.

Theoretical and Practical Implications

The primary goal of this research was to examine the role of commitment to pedagogical quality in instructional technology adoption in a higher education setting. This research assumed that Technology, Content, and Pedagogical Knowledge (TPCK) should not be isolated from each other if good teaching and successful technology implementation were to be achieved (Mishra and Koehler, 2006). Figure 3 displays a summary of variable relationships that resulted from this study. As you can see this illustration is much different from the model hypothesized previously, as the mediator variable relationships have changed.

This model shows ways in which the dependent and independent variable (IV and DV) depend on mediator variables. In fact, none of the variables are "mediators" in the ways I originally hypothesized and seem to play a very different role with the IV and DV altogether. Correlation data (Table 8 and 9) and regression results (Table 10 and 11) suggest these relationships and predictors are much more complex, involving interaction with both the IV and DV. Based on this study's findings, moving each variable and their relationship point was based upon the following: beliefs and categorical variables (academic title, years taught in higher education, and tenure status) are affecting both the IV and DV independently; motives affect just the DV, and perceived adequacy of resources (AoR) was not found to correlate to any other variable.

This study looked at instructional technology adoption models (ITAMs) in relation to the intended audience. Previous research showed little effort has been made to organize these models by their primary features. Three audience categories naturally emerge (non-educational, K-12, and higher education) as an initial way to group ITAMs. Essentially, an ITAM should be relevant to the audience of implementation. Thus, technology adoption models should be tailored to non-educational communities, K-12 educational settings, and higher educational institutions. Through such groupings, ITAMs will be better able to meet the needs of each community by highlighting how they treat teaching and learning differently. Since this study is interested in higher educational institutions, we have learned that higher education has unique goals and qualities for developing successful teaching and learning initiatives (Grosso de Leon, 2001). Thus, higher education ITAMs should be developed within its context.

Practically, this information will aid administrators and instructional technology staff when supporting and assisting faculty in incorporating technology in instruction. By knowing faculty's CPQ, administrators and support staff can tailor adoption strategies and engage faculty further into the adoption process through these commitments. It is this insight into the way each faculty member values teaching and student learning that may be the key to adoption. Most importantly, it will inform faculty on how to identify their own commitments to the profession [education] and how those commitments are related to their acceptance of change or innovation, plus additional variables that affect adoption. Figure 4 shows a working view of how the higher education community can begin to look and to define themselves within the context of their instructional technology adoption and commitments to pedagogical quality.

This 2x2 is a starting point to see the connections between these two variables. Essentially, its goal is to understand how commitments affect readiness to innovate and how readiness to innovate affects commitments. Even further, it initiates the conversation on what engages faculty to change and improve their own teaching. This model provides a simple way to identify

Figure 3. Variable relationships

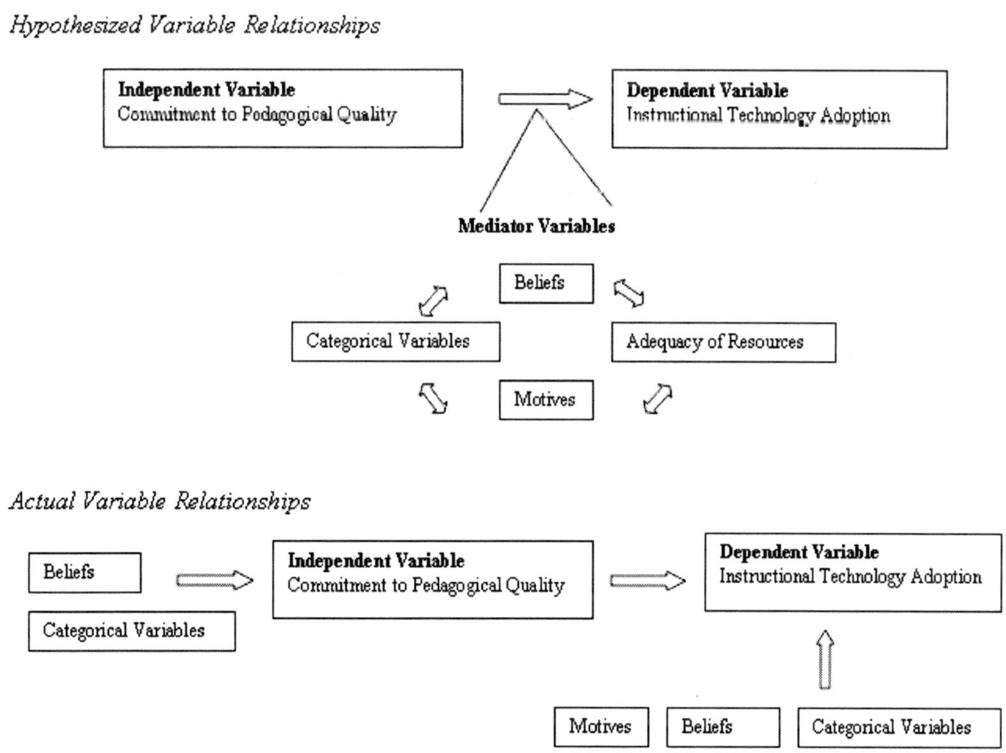

Figure 4. Instructional technology adoption and CPQ 2x2

Instructional Technology Adoption →

CPQ ↓

Low Low	High Low
Low High	High High

where an individual faculty fits among these two variables. This 2x2 does not emerge from my data, but is a useful way to provide a thought-experiment about the relationship between CPQ and technology adoption. Other directionalities were not explored in this study. It is possible, even likely, that the motives and factors that influence technology adoption will interact in complex ways over time. However, my study assumes that there should be a sizable portion of faculty who fall along the diagonal (low-low, and high-high). In spite of the vagaries of my sample, the quality of the CPQ measure, and statistical difficulties (e.g., restriction of range, ceiling effects, etc.), this relationship exists and is worth talking about. For example, faculty who fall in the high-high category maybe considered an individual who is flexible and absorbent to change. Change and benefits of adoption are accepted and they are willing to participate. For those who are high CPQ, but low adoption, the support person could investigate ways to link pedagogical concern with use of technology. These faculty appear to value teaching and student learning, but are resistant to adoption because of obstacles or gaps between the two variables. The low-low faculty maybe individuals who are resistant to change, unwilling to see the benefits, and refuse to participate in best practices. Support staff will need to engage this faculty in both pedagogical knowledge and instructional technology best practices. A low CPQ, high adopter is an oddity, but might be explained by someone who is simply adopting technology for love of technology or for some other valued incentive. As their understanding of their value of teaching and student learning increases, they are able to see the benefits and apply their use of technology to teaching and learning by using best practices. This group and the low-low category need the most training on the importance of teaching and its effects on learning.

With this knowledge, faculty may begin to question what CPQ means for them. Is it the value of teaching and student learning, or do they think about it differently; perhaps in terms of service, scholarship and teaching? Is it the institution's definition, or is it the professors' definition? Essentially, commitment to pedagogical quality has not been looked at in the past nor taken into consideration when change occurs in higher education. By introducing CPQ as a factor in adopting instructional technology, we can begin to develop deeper knowledge of the professoriate. In addition, knowing the relationship and predictive qualities of motives, beliefs and categorical variables will assist in implementation process.

FUTURE RESEARCH DIRECTIONS

There are a number of ways in which this research can be extended. It would be important for future research to clarify the definition of CPQ and develop a set of question that best operationalizes it. The low Cronbach alpha for CPQ, to some extent, was an expected finding, because it was originally hypnotized as a two-fold measure: the value of teaching and the value of student learning.

However a third operation emerged through the factor analysis, the 'value of teaching success'. As these operations define this variable in this study, their presence and depth may be difficult for respondents to express. In addition, there are many possible factors that could explain CPQ's low Cronbach score including number of survey responses; the wording of survey questions; the limitations of a survey as a research instrument; and the faculty sample.

It would be interesting to extend the results of this study to faculty from other higher educational institutions, with a larger sample size (number of respondents to the survey), and varying faculty characteristics. As stated previously, higher education characteristics and the faculty profession are two unique entities which have very different goals and features from other environments (Lucas and Murray, 2002; http://www.nysed.gov/; Wolcott, 1997 and 1998; Camblin, and Steger, 2000). We know that public and private institutions employ faculty for the primary roles of teaching, scholarship (research and publishing), and service (Wergin, 1994; Boyer, 1990). However, within this context, higher educational characteristics (i.e. promotion and tenure policies, mission, administration, etc.) can be very different among institutions and may yield different results.

Another possibility for future research involves the addition of interviews. This methodology would help researchers to understand the meaning behind the survey responses. In general, interview questions should expand upon survey responses and help clarify results/choices. For example, a follow up interview may have provided further details to explain the relationship between CPQ and the intensity of use of particular technologies. Also, measuring faculty's CPQ maybe better surveyed with the addition of interviews. Future research could use a set of standardized questions that adhere to interview protocol techniques to probe the respondent for in-depth information. This qualitative data may prove helpful to the overall quality and robustness of this study. In addition, respondents in this study all participated through the internet and most reported high technology use and high CPQ. Future research might target faculty with low technology use and low CPQ, plus provide hard copy survey's for alternative data collection. In addition, future research should explore the quality of instructional technology adoption. This study only looked for linear relationships and was not sensitive enough to distinguish between a thoughtful and unreflective adoption of instructional technology. Other relationships between instructional technology adoption and CPQ could be explored. It is possible that adoption over time is a much more complex, dynamic, and interactive process than a linear relationship suggests. These factors are worth investigating and would provide further insight into the commitments and professional development needs of faculty.

CONCLUSION

Instructional technology adoption models (ITAMs) were examined in relation to their intended audience and pedagogical qualities. This research indicated little effort has been made in the field to organize these models by their primary features. Three audience categories naturally emerge (non-educational, K-12, and higher education) as an initial way to group ITAMs. Essentially, an ITAM should be written to be audience specific for the purpose of implementation. Thus, models should be tailored to non-educational communities, K-12 educational settings and higher educational institutions. ITAMs will be better able to meet the needs of each community by highlighting how each community treats teaching and learning differently. Since this study was interested in higher educational institutions, we have learned that higher education has specific goals and qualities that are unique to developing successful teaching and learning initiatives. Thus, higher education ITAMs should be developed within its own context.

An extensive statistical analysis was conducted in an effort to examine the role of faculty's commitment to pedagogical quality (CPQ) when adopting instructional technology in higher education. This study found commitment to pedagogical quality (CPQ) does influence the adoption of instructional technology. This is shown as CPQ is measured as a summed variable and then by each question to find relationships and predictors at the item level. The three CPQ survey questions that stood out as predictors of technology adoption included: finding new ways to help students learn, teaching is successful when students demonstrate their learning, and teaching style is more important than content. Beliefs about instructional technology and certain categorical variables (academic title, years taught in higher education, and tenure status) affected both faculty's commitment to pedagogical quality (independent variable) and their adoption of instructional technology (dependent variable). Motives (intrinsic and extrinsic) and faculty teaching in health-related courses also affect the adoption of instructional technology, but the perceived adequacy of resources (AoR) was unrelated to both the independent and dependent variable. If future research can provide support for the results found here, and address the limitations of the current research, the CPQ variable may prove to be a viable tool to further establish successful adoption of instructional technology in higher education.

REFERENCES

Ajzen, I. (1985). From intentions to action: A theory of planned behavior . In Kuhl, J., & Beckman, J. (Eds.), *Action-control: From cognition to behavior* (pp. 11–39). Heidelberg, Germany: Springer.

Bai, H., & Lehman, J. (2003). Impact of a professional development project on university faculty members' perceptions and use of technology. In *Proceedings of World Conference on Educational Multimedia, Hypermedia and Telecommunications 2003* (pp. 1927-1934). Norfolk, VA: AACE.

Barone, C., & Hagner, P. (2001). *Technology-enhanced teaching and learning: Leading and supporting the transformation on your campus*. San Francisco: Jossey-Bass.

Beaudry, A., & Pinsonneault, A. (2005). Understanding user responses to information technology: A coping model of user adaptation. *Management Information Systems Quarterly*, *29*(3), 493–524.

Betts, K. (1998, October). Why do faculty participate in distance education? The technology source. Retrieved from http://ts.mivu.org/default.asp?show=articleandid=6

Boyer, E. (1990). *Scholarship Reconsidered: Priorities of the Professorate*. New York: The Carnegie Foundation for the Advancement of Teaching.

Bradshaw, K. L. (2002). Technology for Teaching and Learning: Strategies for Staff Development and Follow-Up Support. *Journal of Technology and Teacher Education*, 10.

Brase, H., & Brase, P. (2003). *Understanding Statistics: Concepts and Methods* (7th ed.). Boston: Houghton Mifflin.

Buckley, D. (2002, January/February). In the Pursuit of the learning paradigm: Coupling Faculty Transformation and Institutional Change. *EDUCAUSE Review*, 28–38.

Camblin, L., & Steger, J. (2000). Rethinking Faculty Development. *Higher Education*, *39*, 1–18. doi:10.1023/A:1003827925543

Carter-Chapman, R. (2004). *Faculty Technology Survey*. University of Alaska Anchorage, Office of the Vice Provost.

Chism, N. (2004). Using a Framework to Engage Faculty in Instructional Technologies. *EDUCAUSE Quarterly*, *27*(2), 39–45.

Chronicle Careers. The Chronicle of Higher Education, Washington, D.C. 20037, Available online at http://chronicle.com/jobs/.

Covington, M., & Mueller, K. (2001). Intrinsic Verses Extrinsic Motivation: An Approach/Avoidance Reformulation. *Educational Psychology Review*, *13*(2), 157–177. doi:10.1023/A:1009009219144

Cranton, P., & King, K. (2003). Transformative Learning as a Professional Development Goal. *New Directions for Adult and Continuing Education*, *98*, 31–37. doi:10.1002/ace.97

Cronk, B. (2002). *How to use SPSS: A Step-by-Step Guide to Analysis and Interpretation* (2nd ed.). Los Angeles: Pyrczak Publishing.

Davis, F. D., Bagozzi, R. P., & Warshaw, P. R. (1989). User Acceptance of Computer Technology: A Comparison of Two theoretical Models. *Management Science*, *35*(8), 982–1003. doi:10.1287/mnsc.35.8.982

Dewey, J. (1997). *How We Think. Mineola.* New York: Dover Publications.

Diamond, R. (2002). Defining Scholarship for the Twenty-First Century. *New Directions for Teaching and Learning*, *90*, 73–79. doi:10.1002/tl.57

Dolezalek, H. (2004). Comprehensive Analysis of Employer-Sponsored Training in the United States. *Training (New York, N.Y.)*, *41*(10), 20–36.

Dooley, K. E. (1999). Towards a holistic model for the diffusion of educational technologies: An integrative review of educational innovation studies. *Journal of Educational Technology & Society*, *2*(4), 35–45.

Dooly, L. M., Metcalf, T., & Martinez, A. (1999). A Study of Adoption of Computer Technology by Teachers. *Journal of Educational Technology & Society*, *2*(4), 107–115.

Durrington, V., Repman, J., & Valente, T. (2000). Using Social Network Analysis to Examine the Time of Adoption of computer-Related Services among University Faculty. *Journal of Research on Computing in Education*, *33*(1), 16–28.

Dwyer, D., Ringstaff, C., & Sandholtz, J. H. (1990). Teacher Belief and Practices Part 1: Patterns of Change. Apple Classrooms of Tomorrow, Apple Computer, Inc., 1-10.

Earle, R. (2002). The Integration of Instructional Technology into Public: Promises and Challenges. *Educational Technology Magazine, 42*(1), 5-13. Retrieved from http://asianvu.com/bookstoread/etp/earle.pdf

Ertmer, P. A. (1999). Addressing first- and second-order barriers to change: Strategies for technology integration. *Educational Technology Research and Development*, *47*(4), 47–61. doi:10.1007/BF02299597

Feenburg, A. (1991). *Critical Theory of Technology*. New York: Oxford University Press.

Ferguson, P. (2004). Faculty Beliefs about teaching with Technology. Association for Educational Communications and Technology . *Georgia State University, ERIC, ED485069*, 155–166.

Fichman, R. G. (1992). Information Technology Diffusion: A Review of Empirical Research. Proceedings of the Thirteenth International Conference on Information Systems, Dallas, 195-206. http://citeseer.ist.psu.edu/fichman92information.html

Fincher, C. (1998). Teaching and Technological Innovation: the IHE Perspectives. Georgia University Institute of Higher Education, http://service.uga.edu/ihe/. ED429492.

Fishbein, M., & Ajzen, I. (1975). *Beliefs, Attitude, Intention, and Behavior: An Introduction to Theory and Research*. Reading, MA: Addison-Wesley.

Galbo, C. (1998). Helping Adults Learn. *Thrust for Educational Leadership*, *27*(7), 13–17.

Garrison, D. R., & Anderson, T. (2003). *E-Learning in the 21st century: A framework for research and practice*. London: Routledge/Falmer. doi:10.4324/9780203166093

Garrison, D. R., Anderson, T., & Archer, W. (2000). Critical Inquiry in a Text-Based Environment: Computer Conferencing in Higher Education. *The Internet and Higher Education*, *2*(2-3), 87–105. Retrieved from http://communitiesofinquiry.com/. doi:10.1016/S1096-7516(00)00016-6

Geroski, P. A. (2000). Models of Technology Diffusion. *Research Policy*, *29*, 603–625. doi:10.1016/S0048-7333(99)00092-X

Gladhart, M. (2001). Models. Retrieved January 15, 2007, from http://education.wichita.edu/m3/models/teachered/intergrationgrid.htm

Gros, B. (2002). Knowledge Construction and Technology. *Journal of Educational Multimedia and Hypermedia*, *11*(4), 323–343.

Grosso de Leon, A. (2001). *Higher Educations Challenge: New Teacher Education Models for a New Century*. Carnegie Challenge, Carnegie Corporation of New York.

Hagenson, L., & Castle, D. (2003). The Integration of Technology Into Teaching By University College of Education Faculty. In C. Crawford et al. (Eds.), *Proceedings of Society for Information Technology and Teacher Education International Conference 2003* (pp. 947-952). Chesapeake, VA: AACE.

Hagner, P. (2001). Interesting Practices and Best Systems in Faculty Engagement and Support. NLII White Paper, January 25 final report, 1-32.

Hall, G. E., & Hord, S. M. (1987). *Change in schools*. Albany, NY: State University of New York Press.

Huff, S., & Malcolm, M. (1985). Information Technology Assessment and Adoption: A Filed Study. *Management Information Systems Quarterly*, *9*(4), 327–341. doi:10.2307/249233

Jacobsen, D. M. (1998). Adoption Patterns of Faculty who Integrate Computer Technology for Teaching and Learning in higher Education. *ERIC*, *ED428675*, 3–9.

Jacobsen, M. (1997). Bridging the Gap Between Early Adopters' and Mainstream Faculty's use of Instructional Technology. Information Analyses . *Opinion Papers*, *ED423785*, 2–31.

Kersley, G., & Shneiderman, B. (1998). Engagement Theory: A Framework for Technology-Based Teaching and Learning. *Educational Technology*, *38*(5), 20–23.

Kezar, A., & Eckel, P. (2000). Examining the Institutional Transformational Process: The importance of Sensemaking and Inter-related Strategies. *ERIC Clearinghouse*, *ED446720*, 2–46.

King, K., & Lawler, P. (2003). Trends and Issues in the Professional Development of teachers of Adults. *New Directions for Adult and Continuing Education*, *98*, 31–37.

Kotter, J. P. (1996). *Leading change*. Cambridge, MA: Harvard Business School Press.

Kounin, J. S. (1970). *Discipline and Group Management in Classrooms*. New York: Holt, Rinehart and Winston.

Langer, A. (2005). *IT and Organizational Learning: Managing Change through Technology and Education*. New York: Routledge.

Laurillard, D. (2002). *Rethinking University Teaching: A Framework for the Effective Use of Learning Technologies* (2nd ed.). London: RoutledgeFalmer. doi:10.4324/9780203304846

Lee, J. (2001). Instructional support for Distance Education and Faculty Motivation, Commitment, Satisfaction. *British Journal of Educational Technology*, *32*(2), 153–106. doi:10.1111/1467-8535.00186

Lucus, C., & Murray, J. (2002). *New Faculty: A Practical Guide for Academic Beginners*. New York: Palgrave.

Lunenberg, F. (1998). Constructivism and Technology: Instructional Designs for Successful Education Reform. *Journal of Instructional Psychology*, *25*(2), 75–83.

Luppicini, R. (2005). A System Definition of Educational Technology in Society. *Journal of Educational Technology & Society*, *8*(3), 103–109.

Maguire, L. (2005). Faculty Participation in Online Distance Education: Barriers and Motivators. *Online Journal of Distance Learning Administration*, *8*(1), 14.

Major, C., & Palmer, B. (2006). Reshaping teaching and learning: The Transformation of Faculty Pedagogical Content Knowledge. *Higher Education*, *51*, 619–647. doi:10.1007/s10734-004-1391-2

Mann, C., & Stewart, F. (2000). *Internet Communication and Qualitative Research: A Handbook for Researching Online*. London: Sage Publication.

Mars, M., & Ginter, M. (2007). Connecting Organizational Environments with the Instructional Technology Practices of Community College Faculty. *Community College Review*, *34*(4), 324–343. doi:10.1177/0091552107300331

McKenzie, J. (2002). Beyond Toolishness: The Best Ways for Teachers to Learn and Put New Technologies to Good Use. *Multimedia Schools*, *9*(4), 34–39.

Middle Tennessee State University. (2005). Assessment of Instructional Technology Survey. Academic and Instructional Technology Services, http://www.mtsu.edu/~itsurvey

Mishra, P., & Koehler, M. (2006). Technological Pedagogical Content Knowledge: A Framework for Teacher Knowledge. *Teachers College Record*, *108*(6), 1017–1054. doi:10.1111/j.1467-9620.2006.00684.x

Mitchell, M. (1999). Effects of Faculty Motivation in Distributive Education Environments at Institutions of Higher Education. *ERIC*, *ED436155*, 269–274.

Molenda, M., & Sullivan, M. (2002). Issues and Trends in Instructional Technology: Hitting the Plateau. *Educational Media and Technology Yearbook*, *27*, 3–13.

Morris, L. (2004). Changing Institutions and Changing Faculty. *Innovative Higher Education*, *29*(1), 3–6. doi:10.1023/B:IHIE.0000035494.75389.83

New York State Education Department. 89 Washington Avenue, Albany, New York 12234 (http://www.nysed.gov/).

Philips, D. C. (1997). How, Why, What, When and Where: Perspectives on Constructivism in Psychology and Education. *Issues in Education*, *3*(2), 151–195.

Philips, D. C. (2000). *Constructivism in Education*. Chicago: The University of Chicago Press.

Pryor, B., & Pryor, C. (2005). *The School Leader's Guide to Understanding Attitude and Influencing Behavior*. Thousand Oaks, CA: Corwin Press.

Richardson, V. (2003). Constructivist Pedagogy. *Teachers College Record*, *105*(9), 1623–1640. doi:10.1046/j.1467-9620.2003.00303.x

Roberts, F. D., Kelley, C., & Medlin, B. D. (2007). Factors Influencing Accounting Faculty Members' Decision to Adopt Technology in the Classroom. *College Student Journal*, *41*(2), 423–435.

Rockwell, S. K., Schauer, J., Fritz, S. M., & Marx, D. B. (1999). Incentives and Obstacles Influencing Higher Education Faculty and Administrators to Teach Via Distance. *Online Journal of Distance Learning Administration*, *2*(4), 7.

Rogers, E. M. (1962). *Diffusion of Innovation*. New York: Free Press.

Rogers, E. M. (1983). *Diffusion of Innovations* (3rd ed.). New York: Free Press.

Rogers, E. M. (1995). *Diffusion of Innovations* (4th ed.). New York: Free Press.

Rogers, E. M., & Shoemaker, F. (1971). *Communication of Innovations: A Cross-Cultural Approach* (2nd ed.). New York: Free Press.

Russell, A. L. (1996). Six Stages in Learning New Technology. Proceedings of Selected Research and development Presentations at the 1996 National Convention of the Association for Educational Communications and Technology, ED 397 832, 633-641.

Sahin, I. (2005). Understanding Faculty Adoption of Technology Using the Learning/Adoption Trajectory Model: A qualitative Case Study. *The Turkish Online Journal of Educational Technology, 4*(1). Retrieved from http://???

Sahin, I., & Thompson, A. (2007). Analysis of Predictive Factors That Influence Faculty Members' Technology Adoption Level. *Journal of Technology and Teacher Education*, *15*(2), 167–190.

Schifer, C. (2000). Faculty Participation in Asynchronous Learning Networks: A Case Study of Motivating and Inhibiting Factors. *Journal of Asynchronous Learning Networks*, *4*(1), 15–22.

Schoepp, K. (2005). Barriers to Technology Integration in technology-Rich Environment. *Learning and Teaching in Higher Education* [Special issue on Gulf Perspectives], *2*(1). 1-24. Retrieved from http://www.zu.ac.ae/ithe

Sewell, A. (2002). Constructivism and Student Misconceptions. *Australian Science Teachers Journal*, *48*(4), 24–29.

Shea, P. (2007). Bridges and Barriers to Teaching Online College Courses: A Study of Experienced Online Faculty in Thirty-Six Colleges. [JALN]. *Journal of Asynchronous Learning Networks*, *11*(2), 73–128.

Sherry, L., Billig, S., Tavalin, F., & Gibson, D. (2000). New insights in technology adoption in schools. *T.H.E. Journal*, *27*(7), 43–46.

Sherry, L., & Gibson, D. (2002). The path to teacher leadership in educational technology. *Contemporary Issues in Technology & Teacher Education*, *2*(2), 178–203.

Shulman, L. (1987). Knowledge and Teaching: Foundations of the New Reform. *Harvard Educational Review*, *57*(1), 1–20.

Sid, H., & Malcolm, M. (1985). Information Technology Assessment and Adoption: a Field of Study. *Management Information Systems Quarterly*, *9*(4), 327–341. doi:10.2307/249233

Spigner-Littles, D., & Anderson, C. (1999). Constructivism: A Paradigm for Older Learners. *Educational Gerontology*, *25*(3), 203–209. doi:10.1080/036012799267828

Spotts, T. (1999). Discriminating Factors in Faculty Use of Instructional Technology in Higher Education. *Journal of Educational Technology & Society*, *2*(4), 92–99.

Sugar, W., Crawley, F., & Fine, B. (2004). Examining Teachers' Decisions to Adopt New Technology. *Journal of Educational Technology & Society*, *7*(4), 201–213.

Toledo, C. (2005). A Five-Stage Model of Computer Technology Integration Into Teacher Education Curriculum. *Contemporary Issues in Technology & Teacher Education*, *5*(2), 177–191.

University of the State of New York, State Education Department. 8 Washington Ave. Albany, NY 12234. http://www.nysed.gov/

Vygotsky, L. S. (1978). *Mind in Society: The Development of Higher Psychological Processes*. Cambridge, MA: Harvard University Press.

Weinberg, B. A. (2004). Experience and Technology Adoption. The Institute for Study of Labor (IZA), IZA DP No. 1051, 60pg.

Wergin, J. (1994). *Analyzing Faculty Workload*. San Francisco: Jossey-Bass Publishers.

Wertsch, J. (1991). *Voices of the Mind: A Sociocultural Approach to Mediated Action*. Cambridge, MA: Harvard University Press.

Williams, M. (2003). *Making Sense of Social Research*. London: Sage Publication.

Wolcott, L. (1997). *Tenure, Promotion, and Distance Teaching: A Study of faculty rewards and incentives*. Information and Technology, Utah State University.

Wolcott, L. (1998). Faculty Issues Pertaining to Institutional Support and Reward Practices in Distance Education. Presented at the annual meeting of the American Educational Research Association, San Diego, CA: Utah State University.

Wolski, S., & Jackson, S. (1999). Technological Diffusion within Educational Institutions: Applying the Technology Acceptance Model. In J. Price et al. (Eds.), *Proceedings of Society for Information Technology and Teacher Education International Conference 1999* (pp. 1718-1723). Chesapeake, VA: AACE.

Zayim, N., Yildirim, S., & Saka, O. (2006). Technology Adoption of Medical Faculty in Teaching: Differentiating Factors in Adopter Categories. *Journal of Educational Technology & Society*, *9*(2), 213–222.

Zhao, Y., & Cziko, G. (2001). Teacher Adoption of Technology: A perspective Control Theory Perspective. *Journal of Technology and Teacher Education*, *9*(1), 5–30.

ADDITIONAL READING

ASHE. (2008). A Framework for Faculty Growth. *Higher Education Report*, *34*(3), 23–32.

Backhouse, B. (2003). Information and communication technology integration: Beyond the early adopters. *TechTrends*, *47*(3), 5. doi:10.1007/BF02763468

Baldwin, R., DeZure, D., Shaw, A., & Moretto, K. (2008). Mapping the terrain of mid-career faculty at a research university: Implications for faculty and academic leaders. *Change*, *40*(5), 46–55. doi:10.3200/CHNG.40.5.46-55

Bennis, W., & Nanus, B. (1997). *Leaders: Strategies for taking charge*. New York: Harper Collins.

Benson, R., & Brack, C. (2009). Developing the Scholarship of Teaching: What is the Role of E-Teaching and Learning? *Teaching in Higher Education*, *14*(1), 71–80. doi:10.1080/13562510802602590

Bolliger, D., & Wasilik, O. (2009). Factors influencing faculty satisfaction with online teaching and learning in higher education. *Distance Education*, *30*(1), 103–116. doi:10.1080/01587910902845949

Burkman, E. (1987). Factors affecting utilization . In Gagne, R. M. (Ed.), *Instructional Technology: Foundations* (pp. 429–455). Hillsdale, NJ: Lawrence Erlbaum Associates.

Colbeck, C. L. (2002). Assessing institutionalization of curricular and pedagogical reform. *Research in Higher Education*, *43*(4), 397–421. doi:10.1023/A:1015594432215

Diamond, R. M., & Adam, B. E. (Eds.). (1993). *Recognizing faculty work: Reward systems for the year 2000 (New directions for institutional research No. 81)*. San Francisco, CA: Jossey-Bass.

Doppelt, B. (2003). *Leading change toward sustainability*. Sheffield, UK: Greenleaf.

Freire, P. (2007). *Pedagogy of the Oppressed.* New York: Continuum.

Georgina, D., & Hosford, C. (2009). Higher Education Faculty Perceptions on Technology Integration and Training. *Teaching and Teacher Education*, *25*(5), 690–696. doi:10.1016/j.tate.2008.11.004

Glazer, E., Hannatin, M. I., & Song, L. (2005). Promoting technology integration through collaboration and apprenticeship. *Educational Technology Research and Development*, *53*(4), 57–68. doi:10.1007/BF02504685

Keengwe, J., Kidd, T., & Kyei-Blankson, L. (2009). Faculty and Technology: Implications for Faculty Training and Technology Leadership. *Journal of Science Education and Technology*, *18*(1), 23–28. doi:10.1007/s10956-008-9126-2

Kemp, P. (2006). Mimesis in educational hermeneutics. *Educational Philosophy and Theory*, *38*(2), 171–184. doi:10.1111/j.1469-5812.2006.00186.x

Lippitt, G. (1973). *Visualizing change: Model building and the change process*. Fairfax, VA: NTL Learning Resources Corp.

Maslennikova, L. (2008). Key trends in the field of education. *ENews, 8*(4).

McMinn, M. R., Moon, G. W., & McCormick, A. (2009). Integration in the classroom: Ten teaching strategies. *Journal of Psychology and Theology*, *37*, 39–47.

McWilliam, E., & Dawson, S. (2008). Teaching for Creativity: Towards Sustainable and Replicable Pedagogical Practice. *Higher Education*, *56*(6), 633–643. doi:10.1007/s10734-008-9115-7

Murray, J., & Aymer, C. (2009). The Apparent Conflict between Commitment to the Development of the Profession and the Imperatives of the Academy. *Social Work Education*, *28*(1), 81–95. doi:10.1080/02615470802109908

Santo, S., Engstrom, M., Reetz, L., Schweinle, W., & Reed, K. (2009). Faculty Productivity Barriers and Supports at a School of Education. *Innovative Higher Education*, *34*(2), 117–129. doi:10.1007/s10755-009-9098-z

Schrum, L., Thompson, A., Sprague, D., Maddux, C., & McAnear, A. (2005). Advancing the field: Considering acceptable evidence in educational technology research. *Contemporary Issues in Technology & Teacher Education*, *5*(3/4), 202–209.

Sorcinelli, M. D., Austin, A. E., Eddy, P. L., & Beach, A. L. (2006). *Creating the Future of Faculty Development: Learning from the Past, Understanding the Present*. Bolton, MA: Anker Publishing.

Tabata, L., & Johnsrud, L. (2008). The Impact of Faculty Attitudes Toward Technology, Distance Education, and Innovation. *Research in Higher Education*, *49*(7), 625–646. doi:10.1007/s11162-008-9094-7

Youn, T., & Price, T. (2009). Learning from the Experience of Others: The Evolution of Faculty Tenure and Promotion Rules in Comprehensive Institutions. *The Journal of Higher Education*, *80*(2), 204–237. doi:10.1353/jhe.0.0041

KEY TERMS AND DEFINITIONS

Instructional Technology Adoption Models (ITAMs): The theoretical or practical process used when adopting a tool for teaching and learning purposes.

Commitment to Pedagogical Quality (CPQ): Faculty's value of teaching and student learning.

Adoption: Generally defined as the stage in which technology is selected for use by a faculty or organization. Sahin's (2004)

Instructional Technology or Innovation: The new tool being adopted for teaching and learning purposes, in or outside the classroom. Sahin's (2004)

Technology: "the organization of knowledge for the achievement of practical purposes, as well as any tool or technique of doing or making". Luppicini (2005, pg 104)

Model: A pattern, plan, representation, or description designed to show the structure or workings of instructional technology adoption.

Notable Models: Cited by others or have been applied in broad contexts. Particularly, these models substantially contribute to or transform the way faculty adopt technology in education.

Chapter 18 The Momentum of the Technology of the Classroom

Scott Reid
Memorial University of Newfoundland, Canada

ABSTRACT

This paper examines the viability of the concept of "technological momentum" from Thomas Hughes' Technological Systems Theory in the context of the adoption and use of online courses in post-secondary education. A case study approach using qualitative interviews is used to explore the "technological momentum" of the classroom as professors adopt the use of online courses. The findings provide specific examples of how previous classroom practice influences professors' attitudes and practice in relation to the adoption and use of online courses.

INTRODUCTION AND PURPOSE

The adoption of new technology by educators offers many challenges. The adoption and offering of online courses is in many ways impacted by the momentum of the technology which preceded it, the classroom. Technical momentum refers to the "inertia of motion" which large technological systems develop "as organizations and people committed by various interests to the system" support the continuation of the system and work to prevent change (Hughes, 1989, p.76-77). The purpose of this paper is to gain insight into the adoption of online courses by university professors through applying the technological systems theory of change and specifically the concept of technological momentum.

DOI: 10.4018/978-1-61692-854-4.ch018

LITERATURE REVIEW

Universities are often seen as bureaucratic organizations that are slow to change in reaction to outside pressures (Bercuson, Bothwell, & Granatstein, 1997; Daniels, 1996; Laidler, 2002; Miller, Martineau, & Clark, 2000). For some, such as Taylor (2001) and Daniel (1996), this is an incongruous idea. Both noted that while, in many cases, universities are resistant to change they are seen as sources of innovation for society. Many scholarly writers have commented on how with the challenges they face, the social structure at universities will be forced to change (Daniel, 2000; Noam, 1995; Psycharis, 2005; Rajasingham, 2005; Singleton-Jackson & Newsom, 2006). Noam (1995) predicted a "dim future" for universities as new technologies change the three primary functions of a university: the creation of knowledge, the preservation of information, and the transmission of this information to others (teaching). He envisioned a rise of commercial firms that will offer undergraduate and professional education more efficiently than the current university structure. According to Daniel (2000) two realities are setting the agenda for higher education in the "new economy" of the 21st century; lifelong learning and the use of educational technology. Lifelong learning, he claimed, will be the norm and the huge increase in the number of students will place tremendous demands on current educational structures to change. The availability of new technology, and its integration into education, will be factors that help universities meet these new demands for lifelong learning. He sees the rise of "mega-universities" as a possible response to the demands of the new economy. Rajasingham (2005) talked about "virtual universities" as a means of addressing some of the challenges Daniel (2000) outlined. Rajasingham, however, predicted these "virtual universities" will exist at the same time as and work with traditional universities, while also responding to globalization and the use of new educational technology.

Prensky (2001) made the point that the nature of the social system at universities is being altered by advancements in information and communication technology. He contended that "today's students are no longer the people our educational system was designed to teach". While current students are "digital natives" who have spent their lives using computer games, e-mail, cell phones, instant messaging, and other technology, the education system is organized by "digital immigrants" who do not speak the same language or, if they do, speak it with a strong accent. Prensky argued that educators will have to change both teaching methods and content to make learning more meaningful to students. More recently, Prensky (2006) outlined some of the features that will be important for educators in the 21st century. He suggested that educators will have to shift gears and pay attention to how students learn, collaborate more with students in terms of what they teach and how they teach, provide more flexible organizations, integrate digital tools into teaching, as well as provide content that is relevant and up-to-date.

Significant change is required by individual professors as they adopt the use of online courses. McFadden, Marsh, and Price (1999) claimed that the major obstacle to the integration of online courses is that they significantly alter the role of the instructor. Online courses are a disruptive technology in the sense that they require different pedagogical methods, which may not yet be fully understood. In many ways, these methods are a break from the past and require professors to rethink their teaching practice. To add to the disruption, changes have yet to stabilize. Possibilities, such as hybrid courses and programs, video conference courses, the integration of social software and immersive environments are still emerging.

Conrad (2004) conducted interviews with university instructors who were engaged in online teaching for the first time. She identified four areas in which online courses changed instructors' roles: pedagogical, social, managerial, and technical. Conrad observed that professors were experiencing difficulty in adjusting to the role change as they transferred to online teaching. Others, such as Pelz (2004), have also contributed to the development of online pedagogy and provided awareness as to how it is different from in-class instruction. Myers, Bennett, Brown, and Henderson (2004) suggested that younger, less experienced faculty are more likely to adopt new technologies compared to older, more experienced professors. Based on their findings they speculate that while younger professors may be motivated to teach online courses to advance their careers, more experienced faculty require more evidence of the effectiveness of such technology. The offering of online courses is still a relatively new and evolving field of practice. Many authors have pointed out that teachers are still experimenting with this media to uncover the advantages and disadvantages of an online educational environment (Inglis, Lehman, 2006; Ling, & Joosten, 2002; Ostlund, 2005; Shotsberger & Vetter, 2000; Tisdell et al., 2004).

The nature of the online format and the degree of change required to teach that way has been explored by many researchers (Buckingham, 2003; Inglis et al., 2002; Meyer, 2004; Roval & Barnum, 2003; Wilson & Whitelock, 1998). A common finding across this research is that teachers and tutors experience some difficulty due to the lack of feedback provided in the online environment. The main advantage in face-to-face teaching is the immediacy of the response from students, in both language and gesture. Also, students form closer relationships while in class as voice and body language are important in forging these relationships (Wilson & Whitelock). Another issue evident in the literature is the increased amount of time it takes to develop and teach online courses. MacDonald and Thompson (2005) found that offering a quality online course requires a "significant investment of time and energy" (p. 19), particularly in organizations that are still in the process of establishing proper support services. Other researchers have identified some commonly perceived advantages of the online format, including (1) better quality of interactions because more thought is placed into responding, and (2) although the relationship may not be as close, students feel they are part of a broader community of students drawn from various regions and backgrounds (Cavanaugh, 2005; DiBiase, 2004; Lazarus, 2003; Meyer, 2003).

Ketterer and Marsh (2006) predicted that professors and institutions will have to be more flexible in terms of instructional models in light of new information and communication technologies. They claimed that traditional instructional models will be "increasingly problematic" with new technology. This will result in new models being developed to improve service, reach more students, satisfy adult learners, and comply with changing government policy. Archer, Garrison, and Anderson (1999) applied Christensen's (1997) ideas related to the adoption of disruptive technologies to the post-secondary education environment. They speculated that just as "great firms" fail because they do not accept disruptive technologies, traditional universities could fail because of new challenges from organizations offering online courses. As an adaptation of Christensen's strategy of creating an independent entity to develop new technology, Archer et al. suggested using a division of continuing studies or a similar group as an incubator for new technology.

There is also evidence in the literature that some professors are experimenting with non-traditional forms of evaluation or variations of previously used evaluation methods. For example, electronic portfolios (Abrami & Barrett, 2005; Mason, Pegler, & Weller, 2004) and online peer assessment (Wadhwa, Schulz, & Mann, 2006). Other researchers are working to advance the development of various kinds of evaluation software. For example, Attali and Burstein (2006) examined the automated essay scoring system "e-Rater", while Rudner, Garcia and Welch (2006) examined a similar system called "IntelliMetric". Jocoy and DiBiase (2006) found that detecting and combating plagiarism in online courses is a difficult task that needs attention even when students are adult learners.

Literature related to the nature of the change that universities and individual professors have to make as they adopt asynchronous online courses reveals this change to be "discontinuous"; that is, online courses require significant change from previous practice. The literature examined provides a level of understanding regarding how difficult the transition from classroom to online teaching is for many professors. While research has identified specific inhibitors and motivators for adoption, further investigation is still needed.

CONCEPTUAL FRAMEWORK

The Technological Systems Theory of Change has been articulated primarily through the work of Thomas Hughes (1989, 2005). Hughes has written much about the development of technological systems and how these systems influence the construction, acceptance, and use of technological devices. He is credited with having introduced systems theory into the study of the history of technology and has identified a number of patterns, such as the momentum of technology. For example, using the development of the electrical distribution system, he made a number of observations that are useful when examining the development and introduction of other innovations (Hughes, 1989). He recognizes that a technological system can be made up of both physical and nonphysical components. In his case studies of electrical systems, he highlights physical components such as generators, transformers, and transmission lines, as well as nonphysical components such as manufacturing firms, utility companies, investors, a scientific community, and government regulation. Both these physical and nonphysical factors interact to find ways to make the technological system work. While a system can in many ways be self containing, forces from outside can have an impact on the system. For example, in the case of the electrical systems that Hughes studied, changes in oil price, supply stability, and environmental concerns can impact the system that produces and delivers electricity.

Hughes' (1989) observations can be valuable for those who want to direct the development of systems in certain ways. He divides evolving systems into five phases: invention, development, innovation, transfer and growth, and competition and consolidation. It is during the early phases of the system, he observes, that humans have the most autonomy and so change is easier to promote in these phases. Once systems become established, they are difficult to change because of what Hughes calls "systems momentum."As procedures are established within a system and humans have an established interest in perpetuating the system, change becomes more difficult. Also, once investments have been made in physical structures or production facilities it is more difficult to adopt new ways of doing things. There is, as Hughes points out, tremendous pressure within the system to make "continuous" type improvements rather than "radical" or "discontinuous" changes.

METHODOLOGY

A constructivist grounded theory approach was used which incorporates existing theory and literature into the design of the study (Charmaz,2000). It is also a case study involving semi-structured interviews with 32 professors who had taught or were currently teaching online courses at Memorial University of Newfoundland. The findings were transcribed by the researcher and initial observations were made and recorded during the transcription. Data analysis involved the identification of patterns and trends using methods outlined by a number of prominent researchers (Bogdan & Biklen, 1992; Gay & Airasian, 2000; Marshall & Rossman, 1999; Straus & Corbin, 1990).

FINDINGS

The findings from this research illustrate how the dominant existing technology for offering educational opportunities—the classroom—has a momentum within society that impacts the adoption of online courses. Two themes relating to technological momentum and existing technology emerged in this research and will be presented in this paper. First, in exploring professors' views on the future of university teaching, it was noted that their perceptions were based on mindsets founded on previous technologies. Second, professors' views on assessment were sometimes formed based on the affordances of a previous technology and did not take into account the new possibilities in an online environment.

Professors' views on the future of university teaching provide insight into the concept of technological momentum and the connections people have with previously existing technology. The perceptions professors have related to the future of university teaching are significant because not only are these people well informed about what is happening, but they will also most likely be active participants in the decision making process related to future developments. While thinking there would be more courses online in the future, many professors did not want to teach all their courses online. Professors anticipated further changes in technology, program offerings, and the very structure of universities.

Professor 001 explained "everything seems to be moving towards the Web". She thought this was happening because students have trouble getting into the courses they need on campus because of limited space. Offering courses online makes them more accessible. She thought in the future many courses in Masters Programs would be offered online. Indeed, many of the professors interviewed thought the number of online courses would continue to increase, with one professor recognising senior administration "seem to be putting a big effort into the distance courses and online courses" (Prof. 007). Yet, while professors believed online courses would continue to increase in number, many felt that classroom teaching would not disappear because it is so "anchored in society". Professor 009 indicated there are a number of factors, not just improvements in technology, encouraging the adoption of online courses. For example, declining enrolment in some areas and financial constraint are also factors.

Another professor (Prof. 011) said better technology, both hardware and software, would also facilitate the adoption of online courses. He made the point that there will always be some classroom teachers, but they will continue to diminish as the current trend continues:

How many courses are actually taught in the evening and how many of these have gone online? As technology becomes more evident, then more kids come out of the digitized environment. You have [then] got more kids that will be easier to integrate into an online course. (Prof. 011)

Professor 011 contended that the only thing that could hold this back is the university's inability to respond to change quickly enough.

Some, however, thought there was a limit to how many of the university's courses would move to the online format. Professor 023 indicated he would not like to see it go beyond 40 percent of what is required for a program. For him, the interactions that happen in a classroom are "essentially" part of the "pedagogical relationship". While recognizing online courses can augment traditional learning in many ways, Professor 023 was leery of offering whole programs this way. Professor 024 did not think online courses would replace classroom courses in the near future, but predicted that in 10 years technology would have improved to the point where universities will have to re-evaluate what they do. Nonetheless, this professor indicated that some of the courses, because of their content, would still need to be delivered face-to-face but advances in technology might change what is possible:

I can't see our courses, with a heavy design component, totally online. The amount of time which is spent with the students individually to discuss their work and to give them some guidelines and so on, they need face-to-face.... Maybe if the nature of online courses changes dramatically, maybe one of these days, but for the time being I can't see this happening. (Prof 024)

Another professor (Prof. 027) was concerned that with too many courses online students might miss some of the spontaneous interactions and informal intellectual exchange that happens in a classroom. One professor said, while recognizing technology is "shaping and fashioning social interaction," she still believes there is a real need for face-to-face interaction. Professor 031 indicated that while he thought more online courses would be offered in the future he did not see the disappearance of the university. Many professors while recognizing the need for online courses said they would not want to teach all their courses that way. Most thought that classroom courses will exist for the foreseeable future, but the traditional correspondence course may disappear. One professor (Prof. 001) hoped the trend towards online courses would not move to the point where all courses are offered online. While recognizing the need for online courses, her first choice for teaching is the traditional classroom model. One concern with the adoption of more online courses was that there might be a tendency to hire more sessional teachers than full-time professors.

Professor 002 thought some courses are better suited to online delivery than others. As more courses are taught online, he believed there will be a "balance" between what is appropriate for online courses and what should be taught in the classroom. For him, the level of the course is also an important factor in determining if it should be taught online or not:

I would not want to teach university courses online to first year university students. I don't think at that point they have got their feet wet enough. They don't understand the in and the outs and there are too many things going on in their lives. [Online courses] are much better suited for older students who can be self-reliant and responsible. (Prof. 002)

Conversely, other professors say introductory level courses will be the first to go online. These diverging views on what courses should be offered online demonstrates that no clear consensus on these, and many other issues like them, exists.

Professor 014, while she could see more courses going online and more courses having online components, thought there was a limit to the number of courses that could go online. For example, she indicated that in some subject areas things have to be touched and you cannot do that on the computer yet. Another professor (Prof. 018) noted, while he expects there will always be buildings, there will be a lot of changes in teaching styles. She explained universities fulfil many roles other than just being a way of delivering content:

People still need to come together. A university is not just for teaching. It is one very important component of it, but a university is also about research, it is also about experiences. There is a lot to be said for walking the hallowed halls and having your discussions over a cup of coffee and that kind of stuff. (Prof. 018)

Although she expected the number of online courses to increase, Professor 007 would not want them to replace classroom courses completely. She explained why she thinks such a drastic change would be "really sad":

I think the classroom is a pleasant experience; a group of individuals who are all there for the same purpose. If you do enough quality teaching, group facilitation and group interaction is really valuable. (Prof. 007)

Professor 014 believed that as professors become aware of what can be done online and more familiar with the format, more courses will have an online component. Another professor (Prof.

028) explained she would like to mix both online and in class courses as she does not like the idea of students being able to do the whole program online. She suggested including residency requirements and certain courses in a seminar format to encourage interaction.

Professor 005 said he sees the number of online courses increasing because of the focus being placed on them by senior administration at the university. He also believed an increased number of online courses will come as younger faculty, with more accepting attitudes towards technology, take up positions at the university. Other professors noted that not only will there be more online courses, but there will also be the use of new technology such as cell phones or other devices in education. One professor (Prof. 008) thought expectations and attitudes will change as more students who are comfortable with technology enter the system:

These kids who have grown up with [technology] may find it more comfortable to do it with a computer screen. Certainly books are dying away; generally kids get their entertainment today not by reading but from a computer screen. (Prof. 008)

He also explained technology will allow teachers to present material that they could never have presented in the classroom with just a blackboard. For example, he said, "You can draw three dimensional graphics on computers you could never draw on the blackboard". Another professor (Prof. 022) thought it would not be very long before video conferencing with individual students and with whole classes would become common.

Professor 010 suggested the nature of what a university is will change in the future. He contended that there are a lot of potential students who do not want to come and sit in a classroom or live in a residence. The idea of a university as a place where people come together for discussion and interaction will be transformed to a virtual campus. He predicted there will be fewer campuses and students will focus on "a few key big name universities". He said he is unsure how this would impact how students learn; there might be local group discussions or partnership arrangements with smaller local universities to provide supplementary or field work arrangements for students.

Professor 031 predicted there will be greater variety for students in the way courses are offered. He saw this trend developing as on campus students started to take more online courses. He further felt administration will encourage the trend towards online courses in order to avoid overcrowding on campus courses. This approach will require the development of new infrastructure such as a 24 hours a day, 7 days a week help desk for online students. He saw some significant challenges for universities as they prepare to better service this group of students doing online courses.

Professor 010 believed there will be increased competition internationally among universities:

I don't think universities have really tuned into how big a change this actually is in the way operations are going to be. The way things are going ... students will be able to pick and choose from courses all over the world. (Prof. 010)

Similarly, Professor 009 thought universities would be in a more competitive environment in the future. In order to keep existing students and attract new ones, they would have to offer distance learning opportunities. Professor 015 thought people from other provinces would start taking advantage of the online Masters Program in her field in the future. She also expected there will be more international connections being made as well. Professor 029 thought there would be pressure on universities to reduce costs and this might lead to more of an "assembly line" approach that would not be good for education. He predicted as the number of people in society who want to attend university increases, there will be more cost pressures and therefore pressures to change the delivery method.

Several professors also mentioned that new ways of organizing learning might become possible. Professor 010 thought students may be able to work together or on their own using a combination of approaches such as virtual and face-to-face meetings. He was unsure what other combinations or possibilities might exist, but thought universities would be very different in the future. Professor 017 predicted more modular type programs where students will be able to mix and match small units of a larger program. He thought professional groups will start to deliver training programs online and people will move to home schooling with universities providing an accreditation function. He also thought informal groups and settings will be established to bring students together for the social aspects of university. Relationships, friendships, and networks will be established in these groups the way they are now in sorority houses and university clubs. These sorts of groups will be important in dealing with feelings of isolation that students might otherwise get from doing online courses.

The second area examined in this paper where changing educational technology is constrained by societal factors is in the function of assessing student learning. In this instance as well the momentum of the previous classroom technology is evident. One of the points where educational practice directly meets societal factors is when a student leaves an institution to enter the "real world" and has to present their education credentials.

One area of contention is how assessment differs in online and face-to-face classroom courses. While many professors would like to maintain consistency in the assessment methods this sometimes proves to be difficult. Professor 001 asked students to write a term paper in the online course. As there tended to be only a small number of students in her course, marking these papers was manageable. She found it problematic to give an examination online as invigilation centres have to be set up where students can take tests in a monitored environment. These centres need to be set up around the province and, in some cases, outside the province. One problem with this approach is that it takes time for the professors to receive the exams and the cost of doing invigilated exams is significant. In addition, another professor (Prof. 023) expressed concern about the quality of the invigilation in small communities:

Professors outlined various methods of assessment that can be used in online courses, such as multiple choice tests, assignments, mini-assignments, reports, participation, learning logs, peer assessment, and special projects. Some professors changed from using essay questions to multiple choice questions in their assessments because they are easier to administer at a distance over the computer. One professor (Prof. 008) explained that because of the difficulty of sending math equations over e-mail, he had considered switching his exams and assignments to a multiple choice format. Yet, he decided against this since part of the assessment process in his subject area is seeing how students go about solving problems, as well as determining if they can arrive at the correct answer. Professor 043 also found that since there is not the same free flowing exchange of information online as there is in face-to-face; it is hard for professors to work with students on individualized projects.

One method of online assessment that seemed to be increasing in popularity was peer assessment. Professor 004 mentioned she has students prepare mini papers that are posted online for other students to look at and comment on. Although it is not "peer marking", there is an opportunity for "peer response". Similarly, professor 009 explained:

I don't use peer evaluation, but students may [discuss assignments] in discussion forums. They are encouraged to discuss the ideas contained in the assignments of others because they get to read everyone else's assignment. (Prof. 009)

Likewise, another professor (Prof. 011) explained that student assignments for his course are posted where they can be viewed and commented upon by other students.

One professor (Prof. 017) explained that he was experimenting with peer assessment and referred to it as the "democratization of assessment". While there have been years of experimentation with peer assessment, the online format can be used to facilitate the process and make it much easier. Students can upload their assignments for other students to look at and mark. The process of peer assessment may vary. For example, it can be double blind, where the marker does not know whose work they are marking and the student does not know who assessed their work. In this way, students receive the benefit of having a variety of other people comment on their work. This professor has also used "peer input" to provide students with formative assessment on projects for the course he teaches.

Some professors described how they were engaging innovative assessment methods in their online courses. Professor 003 explained he has students create an "imagery script" that involves them explaining their best performance in a particular activity or sport. Before recording their own "imagery script" they have an opportunity to listen to the best examples from previous years online. Another professor (Prof. 006) had students do an "Internet learning log". In this activity, students had to find and evaluate Web-sites pertaining to topics in the course. Students are also asked to complete a case study where they applied the diagnostic skills they had learned in the course and recommended specific action. Another professor (Prof. 015) required her students to keep a journal of the course activities they did in their community. The journals tended to include personal reactions to situations and were kept confidential between the professor and the student. Sometimes students shared part of their experience with the class when they presented a case study for the course. In addition, this professor also used a "local supervisor" who helped the students:

They put them in touch with people who are experienced and work with them once or twice, supervise their teaching projects, give them guidance, evaluate them according to a form we have, and call us if there are any problems. (Prof. 015)

Another example of how professors had considered changing methods of student assessment was evident in their discussions of assigning a grade for participation in the discussion forum. Professor 021 explained that when she taught a course in-class, she gave 10% for participation but in the online format she increased this to 20%. She explained that she expects "a different level of discussion from [the students]". In the discussion forum in the courseware there was no established standard of practice for affording grades for participation. Some professors allocated grades for participation, while others did not. In cases where marks were allotted the percent of the total course grade involved varied greatly. One professor (Prof. 001) explained the first time she taught an online course she did not assign marks for participation in the forum, but in future courses she would in order to encourage participation. Professor 002 explained he had a very structured way of assigning grades for participation in discussion forums:

I give about 10% of the final grade for participation in the discussion forum. To a certain extent that is based on volume, although I try to tailor it.... Part of the mark is for being the first in discussing a question and part of it is for subsequent discussion and keeping the discussion going and that sort of thing. (Prof. 002)

Other professors explained they used the features of WebCT to enable them to compile information about each student's participation in the course. Referring to these records helped professors determine the participation grade for each student.

Professor 040 noted a grade for participation in online courses can be assigned in a more objective way than it is for classroom courses:

You can actually mark the participation in a more clean way online than you can in class; because, after all, if you are just talking about participation in a class session beyond showing up and attending it is a fairly subjective judgement. (Prof. 040)

For one professor (Prof. 006), the mark for participating in the discussion forum initially began as a small allocation of the final grade but has now grown to account for a significant portion (40%) of the grade. Since he taught more than one online course, this professor checked the discussion forum several times a day so students received almost immediate feedback. One professor (Prof. 023) required students to do postings to the class forum at regular intervals as part of the assessment for the course. He explained that having this structure built into the course has been very helpful as it forces students to "stay on top of the readings and [means] they were all at an even point in their readings".

Keeping assessment consistent for both classroom and online versions of the same course was a concern for many professors. Professor 005 explained that there is an expectation on the part of students that requirements in online courses are lower. He believed students saw online courses as being second best and therefore they expected the professor to make the course or the assessment easier. This professor continued to use an invigilated midterm and final exam as a means of assessment, the same as he would do in a classroom course. Professor 029, who also wanted to ensure consistent assessment, administered the same examination in his distance course as in his in-class course. For another professor (Prof. 023), the assessment was adjusted in some ways to account for the locations of the students:

I try to keep [the courses] consistent around content, what I am evaluating. [But] I don't think they should be ... identical, I don't think it is possible to have them identical.... You can't do that online. Your students just don't have access [to the same resources as on campus students], although the Library says they do, they don't have access. So I do a mentor assignment, which would not work on campus. (Prof. 023)

There is evidence in the comments made by professors that the issue of whether or not to maintain consistent evaluation methods between online and classroom courses has become one of contention. Some say consistency is essential, while others regard it as too restrictive and hampering the development of new options that may be more effective for online students.

Some professors contended that plagiarism is more of a concern in online courses than face-to-face courses. To counter this problem, Professor 011 used an open book exam and designed it in such a way to make it difficult for students to plagiarize. Students are asked to answer questions using their own experiences, so it would be difficult for someone else to answer the questions for them. He also used a software package that allows him to scan material and find cases of plagiarism. He suggested that plagiarism is a serious problem at the university, yet it is not being dealt with:

Talk to any student who has been through a business faculty and talk to them about online courses and how they did their last term paper. Don't talk to them as a professor, but chat to a couple of 19 or 29 year olds [and] you will get to see what plagiarism online is all about. (Prof. 011)

This participant felt this was a very serious issue, particularly in professions where public safety is at stake. He suggested that in the near future testing agencies may become more common as an independent way of verifying a person's skills or knowledge in an area.

The findings of this paper provide insight into how previous practice and the momentum of the previous technology sometimes limit the acceptance of the use of features of a new technology. Professors' expectations of the impact of online courses on the future of education show a more restrained expectation than many developers of the technology. Also, professors' views on assessment in online courses demonstrate the difficulty of making the kind of discontinuous change which is often associated with new information and communication technology. Together an examination of professors' views on the future of teaching and assessment in online courses demonstrates the momentum of the technology of the classroom and how it can influence the adoption of online courses.

CONCLUDING COMMENTS

As explained earlier the Technological Systems Theory of change has been articulated primarily through the work of Thomas Hughes who has written many articles and books about the development of technological systems and how these systems as a social factor influence the construction, acceptance, and use of technological devices (Hughes, 1989, 2004). Using the development of the electrical distribution and other system he makes a number of observations which may be useful when examining the development and introduction of other innovations. He recognizes that a technological system can be made up of both human and non-human components. Just as the electrical systems is made up of generators, transformers and transmission lines along with things such as manufacturing firms, utility companies, investors, a scientific community, and government regulation, so does the public education system have it's human and non-human components. All these factors interact together to find ways to make the technological system work. While systems in many ways are self contained, forces outside the system can have an impact on the system. In the case of the electrical systems for example changes in oil prices, supply stability and environmental concerns can impact on the system that has developed to produce, deliver and consume electricity. He divides the history of evolving systems into phases of invention, development, innovation, transfer and growth, competition and consolidation. It is important to note for those who want to shape systems in certain ways, that it is during the early phases that people in a system have the most autonomy. Once systems become established they are very difficult to change because of what Hughes calls a systems momentum. As procedures are established within a system and various people have an established interest in perpetuating the system change becomes more difficult. Also, once investments have been made in physical structures or production facilities it is more difficult to adopt new ways of doing things. There is tremendous pressure within the system to make continuous type improvements rather than radical or discontinuous changes that would threaten the stability of the existing system.

To analysis the introduction of online courses at Memorial University of Newfoundland we are really looking at the public education system. While this research is focussed at one university that university is part of a larger interconnected system of public education which links universities in other provinces and around the world. This system in many ways establishes what university education is and what procedures should be followed in such an education system. These concepts of what quality university education is and what are appropriate procedures are enforced through various methods such as establishing criteria for accreditation of universities, the recognition of degrees and the transferability of credits from one institution to another. Possibly the most effective way which the education system defines what is quality education is through its control of public opinion and the way it is imbedded in the broader

social functions such as professional accreditation and employment practices.

Some of the issues which Hughes approach suggests are looking at critical problems within the system. In the context of Newfoundland and Labrador the critical problems is the traditional model of students travelling to a central point to do courses in a classroom does not work for many people in remote communities around the province. For some younger students who are immersed in the use of the use of technology in other aspects of their lives the classroom based model of the traditional university do not match their lifestyle or meet their expectation of what real learning is. These digital natives as Prensky (2006) refers to them are not impressed with an education system that does not meet their needs. While many of these students need to be verified and accredited by the dominant education system, resistance might come in the form of increased plagiarism and cheating. Such an increase has been mentioned both in the scholarly literature and is evident in the comments of several professors in this research. Another critical problem within the systems is increased competition from private for profit educational institutions and also from corporate universities and in house corporate training. Also, many public universities are taking an entrepreneurial approach to marketing their programs. Such options are placing the public education more in an competitive economic environment than has existed in the past. Comments from professors in this research indicate that many of them are uncomfortable with such a situation but others are embracing such an approach and have ideas about how the university might improve its competitive position.

The concept of technological momentum from Hughes Technological Systems Theory, was evident in the findings of this research. There was an underlying assumption in the comments of many professors that the technology of the classroom was the standard by which all other options should be judged. In many cases the belief expressed by many professors was that classroom teaching was always the best way of teaching but other options which were perceived as less effective would only be undertaken to overcome problems of access. There is evidence from the comments of participants in this research as well as from other sources that university professors are taking actions to protect their professional interests (Blumenstyk, 1999). There is also, evidence that many professors would rather online courses were contained as a continuous type of innovation rather than a radical systems altering innovation. For example many of the professors who supported the offering of online courses for mature professionals who were taking courses from a distance they did not support offering online courses to first year on campus students. Also, many professors while seeing a benefit in offering a limited number of courses online they would not like to see too many go online, they viewed online course as a supplement or add that was acceptable in limited circumstances. However, there were a small minority of professors who believed that online courses had the potential to bring about radical change in the field of education but such change was being hampered by a university system that was slow to change.

The views of professors and the predictions they make about the future of university teaching are much more restrained in comparison to those being made by the developers of the technology such as Kurzweil (2000, 2005). The professors' views on the future of teaching demonstrate how they see a gradual change happening, rather than the more radical departures that some involved with the development of information and communication technology are predicting. This indicates that professors may be in a unique position to understand how societal factors sometimes determine the rate of adoption of a technology. Professors' views on the future of university teaching may be more restrained based on their better understanding of how societal and technical factors interact to determine what change occurs.

Another aspect of Hughes Technological Systems Theory is what it says about the way technological systems evolve. He divides the history of evolving systems into phases of invention, development, innovation, transfer and growth, competition and consolidation. This is significant for this research because some are believe that evolving information and communication technology hold the possibility of leading to the establishment of a whole new system of education. If this is the case and we are at the invention or development phases of the evolution of this system, then these are the early stages where the nature of the system can be shaped. For example, these early stages would be the point where either open source course management systems or private commercial interests controlled packages became the dominate technology. The social shaping of systems which happens at this point will likely determine the nature and operation of the system for a considerable period.

REFERENCES

Abrami, P., & Barrett, H. (2005). Directions for research and development on electronic portfolios 1. *Canadian Journal of Learning and Technology, 31*(3). Retrieved April 18, 2007, from http://www.cjlt.ca/content/vol31.3/abrami.html

Archer, W., Garrison, R., & Anderson, T. (1999). Adopting disruptive technologies in traditional universities: Continuing education as a incubator for innovation. *The Canadian Journal of University Continuing Education, 25*(1). Retrieved April 18, 2007, from http://www.extension.usask.ca/cjuce/eng/Ab251.html

Attali, Y., & Burstein, J. (2006). Automated essay scoring with e-rater. *The Journal of Technology, Learning, and Assessment, 4*(3). Retrieved April 18, 2007, from http://escholarship.bc.edu/jtla/vol4/3/

Bercuson, D., Bothwell, R., & Granatstein, J. (1997). *Petrified campus: The crisis in Canada's universities*. Toronto: Random House Canada.

Blumenstyk, G. (1999, April 5). Union cites Guido Sarducci in ad campaign aimed at distance Education. *The Chronicle of Higher Education*.

Bogdan, R., & Biklen, S. (1992). *Qualitative research for education: An introduction to theory and methods* (2nd ed.). Boston: Allyn and Bacon.

Buckingham, S. (2003). Perspectives on the experience of the learning community through online discussions. *Journal of Distance Education, 18*(2), 74–91.

Cavanaugh, J. (2005). Teaching online: Time comparison. *Online Journal of Distance Learning Administration, 8*(1). Retrieved April 18, 2007, from http://www.westga.edu/~distance/ojdla/

Charmaz, K. (2000). Constructivist and objectivist grounded theory. In Denzin, N. K., & Lincoln, Y. (Eds.), *Handbook of qualitative research* (2nd ed., pp. 509–535). Thousand Oaks, CA: Sage.

Christensen, C. (1997). *The innovator's dilemma: When new technologies cause great firms to fail*. Boston: Harvard Business School Press.

Conrad, D. (2004). University instructors' reflections on their first online teaching experiences. *JALN, 8*(2), 31–44.

Daniel, J. (1996). *Mega-universities and knowledge media: Technology strategies for higher education*. London: Kogan Page.

Daniel, J. (2000). *The university of the future and the future of universities*. Keynote address to Improving University Learning and Teaching: 25th International Conference, Frankfurt, Germany.

DiBiase, D. (2004). The impact of increasing enrolment on faculty workload and student satisfaction over time. *JALN, 8*(2), 45–60.

Gay, L., & Airasian, P. (2000). *Educational research: Competencies and analysis and application*. London: Prentice-Hall.

Hughes, T. (1989). The evaluation of large technological systems. In Bijker, W., Hughes, T., & Pinch, T. (Eds.), *The social construction of technological systems: New directions in the sociology and history of technology*. Cambridge, MA: MIT Press.

Hughes, T. (2005). *Human-built world: How to think about technology and culture*. Chicago, IL: University of Chicago Press.

Inglis, A., Ling, P., & Joosten, V. (2002). *Delivering digitally: Managing the transition to the knowledge media*. London: Kogan Page.

Jocoy, C., & DiBiase, D. (2006). Plagiarism by adult learners online: A case study in detection and remediation. *International Review of Research in Open and Distance Learning, 7*(1). Retrieved April 18, 2007, from http://www.irrodl.org/index.php/irrodl/article/view/242/495

Ketterer, J., & Marsh, G. (2006). Re-conceptualizing intimacy and distance in instructional models. *Online Journal of Distance Learning Administration, 9*(1). Retrieved April 18, 2007, from http://www.westga.edu/~distance/ojdla/

Kurzweil, R. (2000). *The age of spiritual machines: When computers exceed human intelligence*. New York: Penguin Books.

Kurzweil, R. (2005). *The Singularity is near: When humans transcend biology*. New York: Penguin Books.

Laidler, D. (Ed.). (2002). *Renovating the ivory tower: Canadian universities and the knowledge economy*. Ottawa: C.D. Howe Institute.

Lazarus, B. (2003). Teaching courses online: How much time does it take? *JALN*, *7*(3), 47–54.

MacDonald, C. J., & Thompson, T. L. (2005). Structure, content, delivery, service, and outcomes: Quality e-Learning in higher education. *International Review of Research in Open and Distance Learning, 6*(2). Retrieved April 18, 2007, from http://www.irrodl.org/index.php/irrodl/article/view/235/853

Marshall, C., & Rossman, G. (1999). *Designing qualitative research* (3rd ed.). London: Sage.

Mason, R., Pegler, C., & Weller, M. (2004). E-portfolios: An assessment tool for online courses. *British Journal of Educational Technology, 15*(6), 717–727. doi:10.1111/j.1467-8535.2004.00429.x

McFadden, A., Marsh, G., & Price, B. (1999). Why do educators embrace high-cost technologies? *Journal of Distance Learning Administration, 2*(3). Retrieved April 18, 2007, from http://www.westga.edu/~distance/ojdla/.

Meyer, K. (2003). Face-to-face versus threaded discussions: The role of time and higher -order thinking. *JALN*, *7*(3), 55–65.

Meyer, K. (2004). Evaluating online discussions: Four different frames of analysis. *JALN*, *8*(2), 101–114.

Miller, J., Martineau, L., & Clark, R. (2000). Technology infusion and higher education: Changing teaching and learning. *Innovative Higher Education, 24*(3), 227–241. doi:10.1023/B:IHIE.0000047412.64840.1c

Myers, C., Bennett, D., Brown, G., & Henderson, T. (2004). Emerging online learning environments and student learning: An analysis of faculty perceptions. *Journal of Educational Technology & Society*, *7*(8), 78–86.

Noam, E. (1995). Electronics and the dim future of the university. *Science*, *270*, 247–249. doi:10.1126/science.270.5234.247

Ostlund, B. (2005). Stress, disruption and community: Adult learners' experiences of obstacles and opportunities in distance education. *European Journal of Open, Distance and E-Learning*. Retrieved April 18, 2007, from http://www.eurodl.org/materials/contrib/2005/Ostlund.htm

Pelz, B. (2004). (My) Three principles of effective online pedagogy. *JALN, 8*(3), 33–46.

Prensky, M. (2001). Digital natives, digital immigrants. *On the Horizon, 9*(6). Retrieved April 18, 2007, from http://www.marcprensky.com/writing/Prensky

Prensky, M. (2006). Listen to the natives. *Educational Leadership, 63*(4), 8–13.

Psycharis, S. (2005). Presumptions and actions affecting an e-learning adoption by the educational system implementation using virtual private networks. *European Journal of Open, Distance and E-Learning*. Retrieved April 18, 2007, from www.eurodl.org

Rajasingham, L. (2005). The virtual university: From turf to surf-same journey different routes. *European Journal of Open, Distance and E-Learning*. Retrieved April 18, 2007, from www.eurodl.org

Roval, A., & Barnum, K. (2003). On-line course effectiveness: An analysis of student interactions and perceptions of learning. *Journal of Distance Education, 18*(1), 57–73.

Rudner, L., Garcia, V., & Welch, C. (2006). An evaluation of the IntelliMetric essay scoring system. *The Journal of Technology, Learning, and Assessment, 4*(4). Retrieved April 18, 2007, from http://escholarship.bc.edu/jtla/

Shotsberger, P., & Vetter, R. (2000). The handheld Web: How mobile wireless technologies will change Web-based instruction and training. *Educational Technology, 40*, 49–52.

Singleton-Jackson, J., & Newsom, R. (2006). Adapt, adjust, respond: Perspectives on current trends in American colleges and universities. *Higher Education Perspectives, 2*(1). Retrived April 18, 2007, from http://aries.oise.utoronto.ca/highered/

Strauss, A., & Corbin, J. (1990). *Basics of qualitative research: Grounded theory procedures and techniques* (3rd ed.). Newbury Park, CA: Sage.

Taylor, J. (2001). Fifth generation distance education. *Journal of Instructional Science and Technology, 4*(1). Retrieved April 18, 2007, from http://www.usq.edu.au/electpub/e-jist/docs/old/vol4no1/contents.htm

Tisdell, E., Strohschen, G., Carver, M., Corrigan, P., Nash, J., Nelsen, M., & O'Connor, M. (2004). Cohort learning online in graduate higher education: Constructing knowledge in cyber community. *Journal of Educational Technology & Society, 7*(1), 115–127.

Wadhwa, G., Schulz, H., & Mann, B. L. (2006). Effects of anonymity and peer-accountability during online peer assessment. In Mann, B. L. (Ed.), *Selected styles in web-based educational research* (pp. 300–331). Hershey, PA: Idea Group.

Wilson, T., & Whitelock, D. (1998). Changing roles: Comparing face to face and on-line teaching in the light of new technologies. *European Journal of Open, Distance and E-Learning*. Retrieved April 18, 2007, from http://www.eurodl.org

Section 5
Training Teachers

Chapter 19
ICT Ecologies of Learning:
Active Socially Engaged Learning, Resiliency and Leadership

Jenny Arntzen
University of British Columbia, Canada

Don Krug
University of British Columbia, Canada

ABSTRACT

This multiple case study investigates how a cohort of thirty-eight elementary teacher candidates (TC) and a volunteer subgroup of eight teacher candidate researchers (TCR) were prepared to use ICT in their teacher education program (TEP). The authors expected social and cultural relationships would contribute to the formation of these beginning teacher's pedagogical perspectives and practices in relation to ICT. The study examined both TC and TCR uses of ICT from multiple perspectives: as students in the TEP; as teachers in their practicum classrooms; and as research participants. The researchers collected data on how their TEP, and ICT ecologies of learning (ICT-EL) experiences, influenced the formation of TC and TCR ICT perspectives regarding curriculum knowledge (ICT literacies) and pedagogy (ICT practices). This chapter describes the role institutional isomorphism and knowledge and curriculum fragmentation appear to play in the formation of oppositional, or resistant, ICT perspectives. It argues for active socially engaged learning (ASEL), efficacious learning, and critical inquiry as emergent systems that are in a continuous state of formation and change within these institutional contexts.

INTRODUCTION

In 2003, the School District of Philadelphia and Microsoft collaborated to develop a 750-student high school that could serve as a model for 21st-century learning communities around the world. This venture promised to enhance educational practices and promote digital inclusion. The plan was to integrate technology into every area of learning and curriculum. The school would be a collaborative community supported administratively to create engaging content that would be shared and assessed. This School of the Future (SOF) would model ways to generate innovative educational practices and new approaches for learning. The hope was to create a space that

DOI: 10.4018/978-1-61692-854-4.ch019

engaged all participants in passionate and self-responsible learning. With this in mind, students would be prepared to succeed in a digital world and global economy.

The 'closing' of Philadelphia's SOF provides a regrettable example that the integration of information and communication technologies (ICT) is not simply transferrable into educational contexts. Even though the school promised to revolutionize education it was unable to fulfill its mission. Jan Biros, associate vice president for instructional technology support and campus outreach at Drexel University and a former member of the SOF Curriculum Planning Committee, said, "We naively thought, I guess, that by providing a beautiful building and great resources, these things would automatically yield change" (Stansbury, 2009, p. 1).

In a recent study examining the extent to which computer-related technologies were used in schools, Leonard & Leonard (2006) found technology integration remained problematic because many experienced teachers seemed unwilling or unable to incorporate pedagogical changes using ICT into their teaching and learning processes. But this phenomenon is not unique to only experienced teachers. Dawson (2007) found that beginning teachers abandoned their use of ICT during their induction year to fit within unsupportive ICT school situations. In addition, Brown & Warschauer (2006) found that a new teacher's ICT perspective and willingness to continue to use ICT through difficult and unsupported school situations was influenced by their teacher education program (TEP) ICT experiences. Not surprisingly, a teacher's ICT perspectives are connected to a complex web of experiences that include their past and present ICT practices, educational environments, and the cultural specificity of their professional and personal relationships (Albion & Ertmer, 2002).

Over the past 5 years, our research has focused on teacher candidates' (TC) engagements with ICT in their TEP at a large regional university in Canada. We reasoned that if beginning teachers could assume a leadership role as they exited the program, they might be able to help build momentum to change ICT perspectives and practices in educational institutions. Before we began our research, we examined scholarly research to identify conditions that contributed to the formation of beginning teachers ICT perspectives. In this chapter we report on our literature review and the first two years of our three-year study called "ICT Ecologies of Learning (ICT-EL)".

We view ICT ecologies of learning as conceptual positions that acknowledge contextual issues are multi-dimensionally and multi-directionally articulated by experiences, human socially interested agency, and environmental conditions. Research shows that ICT has increased the complexity of people's ways of living (culture), saturating experiences with profound challenges of pedagogical and technological adaptability (Krug & Arntzen, in press; Foucault, 1982; Hall, 1981; Kirsh, 2000). Our definition of ICT ecologies of learning draws from research on ecologies and neuroscience. We articulate active socially engaged learning (ASEL), efficacious learning, and critical inquiry through ecologies as emergent systems that are in a continuous state of formation and change. The emergent formation of a learning ecology is guided by both intrinsic characteristics of the participants and the external conditions they are simultaneously situated within.

In this multiple case study we investigated how a cohort of thirty-eight elementary teacher candidates (TC) and a volunteer subgroup of eight teacher candidate researchers (TCR) were prepared to use ICT in their teacher education program. We expected social and cultural relationships would contribute to the formation of these beginning teacher's pedagogical perspectives and practices in relation to ICT. The TCRs participated in an extended series of collective inquiry processes that led them to investigate and discuss with each other their experiences using ICT in educational contexts. We examined both TC and TCR uses of

ICT from multiple perspectives: as students in the TEP; as teachers in their practicum classrooms; and as research participants. We collected data on how their TEP, and ICT-EL experiences, influenced the formation of TC and TCR ICT perspectives regarding curriculum knowledge (ICT literacies) and pedagogy (ICT practices).

Below we describe several important educational concepts concerning the development of ASEL with ICT such as: problem-based learning, mentoring, cooperative and collaborative learning, communities of practice, and communities of inquiry. We treated each of these educational concepts as continually conditioned within particular social, cultural, historical, and political forces and epistemological positions. We identify characteristics associated with advantages and disadvantages of social learning and meaning-making. Then we describe moments from our research case studies that illustrate how TC's and TCR's ICT perspectives and practices evolved during their academic course work as they accepted, resisted or opposed participation in various socially engaged learning situations. These moments represent only some of the diverse situations TCs and TCRs encountered but serve well to highlight how these experiences contributed to their ICT perspectives. Next, suggestions and recommendations are included based on our research findings. Our future research is leading us to consider how ICT ecologies of learning can be implemented within teacher education programs without becoming prescriptive and institutionalized. In conclusion, we highlight a few significant points regarding participating in, and contributing to, ICT ecologies of learning in a teacher education program. We are interested in TEP cultural formations that instill active socially engaged learning that sustains an interest in life-long critical inquiry.

BACKGROUND: SOCIALLY ENGAGED LEARNING

Research literature articulates a myriad of factors contributing to multiple, shifting affordances and barriers to teacher's engagement with ICT (Brzycki & Dudt, 2005). It seems safe to say there will *never* be ideal conditions for integrating ICT in education. This suggests a need for educators to develop evolving and critical ICT perspectives. Given the complex and dynamic conditions of education, we investigated how teacher candidates might form ASEL relationships that would enable them to continuously conduct critical inquiry about ICT *despite* certain difficulties placed in their way.

Critical Inquiry

Critical inquiry is an *assemblage* (Deleuze & Guattari, 1987) of ideas, theories, and processes. We asked, "Is it possible to conceive of and implement constructivist pedagogies with ICT within a living organization and complex TEP at a large university?" We were aware of research that had studied emerging participatory learning (Jenkins, 2006), that had looked at educators' evolving skills and knowledge (Kellner, 2005) and that examined community based opportunities for teaching, for learning, and for practice (Lave, 1996). Posner (2005) said prospective teachers "do not actually learn from experience as much as [they] learn from reflecting on experience" (p. 21). We wanted to know if it was possible to engage TCs and TCRs in critical inquiry[1] and not just reflective practice. As we conducted a literature review two conditions repeatedly emerged about the complexity of ICT and education: institutional isomorphismand knowledge and curricular fragmentation. Although we acknowledge there are other contextual conditions, we will address these two below.

Institutional Isomorphism

Institutional isomorphism is a re-iterating, reciprocal, emergent phenomenon. DiMaggio and Powell (1983) described three mechanisms of isomorphism: 1) *coercive* (isomorphism that stems from political influence and the problem of legitimacy; 2) *mimetic* (isomorphism resulting from standard responses to uncertainty); and 3) *normative* (isomorphism associated with professionalism). Learning occurs in dynamic spaces, but learning processes are also subject to contextual forces exercised through institutional policies and historical practices. The reproduction of entrenched educational organizational modes of operation is not a new problem. It was reported that the Philadelphia's School of the Future reverted to traditional district assessments and classroom practices as difficulties compounded with leadership, technology, and students' use of ICT (Stansbury, 2009). This reversion was attributed to 'isomorphism', a tendency for innovative schools to eventually conform to the parent model from which it was derived (Levin cited in Stansbury, 2009). Isomorphism refers to a concept of organizational activity as ritual conformity to institutional structures (Scheid-Cook, 1992). According to this theory, educational organizations are environments that actively construct their own realities by creating and defining institutional demands (i.e., the 'institution' of teaching) (Scheid-Cook, 1992). In the province of British Columbia there are 9 TEP operating across a wide geographic region. We found, without exception, that these TEP's had implemented similar responses to ICT: ad hoc, fragmented, non-compulsory course offerings with discipline specific pockets of ICT research taking place in individual departments (Krug & Arntzen, 2009).

Knowledge and Curricular Fragmentation

Our review of literature identified knowledge and curricular fragmentation as a problem. Fragmentation occurs as educational institutions scramble to adopt ICT into their programs without a cohesive, congruent, institutional plan or policy (Coutts, Drinkwater, & Simpson, 2001). Britzman (1991) discussed four areas of knowledge fragmentation in general education: compartmentalization of knowledge, dualism of content and pedagogy, selection of knowledge and interests, and divisions between theory and practice. We found understanding concepts of knowledge and curriculum fragmentation can alert teachers to the importance of issues regarding theory, power, and authority embedded in how and what is taught.

Britzman (1991) extensively studied these issues and contends that the *compartmentalization of knowledge* limits opportunities and possibilities of inquiry. The *dualism of content and pedagogy* has also separated 'what' and 'how' curriculum has been conceptualized and practiced. Britzman identifies three dynamic factors that have influenced educational positions: the elevation of academic scientific knowledge over practice, the value of scientific knowledge over school knowledge, and a belief that scholarly knowledge is more important than practical experience. For some time now, "best practices" have been championed as ways to engage students in meaningful learning of content through tested and proven activities. This kind of knowledge fragmentation and their influences and affects are not always easily recognized and understood. Our point is that it is necessary to develop continuously and carefully a "philosophy of experience" that scrutinizes predefined outcomes and teacher-proof curriculum. Another form of knowledge fragmentation discussed by Britzman (1991) concerns the *selection and politics of knowledge*. Curriculum organization represents a struggle over particular "selective traditions" (Apple, 1982; Williams, 1957).

A fourth form of knowledge fragmentation is the *division of theory from practice*. One prominent misconception is that the process of theorizing is isolated from educational activities and practices of teaching. A popular educational slogan bantered about by some educators at one time or another is the adage "from theory to practice." While meaningful classroom practices should be grounded in scholarly, scientifically researched educational theories, sound educational theories can only emerge from inquiry on empirically-based teaching and learning. Top down positions of educational philosophy should be (re)conceptualized as more dynamic, multidimensional, and multidirectional.

Social Engaged Learning and ICT

Teacher education, ICT, and ASEL have been studied from a variety of perspectives. John Seely Brown, et al. (1989) argues that learning and cognition are fundamentally situated, and the experience within which knowledge was developed and deployed is not separable from constructing knowledge. When observing instruction in the TEP, a common issue concerning ASEL was the assumption instructors made that learning automatically would occur if an appropriate environment was provided (Kao, et al., 2008). However, problems arising from a diffusion of responsibility such as social loafing or free-rider effects were observed when sufficient motivation was not present for the learner (Barron, Kerr, & Miller, 1992). To address this issue some instructors incorporated scripted instructions, but this strategy ran the risk of over-scripting learning processes (Dillenbourg, 2002) making the learning activities dry and technocratic. We wanted to identify ways to address these issues by drawing on past research and applying what we learned in dynamic, contextually complex situations.

Problem-Based Learning

Problem-based learning (PBL) has been shown to enhance work environments for participants and faculty (Albanese, 2000). It draws from case-based education, such as medicine, where participants, working in small groups, are presented with a set of symptoms and charged with the task of diagnosing the patient's condition. Problem-based learning generally deals with hypothetical situations. Three characteristics of problem-based learning include: (1) problems as stimulus for learning; (2) tutors as facilitators; and (3) group work as stimulus for interaction (Dolmans, De Grave, Wolfhagen, & van der Vleuten, 2005). Problem-based learning is considered a means to restructure traditional instructor/student interactions and can emphasize active, self-directed learning by the students, rather than didactic, teacher-directed instruction (Harland, 2002, and Maxwell, Bellisimo & Mergendoller, 2001).

Mentoring

Teacher education programs have a long history of using mentoring to shepherd beginning teachers into the profession (Siebert, Clark, Kilbridge, & Peterson, 2006) Mentoring was commonly conceived of as a one-to-one relationship between an expert and a novice (Clark, et al., 2006; C. A. Morrow & Fredin, 1999; Rose, 2003). Alternate concepts of mentoring attempt to re-align the mentor/mentee relationship in more equitable terms: a multicultural feminist model (Benishek, Bieschke, Park, & Slattery, 2004); co-mentoring support groups (Mullen, Whatley, & Kealy, 1999); dialogic mentoring relationships in adult learning contexts (McDonald & Castleton, 2001); and engagement mentoring for social inclusion (Colley, 2003). When it came to mentoring ICT in teacher education, a couple of interesting studies reported innovative definitions of mentoring. Leh (2005) reported findings from a study that positioned teacher education faculty and teacher candidates in reverse mentoring relationships. In these relationships, the teacher candidate mentored the faculty member to build ICT knowledge and the faculty member mentored the teacher candidate to build pedagogical and content knowledge (Leh, 2005). In another study the mentor teacher contributed pedagogical and classroom management knowledge, the teacher candidate contributed ICT literacies and curriculum knowledge (Margerum-Leys & Marx, 2004).

We found we could not rely on mentoring because the approach placed too much value on higher authority and expert knowledge (Mullen, et al., 1999). Mentoring models carried the risk of re-inscribing unquestioned conservatism (Monaghan & Lunt, 1992). We hypothesized that a more open, analytic, socially engaged, and self-reflexive way of working was needed to foster critical inquiry and collaborative practices than could be provided by one-to-one role modeling or apprenticeship (Monaghan & Lunt, 1992).

Cooperative Learning and Collaborative Learning

Although collaborative learning and cooperative learning are sometimes used interchangeably, they have distinct characteristics. In a collaborative learning relationship learning tasks involve information sharing followed by discussion (Kao, Lin, & Sun, 2008). Collaboration implies negotiation through participants' communicative acts (Dillenbourg & Baker, n/d). Multiple narratives can be used as a means to negotiate meaning, to build a shared representation of a situation for analysis and to problem solve (Soulier & Caussanel, 2002). When engaged in collaborative learning, participants shift from a self-regulated approach to collective processes for the co-construction of shared learning (Jarvela, et al., 2007). This shift can be facilitated by a "scripted collaboration" wherein participants are guided by a set of instructions that outline how participants are expected to perform, interact, and collaborate to solve a problem (Dillenbourg, 2002). Collaborative learning is well-suited for complex, ill-defined, dynamic conditions such as teacher education, ICT, and institutional isomorphism. It functions as a melding of diverse personal histories toward maximizing individual potentials. Participants in collaborative learning engage with their situated conditions and diverse participants to formulate local innovations.

The two important differences between collaborative learning and cooperative learning include: (1) collaborative learning occurs in complex, ill-defined, dynamic conditions, whereas cooperative learning has clearly articulated outcomes and expectations of an end product; (2) collaborative learning functions as a melding of diverse personal histories toward maximizing individual potentials, where as cooperative learning parses out discrete tasks, or spheres of activity, to be accomplished individually, which contribute to the whole group achievement of a task or project.

Communities of Practice

Lave and Wenger (1991) describe communities of practice as informal entities that exist in the perspectives of participants who are united in action and the meanings that action have for them. Embedding learning in experience makes deliberate use of the social and physical contexts available and creates conditions for experience (Collins, Brown, & Newman, date needed in press). Communities of practice are intricately bound by socially constructed webs of perspectives and are significant to what people do (Geertz, 1983). Learning is a process of coming to be, an identity-in-practice (Lave, 1992). Learning viewed as socially engaged is based on an ontological view of people as active beings, in the formation of forging identities through lived experiences in the world (Lave, 1992). Being human is a relational matter, generated in a density of experiences and in the formation of self-identity, social identity, and social relations. People engage with each other as conditions of their existence (Lave, 1996). Wenger (1998) described four components to the formation of a community of practice: (1) meaningful change—individually and collectively; (2) practice as mutual engagement in action that shares historical and social resources, frameworks, and perspectives; (3) competence in community participation recognized as social configurations worth pursuing; and (4) identity created through personal histories formed within learning experiences in the context of the community. These conditions were notably absent in most of the courses we observed within the TEP.

Communities of Inquiry

Communities of inquiry shift participant roles from learners to members of a knowledge building community. Characteristics of learning found in communities of inquiry include: (1) community knowledge advancement rather than individual achievement; (2) knowledge advancement as an idea improved rather than "discovery" of one true or warranted belief; (3) knowledge *of* in contrast to knowledge *about*; (4) discourse as collaborative problem solving rather than argumentation; (5) constructive use of authoritative information; and (6) recognition of the significance of emergent understandings (Scardamalia & Bereiter, 2006). Participants need to be aware of their culturally shaped interpretations within a given situation to become capable of open and critical inquiry, to jointly assess their interpretations, and to engage in negotiating realities (Friedman & Antal, 2005, 2006). Their ability to negotiate realities was recognized as an intercultural attribute that supports developing strategies to address specific contextual conditions (Antal & Friedman, 2008).

CASE STUDY EXAMPLES FROM A TEACHER EDUCATION PROGRAM

Below we describe moments from our research case studies that illustrate institutional isomorphism and curriculum and knowledge fragmentation. We studied how TC's and TCR's ICT perspectives evolved during their academic coursework as they accepted, resisted or opposed participation in various ICT experiences. These moments represent only some of the diverse situations TCs and TCRs encountered but serve well to highlight how these experiences contributed to their ICT perspectives and the formation of their pedagogical practices. We juxtapose examples from the TEP in relation to comments from TC's to understand the formation of opposition and resistant ICT views and represent examples of views of acceptance and the conditions within which they emerged. Through our analysis of the data we discuss solutions and recommendations in relation to ICT ecologies of learning. This theoretical assemblage of concepts is based on our review of research, our research data, and our previous educational experiences. We describe examples of ASEL, efficacious learning, and resiliency, showing instances of TCRs providing ICT leadership with their TEP instructors, their practicum sponsor teachers and in their extended practicum schools.[2]

Research Overview

Our research took place within a two-year elementary TEP at a large university. We employed articulation as a counter-methodology to provide a way to juxtapose diverse contextual conditions and research data within arbitrary moments of closure (Slack, 1996). In this study, articulation was also used to examine relationships among ASEL, ICT, and teacher education.

During the first two years of our study (the entire length of their TEP), eight TCRs participated in a series of critical inquiry sessions. These volunteer TCRs formed a subset from the 38 TC cohort. Our inquiry sessions provided opportunities to discuss and explore issues about pedagogy and curriculum, and served to build TCRs ICT skills and knowledge. The TCRs engaged in research as they worked to develop ICT enhanced lessons, which they taught during their long practicum. The TCRs used video ethnography to record themselves teaching these ICT lessons. These video recordings were reviewed by the TCRs during subsequent inquiry sessions, when they selected seven significant moments of their teaching with ICT for further deliberation. These deliberations were shared amongst the TCRs in later inquiry sessions. As part of these deliberation processes and discussions, the TCRs analyzed and critiqued their own, and each other's, uses of ICT with a focus on pedagogical practice. These conversations extended to discussions, analysis, and critiques of the contextual conditions within the TEP and within their practicum schools.

A significant factor in our research protocol was providing ICT technologies, resources and research support for TCRs. Each TCR received a laptop computer, a digital video camera, and a data projector. They had access to an online server dedicated to the research program, which included social networking software, discussion-forum and weblog. In addition, a range of educational software was loaded on each laptop, and the TCR had opportunities to request additional software and digital devices to support their teaching. There was also a class set of digital cameras available for practicum teaching activities. TCR's were encouraged to ask for in-class support from the research group when teaching an ICT enhanced lesson.

We observed all the classes the TC and TCR attended throughout their first year of the TEP. We facilitated critical inquiry sessions with them during the two years of the TEP. These sessions were designed to instill ASEL and efficacious learning through direct experiences, reflection and observation and deliberation and dialogue. Together we learned how and why to work in collaborative groups. Further afield, we visited all the TCRs practicum schools and met with the TCRs school administrators and sponsor teachers. During these visits we inspected and documented the ICT resources in the schools. At the end of the first year of the TEP, the TC's met with us in small focus groups to complete a questionnaire and discuss characteristics of their ICT experiences in the TEP. These sessions were digitally recorded and transcribed for further analysis. During the long practicum we interviewed the faculty advisors (FA), sponsor teachers (ST) and school administrators (SA) on ICT related policies, practices and perspectives. During the last term of the TEP it was a challenge to carve out time from the TCRs busy TEP schedule for inquiry sessions and other research activities. For example, in the final term of the TEP program, the TCRs (and the rest of their cohort) were in seven face-to-face courses for a total of 21 contact hours a week. In addition to this grueling schedule, the TCRs attended five 2-hour inquiry sessions with us throughout that final term. On the last day of their TEP, the TCRs gathered for a program ending inquiry session and completed a survey, a questionnaire, and participated in deliberation and dialogue about their experiences and possible future ICT leadership.

Institutional Isomorphism

To understand relationships among contextual conditions and the formation of ICT perspectives, we examined research on 'institutional isomorphism'. In 1977 Meyer and Rowan (1977) described how institutional organizations come to employ *a logic of confidence* and *good faith* in place of coordination, inspection and evaluation. They suggested that as organizations expand and become increasingly complex their institutional rules function as myths, which incorporate and gain legitimacy, resources, and stability, in order to enhance survival. They described these organizational structures as isomorphic relationships embedded with myths of the institution (Meyer & Rowan, 1977). Our use of the term isomorphism is not meant to imply a corresponding or causal relationship between agents and their institutional contexts (Morrow & Torres, 1994). In using the term, institutional isomorphism, in the context of a TEP, we refer to a relationship between the teacher candidates as agents, and the social domain of the TEP. Within this domain the TC's were forming their views of acceptance, resistance, and opposition connected with ICT through mediating processes of signification and constitution. Thus, the TC's response to their interpretation of ICT events in the TEP and the formation of their response can only partially represent their ICT perspective of the TEP as an arbitrary moment of closure. We did not perceive this relationship as deterministic; one did not *cause* the other to form. Rather, these *emergent* contexts conditioned individual and collective relationships to occur that enabled the formation of views. Human agency and organizational structures are not static and are re-created in relation to dynamic dimensions of society.

We found examples of *coercive institutional isomorphism* in the formation of ICT perspectives with the TCs. In a survey at the end of the first term of the TEP, one TC wrote, "I did not think I could incorporate much digital technologies in my practicum b/c they are in kindergarten, as digital tech. was quite irrelevant to me" (TC 3-5 #65). At the end of the first year of the program, this concept was re-iterated in a response to a questionnaire during a focus group interview. A TC stated, "I am teaching kindergarten and I feel using technology takes away [from] their fundamental skills e.g. writing, drawing, etc." (TC 15 #146). A different TC added, "I don't know how I could work it into a kindergarten setting. We have 6 computers in our class, but I feel the kids are already on them too much" (TC 16 #147). These responses by TCs were conditioned by authoritative relationships with instructors, who did not model the use of ICT literacy or ICT practices, and by the TC's concern with the legitimacy of using ICT to enhance learning for this age group.

We found *mimetic institutional isomorphism* to be linked with the uncertainty of TCs as they described ICT barriers. A TC stated, "Better and more clear instruction in regards to how to use [ICT], funding for schools, [and] acceptance by teachers" (TC 15-9 #151). A common tension for TCs was an unwritten expectation that they would mimick their sponsor teacher's uncertainty with using ICT. A TC reported, "The one time that I was going to use the Internet for a lesson my teacher said it was unreliable in the school. Also the only way the Internet was used in the computer lab was for simple tasks like crosswords that required no computer skills (TC 4-3 #152)." Most of the TC were unable, or unwilling, to risk projecting an ICT perspective that was contrary to the view of their ST.

A striking moment of *normative institutional isomorphism* (associated with professionalism) took place within the first month of the TEP. In addition to their regular program of courses and school visits during their first term, the TCs attended a weekly guest speaker series. Guest speakers presented on a wide range of topics linked to the concept of diversity in education. The first speaker presented on globalization. At the beginning of her presentation she was asked if she needed an LCD projector. The guest speaker made a dismissive gesture and said, "A good teacher doesn't need to use technology" (Research Notes #48). Later, at the end of the first term of the TEP, a TC commented on teaching and ICT, "Focus on grass roots teaching, ignore it [ICT], ask if it is absolutely necessary that the format be digital" (TC 7-3 #50). At the end of the first year of the TEP, during the TC focus groups, a TC expressed his lack of confidence about using ICT, "My school, I don't feel, is properly equipped, or people don't know enough about it to feel confident using technology, because I feel confident using it myself, but I wouldn't feel confident bringing it into my class." Another TC added, "Same here." These statements indicate a normative, unquestioning perspective that links professionalism with "good teachers do not need to use technology."

ICT Fragmentation

Meyer and Rowan (1977) suggested an organization in an isomorphic relationship with its own myths would fail to employ logic, coordination, or evaluation in its operations. Examples of curriculum and knowledge fragmentation in the TEP lend support to this idea. At the end of the first term of the first year of the TEP the TCs listed some of their experiences of fragmentation in their program. These included ICT face-to-face, hybrid, and online situations. A TC commented, "The various online communities were also frustrating (Ning, WebCT, etc.) [it] would be nice if teachers could agree on one site to use" (TC 2-6 #70). Another TC said, "The fact that we did not have a technology course! It would have been helpful to know more than the basic functions of certain programs, i.e., Powerpoint" (TC 3-6 #71). A different TC struggled with the programs lack of consistency, "Difficult is equal to the horror of doing assignments etc and facing the nightmare of trying to get one format to another, i.e., documents between computers with different editions of word processors or trying to download video for music in a format from a camera to use on a home computer" (TC 5-6 #72). "Overloaded with 'Social Networks' to make life/communication EASIER?!!*!? no thanks" wrote another TC, (TC 7-6 #73). One TC perceived ICT as not valuable because it "segregates students" (TC 7-6 #102). This TC commented further on the experience of fragmentation, "As for this program, I feel too much was injected before the system was ready. It was perceived by us to be sloppy, poorly organized & conducted with very little foresight" (TC 7-7 #102)."

It is fairly easy to interpret views of opposition and resistance to ICT in these TCs' statements. These views emerged after only one term of experiencing curricular and knowledge fragmentation in their TEP. Instructors in the program were also isolated and overworked. There were no ICT guidelines to follow or an articulated ICT policy to provide curriculum organization. The students were not aware of these conditions and felt frustration over the lack of consistency and communication, the intensity of the program schedule, and the lack of collaboration among the instructors and administration. We were surprised to find the absence of any formal ICT plan or policy for the nine British Columbia TEPs. Within the TEP, and across the K-12 TEPs curricula in our study, *good faith* was the standard mode of operation when it came to the inclusion of ICT.

ICT Perspectives

A person's perspective or view is a conceptual, epistemological, spatial and temporal position from which one can 'see' their place and other places within the world. A perspective assumes that a viewer is positioned but that this space is not static. Webster's online dictionary states, "Perspective is the choice of a single view point from which to sense, categorize, measure or codify experience, typically for sharing it with another. It can be interpreted as a visual, audio, or linguistic choice, depending on the sense which is to be addressed and the media used in sharing." hooks used the term "to see" as a powerful way to perceive the subtle and complex web of social relations (hooks, 1990, p. 113). In our working definition, a perspective is not a relativist position but one that is conditioned by particular contextual forces constantly at play.

Views of Resistance and Opposition

The random insertion of ICT within the curriculum of the TEP we studied did not provide for students to gain confidence using ICT in an educational context. Resistant and oppositional perspectives toward using ICT within education can be connected with an institutional failure to employ a comprehensive, coordinated response to ICT engagement in its program. This failure created an absence of programmatic opportunities to discuss the pedagogic and curricular implications of ICT for teaching and learning. Expressions of resistance and opposition were common throughout the TEP. Some TCs entered the program with a certain amount of ICT reluctance pre-formed. For example, in the third week of the TEP we had the TC complete a pre-program survey about their ICT literacies and their attitudes about the role ICT should play in their future as teachers. Out of 38 surveys completed, five students wrote additional comments. Without exception, these comments expressed oppositional views about ICT in education, such as, "Stressing the use of technology pressures families to 'buy into' it. For families that can't afford it, it seems unfair" (TC 8 #153). Another TC commented, "I have many doubts as to my own abilities and the value over true hands-on teaching in the classroom" (TC 18 #154). A TC wrote, "In my future classroom I probably would not use computers regularly in my lessons" (TC 23 #155). "Computers are tools and like all tools, can be misused," penned another TC (TC 26 #156). In addition, "Technology takes away the social [engagement] that schools are supposed to provide to students," cautioned a TC (TC 32 #157). At the end of their first year of the TEP program 54% of the TCs indicated they did not feel well prepared to use ICT for teaching during their extended practicum and 47% of them did not intend to use ICT for teaching during this time.

Other instances of resistance and opposition showed up across the program. An SA at one of the extended practicum schools did not want to have her interview recorded because she was afraid that her ICT knowledge was going to be judged and found lacking in relation to an arbitrary scale (SA 19 #158). An FA wanted to cut her interview short because she couldn't see a connection between the questions about her teaching philosophy and the TC's use of ICT during their practicum, "What does my opinion of collaboration, what does that have to do with what the students did during their practicum?" (FA 23 #159). A ST described the reaction of a staff member who when a Smartboard was introduced, said, "it's just... to learn something again, with the workload... sometimes it is difficult to accept change when you feel it is forced on you" (EST 15 #160). In another instance, after a 30 minute delay to set up a laptop and projector, a FA started off a class session saying, with a tone of frustration, "Technology, this is the drawback, because you never know if everything is going to work, or not, it was working perfectly the other day" (FA 23 #161). Perspectives are not static. Our analysis of these early data from the TEP indicated to us to go back to our research literature review in order to identify ASEL characteristics that might assist a TC to overcome not only using ICT but also how they might support one another.

Views of Acceptance

Based on the early review of our data, we feel confident in saying there was a significant presence of oppositional and resistant views toward ICT in the research group of TC in the TEP. However, we don't want to give the impression that views across the TEP were uniformly similar. Both FAs expressed an accepting perspective during their interviews concerning the importance of ICT, even as they publicly conveyed oppositional or resistant ICT perspectives. One FA said, "It is the only way to go, our students will be at a terrible disadvantage if they are not ready" (FA 23 #163). The other agreed, "there is an imperative to get on board [ICT integration in school practices]" (FA 24 #164). There were TCs who indicated views of acceptance of ICT early in their program. For example, one TC did not plan on using ICT in his practicum, but indicated he would probably use it later in his teaching career (TC 18-5 #162). Another TC expressed awareness of the importance of teaching with and about ICT, "... kids today are living in a digital media age and we need to prepare them in how they can use technologies and warn them about the cautions of using them; we can only teach them if we are taught how to use technologies!" (TC 3-7 #198). One TC commented on a growing awareness of the complexity of bringing ICT into his teaching practices, "It is such a quickly developing and rapidly changing area of knowledge and resources that I find we (including instructors) are all figuring it out together. This can be frustrating when projects are built upon technologies that teachers are unfamiliar with" (TC 22-8 #165).

SOLUTIONS AND RECOMMENDATIONS: ICT ECOLOGIES OF LEARNING

An important pedagogical concept that emerged from of our research was the need for teachers to be active, efficacious and reflexive of their learning. We conceptualized these processes within a conceptual, theoretical, and practical position articulated as ecologies of learning. In this section, we discuss our solutions and recommendations to these conditions. We developed an ICT ecologies of learning research group that included TCs as co-researchers. These TCRs joined us in critical inquiry sessions using ICT for ASEL. The TCRs came to the research from a variety of backgrounds and expertise with ICT. They all had some ICT skills using email, word processing, Internet research, and using it for entertainment. There was a wide range of ICT confidence, from highly motivated and proficient, to not understanding the basic operations of the computer. A common thread of interest amongst the TCRs was a desire to learn how to use ICT for teaching and learning in their professional teaching practice.

Active Socially Engaged Learning

The TCRs experienced ASEL as continuous cycles of critical inquiry that reinforced and questioned previous learning such as the role of the teacher and the role that the learner plays in knowledge generation. When the research technology was distributed to the TCR, they needed to learn how to use the equipment. Their first inquiry session involved designing a lesson to teach each other, and eventually their students, how to use an ICT device or software application of their choice. The first step in this process was to develop a curriculum concept they might teach in an elementary class situation. Through a process of working in pairs to develop these lessons, they taught each other ICT skills and knowledge that would enhance the learning of the concept. As the TCRs became comfortable with teaching each other, it became common for one or more of them to demonstrate short lessons for the group during our inquiry sessions. For example, one TCR had figured out a virtual classroom management strategy for moving files between a Windows Vista and the Mac OS environment. Using the Parallels software application on a MacBook, he gave a detailed demonstration so that the group could access their file and folders between the two operating systems (TCR 4 #104).

Eventually, the TCRs were designing ASEL lessons for their practicum that included the use of ICT. In one instance, a TCR found a site sponsored by the Canadian government that allowed students to access historical documents and trial transcripts. Her idea was to have the students read, interpret, critically analyze, and represent their learning by, "hav[ing] kids look at a series of sites: some documents,... so the kids could piece it together... see what evidence they give more weight... [on a given historical period or historical event]" (TCR 7 #111). Another TCR, "...project[ed] a clip from the TV show 'Flight of the Conchords' for all the kids to see and hear. In it the characters break into a nonsensical French song. At the end, we asked the kids to tell us what they had heard and understood. We watched it 3 or 4 more times and continued this activity" (TCR 4 #133). For a lesson on "Celebrating Diversity" a TCR, "gave them [the students] the option of using a digital camera as either part of the project or to record the [learning] process" (TCR 1 #137). As the TCRs began to experience and recognize the processes of ASEL for themselves, they started to use characteristics of these processes in their own teaching.

Efficacious Learning

ASEL engenders an efficacious approach to critical inquiry. The TCRs took responsibility for contributing to the evolving knowledge of the group and for themselves. In our study, efficacious learning supported TCRs to not be dissuaded by external or internal barriers and challenges to using ICT. One of the TCRs was dyslexic and had difficulty with reading on the computer screen. After the virtual classroom management lesson, she searched and developed a visual representation strategy that would help her remember how the two operating systems were related (TCR 7 #107).

As part of the research, we provided a multi-user blog site for the TCRs to develop an online teaching environment. In one inquiry session, we had the TCRs online at the blog site, where they were exploring the functionality of the blog software and discussing navigation strategies for teaching and learning. One of the TCRs wanted to get her name into the blog header and asked about using a graphics application. At this point the group extended their explorations into photo editing, image manipulation, and designing custom blog headers. During her long practicum, another TCR documented her teaching experiences with a digital camera to communicate with parents about the students learning. She said, "I have been taking lots of pics with my dig[ital] camera–pics of lessons on the board, pics of handouts, posters on the wall… For my own reference…" (TCR 3 #142). She taught herself how to upload images to a secure media library on the research project server and then shared her knowledge with the rest of the research group.

TCRs worked together to solve technology related issues. In one case, two TCR were in side-by-side classrooms during their long practicum. One of them reported they shared equipment and worked together to "troubleshoot a few problems with hardware and software" (TCR 3-2 #166). In another school, a TCR commented, "[TCR 6] was very helpful in setting up and the logistics and planning for bringing the [mobile] Lab into the grade 7 classroom. We talked it out about pairs and procedures, etc" (TCR 7-2 #170). In adopting efficacious learning strategies, TCRs were able to accomplish much more then they could have if they were alone or if they needed to rely solely on the schools technology administrator. They used devices, software, and pedagogical approaches that they would not otherwise have been exposed to, because they began to feel comfortable and confident in their ability to overcome ICT challenges by recognizing the power of critical inquiry linked with efficacious learning.

Resiliency

A significant concept that emerged from the research was the importance of resiliency when using ICT in the contexts of education. Most teachers already employ resilience to adapt to the barriers and challenges that arise in teaching. This sense of confidence seems to be missing when it involves using ICT. We found resilience formed and enhanced TCRs perspectives over extended periods of time and on at least three occasions: (1) TCRs constructed socially engaged learning relationships as an attribute of the TEP and being part of the research group, (2) TCRs drew on ASEL, efficacious learning, and critical inquiry to refine and sustain their own professional education, and (3) TCRs took risks as an informed

ICT leader both in their TEP and during their extended practicum.

With regards to forming ASEL relationships, one TCR reflected on the different experiences he had during his higher education, "In engineering, you feel like a speck of dust, as insignificant as that… in the cohort [in the TEP] you feel part of a community, with its cliques and politics… in [the research group] it was okay to [be yourself], to do the extra work without feeling judged" (TCR 5 #171). Another TCR commented that their participation in the research group had led them to be, "… way more willing to try using new technology" (TCR 4-7a #172). A TCR compared her experience in the research group to experiences in the TEP, "In my [TEP] it was emphasized over and over again how important technology was in the classroom, but frustration among teachers and teacher candidates was evident. [Participation in the research group] gave me confidence and changed my attitude toward learning about technology from apprehensive to interested and excited" (TCR 1-4 #173).

Several of the TCRs also drew on ASEL, efficacious learning, and critical inquiry to refine and sustain their own professional education. The ICT literacies of the SAs could not be generalized across the research group. Even within the same school, three TCRs found their sponsor teachers held very different views about ICT. One TCR said, "In my case, in the primaries, [ICT perspectives were] very archaic. Nobody, generally, takes any progressive steps to learn any of these things. In my classroom… there was one computer, it was very old, it was in a portable, my main concern was trying to hook up the Internet because there was no Internet out there" (TCR 6 #128). This TCR eventually succeeded in getting an Internet connection to the portable. In the same school, another TCR was teaching in a grade 7 class and found her sponsor teacher resistant to her using ICT. She said, "My teacher does not use technology in class. She uses an overhead and occasionally a boom box" (TCR 7 #174). Despite her sponsor teacher's view of using ICT, this TCR reported, "I was very persistent about getting the two in-class computers de-bugged and updated so that they could be used as resources. [This included] some basic applets for math practice, and writing resource of low output learners" (TCR 7-3 #175). A third TCR at this school observed, "The culture at my school is mostly negative. Teachers use any excuse not to get the kids on the computers. If one computer doesn't work, they just write-off the whole lab" (TCR 4 #176). The TCR added, "The teacher's that do use the technology are often very positive and work together to stay up on any issues that might be causing the lab problems" (TCR 4 #177). This TCR's sponsor teacher was part of a small sub-group of teachers in the school who had banded together to learn about ICT. We were careful to not infer a deterministic reading of any individual comments.

TCRs took risks as informed ICT leaders both in their TEP and during their extended practicum, sporadically during the first two years of our research. It appears TCRs were able to apply their resilience with limited success at their sponsor schools during their long practicum. For example, one of the TCRs, who had strong ICT skills, teaching confidence, and a supportive extended practicum ST reported feeling, "… more hesitant to use technology when I was being observed. Our teachers (FAs) warned us that if we used technology it HAD to work perfectly" (TCR 4-4 #182). This was the same TCR who volunteered to teach the other TCRs ICT related lessons during our inquiry sessions. Then again, one of the TCR had a sponsor teacher who was interested in learning from him. He commented, "I have shown my sponsor teacher a couple things with the computer regarding files and folders. [She] was wondering how to get all the pictures that she had downloaded from the school camera from various events into one folder instead of separate folders. It was a simple task of just copying and pasting but she didn't know you could move picture files like this" (TCR 8 #178). Another TCR, "showed [leadership by] creating a class blog. I created it and guided my students and my sponsor teacher through how to use it. I plan to continue to teach my sponsor teacher more about how she can use and continue the blog after I leave" (TCR 1 #179). The topic of ICT leadership showed up in several ST interviews. One ST discussed her resistant view of ICT, "the idea of kids going online and working on blogs alarmed me a little bit for primary because they already don't have enough time to do what the ministry requires us to do" (ST 11 #180). This teacher was able to see the value of teaching with ICT after observing her TCR teach with it. The ST recalled, "She used it to further facilitate the work that we were doing in class…when [she] was doing a book about the pony club… in guided reading…it referred to horses and the [movement] the horses made… [she] could show them, on the computer, what a gallop looked like… otherwise it's just a word and most of the kids, have no idea [what a gallop] is" (EST 11 #181).

It is not possible to represent, in this chapter, the complexity of attributes of ASEL, efficacious learning, and resiliency TCRs learned during this research period. We do hold that this formation includes self and social attributes associated with strength of character, ICT skills and confidence, pedagogical knowledge, and content knowledge. Their resiliency to ICT educational barriers and challenges was conditioned within respectful and caring relationships that helped to overcome some institutional isomorphism and curricular and knowledge fragmentation. At other times, programmatic pressure inhibited TCR's use of ICT. There were many moments that the TCRs extended themselves into areas that they had little authority or control over in order to help another colleague (TC, TCR, sponsor teacher, faculty associate, instructors, and administrators).

FUTURE RESEARCH

We would not characterize the challenges and subsequent outcomes of ICT integration of the Philadelphia School of the Future as a failure. We see this project providing valuable insights into the technological, cultural, and institutional complexities that contribute to the formation of educators' ICT perspectives. Many educators' seek to identify and employ 'best practices' that can be applied in a variety of situations. Our research leads us to suggest that we need to consider that there are no singular 'best practices'; only learning experiences situated and contextually conditioned within arbitrary moments of closure. From this perspective, educational moments within ecologies of learning are emerging, multiple, and infinitely responsive to the diverse contexts within which they are being applied. The disruptive presence of ICT in education is real. Educators' at all levels of the profession need multiple, ongoing, opportunities to engage in critical inquiry within their profession. Educators' will continue to need to adapt to emerging ICT conditions as societal conditions continue to change. We will continue to study how and why evolving methods are needed that make it possible to participate in forming ongoing, constructive, learning relationships.

We have completed the first two years of our three-year study. Our future research will be to stay in contact and continue our critical inquiry with the eight TCR (or, since they recently graduated, teacher researchers). Given the amount of time the TCRs were under the influence of the TEP, in relation to the time they were engaged in building ICT ecologies of learning, we were not able to facilitate remarkable examples of active, socially engaged learning. Creating a model was not our research goal. As the TCRs enter their induction year, we plan to extend our line of critical inquiry further. Although experienced teachers have pedagogical perspectives and practices that they can convey to beginning teachers, we also found beginning teachers could bring forward useful and meaningful ideas for experienced teachers.

CONCLUSION

The difficulties experienced by the TCs in our TEP were not an isolated phenomenon. Education systems formed within the intellectual period of industrialization and a technocratic rationale have severely affected the development of cultural, technological, or systemic capacities to change. The influence of institutional isomorphism in teacher education programs appears to be pervasive and intractable, particularly in relation to teachers' views of acceptance, resistance, and opposition regarding ICT. Needless ICT barriers and challenges are constructed, re-constructed, and co-constructed by contradictions and incongruence's between theories, practices, and programmatic fragmentation. These contextual conditions affect even those teachers who may already have an accepting view of school change. We studied the influences of institutional isomorphism and curricular and knowledge fragmentation in a TEP. Our experience indicates as does our research observations that a teacher's frustration with ICT often results in a view of opposition or resistance toward using ICT. The issue of curricular and knowledge fragmentation is an important developmental dimension in the formation of ICT ecologies of learning. We believe it is the conceptual and practical experiences of ICT ecologies of learning that enabled the TCRs to begin to form the social supports they needed to challenge and contest barriers with solutions drawing from efficacious learning.

Generally there were indications of ICT acceptance, at least at a rhetorical level during our research. All participants engaged with ICT on some level in their personal lives, many made an attempt to use ICT during their TEP. A smaller group used ICT during their practicum, but we observed no opportunities for TCs and TEP instructors connecting it with critical inquiry. Little or no time was provided for investigations into the ethical and moral implications of ICT in professional teaching practices. It appeared that ICT acceptance did not necessarily translate into ICT literacies or practices.

Research in constructivist pedagogy has shown ASEL and self-, and social-relationships make it possible to form a critical perspective to address problems and issues for which there is no single, unifying answer. Our research intervention appears to have helped TCRs form ICT ecologies of learning and begin to contribute to their formation of resiliency and leadership.

The TCR demonstrated many instances of ICT resiliency, as they proceeded through the TEP as partners in research. A number of them indicated their formation of resiliency was a consequence of participating in the research group, in critical inquiry processes, and in the formation of their own ICT ecologies of learning. The preliminary indication of our research suggests a need for the formation of ICT ecologies of learning focused on critical inquiry rather than a model of best practices. All education is situational and any one method will not fit all school conditions (Kiebard, 1988). Beginning teachers have a role to play in providing future leadership by possibly supporting the development of ICT resilience with experienced educators. Educational institutions will only change through initiatives of their constituents. It appears the formation of ICT ecologies of learning could contribute to that transformation. However, this is no small task.

REFERENCES

Adamy, P., & Heinecke, W. (2005). The influence of organizational culture on technology integration in teacher education. *Journal of Technology and Teacher Education*, *13*(2), 233–255.

Albanese, M. (2000). Problem-based learning: why curricula are likely to show little effect on knowledge and clinical skills. *Medical Education, 34*, 729–738. doi:10.1046/j.1365-2923.2000.00753.x

Albion, P. R., & Ertmer, P. A. (2002). Beyond the foundations: The role of vision and belief in teachers' preparation for integration of technology. *TechTrends, 46*(5). doi:10.1007/BF02818306

Anderson, T., Rourke, L., Garrison, D. R., & Archer, W. (2001). Assessing teaching presence in a computer conferencing context. *Journal of Asynchronous Learning Networks, 5*(2).

Antal, A. B., & Friedman, V. J. (2008). Learning to negotiate reality: A strategy for teaching intercultural competencies. *Journal of Management Education, 32*(363).

Apple, M. W. (1982). *Education and power*. New York: Routledge.

Barron, R. S., Kerr, N. L., & Miller, N. (1992). *Group process, group decision, group action*. Bristol, PA: Open University Press.

Bauer, J., & Kenton, J. (2005). Toward technology integration in the schools: Why it isn't happening. *Journal of Technology and Teacher Education, 13*(4), 519–546.

Benishek, L. A., Bieschke, K. J., Park, J., & Slattery, S. M. (2004). A multicultural feminist model of mentoring. *Journal of Multicultural Counseling and Development*, 32.

Boyd, D., Grossman, P. L., Hammerness, K., Hamilton Lankford, R., Loeb, S., & McDonald, M. (2008). Surveying the landscape of teacher education in New York City: Constrained variation and the challenge of innovation. *Educational Evaluation and Policy Analysis, 30*(4), 319–343. doi:10.3102/0162373708322737

Britzman, D. P. (1991). *Practice makes practice: A critical study of learning to teach*. Albany: State University of New York Press.

Brown, D., & Warschauer, M. (2006). From the university to the elementary classroom: Students' experiences in learning to integrate technology in instruction. *Journal of Technology and Teacher Education, 14*(3), 599–621.

Brzycki, D., & Dudt, K. (2005). Overcoming barriers to technology use in teacher preparation programs. *Journal of Technology and Teacher Education, 13*(4), 619–641.

Clark, P., Jamieson, A., Launer, J., Trompetas, A., Whiteman, J., & Williamson, D. (2006). Intending to be a supervisor, mentor or coach? Which, what for and why? *Education for Primary Care, 17*(2), 109–116.

Colley, H. (2003). Engagement mentoring for 'disaffected' youth: A new model of mentoring for social inclusion. *British Educational Research Journal, 29*(4), 521. doi:10.1080/01411920301842

Collins, A., Brown, J., & Newman, S. (1989). Cognitive apprenticeship: teaching the crafts of reading, writing, and mathematics. In Resnick, L. B. (Ed.), *Knowing, learning and instruction: Essays in honor of Robert Glaser* (pp. 453–491). Hillsdale, NJ: Lawrence Erlbaum Associates.

Coutts, N., Drinkwater, R., & Simpson, M. (2001). Using information and communications technology in learning and teaching: A framework for reflection, planning and evaluation in school development. *Teacher Development, 5*(2), 225–239. doi:10.1080/13664530100200135

Cuban, L. (2001). *Oversold and underused: Computers in classrooms*. Cambridge, MA: Harvard University Press.

Dawson, K. (2007). The role of teacher inquiry in helping prospective teachers untangle the complexities of technology use in classrooms. *Journal of Computing in Teacher Education, 24*(1), 5–12.

Deleuze, G., & Guattari, F. (1987). *A thousand plateaus: Capitalism and schizophrenia*. Minneapolis, MN: University of Minnesota Press.

Dillenbourg, P. (2002). Over-scripting CSCL: The risks of blending collaborative learning with instructional design. In Kirschner, P. A. (Ed.), *Three worlds of CSCL. Can we support CSCL?* (pp. 61–91). Heerlen, Netherlands: Open Universiteit Nederland.

Dillenbourg, P., & Baker, M. (n.d.). *Negotiation spaces in human-computer collaborative learning*.

DiMaggio, P. J., & Powell, W. W. (1983). The iron cage revisited: Institutional isomorphism and collective rationality in organizational fields. *American Sociological Review*, *48*(2), 147–160. doi:10.2307/2095101

Dolmans, D. H. J. M., De Grave, W., Wolfhagen, I. H. A. P., & van der Vleuten, P. M. (2005). Problem-based learning: Future challenges for educational practice and research. *Medical Education*, *39*, 732–741. doi:10.1111/j.1365-2929.2005.02205.x

Foucault, M. (1982). The subject and power. In Dreyfus, H. L., & Rabinow, P. (Eds.), *Michel Foucault: Beyond structuralism and hermeneutics* (pp. 208–226). Chicago: The University of Chicago Press.

Friedman, V. J. (2000, July). *The incubator for social entrepreneurship: Creating partnerships for second order social change*. Paper presented at the Annual Conference of the International Society for Third-Sector Research, Dublin, Ireland.

Friedman, V. J., & Antal, A. B. (2005). Negotiating reality: A theory of action approach to intercultural competence. *Management Learning*, *36*(1), 69–86. doi:10.1177/1350507605049904

Friedman, V. J., & Antal, A. B. (2006). Interactive critical reflection as intercultural competence. In Boud, D., Docherty, P., & Cressey, P. (Eds.), *Productive reflection and learning at working* (pp. 120–130). London: Routledge.

Friedman, V. J., & Rogers, T. (2009). There is nothing so theoretical as good action research. *Action Research*, *7*(1), 31–47. doi:10.1177/1476750308099596

Geertz, C. (1983). *Local knowledge: Further essays in interpretive anthropology*. New York: Basic Books.

Grossberg, L. (1992). *We gotta get out of this place: Popular conservatism and postmodern culture*. New York: Routledge.

Gulsecen, S., & Kubat, A. (2006). Teaching ICT to teacher candidates using PBL: A qualitative and quantitative evaluation. *Journal of Educational Technology & Society*, *9*(2), 96–106.

Hall, S. (1981). Notes on deconstructing 'the Popular. In Samuel, R. (Ed.), *People's history and socialist theory* (pp. 227–240). Boston: Routledge and Kegan Paul.

Harland, T. (2002). Zoology students' experiences of collaborative enquiry in problem-based learning. *Teaching in Higher Education*, *7*(1), 6–17. doi:10.1080/13562510120100355

Healy, C. C., & Welchert, A. J. (1990). Mentoring relations: A definition to advance research and practice. *Educational Researcher*, *19*(9), 17–21.

hooks, b. (1990). *Yearning: Race, gender, and cultural politics*. Boston, MA: South End Press.

Hu, W. (2007, May 4). Seeing no progress, some schools drop laptops. *The New York Times*.

Hughes, J. (2005). The role of teacher knowledge and learning experiences in forming technology-integrated pedagogy. *Journal of Technology and Teacher Education*, *13*(2), 277–302.

Jarvela, S., Naykki, P., Laru, J., & Luokkanen, T. (2007). Structuring and regulating collaborative learning in higher education with wireless networks and mobile tools. *Journal of Educational Technology & Society*, *10*(4), 71–79.

Jenkins, H. a. (2006). *Confronting the challenges of participatory culture: Media education in the 21st century*. Chicago: MacArther Foundation.

Johnson, R. T., & Johnson, D. W. (1994). An overview of cooperative learning. In Thousand, J., Villa, A., & Nevin, A. (Eds.), *Creativity and collaborative learning* (pp. 31–44). Baltimore: Brookes Press.

Kao, G. Y. M., Lin, S. S. J., & Sun, C. T. (2008). Beyond sharing: Engaging students in cooperative and competitive active. *Journal of Educational Technology & Society*, *11*(3), 82–96.

Kellner, D. (2006). Technological transformation, multiple literacies, and the re-visioning of education. In Weiss, J., Nolan, J., Hunsinger, J., & Trifonas, P. (Eds.), *The international handbook of virtual learning environments* (pp. 241–268). Dordrecht, Netherlands: Springer. doi:10.1007/978-1-4020-3803-7_9

Kirschner, P. A., Sweller, J., & Clark, R. E. (2006). Why minimal guidance during instruction does not work: An analysis of the failure of constructivist, discovery, problem-based, experiential, and inquiry-based teaching. *Educational Psychologist*, *41*(2), 75–86. doi:10.1207/s15326985ep4102_1

Kirsh, D. (2000). A few thoughts on cognitive overload. *Intellectica*, *1*(30), 19–51.

Krug, D. (2006). Seeds of possibility: Mentoring K–7 educators' ICT ecology of cognition (pp. 10 - 27).

Krug, D. H., & Arntzen, J. (in press). Ecologies of learning: Efficacious learning and ICT pedagogical and technological adaptability. In Mukerji, S., & Tripathi, P. (Eds.), *Cases on technological adaptability and transnational learning: Issues and challenges*. Hershey, PA: IGI Global.

Lave, J. (1992). *Learning as participation in community of practice*. Paper presented at the Annual Meeting of the American Educational Research Association, San Francisco, California.

Lave, J. (1996). Teaching, as learning, in practice. *Mind, Culture, and Activity*, *3*(3), 149–164. doi:10.1207/s15327884mca0303_2

Lave, J., & Wenger, E. (1991). *Situated learning: Legitimate peripheral participation*. Cambridge, UK: Cambridge University Press.

Leh, A. S. C. (2005). Lessons learned from service learning and reverse mentoring in faculty development: A case study in technology training. *Journal of Technology and Teacher Education*, *13*(1), 25–41.

Leonard, L. J., & Leonard, P. E. (2006). Leadership for technology integration: Computing the reality. *The Alberta Journal of Educational Research*, *52*(4), 212.

LeTendre, G. K., Baker, D. P., Akiba, M., Goesling, B., & Wiseman, A. (2001). Teachers' work: institutional isomorphism and cultural variation in the U.S., Germany, and Japan. *Educational Researcher*, *30*(6), 3–15. doi:10.3102/0013189X030006003

Margerum-Leys, J., & Marx, R. W. (2004). The nature and sharing of teacher knowledge of technology in a student teacher/mentor teacher pair. *Journal of Teacher Education*, *55*(5), 421–437. doi:10.1177/0022487104269858

Maxwell, N., Bellisimo, Y., & Mergendoller, J. (2001, March/April). Problem based learning: Modifying the medical school model for teaching high school economics. *Social Studies*, 73–78. doi:10.1080/00377990109603981

McDonald, M., & Castleton, G. (2001). *Mentoring in adult learning contexts: Partners in dialogue*. Melbourne, Australia: Australian National Training Authority.

Meyer, J. W., & Rowan, B. (1977). Institutionalized organizations: Formal structure as myth and ceremony. *American Journal of Sociology*, *83*(2), 340–363. doi:10.1086/226550

Monaghan, J., & Lunt, N. (1992). Mentoring: Person, process, practice and problems. *British Journal of Educational Studies*, *40*(3), 248–263. doi:10.1080/00071005.1992.9973929

Morrow, C. A., & Fredin, B. (1999). *Worksite mentoring guidebook: Practical help for planning and implementing quality worksite learning experiences*. Columbus, Ohio: Ohio State Department of Education.

Morrow, R. A., & Torres, C. A. (1994). Education and reproduction of class, gender, and race: Responding to the postmodern challenge. *Educational Theory*, *44*(1). doi:10.1111/j.1741-5446.1994.00043.x

Mullen, C. A., Whatley, A., & Kealy, W. A. (1999). *Co-mentoring support groups in higher education. HE 031 943*. Washington, DC: US Department of Education.

Posner, G. J. (2005). *Field experiences: A guide to reflective teaching* (6th ed.). New York: Allyn and Bacon.

Pragnell, M. V., Roselli, T., & Rossano, V. (2006). Can a hypermedia cooperative e-learning environment stimulate constructive collaboration? *Journal of Educational Technology & Society*, *9*(2), 119–132.

Prince, M. (2004). Does active learning work? A review of the research. *Journal of Engineering Education*, *93*(3), 223–231.

Roberts, A. (2000). Mentoring revisited: A phenomenological reading of the literature. *Mentoring & Tutoring: Partnership in Learning*, *8*(2), 145–170. doi:10.1080/713685524

Rose, G. L. (2003). Enhancement of mentor selection using the ideal mentor scale. *Research in Higher Education*, *44*(4), 473. doi:10.1023/A:1024289000849

Ross, E. W., Cornett, J. W., & McCutcheon, G. (1992). Teacher personal theorizing and research on curriculum and teaching. In Ross, E. W., Cornett, J., & McCutcheon, G. (Eds.), *Teacher personal theorizing: Connecting curriculum practice, theory, and research*. Albany, NY: State University of New York Press.

Scardamalia, M., & Bereiter, C. (2006). Knowledge building: Theory, pedagogy, and technology. In Sawyer, K. (Ed.), *Cambridge Handbook of the Learning Sciences* (pp. 97–118). New York: Cambridge University Press.

Scheid-Cook, T. L. (1992). Organizational enactments and conformity to environmental prescriptions. *Human Relations*, *45*(6). doi:10.1177/001872679204500601

Schwab, J. J. (1983). The practical 4: Something for curriculum professors to do. *Curriculum Inquiry*, *13*(3), 239–265. doi:10.2307/1179606

Seely Brown, J., Collins, A., & Duguid, P. (1989). Situated cognition and the culture of learning. *Educational Researcher*, 18.

Siebert, C. J., Clark, A., Kilbridge, A., & Peterson, H. (2006). When preserve teachers struggle or fail: Mentor teachers' perspectives. *Education*, *126*(3), 409–422.

Slack, J. D. (1996). The theory and method of articulation in cultural studies. In Morley, D., & Chen, K. H. (Eds.), *Stuart Hall: Critical dialogues in cultural studies. City, ST*. Taylor & Francis.

Soulier, E., & Caussanel, J. (2002). Narrative tools to improve collaborative sense-making. *AAAI Technical Report WS-02-09 Papers from AAAI Workshop, Paolo Bouquet, Chair*. Association for the Advancement of Artificial Intelligence. Menlo Park, California ISBN 978-1-57735-162-7.

Stansbury, M. (2009). School of the future: Lessons in failure. *eSchool News*. Retrieved from http://www.eschoolnews.com/news/top-news/?i=58973

Wenger, E. (1998). *Communities of practice: Learning, meaning, and identity. Cambridge, UK, and New York*. NY: Cambridge University Press.

Williams, R. (1957). Working class culture. *Universities and Left Review, 2*.

ADDITIONAL READING

Anderson, T. D., & Garrison, D. R. (1995). Critical thinking in distance education: Developing critical communities in an audio teleconference context. *Higher Education*, *29*, 183–199. doi:10.1007/BF01383838

Bandura, A. (1982). Self-efficacy in human agency. *The American Psychologist*, *37*(2). doi:10.1037/0003-066X.37.2.122

Banister, S., & Vannatta, R. (2006). Beginning with a baseline: Insuring productive technology integration in teacher education. *Journal of Technology and Teacher Education*, *14*(1), 209–235.

Barak, M., Lipson, A., & Lerman, S. (2006). Wireless laptops as means for promoting active learning in large lecture halls. *Journal of Research on Technology in Education*, *38*(3), 245–263.

Becker, H. J., & Ravitz, J. (1999). The influence of computer and Internet use on teachers' pedagogical practices and perceptions. *Journal of Research on Computing in Education*, *31*(4), 356.

Berger, P. L., & Luckman, T. (1966). *The social construction of reality: A treatise in the sociology of knowledge*. New York: Doubleday.

Bird, T., & Rosaen, C. L. (2005). Providing authentic contexts for learning information technology in teacher preparation. *Journal of Technology and Teacher Education*, *13*(2), 211–231.

Bitner, N., & Bitner, J. (2002). Integrating technology into the classroom: Eight keys to success. *Journal of Technology and Teacher Education*, *10*(1), 95–100.

Cobb, P., McClain, K., Lamberg, T. S., & Dean, C. (2003). Situating teachers' instructional practices in the institutional setting of the school and district. *Educational Researcher*, *32*(6), 13–24. doi:10.3102/0013189X032006013

Dawson, C., & Rakes, G. C. (2003). The influence of principals' technology training on the integration of technology into schools. *Journal of Research on Technology in Education*, *36*(1), 29–49.

Finley, L., & Hartman, D. (2004). Institutional change and resistance: Teacher preparatory faculty and technology integration. *Journal of Technology and Teacher Education*, *12*(3), 319–337.

Garet, M. S., Porter, A. C., Desimone, L., Birman, B. F., & Yoon, K. S. (2001). What makes professional development effective? Results from a national sample of teachers. *American Educational Research Journal*, *38*(4), 915–945. doi:10.3102/00028312038004915

Hayes, D. (2006). Making all the flashy stuff work: The role of the principal in ICT integration. *Cambridge Journal of Education*, *36*(4), 565–578. doi:10.1080/03057640601049256

Jefferies, P. (2003). ICT in supporting collaborative learning : Pedagogy and practice. *Learning, Media and Technology*, *28*(1), 35–48. doi:10.1080/1358165032000156428

Johnson, G. M., & Howell, A. J. (2005). Attitude toward instructional technology following required versus optional WebCT usage. *Journal of Technology and Teacher Education*, *13*(4), 643–654.

Judson, E. (2006). How teachers integrate technology and their beliefs about learning: Is there a connection? *Journal of Technology and Teacher Education, 14*(3), 581–597.

Kilroy, D. A. (2004). Problem based learning. *Emergency Medicine Journal, 21*, 411–413. doi:10.1136/emj.2003.012435

Lai, K. W., Trewern, A., & Pratt, K. (2002). Computer coordinators as change agents: Some New Zealand observations. *Journal of Technology and Teacher Education, 10*(4), 539–551.

Pierson, M. E. (2001). Technology integration practice as a function of pedagogical expertise. *Journal of Research on Computing in Education, 33*(4), 413.

Rakes, G. C., Fields, V. S., & Cox, K. E. (2006). The influence of teachers' technology use on instructional practices. *Journal of Research on Technology in Education, 38*(4), 409–424.

White, M., & Mason, C. (2001). The Mentoring Induction Project: What new teachers need from mentors. *Teaching Exceptional Children, 33*(6), 81.

KEY TERMS AND DEFINITIONS

Active Socially Engaged Learning (ASEL): Draws from constructivist pedagogy–the role the learner plays is facilitated so that the learner is an active contributor to the collective knowledge of the learning group.

Critical Inquiry: A learning process that seeks to understand the taken-for-granted conditions that contribute to perpetuation of institutional dominant-hegemonic perspectives.

Efficacious Learning: Refers to the formation of self-efficacy, the capacity to take responsibility for one's learning needs, and through these self-directed learning activities contribute to the knowledge of the learning group.

ICT Ecologies of Learning: Emerge through ASEL and efficacious learning when a learning group focuses on building ICT pedagogies and practices.

ICT Literacies: Are the accumulated ICT skills and knowledge, pedagogies and curriculum enacted within a professional teaching practice.

ICT Perspectives: are the attitudes and approaches adopted toward ICT by individuals that contribute to their continuing formation of opposition, resistance, acceptance or resilience to the uses of ICT in their professional teaching practice.

ICT Practices: Are active engagements with ICT to enable, enrich, or enhance learning.

Institutional Isomorphism: Refers to the phenomena wherein institutional myths, cultures and practices are re-inscribed through ritual and culture on successive generations.

Knowledge and Curricular Fragmentation: Refers to the phenomena of separating educational activities into discrete, artificial elements that are perceived, and enacted, as autonomous, disconnected elements.

Pedagogical and Technological Adaptability: Refers to the capacity to engage with continuously evolving conditions through critical inquiry and socially engaged learning.

ENDNOTES

1 Our approach to critical inquiry integrated conceptual, iterative, learning processes that included: (1) direct experiences, (2) observations and reflections, and (3) deliberation and dialogue (Kolb, 1984; Birt, Krug, & Sheridan, 1997). This assemblage of critical inquiry processes is not a linear narrative (presented here for the sake of efficiency). Critical inquiry processes are temporal and spatial arbitrary moments of closure that mark historical, social, political, ethical, and cultural contextual conditions. While a record of critical inquiry can mark

moments of learning about cultural practices, it can also be used to partially document the co-emergence of cognitive and experiential learning.

2 Please note these are preliminary interpretations of a limited sample of the entire data set that has been collected over the last two years. These data are providing strong indicators of contents that require further processing to be more fully understood.

Chapter 20
Exploring the Factors to Determine the Competence of Technology Integration for Teacher Candidates

Hae Seong Park
Azusa Pacific University, USA

Joanne Gilbreath
Azusa Pacific University, USA

Daniel Lawson
Azusa Pacific University, USA

Helen Easterling Williams
Azusa Pacific University, USA

ABSTRACT

The purpose of this study is to examine the factors to determine the competence of technology integration for teacher candidates. This study utilized data from a 2006 quick-response survey entitled 'Educational Technology in Teacher Education Programs for Initial Licensure.' Only 1,350 institutions that have teacher education programs for initial licensure were selected. The result of a hierarchical regression revealed that the extent of institutional training programs for technology explain most variation (33%) of the competence of technology integration of teacher candidates. In addition, the more variation of technology programs an institution employs in its program, the more confidence the teacher candidates possess. The result supports findings from previous research as well as supporting some emphasis on professional development design considerations that may be of value to those planning the similar technology trainings.

DOI: 10.4018/978-1-61692-854-4.ch020

BACKGROUND OF THE STUDY

During the past two decades, integration in educational technology has been a leading theme in the area of pre-service teacher education in the United States. There are two major issues associated with the importance of educational technology integration. The first is the accountability movement in the United States which emphasizes student academic achievement. Although contradictory findings on the effectiveness of educational technology exist (Kay, 2006), there is an agreement that the use of educational technology can improve student academic achievement, if it is implemented properly (Protheroe, 2005). The second is an emphasis on educational accountability by the No Child Left Behind (NCLB) Act of 2001. Recently, some researchers have asserted that educational technology may be the remedy to narrowing the achievement gap between majority and minority students. Several researchers (Ba, Tally, & Tsikalas, 2002; Du et al., 2004; Jackson et al., 2005) have stated that technology has a greater impact on academic achievement for the socioeconomically disadvantaged students than others. In addition, Park (2008) has recently determined that the positive impact of computer usage on academic achievement is greater for language minority students than for English-speaking students. Based on recent findings associated with the impact of technology on socioeconomically disadvantaged and language minority students, educators may support the claim that the technology revolution is now one of the most effective and significant resolutions in educational policies.

Due to the collaborative effort of educational policy makers and administrators, computer availability and accessibility in schools have improved. Although the use of instructional technology has become increasingly important in schools, the growth in instructional technology integration has not kept pace with teacher preparation. Relatively few teachers feel that they are prepared. Ineffective teacher education programs are often cited as the reason for this problem (Brinkerhoff, 2006; Fleming, Motamedi, & May, 2007). According to NCES report (2000), only one-third of elementary teachers in the United States felt that they were well prepared for instructional technology teaching. In addition, this report revealed that teachers with less experience in teaching were better prepared and more likely to use computers in the classroom over those who have more experience. One explanation is that a vast majority of today's classroom teachers are digital immigrants (Prensky, 2001). Simply put, the technology tools that are available today have been developed and implemented during the last decade. Digital immigrants have to learn how to integrate them into their pedagogy and instructional delivery system. Digital natives are students who have grown up with technology. They process information in a way that does not fit to the traditional model of learning. Digital immigrants have to "learn" how to use technology, not only in their personal lives, but also in their instructional practices. Therefore, it may be inferred that the enhancement of technology education in teacher education programs is the key to improve educational technology's impact on student achievement. Educators in teacher education programs face a strong challenge in preparing teacher candidates to integrate technology into curriculum and instruction. Several researchers (e.g., ChanLin, 2005; Franklin, 2008; Hanks, 2002) have tried to determine the factors that prevent implementation of technology integration among teachers. Hanks (2002) found environmental and personal factors effecting teacher's utilization of technology. ChanLin (2005) revealed five factors; social impact, curriculum concerns, environmental support, interest and experience, and personal need. Franklin (2008) also discussed availability and access to technology, teacher preparation and training, leadership, and time as the main factors in technology integration. In addition to these factors, some researchers took a different path to conduct their studies and examined negative factors, specifically, barriers that prevent or restrict teachers' integration of technology. Brinkerhoff (2006) grouped a variety of barriers into four categories: resources, institutional and administrative support, training and experience, and attitudinal or personality factors. Although accessibility to resources as a barrier had been gradually overcome, other barriers still remain (Schoepp, 2004).

Rather than embedding technology tools and strategies throughout all pre-service classes, the majority of teacher preparation programs require students to take a specific technology course. The "technology" class focuses primarily on technical skills and applications rather than integration of technology tools into instructional practices (Oakley, 2008). This isolation from regular use of technology in methodology classes lessens the opportunity for new teachers to develop technology-embedded lessons. Thus, there is a disconnection between technology tools and instructional strategies because technology is viewed as a separate skill, or add-on, rather than a normal part of a teacher's tool kit.

Although there is literature to support the inclusion of technology integration for in-service teachers, research reveals that this inclusion for pre-service teachers has only recently emerged (Brinkerhoff, 2006; Fleming, et. al., 2007). More specifically, understanding the factors associated with the practices of pre-service teachers' technology integration remains unclear, although much has been written about modeling and application of educational technology in teacher education programs.

Most institutional studies on school variables have shown that school size impacts many areas of education such as the characteristics of the school, curriculum, and post school outcomes including student perceptions (Bouck, 2004; Koth, Bradshaw, & Leaf, 2008). However, the size and type of institutions have rarely been studied as a factor for technology integration into the curriculum. Based on the above issues, this project was performed to examine the factors that determine the competence of technology integration for teacher candidates. Rather than the opinion of the teacher candidates, the perception of the institutional administrator or faculties was collected. Thus, the level of the analysis in this project is institution. Pre-service teachers and teacher candidates are used interchangeably through this article.

METHODOLOGY

Participants

This study utilized data from a 2006 quick-response survey entitled "Educational Technology in Teacher Education Programs for Initial Licensure." The questionnaires were mailed to all Title IV degree-granting 4-year postsecondary institutions in the 50 states and the District of Columbia. The survey was conducted with persons at the institutions who are most knowledgeable about the role of educational technology in the institution's teacher education programs for initial licensure. Through the telephone follow-up for survey nonresponse, the final response rate was 95 percent. For the purpose of this study, only the institutions that have teacher education programs for initial licensure were selected. The resultant sample was 1,350.

Variables

Dependent Variable

Graduate Competence (COMPETENCE). This measure indicates the overall competence of the graduates for technology integration based on the perception of the institutional survey respondents. This composite variable was computed from four equally weighted, standardized items: to what extent the graduates (a) can construct project-based learning lessons, (b) can recognize when a student needs adaptive technology, (c) have the skills to integrate technology, and (d) have the experience to integrate technology. The variable ranged from 1 (strongly disagree) to 4 (strongly agree) with a Cronbach's Alpha of 0.73 (M= 3.31, SD= 0.45).

Independent Variables

Institution Size (SIZE). This variable indicates the size of institution. There are three levels and the values are 1 (less than 3,000), 2 (3,000 to 9,999), and 3 (10,000 and more).

Institution Type (TYPE). This variable indicates three types of institution: public, private for nonprofit, and private for profit. Two dummy variables for this three category variable were created for the statistical analysis.

Variety of Instructional Technology (VARIETY). This variable indicated the variety of educational technology institutions utilized in their program: multimedia digital content, content-specific software, internet resources and communication tools, integrating technology into instruction, digital portfolios, curriculum plans using technology, achievement assessment using technology, data manipulation, student evaluation using technology, and distance learning. This measure ranged from 0 (none of 10 technologies) to 20 (all of 10 technologies).

Four variables associated with technology training. These variables are: (1) extent of technology training to enhance classroom instruction (TRAIN1); (2) extent of technology training to understand student learning styles (TRAIN2); (3) extent of technology training to assess student progress and challenges (TRAIN3); and (4) extent of technology training to design interventions for individual instruction (TRAIN4).

Six variables associated with barriers. These variables are: (1) availability of technology infrastructure as a barrier (BARRIER1); (2) lack of willingness of supervising teachers to integrate technology (BARRIER2); (3) lack of time for supervising teachers (BARRIER3); (4) lack of training or skills of supervising (BARRIER4); (5) limited skills and knowledge on the part of teacher candidates (BARRIER5); and (6) competing priorities in the classrooms (BARRIER6).

Analytic Strategy

Data analysis for the current project was directed at explicating the association between the perceived barriers and performance of pre-service teachers. To monitor the variations of the patterns for various factors impact on competence of technology integration of pre-service teachers, a hierarchical regression was utilized. In a hierarchical regression, the first model included only the demographic variables for institutions, the second model added variety of technology programs taught in the institutions and the extent of technology trainings, and the third step totaled the variables of barriers into the final model.

Results of the Analysis

To examine the nature of the positive factors and negative factors for the competence of technology integration, descriptive statistics including rank were presented in Tables 1 and 2.

To provide the most valid answer to the main research questions, a hierarchical regression was employed. The first model indicated that institutional size has a negative impact on its graduates' competence of technology integration. Regarding the type of the institution, there is a significant difference of the graduate competence between public and private for profit institutions, while no significant difference exists between public and private for nonprofit institutions. When other variables associated with the technology training and barriers are entered in the sequential models, these patterns are consistent in the second and third models (See Table 3). After controlling the demographic characters of the institutions, adding the variables of the variety of the technology programs and the extent of the technology training into the model, the effect size was dramatically increased (R^2_{change} (Δ) =.33). All variables

Table 1. Rank of the extent of technology training

Variable	Mean	S.D.	Rank
Extent of technology training to enhance classroom instruction (Train1)	3.53	.58	1
Extent of technology training to assess student progress and challenges (Train3)	2.80	.76	2
Extent of technology training to design interventions for individual instruction (Train4)	2.79	.77	3
Extent of technology training to understand student learning styles (Train2)	2.71	.77	4

Table 2. Rank of the barrier of technology integration

Variable	Mean	S.D.	Rank
Competing priorities in the classrooms (Barrier6)	3.13	.86	1
Availability of technology infrastructure (Barrier1)	2.98	.86	2
Lack of training or skills of supervising (Barrier4)	2.84	.85	3
Lack of time for supervising teachers (Barrier3)	2.78	.84	4
Lack of willingness of supervising teachers to integrate technology (Barrier2)	2.57	.83	5
Limited skills and knowledge on the part of teacher candidates (Barrier5)	1.88	.73	6

except the variable for the extent of technology training to assess student progress and challenges displayed significant impact on competence of technology integration of teacher candidates. When the variables for the barriers were added into the model, the same pattern remained.

In the final model, two variables among six variables associated with the technology barriers showed significant impact on the competence of technology integration. They are first limited skills and knowledge on the part of teacher candidates and second competing priorities in the classrooms as a barrier. As anticipated, they have negative effects on the competence level.

CONCLUSION

This study is an exploratory investigation in examining the factors to determine the competence of technology integration of teacher candidates based on the perceptions of college faculties or administrators. The result of the hierarchical regression revealed that the extent of institutional technology training programs explain most variation (33%) of the competence of technology integration of teacher candidates. In addition, the more variation

Table 3. Standardized coefficients for factors to determine graduates competence of technology integration

Variables	Model 1	Model 2	Model 3
Size	-.09**	-.06*	-.06*
Dummy1 (public vs. profit)	.11**	.14**	.12**
Dummy2 (public vs. nonprofit)	-.02	.05	.04
Variety		.19***	.14***
Train1		.23***	.21***
Train2		.12***	.09**
Train3		.07*	.07*
Train4		.19***	.18***
Barrier1			-.05
Barrier2			.01
Barrier3			.01
Barrier4			-.05
Barrier5			-.18***
Barrier6			-.14***
R^2	.02***	.35***	.42***
R^2_{change}	.02***	.33***	.07***

* p<.05, ** p<.01, *** p<.001

of technology programs an institution employs in its program, the more confidence the teacher candidates possess. Although the barriers displayed a sizable additional effect, one institutional barrier related to competing priorities in the classrooms and another personal barrier associated with the limited skills and knowledge of the teacher candidates were significant. It should be noted that teacher candidates may have a greater confidence level when they have experienced that their technology classes are considered more important than other curriculums.

This study confirmed the importance of training and experience for technology integration in the teacher education programs. Among the four types of technology training, the direct training associated with classroom instruction has been done more extensively by the teacher educational programs. Interestingly is the fact that the most perceived barrier and the least perceived barrier remained in the final model of the sequential regression. To reveal the nature of the association between these variables and the competence of teacher candidates, a qualitative research is recommended for future analysis. This study has several limitations. First, it relies on self-reported data from questionnaires. Direct observation and interview of teacher candidates may have provided additional insights into the associations among the variables. Additionally, because this project collected the perception of the person who represents each institution, the loss of the individual variations among actual teacher candidates is another shortcoming.

Despite these limitations, the results support the findings from previous research as well as supporting some emphasis on pre-service teacher program design consideration that may be of value to those planning similar technology training programs. Based on the results of the analysis, we suggest the following three recommendations: (1) There should be a university technology integration teaching strand that is required for all teacher candidates that begins in year one of the teacher education program and progresses throughout the entire program; (2) There should be combined ongoing professional development programs on the inclusion of technology integration in the school curricula for teams of school district teachers and administrators, and university professors; (3) The development and implementation of a university and school district developed coaching model that would be an ongoing support system for school district teachers in technology integration into the teaching curriculum.

REFERENCES

Ba, H., Tally, B., & Tsikalas, K. (2002). *Children's emerging digital literacies: Investigating home computing in low- and middle-income families. CCT reports*. New York: Center for Children & Technology. (ERIC Document Reproduction Service No. ED 477 716).

Bouck, E. C. (2004). How size and setting impact education in rural schools. *Rural Educator*, *25*(3), 38–42.

Brinkerhoff, J. (2006). Effects of a long-duration, professional development academy on technology skills, computer self-efficacy, and technology integration beliefs and practices. *Journal of Research on Technology in Education*, *39*(1), 22–43.

Du, J., Havard, B., Yu, C., & Adams, J. (2004). The impact of technology use on low-income and minority students' academic achievement: Educational longitudinal study of 2002. *Journal of Educational Research & Policy Studies*, *4*(2), 21–39.

Fleming, L., Motamedi, V., & May, L. (2007). Predicting preservice teacher competence in computer technology: Modeling and application in training environments. *Journal of Technology and Teacher Education*, *15*(2), 207–231.

Franklin, C. A. (2008). Factors determining elementary teachers' use of computers. *Principal, 87*(3), 54–55.

Hanks, R. F. (2002, June). *Environmental and Personal Factors Effecting K-12 Teacher Utilizatio of Technology*. Paper presented at the annual meeting of National Educational Computing Conference, San Antonio, Texas.

Jackson, L. A., von Eye, A., Biocca, F., Barbatsis, G., Zhao, Y., & Fitzgerald, H. (2005). How low-income children use the Internet at home. *Journal of Interactive Learning Research, 16*(3), 259–271.

Kanaya, T., Light, D., & Culp, K. M. (2005). Factors influencing outcomes from a technology-focused professional development program. *Journal of Research on Technology in Education, 37*(3), 313–329.

Kay, R. H. (2006). Evaluating strategies used to incorporate technology into preservice education: A review of the literature. *Journal of Research on Technology in Education, 38*(4), 383–408.

Koth, C. W., Bradshaw, C. P., & Leaf, P. J. (2008). A multilevel study of predictors of student perceptions of school climate: the effect of classroom-level factors. *Journal of Educational Psychology, 100*(1), 96–104. doi:10.1037/0022-0663.100.1.96

Lih-Juan, C. (2005). Development of a questionnaire for determining the factors in technology integration among teachers. *Journal of Instructional Psychology, 32*(4), 287–292.

Oakley, C. (2008). *Preparing future teachers for 21st century learning: Partnerships that enhance the capacity of pre-service education* [White Paper]. City, ST: Intel Corporation.

Oberlander, J., & Talbert-Johnson, C. (2007, February). *Envisioning the Foundations of Technology Integration in Pre-service Education*. Paper presented at the annual meeting of the Association for Teacher Education, San Diego, California.

Park, H. S. (2008). The impact of technology use on Hispanic students' mathematics achievement within family and school contexts: Subgroup analysis between English- and non-English speaking students. *Journal of Educational Computing Research, 38*(4), 553–568. doi:10.2190/EC.38.4.d

Rogers, P. L. (2000). Barriers to adopting emerging technologies in education. *Journal of Educational Computing Research, 22*(4), 455–472. doi:10.2190/4UJE-B6VW-A30N-MCE5

Swain, C. (2006). Preservice teachers self-assessment using technology: Determining what is worthwhile and looking for changes in daily teaching and learning practices. *Journal of Technology and Teacher Education, 14*(1), 29–59.

Chapter 21
Access and Advancement:
Teacher Transformation and Student Empowerment through Technology Mentoring

Steven D'Agustino
Fordham University, USA

Kathleen P. King
University of Southern Florida, USA

ABSTRACT

This research studied a professional development technology mentoring program serving approximately 500 K-12 teachers in New York City. The teacher training model, designed to improve student outcomes through the integration of technology into instruction, employed school visits by professional development technology mentors, training workshops and an online collaboration environment for participants. With a theoretical basis in transformative learning, the model focused on developing relationships of trust between teachers and professional developers. Findings in the paper discuss how to improve student performance in mathematics and English Language Arts through technology integration and teacher competence in teaching with technology, and they provide new insights into the potential for professional development initiatives incorporating similar perspectives and practices.

INTRODUCTION

With financial support from the Title IID Enhancing Education through Technology Grant (EETT), a large k-12 region in the New York City public school system and a major university's research center conducted a professional development project. This unique professional development initiative was designed to improve student learning and achievement by changing teacher practice through technology-integration. By utilizing the requirements of the grant, the initiative targeted schools having high levels of low-income students and evidence of poor school performance, and was designed to assist students in accessing technology in instructional settings.

It is well documented through federally and privately funded research projects that the integration of technology lags behind expectations in historically underserved communities (Solomon, Allen & Resta, 2003; National Telecommunications and Information Administration (NTIA),

DOI: 10.4018/978-1-61692-854-4.ch021

1999, 2004). This grant project's funding stream and the resulting project were specifically designed to address the issues of promoting student technology literacy and increasing achievement in mathematics and English Language Arts.

The project is firmly grounded in research which demonstrates that technology integration is effective at improving student performance (Vannatta & Fordham, 2004; Schacter, 1999). Regarding the model of how to approach the professional development successfully, research by King (1998, 2003, 3005) served as the foundation as it revealed an effective model which supports teacher professional development in learning new technologies, overcoming fear and hesitancy in using technology, changing teacher practice and in effecting change in teacher's educational perspectives.

This initiative engaged 500 teachers in 7 different cycles or cohorts. (There were 55 in Cycle 1; 82 in Cycle 2; 103 in Cycle 3; 76 in Cycle 4; 83 in Cycle 5, 82 in Cycle 6, and 19 in Cycle 7). Across the three years of the project, all told 114 schools in Bronx New York were represented by these 500 teachers. This approach reveals that part of the design of the project was to expand the population of teachers and schools who participated in this professional development initiative over time. This strategy was used to promote, sustain and scale systemic change within the schools across the participating district.

Teachers were visited on a weekly basis for nine months by a professional developer and attended ten training sessions off-site. Research has shown that professional development can be effective in moving teachers toward greater technology integration (Bailey & Pownell, 1997; Ertner, Gopalakrishnan & Ross, 2000; Ross,) and that such training promotes the use of technology as both an instructional tool (Atkins, 2000; Casey & Rakes, 2002; Martin & Lundstrom, 1988; Smith, 1998) and a transformation of paradigms or perspectives of teaching (King, 2005; Jonassen, Howland, Mara, & Crismond, 2007).

Research conducted about this substantial opportunity to provide change in professional development model, perspectives and delivery across 114 schools afforded a rich source of data. The following research questions are the focus of this paper's discussion about the teacher change and technology-integration project

- To what extent does project participation improve the academic performance of students?
- To what extent does project participation improve students' technology literacy?
- To what extent does project participation increase teachers' integrated uses of technology for classroom instruction?

The objectives of the instructional technology professional development project were:

- Improve student achievement in math and ELA.
- Increase teacher use of technology in classrooms settings with students
- Increase student use of technology in classroom settings

THEORETICAL FRAMEWORK

The funding agency's primary focus for this project of technology integration was increase to student technology literacy and improved student achievement. The theoretical basis for this work is in the field of adult learning, and more specifically transformative learning (King, 2002; Mezirow, 1978; 1990; Mezirow & Associates, 2000; O'Sullivan, 1999). Transformative learning is the theory of adult learning which emerged from the work of Jack Mezirow (1978) to explain the dramatic changes in worldview, paradigms and "meaning perspectives" among women returning to college. It is closely related to the work of Mezirow's contemporary Paulo Freire (1973,

1980). However while Freire's radical pedagogy focuses on dramatic social change against oppressing forces (1980) through the educational transformation; Mezirow's model emphasizes personal change: the individual.

The research on the topic has continued across many contexts of adult learning. Over the years King has been recognized as one of the most prominent researchers on this topic in particularly using large groups in which to examine trends and impact (Taylor, 2000). In order to understand the needs of adult learners better and to create better instructional approaches, some of the transformative learning contexts which have been include not only higher education (Cranton, 1994; King, 1997), but also ESL students (King, 2000), adult basic learners (King & Wright, 2003), and teachers and professors learning technology (King, 1998, 2002, 2003, 2005) to name some areas related to this study.

The theory of transformative learning uses as a pivotal point the "disorienting dilemma" of the adult learner which precipitates a need to re-examine their values, assumptions and perspectives. At this point in time, the world is out of order for them; they are frustrated and sometimes emotionally overwrought. In the case of technology learning this disorienting dilemma has been identified by King (2002, 2005) to variously the fear of learning technology, frustration with past experiences, a sense of being out of touch with the world or their students, a desire to master new innovations for instructional application, mandates for learning or overbearing pressures and demands by others for them to learn.

The ten stages of the transformative learning model were modified by King's research as she examined how teachers experienced perspective transformations while learning instructional technology. Her modified model has 8 stages (King, 2002) which focus on the learner overcoming fear, being comfortable with testing and exploring, then reaching an exploration stage and finally independence and discoveries. She clearly states that this is a dynamic process which is continuous, can proceed back and forth between stages and that with different learning experiences, new situations and new technologies to learn, adults may engrain many transformative learning experiences.

Major characteristics of King's (2002) model further clarify the facts that a supportive, nurturing learn-centered environment is need to support the teachers taking the risk of learning. Also the work demonstrates that teachers and learners alike need to ignore preconceived timeframes. In fact a characteristic phrase used in this study and among our mentors echoed this premise frequently: "No one is behind or ahead in the schedule of learning instructional technology. You are always right on time."

This foundation demonstrates several significant points including, if students are to learn in technologically integrated environments, developing teacher skill and comfort in teaching with technology is an essential first step (Archambault, Kulikowich, Brown & Rezendes, 2002, Marx, Blumenfeld, Krajcik & Soloway, 1998). In addition the model of transformative learning provides a robust framework through which to understand teacher learning as adult learning. Rather than solely focusing on the product of teachers' learning as being increased student performance, transformative learning looks to the adult learner- how will teacher learning impact the personal and professional lives of the educator? In which ways are the teachers' perspectives of education changed through this learning experience? How does the situation of learning technology create teachable opportunities for these instructors so they can better understand themselves as learners and therefore their learners' needs? (King, 2003, 2004)

Operationally this theoretical framework guides the professional development design and learning environment. Our focus has been one of nurturing supporting and mentoring the teachers who participated in the project. We focused on supporting them in their learning as professionals and sought to understand them as individuals and professional with specific needs and valid questions. (King, 2005)

The theoretical model that framed the model of professional development in the project is based upon a further development of King's research: the *Transformative Learning Opportunities Model* (TLOM) (King, 2005) and it's underpinning research. In a collaborative and reflective approach, educators initiate, develop and sustain relationships with teachers designed to uncover opportunities for professional learning and growth that are shaped by the context in which the learning occurs. TLOM occurs in two simultaneous layers. In Layer 1, thinking centers on the question: *what does the learner experience?* Teachers and professional developers progress through phases of building safety and trust, determining needs and expectations, and creating learning experiences. In Layer 2, thinking centers on the question: *How does the professional developer prepare?* This requires the professional developer to engage in her own learning and growth during the effort through journaling and self-assessment. Next, the professional developer determines learner needs, begins to understand the context and challenges, identifies resources and modifies the environment. The final stage is practice, during which the professional developers continues to build trust, reflects and refines methods.

As the TLOM model was the theoretical base of the professional development engaged in by the participants it included several specific characteristics for this context of teachers leaning instructional technology. A major characteristic of this design was the amount of time invested by everyone in this learning experience. Substantial change in people's attitudes, behavior and performance were targeted, and substantial time and effort needed to be invested. The TLOM for professional development required time for teachers and professional developers to form relationships of mutual trust and support as an integral part of the instructional change process. Specifically in this program, participating teachers attended ten training sessions off-site for a total of 36 hours of professional development workshops. These workshops modeled technologically integrated lessons to aid participants in the development of mental models. Teachers also received 20 weekly visits from a professional developer at their school site. A few of the important premises which were communicated in this program design include: change does not happen quickly, we are providing long-term mentoring for you, and we need teacher commitment to the project.

Improving Technology Integration

The project outcomes focused on technology integration leading to student technology literacy and ultimately improving student achievement. Experience has shown (Hooper & Rieber, 1994; King, 2002; Jonassen et al, 2007) that teachers learning new technologies first test them on their own, and then use them with their students, before fully incorporating them into their teaching and learning. Specifically, it was expected, as a result of this project, teachers would learn new instructional technology strategies and begin to apply them to their classroom instructional practices. Students would then experience increased and enhanced instructional technology activities and engage in instructional technology project-based learning. Changes in instructional practice and student-centered, project-based learning are then expected to result in students achieving at higher levels. To accomplish this, the project model offered a program of professional development incorporating four promising practices, that when implemented together increase teachers' effective uses of technology.

The Project Model

The underlying premise of the professional development initiative is that the integration of technology in classrooms and schools requires that teachers substantially transform how they understand, view, plan, and practice teaching with their students, as well as how they approach their own learning. To achieve this kind of transformation, the project model developed and employed a four-pronged approach to professional development—modeling, mentoring, membership and materials. Each professional development cycle covered a 9-month period in which the participants were provided with all the elements of the model simultaneously.

- **Modeling:** Teachers attended monthly, whole-group, professional development workshops at Fordham University where they were introduced to different technology applications for the classroom. These professional development sessions took a variety of forms and included exposure to new technologies, demonstrations of technology applications for the classroom, modeling an actual lesson, long-term planning, and teacher presentations of their work.
- **Exposure to New Technologies:** Brief presentations of technology devices, how they operate and can be used in the classroom (e.g., digital cameras, projectors, others).
- **Demonstrations of Technology Applications for the Classroom:** Longer presentations of how to use specific technology applications. These included professional developer and leader-led sessions. Where teachers had used the technologies in their classrooms they were invited to share their work with the project group of teachers. Examples of technology applications shared in this category included, WebQuests, designing teacher websites, and using PowerPoint® for report presentations.
- **Modeling an Actual Lesson:** Teachers participated in a lesson that professional developer facilitated. Those demonstrating the entire process of lesson plan design, delivery, facilitation strategies, instructional techniques, and evaluation.
- **Long-Term Planning:** teachers examined what they want to accomplish over the year in relation to their students' needs and resources; or teachers plan how they will pass on what they have learned to their colleagues.
- **Group Presentations:** teachers presented and discussed the activities they had tried in their classrooms and discussed the processes and outcomes with the larger group.
- **Mentoring:** Participants received weekly site visits by their assigned professional developer. During these visits, teachers worked with their mentors to identify and develop instructional activities for their students. The mentoring component provided the opportunity for the teachers to adapt the instructional activities from the workshops to their particular school and class contexts.
- **Membership:** The first two years of the course teachers were enrolled in a credit-bearing online course that provided a theoretical and research base for the project. The online learning environment used was Blackboard.com. A powerful aspect of this course directly relates to the transformative leaning theoretical basis of this project: dialogue and discourse. The online course and discussion board environment was a democratic process (Shor, 1992) which provided teachers continuous access to information, to their mentors, and to one another. The online community established by the course discussion board enabled teachers to share ideas and resources and to reflect upon the readings. The online course included assignments for teachers to complete. However, in year three this

course was discontinued due to federal budget cuts.

- **Materials:** Each teacher in the project received a laptop. Providing teachers with computers was intended to act as an incentive for participation, but more importantly it allowed teachers to test and experiment with the ideas they were learning throughout the program immediately. Upon completion of the program schools received an additional set of laptops and a laptop cart. These allowed the teachers to better implement what they had learned with their students. In year three, due to federal budget cuts, schools did not receive additional incentive computers, although all teachers received a laptop.

METHODOLOGY

The research employed both quantitative and qualitative sources of data to determine characteristics of the learning experiences and to measure progress against the project's goals. Data sources for the research and evaluation included:

- Site visits to schools which include classroom observations and interviews with participating teachers.
- Surveys of participating teachers
- Observations of professional development workshops
- Focus group interviews with the project's professional development staff
- Focus group interviews with teachers
- Analysis of student performance and demographic data
- Analysis of programmatic data
- Analysis of teacher and student artifacts

In an effort to demonstrate teacher perceptions of their use of technology during instruction and their own technology skill and comfort, a web-based survey was administered to all participants pre- and post- project. These responses were collected and analyzed to determine if teachers expressed greater confidence in their ability to teach using technology and their perceptions of their technical skills. The current research used a mixed-methods approach to research the current questions (Creswell, 1998, 2003). Based on prior experience with these formats in large scale teacher professional development research (King, Melia & Dunham, 2005), a new online survey instrument which specifically addressed teacher technology learning, efficacy and change, was developed, vetted and used (Fowler, 1995; Rea & Parker, 2005). The survey included a variety of question types including Likert scale, multiple-choice, and open ended. Data was anonymously gathered online and collected in a database. Professional development observations and focus groups were also conducted.

Site Visits and Observations

Over the first two years of the project, the evaluation team visited teachers from Cycles 1, 2, and 3 in the project twice (once toward the beginning and once toward the end) during their nine-month professional development cycle. However, due to the expanded professional development program in year 2 coinciding with a decrease in the evaluation budget in that same year, Cycle 4 and 5 teachers received only 1 visit at the end of their participation period. In year three, due to additional decreases in the evaluation budget, there were no classroom observations of Cycle 6 teachers. Instead these teachers participated in focus group interviews (see below).

For Cycles 1 through 5, each classroom visit consisted of a classroom observation and an interview with the teacher. In developing the classroom observation instrument we drew upon the work of experts in the field including Horizon Research (2004), developers of exemplary instructional practices classroom observation protocols for the National Science Foundation's (NSF) Local Systemic Change (LSC) Initiative, and the International Society for Technology in Education (ISTE) Standards. The observation lasted one class period. The teacher interview contained questions to elicit background information on the lesson being observed, provide an overview of how teachers have used technology in their instruction, and obtain teachers' feedback on their experiences with the professional development activities. The interviews took approximately 30 minutes and detailed notes were taken of the responses. For each cycle the evaluation team selected a sample of approximately 50 teachers for visits. An average of 36 classroom observations and 49 interviews were conducted in Cycles 2 through 5.

Focus Group Interviews

The researchers conducted focus group interviews with Cycle 6 participants. In these interviews teachers were asked to describe how they have used technology in their instruction and their experiences with the professional development activities. The focus groups were conducted during part of the teachers' monthly workshops. Four focus groups were conducted with a total of 31 teachers. Each focus group was approximately 45 minutes.

Teacher Surveys

All teachers participating in the project completed an online survey during their orientation sessions and their final professional development sessions. The survey contained a self-report of participants' technology expertise, and also contained questions about their attitudes toward and uses of educational technology, their instructional strategies in English language arts and mathematics, and their attitudes toward professional development. Items for this survey were adapted from the Computer Attitude Questionnaire developed by the Texas Center for Educational Technology (University of North Texas) and from survey instruments used in the Academy for Educational Development's (2002) National Writing Project Evaluation. The computer attitude component of the survey and several other items were revised in year 2. Participants in Cycles 4, 5, and 6 received the revised version of the online survey.

In year 1, the baseline surveys were administered to teachers in Cycles 1, 2, and 3, and post-surveys to participants in Cycle 1. In year 2, baseline surveys were administered to Cycles 4 and 5 and post-surveys to Cycles 2, 3, 4 and 5. In year three, baseline and post-surveys to Cycle 6. Survey responses are seen in Table 1.

Analysis

All gathered data was analyzed by the research team in order to ensure confidentiality and rigor in research methodology. Demographic data and objective responses were totaled for descriptive statistics. Frequencies, means, ranges, and percentages, where applicable, were determined for relevant responses (Borg, Gall, & Borg, 1996). Additional analyses were tested for relevance of inferential statistics as appropriate.

Free responses, verbatim and interview data regarding transformative learning, teacher em-

Table 1. Online survey responses by cycle: baseline and post project

Respondent Group	N
Cycle 1 (baseline)	58
Cycle 1 (post)	60
Cycle 2 (baseline)	85
Cycle 2 (post)	59
Cycle 3 (baseline)	105
Cycle 3 (post)	105
Cycle 4/5 (baseline)	115
Cycle 4/5 (post)	88
Cycle 6 (pre)	60
Cycle 6 (post)	46

powerment and impact of the training were evaluated for recurrent and emergent themes separately. Identifying the themes of transformative learning is one strand of this data set at this point in time and the researchers preserved all data. The qualitative analysis and coding method used in this research study was that of determining emergent themes by constant comparison (Borg, Gall, & Borg, 1996; Creswell, 1998) and pursued until the data had been theoretically saturated (Borg, Gall, & Borg, 1996). That is, analysis by constant comparisons was continued until all data was analyzed for possible themes and the occurrence of each theme in all of the data.

Findings

Teachers' Responses to Professional Development

Overall, the professional development sessions were generally well attended, well received, and appeared to benefit the teachers. Importantly, survey findings indicated that teachers attributed their change in instructional technology knowledge to the professional development they received in the program. Teacher surveys, interviews, observations, and work samples all provided evidence of participants' application of the knowledge and skills they had acquired throughout the professional development program. Furthermore, teacher surveys and individual interviews provide testimony to the personal and professional benefits of the program that go beyond increases in technology skill. Teachers expressed a sense of pride in their accomplishments. They felt they had become better teachers. They furthered their experience by taking on leadership roles in their schools or by continuing to pursue instructional technology education on their own. The following sections of this paper present details which illustrate this initial brief overview of the findings.

Teacher Technology Integration Data

A total of 218 teachers were surveyed with the web-based instrument developed for the project the *Technology Skills Self Assessment Profile* during their first professional development workshop and their final one. A pre- post analysis revealed that, as a group, 93% of all participants increased their technology skill level score. Teachers reported a significant increase in knowledge from pre to post project participation on all 18 technology skills that were identified on the survey (e.g., basic computer operation, webpage construction, etc.). Teachers also reported significantly greater confidence in their ability to use technology as well as using more technology in their classrooms. Overall, 78% of teachers reported an increase in implementing the New York State Learning and ISTE Technology. 69.4% of teachers indicated the amount of time their students were using computers in their classrooms had increased. 51.9% of the teachers reported that their students were using more technology in a more integrated way–that is, in the classroom rather than in a computer lab in ways directly connected to acquiring content area knowledge and skills.

Individual teacher interviews, classroom observation data and samples of student work were analyzed to determine how teachers were meeting their technology integration goals. A pre- post analysis of observations of classroom instruction and interviews with teachers revealed that at the beginning of the program approximately 20% of teachers were at the initial level of technology integration, meaning that they were not using technology in any way related to instruction. And by the end of the program only 2% of the teachers were still rated at this level. From the beginning of the program to the completion of the program the percentage of teachers went from 27 to 48 of those rated at the highest level of technology integration, meaning that they appropriately and intentionally used technology for certain instructional tasks.

Classroom Observation Data

A total of 82 classrooms were observed at the beginning and again at the end of the project. At the beginning of the program about 32% of these classrooms were rated as having the lowest level of student technology literacy, meaning that students were not using technology. By the end of the program about 18% of the classrooms were rated at this level, meaning that 14% of observed classes were no longer at the lowest level of technology integration. Additionally by the end of the project, percentages of classrooms using technology at the highest level of student technology literacy, meaning that students were using technology appropriate to the ISTE Technology Standards (2002) for that grade level and infused in content areas went from 22% to 31%; an improvement of 9% even in the highest category. These results demonstrate the impact of the teacher professional development on teacher performance and student technology use in the classroom.

Technology Integration

A total of 218 teachers from Cycles 1 through 6 were surveyed with the Technology Skills Self Assessment Profile during their first professional development workshop and their final one. A pre-post analysis revealed that:

- More than 80% of the teachers within each cycle increased their overall technology skill level score. As a group, 93% of all participants increased their score.
- Teachers reported a significant increase in knowledge from pre to post surveys on all 18 technology skills that were identified on the instrument (e.g., basic computer operation, webpage construction, etc.).
- Teachers reported significantly greater confidence in their ability to use technology.
- Teachers reported a significant increase in implementing the New York State and ISTE technology standards. Overall 78% of teachers reported an increase with a range of 70% to 95% over the 6 cycles.
- Teachers reported using more technology in their classrooms.
- Teachers reported a lack of student access to computers and a lack of administrative support as the two main barriers to technology integration and student use of technology.

At the beginning of the program about 20% of Cycle 2 and 3 teachers were at the initial level of technology integration, meaning that they were not using technology. By the end of the program about 2% of Cycle 2 and 3 teachers were rated at this level. Similarly, about 2% of Cycle 4 and 5 teachers were at this initial level at the end of the program. Overall, level 1 was the highest level of technology integration reached for about 3% of all teachers in Cycles 2-4 over the course of the program (7 out of 206).

At the beginning of the program about 27% of Cycle 2 and 3 teachers were rated to be at the highest level of technology integration, meaning that they appropriately and intentionally use technology for certain instructional tasks, which they would not be able to accomplish otherwise. By the end of the program, 48% of Cycle 2 and 3 teachers fit this category. About 37% of Cycle 4 and 5 teachers demonstrated technology usage patterns that would place them at this level by the time they completed their program.

Workshop Participation and Satisfaction

Teachers received at least 10 sessions (4 full-day sessions and 6, 2-hour evening sessions) of professional development at Fordham University. The workshops were generally well attended with about 70% to 75% of the teachers attending, on average.

Teacher Interview Feedback

Results of focus group interviews with 31 Cycle 6 teachers provided information on how teachers felt about the workshops in year three–what they felt helped them, and what they would like to change. Teachers overwhelmingly described the workshops as useful and mentioned several types of benefits they derived from them. A key benefit of the workshops, according to the teachers, was the many instructional ideas that were presented to them. The workshops were presented in such a way that teachers were not just introduced to an application (such as Excel or PowerPoint), but they experienced (as their students would) the implementation of the lesson in the context of the workshop. Teachers considered the "hands-on" sessions, where they had the opportunity to go through a lesson using the computers themselves to be the most productive.

Professional Development Mentor

Teachers in the program received a weekly site visit from a professional development mentor. Mentors were assigned to schools based on an effort to match mentor skill sets with schools' grade level and subject area needs. The mentors met with the teachers individually during a planning period. Over the course of the project, participants received an average of about 20 visits. The nature of these visits differed depending on the teacher, the mentor and the goal of the visit. For example, mentors would typically meet with teachers individually, or as a group, during their preparation periods. Other times, mentors might observe a teacher's classroom. Occasionally, mentors might demonstrate a lesson integrating technology in the teachers' classroom.

Teachers described the support they received from the mentor as largely positive and the strongest component of the program. Participants found that the mentors were responsive to questions and were concerned about meeting their learning needs and those of students. They reported feeling highly supported by their mentors and described how their mentors encouraged and motivated them. Teachers found the role of the mentor to be useful in helping them think more about open-ended questions and broader learning goals for students. Some teachers indicated that their mentor would act as their advocate. This included getting teachers better access to the technology resources in the school, or stressing that it was important for the teachers to attend the monthly workshops.

These responses are consistent with those of teachers who attended the program in previous years. In year two, of the teachers interviewed who commented on their satisfaction with their mentors (158), 81% described the experience positively. Overall, the teachers' responses indicated that the mentors played a critical role in their learning process. Some teachers indicated that they would never have been able to accomplish what they had without their mentor.

On-Line Instruction Using Blackboard

In years one and two teachers had access to an on-line instructional course on Blackboard throughout the program. The site contained articles that provided a theoretical base for the overall program and the individual workshops. Teachers were encouraged to read and comment upon the articles by responding to specific questions posed by the professional development staff. The site also contained instructional materials created by the professional development staff that was used in the workshops, as well as materials created by teachers in the program. Other resources included links to a number of educational sites. Teachers had email access through Blackboard and could communicate with the other teachers in their cycle and the professional development staff individually or globally by posting comments on the discussion board.

Of the teachers who commented on their satisfaction with Blackboard (69) during individual interviews, only 45% described the experience positively; while 39% expressed negative attitudes. The remaining participants had neutral or mixed responses to Blackboard. The aspect of Blackboard that teachers seemed to like best was that it provided excellent resources and a chance to share ideas with their colleagues and professional developers.

Teacher Survey Findings on Professional Development

Pre-post surveys were administered to assess the extent to which participants felt the professional development they received throughout the program had an impact upon their teaching. During the first workshop session teachers completed a 27-item survey on their professional development experiences. Participants felt that the professional development they received in the project helped them to increase their technology knowledge and skills to a significantly greater degree than what they had received prior to the program. They also reported that it helped them to understand and integrate the technology standards, which is an important factor in effective technology integration.

Changes in Teachers' Self-Reported Knowledge of Technology

Approximately 218 teachers across all cycles completed both the pre- and post-administrations of the Technology Skills Self Assessment Profile. The data analyses demonstrate that for each cycle more than 80% of the teachers increased their overall technology skill level score. As a group, 93% of all participants increased their score (Please see Table 2.)

Changes in Teachers' Self-Reported Attitudes toward Technology

Across all cycles, teachers reported greater self-confidence in their ability to use computers by the end of their program. This was particularly apparent for teachers in cycles 4, 5 and 6 who started out with notably lower reported levels of confidence than the other teachers. Teachers in cycles 1-3 also reported that they enjoyed using computers more. Teachers in cycles 4-6 reported significantly greater confidence in managing technology on their own, and getting support for technology questions or problems at their school. They also received a great deal of validation from the program and their peers throughout the course of the program.

Cycle 4-6 teachers were also less likely to agree that using computers would increase efficiency and productivity. This may reflect that in the beginning technology integration takes more planning, particularly in schools where there is not easy access to computers for students. These items, in part, contributed to an overall decrease in attitudes toward technology by the end of the program fort teachers in cycles 4-6.

Table 2. Teacher increases in technology skill level

		Cycle					Total
		1	2	3	4/5	6	
Did not increase	Count	2	5	5	3	0	**15**
	%	6.3%	10.2%	11.9%	5.0%	.0%	**6.9%**
Increased	Count	30	44	37	57	35	**203**
	%	93.8%	89.8%	88.1%	95.0%	100.0%	**93.1%**
Total	**Count**	**2**	**49**	**42**	**60**	**35**	**218**
	%	**0.0%**	**100.0%**	**100.0%**	**100.0%**	**100.0%**	**100.0%**

Changes in Teachers' Implementation of Technology Standards

Over the course of the project, teachers obtained a significantly greater understanding of both the New York State and ISTE technology standards. Their implementation of those standards also increased significantly. At the outset of the project, teachers, on average, reported that they "rarely" implemented the standards. At the end of the program their implementation increased to about "half the time."

In terms of the percentage of teachers who increased their implementation of standards, overall 78% of teachers reported an increase with a range of 70% to 95% over the cycles. As shown in Table 3, teachers increased their implementation of the technology standards as a result of participation in the project.

Implications for Teacher Integration

Based upon multiple sources of evidence including teacher survey data, interviews, observation and a review of artifacts, the teachers in the program significantly increased their level of technology integration over the course of the program. Teachers increased their reported knowledge of technology skill and had more confidence in their abilities to integrate technology. Teachers not only increased their technology use but changed how they used it over time, with it becoming more and more integrated into their instruction. The two main factors that appear to affect changes in technology integration over time was level of expertise at the beginning of the program and, possibly, student access to computers. A sizable number of teachers already had a high level of technology integration at the beginning of the program. Also, students access to technology varied across the Cycles observed. It would be difficult for teachers to reach the highest level of technology integration if their students do not have regular access to computers. The next section will address how teachers' technology knowledge and skill set carries over into classroom instruction.

Teacher Reports of Student Technology Use

As part of the pre/post survey, teachers were asked to estimate the number of hours per week their students used computers in the classroom on a scale of 0 to more than 21. The results in Table 4 show that, overall, the percentage of teachers who did not use technology (i.e. 0 hours per week) decreased by more than half, from 45% to 20%. Increases were also noted in each separate category.

Examining increases in number of hours by matching individual teachers pre- to post (Table 4), we found that over the course of the program, more than two-thirds of all the teachers (69.4%) indicated the amount of time their students were using computers in their classrooms had increased.

Teachers also rated the level of integration of students' technology on a scale of 1 (*I never or rarely require the use of technology to complete*

Table 3. Teachers' implementation of technology standards

		Cycle					Total
		1	2	3	4/5	6	
Did not increase	**Count**	1	12	8	15	7	**43**
	%	4.8%	30.0%	20.0%	25.0%	20.0%	**21.9%**
Increased	**Count**	20	28	32	45	28	**153**
	%	95.2%	70.0%	80.0%	75.0%	80.0%	**78.1%**
Total	**Count**	**21**	**40**	**40**	**60**	**35**	**196**
	%	**100.0%**	**100.0%**	**100.0%**	**100.0%**	**100.0%**	**100.0%**

Table 4. Increases in student technology use per week

		Cycle					Total
		1	2	3	4	6	
Did not increase	Count	9	15	9	15	7	**55**
	%	31.0%	37.5%	23.7%	29.4%	31.8%	**30.6%**
Increased	Count	20	25	29	36	15	**125**
	%	69.0%	62.5%	76.3%	70.6%	68.2%	**69.4%**
Total	Count	**29**	**40**	**38**	**51**	**22**	**180**
	%	**100.0%**	**100.0%**	**100.0%**	**100.0%**	**100.0%**	**100.0%**

assignments.) to 5 (*My students independently experiment with different software and technologies.*) The percentage of teachers who reported that their students do not use technology decreased from 34% to 7% over the course of the project. Students' regular use of the internet and software increased from 17 to 32%.

Matching pre- post survey responses, we found that that over the course of the project, more than half (51.9%) of the teachers reported that their students were using more technology in a more integrated way.

Observed Student Technology Use

A total of 147 cycle 1, 2, and 3 teachers' classrooms were observed using a technology integration rubric (Northwest Regional Educational Laboratory, 2004) after participating in the program for three months, and 99 teachers were observed at the end of the 9-month period (class trips, testing, and absenteeism decreased the numbers of observable classrooms in the follow-up visits). The majority of the observations took place in the classroom, 78% during the first visit and 80% during the second. Fewer observations took place in computer labs (17% and 12%). In most cases (65% for both administrations) there were two or fewer computers in the room during the observed lesson.

A pre- post analysis revealed that after 6 months, more students of cycles 1, 2, and 3 teachers were using technology in the classroom independently and with a greater level of skill. More students were observed using technology in an integrated way. The technology skills they were learning were imbedded in the content of the lessons and focused on curricular goals; the technology enhanced the overall lesson.

Sixty-three cycle 4 and 5 teachers' classrooms were observed in the spring of 2006, toward the end of their participation in the program. The observations took place predominantly in classrooms (82%), and to a much lesser extent in computer labs (11%). Seventy-three percent of the classrooms observed had 2 or fewer computers.

The findings show lower levels of integrated technology usage among students of cycle 4 and 5 teachers than those of cycles 1 to 3. One explanation is that some of the cycle 1 to 3 schools had received their student laptops by the time of the second observation, while none of the cycle 4 and 5 schools had. However, in several cases, the cycle 4 and 5 students' technology level at the end of the program was lower than those observed from cycles 1 to 3 at pre-testing. One explanation is that cycle 4 and 5 teachers had reported themselves to be somewhat less "tech savvy" than the other cohorts. Observation findings indicated that the most common technology applications used by students were word processing, Internet, simulation/games, and PowerPoint presentations, which is consistent with teachers' reports of technology use.

Student Technology Literacy

A total of 218 teachers from Cycles 1 through 6 were surveyed during their first professional development workshop and their final one. A pre- post analysis revealed that:

- More than two-thirds of all the teachers (69.4%) indicated the amount of time their students were using computers in their classrooms had increased.
- More than half (51.9%) of the teachers reported that their students were using more technology in a more integrated way.

A total of 147 Cycle 1, 2, and 3 teachers' classrooms were observed using a technology integration rubric (Northwest Regional Educational Laboratory, 2004) after participating in the program for three months and 99 teachers were observed at the end of the 9-month period. A pre/post analyses revealed the following:

- Students were observed using technology more, using it more in integrated ways, and with greater skill over the project period.

Individual teacher interviews, classroom observation data and samples of student work were reviewed to assess how teachers were meeting student technology literacy goals. A total of 59 Cycle 2 teachers' classrooms and 56 Cycle 3 teachers' classrooms were observed at the beginning of the program. At the end of program, 47 Cycle 2 classrooms and 35 Cycle 3 classrooms were visited again. Also interviewed and/or observed at the end of their program were 86 Cycle 4 and 5 teachers. A pre- post analysis revealed the following:

At the beginning of the program about 32% of Cycle 2 and 3 classrooms were rated as having the lowest level of student technology literacy, meaning that students were not using technology. By the end of the program about 18% of the classrooms were rated at this level. Almost a third (32%) of Cycle 4 and 5 teachers' classrooms were rated as not using technology by the time their program ended. Overall, there was minimal student technology use for almost a quarter of classrooms across all four cycles over the course of the program (49 out of 206).

At the beginning of the program 22% of Cycle 2 and 3 classrooms were rated as having the highest level of student technology literacy, meaning that students were using technology appropriate to the ISTE technology standards for that grade level and infused in content areas. By the end of the program about 31% of the classrooms were rated at this level. A somewhat smaller %age of Cycle 4 and 5 classrooms (28%) fit this category, as well. Across all four cycles, almost a third of the classrooms (32%) could be described as fitting the highest level of student technology literacy.

The findings of teacher surveys, classroom observations, and professional developer interviews indicate that students' lack of access to computers is the number one factor impeding student technology use and ultimately their development of technology literacy. Students' regular access to working, up-to-date computers varied across schools, but was a challenge in most schools in the program.

Classroom observations and ratings based on multiple sources of evidence demonstrated that student technology literacy increased over the course of the project. Comparing the earlier ratings of teacher levels of technology integration with ratings of student technology literacy shows that as teachers grow in their level of integration, students' technology literacy begins to increase. This is to be expected.

Student Achievement

This research provides two levels of analysis of student achievement. First, it reports overall achievement of students in grades 3 to 8 who attended participating schools as compared to students in Region 2 schools that were not part of the program. Second, it examines the academic progress of individual students whose teachers participated in the professional development program compared to students in the same schools whose teachers did not participate.

Over the three years of the project, more of the lowest performing students (Level 1) improved on the ELA test in participating schools than non-participating schools in the same districts. Also the percentages of students who met or exceeded standards (levels 3 and 4) increased at a greater rate in participating schools. Mathematics achievement showed similar results. The percentages of Level 1 students decreased by somewhat more in participating schools than in non-participating schools. At the same time, the percentage of students meeting and exceeding standards increased more in participating schools and non-participating schools.

After 1 year of teachers participating in the project, students increased, on average, 3 percentage points on their ELA exam. The lowest achieving students (Level 1) made the greatest gains of 6 percentage points. In Math, students increased, on average, 4.2 percentage points, with the lowest achieving students again making the greatest gains of 7 percentage points. These gains cannot necessarily be attributed to the program because there were no significant differences between participants and non-participants. Due to changes in the 2006 achievement tests, year-two gains could not be reported.

By the second year of the program the academic performance of high school students whose teachers participated in the program exceeded those students whose teachers did not participate. The results revealed significant positive differences in the performance of participants vs. non-participants on the 2006 ELA and Math A Regents exams for students whose teachers participated in 2004/2005. It also showed significant positive differences in the performance of participants vs. non-participants on the 2006 ELA, Math A, Global Studies, Biology, History and Government, and Earth Science for students whose teachers participated in 2005/06.

Overall, the student achievement results, while quite promising, do not provide conclusive evidence that the project alone had a significant, positive impact on student performance over grades 3 to 12. The logic model for the project assumes that increased technology literacy will lead to increases in student achievement. By the end of the second year student use of technology had increased, but the majority of the classrooms that were impacted by the program still had not integrated instructional technology on a regular basis. One may see greater differences in student achievement outcomes as student technology access and use continue to increase.

CONCLUSION AND RECOMMENDATIONS

Enabling students in urban, underserved schools to access technology in meaningful and authentic ways has been an ongoing area of critical concern. As with any educational innovation, teachers are at the forefront of the change process and yet the difficulties of changing teacher practice are well-known (Cranton, 2000; Darling-Hammond, Bransford, LePage, Hammerness, Duffy, & 2005; Jonassen et al, 2007; King 2002; King, Melia & Dunham, 2005).

When coupled with the inadequate infrastructure of many urban schools, transforming learning environments through the integration of technology can seem insurmountable. However, the nature of contemporary society and the promise of a technologically dependent future demand that all students receive access to technology in school (Darling-Hammond, et al., & Duffy, 2005; Gura, 2005). Other instructional innovations, no matter how urgent, do not carry the significance for students that the inability to access technology will for their futures–technology access is a matter of social justice as well as educational improvement.

Traditionally, as teachers operate at the technical core of teaching and learning in schools, they are often left on their own to implement educational advancements to the best of their ability. The success of this model is grounded in its approach to teachers as adult learners and providing knowledgeable, substantial and friendly professional support. This professional development model's research results demonstrate that teachers can change learn instructional technology, change their classroom instructional practices, and engage their students in technology appropriate activities for instruction. However we recognize the significant investment in terms of time, resources and content.

The model also highlights valuing and determining the varying contexts of schools and teachers' classrooms and dynamically addresses those needs in each step of the way. This model is not a "one-size fits all" solution. This model and the professional development rely heavily on the expertise of the professional development team gaining support of the school leadership and collaborating with the teachers involved. The project is also not a "quick-fix" solution. Substantial gains were made in teacher learning, expertise and practice in part because this project provided sustained teacher support over an entire school year.

Encouraging findings for schools, teachers and professional developers herein include evidence of viable strategies, direction and complete model for serving the professional learning needs of teachers, to effect change in the instructional process and to integrate instructional technology and teaching and learning standards into the classroom. Future research of the model could focus on additional contexts, rural, specialized schools or individual instructional technology methods.

Future analysis of this data will present discussions about the participants' perceptions of their changes and their experiences. Better understanding teachers' needs can greatly assist all professional developers and administrators in meeting these needs and providing the resources they most critically need.

AUTHOR NOTE

This professional development initiative and research project was funded by a grant from Title IID, Enhancing Education through Technology of the US Department of Education's No Child Left Behind Act.

The authors wish to express appreciation to Dr. Jody Imbimbo and her evaluation team at Design & Development Resources for Education and the Arts for their assistance in the design and delivery of the evaluation and data.

REFERENCES

Archambault, F., Kulikowich, J., Brown, S., & Rezendes, G. (2002). Developing performance assessments to measure teacher competency in the use of educational technology. Paper presented at the Annual Meeting of the Educational Research Association, New Orleans, LA.

Atkins, N. E., & Vasu, E. S. (2000). Measuring knowledge of technology usage and stages of concern about computing: A study of middle school teachers. *Journal of Technology and Teacher Education*, *8*(4), 279–302.

Bailey, G. D., & Pownell, D. (1997). Technology staff development and support programs applying Abraham Maslow's hierarchy of needs. *Learning and Leading with Technology*, *26*(3), 47–64.

Brookfield, S. (1987). *Developing critical thinkers*. San Francisco: Jossey-Bass.

Brookfield, S. (1999). *Discussion as a way of teaching*. San Francisco: Jossey-Bass.

Casey, H. B., & Rakes, G. C. (2002). An analysis of the influences of technology training on teacher stages of concern regarding the use of instructional technology in schools. *Journal of Computing in Teacher Education, 18*(4), 124–132.

Cranton, P. (1994). *Understanding and promoting transformative learning*. San Francisco: Jossey-Bass.

Cranton, P. (2000). Individual differences and transformative learning. In Mezirow, J. (Eds.), *Learning as transformation* (pp. 181–204). San Francisco: Jossey-Bass.

Creswell, J. (1998). *Qualitative inquiry and research design*. Thousand Oaks: Sage.

Creswell, J. (2003). *Research design* (2nd ed.). Thousand Oaks, CA: Sage.

Darling-Hammond, L., Bransford, J., LePage, P., Hammerness, K., & Duffy, H. (2005). *Preparing teachers for a changing world*. San Francisco: Jossey-Bass.

Dean, G. J. (1994). *Designing instruction for adult learners*. Malabar, FL: Krieger.

Ertmer, P. A., Gopalakrishnan, S., & Ross, E. M. (2000). *VisionQuest: Helping teachers achieve technology integration*. Paper presented at the annual meeting of the Society for Information Technology and Teacher Education, San Diego, CA.

Fowler, F. J. (1995). *Improving survey questions: Design and evaluation*. Thousand Oaks, CA: Sage.

Freire, P. (1973). *Education for critical consciousness*. New York: Continuum.

Freire, P. (1980). *Pedagogy of the oppressed*. New York: Continuum.

Gall, M., Borg, W., & Gall, J. (1996). *Educational research: An introduction* (6th ed.). White Plains, NY: Longman.

Gura, M. (2005). *Recapturing technology for education: Keeping tomorrow in today's classrooms*. Lanham, MD: Scarecrow Education.

Hooper, S., & Rieber, L. P. (1995). Teaching with technology. In Orstein, A. C. (Ed.), *Teaching:Theory into practice* (pp. 154–170). Boston: Allyn and Bacon.

International Society for Technology in Education. (2002). *NETS Project*. Eugene, OR: ISTE Publications.

Jonassen, D., Howland, J., Mara, R., & Crismond, D. (2007). *Meaningful learning with technology* (3rd ed.). Upper Saddle River, NJ: Prentice Hall.

King, K. P. (1997). Examining learning activities and transformational learning. *International Journal of University Adult Education, 36*(3), 23–37.

King, K. P. (1998). *A guide to perspective transformation and learning activities: The Learning Activities Survey*. Philadelphia: Research for Better Schools. Retrieved from http://www.transformationed.com

King, K. P. (1999, Fall). Unleashing technology in the classroom: What adult basic education teachers and organizations need to know. *Adult Basic Education: An Interdisciplinary Journal for Adult Literacy Educators, 9*(3), 162–175.

King, K. P. (2000, Summer). The adult ESL experience: Facilitating perspective transformation in the classroom. *Adult Basic Education: An Interdisciplinary Journal for Adult Literacy Educators, 10*(2), 69–89.

King, K. P. (2002). *Keeping pace with technology: Educational technology that transforms* (*Vol. 1*). Cresskill, NJ: Hampton Press.

King, K. P. (2005). *Bringing transformative learning to life*. Malabar, FL: Krieger Publishing.

King, K. P., Melia, F., & Dunham, M. (2005). Update Anytime Anywhere- Finding our way: Better understanding the needs and motivations of teachers in online learning. *International Journal of Information and Communication Technology Education*, *1*(4), 57–70.

King, K. P., & Wright, L. (2003, Summer). New perspectives on gains in the ABE classroom: Transformational learning results considered. *Adult Basic Education: An Interdisciplinary Journal for Adult Literacy Educators*, *13*(2), 100–123.

Lawler, P. A., & King, K. P. (2000). *Preparing for effective faculty development*. Malabar, FL: Krieger.

Martin, R., & Lundstrom, K. (1988). Attitudes of vocational home economics teachers toward computers. *Journal of Vocational Education Research*, *13*, 83–93.

Marx, R. W., Blumenfeld, P. C., Krajcik, J. S., & Soloway, E. (1998). New technologies for teacher professional development. *Teaching and Teacher Education*, *14*, 35–52. doi:10.1016/S0742-051X(98)00059-6

Mezirow, J. (1990). *Fostering critical reflection in adulthood*. San Francisco: Jossey-Bass.

Mezirow, J. (1997). Transformative learning: Theory to practice. In P. Cranton (Ed.). *Transformative learning in action: New Directions in Adult and Continuing Education* (No. 74, pp. 5-12). San Francisco: Jossey-Bass.

Mezirow, J. (Eds.). (2000). *Learning as transformation*. San Francisco: Jossey-Bass.

National Telecommunications and Information Administration (NTIA). (1999). Falling through the net. Washington, DC: U.S. Department of Commerce. Retrieved March 25, 2005, from http://www.ntia.doc.gov/ntiahome/fttn99/contents.html

National Telecommunications and Information Administration (NTIA). (2004). A nation online: Entering the broadband age. Washington, DC: U.S. Department of Commerce. Retrieved February 25, 2007, from http://www.ntia.doc.gov/reports/anol/NationOnlineBroadband04.htm

New York City Department of Education. (2006). The 2005-2006 Annual School Reports. Retrieved July 29, 2007, from http://schools.nyc.gov/daa/schoolreports/

New York State Department of Education. (n.d.). *New York State learning standards*. Retrieved July 30, 2007, from http://www.emsc.nysed.gov/ciai/cores.htm#3ela

Northwest Regional Educational Laboratory. (2004) *OPTIC- Observation Protocol for Technology Integration in the Classroom*. Portland, OR: Author. Retrieved June 26, 2006, from http://www.netc.org/images/doc/observation.continuum.doc

O'Sullivan, E. (1999). *Transformative learning* London: Zed Books.

Pilling-Cormick, J. (1997). Transformative and self-directed learning in practice. In P. Cranton (Ed.), *Transformative learning in action: New Directions in Adult and Continuing Education* (No. 74, pp. 69-78). San Francisco: Jossey-Bass.

Rea, L. M., & Parker, R. A. (2005). *Designing and conducting survey research: A comprehensive guide*. San Francisco: Jossey-Bass.

Schacter, J. (1999) *The impact of educational technology on student achievement: What the most current research has to say*. Retrieved July 1, 2007, from http://www.mff.org/pubs/ME161.pdf

Shor, I. (1992). *Empowering education: Critical teaching for social change*. Chicago: University of Chicago Press.

Smith, P. L. H. (1998) *The impact of a computer enhanced instruction staff development program on elementary teachers' self efficacy and outcome expectancy in the use of computers*. Unpublished doctoral dissertation, Georgia State University.

Solomon, G., Allen, N., & Resta, P. (2003). *Toward digital equity*. New York: Allyn and Bacon.

Taylor, E. W. (2000). Analyzing research on transformative learning theory. In Mezirow, J. (Eds.), *Learning as transformation: Critical perspectives on a theory in progress* (pp. 29–310). San Francisco, CA: Jossey-Bass.

Vannatta, R. A., & Fordham, N. (2004). Teacher dispositions as predictors of classroom technology use. *Journal of Research on Technology in Education*, *36*(3), 253–271.

KEY TERMS AND DEFINITIONS

Transformative Learning: The expansion of consciousness through the transformation of how one sees the world and measures their own individual capacities.

Teacher Professional Development*:* A method of improving teacher's methodological skills and content area knowledge with the end goal of improving student academic outcomes through conferences: workshops, lectures, discussions and hands on workshops.

Technology Literacy: The ability to use, manage, assess, and understand technology.

Technology Access: Related to issues of social equity, the ability of historically underserved populations and communities to access current and emerging technologies.

Chapter 22
Bringing the Village to the University Classroom:
Uncertainty and Confusion in Teaching School Library Media Students in the Design of Technology Enhanced Instruction

Joette Stefl-Mabry
State University of New York Albany, USA

William E.J. Doane
Bennington College, USA

Michael S. Radlick
Institute for Research on Learning Technology Visions, USA

ABSTRACT

This chapter highlights critical lessons learned during the past six years during the development of a capstone graduate educational technology course, teaching School Library Media (SLMS) pre-service students how to develop learner centered, knowledge centered and assessment centered Web-based learning tools; in short, to enable them to become change agents in their educational communities. A large northeastern University has cultivated educational partnerships that bring together University students with their professional, in-service, PreK-12 counterparts to explore issues of technology in education, pedagogy, theory, curriculum, information literacy, assessment, and evaluation. Unlike traditional courses with prepackaged academic assignments, this course engages school library media specialists with real-world teaching and learning situations that are frequently ill-structured, often chaotic, and collaboratively defined by the learning needs of all participants (PreK-12 through university; in-service and pre-service). The strengths and weaknesses of the course are candidly discussed with recommendations for improvement.

DOI: 10.4018/978-1-61692-854-4.ch022

INTRODUCTION

The Challenge of Designing Technology Enhanced Instruction

In this chapter, we discuss two aspects of the collaborative design of technology enhanced PreK-12 instruction. First, students at university—both undergraduate and graduate—find it challenging to design appropriate instructional tools using computing technologies that will meet the needs of PreK-12 students, given the dynamic and uncertain learning needs of the intended audience. Second, students at university find it challenging, themselves, to use computing technologies to support their own learning and collaboration processes, sometimes devolving instead into a type of *grin and bear it* cooperative process.

These issues have importance for the design of teacher training programs and, in particular, for the use of technology in education. One of the few absolutes in education is our awareness that "teachers teach the way they were taught to teach" (Sarason, 2004, p. 72). If we are to expect our future educators to integrate technology tools effectively into the curricula both as an object of study and as a learning tool to support their charges in years to come, then we must work to do the same for our own learning and teaching efforts.

School Library Media Specialists as Change Agents

"Change agentry" is acclaimed to be "an essential role for Library Media Specialists" (Hughes-Hassell & Harada, 2007, p. 3), therefore it benefits us, as university faculty responsible for the professional educational training of school library media specialists (SLMS), to develop curricula that promote leadership by focusing on the "organic relationship between schooling and the community" (Macedo, 2006, p. 140). Schools are affected by the socio-cultural and political landscape of the society within which they exist (Hughes-Hassell & Harada, 2007; Macedo, 2006). "Successful change requires every person working in a school to be committed to change and to strive for individual and collective improvement" (Hughes-Hassell & Harada, 2007, p. 3). But how do we structure learning experiences at the graduate level to encourage SLMS to develop moral purpose and make a difference in the life-choices of all students and contribute toward "education's societal development and democracy" (Fullan, 1999)?

Schools of education[1] cannot succeed in preparing future teachers for leadership positions and for being agents of change if they continue to advocate the use of neatly packaged instructional programs that are presented as the panacea for difficulties students face in the acquisition of prepackaged knowledge (Macedo, 2006, p. 152).

The reality that we, as educators need to confront, understand and proactively address is that the instrumental approach to literacy, whether in its lowest form of "a competency-based skills-banking approach" or its highest form "acquired through the university in the form of professional specialization" share a common characteristic: "They both prevent the development of the critical thinking that enables one to 'read the world' critically and to understand the reasons and linkages behind the facts" (Macedo, 2006, p. 16).

There is no such thing as a neutral education process. Education either functions as an instrument which is used to facilitate the integration of generations into the logic of the present system and bring about conformity to it, or it becomes the 'practice' of freedom', the means by which men and women deal critically with reality and discover how to participate in the transformation of their world (Paulo Freire, speech at Northeastern University, March 16, 1994 as cited by Herbert, 1998, p. 57).

Most educators would agree that the educational system currently in place in the United States is not working.

The public school systems in virtually every large city are collapsing: dropout rates hover well above 50 percent, truancy is the norm rather than the exception, violence is common, students struggle for basic literacy, often without success, a great deal of teaching is uninspired, and the physical condition of schools is a disgrace... These are the "Savage Inequalities[2]" (Cookson, 1994, pp. 2-3)

The majority of learners, from Pre-K through university in the United States, have come to view learning as producing a product (or a series of products) that are almost always tangible in nature. Rarely do educators critically reflect upon their teaching and learning as a continuous, iterative process. Seldom are students asked to provide input into the learning process, even though learning experiences are designed for them as the end-user. In truth, educators determine *a priori* what students are expected to learn regardless of whether what is taught is relevant or connected to students' lived experiences. Students feel disconnected and alienated in school (Stefl-Mabry, Doane, & Radlick, 2009), where they find neither meaning nor relevancy. Yet "meaning must be accomplished at every level of the system... [and] if it is not done at the level of the student, for the vast majority of students, all is lost" (Fullan, 2007, p. 187). Meaning matters, regardless the age of student. Meaning is essential to learning and yet what do we know about how teachers and/or school library media specialists learn?

Research on Teacher and SLMS Learning

Though noting "the word or concept of learning has the highest of all word counts in the diverse literatures in education" (2004, p. x) Sarason explains that defining learning is not easily done:

...the word or concept of learning is not only lacking in substance but also has the characteristics of an inkblot; in addition, the relationship of those characteristics to actions is illogical, confusing, and self-defeating. ...unless and until research provides a credible basis for distinguishing between contexts of productive and unproductive learning in the classroom, educational reform will be fruitless (2004, p. viii).

"Teacher learning is relatively new as a research topic, so there is not a great deal of data on it" (J. D. Bransford, Brown, & Cocking, 2000, p. 190). There exists less, if any, research that focuses on the learning of school librarian media specialists (SLMS). The authors of this paper were unable to locate any research related to *how* SLMS learn. We do know however, that "teachers [and SLMS] teach the way they were taught to teach, and the nature and power of the school culture reinforce what they were taught in preparatory programs" (Sarason, 2004, p. 72). Since SLMS are tasked to be change agents (Hughes-Hassell & Harada, 2007) and leaders (AASL, 2008; Doll, 2005; Harada, 2003; Hartzell, 2001; K. Latrobe, 1998; Lowe, 2000; Shannon, 2002), who teach information literacy[3] not only to students from PreK-12, but also to teachers, administrators, and community members (Carver, 1986; Craver, 1994; Doll, 2005; Harada, 2003; Haycock, 1999; Kuhlthau, 1989; K. H. Latrobe, 1998; Lowe, 2000; Stefl-Mabry & Lynch, 2006; Weil, 2008; Woolls, 1995), and we, at the graduate level prepare SLMS for professional practice, we need to focus our attention on how SLMS learn and in particular how SLMS learn to design technology enhanced instruction.

What do we Mean by Learning?

Sarason (2004) has long predicted that "...educational reforms, resting as they do on a superficial conception of learning, will continue to be disappointing" adding that

"...the failures of the educational reform movement should have alerted us a long time ago to the possibility that our conception of learning and its contexts is part of the problem" (p.viii).

No one, educators or otherwise, has ever said that schools are places where teachers learn. I have long regarded it as a glimpse of the obvious – that teachers cannot be expected to create and sustain a context of productive learning for children, if such a context does not exist for teachers. And such a context hardly exists for teachers. In many schools it exists not at all...(Sarason, 2004, p. ix).

This paper represents a first step toward making school library media specialists' learning visible. For the purposes of this paper, we have defined learning as "the work" (Fullan, 2008, p. 75): the work our students at the university do in conjunction with each other and their PreK-12 learning partners (teachers and SLMS); the work of the PreK-12 students; and yes, the work that we, as university faculty, do as well for:

Learning is not a thing. Learning is a process that occurs in an interpersonal and group context, and it is always composed of an interaction of factors to which we append labels such as motivation, cognition, emotion or affect, and attitude. Neither singly nor in their interactions is the strength of these factors ever zero. Direct observation of the learner can give us a limited albeit important, picture of the factors always part of the learning process. How we intuit or deduce the role of the factors depends on the psychological-conceptual sophistication of the teacher (Sarason, 2004, p. vii).

BRINGING THE VILLAGE TO THE UNIVERSITY CLASSROOM: UNCERTAINTY AND CONFUSION

Previous Course Design

The specifics of the development of the early years of this transgenerational pedagogical model have been presented in several publications ((Stefl-Mabry, 2004; Stefl-Mabry, Doane, Radlick, & Theroux, 2007; Stefl-Mabry & Lynch, 2004; Stefl-Mabry & Powers, 2004; Stefl-Mabry, Powers, & Doll, 2006; Stefl-Mabry & Powers-Goodall, 2005; Stefl-Mabry, Radlick, Doane, & Theroux, 2007; Stefl-Mabry, Theroux, & Radlick, 2005). This chapter will briefly review the course's history and focus on the 2007-2008 semesters, highlighting emergent learning patterns and pedagogical concerns that appear to have consistency over time.

In brief, the course, IST673, began in the fall of 2002 (then called *ISP523L, Fundamentals of Technology for School Libraries*). The lead author, never a proponent of teaching technology skills in isolation, decided to improve student and faculty productivity by connecting SLMS graduate students to in-service PreK-12 professionals to provide them the opportunity to collaborate, lead, and integrate technology effectively for the most important end-user in education—the PreK-12 student. Later iterations of the course (and its change in title) reflected the need to provide SLMS students with experience in the assessment and evaluation of instruction. The new course is now called: *IST673 School Library Media: Technology, Theory, Application & Assessment* and connects graduate and undergraduate students with in-service educators from local PreK-12 school districts to design, develop, deploy, and assess Web sites developed for use in participating PreK-12 schools (Doane & Stefl-Mabry, 2009).

Students are asked to generate a range of reflective evaluations of their experiences including an early-semester questionnaire exploring their expectations of their learning environment and teaching strengths, weekly reflections on the collaborative development experience, on-going journals of their observations of PreK-12 classrooms, and end-of-semester course evaluations. The remainder of this chapter will explore our observations based on student reflections from these sources.

Evolution of the New Design

Although early iterations of the new course concentrated on bringing together pre-service and in-service educators (along with undergraduate students studying Web development), each semester has provided the faculty with new understandings of the science of learning. "The emerging science of learning underscores the importance of rethinking what is taught, how it is taught, and how learning is assessed" (J. D. Bransford et al., 2000, p. 13), thus the present iteration of the course reflects a learner centered, knowledge centered and assessment centered learning environment. Students in the course reflect on their experiences both as a student and as a paraprofessional. As such, they are asked to consider the role of the learner in the classroom, to identify the information that is to be the focus of instruction, to select technologies that will enhance the curriculum and, equally important, are appropriate for the user, and to assess to what degree learning goals have been attained.

Early-Semester Expectations

At the beginning of the semester, SLMS students were asked to fill out a questionnaire and reflect upon themselves as learners and teachers. The purpose of this survey was to focus on students' individual strengths, interests and needs "to make students' thinking visible" (Darling-Hammond & Bransford, 2005, p. 37). Highlights of the results of the questionnaire reveal SLMS, as learners need:

- A learning environment in which to ask questions and be creative: "An emotionally safe environment where I can feel o.k. asking for help, I can make mistakes, I can take risks."
- A learning environment in which they understand the purpose of what they are learning: "To know how what I'm learning pertains [sic] to me and why I need to know it."
- A learning environment with little or no uncertainty: "Clearly defined goals and the means to achieve them."
- A variety of ways to receive and process information: "I like to hear the information, see the information and put it into my own words. I want the opportunity to be a visual, audio, and kinetic learner."
- Time to accomplish learning goals: "Sufficient time to consider and complete tasks."

Results provided the faculty with insight into structuring learning experiences for the class and for individual learners during the semester.

The majority of students enrolled in the class stated that they were most comfortable in learning environments that are predictable and highly organized. The course, however, embodies a problem-based learning (PBL) environment and uncertainty is a common feature of PBL environments. We assured students that collaboration is "both a *learning process* and a *learning outcome*" (Remedios, Clarke, & Hawthorne, 2008, p. 2) and warned that the instructional and learning needs of the PreK-12 learning partners would not be something that we would be able to predict with certainty, nor could *we* or would *we,* as faculty, outline the specific parameters of the "project" for them. The design, development, deployment, and assessment of the project was something that the SLMS graduate students were going to have to *learn* (over the course of the semester) as they worked with their peers, the undergraduate students, and Pre-K-12 partners (educators and students alike). This did little to dispel their initial anxiety and frustration. This was a new learning environment for them and in order for them to learn they had to "learn in context", for as Fullan explains "...you can achieve consistency and innovation only through deep and consistent *learning in context*...Learning on the job, day after day, is the work" (2008, p. 86).

In addition to students' desire to engage only in well-defined tasks, students also indicated an expectation that the course would involve substantial acquisition of technical skills (i.e., how to use Web development software, file uploading tools, etc.). Early versions of the course did indeed focus more on developing technology skills but over time, it became clear that the focus on technology was but a small part of what SLMS needed to learn in order to become effective teacher-librarians (Haycock, 1997, 1999, 2003). Technological skills acquired in one semester were guaranteed to become obsolete by the time SLMS graduate the program and begin working in their schools. Merely providing technology skills prevented students from wrestling with deeper questions than *which technology is better than others*, a question analogous to asking which tool is best—a hammer, or a screwdriver? "In teaching as in carpentry, the selection of tools depends on the task at hand and the materials and students one works with" (J. Bransford, Brophy, & Williams, 2000, p. 22). We wanted SLMS to develop projects based upon the needs of teachers and students, modeling their future day-to-day professional responsibilities. Thus, the SLMS students were tasked to develop technology-enhanced instruction based upon the information needs of a PreK-12 classroom, select information resources, and teaching strategies – mediated by subject matter, grade level, and desired outcome in order to be "purposeful" (J. D. Bransford et al., 2000, p. 23).

Despite the faculty's attempts (written and verbal) to explain that the course was *not* about technology, but how to integrate technology effectively into PreK-12 curriculum, University students continued to expect to be taught basic technology skills. (This despite the fact that they are required to take as a prerequisite two technology-focused courses). This may be because technology courses are more linear and their assignments more predictable. Undoubtedly, the task of providing effective and appropriate instructional resources for real PreK-12 students was neither easily defined, nor quickly resolved in a linear fashion.

Lastly, another core competency for SLMS to develop was how to design, assess and evaluate educational environments to optimize students' learning. There are different types of assessments and they serve different purposes (Darling-Hammond & Bransford, 2005; Dean, 2001; University of Missouri, 2008). While most people think about assessments as *summative assessments* (standardized tests, final exams and unit exams) information revealed from these, although important, comes too late to provide help, support, or guidance when students are engaged in the learning process. *Formative assessments,* used for the purpose of improving teaching and learning, involve making students' thinking visible *as they progress through the course,* giving teachers and students the ability to monitor progress (J. Bransford et al., 2000, p. 24). Thus, incorporation of meaningful formative assessment in the curriculum is essential to inform instructional design in the PreK-12 setting.

Weekly Reflections on the Collaboration Process

Our students came to class prepared to complete traditional academic assignments in the same fashion that they always had: listen, read, write, regurgitate; a process common to many students in the United States of America. American students are trained for this predictable model of superficial learning and assessment (Fullan, 2008) during their PreK-12 and undergraduate classroom experiences (Macedo, 2006; Roosevelt,

2009). When informed that, for this course, their project would be defined by the curricula, and the information and developmental learning needs of Pre-K-12 educators and their students, many of the SLMS students struggled during the first few weeks of the semester as they began to understand that *collaboration,* too, is a process that takes practice and patience. Each week, students completed an online self-assessment that required them to consider such issues as the progress of the planning and development of the project, interpersonal dynamics, and other significant events in the project development (Doane & Stefl-Mabry, 2009). This modeling of the use of technology to support teaching and learning is an important part of our process. By using technology to support our students, we implicitly train them to use technology to support their future students, as well. These formative assessments provided us an opportunity to witness the progress of each group and provide "just in time" learning experiences for our students. These self-assessments revealed that early in the semester the anxiety for some groups was almost palpable:

Collaboration between [sic] our group (grads/undergrads) is fine, but the collaboration between grad students/teachers is awful.

We are a week behind due to the confusion regarding our classroom teachers and subject matter.

[Name of SLMS graduate student] and I work very well together; our frustration is not with each other, but with the overwhelming confusion about how to put this project together and have it be meaningful for everyone involved.

The message behind these words is clear: the SLMS graduate students were anxious to move forward and "get their job done". Thinking deeply about integrating technologies with effective learning experiences is a process that takes time and careful reflection, and as the semester progresses most groups come to understand it is a valuable process that cannot be rushed:

We all had a lot of ideas and thought that they would work, but then had to adjust everything once we got together with [the teacher], who had a different idea in her head that was new to us. Once she laid out her vision, we were able to collaborate on ideas to enhance it. We think we are finally on the right track!

The groups that were most successful, in terms of quality of projects and understanding of the learning process, became "knowledge builders" (Bereiter & Scardamalia, 2003). "Knowledge Building" may be defined simply as "creative work with ideas that really matter to the people doing the work" (Bereiter & Scardamalia, 2003, p. 13). These were groups that attended to the instructional needs of *all* learning partners. They asked PreK-12 students what they knew and what they wanted to learn, and were intentional in their design of instructional technologies. They developed formative assessments to gauge the effectiveness of their teaching and the students' learning. They were reflective practitioners who took responsibility for their own learning.

I was in the school three days this week and worked with the librarian and both of my classroom teachers. Confusion was definitely decreased and confidence has been raised.

Our group is becoming more confident and I think that we left today's meeting with the teachers feeling really good about our progress. Everyone seems to be very motivated and willing to put in the extra effort to make this project a success.

It seems clear from student self-reports that increased contact with classroom teachers and with PreK-12 students offers SLMS a better understanding of the learning needs of the students and the instructional goals of the teachers. Groups that experienced the greatest difficulty were those that reported that they independently created solutions with little or no interaction with their learning partners. These same groups were later frustrated when their efforts proved ineffective in the PreK-12 classroom. We take this to mean that our graduate students did not *know* their learners or *understand* their needs. Confusion and anxiety remained high when graduate students adopted a "get the job done" mentality, rather than building a learning partnership with the PreK-12 educators.

I now understand that the real learning is the process. The product is really just a by-product. If I knew in January what we know today, our final project would be the best ever produced. But in a way we have come up with something better than a project, and that is a satisfying process.

The course is purposefully designed to mirror the day-to-day professional practice of the SLMS in that it requires that teams work together in order to marshal their unique skills toward the building of Web sites; no one person within the partnership possesses the full range of skills and information necessary to be successful. Yet, for many SLMS graduate students, this is their first experience actually engaging in this type of professional practice in real world conditions and the often chaotic and unpredictable world of the PreK-12. They expect to be given a set of explicit assignments along with clearly defined expectations for each assignment. Although the SLMS graduate students come to the course having learned about collaboration and the theory behind it and they can articulate orally and in writing that collaboration will be a vital part of their work as SLMS practitioners, for the majority, this is the first experience in actually *collaborating*.

On-Going Observation Journals

Working collaboratively requires one to observe others and to be oneself observed in a professional setting. Fullan, citing Richard Elmore (2004) agrees "the problem [is that] there is almost no opportunity for teachers to engage in continuous and substantial learning about their practice in the setting in which they actually work, observing and being observed by their colleagues in their own classrooms and classrooms of other teachers in other schools confronting similar problems of practice" (2008, p. 86).

Toward this end, graduate SLMS are expected to spend at least two hours each week in the PreK-12 classroom working with and observing the teachers and students. They maintain journals of their observations that are intended to help them identify challenging as well as rewarding aspects of the PreK-12 classroom and to reflect on teaching practice—both that of their learning partners and their own. These journals have revealed a number of recurring themes related to collaboration and expectations about the course.

Although "conflict and diversity are our friends" (Michael Fullan, 1993, p. 18 as cited by Hughes-Hassell & Harada, 2007, p. 7) many students found it difficult to work together as a collaborative group. Most groups learned to at least cooperate[4], and some groups harnessed collective knowledge and learned to work collaboratively[5]. One student's reflections spoke directly to this issue:

The area in which I've had to consistently mark myself low in self-assessments is the 'works well with others' category. My trouble with group projects wasn't caused by antisocial behavior but, rather, having grown accustomed to a very particular way of thinking, working and organizing. I had always been of the grin and bear it school of thought when it comes to working in a group, but as I've gotten older, I have started to see group projects as a learning experience.

This (perhaps late in life) epiphany was an important one to have, because collaboration and cooperation are essential parts of working in a school. Callison and Preddy (2006), note the positive aspects of working collaboratively with other teachers. Each teacher in a collaborative group brings their personal knowledge and passion, and the end result is deeper and more powerful than it would be if one teacher worked by himself/herself, which directly benefits the students" (Harlen, 2009).

This level of reflection is highly beneficial to the student and to us, as educators, as we continue to work toward understanding the challenges facing SLMS students. Still, we find that a minority of SLMS student observations lack the depth or truly reflective tone that would allow them to become reflective practitioners. Students have expressed difficulty and, in some cases, resistance to working with PreK-12 populations that don't share the student's social or economic background.

After meeting with our project teacher, I realized that I know jack about inner city kids. Even the poorest kids from the most awful family situations where I live use computers fairly well. And I know even less about their culture. I have a feeling a lot of my group's original project ideas were geared for middle class ninth graders. Not ninth graders whose classmates get executed on the street.

When students view team work as cooperative, *grin and bear it* sorts of endeavors, rather than as collaborative, *we're all in this together* experiences, the resulting projects are less well constructed, less coherent, and often fail to address PreK-12 learners' needs, as reported by the assessment instruments embedded within the projects.

End of Semester Course Evaluations

By mid semester, at least a quarter of the students would plead: "Please just tell us what you want. What should the curriculum projects look like at the end?" "What types of information resources should we include and how many is enough?" Clearly the educational process for most students has taught them that to be "successful" academically they need to follow a prescribed formula: attend class, listen to lectures, do the readings, and complete assignments according to the mandates outlined by the instructor. Thinking critically, reflectively, and independently is, for many of our students, a formidable experience. In addition, being required to provide evidence of their instructional practice (formative and summative assessment) is something many students felt was not within their professional purview. This, despite the fact that "all the research evidence points clearly to this dimension [instructional] of the school librarian's role as a primary enabler of learning outcomes" and is a "theme of school library conferences and publications across the world" (Hughes-Hassell & Harada, 2007, p. 62). Our students have certainly been exposed to the current research in the field and have completed the requisite term papers in their core courses, but sadly, some still have not internalized those beliefs into their own world views.

Course evaluations are typically gathered during the last two weeks of the semester, when students are writing reports about their project, analyzing their assessment data, and getting ready to present their findings. They reveal students' high level of anxiety and frustration. Some have written: "This course was one of the hardest courses I have ever taken" and "This has taught me nothing about school libraries". On a related note, one undergraduate student critiqued the course noting, "[the course] didn't teach us anything! We had to learn it on our own!!" Such comments might be cause for concern, were it not for the strong positive feedback we get from many of the same students in later months (discussed below).

As faculty we must concern ourselves with the question of how our students will perform professionally and create environments for them to experience the complexity of real-world instructional design and technology development experiences. Will they become the "active, and not passive" SLMS that the field calls for (Harada, 2003; Hughes-Hassell & Harada, 2007)? We believe one capstone course is not enough. We need to be developing curricula together with our students, PreK-12 in-service teachers, administrators, community members, and PreK-12 students that will enable pre-service educators to see learning and instructional design as a process, rather than a product. Students need to have the space and time to understand learners' needs in order to be able to design instruction to meet those needs successfully. The development of this course—over six years in the making— is but one step in that direction. More needs to be done to ensure that the educational training and professional development of SLMS is meaningful and effective. We cannot and should not say that it is effective without providing evidence to support such statements. Just as we hold our students accountable for *learning,* so we too should be held accountable for *teaching* and we cannot do that unless we know more about how SLMS and teachers *learn.*

Student Reactions after Being In-Service

Much like the pain of any creative process, perhaps, after students graduate from the program there appears to be little memory of the discomfort of the learning experience. Instead, SLMS who stay in touch—no doubt a biased group—volunteer to be in-service partners for subsequent IST673 students and many undergraduates apply to our graduate level SLMS program. Many students proclaim that the course was "one of the best learning experiences of their lives". There appears to be a need for students to put some distance between themselves and the learning experience in order to process their experience, as reflected in an unsolicited email received from a former student:

Another example of how YOU empower individuals in our field... Your pushing of reading scholarly articles, presentations by various people in the field of information and networking has kept me alive in what was a stagnant situation where I work. New scenario - a strong advocate of librarians is hired as our new superintendent, [name omitted]. He immediately makes it clear that his 1st priority with our new budget is LIBRARIES AND TECHNOLOGY. In less than 2 weeks after school began, he requested to meet with me, the high school librarian and respective [administrators]. The dialogue was phenomenal - dynamic... targeted right at where we SHOULD BE (but obviously are not) and then he asked that each librarian to give him a near-term and long range plan for our respective media centers. I have attached my plan which is representative of all you drove us to do in your classes. I believe it will materialize because the superintendent is on the same page as you pushed with us.

Although most graduates go on to be successful practitioners—and several have assumed leadership roles in state and local school library and educational organizations— we must acknowledge that for some, our course design and, perhaps, the professional responsibilities of the emerging 21st century teacher-librarian may indeed be overwhelming.

CONCLUSION

"One of the hallmarks of the new science of learning is its emphasis on learning with understanding" (J. D. Bransford et al., 2000, p. 8). It is easy to be misled by the simplicity of the words "learning with understanding". In actuality, creating an environment that fosters learning for understanding is complex and difficult. It requires reflective and intentional practice on the part of faculty teaching the course, frequent formative assessment, and a willingness to engage students as partners in the learning process. The very technologies we are teaching our students *about* can be used to facilitate their learning and our teaching. Successful use of collaboration tools such as wikis, blogs, and dynamic online surveys foster in students an expectation that technology can be supportive of education, rather than serve as a barrier to it.

How can we expect the SLMS to be a "collaborator, change agent, and leader" promoting and implementing programs "that will help prepare students to be effective users of ideas and information" (AASL, 2008), if they never experience such learning experiences themselves? We need, as faculty who teach SLMS and teachers, to know more about how our students learn if we, as faculty, are to provide graduate students with meaningful educational experiences. The course described in this chapter is but a small step in that direction.

REFERENCES

AASL. (2008). Learning about the Job [What does a school library media specialist do?]. Retrieved July 31, 2008, from http://www.ala.org/ala/aasl/aasleducation/recruitmentlib/learningabout/learningabout.cfm

Angeley, R., & Purdue, J. (2000). Information literacy: an overview [Electronic Version]. *Dialogue Home*. Retrieved November 30, 2009, from http://pandora.cii.wwu.edu/dialogue/issue6.html

Bereiter, C., & Scardamalia, M. (2003). Learning to work creatively with knowledge. In De Corte, E., Verschaffel, L., Entwistle, N., & van Merrienboer, J. (Eds.), *Unravelling basic components and dimensions of powerful learning environments*. Toronto, Canada: EARLI.

Bransford, J., Brophy, S., & Williams, S. (2000). When Computer Technologies Meet the Learning Sciences: Issues and Opportunities. *Journal of Applied Developmental Psychology*, *21*(1), 59–84. doi:10.1016/S0193-3973(99)00051-9

Bransford, J. D., Brown, A. L., & Cocking, R. R. (2000). *How people learn: Brain, mind, experience and school*. Washington, DC: National Research Council National Academy Press.

Carver, K. W. (1986). The changing instructional role of the high school library media specialist: 1950-84; A survey of professional literature, standards, and research studies. *School Library Media Quarterly*, *14*(4), 183–191.

Cookson, P. W. J. (1994). *School choice: The struggle for the soul of American education*. New Haven, CT: Yale University Press.

Craver, K. W. (1994). *School library media centers in the 21st century: Changes and challenges*. Westport, CT: Greenwood Press.

Darling-Hammond, L., & Bransford, J. D. (Eds.). (2005). *Preparing teachers for a changing world: What teachers should learn and be able to do*. Somerset, NJ: Jossey-Bass.

Dean, C. D. (2001). They Expect Teachers to Do That? Helping Teachers Explore and Take Ownership of Their Profession. In Levin, B. B. (Ed.), *Energizing Teacher Education and Professional Development with Problem-Based Learning* (pp. 8–23). Alexandria, VA: Association for Supervision and Curriculum Development.

Doane, W. E. J., & Stefl-Mabry, J. (2009). Transgenerational problem-based Web development learning experience. In Tan, O. S. (Ed.), *Problem-based learning and creativity*. Singapore: Cengage Learning Asia Pte Ltd.

Doll, C. A. (2005). *Collaboration and the School Library Media Specialist*. Location: Scarecrow Press.

Fullan, M. (1999). *Change forces: The sequel*. Philadelphia: Falmer Press.

Fullan, M. (2007). *The new meaning of educational change* (4th ed.). New York: Routledge.

Fullan, M. (2008). *The six secrets of change.* Somerset, NJ: Jossey-Bass.

Harada, V. H. (2003). Taking the lead in developing learning communities. *Knowledge Quest: Journal of the American Association of School Librarians, 31*(2), 12–16.

Harlen, M. (2009). IST673 Wiki Weekly Reflections.

Hartzell, G. N. (2001). The implications of selected school reform approaches for school library media services. *School Library Media Research, 4.*

Haycock, K. (1997). Working together to improve student achievement, kindergarten through college. *The Educational Record, 78,* 10–18.

Haycock, K. (1999). *Foundations for effective school library media programs.* Englewood, CO: Libraries Unlimited.

Haycock, K. (2003). *The crisis in Canada's school libraries: The case for reform and reinvestment.* Toronto, Canada: Association of Canadian Publishers and Canada Heritage.

Herbert, M. (1998). *Education as a social institution and ideological process.* City, Country: Waxmann Verlag.

Hughes-Hassell, S., & Harada, V. H. (2007). *School reform and the school library media specialist.* Westport, CT: Libraries Unlimited.

Kozol, J. (1991). *Savage inequalities: Children in America's schools* (1st ed.). New York: Crown Publishers.

Kuhlthau, C. C. (1989). Information search process: A summary of research and implications for school library media programs. *School Library Media Quarterly, 18*(1), 19–25.

Latrobe, K. (1998). *The emerging school library media center: Historical issues and perspectives.* Englewood, CO: Libraries Unlimited.

Latrobe, K. H. (1998). *The emerging school library media center: Historical issues and perspectives.* Englewood, CO: Libraries Unlimited.

Lowe, C. A. (2000). *The role of the school library media specialist in the 21st century* [Electronic Version]. ERIC Digest.

Macedo, D. (2006). *Literacies of power: What Americans are not allowed to know.* Boulder, CO: Westview Press.

Remedios, L., Clarke, D., & Hawthorne, L. (2008). Framing collaborative behaviors: Listening and speaking in problem-based learning. *The Interdisciplinary Journal of Problem-Based Learning, 2*(1), 1–20.

Roosevelt, M. (2009, Month day). Student expectations see as causing grade disputes. *The New York Times,* 1.

Sarason, S. (2004). *And what do you mean by learning?* Portsmouth, NH: Heinemann.

Shannon, D. (2002). The education and competencies of school library media specialists: A review of the literature. *School Library Media Research, 5.*

Stefl-Mabry, J. (2004). Learning made real: Collaborative work, shared Assessment. *Knowledge Quest. Journal of the American Association of School Librarians, 32*(5).

Stefl-Mabry, J., Doane, W. E. J., & Radlick, M. S. (2009, April 13 - 17). *Seen and still not heard: What students voices reveal about teachers and technology.* Paper presented at the American Educational Research Association, San Diego, CA.

Stefl-Mabry, J., Doane, W. E. J., Radlick, M. S., & Theroux, P. (2007). Redefining schools as learning organizations: A model for trans-generational teaching and learning. *International Journal of Teaching and Learning in Higher Education, 19*(3).

Stefl-Mabry, J., & Lynch, B. L. (2004). A teaching hospital approach to graduate course design and implementation: Authentic project-based curricula and school library media graduate students.

Stefl-Mabry, J., & Lynch, B. L. (2006). *Knowledge communities: Bringing the village into the classroom*. Lanham, MD: Scarecrow Press.

Stefl-Mabry, J., & Powers, J. G. (2004). Learning Pathways Project: Collaborative Multidirectional Learning.

Stefl-Mabry, J., Powers, J. G., & Doll, C. (2006). Creating and sustaining problem-based partnerships among graduate, undergraduate, and K-12 learners: Opportunities and challenges. *Journal of Educational Technology Systems, 34*(2), 131–153. doi:10.2190/4DMJ-85B4-GMH7-GEQB

Stefl-Mabry, J., & Powers-Goodall, J. (2005). A model of problem-based learning higher education curricula: Creating learning pathways. The Twelfth International Conference on Learning Faculty of Education at the University of Granada from 11-14 July 2005. *The International Journal of Learning*.

Stefl-Mabry, J., Radlick, M., Doane, W. E. J., & Theroux, P. (2007). Redefining schools as learning organizations: A model for trans-generational teaching and learning. *International Journal of Teaching and Learning in Higher Education*.

Stefl-Mabry, J., Theroux, P., J., & Radlick, M. S. (2005). *Examining data from multiple perspectives: A gestalt approach to library information science & educational research*. Philadelphia, PA: Treasure Mountain #12 (AASL Research Group).

University of Missouri. (2008). Evaluation, assessment, grading, norming. In *Teaching at Mizzou: A guide for new faculty, graduate instructors and teaching assistants 2008*. Columbia, MO: University of Missouri.

Weil, E. (2008). Meet your new school library media specialist [Electronic Version]. *Scholastic Administrator*. Retrieved March 12, 2008, from http://www2.scholastic.com/browse/article.jsp?id=3748779&print=2

Woolls, B. (1995). The role of library media services in future schooling: The future of the school library media center. [SLMA]. *School Library Media Annual, 13*, 54–59.

KEY TERMS AND DEFINITIONS

Assessment (in Education): Judgments made about the degree of attainment of intended learning outcomes by learners. Assessments of student learning may be formative (conducted during instruction) or summative (conducted following completion of instruction). See "Formative Assessment" and "Summative Assessment"

Cooperation: A division of responsibilities among group members with the expectation that their individual efforts will be integrated at a later date. Cooperation processes differ from collaboration processes, although the intended outcomes may be the same.

Collaboration: Beyond simple cooperation, collaboration includes active sharing of knowledge and skill building among group members and a mutual commitment to work on projects for shared benefit.

Critical Thinking: The ability to perceive the world, analyze, synthesize, and evaluate what one learns, and understand the underlying reasons for and relationships among phenomena.

Evaluation (in Education): Judgments made about outcomes related to professional practice or program goals. For example, one evaluates the effectiveness of teaching, execution of an instructional plan, or the attainment of specified graduation rates. Evaluation may be either formative (conducted during the activity of interest) or summative (conducted following completion of the activity of interest). Evaluation is to be distinguished from assessments of student learning.

Formative Assessment: Formative assessments provide information about individual learners so that the learner and teacher can target and adjust subsequent learning activities to meet the learner's needs. For example, a self-, peer-, or teacher-assessment of student progress during a learning activity. See "Assessment".

Information Literacy: An engagement with information technologies and information sources with a critical perspective, as opposed to passive, non-critical consumption of information.

Problem-Based Learning (PBL): A collaborative, student-centered instructional strategy in which learners are confronted with a problem—possibly loosely defined—and must identify what learning resources and activities they need to marshal in order to successfully address the problem. Pioneered at McMaster University, Hamilton, Ontario, Canada.

School Library Media Specialist/Student (SLMS): Teacher-librarians who actively engage with students, teachers, administrators, parents, and community members to marshal media resources from the school, community, and the world-at-large in order to address student learning needs and support the PreK-12 curriculum. *Specialist* generally refers to in-service SLMS, while *student* refers to pre-service SLMS.

Summative Assessment: Summative assessments provide information about individual learners' final degree of attainment of intended learning outcomes after learning activities are completed. For example, end of chapter tests, end of unit exams, and other post-instruction assessments. See "Assessment".

ENDNOTES

1 indeed, anyplace where teachers are trained, regardless of the formal or informal nature of the experience.

2 (Kozol, 1991)

3 "Information literacy implies a critical engagement with technology and information sources, not simply using them unquestioningly (Angeley & Purdue, 2000, p. 1).

4 Cooperation generally involves a division of responsibilities among the group members with the expectation that their individual efforts will be integrated at a later date.

5 Collaboration moves beyond simple cooperation to include shared knowledge and skill building and a mutual effort to work on project products for shared benefit.

Chapter 23
Preparing Teachers to Integrate Technology Effectively:
The Case of Higher-Order Thinking Skills (HOTS)

Drew Polly
University of North Carolina at Charlotte, USA

ABSTRACT

Technology has the greatest impact on student learning outcomes when students complete technology-rich activities that also develop their higher-order thinking skills (HOTS). This chapter presents findings from a study that examined two lesson plans from 74 first-year teachers who were learning how to plan technology-rich instruction focused on students' HOTS. Findings indicate that teachers' lesson plans did not address students' HOTS and rated low on the Level of Technology Integration (LOTI) scale. Further, teachers' use of an indirect instruction lesson plan format that promoted student discovery was associated with higher levels of HOTS and technology use. Implications and future trends for both practice and research are also shared.

INTRODUCTION

Technology Integration

Technology integration continues to be a popular topic to discuss among scholars, policy makers and educators. While the influence of technology on student learning has yielded mixed results, many maintain that educational technologies hold the key to improving student achievement (Bransford, Brown, & Cocking, 2000; U.S. Department of Education [USDE], 2004) and the future of our nation (Friedman, 2005; Gladwell, 2002). While research has yielded mixed results on the influence of technology on learning, numerous studies highlight the need for technology-rich learning activities to also develop students' higher-order thinking skills (HOTS) (e.g., Mann, Shakeshaft, Becker, & Kottkamp, 1999; Ringstaff & Kelley, 2002; Roschelle, Pea, Hoadley, Gordin, & Means, 2001; Schacter, 1999; Wenglinsky, 1998). It has proven problematic for researchers to establish relationships between technology and student

DOI: 10.4018/978-1-61692-854-4.ch023

learning without accounting for the manner in which technology is used (Roschelle et al., 2001).

In a large-scale analysis of data from the National Assessment for Education Progress, Wenglinsky (1999) found that technology use was only associated with gains in student learning in the context of activities that developed students' higher-order thinking skills. This finding has been confirmed with other research about technology-rich authentic learning environments (Cognition and Technology Group at Vanderbilt [CTGV], 1997), reading programs (Knezek & Christensen, 2007) science inquiry environments (Dunleavy & Hienecke, 2007), and mathematics problem solving (Bransford, Brown, & Cocking, 2000; Polly, 2008-a). Other studies indicate that technology impacts learning positively when associated with learner-centered activities, such as when students use technology to facilitate problem solving, conceptual development, and critical thinking (CTGV, 1997; Means, 1994; Ringstaff & Kelley, 2002; Wenglinsky, 1998).

Therefore, if educational technologies are going to impact student learning, the use of these must be embedded in activities where technology serves as a tool to support learning (Jonassen & Reeves, 1996; ISTE, 2008), and develop students' higher-order thinking skills (Bransford, Brown, & Cocking, 2000; ISTE, 2008).

Higher-Order Thinking Skills

Higher-order thinking skills (HOTS) are not new to education. In 1956, Benjamin Bloom and some of his colleagues created Bloom's Taxonomy, which categorized types of educational tasks according to cognitive difficulty. Students' actions were the focal point of the taxonomy.

Marzano (1988) modified Bloom's Taxonomy with his own framework. Most recently, Anderson and Krawthwohl (2000), two of Bloom's co-authors, revised the original Bloom's Taxonomy. The taxonomy lists the process of Creating at the highest level. Creating, is the process of "putting elements together to form a coherent or functional whole; reorganizing elements into a new pattern or structure" (Anderson and Krawthwohl, 2000). This process of creating serves as a natural fit with educational technology and the advancements of the past few decades, where scholars have advocated for students to learn content by building and creating representations of knowledge (Harel & Papert, 1991; Kafai & Resnick, 1996).

Recommendations for reforming PK-12 schools include developing students' HOTS, in addition to teaching from a more learner-centered manner (Bransford, Brown, & Cocking, 2000; Cornelius-White & Harbaugh, 2009; McCombs, 2003; McCombs & Whisler, 1997). McCombs and Whisler (1997) published recommendations (see Table 1) for K-12 schools based off the empirically-based learner-centered principles published by the American Psychological Association (APA Work Group, 1997). According to McCombs and Whisler (2003), teachers should:

- Pose tasks that were relevant to learners,
- Allow students to direct their learning and take more ownership of tasks
- Promote reflection
- Embed assessment within a task
- Allow resources such as technology to be used to support learning,
- Facilitate learning during class,
- And create a positive environment that encourages collaboration.

While research indicates that learner-centered instruction contributes to gains in student learning outcomes (Cornelius-White, 2007), there have been barriers teaching in this manner. Research shows that teachers struggle to teach in ways that are learner-centered and focus on students' HOTS (Fishman, Marx, Best, & Tal, 2003; Schneider, Blumenfeld, & Krajcik, 2005). In some cases, teachers reverted to traditional approaches when

Table 1. K-12 Learner-centered environments (Adapted from McCombs & Whisler, 1997)

Characteristic	Learner-centered tasks	Learner-Centered Principles (APA Work Group, 1997)
Relevant	Personally relevant to students' lives and build upon prior experience or prior knowledge.	The learning of complex subject matter is most effective when learners construct meaning from information and experience (Principle 1). The successful learner can link new information with existing knowledge in meaningful ways (Principle 3). An individual's motivation is influenced by their beliefs and interests (Principle 7), the learner's creativity and curiosity (Principle 8), and their background and experiences (Principles 10, 12 and 13).
Student-directed	Designed so that learners have ownership of the tasks they are completing, have, are able to choose their approach and have some influence about how the products of the task are represented.	An individual's motivation is influenced by their beliefs and interests (Principle 7), the learner's creativity and curiosity (Principle 8), and their background and experiences (Principles 10, 12 and 13).
Reflective	Reflective and allow learners to refine their understanding and make connections between concepts or approaches used to complete the task.	Higher order strategies for selecting and monitoring mental operations facilitate creative and critical thinking (Principle 5).
Assessment	Aligned with assessment so that learning is evaluated in the context of the task.	Setting appropriately high and challenging standards and assessing the learner as well as learning progress–including diagnostic, process, and outcome assessment–are integral parts of the learning process (Principle 14).
Technology-rich	Able to be supported with technology that allows students to gather information, explore concepts, collaborate with peers or represent knowledge.	Learning is influenced by environmental factors, including culture, technology, and instructional practices (Principle 6).
Facilitated	Facilitated by teachers or peers that model, scaffold student learning and facilitate the completion of the tasks.	The successful learner, over time and with support, can create meaningful, coherent representations of knowledge (Principle 2).
Collaborative	Implemented in a manner that allows students to collaborate and share ideas with one another.	Social interactions, interpersonal relations, and communication with others all provide opportunities for learning (Principle 11).

confronted with time constraints, unfamiliar content, and problems with technology (Schneider et al., 2005; Stein, Grover & Henningsen, 1996). Teachers in the *Jasper Woodbury* project posed pre-designed tasks that required students to view an *adventure* on a video-disc, identify needed information, determine how to examine a task, and apply their solutions to an immediate sub-problem (CTGV, 1997). Classroom observations suggested that many teachers were reluctant to depend on the pre-packaged materials or allow their students to take responsibility for their learning (CTGV, 1997). Others modified Jasper tasks by providing drill-and-practice worksheets that addressed the same skills embedded in the video scenarios.

In order for technology to be effectively used to develop students' HOTS, teacher education and professional development programs must adequately prepare preservice and inservice teachers to adequately integrate technology in a learner-centered manner that develops students' HOTS. I present findings from a study done with inservice teachers who are taking an introduction to teaching course focused on designing instruction and technology integration. After presenting the findings, I follow with by highlighting implications and future trends related to the integration of educational technologies.

METHODOLOGY

Research Questions

The current study is driven by the following research questions:

1) To what extent (and how) do participants' lesson plans develop students' higher-order thinking skills?
2) To what extent (and how) do participants' lesson plans integrate technology in a way that develops students' higher-order thinking skills?

Participants

The study examined the work samples of 74 in-service teachers enrolled in an introductory course focused on designing instruction and technology integration during the Spring, 2008 and Spring, 2009 semesters. Twenty-three teachers took the course in Spring, 2008 and 51 teachers took the course in Spring, 2009. All participants were elementary school teachers in the Teach for America program, which places college graduates in high-need schools after an intense 6-week program on teaching. As part of their agreement with Teach for America, all students enrolled in this course. The author was the course instructor.

Data Sources and Course Description

For the present study, participants' lesson plans were the primary data source. Table 2 shows how the various data sources were analyzed for each research question. In the course teacher-participants created two lesson plans and a number of technology-rich projects, including a WebQuest and an educational game built using PowerPoint. Participants also learned about multiple intelligences, learning theories and higher-order thinking skills, and were expected to apply that knowledge while creating their different artifacts.

Lesson planning included two different formats, direct instruction, which is a more traditional teacher-centered format. While the formats, teacher input, guided practice and independent practice are included, teachers were encouraged to design learner-centered activities that taught and reinforced the concepts in an engaging manner.

The other format, indirect instruction is more geared towards inquiry-based lessons and students' explorations. The phases Engage and Explore advocate beginning the lesson with activities that capture students' attention and allow them to discover and inquire about concepts through experiments, problem solving or research tasks.

Data Analysis

Analytical framework. Data analysis was informed by an interpretivist lens that examined each lesson plan as the unit of analysis. Interpretivists strive to analyze data in order to interpret or explain certain situations or experiences (Guba & Lincoln, 1994). In this case, teacher-participants' lesson planning was the experience of primary interest.

Analytic procedures. The interpretivist lens influenced the use of inductive analysis methodologies (Bogden & Biklen, 2003). All data analysis was done by the author using a spreadsheet to organize the data and coded units. For question one, lesson plans were analyzed with a focus on

Table 2. HOTS based on instructional objective

Level	Frequency	Percentage
Remember	1	0.68%
Understand	22	14.86%
Apply	109	73.65%
Analyze	8	5.41%
Evaluate	2	1.35%
Create	6	4.05%

student performance. During each lesson plan, teacher-participants detailed out the student performance in the instructional objective as well as in the narrative of the lesson plan. The performances were analyzed using revised Bloom's Taxonomy (Anderson & Krathwohl, 2000). As described earlier, the revised Bloom's Taxonomy characterized tasks and students' performances according to cognitive difficulty. Anderson and Krathwohl (2000) thoroughly described and provided examples of the various levels of the taxonomy, which guided the analysis.

For question two, lesson plans were analyzed with a focus on how technology supported the student performance. All lesson plans were to include technology in the lesson. The technology use in each lesson plan was analyzed using the Level of Technology Integration ([LOTI}; Moersch, 2001). The LOTI scale was developed to quantitatively describe how teachers were using technology in their classroom (Moersch, 2001). Tasks that rate high on the scale are authentic, problem-based activities that embody components of learner-centered instruction.

Data analysis included two rounds. In the first round, the author read each lesson plan making notes about the level of HOTS in the plan. During the second round, the researcher attended to how technology was used in the lesson. When the author analyzed lessons and was uncertain about the level of HOTS or LOTI level, the examples provided in the frameworks (Anderson & Krawthwohl, 2000; Moersch, 2001) were revisited to compare the examples to the plans. Following the two rounds of analysis, the researcher analyzed the frequency of lessons based on levels of HOTS and LOTI levels.

The findings section presents frequencies and percentages for the level of HOTS and the LOTI levels. For each of the research questions, Independent Chi-square tests (Creswell, 2002) were run to examine the relationship between the lesson plan format and the levels of HOTS and LOTI levels. The results of those tests are also presented.

FINDINGS

Question One: Higher-Order Thinking Skills in Lesson Plans

Students' lesson plans varied in terms of the higher-order thinking skills (HOTS) that were included. Variation occurred in terms of the levels of HOTS across plans, but also in terms of the HOTS described in the instructional objective and those described in the narrative of the lesson plan. Trends that existed are described below.

Variation across plans. Tables 2 and 3 describe the Out of the 148 lesson plans that were evaluated, only six (4.05%0 were found to rate at the Create level using the revised Bloom's Taxonomy. Based on the instructional objective and the narrative of the lesson plan, a majority of the lessons (109, 73.65% based on the instructional objective and 84, 56.76% based on the narrative) involved students applying information that they were learning.

Variation within a plan. As detailed in Tables 2 and 3, variations existed between the level of HOTS within a lesson plan. The instructional objectives indicated that students would be applying information and taking concepts that they learned and using the information in various ways to reinforce their learning. However, the narrative

Table 3. HOTS based on narrative of lesson plan

Level	Frequency	Percentage
Remember	1	0.68%
Understand	48	32.43%
Apply	84	56.76%
Analyze	8	5.41%
Evaluate	1	0.68%
Create	6	4.05%

Table 4. Levels of HOTS based on instructional objective and lesson plan format

HOTS Level	DI Plans	Percentage DI	Ind. Plans	Percentage Ind.
Remember	1	0.68%	0	0.00%
Understand	18	12.16%	4	2.70%
Apply	51	34.46%	58	39.19%
Analyze	2	1.35%	6	4.05%
Evaluate	1	0.68%	1	0.68%
Create	1	0.68%	5	3.38%

of the lesson plans indicated that students would be summarizing and comparing concepts, which is on the Understand level of the revised Bloom's Taxonomy.

Variation between direct and indirect instruction. After analyzing all of the lesson plans as one set, plans were then analyzed based on format, in order to compare plans using the direct instruction and the indirect instruction format. Tables 4 and 5 show the frequency and percentages for levels of HOTS based on the lesson plan formats.

Based on the analysis of both the instructional objective and the narrative, indirect instruction lesson plans had more lesson plans that included HOTS.

A Chi-squared test of independence was conducted to examine the relationship between lesson plan format and HOTS in the instructional objective. There was a significant relationship between these variables, *X2* (5, N = 148) = 15.03, *p=0.01*. Therefore, the indirect instruction format led to statistically significant higher instances of HOTS in the lessons.

A Chi-squared test of independence was conducted to examine the relationship between lesson plan format and HOTS in the lesson plan narrative. There was a significant relationship between these variables, *X2* (5, N = 148) = 16.71, *p<0.01*. In the case of the lesson plan narrative, the indirect instruction format led to statistically significant higher instances of HOTS in the lessons.

Question Two: Use of Technology to Develop HOTS

An analysis of lesson plans and the planned technology use indicated that a few technologies were primarily used during lessons. Further, most of the technologies rated at the Exploration level (Level 2) on the Level of Technology Integration (LOTI) scale. Table 6 lists the LOTI Levels for the lesson plans. Eighty-four lesson plans (56.76%) used technology and the Awareness

Table 5. Levels of HOTS based on narrative and lesson plan format

Level	DI Plans	Percentage DI	Ind. Plans	Percentage Ind.
Remember	1	0.68%	0	0.00%
Understand	34	22.97%	14	9.46%
Apply	36	24.32%	48	32.43%
Analyze	2	1.35%	6	4.05%
Evaluate	0	0.00%	1	0.68%
Create	1	0.68%	5	3.38%

Table 6. LOTI levels in lesson plans

LOTI Level	Frequency	Percentage
Non-use (0)	0	0.00%
Awareness (1)	84	56.76%
Exploration (2)	46	31.08%
Infusion (3)	14	9.46%
Integration (4)	4	2.70%
Expansion (5)	0	0.00%
Refinement (6)	0	0.00%

level. Most of these lesson utilized technology to show a PowerPoint or YouTube video to students in ways that were not seamlessly integrated into the lesson. In essence, the lesson could have been taught without the technology. Forty-six lessons (31.08%) used technology to support drill and practice or lower-level knowledge development (Exploration level). The eighteen tasks that rated higher on the LOTI scale (14 Infusion lessons and 4 Integration lessons) allowed students to research information on the Internet or use technology to create products based on what they were learning.

Table 7 describes the LOTI levels based on the format of each lesson plan. A majority of the lesson plans at the awareness level used technology to present information to students. In the cases of the direct instruction (DI) plans, this presentation occurred towards the beginning of the lesson. For the indirect instruction plans, this presentation occurred after students had completed a student-centered activity. Similarly to levels of HOTS, indirect instruction lesson planning format was associated with higher-level uses of technology integration.

A Chi-squared test of independence was conducted to examine the relationship between lesson plan format and HOTS in the instructional objective. There was a significant relationship between these variables, $X2(3, N = 148) = 16.079, p<0.01$. Therefore, the indirect instruction format led to statistically significant higher instances of HOTS in the lessons.

DISCUSSION

The findings presented from this study have many implications that warrant further discussion. These are detailed below.

Variation across Lessons for HOTS and LOTI Levels

While variation across lessons for both HOTS and LOTI was to be expected, the multitude of lower-level lessons was concerning. Both groups of participants had spent time examining the revised Bloom's Taxonomy and brainstorming instructional objectives and technology-rich lessons to support students' development of HOTS. However, when given the opportunity to plan their own lessons, students primarily designed lessons

Table 7. LOTI levels based on lesson plan formats

Level	DI Plans	Percentage DI	Ind. Plans	Percentage Ind.
Non-use (0)	0	0.00%	0	0.00%
Awareness (1)	53	35.81%	31	20.95%
Exploration (2)	18	12.16%	28	18.92%
Infusion (3)	2	1.35%	12	8.11%
Integration (4)	1	0.68%	3	2.03%
Expansion (5)	0	0.00%	0	0.00%
Refinement (6)	0	0.00%	0	0.00%

that did not develop students' HOTS and used technology in ways that did not rank high on the LOTI scale. There may be several reasons for this.

First, despite having the intense institute on teaching, participants anecdotally reported that the idea of Bloom's taxonomy and LOTI levels was new to them when the course started. As in the case of most teacher learning opportunities, these ideas require adequate time and opportunities for students to be able to successfully perform them independently (Orrill, 2001; Richardson, 1990).

Also, participants were told to create their lesson based on the North Carolina state standards. Part of the coursework was to map state standards to the revised Bloom's Taxonomy and plan from there. In essence, if teachers chose standards that did not align with the higher levels of Bloom's Taxonomy, then there is little reason to expect the lessons to develop students' HOTS. Teachers should design instruction to meet their state standards, not based on their ideal for HOTS (Anderson & Krathwohl, 2000).

The relationship between levels of HOTS and LOTI levels confirms prior research (Polly and Ausband, in press). In a prior study, while teachers were designing WebQuests, those tasks that were low in levels of HOTS were also low on the LOTI scale. In that study, researchers found that while teachers were eager to integrate technology into their classroom, there were misconceptions about what constituted technology-rich activities that developed students' HOTS.

Variations within a Lesson for HOTS

Participants' lessons also revealed discrepancies between HOTS in the instructional objective and the narrative of the lesson plan. In the instructional objective, participants used terminology and language with connotations of applying and making use of knowledge. However, the analysis of the lesson plan narratives found that students were merely summarizing and comparing, which is classified as the Understand level of the revised Bloom's Taxonomy. One reason for this might have been the difference in the amount of detail. The instructional objective was brief and did not elaborate greatly on students' actions, as the narrative did.

Further, the discrepancy could also be explained by participants' intent to develop students' HOTS without a strong conceptual understanding of how that would appear within a lesson plan. Studies on reform-based teaching (e.g., Peterson, 1990; Polly, 2006; Schneider et al., 2005) found that teachers report an intention to develop students' HOTS, but in fact they lack the knowledge of content and pedagogy to adequately plan and teach in this manner. In this case, since the participants were first-year teachers that were new to considering HOTS, there could be a disconnection between participants' understanding of HOTS and what they were taught in the course.

Influence of Lesson Plan Format

While the levels of HOTS and LOTI levels were overall not very high, there were statistically significant differences between the HOTS and LOTI levels based on lesson plan formats. This finding offers promise as a way to support teachers' design of learner-centered instruction that will develop HOTS and integrate technology in effective ways. For both the HOTS and LOTI levels, teachers' lesson plans rated higher when they used the indirect instruction format.

Based on the neo-Vygotskian idea of assisted performance (Tharp & Gallimore, 1988), the lesson plan format served as a type of scaffold to support teachers' planning. While the idea of having students explore concepts before explaining content to them is quite contrary to typical views of teaching, this indirect instruction lesson plan format supported teachers' planning of HOTS and higher LOTI levels than the direct instruction plan. However, prior studies found that teachers' efforts to implement learner-centered instruction have been facilitated through planning supports (Polly, 2008-b; Silver & Stein, 1996).

Limitations of the Study

The goal of this study was to provide a thorough description of one experience, in which beginning teachers created lesson plans that included both HOTS and technology. The goals of this study were not to provide generalizable findings or make universal claims about the lesson planning practices of elementary education teachers in general. That being said, this study does have limitations. Primarily, since the data source of interest were participants' lesson plans, no data was collected on participants' actual teaching practices or their beliefs about HOTS or technology use. Future studies might extend this research by collecting data from teachers' plans as well as teachers' classroom practices. Further, future research might collect pre-course work samples and examine the influence of the course on participants' planning practices.

FUTURE TRENDS

Future trends and implications based on this study have been split into sections specifically relating to practice and research. They are detailed below.

Implications for Practice

Technology integration in the context of content. In recent years, the idea of technological, pedagogical and content knowledge (TPACK) has been advanced to describe the complex knowledge associated with effective technology integration (Mishra & Koehler, 2006; Neiss, 2005; Polly & Brantley-Diaz, 2009; Polly & Mims, 2009;). The primary premise of the TPACK framework is that effective technology integration, that which develops student's higher-order thinking skills (HOTS) includes knowledge related to the content being taught, sound pedagogies, and technological knowledge.

The TPACK framework provides basis for content-specific learning opportunities for both inservice and preservice teachers. In essence, stand-alone programs that teach technological tools or research-based pedagogies without explicit connections to content are not as powerful as those opportunities that integrate knowledge of all three areas. Mishra and Koehler (2005, p. 1025) stated, "True technology integration is understanding and negotiating the relationships between these three components of knowledge." This idea of integrating technology, pedagogy and content into every learning opportunity for teachers has implications for both professional development and teacher education programs.

Professional development. Preparing inservice teachers to effectively integrate technology in ways that develop students' higher-order thinking skills (HOTS) in a way that addresses the TPACK model is not a one-size fits all model. Practicing teachers vary widely on continua of knowledge related to technology, content and pedagogy. Therefore, a prescribed or scripted professional development program will not meet the needs of all teachers compared to those programs that are more open-ended and allow for individualization.

Based on the APA *Learner-centered Principles* mentioned earlier, learner-centered approaches to professional development include activities relevant to teachers, allow teachers to have ownership of their learning, promote collaboration among teachers, and are comprehensive and ongoing as opposed to typical models of one or two-day learning opportunities (Polly, 2006; National Partnership for Excellence and Accountability for Teaching, 2000).

For professional development projects that are specifically focused on designing technology-rich instruction and that will develop students' HOTS, teachers should participate in a type of needs analysis. This process will include the examination of student learning outcomes or concepts that are troublesome to teach. After identifying these instructional problems, teachers should work with other teachers and professional developers to identify ways, including both pedagogies and technological resources that could enhance the teaching of the identified concepts. Building in its ongoing and comprehensive components, effective professional development programs would allow teachers to use their classroom as a learning laboratory to implement the planned lessons, and then reflect on the lessons by examining artifacts of practice, such as student work samples or videos of their classroom practices. This approach has been employed in various forms to support technology integration (Lawless & Pellegrino, 2007).

Teacher education. Developing preservice teachers' TPACK and capacity to integrate technology-rich tasks in ways that also build students' HOTS are different than professional development programs in a variety of ways. The most significant difference is that most preservice teachers lack the classroom experience and knowledge of pedagogies that inservice teachers have. In recent years, preservice teachers that are traditional college students (between 18 and 22 years old) are what Prensky (2001) refers to as digital natives; that is, when they attended K-12 schools, they had access to and used various educational technologies. In some cases, these digital natives have much more technological knowledge than the inservice teachers currently working in schools. In terms of content knowledge, there is no substantial difference between content known by preservice and inservice teachers.

While preservice teachers only significant deficiency to inservice teachers is pedagogical knowledge, the TPACK model accounts for preservice teachers to deepen their knowledge of pedagogy related to content, pedagogy related to technology, and lastly pedagogy related to both content and pedagogy, which is the construct of technological pedagogical and content knowledge. In that spirit, teacher education programs, like professional development programs, need to provide learning opportunities that address knowledge of all components within the TPACK model.

Schrum (1999) cited three ways that preservice teachers learn about integrating technology: the educational technology course, methods courses, and technology-rich field experiences. Out of those three opportunities, the development of preservice teachers' TPACK is largely influenced by the latter two: the methods courses and field experiences. Teacher educators who teach methods courses, such as reading education and mathematics education, must provide preservice teachers with rich experiences to learn about technology-rich activities that also develop students' HOTS. Prior studies have found that video cases of technology integration helped to provide examples of technology-rich teaching (Krueger, Boboc, Smaldino, Cornish, & Callahan, 2004).

Teacher education programs must also find effective integrators of technology in local schools to match preservice teachers up with. Faculty at the University of Nevada at Las Vegas found that despite intentions to focus on technology integration, preservice teachers did not see effective examples in their field experiences, and reported that technology integration was not an important focus of their career development (Strudler, Archambault, Bendixen, Anderson, & Weiss, 2003). A synthesis of research from the U.S. Department of Education's Preparing Tomorrow's Teachers to Teach with Technology initiative indicated that the most effective programs developed TPACK comprehensively in all three ways that Schrum discussed (Mims, Polly, Shepherd, & Inan, 2006).

Implications for Research

The current study also has implications for research in the areas of teacher learning and educational technology.

Teacher learning. Guskey (2000) calls for multi-level, multi-data evaluations of programs that provide opportunities for teacher learning. These levels include teachers' reactions to their experiences, teachers' knowledge and skills, teachers' instructional practices, influence of the program on the school and school district, and student learning outcomes. While this study provides valuable information about teachers' experiences planning technology-rich activities, future studies should build on this exploratory work by collecting multiple data sources and attempting to make connections between Guskey's various levels of evaluation.

Two connections between levels are of great interest as a follow-up to this current study. First, researchers should analyze connections between teachers' lesson plans and their instructional practices. This type of studies would provide further information to the observed disconnection between teachers' level of HOTS in their instructional objective and the narrative of the lesson plan. Second, future studies should examine the impact of teachers' instructional practices and student learning outcomes (Suppovitz, 2001). The gold standard of educational research is the empirical connection between teachers' practices and student learning outcomes (Yoon, Duncan, Lee, Scarloss, & Shapley, 2007), and future studies should strive to examine the connection between those factors.

Educational technology. Future work that builds on this study has promise to advance knowledge in the field of educational technology. While numerous studies have attempted to link technology use to student learning outcomes (Roschelle et al., 2001), few studies have examined teachers' instructional plans in relation to students' HOTS and LOTI levels. Subsequent studies should continue to develop this program of research by examining how teachers' plan to integrate technology into their classroom, how teachers actually integrate technology, and the impact of their instruction on student learning outcomes.

Along the same lines, future studies should examine how reforms in both teacher education and professional development programs influence teachers' classroom practices and student learning outcomes. Specific research on programs can advance the field by using a framework such as TPACK, and examining how to best deepen teachers' knowledge of the various TPACK components.

CONCLUSION

Technology-rich instruction must develop students' higher-order thinking skills, if technology is going to impact student learning outcomes. The findings described here indicate that beginning teachers experienced difficulty planning technology-rich lessons that rated high on both scales of HOTS and technology integration. However, the indirect instruction format for planning provided a scaffold to help students begin to incorporate more HOTS into their lessons. Future efforts in both teacher education and professional development programs should use the TPACK model as a framework to design learning opportunities that address knowledge related to technology, pedagogies and content, and the intersection of all three domains.

REFERENCES

Anderson, L. W., & Krathwohl, D. (Eds.). (2000). *A taxonomy for learning, teaching and assessing: A revision of Bloom's taxonomy of educational objectives*. New York: Longman.

Bloom, B. S., & Krathwohl, D. R. (1956). *Taxonomy of educational objectives: The classification of educational goals, by a committee of college and university examiners. Handbook I: Cognitive domain*. New York: Longmans and Green.

Bogden, R. C., & Biklen, S. K. (2003). *Qualitative research for education: An introduction to theories and methods*. Boston, MA: Allyn and Bacon.

Borko, H. (2004). Professional development and teacher learning: Mapping the terrain. *Educational Researcher, 33*(8), 3–15. doi:10.3102/0013189X033008003

Bransford, J. D., Brown, A., & Cocking, R. (Eds.). (2000). *How people learn: Mind, brain, experience and school (Expanded Edition)*. Washington, DC: National Academy Press.

Church, A. (2008). *Bloom's taxonomy, Bloom's digitally*. Retrieved April 4, 2009, from http://www.techlearning.com/article/8670

Cognition and Technology Group at Vanderbilt. (1997). *The Jasper Project: Lessons in curriculum, instruction, assessment, and professional development*. Mahwah, NJ: Erlbaum.

Cornelius-White, J. D. (2007). Learner-centered teacher-student relationships are effective: A meta-analysis. *Review of Educational Research, 77*, 113–143. doi:10.3102/003465430298563

Cornelius-White, J. H. D., & Harbaugh, A. P. (2009). *Learner-centered instruction: Building relationships for student success*. Thousand Oaks, CA: Sage.

Creswell, J. (2002). *Research design: Qualitative, quantitative and mixed methods* (2nd ed.). Thousand Oaks, CA: Sage.

Dunleavy, M., & Heinecke, W. F. (2007). The impact of 1:1 laptop use on middle school math and science standardized test scores. *Computers in the Schools, 24*, 7–22. doi:10.1300/J025v24n03_02

Elmore, R. (2002). *Bridging the gap between standards and achievement*. Washington, DC: The Albert Shanker Institute.

Fishman, B. J., Marx, R. W., Best, S., & Tal, R. T. (2003). Linking teachers and student learning to improve professional development in systemic reform. *Teaching and Teacher Education, 19*(6), 643–658. doi:10.1016/S0742-051X(03)00059-3

Friedman, T. (2005). *The world is flat: A brief history of the twenty-first century*. New York: Farrar, Straus and Giroux.

Garet, M., Porter, A., Desimone, L., Briman, B., & Yoon, K. (2001). What makes professional development effective? Analysis of a national sample of teachers. *American Educational Research Journal, 38*(4), 915–945. doi:10.3102/00028312038004915

Gladwell, M. (2002). *The tipping point: How little things can make a big difference*. New York: Back Bay.

Guba, E. G., & Lincoln, Y. S. (1994). Competing paradigms in qualitative research. In Denzin, N. K., & Lincoln, Y. S. (Eds.), *Handbook of Qualitative Research* (pp. 105–117). City.

Guskey, T. R. (2000). *Evaluating professional development*. Thousand Oaks, CA: Corwin Press.

Harel, I., & Papert, S. (Eds.). (1991). *Constructionism*. Norwood, NJ: Ablex.

Huntley, L., & Greever-Rice, T. (2007). *Analysis of 2005 MAP results for eMINTS students*. Retrieved June 27, 2009, from http://www.emints.org/evaluation/reports/

International Society for Technology in Education. (2008). *Technology and student achievement: The indelible link*. Retrieved June 28, 2009, from http://www.iste.org/Content/ NavigationMenu/Advocacy/Policy/59.08-PolicyBrief-F-web.pdf

Jonassen, D. H., & Reeves, T. C. (1996). Learning with technology: Using computers as cognitive tools. In Jonassen, D. H. (Ed.), *Handbook of research on educational communications and technology* (pp. 693–719). New York: Macmillan.

Kafai, Y., & Resnick, M. (Eds.). (1996). *Constructionism in practice: Designing, thinking, and learning in a digital world*. Mahwah, NJ: Erlbaum.

Knezek, G., & Christensen, R. (2007). Effect of technology-based programs on first- and second-grade reading achievement. *Computers in the Schools, 24*, 23–41. doi:10.1300/J025v24n03_03

Krueger, K., Boboc, M., Smaldino, S., Cornish, Y., & Callahan, W. (2004). InTime impact report: What was InTime's effectiveness and impact on faculty and preservice teachers? *Journal of Technology and Teacher Education, 12*(2), 185–210.

Lawless, K. A., & Pellegrino, J. W. (2007). Professional development in integrating technology into teaching and learning: Knowns, unknowns, and ways to pursue better questions and answers. *Review of Educational Research, 77*(4), 575–614. doi:10.3102/0034654307309921

Mann, D., Shakeshaft, C., Becker, J., & Kottkamp, R. (1999). *West Virginia's basic skills/computer education program: An analysis of student achievement*. Santa Monica, CA: Milken Family Foundation.

Marzano, R. J., Brandt, R. S., Hughese, C. S., Jones, B. F., Presseisen, B. Z., Stuart, C., & Shhor, C. (1988). *Dimensions of Thinking*. Alexandria, VA: Association for Supervision and Curriculum Development.

McCombs, B. L. (2003). A framework for the redesign of K-12 education in the context of current educational reform. *Theory into Practice, 42*(2), 163–167. doi:10.1207/s15430421tip4202_2

McCombs, B. L., & Whisler, J. S. (1997). *The learner-centered classroom and school: Strategies for increasing student motivation and achievement*. San Francisco: Jossey-Bass.

Means, B. (1994). *Technology and education reform*. San Francisco: Jossey-Bass.

Mims, C., Polly, D., Shepherd, C., & Inan, F. (2006). Examining PT3 projects designed to improve preservice education. *TechTrends, 50*(3), 17–24. doi:10.1007/s11528-006-7599-5

Mishra, P., & Koehler, M. J. (2006). Technological Pedagogical Content Knowledge: A framework for teacher knowledge. *Teachers College Record, 108*(6), 1017–1054. doi:10.1111/j.1467-9620.2006.00684.x

Moersch, C. (2001). Next steps: Using LOTI as a research tool. *Learning and Leading with Technology, 29*(3), 22–26.

National Partnership for Excellence and Accountability in Teaching (NPEAT). (2000). *Revisioning professional development: What learner-centered professional development looks like*. Oxford, OH: Author. Retrieved April 4, 2009, from http://www.nsdc.org/library/policy/npeat213.pdfNiess, M. L. (2005). Preparing teachers to teach science and mathematics with technology: Developing a technology pedagogical content knowledge. *Teaching and Teacher Education, 21*, 509-523.

Orrill, C. H. (2001). Building learner-centered classrooms: A professional development framework for supporting critical thinking. *Educational Technology Research and Development, 49*(1), 15–34. doi:10.1007/BF02504504

Penuel, W., Fishman, B., Yamaguchi, R., & Gallagher, L. (2007). What makes professional development effective? Strategies that foster curriculum implementation. *American Educational Research Journal, 44*(4), 921–958. doi:10.3102/0002831207308221

Peterson, P. L. (1990). Doing more of the same: Cathy Swift. *Educational Evaluation and Policy Analysis, 12*(3), 261–280.

Polly, D. (2006). *Examining the influence of learner-centered professional development on elementary mathematics teachers instructional practices, espoused practices, and evidence of student learning*. Unpublished Doctoral Dissertation, University of Georgia, Athens, GA.
Polly, D. (2008-a). Modeling the influence of calculator use and teacher effects on first grade students' mathematics achievement. *Journal of Technology in Mathematics and Science Teaching, 27*(3), 245-263.

Polly, D. (2008, Month day). Supporting standards-based mathematics in elementary classrooms. Paper presented at the Annual Conference of the School Science and Mathematics Association, Raleigh, NC.

Polly, D., & Ausband, L. (in press). Developing higher order thinking skills through WebQuests. *Journal of Computing in Teacher Education*.

Polly, D., & Brantley-Dias, L. (2009). TPACK: Where do we go now? *TechTrends*, *53*(5), 46–47. doi:10.1007/s11528-009-0324-4

Polly, D., & Mims, C. (2009). Designing professional development to support teachers' TPACK and integration of Web 2.0 technologies. In Kidd, T. T., & Chen, I. (Eds.), *Wired for Learning: Web 2.0 Guide for Educators* (pp. 301–316). City.

Prensky, M. (2001). Digital natives, digital immigrants. *Horizon*, *9*(5), 1–6. doi:10.1108/10748120110424816

Richardson, V. (1990). Significant and worthwhile change in teaching practice. *Educational Researcher*, *19*, 10–18.

Ringstaff, C., & Kelley, L. (2002). *The learning return on our educational technology investment*. San Francisco: WestEd.

Roschelle, J., Pea, R., Hoadley, C., Gordin, D., & Means, B. (2001). Changing how and what children learn in schools with computer-based technologies. *The Future of Children*, *10*(2), 76–101. doi:10.2307/1602690

Schacter, J. (1999). *The impact of education technology on student achievement: What the most current research has to say*. Santa Monica, CA: Milken Exchange on Education Technology.

Schneider, R. M., Krajcik, J., & Blumenfeld, P. (2005). Enacting reform-based science materials: The range of teacher enactments in reform classrooms. *Journal of Research in Science Education*, *42*(3), 283–312.

Schrum, L. (1999). Technology professional development for teachers. *Educational Technology Research and Development*, *47*(4), 83–90. doi:10.1007/BF02299599

Silver, E. A., & Stein, M. K. (1996). The QUASAR project: The "revolution of the possible" in mathematics instructional reform in urban middle schools. *Urban Education*, *30*(4), 476–521. doi:10.1177/0042085996030004006

Stein, M. K., Grover, B. W., & Henningsen, M. (1996). Building student capacity for mathematical thinking and reasoning: An analysis of mathematical tasks used in reform classrooms. *American Educational Research Journal*, *33*, 455–488.

Strudler, N., Archambault, L., Bendixen, L., Anderson, D., & Weiss, R. (2003). Project THREAD: Technology helping restructure educational access and delivery. *Educational Technology Research and Development*, *51*(3), 41–56. doi:10.1007/BF02504517

Supovitz, J. A. (2001). Translating teaching practice into improved student achievement. In Fuhrman, S. (Ed.), *National Society for the Study of Education Yearbook*. Chicago, IL: University of Chicago Press.

Tharp, R., & Gallimore, R. (1988). *Rousing minds to life: Teaching, learning, and schooling in social context*. New York: Cambridge University Press.

U.S. Department of Education. (2004). Toward a new golden age in American education--How the internet, the law and today's students are revolutionizing expectations: National Educational Technology Plan. Retrieved June 28, 2009, from http://www.ed.gov/about/offices/list/os/technology/plan/2004/plan.pdf

Wenglinsky, H. (1998). Does it compute? The relationship between educational technology and student achievement in mathematics. *Educational Testing Service Policy Information Center*. Retrieved June 25, 2009, from www.mff.org/pubs/ME161.pdf

Work, A. P. A. Group of the Board of Educational Affairs (1997). *Learner-centered psychological principles: A framework for school reform and redesign*. Washington, DC: Author.

Yoon, K. S., Duncan, T., Lee, S. W. Y., Scarloss, B., & Shapley, K. (2007). *Reviewing the evidence on how teacher professional development affects student achievement* (Issues & Answers Report, REL 2007–No. 033). Washington, DC: U.S. Department of Education, Institute of Education Sciences, National Center for Education Evaluation and Regional Assistance, Regional Educational Laboratory Southwest. Retrieved December 31, 2008, from: http://ies.ed.gov/ncee/edlabs

KEY TERMS AND DEFINITIONS

Bloom's Taxonomy: A framework to describe students' actions based on the level of cognitive demand published by Bloom and his colleagues in 1956.

Direct Instruction: A format for planning lessons that promotes the direct teaching of information. The plan includes the phases Focus/Review, Teacher Input, Guided Practice, Independent Practice and Closure.

Indirect Instruction: A format for planning lessons that promotes students' discovery of information. The plan includes the phases Engage, Explore, Explain, Elaborate and Evaluate.

Learner-centered Principles: Fourteen research-based principles developed in 1997 by a task force of the American Psychological Association.

Level of Technology Integration: A framework developed by Moersch in 2001 to describe how technology is integrated into K-12 schools.

Revised Bloom's Taxonomy: A revision of the original Bloom's Taxonomy published by Anderson and Krathwohl in 2000.

Technological Pedagogical and Content Knowledge (TPACK): A framework developed by Mishra and Koehler in 2006, based off of earlier work (Neiss, 2005) that associates technology integration with knowing about technology, pedagogies and content, and the intersection of those three components.

Chapter 24
Developing an Online Mentoring Program for Beginning Teachers

Nancy K. Gagen Clouse
University of Montana, USA

Sandra R. Williams
University of Montana, USA

Roberta D. Evans
University of Montana, USA

ABSTRACT

If schools are to retain well-qualified and much needed new teachers, it is important that teachers are provided a variety of resources for helping them through the transition from pre-service education to the classroom. An electronic mentoring program that provides school administrators and teachers a connection to a wide spectrum of professional contacts without the constraints of time and distance can be a valuable tool for the retention and professional development of this precious human resource. The leadership role for an electronic mentoring program calls for a unique combination of in-depth knowledge of the developmental needs of beginning teachers, a plan for development of an online program based on knowledge of the necessary program components, an understanding of professional development and adult learning, skills to effectively communicate online, and the ability to work in a collaborative, facilitative, and ever-changing environment.

INTRODUCTION

This chapter focuses on the program development of an innovative approach to mentoring, known as online or electronic mentoring, to assist beginning teachers during the transition into the classroom. Online mentoring is a fairly new concept, particularly as a support for beginning teachers, and little research that has been done in this area, especially in regard to program administration and leadership issues. It is also a concept that meets resistance among many educators, who believe that mentoring requires a more personal, face-to-face approach to be effective. This chapter will discuss the findings of a study entitled *The Leadership Role in Online Support Programs for Beginning Teachers* (Clouse, 2008). This study examined both the program development and

DOI: 10.4018/978-1-61692-854-4.ch024

leadership strategies involved in the administration of online mentoring programs for beginning teachers. The methodology used a qualitative research design employing an inductive process to develop a grounded theory. Data, gathered via telephone interviews with administrators of past and present electronic support programs for new teachers, were coded to identify, organize, and relate categories and themes. From the emerging themes, propositions were formulated to support a grounded theory of leadership for the administration of electronic support programs for new teachers.

The objectives of the chapter are to present the issues related to the development of these types of mentoring programs, the leadership strategies involved, as well as challenges, successes and advice of program administrators who developed and implemented online mentoring programs. This information can be helpful to educational leaders involved with mentoring and the professional development of both beginning and veteran teachers, by providing insight into an alternative approach to support such efforts.

BACKGROUND

Since the early 1990s, the annual number of teachers leaving the profession has surpassed the number of those entering by an increasing amount (Darling-Hammond, 2003). Teacher attrition, which is particularly high among teachers in their first few years of service, is the primary problem. Data suggest that 40 to 50% of all beginning teachers exit the profession within the first five years. Not only are there high costs associated with teacher exits, high turnover of teachers causes staffing problems due to the lack of commitment, continuity, and cohesion among employees. Consequently, this can adversely affect school environment and student performance (Ingersoll & Smith, 2003).

There is an emerging consensus among educators and policymakers that the retention of new teachers is dependent on effective mentoring and induction programs (Feiman-Nemser, 2003). However, not all school districts have the resources to establish formal mentoring programs, particularly smaller districts in rural areas. This calls for alternative forms of induction and mentoring support. An alternative kind of mentoring, called electronic mentoring, could help school districts provide their teachers the benefits of mentoring despite their lack of resources. Electronic mentoring or e-mentoring uses electronic communications, such as e-mail and online discussion groups, to connect mentors with protégées without constraints of time or place (Single & Muller, 2003). A well-structured electronic mentoring program could serve a relatively large number of teachers and sites and provide needed support to beginning teachers in districts that are unable to provide adequate on-site mentoring.

The research study entitled *The Leadership Role in Online Support Programs for Beginning Teachers* (Clouse, 2008) explored this innovative approach of electronic or online mentoring to help beginning teachers with the transition into the classroom. Many of these programs have shown encouraging reports of satisfaction by program participants and possible support in retention efforts (Merseth, 1990; Redmond, 2002; Johnson, Clift, & Klecka, 2002; Abbott, 2003). However, e-mentoring is not quite as simple to implement as it may seem (Harris, O'Bryan, & Rotenberg, 1996; Johnson et al., 2002). E-mentoring is a fairly new concept, particularly as a support for beginning teachers; and there is limited research in this area, especially in regard to program administration and leadership issues. Clouse's (2008) study examined how organizations developed and administered these kinds of online support programs for new teachers and explored the leadership traits of administrators of these programs. This study investigated these programs from the perspective of the program administrators to uncover the challenges and successes they experienced during the development and implementation of their e-mentoring programs.

The literature pertaining to online mentoring programs is still rather limited and the research for online support programs for new teachers is even more so. Much of the literature discussed next is garnered from research on face-to-face mentoring and online mentoring in a variety of areas including business, industry, and education. As such, most of the information providing a context for online mentoring comes from a wide variety of areas including new teacher needs, mentor program development, technology and online communications, professional development, adult learning, change, and leadership theory.

New Teacher Needs

To properly address how to support new teachers through the transition from pre-service to in-service teaching, educational leaders must recognize the needs of new teachers. Research indicates that the major concerns of most new teachers include classroom management, student motivation, meeting individual student needs, assessment and evaluation of learning, and working effectively with parents (Britton, Paine, & Raizen, 1999; Kurtz, 1983; Veenman, 1984). The first years of teaching should be viewed as a phase in learning to teach, and new teachers must be surrounded by a professional culture that supports teacher learning (Feiman-Nemser, 2003). A new teacher induction program that focuses on teacher training, support, and retention is the best way to support, develop, and cultivate an attitude of lifelong learning in beginning teachers (Breaux & Wong, 2003). Studies show that induction and mentoring programs can be particularly effective in the retention of beginning teachers after their first year (Ingersoll & Smith, 2003). The benefits of mentoring include: (a) acclimation of faculty to the school culture, (b) enhancement of effective teaching, (c) increased job satisfaction, (d) vitality, (e) scholarly productivity, (f) collegiality, and (g) retention (Cunningham, 1999). Clearly, induction programs are a wise investment in the ongoing training, support, and retention of beginning teachers. Unfortunately, many schools do not have the financial or personnel resources to provide effective induction and mentoring support to their new faculty. There is a need for alternative approaches to accommodate those teachers who do not find the support they need in their local communities. This is when the use of an online mentoring program might be considered to provide this much needed support.

Benefits of Online Mentoring Programs

Using electronic communications within an online support program provides a flexible, asynchronous environment that is independent of time and place, so schedules and geographic locations do not dictate meetings (Single & Muller, 2001). Research supports that many of the benefits associated with face-to-face mentoring are also provided with e-mentoring (Kram, 1983; Scandura & Williams, 2001); yet the benefits of e-mentoring can go beyond those of face-to-face mentoring. These benefits may include (a) the development of more open and supportive relationships because the difference between higher and lower status is concealed; (b) more time to compose thoughtfully written messages (Single & Muller, 2001); (c) the opportunity to learn from outside of familiar networks, affording one access to varied information (Single & Single, 2004); (d) impartial mentors who are not in a position to assess or judge, allowing for more trusted and open mentoring relationships (Boyle & Boice, 1998; Diehl & Simpson, 1989; Hew & Knapczyk, 2007; Single, P. B., Muller, Cunningham, Single, R. M., Carlson, 2003); (e) discussions that offer personal and emotional support and reduced feelings of isolation (Merseth, 1990); and (f) development of both subject matter and technology skills, as well as a connection to the professional community (Redmond, 2002). Electronic mentoring does have some unique challenges, however, particularly in relation to the use of online communications. In order to sustain participation, mentors and protégés need to have a feeling of safety and trust in their online interactions. Any breach in trust and confidence of the security of the online environment will most likely reduce participation (Cheng, Clift, & Klecka, 2003).

Developing Online Mentoring Programs

The program development of an electronic mentoring program includes planning, recruitment, matching, orientation and training, coaching, and evaluation. Program planning requires the development of clearly articulated goals and anticipated outcomes (Single & Muller, 2001). Recruitment of both mentors and mentees is a critical part of a mentoring program; participants may be recruited online as well as in person (Single & Muller, 2001). Matching strategies might utilize assigned matches generated from database records or allow participant choice based on personality profiles (Single & Muller, 2001).

Orientation and training within an e-mentoring program needs to provide an overview of the program, clarify the roles of the participants—including responsibilities and expectations of their participation—and discuss how to handle a variety of situations (MENTOR, 2002). Training occurs at the onset of the mentoring program and usually focuses on mentors, but can include mentees. Coaching occurs throughout the electronic mentoring program and includes discussion topics and mentoring tips. This can be delivered face-to-face or online for both mentors and mentees (Single & Muller, 2001). Research suggests that regular contact between program staff and participants motivates and encourages participants to stay involved with the program (Boyle & Boice, 1998). To ensure quality and effectiveness, a program evaluation plan that measures program progress and expected outcomes needs to be developed and should include a plan for reflection and dissemination of findings (MENTOR, 2003).

Professional Development and Adult Learning Theory

Professional development should be viewed as a process of change and needs to include strategies that will facilitate the success of the staff development effort (Southwest Educational Development Laboratory, 1994). Providing staff development that is user-driven is consistently recommended when designing professional development programs (Guskey, 1994; Lawrence, 1974; Orlich, 1989). In addition, an understanding of adult learning theory is important in the knowledge base for designing professional development. Professional development leaders need to recognize and address a variety of adult learning styles in regard to the services provided to both new teachers and mentors. Programs should provide professional development opportunities that give participants choices, provide practical and immediately applicable information, and allow self-direction, collaboration, and reflection (Brookfield, 1986; Cranton, 1994; Knowles, 1980, 1984; Mezirow, 1981, 1990).

Building Online Relationships

Building distance relationships presents special challenges to online mentoring partners. Once a connection is made, a relationship needs to be formed, and common ground must be established. From this, common understandings then flow, which become the basis of the relationship. Mentoring relationships are embedded in context; therefore, mentoring partners must communicate expectations and establish processes and ground rules that will work in the context of their relationship (Zachary, 2000). Communication via electronic mail differs from other forms of interchange because it is primarily text-based, asynchronous, and includes participants who are often widely geographically dispersed. Because it lacks the full range of audible and visual information of face-to-face exchanges, it requires different strategies for interaction to realize maximum benefits. Two strategies to address these barriers include establishing a regular "rhythm" of exchanging messages to maintain a two-way flow of conversation and providing a balance of shared academic and personal information (Harris et al., 1996). In addition to one-on-one communications, the use of electronic versions of group meetings can provide a sense of involvement and opportunities for discussion topics, advice, and additional points of view (Single & Muller, 2001). This community building helps develop a sense of belonging among participants by providing opportunities for interactions outside of the one-on-one mentoring. These opportunities seem to increase participant involvement with the program as well as involvement within their organization or field (Headlam-Wells, Gosland, & Craig, 2006; Single & Single, 2004).

Leadership Theories Related to Program Development

An understanding of various leadership theories and characteristics helps in identifying one's style of leadership. A number of leadership theories may be foundational in identifying the leadership styles of those who administer electronic mentoring programs. These theories include a collaborative style in which leaders delegate authority, support subordinates to develop ideas and decision-making skills, and function as a team (McGregor, 1960). Also relevant is a transformational leadership style (Burns, 1978; Leithwood, Steinback, & Raun, 1993) in which leaders help team members develop a collaborative culture, problem solve together, foster staff development, map new directions for the program, and respond to organizational change. Program leaders may also identify the need to use reflective practice (Schön, 1983; Sergiovanni, 1991) by researching, experimenting, and sharing insights throughout the process of directing their programs. A facilitative leadership style (Hord, 1992) sees program leaders in a role to move their programs forward by guiding and supporting their team members. The ability to be flexible and modify their leadership style according to various situations (Hersey & Blanchard, 1977, 1982) may also identify program leaders. Because it often defies the traditional paradigm, implementing an innovative program such as online mentoring, can be challenging. Therefore, an understanding of the change process is important to help in the facilitation of program development and administration. Some of the aspects of this process are (a) including others in the formation of the vision; (b) allowing those involved to work out their own meaning and form a position; (c) realizing conflict is inevitable; (d) accepting that change takes time; (e) understanding there are many reasons for lack of implementation; (f) having a plan to affect implementation; and (g) not expecting everyone to change (Fullan, 1991).

LEADERSHIP FOR ONLINE MENTORING PROGRAMS

The leadership role for an online mentoring program requires a combination of specific skills, knowledge, and experience to oversee such an innovative support program. Analysis of the data collected from the semi-structured interviews of Clouse's (2008) study revealed interrelationships between five subcategories: (a) Needs and Benefits of Participants, (b) Program Development, (c) Professional Development, (d) Technology Considerations, and (e) Leadership Strategies. These subcategories are further described below within the context of past and current online mentoring programs.

Needs and Benefits of Participants

Online mentoring programs must try to address the needs of new teachers, the mentors, and the institutions they serve. These needs occur at many levels of development for these participants. Benefits are realized in a variety of ways and in a variety of degrees for each of these different program participants.

New Teachers

Leaders of online support programs for beginning teachers try to address the pedagogical, emotional, social, and programmatic needs of new teachers. Programs are designed to provide online support in the pedagogical areas of classroom management, content, methodology, standards, cyclical issues, and reflective practice. New teachers are given emotional support by providing an empathetic and encouraging environment to build confidence and empower them to problem solve, as well as develop leadership skills. Program leaders seek to provide social support to new teachers by reducing feelings of isolation and building their pool of resources by connecting them with other new teachers, experienced teachers, and education and research professionals. By providing these connections outside of their classrooms, the programs can provide new teachers another perspective of their teaching environment and situations. Leaders build programmatic support into the online programs by providing services based on not only what they anticipate to be new teachers' needs, but what participants actually request. These services include (a) program flexibility that constantly adjusts to changing needs of participants; (b) 24/7 access to resources; (c) anonymity of participants; (d) a non-evaluative, confidential, and secured environment; (e) resources specific to a particular site; and (f) technical assistance in using the online environment.

Mentors

Program leaders support the mentors of these online programs by providing the opportunity for them to (a) reflect on their practice; (b) make new connections to a broader professional community; (c) give back to the profession; and (d) experience professional and personal growth by participating in this new approach to mentoring. Program leaders also find they need to address the times when mentors experience frustration and apprehension with using a non-face-to-face mentoring program. Leaders need to assist mentors through issues regarding using the technology and address their resistance and encourage their adaption to a new method of mentoring.

Institutions

Schools participating in these online support programs also benefit from the professional growth and leadership development of their new teachers and mentors. Program leaders anticipate involvement in these online support programs can benefit the institutions by providing opportunities for leadership development and grant acquisition, increased retention of new and experienced teachers, and the eventual trickle-down effect of improved student achievement. Some programs report their schools have seen improvements in teacher retention that may be connected to participation in the online programs. It is the hope of program leaders that these programs can make a difference in the retention efforts of their new teachers and, eventually, student achievement. For the present, however, program leaders are encouraged by the comments received from many of their new teacher participants expressing how valuable this support is to them.

Program Development

It is important to articulate the organization's needs and goals for an online support program. Careful planning in the design and development of the program is imperative, including researching other similar programs. Areas of development include initial and ongoing program planning, services to offer, selection of personnel, recruitment of participants, matching mentors and mentees, training of participants, program evaluation, and funding.

Planning

The leaders of online support programs develop and implement these programs to try to meet the needs of new teachers in an effort to (a) increase teacher retention; (b) address teacher shortages in high demand content areas; (c) provide continuing support to graduates of teacher education programs; (d) meet an induction program mandate; and (e) fulfill a personal commitment to help new teachers. Program leaders use a highly collaborative approach in the planning and development of their programs and integrate best practices of other online and face-to-face mentoring programs by researching what other programs have done. Those looking to develop a program might consider a blended model that utilizes both face-to-face and online support. Many program leaders establish an advisory committee in an effort to get input from a variety of stakeholders to help guide their decision making. Leaders emphasize the importance of defining the purpose of the program, articulating the program goals, carefully designing a plan to reach those goals, and developing an evaluation strategy. They also caution that, as in most new program implementation, even with careful planning there will always be unanticipated problems and a need to make changes accordingly.

Services

Leaders structure their programs to provide a variety of services for participants. Online services provided by these programs often include (a) one-to-one communications; (b) group communications via discussion areas (asynchronous) and live chats (synchronous); (c) content area resources; (d) pedagogical resources; (e) frequently asked questions; (f) instructional modules; (g) lesson plan builders; (h) document share ability; and (i) links to district policies, state standards, and credentialing information. Programs may be structured as one-to-one mentoring or group mentoring and may serve new and pre-service teachers from local areas, nationally, and even internationally. The length of time that support is provided can vary from the first year up until the fifth year of teaching. Programs need to be structured to provide a confidential and safe online environment that does not allow access by school administrators or the general public.

Personnel

Programs may range anywhere from one to a team of people to administer the operations such as recruitment, training, facilitation, and technology. Depending on the size of the program, the program administrator may have some of these specific responsibilities in addition to overseeing the overall functioning of the program. Many program leaders believe it would be very difficult for an online support program to be run by one individual; they posit that a collaborative team effort is the best model. Leaders emphasize the importance of finding the right people to work in this kind of program: those who have a broad range of educational backgrounds and are dedicated to supporting new teachers.

Recruiting

Program leaders generally recruit mentors on a volunteer basis and select them based on their qualifications of excellent teaching and a desire to mentor new teachers. Mentors are often paid a stipend. Mentees are also recruited on a mostly volunteer basis and are either new teachers of a school district served by an online program or graduates or pre-service students of a teacher education program that provides this service. Mentees are sometimes given a monetary stipend for participation, although other incentives are often available such as continuing education credits, advanced certification, and use of equipment for connectivity. The degree of participation is primarily mentee-driven on an as-needed basis. Some programs, however, request a minimum requirement for participation, such as a weekly or monthly communication.

Matching Strategies

Programs use a variety of matching strategies based on the mentoring structure, the parameters of the program, the availability of mentors, and the needs of the mentees. Programs might use one-to-one matches, one-to-several (perhaps 2-6 mentees), or group mentoring, with one mentor having up to 20 mentees. Some programs assign mentees to mentors, while other programs allow mentees to self-select their mentor or group. Programs might provide personality and professional profiles of mentors to help in the self-selection process; there are software programs available to assist with this task. Much of the matching is usually according to grade level or content area. Program leaders whose programs assign matches believe they can make very good choices for mentees based on requests made by the mentees. On the other hand, leaders of programs that provide self-selection of mentors or mentor groups find they provide mentees an important opportunity to make a choice that meets their own individual needs.

Training

Programs need to define roles and expectations and provide participants training specific to their role in the program. Program leaders emphasize the importance of basing the training on feedback from participants who indicate what they need and when. Training common to all participants usually includes: (a) guidelines of the online mentoring program; (b) use of the technology specific to the program (i.e., e-mail, discussion board, website navigation); (c) e-mail etiquette; and (d) building online relationships. Training specific to mentors may include: (a) being a mentor; (b) the nature of the new teacher; (c) teacher socialization; (d) teacher development and leadership; (e) peer coaching; and (f) questioning strategies. Training provided to mentees may include: (a) classroom management; (b) organizing the classroom; (c) literacy issues; and (d) how to be mentored. Training may be face-to-face, online, or a combination of both depending on the resources of the program and the needs of the participants. Many program leaders believe that training on an as-needed basis is a more productive approach and less demanding on the busy schedules of mentors and new teachers.

Program Evaluation

Formative data is used to make ongoing adjustments to the program to better meet participant needs. Most program leaders believe that participants' satisfaction with the support they receive from the program is the most important indicator of program success. Programs need to collect data on retention of their participants in the teaching profession, particularly if new teacher retention is a goal of the program. Programs that have retention data have reported some increases in retention of new teachers, but program leaders are not yet confident in directly linking participation in the online support to the increase in retention—although they see it as a possible contributing factor. Most programs do not yet track connections to improved teacher efficacy and student achievement due to participation in an online support program; but leaders realize this is another outcome they need to eventually track to validate continued funding. Program leaders usually need to provide reports on the progress and evaluations of their programs to their funding sources. By sharing their experiences regarding their online support programs in published journal articles and presentations at professional conferences, program administrators can help build networks with other mentoring programs and provide valuable professional development for those involved in administering these unique mentoring initiatives.

Funding

Program leaders find they need to seek funding from multiple sources, both internal and external, and the search for continued funding is an ongoing challenge. Funding most often comes from grants and foundations, but some may come from the institutions or state funds. Leaders see the potential of online support as an extension of traditional induction for school districts and an opportunity to provide outreach to graduates of teacher education programs. As such, perhaps in the future more consistent funding can be secured for these programs as part of overall new teacher support systems.

Professional Development

Online support programs can provide a variety of professional development opportunities for new teachers. Many programs offer other services beyond the online environment including face-to-face mentoring and site-based workshops. Most new teachers who use online mentoring use it as a supplement to the other supports they have available. However, some programs in Clouse's (2008) study reported that some of their new teachers had only the online mentoring as their support or often stated this was their most important support. Some programs are also designed to meet a mandate or standard for new teacher induction or offer the ability for participants to earn credits toward advanced certification or credentialing, providing the type of advancement often desired through professional development opportunities.

Participation in an online support program is usually on a voluntary basis and usually there is some choice of when and how often participants engage in online activities. This provides participants the flexibility of time and place and choices in the level and type of services in which they can engage. Programs generally take requests and make changes to their programs as a result of teacher input regarding content and delivery. This provides participants a sense of ownership in the programs since their input is requested and used to improve program services. Such approaches demonstrate best practices of professional development by providing participants choices in the type of support they believe they need (Guskey, 1994; Lawrence, 1974; Orlich, 1989).

Online mentoring programs address a variety of adult learning styles and principles including self-directed learning, collaboration, practical application of useable knowledge, problem-solving, and reflective practice (Brookfield, 1986; Cranton, 1994; Knowles, 1980, 1984; Mezirow, 1981, 1990). Although online support can meet many learning styles, not all participants find their needs met and some may believe it lacks a human or personal connection. Some participants may be very comfortable with the technology of an online support system, while others may be afraid, resistant, or even resentful of it.

Technology Considerations

Access to the Internet is a critical requirement for participants since they use either e-mail or online discussions and, oftentimes both, for their online communication. Programs may provide asynchronous and/or synchronous discussions for group support and as a means to model appropriate online support behavior. Video conferencing can provide another option for both communication and training sessions. Programs may provide hardware to the participants or require them to have their own computers and access to the Internet. Technical assistance should be made available to participants, either from the staff of the online support program or combined with technical support from the participant's site. Online support programs need to utilize software that supports the services their programs offer. Software may be commercially available (i.e., course management systems such as Blackboard) or may include programs that are customized for a particular online support system. It is also important to provide instructional and other professional resources online so that participants have easy 24/7 access to these resources.

Those looking to offer an online mentoring program must realize the need for specific skills in developing supportive relationships online. These skills combine methods used in a face-to-face setting as well as methods that help to overcome the sometimes impersonal nature or limited abilities of online communications. These skills include (a) using a tone within the communications that conveys genuine interest and understanding; (b) being responsive in a timely manner; (c) providing guidance to help mentees realize their own solutions; (d) recognizing when a direct suggestion is needed; and (e) providing a balance of academic and personal information sharing. Leaders of these programs believe that online communication has the potential to create a sense of community among people who would otherwise not be able to meet due to time and distance issues. They find, however, that just getting people together online is not enough and advise that these relationships need to be developed and tended to build trusting, meaningful bonds. Therefore, facilitators play a key role in the success of the online communications by feeding questions, promptly responding to inquiries, and maintaining open lines of discussion among participants. Leaders realize that they, too, need to provide the necessary leadership and guidance to help their participants realize the potential of an online professional learning community.

Leadership Strategies

There are a number of leadership issues to consider throughout the development and implementation of an online mentoring program. Program administrators find that specific knowledge, skills, and styles are instrumental in providing leadership for these programs. As with any innovative program, there are a number of challenges to address and the need to guide participants through a new way of doing business requires the ability to facilitate change.

Program Leadership Skills

Important skills and knowledge of program leaders include experience as a classroom teacher, understanding new teacher needs, and knowledge of mentoring and professional development. These leaders need to have an understanding of the unique experience of the first years of teaching and must recognize the many challenges of the beginning teacher. Program leaders must also have the willingness to acquire new knowledge necessary to work in an innovative and developing program such as online mentoring. These leaders need to have the ability and willingness to effectively use technology in online communications. They must be very organized, detail-oriented, open to new ideas, flexible, and continuously responsive to the challenge of meeting the needs of program participants. Leaders also need to remember to have considerable patience to give the program time to evolve.

Leadership Styles

The leadership style that program administrators most identify with is a collaborative, team-building approach that empowers members to do their jobs. Yet, leaders must still stay informed and be involved. The importance of listening, reflecting, and responding to program participants—characteristic of reflective practice—is also important for program leaders. They need to be able to move their organization forward through the change process by providing assistance in implementation through building capacity and empowerment among members. Program leaders need to be able to respond to change by being open to new ideas and flexible with requests of the various stakeholders involved in the program in an effort to best meet the needs of its constituents. They can help program participants and personnel adjust to the idea of this new method of mentoring by modeling supportive behavior, both online and face-to-face, and continually advocating for the program. Program leaders are advised to get support from the top of their organization, but plan from the bottom to establish buy-in and a sense of ownership among those involved.

Program Challenges

There are a number of current and future challenges with these online support programs such as engaging participants, promptly responding to constantly changing needs, scaling up, and securing funding. Leaders need to continue to consider ways to reliably assess and evaluate whether these online support efforts are making a difference in teacher effectiveness, retention, and student achievement. Program leaders must realize that in order to improve and expand future services they need to seek continued funding. However, the ability to sustain the programs and funding are also going to depend upon their ability to show that these programs are providing positive results in teaching and learning.

FUTURE RESEARCH DIRECTIONS

Based on the findings of Clouse's (2008) study, there are a number of implications for the future of online mentoring programs for beginning teachers and areas that call for further research. These implications include those for practitioners working in the area of new teacher support and implications for future studies regarding specific areas of online support for new teachers.

Implications for Practitioners

Research findings presented in this chapter have a number of implications for those practicing in the area of new teacher support. These may include school administrators, teacher mentors, the new teachers themselves, and those within higher education in the field of teacher preparation. These findings are twofold: (a) providing a broad view of how online support programs for beginning teachers are developed, administered, and sustained, and (b) describing the leadership styles and challenges of overseeing such programs. School administrators might consider this kind of program as a relatively economical way to provide quality induction support to a large number of teachers over a wide geographical area. Teacher mentors and new teachers may see this as a convenient and flexible support system that provides confidential, practical support on an as-needed basis. Those working in higher education may find an online support program a practical way to provide outreach for graduates of their teacher education programs. Although these programs may appear simple enough to develop and even seem to provide "one-stop shopping" for anytime support for new teachers, it is clear that there are a number of issues and challenges that practitioners must heed when considering this type of venture. These challenges include the logistics of the type of services to provide, time commitments of all parties involved, maintaining participation, funding, and ultimately improving teacher retention.

These online programs show considerable promise for providing support to new teachers as well as establishing online learning communities of practice for all education professionals. However, they must be carefully developed and tended, just as any mentoring relationship. The advice given by a number of program administrators was to bc patient with the development and progress of the program. Any new idea takes time to process—time to catch on. One program leader emphasized that it is important to have the vision, but realize that it does take time build an effective and well-utilized program.

Implications for Future Studies

The use of online support systems or electronic mentoring is a fairly new idea in the area of beginning teacher support. Programs are not highly visible, nor easy to find. The research and subsequent publications on these specific types of online programs is rather limited, although the interest in them appears to be growing. Clouse's (2008) study found that those working with these programs are very curious about what others are doing and anxious to find ways to collaborate and network with one another. Based on the findings within that study, the following are areas that are particularly lacking in information and further research would help others who are considering implementing an online support program.

Requirements for Participant Online Engagement

Setting specific requirements for participants to engage online was an issue of debate for some participants in Clouse's (2008) study. Some programs believed that participants should have the choice of participating only when they needed help, while other programs required participants to engage in online communications a certain number of times per week, month, etc. The question that emerged from this discussion was whether evaluations were indicating a true measure of useful engagement because participants were getting online when they felt they needed the support or because they needed to fulfill a program requirement for participation. An examination of the satisfaction levels of those who have requirements versus those who do not, to see if there is any difference in participants' perceived value of the online support experience, would shed some light on this debate.

Technology for Online Support Systems

There are many online communications systems and software programs available that can support the technological requirements of an online mentoring program. Some software is available commercially and widely used, such as Blackboard and TaskStream. Membership to online learning communities, such as Tapped In, can provide a means to host an online mentoring program and provide the technical support many districts lack. However, the cost of some of these memberships can be significant. Some programs have been developed specifically for a particular e-mentoring program and use open source coding to make it customized to the user's needs. Moodle, a free, open source program could be another option to deliver an online support program. A study examining the various technologies online support programs have used, including features, costs, pros and cons would be helpful to those looking to make decisions regarding the technology for their programs, whether starting a new program or updating a current one.

The Role of the Facilitator

Although many involved with online support programs indicated that facilitation of the online communications is the key to success of these programs, there is really little research on the specific role of the facilitator for new teacher online support. Further exploration of the role of the facilitator and best practices of facilitation for these programs would provide an important contribution to establishing effective practice in online facilitation of these support programs for new teachers.

Measuring Program Effectiveness

Although nearly every program in Clouse's (2008) study cited teacher retention as a primary impetus for their programs, no one had a reliable system in place to track retention, let alone to find a definite relationship to participation in the program. Programs also did not have systems to measure teacher effectiveness or student achievement that may be related to participation in these programs. These will be difficult evaluations to make, but they will eventually be needed to justify these kinds of programs and sustain their support from both a fiscal and philosophical standpoint. It will be a continuous challenge to bring attention to online mentoring and engage people to participate to help secure the future of these kinds of programs. One program leader described e-mentoring as in the early adoption phase and whether it will be completely embraced is still open to question. Those working within this new medium need to continue to try to understand its strengths and limitations in an effort to explore its potential.

The opportunity for research in these online support systems for new teachers really is quite open. This is a new frontier in new teacher induction and support, and it has generated excitement as well as frustration among those trying it. It is hoped that Clouse's (2008) study will help fill some of the void in the research and perhaps be a springboard for future studies in this area.

CONCLUSION

This chapter provides a broad view of online mentoring programs for new teachers by describing program components and development issues as well as leadership skills and styles needed to run these programs. Based on the descriptions of the requisite knowledge, skills, and leadership styles provided, Clouse (2008) posits that the leadership role of online support programs for beginning teachers requires the following:

- An understanding of the unique needs of new teachers
- A collaborative and comprehensive program development plan based on knowledge of the necessary program components
- An understanding of professional development and adult learning
- Skills to effectively communicate and build relationships online
- The ability to work in a collaborative, facilitative, and ever-changing environment

Developing an Online Support Program for New Teachers

A rather wide variety of program features were presented in this chapter, yet the purpose and goals of most programs are very similar. It is suggested that those considering an online support program should look at other programs, both face-to-face and online, as well as programs outside of education, to help them in their development stages. Many programs leaders suggest using design teams and advisory boards that include stakeholders at a variety of levels. It is also suggested that all possible funding sources should be considered to support these programs.

Leaders of these programs emphasized the need to establish goals for the program and decide early on how to evaluate outcomes. Programs need to provide a secure, reliable, and non-evaluative environment for support and collaboration among new and experienced teachers. Program goals should address new teachers' pedagogical, emotional, social, and programmatic needs. Programs should be designed to request continual feedback from participants at all levels to make sure they are meeting needs and expectations. It is important that programs meet the actual needs—not just the assumed needs—of participants. A continuous cycle of formative evaluation will help assess goals and direct leaders in making changes to programs.

Voluntary participation of both mentors and mentees is highly advised among program leaders. Providing a stipend to mentors is recommended, as is some type of stipend or incentive for mentees. Incentives might include the use of a laptop computer, payment for professional membership fees or a conference registration, or earning continuing education credits. Training of participants to clarify roles and expectations and to ensure necessary technology skills should be provided early on. It is also suggested that guidance be provided regarding effective online communication and building relationships. This can be accomplished by modeling appropriate online communications through the use of a facilitator and should be on-going and on an as-needed basis. It is also advised that an online support program be a value-added part of professional development, not just an added responsibility to the already busy schedules of new teachers. This could be accomplished by providing the opportunity for participants to receive continuing education credits or credit toward advanced certification or credentials.

It is advised that technology decisions be made later in the development process of an online mentoring program. It is most important to establish the goals and services of the program first and the technology decisions will fall into place. This follows a primary principle of instructional technology design: don't let technology guide the instructional or, in this case, program decisions (Maurer & Davidson, 1998). There are a number of commercial software programs as well as open source programs available that can support the functions of these systems. It will just be a matter of deciding what technology fits with the goals of the online support program.

There is the potential that online support can be an extension of traditional induction for school districts and an opportunity to provide outreach to graduates of teacher education programs. These systems can also provide access to a larger professional learning community and provide important networks to educators at all levels. As such, perhaps in the future more consistent funding can be secured for these programs as part of overall new teacher support systems.

Leadership Style for Online Support Systems for New Teachers

Leaders of online support programs describe the need for a leadership style that is collaborative, team-oriented, and uses a collegial problem-solving approach. Program leaders believe it is very important to empower team members in an effort to strengthen this team approach. Leaders find they need to be informed at all levels but also need to trust in their team's abilities and resist trying to micromanage. The ability to be flexible and open to suggestions and possibilities is also very important. It is imperative that program leaders be able to embrace change and help guide others through the change process. These online programs are often initially met with apprehension, and the leaders are the ones who must guide the way into this new territory. Leaders can help program participants and personnel adjust to the idea of this new way of mentoring by modeling supportive behavior, both online and face-to-face, and continually advocating for the program. Leading by example can set the tone for progress, growth, and success of these programs. Clouse (2008) found that the people who are developing and maintaining these online support programs are excited and committed to providing a service to new teachers that they hope will have a positive impact on their teaching careers.

The leadership role for online mentoring programs is still evolving, yet a number of assertions can be made to help better understand what skills, knowledge, and leadership traits seem to work well in the development and administration of these programs. The leadership needed for these online programs is a unique combination of a professional educator, mentor, tech-savvy communicator, and collaborative and facilitative leader.

Leaders of online support programs for new teachers need to accept the challenges of running these programs and securing the future of them. Many program leaders see this as, potentially, the future of how "we do business" in the area of teacher induction. However, consistent and sustained funding is a primary and ongoing challenge to continue these programs. To keep programs in operation and sustain funding, it will be imperative that programs show a link to effective teaching, retention, and student achievement due to participation in an online support program. In addition, the need to collaborate with other programs is important in the effort to strengthen the practice and to advance research in this area. These responsibilities of sustenance will lie squarely on the shoulders of program leaders, and these leaders will need to advocate and be the champion for their programs.

REFERENCES

Abbott, L. D. (2003). Novice teachers' experiences with telementoring as learner-centered professional development. Available from Dissertations and Theses database. (UMI No. 3116246)

Boyle, P., & Boice, B. (1998). Systematic mentoring for new faculty teachers and graduate teaching assistants. *Innovative Higher Education*, *22*(3), 157–179. doi:10.1023/A:1025183225886

Breaux, A. L., & Wong, H. K. (2003). *New teacher induction: How to train, support, and retain new teachers*. Mountain View, CA: Harry K. Wong Publications, Inc.

Britton, E., Paine, L., & Raizen, S. (1999). *Middle grades mathematics and science teachers' induction in selected countries: Preliminary findings*. Washington, DC: National Center for Improving Science Education, WestEd.

Brookfield, S. (1986). *Understanding and facilitating adult learning*. San Francisco: Jossey-Bass.

Burns, J. M. (1978). *Leadership*. New York: Harper and Row.

Cheng, Y. M., Clift, R. T., & Klecka, C. L. (2003, June). *Supporting new teachers across school districts: Learning from on-going, internal evaluation* [Electronic version]. Paper presented to the Second Annual Illinois Education Research Conference, Urbana, IL. Retrieved from http://??? Clouse, N. K. (2008). The leadership role in online support programs for beginning teacher. Available from Dissertations and Theses database. (UMI No. 3288939)

Cranton, P. (1994). *Understanding and promoting transformative learning*. San Francisco: Jossey-Bass.

Cunningham, S. (1999). The nature of workplace mentoring relationships among faculty members in Christian higher education. *The Journal of Higher Education*, *70*(4), 441–463. doi:10.2307/2649310

Darling-Hammond, L. (2003). Keeping good teachers: Why it matters, what leaders can do. *Educational Leadership*, *60*(8), 7–13.

Diehl, P. F., & Simpson, R. D. (1989). Investing in junior faculty: The teaching improvement program (TIPs). *Innovative Higher Education*, *13*, 147–157. doi:10.1007/BF00889746

Feiman-Nemser, S. (2003). What new teachers need to learn. *Educational Leadership*, *60*(8), 25–29.

Fullan, M. G. (1991). *The new meaning of educational change*. New York: Teachers College Press.

Guskey, T. R. (1994, April). *Professional development in education: In search of the optimal mix*. Paper presented at the annual meeting of the American Educational Research Association, New Orleans, LA.

Harris, J., O'Bryan, E., & Rotenberg, L. (1996). It's a simple idea, but it's not easy to do: Practical lessons in telementoring. *Learning and Leading with Technology, 24* (2), 53-57. Retrieved March 30, 2004, from http://emissary.wm.edu/templates/content/publications/October96LLT.pdf

Headlam-Wells, J., Gosland, J., & Craig, J. (2006). Beyond the organization: The design and management of e-mentoring systems [Electronic version]. *International Journal of Information Management, 26*, 372–385. doi:10.1016/j.ijinfomgt.2006.04.001

Hersey, P., & Blanchard, K. H. (1977, 1982). *Management of organizational behavior: Utilizing human resources.* Englewood Cliffs, NJ: Prentice-Hall.

Hew, K. F., & Knapczyk, D. (2007). Analysis of ill-structured problem solving, mentoring functions, and perceptions of practicum teachers and mentors toward online mentoring in a field-based practicum [Electronic version]. *Instructional Science, 34*, 1–40. doi:10.1007/s11251-006-9000-7

Hord, S. M. (1992). *Facilitative leadership: The imperative for change.* Austin: Southwest Educational Development Laboratory. Retrieved April, 11, 2005, from http://www.sedl.org/change/facilitate/

Ingersoll, R. M., & Smith, T. M. (2003). The wrong solution to the teacher shortage [Electronic version]. *Educational Leadership, 60*(8), 30–33.

Johnson, N. L., Clift, R. T., & Klecka, C. L. (2002, August). *Novice Teacher Support Project (NTSP): Following program participants.* Presentation to the Association of Teacher Educators, Williamsburg, VA.

Knowles, M. S. (1980). *The modern practice of adult education: From pedagogy to andragogy* (2nd ed.). Chicago: Association/Follett.

Knowles, M. S. (1984). *Andragogy in action: Applying modern principles of adult learning.* San Francisco: Jossey-Bass.

Kram, K. E. (1983). Phases of the mentor relationship. *Academy of Management Journal, 26*(4), 608–625. doi:10.2307/255910

Kurtz, W. H. (1983). Identifying their needs: How the principal can help beginning teachers. *NASSP Bulletin, 67*(459), 42–45. doi:10.1177/019263658306745908

Lawrence, G. (1974). *Patterns of effective in-service education: A state of the art summary of research on materials and procedures for changing teacher behaviors in in-service education.* Tallahassee: Florida State Department of Education. Retrieved from ERIC database (ED 176 424).

Leithwood, K. A., Steinback, R. S., & Raun, T. (1993). Superintendent's group problem-solving process. *Educational Administration Quarterly, 29*(3), 364–391. doi:10.1177/0013161X93029003008

Maurer, M. M., & Davidson, G. S. (1998). *Leadership in instructional technology*. Upper Saddle River, NJ: Prentice Hall.

McGregor, D. (1960). *The human side of enterprise.* New York: McGraw-Hill.

Mentor /National Mentoring Partnership. (2003). *Elements of effective practice* (2nd ed). Retrieved March 31, 2004, from http://www.mentoring.org/common/effective_mentoring _practices/effective_mentoring_practices.adp?Menu=nav_left_resources.adp&Preload=resources

Mentor/National Mentoring Partnership. (2002). *Elements of effective practice for e-mentoring.* Retrieved March 22, 2004, from http://www.mentoring.org/common/effective _ementoring/effective_ementoring.adp?Menu=nav_left_run.adp&Preload=resources

Merseth, K. K. (1990, April). *Beginning teachers and computer networks: A new form of induction support* [Electronic version]. Paper presented at the annual meeting of the American Educational Research Association, Boston, MA. Retrieved from http://??? Mezirow, J. D. (1981). A critical theory of adult learning and education. *Adult Education, 32*(1), 3–24.

Mezirow, J. D. (1990). *Fostering critical reflection in adulthood. A guide to tranformative and emancipatory learning*. San Francisco: Jossey-Bass.

Orlich, D. C. (1989). *Staff development: Enhancing human potential*. Boston: Allyn and Bacon.

Redmond, P. A. (2002). Building a community of practice: A case study of technology augmented mentoring for new teachers. Available from Dissertations and Theses database. (UMI No. 3059402)

Scandura, T. A., & Williams, E. A. (2001). An investigation of the moderating effects of gender on the relationships between mentoring initiation and protégé perceptions of mentoring functions. *Journal of Vocational Behavior*, *59*, 342–363. doi:10.1006/jvbe.2001.1809

Schön, D. (1983). *The reflective practitioner: How professionals think in action*. New York: Basic Books.

Sergiovanni, T. J. (1991). *The principalship: A reflective practice perspective*. Boston: Allyn & Bacon.

Single, P. B., & Muller, C. B. (2001). When email and mentoring unite: The implementation of a nationwide electronic mentoring program. In L. Stromei (Ed.), *Implementing successful coaching and mentoring programs* (pp. 107-122). Cambridge, MA: American Society for Training & Development (ASTD) In Action Series.

Single, P. B., & Muller, C. B. (2003, under review). *Electronic mentoring programs: a model to guide practice and research.*

Single, P. B., Muller, C. B., Cunningham, C. M., Single, R. M., & Carlsen, W. S. (2003, forthcoming). Inter-organizational connections, the value of impartial advisors, and increased self-confidence: Research from a large-scale e-mentoring program.

Single, P. B., & Single, R. M. (2004, in press). E-mentoring and telementoring: Review of research. In F. K. Kochan & J. T. Pascarelli (Eds.), *Technological aspects of mentoring*. Greenwich, CT: Information Age Press. Retrieved on March 31, 2004, from www.uvm.edu/~pbsingle

Southwest Educational Development Laboratory. (1994). *Staff development and change process: Cut from the same cloth.* Austin, TX: Southwest Educational Development Laboratory. Retrieved April 11, 2005, from http://www.sedl.org/change/issues42.html

Veenman, S. (1984). Perceived problems of beginning teachers. *Review of Educational Research*, *54*, 143–178.

Zachary, L. J. (2000). *The mentor's guide: Facilitating effective learning relationships*. San Francisco, CA: Jossey-Bass.

ADDITIONAL READING

Abbott, L. D. (2003). Novice teachers' experiences with telementoring as learner-centered professional development. Available from Dissertations and Theses database. (UMI No. 3116246)

Bennett, D., Hupert, N., Tsikalas, K., Meade, T., & Honey, M. (1998). *Critical issues in the design and implementation of telementoring environments*. City: Center for Children and Technology. Retrieved March 30, 2004, from http://www2.edc.org/CCT/publications _report.asp

Bierema, L. L., & Merriam, S. B. (2002). E-mentoring: Using computer mediated communication to enhance the mentoring process. *Innovative Higher Education*, *26*(3), 211–227. doi:10.1023/A:1017921023103

Cheng, Y. M., Clift, R. T., & Klecka, C. L. (2003, June). *Supporting new teachers across school districts: Learningfrom on-going, internal evaluation* [Electronic version]. Paper presented to the Second Annual Illinois Education Research Conference, Urbana, IL. Retrieved from http://??? Cummings, J. N., & Finholt, T. A. (1996). *Understanding communications as mentoring moves online.* Paper presented at the annual meeting of the American Psychological Society, San Francisco, CA.

DeWert, M. H., Babinski, L. M., & Jones, B. D. (2003). Safe passages: Providing online support to beginning teachers. *Journal ofTeacher Education, 54*(4), 311–320. doi:10.1177/0022487103255008

Eisenman, G., & Thorton, H. J. (April, 1999). Telementoring: Helping new teacher through the first year. *Technological Horizons in Education Journal Online*. Retrieved November 24, 2002, from http://www.thejournal.com/magazine/vault/articleprintversion.cfm?aid=2065

Ensher, E. A., Heun, C., & Blanchard, A. (2003). Online mentoring and computer-mediated communication: New directions in research [Electronic version]. *Journal of Vocational Behavior, 63*, 264–288. doi:10.1016/S0001-8791(03)00044-7

Fulop, M. (2002). *Assessing the potential of e-mentoring: A survey of current issues.* Retrieved April 2, 2004, from http://www.nwrel.org/mentoring/panel.html

Fulop, M. (2003) *Mentoring program development: A start-up toolkit.* Portland, OR: National Mentoring Center. Retrieved March 30, 2004, from http://www.nwrel.org/mentoring

Hamilton, B. A., & Scandura, T. A. (2003). E-mentoring: Implications for organizational learning and development in a wired world. [from http://www.sciencedirect.com]. *Organizational Dynamics, 31*(4), 388–402. Retrieved January 14, 2005. doi:10.1016/S0090-2616(02)00128-6

Harris, J., O'Bryan, E., & Rotenberg, L. (1996). It's a simple idea, but it's not easy to do: Practical lessons in telementoring. *Learning and Leading with Technology, 24* (2), 53-57. Retrieved March 30, 2004, from http://emissary.wm.edu/templates/content/publications/October96LLT.pdf

Headlam-Wells, J., Gosland, J., & Craig, J. (2006). Beyond the organization: The design and management of e-mentoring systems [Electronic version]. *International Journal of Information Management, 26*, 372–385. doi:10.1016/j.ijinfomgt.2006.04.001

Herrington, A., Herrington, J., Kervin, L., & Ferry, B. (2006). The design of an online community of practice for beginning teachers. *Contemporary Issues in Technology & Teacher Education, 6*(1), 120–132.

Hew, K. F., & Knapczyk, D. (2007). Analysis of ill-structured problem solving, mentoring functions, and perceptions of practicum teachers and mentors toward online mentoring in a field-based practicum [Electronic version]. *Instructional Science, 34*, 1–40. doi:10.1007/s11251-006-9000-7

Kasprisin, C., Single, P., Single, R., Ferrier, J., & Muller, C. (2008, May). Improved mentor satisfaction: Emphasising protégé training for adult-age mentoring dyads. *Mentoring & Tutoring: Partnership in Learning, 16*(2), 163–174.. doi:10.1080/13611260801916424

Klecka, C. L., Cheng, Y. M., & Clift, R. T. (2004, Fall). Exploring the potential of electronic mentoring [Electronic version]. *Action in Teacher Education, 26*(3), 2–9.

Klecka, C. L., Clift, R. T., & Thomas, A. (2002) Proceed with caution: Introducing electronic conferencing in teacher education. *Critical Issues in Teacher Education, 9*, 28-37. Retrieved March 16, 2003, from http://ntsp.ed.uiuc.edu/ElectronicMentoring/Resources.html

MENTOR/National Mentoring Partnership. (2002). *Elements of effective practice for e-mentoring.* Retrieved March 22, 2004, from http://www.mentoring.org/common/effective _ementoring/effective_ementoring.adp?Menu=nav_left_run.adp&Preload=resources

Merseth, K. K. (1990, April). *Beginning teachers and computer networks: A new form of induction support* [Electronic version]. Paper presented at the annual meeting of the American Educational Research Association, Boston, MA. Retrieved from http://??? Novice Teacher Support Project. (2002). *Electronic mentoring handbook.* Urbana, IL: University of Illinois at Urbana-Champaign. Retrieved April 15, 2003, from http://ntsp.uiuc.edu

O'Neill, D. K., & Harris, J. (April, 2000). *Is everybody happy? Bridging the perspective and developmental needs of participants in telementoring programs.* Paper presented at the annual meeting of the American Educational Research Association, New Orleans, LA. Retrieved January 27, 2005, from http://www.learningrelationslab.org/

Redmond, P. A. (2002). Building a community of practice: A case study of technology augmented mentoring for new teachers. Available from Dissertations and Theses database. (UMI No. 3059402)

Sweeny, B. (2003). Lessons learned in using technology to better support new teachers. In Hulett, E. C., Milyard, C., Tanner, J., & Miller, P. D. (Eds.), *Tracks to the future: Integrating technology into today's schools. City: New Mexico Association for Supervision and Curriculum Development.*

Williams, J., & Warren, S. (2007, Summer). E-Mentoring: Supporting First-Year Educators and Rejuvenating Veteran Teachers. [from Academic Search Premier database.]. *Delta Kappa Gamma Bulletin, 73*(4), 9–39. Retrieved July 15, 2009.

KEY TERMS AND DEFINITIONS

Asynchronous: An event (discussion) happening at different times.

Beginning or New Teacher: A teacher in the first three years of the profession.

Discussion Board: An online area in which participants can engage in text-based discussions of various issues.

E-Mentoring: A mentoring relationship that is established between a mentor and protégé or mentee, using electronic communications, such as email, discussion boards, video conferencing, blogs, or social networking services.

Facilitator: The person who monitors and facilitates online discussion boards and synchronous chats

Mentor: A more skilled and experienced person (teacher) who works with a partner (mentee or protégé) offering emotional support, direct assistance with career and professional development, and role modeling.

Mentee: A less skilled and experienced person (beginner teacher) who receives guidance, support, and feedback from a mentor.

Synchronous: An event (discussion) happening in real time.

Chapter 25
Electronic Portfolios in the Professional Development of Educators

Greg Sherman
Radford University, USA

Al Byers
National Science Teachers Association, USA

ABSTRACT

This chapter presents an overview of current electronic portfolio options available to practicing educators, emphasizing the different roles portfolios play within the professional development process. Available features within a variety of free and subscription web-based portfolio services are compared and the use of specific portfolio options within different professional development environments such as university graduate programs are profiled. Using a case study-like approach, the chapter details the use of the National Science Teachers Association's (NSTA) Learning Center, a collection of resources available to teachers that includes a web-based professional development plan and portfolio tool. The chapter concludes with a reflection on the different ways in which professional organization resources like the NSTA's PD Plan and Portfolio Tool can be used in the near future to continually improve the professional practice of educators.

INTRODUCTION: SUSAN CHILDRESS'S BIG SUMMER

Prairie View High School is a small, rural school serving the farm and ranch communities populating Phillips County in the north-central region of Kansas. It is near the geographic center of the United States, and most of the faculty members who teach at Prairie View grew up in this heartland and have been teaching at the school for many years.

DOI: 10.4018/978-1-61692-854-4.ch025

Susan Childress, however, has only been a science teacher at Prairie View for the past five years. And like many science teachers in small, rural high schools across America, she teaches more than one science subject. Since joining the other two teachers constituting the small science department at Prairie View, Ms. Childress has taught both biology as well as physical science courses. Although she is certified to teach secondary education biology in Kansas, she has taken enough undergraduate and graduate physical science coursework to feel comfortable with high school physical science content. But this year, Ms. Childress agreed to teach an Earth science class in addition to her biology and physical science courses. It was only after she agreed to teach the course that she realized she had never actually taken a single course in any Earth science content area. Not in college. Not even in high school. In fact, after spending part of her summer break examining curriculum guidelines as well as state standards, Ms. Childress realized that there were quite a few areas of Earth science that she would need to learn more about before she would feel comfortable teaching the course.

Ms. Childress could not take an Earth science graduate course during the summer break before school started because she only had enough time and money to accommodate two courses she needed to fulfill requirements of a state university educational leadership graduate program. She chose to be part of this program not only because she was interested in school administration, but also because the graduate program administrators encouraged her to join with other teachers from Phillips County as a cohort; many of the courses were offered to this group via distance learning technologies or on-site at the district offices after school. This was important to Ms. Childress because the main university campus was over 200 miles from where she lived.

Since she could not take any Earth science coursework over the summer, Ms. Childress identified a variety of Earth science content resources and experiences that she wanted to review and participate in over the summer, including selected journal article and text readings, online seminars and workshops, and even a visit to a natural history museum. In her evaluation report at the end of the spring semester, Ms. Childress articulated the goals she envisioned for the upcoming school year. These goals included the development of content-rich, inquiry-based science lessons based in part on her plans to acquire more Earth science content over the summer. When she communicated these goals to her building administrator, he was pleased to learn that she was planning both formal and informal experiences designed to help her improve her Earth science content. He asked Ms. Childress to carefully document her accomplishments, because he was under some pressure to report the steps taken to ensure that she was qualified to teach Earth science in the fall.

In addition to her educational leadership coursework and Earth science learning experiences, Ms. Childress also hoped to spend part of her summer organizing the materials needed to continue her work toward national board certification in science. She started this journey the previous year, and although it had been a difficult process at times, she committed herself to using the national certification experience as an important means toward improving her professional practice.

Graduate school. Earth science instruction. National Board Certification. Susan Childress's summer looked quite busy indeed. And it hadn't even started yet. During the hectic summer, Ms. Childress expected to learn many things that would help her improve her professional practice for the subsequent school year. But one of the most unexpected things she experienced during this time was the tremendous support she received through the use of electronic portfolios within many of her endeavors.

The purpose of this chapter is to briefly discuss the role of electronic portfolios in the preparation and continual improvement of professional educators like Susan Childress. This chapter will provide a summary of popular electronic portfolio options for professional educators, and it will profile an innovative tool developed by the National Science Teachers Association (NSTA) that has the potential to support the efforts of teachers such as Ms. Childress to plan and manage professional development experiences and resources. The chapter concludes with a brief discussion about the future of electronic portfolios in the professional development of teachers.

BRIEF OVERVIEW OF PROFESSIONAL DEVELOPMENT IN EDUCATION

Professional educators like Ms. Childress, as well as other professionals such as doctors and lawyers, must regularly engage in activities designed to help them continually improve their practice as well as maintain their professional credentials. Continuing education experiences common to many different types of professionals include reading journals and other professional publications, attending professional organization conferences, and participating in employer-sponsored workshops. Unlike doctors and lawyers, however, teachers and administrators often pursue advanced graduate degrees as a means of obtaining continuing education professional development experience. Most states, in fact, require teachers to include graduate coursework in their recertification plans. For example, Kansas requires teachers without advanced degrees to earn a minimum of 160 professional development points within an approved individual professional development plan during the first five years of practice that includes at least 80 points for college credit, where one hour of professional development or college credit equals 20 points (Kansas State Department of Education 2008).

It is likely that the education-related graduate courses in which most teachers enroll are administered through nationally accredited programs. Many colleges and universities in America are accredited by the National Council for Accreditation of Teacher Education (NCATE). The standards by which NCATE evaluates various graduate programs include professional organization standards (e.g., International Reading Association standards for graduate reading programs, NSTA standards for science educators, etc.), as well as general programmatic standards outlined in the Interstate New Teacher Assessment and Support Consortium's (INTASC) *Model Standards for Beginning Teacher Licensing, Assessment and Development* (Council of Chief State School Officers 1992). These standards address knowledge, dispositions, and performances associated with understanding specific content and content pedagogy, meeting the needs of diverse learners, promoting critical-thinking skills and constructive collaboration efforts, designing and assessing effective instructional experiences, and implementing continuous improvement methods into educators' professional practice.

As described in the Kansas requirements for recertification, educators may also choose to participate in professional development experiences designed and facilitated through state or local education agencies such as school districts. Such professional development experiences often include summer or after-school workshops designed to facilitate specific education-related goals. These workshops might reflect single, stand-alone sessions, or they might involve recurring support experiences lasting throughout an entire year. The data in Table 1 represent specific types of professional development activities reported by a sizable sample of teachers within the National Center for Educational Statistic's 1999–2000 Schools and Staffing Survey (Choy, Chen, and Bugarin 2006).

Like 30 percent of her peers across the United States, Ms. Childress is directing most of her professional development efforts toward earning a degree and advanced certification. As indicated, she does not plan to enroll in university coursework to help her better prepare for teaching Earth science. Her efforts in better preparing for teaching Earth science will focus on activities outside formal coursework. She may choose to participate in any available workshops, or she may choose to collect resources on her own and work independently toward her preparation. However, she will need to be mindful about selecting professional development experiences that will result

Table 1. Percentage of teachers participating in various professional development activities during 1999–2000

Type of Professional Development Activity	*% of Survey Respondents**
Workshops, conferences, or training	93.8
Regularly scheduled collaborative research on a topic of interest	72.6
Individual or collaborative research on a topic of interest	46.5
Mentoring and/or peer observation and coaching	41.9
Observational visits to other schools	34.4
University courses for recertification or advanced certification	30.3
Networks of teachers	24.6
University courses in the main assignment field	22.7
Workshops, conferences, or training as a presenter	21.4
Any of these activities	98.3

*Data from the 1999–2000 Schools and Staffing Survey (SASS): 52,400 teachers.

in effective support. Generally, the characteristics of effective professional development in education have been identified as addressing content designed to enhance content and pedagogical knowledge, providing sufficient time and resources to accomplish individual professional development goals, promoting collegiality and collaborative exchange, and providing structured and purposeful evaluation of the professional development experience (Gusky 2003). Formal graduate courses typically incorporate such strategies into the experience, but informal professional development experiences may lack one or more of these elements.

Luckily, Ms. Childress plans to manage her informal science-related professional development using resources from the National Science Teachers Association that will help her integrate effective professional development strategies into her experiences. Central to NSTA's set of professional development resources is an electronic portfolio system that encourages organization, reflection, and communication with others about Ms. Childress's professional development plans, challenges, and accomplishments. This electronic portfolio system, which includes a number of features from various popular electronic portfolio products, will be discussed in greater detail later in the chapter. To better understand NSTA's resources, the next section provides a brief overview of some of the different electronic portfolio programs currently available online.

CURRENT STATUS AND ROLE(S) OF ELECTRONIC PORTFOLIO USE IN PD FOR TEACHERS IN NORTH AMERICA

Portfolios in education typically represent collections of the portfolio developer's work, and tangible products of the work included in portfolios are often referred to as "artifacts." The specific nature of an individual portfolio generally depends on its purpose. "Learning" portfolios are often used to organize works-in-progress and may include a variety of features designed to aid in the development of quality artifacts. "Assessment" portfolios often include artifacts that are collected and displayed in accordance with clearly defined evaluation criteria, while "showcase" portfolios may represent a collection of artifacts selected by the portfolio developer as a representation of her or his best work. Of course, individual portfolios may serve a variety of purposes and include works-in-progress, criterion-referenced artifacts, and samples of best practice. In addition to selected artifacts, many portfolios also include features designed to illustrate the growth of a learner over time. Such features might include a sampling of artifacts across a semester or year, complete with written reflections about the development process for each artifact collection and discussions about future projects and learning goals based on past accomplishments (Barrett 2003).

With the advent of personal computers and networked computing technologies, opportunities to create digital electronic portfolios have flourished. In addition to the more traditional roles of portfolios, electronic portfolios add new roles and features to the portfolio development and presentation process. Most notably, artifacts presented within electronic portfolios must be developed or converted to digital format. This generally necessitates the learning and/or application of skills associated with using various computer applications. Although this may add a certain degree of difficulty to artifact development for some learners, digital formatting also provides learners with opportunities to include artifacts that may not be presented in a more traditional paper-based collection of work. For example, digital video and audio can be integrated into an electronic portfolio with relative ease.

In addition to providing a mechanism for easily presenting multimedia artifacts, electronic portfolios also provide an opportunity to establish a "connected" portfolio in ways that were unthinkable before computers (Barrett 2003). Web-based electronic portfolios, for instance, enable learners to share their artifacts with the world and collect feedback from parents, teachers, experts, and even other students. Artifacts can include links to related material developed by others, and links to detailed reflections about each artifact can be included as well.

POPULAR ELECTRONIC PORTFOLIO SYSTEMS

Electronic portfolios can be developed using any number of computer software applications. The simplest type of portfolio might consist of a folder on an individual computer that contains files such as word processing documents and images. These types of basic electronic portfolios represent organized collections of files that can be copied to a CD-ROM disk and distributed to any stakeholders needing to view, and perhaps evaluate, the artifacts. Teachers wishing to develop portfolios that are accessible on the web can take advantage of many free or inexpensive file management services that allow individuals to access files online. Google provides users free resources such as web space, document development, and file storage tools that enable users to create web pages, word processing documents, spreadsheets, and multimedia presentation files. These files are stored within an online account and can be made accessible to selected individuals or anybody online.

Though collecting and organizing digital artifacts can be accomplished using applications and web-based tools designed to aid in the development of different types of files in general, there are a number of web-based services that have been developed to support the creation and management of electronic portfolios; many specifically designed for educators. Currently, two of the more popular electronic portfolio systems designed for educators include Livetext (http://www.livetext.com) and TaskStream's *Learning Achievement Tools* (http://www.taskstream.com). These products have many features in common, probably because they were both designed to serve the needs of similar target populations. TaskStream's products and services have been designed to support the professional development of both preservice and inservice professional educators, while LiveText was designed to meet the specific needs of teacher preparation programs within colleges of education. Because both products were designed to meet the needs of educators as well as personnel involved in managing the professional development process, both products include the ability to align portfolio artifacts with specific standards and report on performances at the individual, class, and programmatic levels. Additionally, these products include features that enable them to be implemented within courses that constitute well-defined preservice or inservice programs.

The information presented in Table 2 displays some of the specific features available in TaskStream, Livetext, and eight additional electronic portfolio products. The features in Table 2 are categorized into groups reflecting specific roles that portfolios in general can play within various types of programs, including Presentation/Artifact Creation Tools, File Management, Artifact Assessment, Reporting, Communication, Instructor Control, and Course Management. Also included in Table 2 are features indicating whether a user's portfolio can be downloaded in a single folder to a local computer and whether an annual subscription fee is required.

All the electronic portfolio tools presented in Table 2 include some common features, regardless of their role or target audience. For example, all of the tools are web-based applications requiring the users to access features through a web browser such as Internet Explorer, Safari, or Firefox. Likewise, all the products presented in Table 2 include some type of web-based tool enabling the user to develop basic web pages. These pages could include links to portfolio artifacts developed in other applications (such as Microsoft Word or PowerPoint), or the web page itself could be the artifact. In addition, all the electronic portfolio tools listed in Table 2 include the ability to upload files into the web space defining the portfolio. But only those tools designed to aid preservice or inservice education programs include options that facilitate group or course membership. Such options include specific features in the categories of artifact assessment, reporting, course management instructor control (including group management features designed to control access to portfolio development tools and viewing privileges), and the communication features of e-mail, chat, and electronic bulletin boards.

GRADUATE PROGRAM ELECTRONIC PORTFOLIO EXAMPLE: LIVETEXT

When Susan Childress was accepted into an educational leadership graduate program, she was informed that she would need to purchase a subscription to LiveText in order to develop an electronic portfolio that would include a number of artifacts aligned with the professional standards defined by the Educational Leadership Constituent Council (ELCC). The subscription fee of $89 included access to the online portfolio system for the entire time she would be a graduate student in the educational leadership program, as well as an additional year following her completion of the program.

During the first course she took in the program, Ms. Childress was provided with a detailed description of the different assignments that would need to be included in her LiveText portfolio, not only for the class in which she was enrolled, but for all the courses she would be taking throughout the certification program. She was informed that one of the primary reasons the program directors decided to use the LiveText system was to enable them to ensure that all the educational leadership skills described by the ELCC would be addressed throughout the program, and also to aid in the accreditation process by enabling the program coordinators to provide easy access to artifacts representing evidence that all students have learned and applied targeted skills.

Learning how to manage work within an online system like LiveText did add some additional work, not to mention anxiety, to Susan Childress's graduate school experience. However, once she figured out how to negotiate the LiveText space, Ms. Childress began to see the real benefits of having an online electronic portfolio resource like LiveText. Within this system, she has been able to store and organize all her work from her different courses, and the evaluations of her assignments have been matched with professional

Table 2. Popular electronic portfolio product options by category

Category	*Option*	KEEP Toolkit[1]	OSP/ Sakai[2]	LiveText[3]	FolioTek[4]	Chalk & Wire[5]	ePortaro[6]	Epsilen[7]	FolioLive[8]	iWebfFolio[9]	TaskStream[10]
Target Population	K–5	·	·		·	·	✓				
	6–12	·	✓		✓	·	✓	✓			
	College	✓	✓	✓	✓	✓	✓	✓	✓	✓	✓
	Professional	✓	✓		✓	✓	✓	✓	✓	✓	✓
Artifact Organization	Web Page	✓	✓	✓	✓	✓	✓	✓	✓	✓	✓
	Linked External Files	✓	✓	✓	✓	✓	✓	✓	✓	✓	✓
	Website [Linked Pages]	✓	✓	✓	✓	✓	✓	✓	✓	✓	✓
	Multiple Portfolios	✓	✓	✓	✓	✓	✓		✓	✓	✓
	File Management View	·	✓	·	✓		✓	✓			
Presentation/ Artifact Creation Tools	Web-Based	✓	✓	✓	✓	✓	✓	✓	✓	✓	✓
	Forms Driven	✓	✓	✓		✓		✓	✓	✓	✓
File Management	Upload Files	✓	✓	✓	✓	✓	✓	✓	✓	✓	✓
	Attached File Descriptions		✓		✓			✓			
	View Folder Structure		✓		✓			✓			
Artifact Assessment	Rubrics			✓	✓	✓				✓	✓
	Comments			✓	✓	✓	✓			✓	✓
Reporting	Student Performance by Standard		✓	✓	✓	✓				✓	✓
	Group Performance by Standard			✓	✓	✓					✓
	Export Data to Spreadsheet			✓	✓	✓					✓

continued on following page

Table 2. continued

Category	*Option*	**KEEP Toolkit[1]**	**OSP/ Sakai[2]**	**LiveText[3]**	**FolioTek[4]**	**Chalk & Wire[5]**	**ePortaro[6]**	**Epsilen[7]**	**FolioLive[8]**	**iWebfFolio[9]**	**TaskStream[10]**
Communication	E-Mail		✓		✓			✓	✓		✓
	IM/Chat		✓		✓						✓
	Bulletin Board		✓					✓			✓
	Announcements		✓								✓
	Blog							✓			
Instructor Control	Enrollment/Roles		✓	✓	✓				✓		✓
	Artifact Template(s)		✓	✓	✓					✓	✓
	Assessment Template(s)			✓	✓						✓
Course Manage-ment	Announcements		✓								✓
	Course Resources										✓
Export Portfolio	Single.ZIP file	✓		✓	✓	✓		✓	✓		
Subscription	NO Annual Fee	✓	✓					✓			

1. http://www.cfkeep.org
2. http://www.theospi.org
3. http://www.livetext.com
4. http://www.foliotek.com
5. http://www.chalkandwire.com
6. http://www.eportaro.com
7. http://www.epsilen.com
8. http://www.foliolive.com
9. http://www.nuventive.com/products_iwebfolio.html
10. http://www.taskstream.com

Figure 1. LiveText listing of work samples

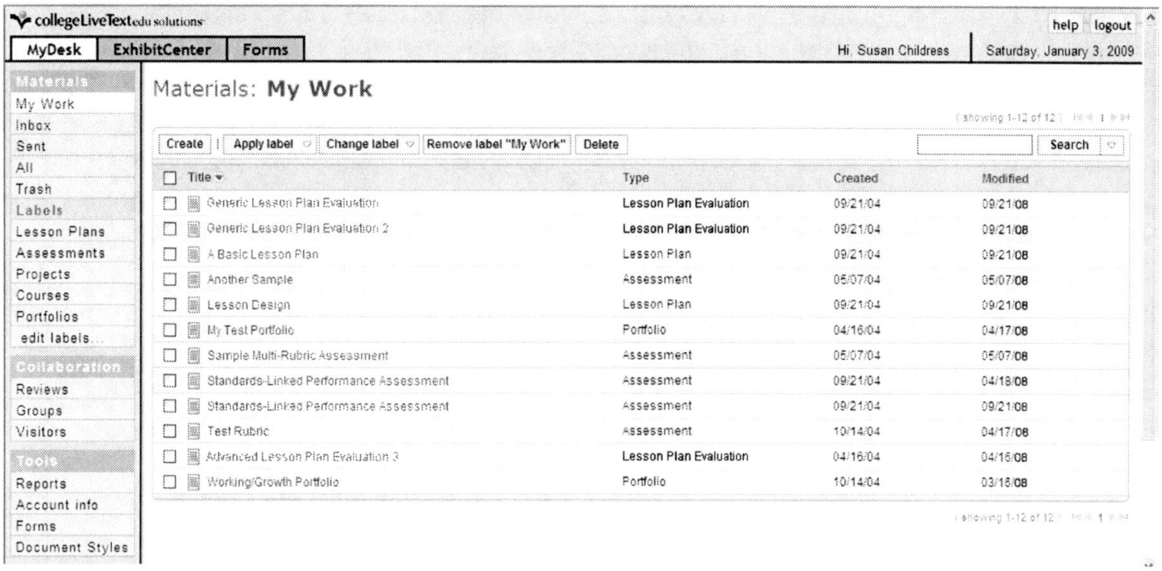

competencies from the ELCC standards. Figure 1 presents a listing of some of her work samples within one of Livetext's menu windows.

As she progressed through the educational leadership program, Ms. Childress's LiveText account helped her organize all the work she needed to complete. Additionally, the program's emphasis on aligning coursework with national standards provided Ms. Childress with a conceptual "big picture" that continues to enable her to know what she is expected to learn at all times. And the feedback she receives through the online system provides her with detailed knowledge regarding her personal progress.

The LiveText electronic portfolio system organizes, manages, and presents Susan Childress's work associated with learning skills needed to become an effective educational leader. As previously indicated, however, she also possesses professional needs in the area of science education that will not be fully supported through her educational leadership program. In her effort to identify resources that might help her feel more comfortable heading into a year of science instruction that includes Earth science, Ms. Childress looked to NSTA, the world's largest association of science educators, for assistance and found an electronic portfolio system that will provide her with a tremendous amount of support in accomplishing her science-related professional development goals.

SCIENCE INSTRUCTIONAL PROFESSIONAL DEVELOPMENT ELECTRONIC PORTFOLIO EXAMPLE: NSTA

As Susan Childress was compiling resources to help her address Earth science content needs, she recalled an e-mail message from NSTA announcing the release of a series of online tools designed to help with professional development. The announcement indicated that the professional development tools resided in an online section of NSTA's website call the "NSTA Learning Center" (http://learningcenter.nsta.org).

One of the primary purposes of the NSTA Learning Center is to provide access to many of its science educator resources, including digital copies of articles from NSTA's many journals, chapters from books published by NSTA Press, online web seminars, and instructional science content learning experiences called "Science Objects" that comprise complete, self-directed courses called "SciPacks." All these professional development resources can be accessed from the NSTA Learning Center by selecting all titles by resource type, subject, grade level, or individual state science standards. In addition to providing access to science content-related resources, the NSTA Learning Center also provides a number of tools designed to help professional science educators plan and manage professional development experiences.

One such tool, the PD Indexer, allows users to select specific content assessments and, based on the results of these private online multiple-choice tests, diagnose their personal professional development needs and select from a number of recommended resources and opportunities in specific areas of need in science content knowledge. Recommended resources might include specific NSTA Press articles, book chapters, Science Objects, or live online classes, archived web seminars, or face-to-face learning opportunities. These resources and opportunities may then be added to a user's library, which represents another NSTA Learning Center professional development tool. The My Library tool enables users to organize NSTA resources into categories and collections, providing easy access to all online NSTA resources. Individual resources as well as resource collections can be easily annotated with notes and shared with others as well.

Using the many tools available, Ms. Childress was able to rapidly identify a collection of resources that addressed specific Earth science content, and she planned to spend part of her summer reviewing the material in an effort to feel more comfortable with the Earth science content she planned to teach in the fall. But it was the NSTA Learning Center's PD Plan and Portfolio (PDPP) Tool that really helped her organize her resources and plan strategies for accomplishing her personal PD goals. One of the important ways in which the PDPP tool helps all users clearly identify and articulate their own professional development needs and goals is to encourage them to reflect upon goal categories that might represent areas in which they want to improve their professional practice. These PDPP categories include:

- My Content Knowledge
- My Content Pedagogy
- My Assessment/Evaluation Skills
- My Technology Skills
- My Management Skills
- Impact on Student Learning

After selecting a time frame and goal categories, the tool provides an easy-to-navigate file folder interface that helps users easily define specific goals and identify evidence related to accomplishing those goals. Figure 2 presents a view of the file management features within the PDPP tool.

Developing a professional development goal is further supported through the structure of the online professional development goal creation form. This form encourages teachers to create a goal statement as well as reflect on the reasons why the goal was selected. Additionally, the form provides links to websites that present professional goals and objectives that might be included as part of the overall goal.

By selecting a goal within one of the folders, the NSTA PDPP tool provides an easy way to define specific action items that may help teachers accomplish the identified goal. Some action items are suggested, and in many cases, these suggested resources are available through NSTA. Depending on the type of goal, action items might include participating in a web seminar, completing a Science Object, or participating in a course or workshop. Teachers can also define their own specific action items as well. The form also encourages teachers to justify how the identified action item will support

Figure 2. File management features of the NSTA PDPP tool

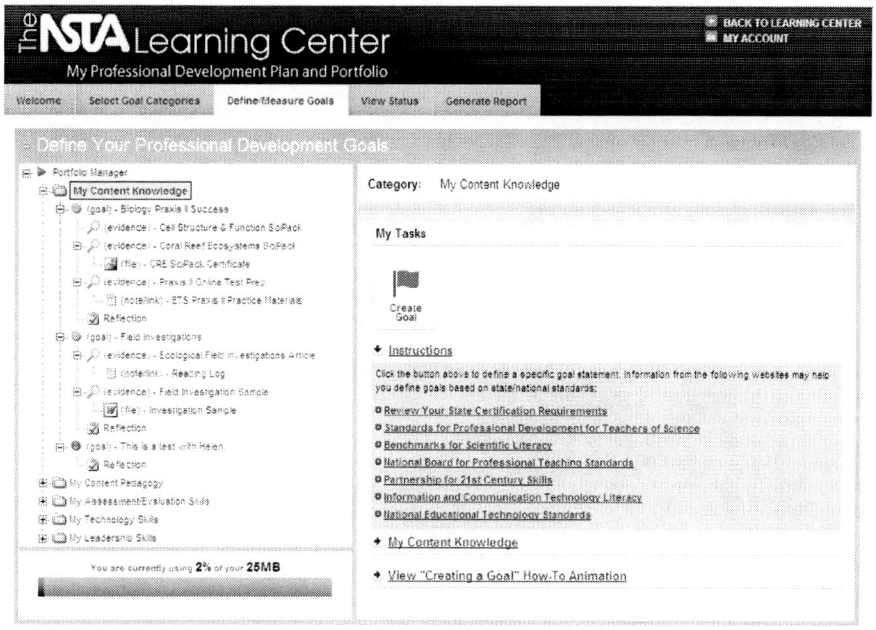

accomplishing the specified goal. Additionally, teachers must describe the file or files that will be included in the portfolio constituting evidence that the selected action item has been successfully completed. Figure 3 presents the PDPP form used to enter information about specific action items.

All planned action items and evidence appear in the file management system. Selecting one of the entries enables teachers to easily upload an evidence file or create a note or web link that might constitute evidence of action item completion (such as a link to a book discussion blog, or a note detailing the amount of time spent reading professional journals).

The NSTA PDPP tool makes it easy to quickly reflect on the status of goal accomplishments. A status page presents basic information about a teacher's goals, including expected finish dates and whether they are past due. Figure 4 presents a sample of this status screen, accessible from within the PDPP tool.

The status of a teacher's goals is also communicated within another one of the NSTA Learning Center's PD tools, the My Calendar tool. Upcoming events, including PD Indexer goal completion dates, are displayed on the NSTA Learning Center's home page when a user logs into the site.

To "complete" a goal, evidence for each action item must be copied to the portfolio, and a reflection statement must be completed. In this reflection, teachers summarize what they accomplished, why it was important to them, and how accomplishing the goal will affect their future practice. Additionally, teachers have opportunities to describe subsequent professional development activities they might choose to experience as a result of accomplishing a specific goal. Websites can also be added to the goal reflections, providing easy access to resources that might support future professional development efforts.

Once goals have been completed for a specified period of time, teachers may wish to generate a written report to document goals, evidences of successful action item completion, and personal reflections. This report can be easily generated by

Figure 3. PDPP action item information form

selecting all the items to be included from the file management window, and then simply selecting the "Generate Report" button. Figure 5 presents a sample of what the report generation window might look like for an individual teacher.

Selecting the "Generate report" button results in the creation of a nicely laid out document presented in PDF format. This report file can be saved, printed, or e-mailed. Figure 6 presents a sample of the report format.

After examining all the features of the NSTA PDPP tool as well as all the features of the other tools available within NSTA's Learning Center, Ms. Childress felt nicely supported as she entered into a very busy season of professional development. Using the PD Indexer, she could identify specific resources addressing Earth science content with which she felt she needed to become more familiar. She could then use the PDPP tool to articulate specific professional development

Figure 4. PDPP sample goal status screen

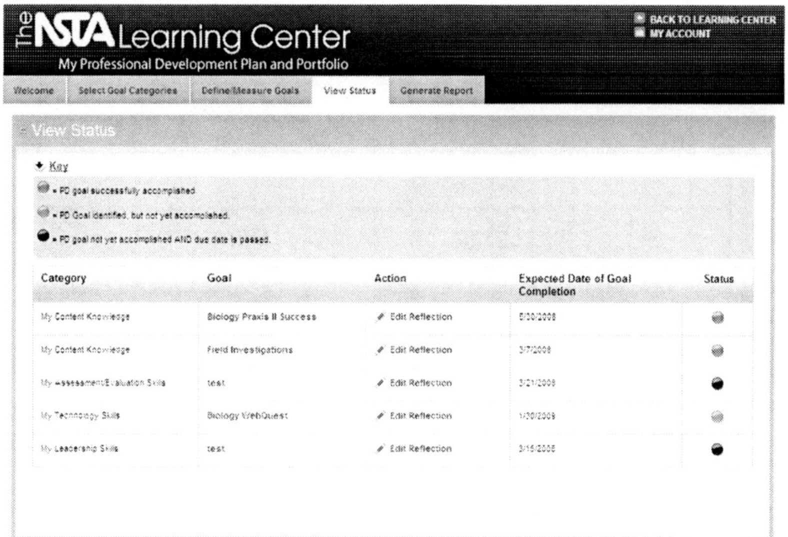

goals in the area of content knowledge. Following her completion of SciPacks and perhaps reading a few articles of book chapters related to Earth science, she could upload certificates of completion or reading logs into her PDPP space. And at the beginning of her new school year, she could even send a PDF copy of her portfolio to her principal in support of her own professional development plan for the upcoming year. This would also aid her principal in communicating to others about her qualifications for teaching Earth science.

Figure 5. Sample PDPP report generation window

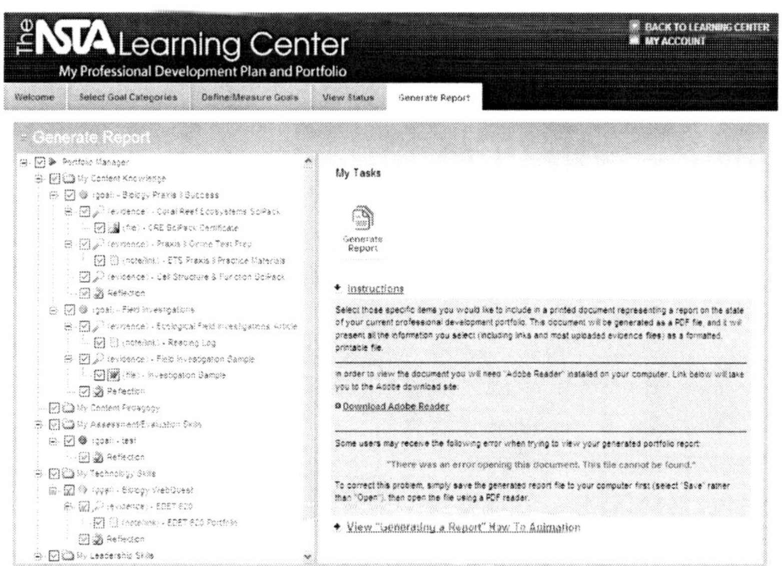

Figure 6. Sample PDPP report format

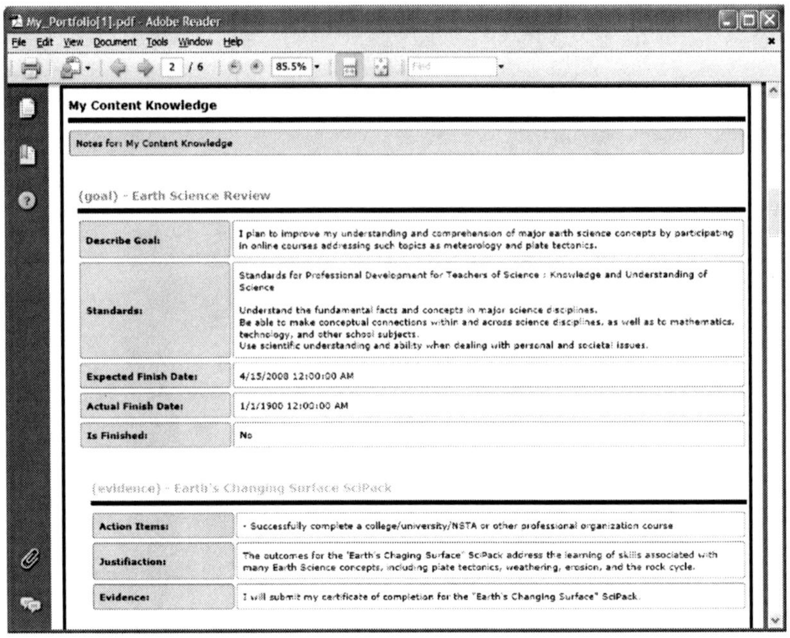

CONCLUSION: PUTTING IT ALL TOGETHER FOR TOMORROW

There are ostensibly just a few common roles that electronic portfolios currently play in the professional development of preservice and inservice educators, yet there are a multitude of technology options to support the creation and presentation of digital portfolio material. In the case of Susan Childress, the two different types of electronic portfolio environments she encountered provided organization, access to resources, opportunities to assess artifacts online, and the ability to easily generate reports of her accomplishments. A number of commercially available products have been designed to support education students at the undergraduate and graduate level, and the example of LiveText used to help organize and support the educational leadership program in which Ms. Childress is enrolled illustrates how a commercial electronic portfolio product might be used in a typical university program. The LiveText tool enables program faculty to develop standards-aligned assignments and assessment rubrics. It also enables students like Ms. Childress to contribute work in digital format within an organized system that communicates program expectations at all times and affords students, program faculty, and other stakeholders a platform for easily communicating about works-in-progress and finished artifacts representing the application of clearly defined skills, knowledge, and dispositions.

NSTA's Learning Center provides more direct support for the individual professional development needs of science teachers by providing access to resources and opportunities addressing science content and teaching. The PDPP tool within the NSTA Learning Center further advances the development of inservice teachers by encouraging them to articulate personal goals in such areas as content knowledge, content pedagogy, technology skills, and classroom management. This electronic portfolio environment provides a structure for

- Identifying and calendaring action items,
- Defining digital artifacts that will reflect successful completion of action items,

- Formally reflecting on the accomplishment of specific goals by summarizing the experiences and communicating why the goal accomplishment was important in the journey of continual improvement, and
- Articulating what a teacher will do subsequent to accomplishing the goal and continuing down the road of professional growth and development.

Graduate school requirements and the need to enhance Earth science knowledge represent two important professional development challenges facing Susan Childress. A third area of formal professional development that Ms. Childress needs to manage involves her desire to gain national board certification in science instruction. Within this process, Ms. Childress will need to provide evidence that she possesses master educator characteristics defined by the National Board for Professional Teaching Standards (NBPTS). These characteristics include (NBPTS 2002a):

1. Teachers are committed to students and their learning.
2. Teachers know the subjects they teach and how to teach those subjects to students.
3. Teachers are responsible for managing and monitoring student learning.
4. Teachers think systematically about their practice and learn from experience.
5. Teachers are members of learning communities.

The primary means of communicating evidence that she has demonstrated these traits is a portfolio that must be submitted to the national board for review (NBPTS 2002b). This portfolio must include four distinct artifacts: one classroom-based entry with accompanying student work, two classroom-based entries that require video recordings of interactions between Ms. Childress and her students, and one documented "accomplishments" entry that provides evidence of accomplishments outside of the classroom and how such work affected student learning. Each entry requires some direct evidence of teaching as well as a commentary describing, analyzing, and reflecting on this evidence.

Currently, the entire NBPTS portfolio must be submitted as paper documents along with video evidence (videotape or DVD). There is no doubt that the NBPTS organization will eventually enact procedures for entries to be submitted in digital format via online technologies (including online video access). But for now, Ms. Childress will comply with existing parameters for submission. However, the artifacts and reflections she collects within her LiveText and NSTA PDPP portfolios may help provide her with some of the evidence she needs to complete her NBPTS portfolio requirements. For example, she may include a goal in her NSTA PDPP portfolio that addresses science content pedagogy, and she may decide to enroll in a series of NSTA web seminars, or a more formally structured NSTA online short course that teach inquiry-based strategies for effective science instruction. Based on her participation in these web seminars or short courses, as well as applications in her own classroom, Ms. Childress may choose to include in her online portfolio digital copies of certificates of web seminar or course completion, as well as images, work samples, and pretest/posttest data from her own students as evidence that she successfully met her goal to improve her science pedagogy skills. At any time, she can generate a paper-based report from her NSTA PDPP that presents her goals as well as all evidence files and reflections. This document can then be used to support her NBPTS portfolio artifact requirements.

The use of resources from NSTA to help Ms. Childress define and accomplish her professional development goals is indicative of the type of support any professional organization should provide its members. Technology-based products such as NSTA's Professional Development Plan and Portfolio tool can be used free by any teacher, but the PDPP connections to science-related digital resources make it an ideal professional development companion for teachers of science at the K–12 grade levels. Although no other professional organizations for educators currently offer such support mechanisms, it is likely most professional organizations will provide such services to its members in the future.

And as these professional organization resources become more flexible and refined, they just might end up taking the place of commercial electronic portfolio products used by teacher preparation institutions. After all, it is the professional organization standards that are being assessed within the accreditation process. And encouraging more teachers to become involved in professional organizations earlier in their careers may very well move the entire teaching profession in the direction of continuous improvement and innovation that most, if not all, professional organizations have been working toward for many years.

REFERENCES

Barrett, H. (2003). Electronic portfolios. In Kovalchick, A., & Dawson, K. (Eds.), *Education and technology: An encyclopedia* (pp. 271–276). Santa Barbara, CA: ABC-Clio.

Choy, S. P., Chen, X., & Bugarin, R. (2006). *Teacher professional development in 1999–2000: What teachers, principals, and district staff report* (NCES 2006-305). Washington, DC: National Center for Education Statistics, U.S. Department of Education.

Council of Chief State School Officers. (1992). Model standards for beginning teacher licensing, assessment and development: A resource for state dialogue developed by Interstate New Teacher Assessment and Support Consortium (INTASC). Retrieved November 1, 2008, from http://www.ccsso.org/content/pdfs/corestrd.pdf

Gusky, T. (2003). What makes professional development effective? *Phi Delta Kappan*, *84*(10), 748–750.

Kansas State Department of Education. (2008). Regulations and standards for Kansas educators..

National Board for Professional Teaching Standards. (2002b). *Adolescence and young adulthood science for teachers of students ages 14–18+ Portfolio Instructions.* Arlington, VA: NBPTS.

National Board for Professional Teaching Standards (NBPTS). (2002a). *What teachers should know and be able to do.* Arlington, VA: NBPTS.

KEY TERMS AND DEFINITIONS

Electronic Portfolio (e-Portfolio, digital portfolio): A collection of evidence assembled and managed within non-print media, usually some type of web-based environment. Such evidence may include text, links to computer files, digital images, audio and/or video files, blog entries, and hyperlinks to other web-based content. Although they can play many roles, most electronic portfolios represent learning records that provide actual evidence of educational goal achievement.

Professional Development: The improvement of those skills, knowledge or dispositions (attitudes) needed to succeed in a particular profession, usually through some form of continuing educational experiences.

Chapter 26
Teaching in the Future:
A Blueprint for Faculty Development

David S. Stein
The Ohio State University, USA

Constance E. Wanstreet
The Ohio State University, USA

ABSTRACT

Based on an intellectual exercise that guided projections of the classroom environment in 2020 and beyond, this chapter envisions a future where fewer faculty are affiliated with only one institution and more are independent scholars. Faculty will serve as knowledge-brokers, and learners will assemble their own cohort of scholars and other learners around similar inquiry projects. Tools to facilitate learning will include personal learning environments and computer-based instructional agents. Social practices will include learning content in the context of doing the work and jointly coming to agreement about what constitutes mastery of the subject matter. Faculty development must attend to the interactions among tools, participants, social practices, learning in community, and the learning outcome.

INTRODUCTION

"It's not the responsibility of working adults to modify their lives to fit an educational format, but rather up to the colleges to mold their programs to fit the changing needs of adults and parents like me. For example, offering flexible class times [and] online courses...are ways in which colleges can help working adults go to school." –Melanie, Adult Learner, Central Ohio

"Distance learning is important, but we are committed to current curriculum and what it offers."—Garry, Associate Dean, Central Ohio University

Melanie, an adult learner in central Ohio, is working with two universities to complete her bachelor's degree. She calls for universities to offer flexible class times and online courses to meet the needs of adult learners (Dick, 2009). Melanie is, in effect, creating her own learning plan from the educational options available to her. Garry is an associate dean for a large midwestern

DOI: 10.4018/978-1-61692-854-4.ch026

university that does not specifically address the individual needs of self-directed adult learners such as Melanie. Garry's institution is committed to traditional face-to-face instruction, without which, he contends, students "miss a great deal" (Borgia, 2008). For now, Garry's institution is actively resisting Melanie's request for a flexible learning environment.

Let us imagine the classroom environment in 2020 and beyond. More students will study online from multiple universities, as Melanie is doing now (Chronicle Research Services, 2009). Personalized learning plans will provide learning experiences based on individual needs (KnowledgeWorks Foundation, 2006). Faculty members will become independent of universities, attracting students in an international marketplace (Brown, 2001; Levine, 2000). Despite Garry's resistance, most courses of study in higher education will have an online component; and students learning via computer-mediated technologies will outnumber those who are sitting in classroom seats for the majority of their education (Levin, 2002). Most learners will have been born in a technological age different from the age in which most instructors have been trained. How will faculty work in this environment?

This chapter presents a blueprint for faculty to develop skills in support of the classroom environment in 2020 and beyond. The chapter addresses the following questions:

- What technological and pedagogical trends are emerging that will change the notion of the classroom space?
- What characteristics will participants in the learning process bring to the effort?
- In what ways will the pedagogical mindset of faculty need to change regarding their role in the learning process?

The chapter begins with a discussion of the art of futuring, an intellectual exercise that forecasts possibilities for future events. We will then present a faculty development framework derived from major ideas of activity theory. In this framework, we posit a learner-controlled, highly interactive, collaborative, and constructivist environment. We conclude the chapter by integrating our forecasts with the theoretical framework and evaluating our futuring exercise against the criteria for good forecasts.

BACKGROUND: LEARNING IN 2020 AND BEYOND

Universities are thought to have been stable learning organizations, slow to react to changing technologies. The idea of traditional learner-faculty interactions is the image of the philosopher flanked by a small group of students receiving wisdom. Yet that image is not true to the innovations that have changed the way many learners and teachers interact. Even in the Socratic dialogues, the role of the instructor was to challenge, push, and improve the critical and reflective thought process using the dialogic process. Certainly, the printing press provided alternative viewpoints to those argued by the master instructor. The development of mass instruction through the publicly supported school democratized learning and required new technologies to reach and engage large numbers of students. However, the skills of instruction may not have changed as dramatically as the technology used to support instruction.

Dirr (1999) suggests that higher education is entering the fourth phase of a technological development that began with correspondence courses in the 19th century, moved to radio in the early 20th century, progressed to televised learning opportunities in the mid-20th century, and entered the age of the Internet in the late 20th century. We can project the influence of the Internet on learning environments in 2020 and beyond through a process called futuring.

The Art of Futuring

We consider futuring an intellectual pursuit that involves anticipating the shape of tomorrow. As an intellectual pursuit, futuring combines imagination with present realities to paint images of possibilities. Futuring involves studying the past and present for events, trends, and technologies and envisioning the possible directions and impacts at a given future time. Of course, the more distant the future, the more imagining one might use to picture the future.

The art of futuring involves developing scenarios that present alternative possibilities and assessing those possibilities in terms of the probable impact that events might have on the situation. Statements about the future reflect possibilities, not predictions. In futuring, we can consider what might happen if events continue without any interventions (i.e., a primary forecast) or what might happen if events change in a particular direction (i.e., a secondary forecast); or we can make statements about the future based on a study of the forces and consider the most likely occurrences (i.e., a tertiary forecast) (Fowles, 1978). A good forecast can alert us to possibilities. Based on a set of criteria, we might prepare for the likelihood of a certain future, always noting that we could be wrong.

Attributes of a good forecast include clarity (i.e., clear assumptions and a specified time period); plausibility (i.e., internal consistency and basis in events that have happened or may possibly happen given the available technology and knowledge); imagination (i.e., intuitive leaps from which possibilities emerge); and justification (i.e., arguments building from the known to the unknown based on reason, literature, practices, emerging events, and data when possible) (Kauffman, 1976).

Seeding the Future

In 2002, Levin projected that the idea of schooling would change to that of tele-learning in more collaborative settings. Learners would be involved in tele-taskforces and engage in presentations. Certainly, course platforms in use by many universities have enabled students to participate and learn in a variety of different spaces through collaboration and engagement with each other and the instructor.

Howell, Williams, and Lindsay (2003) reviewed the literature and identified 32 trends affecting distance education to help higher education administrators plan for technologically dominated learning environments. Trends include the need for faculty development in the context of online environments rather than conventional classroom methods. Other trends include providing flexibility around learner needs rather than around faculty-driven knowledge in the structure of programs, shifting the academic emphasis from course completion to competency, accommodating new models of educational providers, and designing for versatile and ubiquitous technology.

Even at the high school level, a challenge to the traditional ways of learning is emerging. Szep (2008) reported on a high school that has eliminated textbooks in favor of online resources and uses multicompetency-level classrooms in which student progress is tracked electronically. With mediated instruction, teachers can invest time in developing individual learners rather than in presenting content. Szep's news report presents data suggesting that 50% of high school courses will be taught online by 2019. In 2008, 1% of courses were taught online. The article suggests three trends: outsourcing of curriculum design, delivering courses online, and providing individualized guidance based on learner performance.

Scenarios of the Future

In this futuring exercise, we present scenarios that describe changes in the classroom, the major learning space. We are going beyond course management systems, which to us resemble classrooms reconstructed in an electronic environment. In most cases, the CMS still brings learners together with an instructor who is the subject matter expert and the course manager. What happens to "the classroom" when we escape the physical and electronic walls? What do learning and teaching look like when we enter an *edunetworked* space that is mobile, learner-controlled, learner-centered, and always connected. We define *edunetworked* as the connections learners establish with other learners, subject matter experts, and a learning manager (i.e., a credentialing authority). Learners can build their own teams across university boundaries in pursuit of academic goals.

Scenario One: Faculty Role

The learning environment will blend physical and virtual instruction, which will take place simultaneously. Learners and teachers will be connected through electronic tools as well as in physical space. Instructors and learners will cross physical borders and will interact in real time. Multiple instructors will be present at different points in the learning session because the need for expertise in specific content areas will be required. The primary instructor will serve as the conduit for connecting content, learners, and instructors, as needed. Information will be everywhere and will be accessible immediately. Increased numbers of adults will pursue advanced degrees and will obtain those degrees at a distance from their degree-granting institution. The classroom as we presently think of it, as a physical space used for a single learning encounter, will be redesigned as a learning community space for learners within a geographic area to come together in person when appropriate. Learning sessions will be global, available anytime and anyplace, to anyone who has access to the technology. In this scenario, how will faculty prepare for and teach in that environment?

Scenario Two: Learner Role

To illustrate how faculty should be prepared to teach, we offer a glimpse into a typical learner in the future. Jane is a graduate student at a major university. She uses a personal learning environment (PLE) to control and manage her own learning. Jane's university has created an academic program in which learners set their own learning goals and carry them out using both internal and external resources. Jane meets weekly with her advisor and quarterly with her committee; but essentially, she is in charge of her own learning, free to enroll in those courses that meet her learning goals. Jane and her university know that this is only one stop in her lifetime of learning.

Jane (and her learning) are at the center of her PLE. The device has a management function that organizes her course materials, tracks her assignment submissions, provides a calendar, and includes a synchronous meeting space. Her PLE uses animated computer-based instructional agents, similar to intelligent avatars, to represent her in virtual courses whether she herself is present or not. Jane's personal blog has an aggregator that allows her to browse the latest postings in her courses, messages from her instructors and other students, and information from her external networks. Her aggregator identifies the information that is pertinent to her learning pursuits. Jane begins each day by accessing her PLE and checking for updates. Much of her learning takes place by creating posts and links, as well as synthesizing and commenting on posts on other blogs. As part of this process, Jane identifies and copyrights her own contributions so that they are known as her intellectual property. In this scenario, how will learners function independently and interdependently in their learning environment?

FACULTY DEVELOPMENT FRAMEWORK

Faculty development involves organized support in the areas of teaching, scholarship, and community and professional engagement (Sorcinelli, Austin, Eddy, & Beach, 2006). Faculty development programs are used to manage change, help increase instructional strengths and skills, and put knowledge into practice (Schlager & Fusco, 2004; Bligh, 2005). Although activities may include leadership development and insight into the values and culture of the educational institution (Wilkerson & Irby, 1998), this chapter will focus on orienting faculty to the changing nature of their role as instructors in a networked environment and how they can excel in that role.

The conceptual framework for faculty development resembles the characteristics of the environment in which instruction will take place. The use of electronic tools and the availability of information will create a learning environment that is highly interactive, collaborative, and constructivist. Activity theory is well-suited for a constructivist, collaborative learning environment.

Figure 1. The blueprint for faculty development is highly interactive, collaborative, and constructivist

Activity theory is a form of sociocultural analysis that focuses on activity systems: collective human constructions, such as family, a workplace, an advocacy group, a school, discipline, or course of study (Engström, 1987). Activity theory provides a lens for analyzing change (Engström, Miettinen, & Punamaki, 1999). Elements of an activity system include the object of the action, the subject (i.e., the person or group performing the action), artifacts (i.e., signs and tools used to perform the action), rules, community, and division of labor (Engström, 1987). Activity theory links the individual with the social structure through dialogue while carrying out an activity (Lektorsky, 1999).

In educational settings, activity theory has been used as a conceptual framework to evaluate learning technologies (Scanlon & Issroff, 2005; Waycott, Jones, & Scanlon, 2005) and to analyze learning processes and outcomes for the purpose of designing instruction (Jonassen, 2000). As such, activity theory can provide guidance on the design of a faculty development framework. Lektorsky (1999, p. 68) calls for new versions of activity theory that account for "interhuman communication," which involves reflection and consideration of others' perspectives. In that spirit, we envision the teaching environment of the future as having the following activity elements: tools, participants, social practices, learning in community, and outcomes. Figure 1 illustrates the components of the conceptual framework.

Activity System Elements

- *Tools* refer to internal or external mediating artifacts that help achieve the outcomes of the activity. Examples are synchronous and asynchronous technology, books, online resources and learning theories, and self-concepts.
- *Participants* refer to the individual or group whose point of view is taken in the analysis of the activity or to the animated

computer-based instructional agent that represents the individual's point of view.

- *Social Practices* regulate actions and interactions within the activity system and address how tasks are divided among community members. Social practices will be built around faculty serving as knowledge-brokers and working with learners to identify and develop competencies related to subject matter.
- *Learning Community* is comprised of one or more people who share the objective with the subject. Learning in community means being engaged in the task of knowledge building around inquiry rather than knowledge acquisition and retention.
- *Outcome* is the target of the activity within the system. It refers to the problem space at which activity is directed. An example might be the problem of changing a traditional course into a Web-based course. The problem is shaped or transformed into outcomes with the help of mediating instruments, tools, and signs.

In an educational activity system, people construct meaning, the object of learning, through interactions with others. They then create outcomes using tools or artifacts. In the activity system of an online course, for example, the course Web site with its discussion boards, chat rooms, e-mail, and other tools of technology are used by the instructor and by learners to produce course outcomes, such as research, presentations, projects, or papers.

An Activity System for 2020 and Beyond

In the edunetworked environment, the classroom becomes a space where learners, subject matter experts, and software are connected in a knowledge-building environment. The classroom is no longer a bounded, physical space. In 2010, the virtual classroom is under the direction of a single instructor who is responsible for content delivery, feedback, and evaluation, and who has the power and authority to determine what is acceptable knowledge and appropriate levels of learning. In 2020, the classroom will be a space for learning communities to gather resources, share ideas, and address issues generated by collaborators focused on a relevant inquiry related to a subject matter concern.

In terms of teaching and learning in the future, the activity system framework can help redefine the role of the faculty from being the primary source of content to managers of teams and facilitators of learning experiences. Faculty will help students organize their curriculum, achieve literacy regarding online sources, and operate in a fluid, ambiguous environment. The framework also can help redefine the role of the learner from being a recipient of the instructor's knowledge to an active learner at the center of the learning activity.

Tools

Instruction is shaped by the interaction of tools, learners, and the instructor. Tools include any device that mediates or shapes the instructional interaction, such as synchronous and asynchronous technology, books, online resources, group size, online learning theories, and self-concepts. In 2020 and beyond, learning spaces will be built on the idea of the personal learning environment (PLE). In 2010, tools are available for the construction of personal learning spaces. However, because most instruction is still carried out in physical classrooms or course management systems that are controlled and directed within the confines of an institution, the idea has not received much attention until changes in the educational landscape will prompt a change in the approach to education. The change will be brought about by the inevitable decline of full-time learners and the shift from full-time to part-time working students who need flexible and portable ways to continue their studies while integrating work, family, and community.

The PLE allows a learner to have a portfolio of knowledge in one place that includes formal, nonformal, informal, and incidental learning experiences. All sources of learning can be combined to help learners address their needs. The learning recorded in the portfolio will be used to credential the experience (Attwell, 2007). Unlike course management systems that belong to an institution, a PLE is created by the learner who selects the tools needed to acquire, share, comment, and collaborate. The platform belongs to the learner, is available at all times throughout the learning life of the learner, and can integrate work, school, and other learning needs. The PLE can connect with institutional systems as well as PLEs maintained by others in virtual learning spaces. Intelligent agents that reside in the PLE respond to the learning patterns of the user and begin to shape the way learners think about learning. Aggregators capture ideas from sources throughout the Internet working on an issue and, using a thought-like process, distill and integrate the streams into a coherent document that reflects the learner's writing and thinking style (Hewitt, 2004). The PLE becomes the space in which learners communicate, create, consume, reshape, and collaborate. PLEs may take various forms and use different tools. However, PLEs share similar characteristics: the spaces belong to the learner, have global reach, are smart and comprehensive in function, and integrate with other systems (Schneider, 2009).

Tools constantly change, and in the process they change how we teach and learn. For example, technologies such as Internet2, social networking sites, wikis, and virtual environments extend constructivist learning environments beyond our geographical boundaries. In 2020 and beyond, academic materials will include files from conferences, personal thoughts on electronic diaries, blogs, journals, current discussions and other informal learning materials all a click or RSS-type feed away. Experience with social networking sites and micro-blogging technologies will provide learners with the skills to seek more control over the tools used for learning and to receive feedback within seconds (Diannekrause, 2009). Mobile computers, including cell and smart phones, will display animations, support language lessons, and be used for polling. Instructors will need to know how to combine tools to achieve the desired learning outcomes.

Participants

Participants in the classroom of 2020 will include humans and computer-based instructional agents. Intelligent, embodied agents will "reside in the learning environment by appearing as animated 'humanlike' characters, which allows them to exploit...communication typically reserved for human-human interaction" (Atkinson, 2002, p. 416). Faculty, learners, and embodied agents will each have roles in the learning process. Faculty will focus on the learning process rather than on imparting their knowledge. Scholars and others will be affiliated with multiple institutions. These independent scholars will use their knowledge, commentaries, ideas, and expertise in a field of inquiry as marketing tools. With the help of intelligent agents, learners will assemble their own cohort of scholars and other learners based on shared interests (Brown & Duguid, 1996; Yang, Wang, Shen, & Han, 2007). Learners will build knowledge by bringing global sources on the Internet into the class to add content and challenge instructors and one another. Intelligent agents will scan files for information relevant to the inquiry and disseminate content to others for verification. Agents will choose and integrate the learning tools that are most appropriate for the inquiry currently under way and reconfigure them for mobile devices if necessary.

In 2010, intelligent agents are in the nascent stages and are used predominately as substitute tutors responding to frequently asked questions. In 2020 and beyond, these agents can be expected to work on behalf of both instructors and learners. For instructors, agents can respond to questions, send deadline reminders, and potentially grade assignments (Li, 2007). Instructors may have solely a digital presence in the classroom (Hai-Jew, 2007) and may interact with learners through the students' embodied agents (Mahmood & Ferneley, 2006). For example, a learner may dispatch agents to multiple courses simultaneously. The agents could represent the learner based on previous learning behaviors and report filtered content back to the learner based on learner needs. Intelligent agents can help students build cohorts by identifying learners with similar interests and experiences (Li, 2007; Yang et al., 2007). In addition, agents can track work progress and help the learner develop study skills (Li, 2007).

Faculty will help learners manage this complex, media-rich environment by orchestrating multiple views and pulling them together coherently. As faculty change their mindset from being the primary source of information to guiding students in critically selecting content, what faculty say will become less important than what they do to help generate critical thought. For their part, learners will receive guidance instantly from international scholars, join teams of inquirers from around the world, and work on their academic journey anywhere. Learners will be able to knit together formal and informal learning resources to complete an inquiry. How learners form their study teams and what the team learned about the inquiry will become more important than any single individual with whom learners study.

Social Practices

The model of learning in 2020 will be built on the following elements: Higher education faculty will be known as knowledge-brokers who will work with learners to produce a set of competencies related to subject matter. Learning will be situated in context; i.e., content will be found and applied in the doing of the work. An instructor and learner will develop a learning contract specifying what an acceptable product might look like (Knowles, 1986). Agreement about good scholarship or mastery of subject matter will be embedded in issues generated by the learner (Vella, Berardinelli, & Burrow, 1998). Together with faculty, individual learners or groups will determine competencies that need to be developed, specify the particular objectives for inquiry, identify potential learning resources, determine what might constitute evidence of accomplishment, and agree on a means for validation.

As a knowledge-broker, the faculty member will serve as a link to others who have or may have similar interests in the issue. The idea of curriculum becomes learner-centered and learner-controlled, with the goal of creating "highly developed individuals, providing them with the skills to continue creating learning experiences, digest current knowledge, and create new knowledge within the curriculum itself" (Emes & Cleveland-Innes, 2003, p. 47). The notion of learner control is similar to the idea of self-direction in adult learning. Self-direction does not imply isolation in learning but includes the learner both individually and collectively in making curricula decisions, including planning, conducting and assessing the experience (Brockett & Hiemstra, 1991; Delaney, 1999).

In 2020 and beyond, the further development of collaborative tools and the ability of learners and intelligent agents to configure tools will shift how learning occurs and how higher education will regard the learning process. This includes how knowledge is represented by the learner; what is credible as knowledge; where knowledge resides; and what it means to make meaning from various information sources, including text, graphics, and images. The tools will require learners to knit together various forms of content to address an issue in a scholarly and creative manner. The ability to work with content rather than to retain content will demonstrate mastery in an area of inquiry (Farmer, 2006; Emes & Cleveland-Innes, 2003; Lave, 1988).

Social practices regulate actions and interactions within the activity system. Instructors will need to understand how learners interact with their computers and one another. They will need to help learners manage text-based and voice-based interactions to promote critical thought and deep learning. This involves skill in coaching discussion groups, providing feedback on the quality of online discussion, and offering guidance on expressing oneself online through text and paralanguage.

Learning Community

Learning will take place in academic communities that recognize that learners are co-producers of knowledge. These communities are based on the idea that social groupings can facilitate individual and collective learning. Learning in community means acquiring new basic skills, including the ability to work in groups with persons of various backgrounds; to communicate effectively, both orally and in writing; to combine independent and interdependent work to produce a meaningful outcome; and to use social networking and collaborative software. Learning in community means being engaged in the task of knowledge building around inquiry rather than being engaged in knowledge acquisition and retention.

Intelligent agents will bring together learners who wish to work on the same inquiry-based project (Yang et al., 2007). An inquiry-based project is a set of questions generated from a content area that has relevance to the practice lives of the learners and which meets competencies for mastering content knowledge in a situated context (Schlager & Fusco, 2004). Learners on inquiry-based projects will be guided by those who have expertise in the particular field of inquiry. Their learning community will form and re-form based on the nature of the project (Barab, Kling, & Gray, 2004).

Outcome

In 2010, courses were focused on content dissemination and acquisition decontextualized from the daily lives of the learners. In 2020, courses will be a set of knowledge demonstrations (Bousquet, 2009). Instruction will help students connect their experience of learning to real-world applications. Faculty and learners alike will assess and monitor the validity of content from multiple channels to achieve learning outcomes.

Between 2005 and 2010, changes were occurring not only in the uses and forms of online technologies for learning but in the nature of learning itself. The intersection of advances in the way learners could communicate using technology and the call for greater collaboration in the way the university functions resulted in changes in how teaching and learning were beginning to be conceptualized and actualized in practice. Pedagogical practice in the first decade of the 21st century had not kept up with changes in technology:

> *For years...it has been part of the underlying set of pedagogical intentions to design online courses utilizing the individual student's perspectives and knowledge and engaging students in interactive collaboration and shared knowledge building. This ambition has not been realized. (Sorensen, 2005, p. 446)*

In 2005, Sorensen presented a model of collaborative education occurring in Northern Europe citing a case in which one university provided administrative support while four other universities collaboratively developed a teacher education curriculum for delivery online. The approach, known as Problem-Oriented Project Pedagogy (POPP), was based on the notion that knowledge building was the outcome of an educational experience. This was the beginning of a different approach to using technology in the support of learning.

By 2010, some leaders in higher education called for greater levels of collaboration within and outside institutions to server learners better. Financial constraints, safety concerns, the cost of maintaining student services, and the intellectual challenge of dealing with complex social issues rendered the notion of rugged individuality as an outmoded notion, including the model of the individual scholar (Kezer & Lester, 2009). The emerging university would be stressing collaboration in daily work processes and in learning. Learning would be an active, engaged inquiry centering on the experiences and collective issues of groups rather than a recitation of content and individual attainment (Fullen & Scott, 2009).

Knowledge building is the creative act of adding to the intellectual and practical knowledge possessed by a community working on projects deemed important by that community. Knowledge building adds to the communal way of seeing the world, while learning adds only to an individual's repertoire of perspectives (Lipponen, 2000). The Twitter micro-blogging service has shown us how powerful and intriguing connections are and how we might engage in critical reflection and critical analysis of thought and action (Johnson, 2009). Our thought will be expanded by interactions with those with whom we work at a distance, everywhere, anywhere, and anytime.

FUTURE RESEARCH DIRECTIONS

In this chapter, we have used a technique called futuring to forecast how the notion of the classroom may change. A good forecast is clear, plausible, justifiable, and imaginative (Kauffman, 1976). Regarding clarity, we have specified a time period of 2020 and beyond and have based our framework on activity theory, which has assumptions about the importance of working collectively on goals determined by the group and using appropriate tools and social practices to achieve an outcome. We addressed the second criterion of a good forecast, plausibility, by basing our scenarios on technology that is in the development stages or is already available. In addition, our pedagogy is based on constructivism, an approach widely discussed if not pervasively practiced. Regarding justifying our forecast, we have built our arguments on extant theory, literature, and practice as well as on emerging trends. Building from those seeds planted in the past, we made intuitive leaps to imagine the possibilities that may bloom for future learning environments.

Although events may unfold in multiple ways, empirical studies that examine future learning environments are not considering how the future may change by applying Kauffman's (1976) criteria. Clark and Choi (2005) have sounded a warning about how studies of tools in future learning environments are designed. We suggest that researchers add the criteria of clarity, plausibility, justification, and imagination when projecting changes to the participants, tools, practices, and outcomes in future learning communities.

CONCLUSION

Based on an intellectual exercise that guided our projections of the classroom environment in 2020 and beyond, we envision a future with fewer faculty affiliated with only one institution and more independent scholars. As knowledge-brokers, faculty will recognize that knowledge exists outside themselves (Emes & Cleveland-Innes, 2003). Learners will assemble their own cohort of scholars and other learners, and they will use personal learning environments and intelligent agents to facilitate their inquiry. Such tools will respond to what faculty and other learners are doing and influence how they will carry out the learning process. Social practices will include learning content in the context of doing the work and jointly coming to agreement about what constitutes mastery of the subject matter.

Faculty development must attend to the interactions among tools, participants, social practices, learning in community, and the learning outcome.

Technological tools, the subject of a robust literature (Jonassen & Reeves, 1996, Kim & Reeves, 2007; Lajoie, 2000), represent only one of the elements in the faculty development model. The combination of and interaction among tools, participants, social practices, community, and the outcome create an environment for a meaningful educational experience.

Educational deficits will still exist for some individuals in 2020 and beyond. We realize our future vision may have unintended consequences that may hinder learning for those who have not yet developed into engaged independent and interdependent learners (Grow, 1991). Faculty will need to be sensitive to the stages of self-direction and learner control and adjust their pedagogy accordingly.

The most significant barriers may include faculty who resist changing their mindset about what constitutes an appropriate role and administrators such as Garry, the associate dean mentioned at the beginning of the chapter, who resist changing their mindset about what constitutes a worthwhile learning environment. As long as those mindsets are at odds with what learners like Melanie expect in terms of flexibility and control, the activity system we propose will remain a possibility and not a certainty.

ACKNOWLEDGMENT

The authors thank Lynn A. Trinko for her development of the personal learning environment scenario.

REFERENCES

Atkinson, R. K. (2002). Optimizing learning from examples using animated pedagogical agents. *Journal of Educational Psychology*, *94*, 416–427. doi:10.1037/0022-0663.94.2.416

Attwell, G. (2007). The personal learning environment: The future of eLearning? *eLearning Papers*, 2(1). Retrieved July 27, 2009, from http://www.elearningpapers.eu

Barab, S. A., Kling, R., & Gray, J. H. (2004). Introduction: Designing for virtual communities in the service of learning. In Barab, S., Kling, R., & Gray, J. (Eds.), *Designing virtual communities in the service of learning* (pp. 3–15). New York: Cambridge University Press.

Bligh, J. (2005). Faculty development. *Medical Education*, *39*, 120–121. doi:10.1111/j.1365-2929.2004.02098.x

Borgia, N. (2008, November 12). Online law degrees not expected to come to Ohio any time soon. *The Daily Reporter*, *162*, A1.

Bousquet, M. (2009, July 10). The faculty of the future: Leaner, meaner, more innovative, less secure. *The Chronicle of Higher Education*, *55*(41), B24.

Brockett, R., & Hiemstra, R. (1991). *Self-direction in adult learning*. New York: Routledge.

Brown, J. S. (2001). *Learning in the digital age*. Retrieved July 5, 2009, from http://www.johnseelybrown.com/learning_in_digital_age-aspen.pdf

Brown, J. S., & Duguid, P. (1996, July/August). Universities in the digital age. *Change*, *28*(4), 11–20. doi:10.1080/00091383.1996.9937757

Chronicle Research Services. (2009). *The college of 2020: Students*. Retrieved June 23, 2009, from https://chronicle.com/subscribe/singlecopies/college2020non

Clark, R. E., & Choi, S. (2005). Five design principles for experiments on the effects of animated pedagogical agents. *Journal of Educational Computing Research*, *32*(3), 209–225. doi:10.2190/7LRM-3BR2-44GW-9QQY

Delaney, J. G. (1999). *What are learner-centered schools?* Retrieved September 8, 2008, from http://www.mun.ca/educ/faculty/mwatch/win99/delaney.htm

Diannekrause. (2009, April 17). Twitter useful for education [Web log message]. Retrieved from http://diannekrause.edublogs.org/2009/0407/twitter-useful-for-education

Dick, M. (2009, June 23). Colleges must yield to people's schedules. *The Columbus Dispatch, 138*, A10.

Dirr, P. J. (1999). Distance and virtual learning in the United States. In Farrell, G. M. (Ed.), *The development of virtual education: A global perspective* (pp. 23–48). Vancouver, BC: The Commonwealth of Learning.

Emes, C., & Cleveland-Innes, M. (2003). A journey toward learner-centered curriculum. *Canadian Journal of Higher Education, 33*(3), 47–70.

Engström, Y. (1987). *Learning by expanding: An activity-theoretical approach to developmental research.* Helsinki: Orienta-Konsultit.

Engström, Y., Miettinen, R., & Punamaki, R. L. (1999). *Perspectives on activity theory.* Cambridge: Cambridge University Press.

Farmer, J. (2006). The inevitable personal learning environment post. Retrieved March 13, 2009, from http://incsub.org/blog/2006/the-inevitable-personal-learning-environment

Fowles, J. (1978). *Handbook of futures research.* Westport, CT: Greenwood Press.

Fullen, M., & Scott, G. (2009). *Turnaround leadership for higher education.* San Francisco: Jossey-Bass.

Grow, G. (1991). Teaching learners to be self-directed. *Adult Education Quarterly, 41*(3), 125–149. doi:10.1177/0001848191041003001

Hai-Jew, S. (2007). F2F and online "live personalization" of learning and implications for learning object repositories and automated eLearning (A survey and analysis). *Journal of Interactive Instruction Development, 19*(4), 19–39.

Hewitt, J. (2004). An exploration of community in a knowledge forum classroom: An activity system analysis. In Barab, S., Kling, R., & Gray, J. (Eds.), *Designing virtual communities in the service of learning* (pp. 210–238). New York: Cambridge University Press.

Howell, S. L., Williams, P. B., & Lindsay, N. K. (2003). Thirty-two trends affecting distance education: An informed foundation for strategic planning. *Online Journal of Distance Learning Administration, 6*(3), 8–26.

Johnson, S. (2009). How twitter will change the way we live. *Time, 173*(23), 32–37.

Jonassen, D. H. (2000). Revisiting activity theory as a framework for designing student-centered learning environments. In Jonassen, D. H., & Land, S. (Eds.), *Theoretical foundations of learning environments* (pp. 89–122). Mahwah, NJ: Erlbaum.

Jonassen, D. H., & Reeves, T. C. (1996). Learning with technology: Using computers as cognitive tools. In Jonassen, D. H. (Ed.), *Handook of research for educational communications and technology* (pp. 693–719). New York: Macmillan.

Kauffman, D. (1976). *Teaching the future.* Palm Springs, CA: ETC Publications.

Kezar, A., & Lester, J. (2009). *Organizing higher education for collaboration.* San Francisco: Jossey-Bass.

Kim, B., & Reeves, T. C. (2007). Reframing research on learning with technology: In search of the meaning of cognitive tools. *Instructional Science, 35*, 207–256. doi:10.1007/s11251-006-9005-2

KnowledgeWorks Foundation. (2006). *2006-2016: Map of future forces affecting education*. Palo Alto, CA: Institute for the Future and KnowledgeWorks Foundation.

Knowles, M. S. (1986). *Using learning contracts*. San Francisco: Jossey-Bass.

Lajoie, S. P. (2000). *Computers as cognitive tools: No more walls* (*Vol. 2*). Mahwah, NJ: Erlbaum.

Lave, J. (1988). *Cognition in practice: Mind, mathematics and culture in everyday life*. New York: Cambridge University Press. doi:10.1017/CBO9780511609268

Lektorsky, V. A. (1999). Activity theory in a new era. In Engström, Y., Miettinen, R., & Punamaki, R. L. (Eds.), *Perspectives on activity theory*. Cambridge: Cambridge University Press.

Levin, J. (2002). A 2020 vision: Education in the next two decades. *Quarterly Review of Distance Education*, *3*(1), 110–117.

Levine, A. (2000). The future of colleges: Nine inevitable changes. *The Chronicle of Higher Education*, *47*(9), B10.

Li, X. (2007). Intelligent agent-supported online education. *Decision Sciences Journal of Innovative Education*, *5*, 311–331. doi:10.1111/j.1540-4609.2007.00143.x

Lipponen, L. (2000). Towards knowledge building: From facts to explanations in primary students' computer-mediated discourse. *Learning Environments Research*, *3*, 179–199. doi:10.1023/A:1026516728338

Mahmood, A. K., & Ferneley, E. (2006). Embodied agents in e-learning environments: An exploratory case study. *Journal of Interactive Learning Research*, *17*(2), 143–162.

Scanlon, E., & Issroff, K. (2005). Activity theory and higher education: Evaluating learning technologies. *Journal of Computer Assisted Learning*, *21*(6), 430–439. doi:10.1111/j.1365-2729.2005.00153.x

Schlager, M. S., & Fusco, J. (2004). Teacher professional development, technology, and communities of practice: Are we putting the cart before the horse? In Barab, S., Kling, R., & Gray, J. (Eds.), *Designing virtual communities in the service of learning* (pp. 120–153). New York: Cambridge University Press.

Schneider, D. (2009). Personal learning environment. Retrieved March 13, 2009, from http://edutechwiki.unige.ch/en/Persnal_learning_environment

Sorcinelli, M. D., Austin, A. E., Eddy, P. L., & Beach, A. L. (2006). *Creating the future of faculty development: Learning from the past, understanding the present*. Bolton, MA: Anker Publishing.

Sorensen, E. (2005). Networked eLearning and collaborative knowledge building: Design and facilitation. *Contemporary Issues in Technology & Teacher Education*, *4*, 441–455.

Szep, J. (2008, July 7). Technology reshapes America's classrooms. *Reuters*. Retrieved July 20, 2009, from http://www.reuters.com/article/topNews/idUSN2547885520080707?feedType=RSS&feedName=topNews

Vella, J., Berardinelli, P., & Burrow, J. (1998). *How do they know they know? Evaluating adult learning*. San Francisco: Jossey-Bass.

Waycott, J., Jones, A., & Scanlon, E. (2005). PDAs as lifelong learning tools: An activity theory based analysis. *Learning, Media and Technology*, *30*(2), 107–130. doi:10.1080/17439880500093513

Wilkerson, L., & Irby, D. M. (1998). Strategies for improving teaching practices: A comprehensive approach to faculty development. *Academic Medicine, 73*(4), 387–396. doi:10.1097/00001888-199804000-00011

Yang, F., Wang, M., Shen, R., & Han, P. (2007). Community-organizing agent: An artificial intelligent system for building learning communities among large numbers of learners. *Computers & Education, 49*, 131–147. doi:10.1016/j.compedu.2005.04.019

ADDITIONAL READING

Akhras, F. N., & Self, J. A. (2000). Modeling the process, not the product, of learning. In Lajoie, S. P. (Ed.), *Computers as cognitive tools: No more walls* (*Vol. 2*, pp. 3–28). Mahwah, NJ: Erlbaum.

Anderson, J. R., Corbett, A. T., Koedinger, K. R., & Pelletier, R. (1995). Cognitive tutors: Lessons learned. *Journal of the Learning Sciences, 4*(2), 167–207. doi:10.1207/s15327809jls0402_2

Baylor, A. L. (2002). Agent-based learning environments as a research tool for investigating teaching and learning. *Journal of Educational Computing Research, 26*(3), 249–270. doi:10.2190/PH2K-6P09-K8EC-KRDK

Carter, A. (1995). Developing faculty training for interactive distance education. *Innovations in Education and Training International, 32*(2), 147–152.

Craig, S. D., Gholson, B., & Driscoll, D. M. (2002). Animated pedagogical agents in multimedia educational environments: Effects of agent properties, picture features and redundancy. *Journal of Educational Psychology, 94*, 428–434. doi:10.1037/0022-0663.94.2.428

De Simone, C. (2006). Preparing our teachers for distance education. *College Teaching, 54*(1), 183–184. doi:10.3200/CTCH.54.1.183-184

Diaz, V., Garrett, P. B., Kinley, E. R., Moore, J. F., Schwartz, C. M., & Kohrman, P. (2009). Faculty development for the 21st century. *EDUCAUSE Review, 44*(3), 46–55.

Engström, Y. (2008). *From teams to knots: Activity-theoretical studies of collaboration and learning at work.* New York: Cambridge University Press. doi:10.1017/CBO9780511619847

Irani, T. (2001). Going the distance: Developing a model distance education faculty training program. *Campus Technology.* Retrieved June 18, 2009, from http://campustechnology.com/articles/38638_4/

Johnson, W. L., Rickel, J. W., & Lester, J. C. (2000). Animated pedagogical agents: Face-to-face interaction in interactive learning environments. *International Journal of Artificial Intelligence in Education, 11*, 47–78.

Moreno, R. E., Dow, G. T., & Mayer, S. (2003). Multimedia learning in an interactive self-explaining environment: What works in the design of agent-based microworlds? *Journal of Educational Psychology, 95*, 806–813. doi:10.1037/0022-0663.95.4.806

Resta, P., & Laferriere, T. (2007). Technology in support of collaborative learning. *Educational Psychology Review, 19*, 65–83. doi:10.1007/s10648-007-9042-7

Sampson, D., Karagiannidis, C., & Kinshuk, C. (2002). Personalised learning: Educational technological and standardisation perspective. *Interactive Education Multimedia, 4*, 24–39.

Vella, J. (1994). *Learning to listen, learning to teach: The power of dialogue in educating adults.* San Francisco: Jossey-Bass.

KEY TERMS AND DEFINITIONS

Activity Theory: A form of sociocultural analysis that focuses on activity systems such as workplaces and courses of study.

Faculty Development: Activities that help manage change, improve teaching performance, and put knowledge into practice.

Learning Community: One or more people who share the objective with the subject.

Outcome: The target of the activity within the system.

Participants: Individuals whose point of view is taken in the analysis of the activity or the animated computer-based instructional agent that represents the individual's point of view.

Social Practices: Actions and interactions within the activity system that address how tasks are divided among community members.

Tools: Mediating artifacts that help achieve the outcomes of the activity.

Compilation of References

AASL. (2008). Learning about the Job [What does a school library media specialist do?]. Retrieved July 31, 2008, from http://www.ala.org/ala/aasl/aasleducation/recruitmentlib/learningabout/learningabout.cfm

Abbott, L. D. (2003). Novice teachers' experiences with telementoring as learner-centered professional development. Available from Dissertations and Theses database. (UMI No. 3116246)

AbilityNet. (2008, January 18). Social networking sites lock out disabled users. Retrieved January 31, 2009, from http://www.abilitynet.org.uk/enation85

Abrami, P., & Barrett, H. (2005). Directions for research and development on electronic portfolios 1. *Canadian Journal of Learning and Technology, 31*(3). Retrieved April 18, 2007, from http://www.cjlt.ca/content/vol31.3/abrami.html

Academy of American Poets. (1997-2009). Ekphrasis: Poetry confronting Art. Retrieved March 15, 2009, from http://www.poets.org/viewmedia.php/prmMID/5918

Adam, L. (2003). Information and communication technologies in higher education in Africa: Initiatives and challenges. *Journal of Higher Education in Africa* (JHEA/RESA), *1*(1),195–2210.

Adamy, P., & Heinecke, W. (2005). The influence of organizational culture on technology integration in teacher education. *Journal of Technology and Teacher Education, 13*(2), 233–255.

Ajzen, I. (1985). From intentions to action: A theory of planned behavior. In Kuhl, J., & Beckman, J. (Eds.), *Action-control: From cognition to behavior* (pp. 11–39). Heidelberg, Germany: Springer.

Akudolu, L. (2007) The place of ICT in the successful implementation of the education reform under NEEDS and Millennium Development Goals (MDGs). Paper presented at the *ANCOPSS (All Nigeria Conference of Principals of Secondary Schools) 2006/2007 Mandatory Continuing Professional Training (MCPT) for Principals of South East Zone*, Awka, Nigeria, January 2007. Retrieved July 22, 2007, from http://www.lilianrita.com/lr3/INTRODUCTION%20NATION.pdf

Albanese, M. (2000). Problem-based learning: why curricula are likely to show little effect on knowledge and clinical skills. *Medical Education, 34*, 729–738. doi:10.1046/j.1365-2923.2000.00753.x

Albion, P. R., & Ertmer, P. A. (2002). Beyond the foundations: The role of vision and belief in teachers' preparation for integration of technology. *TechTrends, 46*(5). doi:10.1007/BF02818306

Allen, E., & Seaman, J. (2008). *Staying the course: Online education in the United States*. Needham, MA: Sloan-C.

American Federation for the Blind. (2008). Are social networking sites accessible to people with vision loss? Retrieved from January 31, 2009, from http://www.afb.org/Section.asp?SectionID=57&TopicID=167&DocumentID=3153

Anderson, B. (2006). Writing power into online discussion. *Computers and Composition, 23*, 108–124. doi:10.1016/j.compcom.2005.12.007

Anderson, T., Rourke, L., Garrison, D. R., & Archer, W. (2001). Assessing teaching presence in a computer conferencing context. *Journal of Asynchronous Learning Networks*, *5*(2).

Anderson, L. W., & Krathwohl, D. (Eds.). (2000). *A taxonomy for learning, teaching and assessing: A revision of Bloom's taxonomy of educational objectives*. New York: Longman.

Anderson, R., & Dexter, S. (2000). *School technology leadership: Incidence and impact*. Center for Research on Information Technology and Organizations, University of California Irvine. Available from http://www.crito.uci.edu/tlc/findings/report_6

Angeley, R., & Purdue, J. (2000). Information literacy: an overview [Electronic Version]. *Dialogue Home*. Retrieved November 30, 2009, from http://pandora.cii.wwu.edu/dialogue/issue6.html

Annetta, L. A., & Holmes, S. (2006). Creating presence and community in a synchronous virtual learning environment using avatars. *International Journal of Instructional Technology & Distance Learning*, *3*(8), 31–47. Retrieved February 7, 2007, from http://www.itdl.org/Journal/Aug_06/article03.htm

Antal, A. B., & Friedman, V. J. (2008). Learning to negotiate reality: A strategy for teaching intercultural competencies. *Journal of Management Education*, *32*(363).

Apple, M. W. (1982). *Education and power*. New York: Routledge.

Aragon, S. R. (2003). Creating social presence in online environments. *New Directions for Adult and Continuing Education*, *100*, 57–68. doi:10.1002/ace.119

Archambault, F., Kulikowich, J., Brown, S., & Rezendes, G. (2002). Developing performance assessments to measure teacher competency in the use of educational technology. Paper presented at the Annual Meeting of the Educational Research Association, New Orleans, LA.

Archer, W., Garrison, R., & Anderson, T. (1999). Adopting disruptive technologies in traditional universities: Continuing education as a incubator for innovation. *The Canadian Journal of University Continuing Education*, *25*(1). Retrieved April 18, 2007, from http://www.extension.usask.ca/cjuce/eng/Ab251.html

Argyris, C., & Putnam, R. (1985). *Action science: Concepts, methods, and skills for research and intervention*. San Francisco: Jossey - Bass.

Association of African Universities. (2000). Guidelines for institutional self-assessment of ICT maturity in African universities.

Association of College and Research Libraries. (2000). *Information literacy competency standards for higher education*. Retrieved June 24, 2009, from http://www.ala.org/ala/mgrps/divs/acrl/standards/informationliteracycompetency.cfm#ildef

Atkins, N. E., & Vasu, E. S. (2000). Measuring knowledge of technology usage and stages of concern about computing: A study of middle school teachers. *Journal of Technology and Teacher Education*, *8*(4), 279–302.

Atkinson, S., & Burden, K. (2007). *Virtuality, veracity and values: Exploring between virtual and real worlds using the 3V model. ICT: Providing choices for learners and learning: ASCILITE 2007*. Singapore: Ascilite.

Atkinson, R. K. (2002). Optimizing learning from examples using animated pedagogical agents. *Journal of Educational Psychology*, *94*, 416–427. doi:10.1037/0022-0663.94.2.416

Attali, Y., & Burstein, J. (2006). Automated essay scoring with e-rater. *The Journal of Technology, Learning, and Assessment*, *4*(3). Retrieved April 18, 2007, from http://escholarship.bc.edu/jtla/vol4/3/

Attwell, G. (2007). The personal learning environment: The future of eLearning? *eLearning Papers*, 2(1). Retrieved July 27, 2009, from http://www.elearningpapers.eu

August, D., & Shanahan, T. (Eds.). (2006). *Developing literacy in second-language learners: Report of the National Literacy Panel on language-minority children and youth. The Center for Applied Linguistics*. Mahwah, NJ: Erlbaum.

Ba, H., Tally, B., & Tsikalas, K. (2002). *Children's emerging digital literacies: Investigating home computing in low- and middle-income families. CCT reports*. New York: Center for Children & Technology. (ERIC Document Reproduction Service No. ED 477 716).

Badke, W. (2008, November/December). Ten reasons to teach information literacy for credit. *Online*, 47-49.

Baguma, I., & Ssewanyana, J. K. (2008). A Simulation Modeling-Based Investigation of the Impact of IT Infrastructure on Business Process Reengineering. [Special Issue]. *International Journal of Computing and ICT Research*, *1*(1).

Bahr, P. R. (2009). College hopping: Exploring the occurrence, frequency, and consequences of lateral transfer. *Community College Review*, *36*(4), 271–298. doi:10.1177/0091552108330903

Bai, H., & Lehman, J. (2003). Impact of a professional development project on university faculty members' perceptions and use of technology. In *Proceedings of World Conference on Educational Multimedia, Hypermedia and Telecommunications 2003* (pp. 1927-1934). Norfolk, VA: AACE.

Bailenson, J. N., Yee, N., Merget, D., & Schroeder, R. (2006). The effect of behavioral realism and form realism of real-time avatar faces on verbal disclosure, nonverbal disclosure, emotion recognition, and copresence in dyadic interaction. *Presence (Cambridge, Mass.)*, *15*(4), 359–372. doi:10.1162/pres.15.4.359

Bailey, G. D., & Pownell, D. (1997). Technology staff development and support programs applying Abraham Maslow's hierarchy of needs. *Learning and Leading with Technology*, *26*(3), 47–64.

Baker, S. C., Wentz, R. K., & Woods, M. M. (2009). Using virtual worlds in education: Second Life® as an educational tool. *Teaching of Psychology*, *36*(1), 59–64. doi:10.1080/00986280802529079

Bandura, A. (1986). *Social Foundations of Thought and Action*. Englewood Cliffs, NJ: Prentice-Hall.

Bandura, A. (1997). *Self-efficacy: The exercise of control*. New York: W.H. Freeman.

Barab, S., Dodge, T., & Thomas, M. (2007). Our designs and the social agendas they carry. *Journal of the Learning Sciences*, *16*(2), 263–305.

Barab, S., Kling, R., & Gray, J. H. (Eds.). (2004). *Designing for virtual communities in the service of learning*. Cambridge, UK: Press Syndicate of the University of Cambridge.

Barab, S., Thomas, M., Dodge, T., Carteaux, R., & Tuzun, H. (2005). Making learning fun: Quest Atlantis, a game without guns. [from http://inkido.indiana.edu/research/onlinemanu/papers/QA_ETRD.pdf]. *Educational Technology Research and Development*, *53*(1), 86–107. Retrieved July 3, 2005. doi:10.1007/BF02504859

Barab, S. A., Kling, R., & Gray, J. H. (2004). Introduction: Designing for virtual communities in the service of learning. In Barab, S., Kling, R., & Gray, J. (Eds.), *Designing virtual communities in the service of learning* (pp. 3–15). New York: Cambridge University Press.

Barefoot, B. O. (2004). Higher education's revolving door: Confronting the problem of student drop out in US colleges and universities. *Open Learning: The Journal of Open and Distance Learning*, *19*(1), 9–18.

Barker, J. (Writer). (1993). Discovering the future series: Paradigm pioneers.

Barone, C., & Hagner, P. (2001). *Technology-enhanced teaching and learning: Leading and supporting the transformation on your campus*. San Francisco: Jossey-Bass.

Barrett, H. (2003). Electronic portfolios. In Kovalchick, A., & Dawson, K. (Eds.), *Education and technology: An encyclopedia* (pp. 271–276). Santa Barbara, CA: ABC-Clio.

Barron, R. S., Kerr, N. L., & Miller, N. (1992). *Group process, group decision, group action*. Bristol, PA: Open University Press.

Basque, J., Dore, S., & Henri, F. (2000). Facilitating a Techno-pedagogical Change in higher education: lessons from the SAVOIR and AMETIST projects. In *Proceedings of the XVIIIth Conference of the International Council for Innovation in Higher Education,* November 5-9, 2000, Quebec, Canada.

Bateman, P. (2006, November 19-2?). Bandwidth Connectivity and Management. Paper presented at the *Frontiers of Knowledge Conference*, University of Cape Town, South Africa. Retrieved on Dec. 27, 2009, from http://www.foundationpartnership.org/pubs/leaders/assets/papers/BatemanSession7Part1.pdf

Bauer, J., & Kenton, J. (2005). Toward technology integration in the schools: Why it isn't happening. *Journal of Technology and Teacher Education, 13*(4), 519–546.

Bauerlein, M. (2008). *The dumbest generation: How the digital age stupefies young Americans and jeopardizes our future*. New York: Penguin.

Bazerman, C. (2008). *Writing realities, changing realities. CCCC Call for Program Proposals*. Urbana, IL: NCTE.

Bean, J. C. (2001). *Engaging ideas: The professors guide to integrating writing, critical thinking, and active learning in the classroom*. San Francisco: Jossey-Bass.

Beaudry, A., & Pinsonneault, A. (2005). Understanding user responses to information technology: A coping model of user adaptation. *Management Information Systems Quarterly, 29*(3), 493–524.

Becker, H. J. (2000). Findings from the teaching, learning, and computing survey: Is Larry Cuban right? *Education Policy Analysis Archives, 8*(51). Retrieved June 19, 2009, from http://epaa.asu.edu/epaa/v8n51

Belenky, M. F., Clinchy, B. M., Goldberger, N. R., & Tarule, J. M. (1997). *Women's ways of knowing: The development of self, voice, and mind (10th Anniversary Edition)*. New York: Basic Books.

Bell, D. (2009). Learning from Second Life. *British Journal of Educational Technology, 40*(3), 515–525. doi:10.1111/j.1467-8535.2009.00943.x

Benek-Rivera, J., & Mathews, V. E. (2004). Active learning with Jeopardy: Students ask the questions. *Journal of Management Education, 28*(1), 104–118. doi:10.1177/1052562903252637

Benishek, L. A., Bieschke, K. J., Park, J., & Slattery, S. M. (2004). A multicultural feminist model of mentoring. *Journal of Multicultural Counseling and Development,* 32.

Benson, H. C. (2000). *Socratic Wisdom*. New York: Oxford University Press.

Bente, G., Ruggenberg, S., Kramer, N. C., & Eschenburg, F. (2008). Avatar-mediated networking: Increasing social presence and interpersonal trust in net-based collaborations. *Human Communication Research, 34*(2), 287–318. doi:10.1111/j.1468-2958.2008.00322.x

Bercuson, D., Bothwell, R., & Granatstein, J. (1997). *Petrified campus: The crisis in Canada's universities*. Toronto: Random House Canada.

Bereiter, C., & Scardamalia, M. (1987). *The psychology of written composition*. Hillsdale, NJ: Lawrence Erlbaum Associates.

Bereiter, C., & Scardamalia, M. (2003). Learning to work creatively with knowledge. In De Corte, E., Verschaffel, L., Entwistle, N., & van Merrienboer, J. (Eds.), *Unravelling basic components and dimensions of powerful learning environments*. Toronto, Canada: EARLI.

Berg, J., Berquam, L., & Christoph, K. (2007, March/April). Social networking technologies: A poke for campus service. *EDUCAUSE Review*, 32–42.

Betts, K. (1998, October). Why do faculty participate in distance education? The technology source. Retrieved from http://ts.mivu.org/default.asp?show=articleandid=6

Black, R. W. (2006). Language, culture, and identity in online fanfiction. *E-learning, 3* (2), 170-184. Retrieved May 10, 2008, from http://dx.doi.org/10.2304/elea.2007.4.4.384

Blakely, L. (2008). I'm majoring in facebook, how about you? Retrieved Janurary 31, 2009, from http://money.cnn.com/2007/10/08/magazines/fortune/blakely_facebook.fortune/index.htm

Bligh, J. (2005). Faculty development. *Medical Education, 39*, 120–121. doi:10.1111/j.1365-2929.2004.02098.x

Bloom, B. S., & Krathwohl, D. R. (1956). *Taxonomy of educational objectives: The classification of educational goals, by a committee of college and university examiners. Handbook I: Cognitive domain*. New York: Longmans and Green.

Blumenstyk, G. (1999, April 5). Union cites Guido Sarducci in ad campaign aimed at distance Education. *The Chronicle of Higher Education*.

Boellstorff, T. (2008). *Coming of age in Second Life®. An anthropologist explores the virtually human*. Princeton, NJ: Princeston University Press.

Bogden, R. C., & Biklen, S. K. (2003). *Qualitative research for education: An introduction to theories and methods*. Boston, MA: Allyn and Bacon.

Bonk, C. J., & King, K., S. (1998). *Electronic collaborators*. Mahwah, NJ: Erlbaum.

Bonwell, C. C., & Eisen, J. A. (1991). Active learning: Creating excitement in the classroom (ASHE-ERIC Higher Education Report No. 1). Washington, DC: George Washington University.

Borgatti, S. P., Everett, M. G., & Freeman, L. (1999). *UCINET V. Software for social network analysis*. Harvard, MA: Analytical Technologies.

Borgia, N. (2008, November 12). Online law degrees not expected to come to Ohio any time soon. *The Daily Reporter*, *162*, A1.

Borko, H. (2004). Professional development and teacher learning: Mapping the terrain. *Educational Researcher*, *33*(8), 3–15. doi:10.3102/0013189X033008003

Bouck, E. C. (2004). How size and setting impact education in rural schools. *Rural Educator*, *25*(3), 38–42.

Bousquet, M. (2009, July 10). The faculty of the future: Leaner, meaner, more innovative, less secure. *The Chronicle of Higher Education*, *55*(41), B24.

Boyd, D., Grossman, P. L., Hammerness, K., Hamilton Lankford, R., Loeb, S., & McDonald, M. (2008). Surveying the landscape of teacher education in New York City: Constrained variation and the challenge of innovation. *Educational Evaluation and Policy Analysis*, *30*(4), 319–343. doi:10.3102/0162373708322737

Boyd, D. M., & Ellison, N. (2007). Social network sites: Definition, history, and scholarship. *Journal of Computer-Mediated Communication, 13*(1), article 11. Retrieved January 31, 2009, from http://jcmc.indiana.edu/vol13/issue1/boyd.ellison.html

Boyer, E. (1990). *Scholarship Reconsidered: Priorities of the Professorate*. New York: The Carnegie Foundation for the Advancement of Teaching.

Boyle, P., & Boice, B. (1998). Systematic mentoring for new faculty teachers and graduate teaching assistants. *Innovative Higher Education*, *22*(3), 157–179. doi:10.1023/A:1025183225886

Bradshaw, K. L. (2002). Technology for Teaching and Learning: Strategies for Staff Development and Follow-Up Support. *Journal of Technology and Teacher Education*, 10.

Brady, L., Singh-Corcoran, N., Dadisman, J. A., & Diamond, K. (2009). A collaborative approach to information literacy: First-year composition, writing center, and library partnerships at West Virginia University. *Composition Forum, 19*. Retrieved January 29, 2009, from http://compositionforum.com/issue/19/west-virginia.php

Bransford, J., Brophy, S., & Williams, S. (2000). When Computer Technologies Meet the Learning Sciences: Issues and Opportunities. *Journal of Applied Developmental Psychology*, *21*(1), 59–84. doi:10.1016/S0193-3973(99)00051-9

Bransford, J. D., Brown, A. L., & Cocking, R. R. (2000). *How people learn: Brain, mind, experience and school.* Washington, DC: National Research Council National Academy Press.

Brase, H., & Brase, P. (2003). *Understanding Statistics: Concepts and Methods* (7th ed.). Boston: Houghton Mifflin.

BraveTree Productions LLC. n.d, [Computer Software]. Eugene, OR.

Breaux, A. L., & Wong, H. K. (2003). *New teacher induction: How to train, support, and retain new teachers.* Mountain View, CA: Harry K. Wong Publications, Inc.

Brinkerhoff, J. (2006). Effects of a long-duration, professional development academy on technology skills, computer self-efficacy, and technology integration beliefs and practices. *Journal of Research on Technology in Education*, *39*(1), 22–43.

Britton, E., Paine, L., & Raizen, S. (1999). *Middle grades mathematics and science teachers' induction in selected countries: Preliminary findings.* Washington, DC: National Center for Improving Science Education, WestEd.

Britzman, D. P. (1991). *Practice makes practice: A critical study of learning to teach.* Albany: State University of New York Press.

Brockett, R., & Hiemstra, R. (1991). *Self-direction in adult learning.* New York: Routledge.

Brookfield, S. (1987). *Developing critical thinkers.* San Francisco: Jossey-Bass.

Brookfield, S. (1999). *Discussion as a way of teaching.* San Francisco: Jossey-Bass.

Brookfield, S. (1986). *Understanding and facilitating adult learning.* San Francisco: Jossey-Bass.

Brown, J. S. (2000, March/April). Growing up digital: how the web changes work, education, and the ways people learn. *Change*, *32*(2), 11–20. doi:10.1080/00091380009601719

Brown, J. S., Collins, A., & Duguid, S. (1989). Situated cognition and the culture of learning. *Educational Researcher*, *18*(1), 32–42.

Brown, D., & Warschauer, M. (2006). From the university to the elementary classroom: Students' experiences in learning to integrate technology in instruction. *Journal of Technology and Teacher Education*, *14*(3), 599–621.

Brown, J. S., & Duguid, P. (1996, July/August). Universities in the digital age. *Change*, *28*(4), 11–20. doi:10.1080/00091383.1996.9937757

Brown, C., et al. (2008). The Impact of South Africa's ICT Infrastructure on Higher Education. In Remenyi., *Proceedings of the 3rd International Conference of E-Learning.* Cape Town, South Africa. Academic Publishing Limited.

Brown, J. S. (2001). *Learning in the digital age.* Retrieved July 5, 2009, from http://www.johnseelybrown.com/learning_in_digital_age-aspen.pdf

Brown, L. (2008, March 6). Student faces facebook consequences. *The Toronto Star.* Retrieved January 31, 2009, from http://www.thestar.com/News/GTA/article/309855

Bruffee, K. A. (1999). *Collaborative learning: higher education, interdependence, and the authority of knowledge* (2nd ed.). Baltimore: Johns Hopkins University Press.

Bruner, J. (1978). The role of dialogue in language acquisition. In Sinclair, A., Jarvelle, R. J., & Levelt, W. J. M. (Eds.), *The child's concept of language.* New York: Springer Verlag.

Brzycki, D., & Dudt, K. (2005). Overcoming barriers to technology use in teacher preparation programs. *Journal of Technology and Teacher Education*, *13*(4), 619–641.

Buckingham, S. (2003). Perspectives on the experience of the learning community through online discussions. *Journal of Distance Education*, *18*(2), 74–91.

Buckley, D. (2002, January/February). In the Pursuit of the learning paradigm: Coupling Faculty Transformation and Institutional Change. *EDUCAUSE Review*, 28–38.

Burgoon, J. K., & Hale, J. L. (1987). Validation and measurement of the fundamental themes of relational communication. *Communication Monographs*, *54*, 19–41. doi:10.1080/03637758709390214

Burnett, R., & Marshall, P. D. (2003). *Web theory: An introduction*. London: Routledge.

Burns, J. M. (1978). *Leadership*. New York: Harper and Row.

Bussu, B. (2004). The Open University of Tanzania: The African Virtual University (AVU). In UNESCO Institute for Information Technologies in Education (IITE), *Information and Communication Technology Usage in Higher Distance Education in Sub-Saharan Africa*. Moscow: UNESCO Institute.

Bylin, K. (2009). Minds for the future: Why digital immersion matters. Hypebot. Retrieved October 21, 2009, from http://www.hypebot.com/hypebot/2009/10/minds-for-the-future-why-digital-immersion-matters.html

Caggiano, M. E., Audet, R., & Abegg, G. (1995, April). *A Pilot study of an electronic community of interdisciplinary secondary science teachers*. Paper presented at the Annual Meeting of the National Association for Research in Science Teaching, San Francisco, CA.

Callon, M. (1991). Techno-Economic Networks and Irreversibility. In Law, J. (Ed.), *A Sociology of Monsters: Essays on Power, Technology and Domination (pp. ##-##)*. New York: Routledge.

Camblin, L., & Steger, J. (2000). Rethinking Faculty Development. *Higher Education*, *39*, 1–18. doi:10.1023/A:1003827925543

Campbell, R. J., Robinson, W., Neelands, J., Hewston, R., & Mazzoli, L. (2007). Personalized learning: Ambiguities in theory and practice. *British Journal of Educational Studies*, *55*(2), 135–154. doi:10.1111/j.1467-8527.2007.00370.x

Carboni, L. W. (1999). *How might an online discussion forum support teachers' professional development in mathematics? A first look.* Paper presented at the Annual Meeting of the Association of Mathematics Teacher Educators, Chicago, IL.

Carlsson, L. (2000). Policy Networks as Collective Action. *Policy Studies Journal: the Journal of the Policy Studies Organization*, *28*(3), 502–520. doi:10.1111/j.1541-0072.2000.tb02045.x

Carnevale, D. (2006). College tries to be cool but runs afoul of facebook. *The Chronicle of Higher Education*, *54*(4), 67.

Carnoy, M. (1999). *Globalization and Educational Reform: What Planners Need to Know*. Paris: UNESCO.

Carpenter, S. (2008). CDA protects Myspace from underage user's negligence claim. Retrieved January 31, 2009, from http://privacylaw.proskauer.com/tags/social-networking/

Carr, P. (2001). Changing the culture. *For a Change*. Retrieved from http://findarticles.com/p/articles/mi_m0KZH/is_3_14/ai_30122398

Carter, H., Fougler, T., & Ewbank, A. D. (2008, May). Have you googled your teacher lately: Teachers' use of social network sites. *Phi Delta Kappan*, 681–685.

Carter-Chapman, R. (2004). *Faculty Technology Survey*. University of Alaska Anchorage, Office of the Vice Provost.

Carver, K. W. (1986). The changing instructional role of the high school library media specialist: 1950-84; A survey of professional literature, standards, and research studies. *School Library Media Quarterly*, *14*(4), 183–191.

Carvin, A. (2000). E-Rate 101: How the Program Works. In Carvin, A. (Ed.), *The E-Rate in America: A Tale of Four Cities*. Washington, DC: The Benton Foundation.

Casey, H. B., & Rakes, G. C. (2002). An analysis of the influences of technology training on teacher stages of concern regarding the use of instructional technology in schools. *Journal of Computing in Teacher Education*, *18*(4), 124–132.

Castelli, L., & Tomelleri, S. (2008). Contextual effects on prejudiced attitudes: When the presence of others leads to more egalitarian responses. *Journal of Experimental Social Psychology*, *44*(3), 679–686. doi:10.1016/j.jesp.2007.04.006

Castells, M. (2000). *The Rise of the Network Society*. Oxford: Blackwell Publishers.

Castells, M. (2004a). *End of Millennium*. Oxford: Blackwell Publishers.

Castells, M. (2004b). *The Power of Identity*. Oxford: Blackwell Publishers.

Castells, M. (1994). The University System: Engine of Development in the New World Economy. In Salmi, J., & Verspoor, A. M. (Eds.), *Revitalizing Higher Education (pp. ##-##). Location?*IAU Press/Pergamon Press.

Cavanaugh, J. (2005). Teaching online: Time comparison. *Online Journal of Distance Learning Administration, 8*(1). Retrieved April 18, 2007, from http://www.westga.edu/~distance/ojdla/

Central Intelligence Agency. (2008). *The World FactBook*. Retrieved January 12, 2009, from https://www.cia.gov/library/publications/the-world-factbook/geos/et.html

Chao, S. J., Stigler, J. W., & Woodward, J. A. (2000). The effects of physical materials on kindergartners' learning of number concepts. *Cognition and Instruction*, *18*(3), 285–316. doi:10.1207/S1532690XCI1803_1

Charmaz, K. (2000). Constructivist and objectivist grounded theory. In Denzin, N. K., & Lincoln, Y. (Eds.), *Handbook of qualitative research* (2nd ed., pp. 509–535). Thousand Oaks, CA: Sage.

Chen, S. J. (2007). Instructional design strategies for intensive online courses: An Objectivist- Constructivist blended approach. *Journal of Interactive Online Learning*, *6*(1), 72–86.

Cheng, Y. M., Clift, R. T., & Klecka, C. L. (2003, June). *Supporting new teachers across school districts: Learning from on-going, internal evaluation* [Electronic version]. Paper presented to the Second Annual Illinois Education Research Conference, Urbana, IL. Retrieved from http://??? Clouse, N. K. (2008). The leadership role in online support programs for beginning teacher. Available from Dissertations and Theses database. (UMI No. 3288939)

Chenoweth, N. A., & Hayes, J. R. (2001). Fluency in writing: Generating text in L1 and L2. *Written Communication*, *18*, 80–98. doi:10.1177/0741088301018001004

Chin, G., Myers, J., & Hoyt, D. (2002). Social networks in the virtual science laboratory. *Communications of the ACM*, *45*(8), 87–92. doi:10.1145/545151.545156

Chism, N. (2004). Using a Framework to Engage Faculty in Instructional Technologies. *EDUCAUSE Quarterly*, *27*(2), 39–45.

Choy, S. P., Chen, X., & Bugarin, R. (2006). *Teacher professional development in 1999–2000: What teachers, principals, and district staff report* (NCES 2006-305). Washington, DC: National Center for Education Statistics, U.S. Department of Education.

Christensen, C. (1997). *The innovator's dilemma: When new technologies cause great firms to fail*. Boston: Harvard Business School Press.

Chronicle Careers. The Chronicle of Higher Education, Washington, D.C. 20037, Available online at http://chronicle.com/jobs/.

Chronicle Research Services. (2009). *The college of 2020: Students*. Retrieved June 23, 2009, from https://chronicle.com/subscribe/singlecopies/college2020non

Church, A. (2008). *Bloom's taxonomy, Bloom's digitally*. Retrieved April 4, 2009, from http://www.techlearning.com/article/8670

Clark, P., Jamieson, A., Launer, J., Trompetas, A., Whiteman, J., & Williamson, D. (2006). Intending to be a supervisor, mentor or coach? Which, what for and why? *Education for Primary Care*, *17*(2), 109–116.

Clark, R. E., & Choi, S. (2005). Five design principles for experiments on the effects of animated pedagogical agents. *Journal of Educational Computing Research*, *32*(3), 209–225. doi:10.2190/7LRM-3BR2-44GW-9QQY

Cognition and Technology Group at Vanderbilt. (1997). *The Jasper Project: Lessons in curriculum, instruction, assessment, and professional development*. Mahwah, NJ: Erlbaum.

Cohen, J. A., & Castner, M. H. (2000). Technology in classroom design: A faculty perspective. In Lloyd, L. (Ed.), *Teaching with Technology: Rethinking Tradition* (pp. 1–20). Medford, NJ: Information Today.

Cole, M., & Derry, J. (2005). We Have Met Technology and It Is Us. In Sternberg, R. J., & Preiss, D. (Eds.), *Intelligence and Technology: The Impact of Tools on the Nature and Development of Human Abilities (pp. ##-##)*. Mahwah, NJ: Erlbaum.

Cole, M. (1993, April). Vygotsky and writing: Reflections from a distant discipline. Paper presented at the Annual Conference on College Composition and Communication, San Diego, CA.

Colley, H. (2003). Engagement mentoring for 'disaffected' youth: A new model of mentoring for social inclusion. *British Educational Research Journal*, *29*(4), 521. doi:10.1080/01411920301842

Collins, A., & Halverson, R. (2009). *Rethinking Education in the Age of Technology: The Digital Revolution and Schooling in America*. New York: Teachers College Press.

Collins, A., Brown, J. S., & Holum, A. (1991). Cognitive apprenticeship: Making thinking visible. *American Educator*, *15*(3), 6–12, 38–46.

Collins, A., Brown, J., & Newman, S. (1989). Cognitive apprenticeship: teaching the crafts of reading, writing, and mathematics. In Resnick, L. B. (Ed.), *Knowing, learning and instruction: Essays in honor of Robert Glaser* (pp. 453–491). Hillsdale, NJ: Lawrence Erlbaum Associates.

Collis, B., & Moonen, J. (2001). *Flexible learning in a digital world*. London: Kogan Page.

Conrad, D. (2004). University instructors' reflections on their first online teaching experiences. *JALN*, *8*(2), 31–44.

Cookson, P. W. J. (1994). *School choice: The struggle for the soul of American education*. New Haven, CT: Yale University Press.

Cooper, D. (2001, Fall). The South African 'National Plan for Higher Education', 2001. *International Higher Education Newsletter.* Retrieved June 25, 2009, from http://www.bc.edu/bc_org/avp/soe/cihe/newsletter/News25/text004.htm

Coppola, E. M. (2004). *Powering up: Learning to teach well with technology*. New York: Teachers College Press.

Cornelius-White, J. D. (2007). Learner-centered teacher-student relationships are effective: A meta-analysis. *Review of Educational Research*, *77*, 113–143. doi:10.3102/003465430298563

Cornelius-White, J. H. D., & Harbaugh, A. P. (2009). *Learner-centered instruction: Building relationships for student success*. Thousand Oaks, CA: Sage.

Council of Chief State School Officers. (1992). Model standards for beginning teacher licensing, assessment and development: A resource for state dialogue developed by Interstate New Teacher Assessment and Support Consortium (INTASC). Retrieved November 1, 2008, from http://www.ccsso.org/content/pdfs/corestrd.pdf

Council of Higher Education. South Africa. (2001). Developing African Higher Education. Retrieved June 8, 2009, from http://www.nepad.org/2005/files/documents/22.pdf

Coutts, N., Drinkwater, R., & Simpson, M. (2001). Using information and communications technology in learning and teaching: A framework for reflection, planning and evaluation in school development. *Teacher Development*, *5*(2), 225–239. doi:10.1080/13664530100200135

Covington, M., & Mueller, K. (2001). Intrinsic Verses Extrinsic Motivation: An Approach/Avoidance Reformulation. *Educational Psychology Review*, *13*(2), 157–177. doi:10.1023/A:1009009219144

Cox, M. D. (2004, Spring). Introduction to faculty learning communities. *New Directions for Teaching and Learning*, *97*, 5–23. doi:10.1002/tl.129

Cox, M., Preston, C., & Cox, K. (1999, September 2-5). *What factors support or prevent teachers from using ICT in their classrooms?* Paper presented at British Educational Research Association Annual Conference, University of Sussex, Brighton, UK.

Cranton, P., & King, K. (2003). Transformative Learning as a Professional Development Goal. *New Directions for Adult and Continuing Education*, *98*, 31–37. doi:10.1002/ace.97

Cranton, P. (1994). *Understanding and promoting transformative learning*. San Francisco: Jossey-Bass.

Cranton, P. (2000). Individual differences and transformative learning. In Mezirow, J. (Eds.), *Learning as transformation* (pp. 181–204). San Francisco: Jossey-Bass.

Craver, K. W. (1994). *School library media centers in the 21st century: Changes and challenges*. Westport, CT: Greenwood Press.

Creswell, J. (1998). *Qualitative inquiry and research design*. Thousand Oaks: Sage.

Creswell, J. (2003). *Research design* (2nd ed.). Thousand Oaks, CA: Sage.

Creswell, J. (2002). *Research design: Qualitative, quantitative and mixed methods* (2nd ed.). Thousand Oaks, CA: Sage.

Cronk, B. (2002). *How to use SPSS: A Step-by-Step Guide to Analysis and Interpretation* (2nd ed.). Los Angeles: Pyrczak Publishing.

Crook, C. (1996). *Computers and the collaborative experiences of learning*. London: Routledge.

Cross, M., & Adam, F. (2007). ICT Policies and Strategies in Higher Education in South Africa: National and Institutional Pathways. *Higher Education Policy*, *20*(1), 73–95. doi:10.1057/palgrave.hep.8300144

Cross, K. P. (1981). *Adults as Learners*. San Francisco: Jossey-Bass.

Crum, C. (2008). How many sites are on the internet? *Webpronews*. Retrieved June 22, 2009, from http://www.webpronews.com/topnews/2008/11/04/how-many-sites-are-on-the-internet

Csikszentmihalyi, M. (1996). *Creativity flow and the psychology of discovery and invention*. New York: HarperCollins Publishers.

Cskiszentmihalyi, M. (1978). Intrinsic Rewards and emergent motivation. In Lepper, M. R., & Greene, D. (Eds.), *The hidden costs of rewards: New perspectives on the psychology of human motivation* (pp. 205–216). Hillsdale, NJ: Erlbaum.

Cuban, L. (2001). *Oversold & underused: Computers in the classroom*. Cambridge, MA: Harvard University Press.

Cuban, L., Kirkpatrick, H., & Peck, C. (2001). High access and low use of technology in high school classrooms: Explaining the apparent paradox. *American Educational Research Journal*, *38*(4), 813–834. doi:10.3102/00028312038004813

Cummins, J. (2000). *Language, power, and pedagogy: Bilingual children in the crossfire*. Buffalo, NY: Multilingual Matters Ltd.

Cunningham, S. (1999). The nature of workplace mentoring relationships among faculty members in Christian higher education. *The Journal of Higher Education*, *70*(4), 441–463. doi:10.2307/2649310

Cunningham, M., Kerr, K., McEune, R., Smith, P., & Harris, S. (2003). *Laptops for teachers: An evaluation of the first year of the initiative (ICT in Schools Research and Evaluation Series No. 19)*. Becta/DfES

Dale, R., Robertson, S., & Shortis, T. (2004). 'You can't not go with the technological flow, can you?': Constructing 'ICT' and 'teaching and learning.'. *Journal of Computer Assisted Learning, 20*, 456–470. doi:10.1111/j.1365-2729.2004.00103.x

Dalgarno, B. (2002). The potential of 3D virtual learning environments: a constructivist analysis. *E-Journal of Instructional Science and Technology, 5*(2). Retrieved November 24, 2004, from http://www.usq.edu.au/ electpub/e-jist/docs/Vol5_No2/dalgarno_frame.html

Daniel, J. (1996). *Mega-universities and knowledge media: Technology strategies for higher education*. London: Kogan Page.

Daniel, J. (2000). *The university of the future and the future of universities*. Keynote address to Improving University Learning and Teaching: 25th International Conference, Frankfurt, Germany.

Darling-Hammond, L., Bransford, J., LePage, P., Hammerness, K., & Duffy, H. (2005). *Preparing teachers for a changing world.* San Francisco: Jossey-Bass.

Darling-Hammond, L., & Bransford, J. D. (Eds.). (2005). *Preparing teachers for a changing world: What teachers should learn and be able to do*. Somerset, NJ: Jossey-Bass.

Darling-Hammond, L. (2003). Keeping good teachers: Why it matters, what leaders can do. *Educational Leadership, 60*(8), 7–13.

Davis, F. D. (1989). Perceived usefulness, perceived ease of use, and user acceptance of information technology. *Management Information Systems Quarterly, 13*(3), 319–340. doi:10.2307/249008

Dawson, K. (2007). The role of teacher inquiry in helping prospective teachers untangle the complexities of technology use in classrooms. *Journal of Computing in Teacher Education, 24*(1), 5–12.

de Frietas, S., & Newmann, T. (2009). The use of 'exploratory learning' for supporting immersive learning virtual environments. *Computers & Education, 52*, 343–352. doi:10.1016/j.compedu.2008.09.010

De la Paz, S. (1999). Composing via dictation and speech recognition systems: Compensatory technology for students with learning disabilities. *Learning Disability Quarterly, 22*, 173–182. doi:10.2307/1511284

Dean, G. J. (1994). *Designing instruction for adult learners*. Malabar, FL: Krieger.

Dean, C. D. (2001). They Expect Teachers to Do That? Helping Teachers Explore and Take Ownership of Their Profession. In Levin, B. B. (Ed.), *Energizing Teacher Education and Professional Development with Problem-Based Learning* (pp. 8–23). Alexandria, VA: Association for Supervision and Curriculum Development.

Dede, C. (2004). Enabling distributed learning communities via emerging technologies-part one. *T.H.E. Journal, 32*(2), 12–22.

Dede, C. (2005). Planning for neomillinnial learning styles. *EDUCAUSE Quarterly, 1*, 7–12.

Dede, C. (1998). Six Challenges for Education Technology. Retrieved June 13, 2009, from www.virtula.gmu.edu/pdf/ASCD.pdf

Dede, C., & Barab, S. (2009) Emerging technologies for learning sciences: A Time of rapid advances. *Journal of Science Education and Technology*. Retrieved September 2, 2009 from http://resources.metapress.com/pdf-preview.axd?code=061561872p271487&size=largest

Dede, C., Nelson, B., Ketelhut, D. J., Clarke, J., & Bowman, C. (2004). Design-based research strategies for studying situated learning in a multi-user virtual environment. In *Proceedings of the Sixth International Conference on the Learning Sciences* (pp. 158-165). Mahweh, NJ: Erlbaum. Retrieved May 20, 2005, from http://muve.gse.harvard.edu/muvees2003/documents/dedeICLS04.pdf

Delaney, J. G. (1999). *What are learner-centered schools?* Retrieved September 8, 2008, from http://www.mun.ca/educ/faculty/mwatch/win99/delaney.htm

Deleuze, G., & Guattari, F. (1987). *A thousand plateaus: Capitalism and schizophrenia*. Minneapolis, MN: University of Minnesota Press.

Dennen, V. P. (2005). From message posting to learning dialogues: Factors affecting learner participation in asynchronous discussion. *Distance Education*, *26*(1), 127–148. doi:10.1080/01587910500081376

Department of Education. (1997). *Education White Paper 3: A Program for Higher Education Transformation*. Pretoria.

Department of Education. (2003). White Paper on e-Education: Transforming Learning and Teaching through Information and Communication Technologies (ICTs). GOVERNMENT GAZETTE, 26 AUGUST 2004

Dewey, J. (1997). *How We Think. Mineola*. New York: Dover Publications.

Dewey, J. (1916). *Democracy and education*. Retrieved on July 14, 2009, from http://www.ilt.columbia.edu/publications/Projects/digitexts/dewey/d_e/chapter06.html

Diamond, R. (2002). Defining Scholarship for the Twenty First Century. *New Directions for Teaching and Learning*, *90*, 73–79. doi:10.1002/tl.57

Diannekrause. (2009, April 17). Twitter useful for education [Web log message]. Retrieved from http://diannekrause.edublogs.org/2009/0407/twitter-useful-for-education

DiBiase, D. (2004). The impact of increasing enrolment on faculty workload and student satisfaction over time. *JALN*, *8*(2), 45–60.

Dick, M. (2009, June 23). Colleges must yield to people's schedules. *The Columbus Dispatch*, *138*, A10.

Diehl, P. F., & Simpson, R. D. (1989). Investing in junior faculty: The teaching improvement program (TIPs). *Innovative Higher Education*, *13*, 147–157. doi:10.1007/BF00889746

Dillenbourg, P. (2002). Over-scripting CSCL: The risks of blending collaborative learning with instructional design. In Kirschner, P. A. (Ed.), *Three worlds of CSCL. Can we support CSCL?* (pp. 61–91). Heerlen, Netherlands: Open Universiteit Nederland.

Dillenbourg, P. (2000). Virtual Learning Environments. EUN Conference 2000: Learning in the New Millennium: Building New Education Strategies for Schools. Retrieved November 24, 2004, from http://tecfa.unige.ch/tecfa/publicat/dil-papers-2/Dil.7.5.18.pdf

Dillenbourg, P., & Baker, M. (n.d.). *Negotiation spaces in human-computer collaborative learning*.

Dillenbourg, P., Baker, M., Blaye, A., & O'Malley, C. (1996). The evolution of research on collaborative learning. In E. Spada & P. Reiman (Eds.), *Learning in humans and machine: Towards an interdisciplinary learning science* (pp. 189-211). Oxford: Elsevier. Retrieved November 1, 2004, from http://tecfa.unige.ch/tecfa/publicat/dil-papers-2/Dil_7_1_10.pdf

Dillon, S. (2009, May 28). New push seeks to end need for pre-college remedial classes. *The New York Times*. Retrieved from http://www.nytimes.com/2009/05/28/education/28remedial.html

DiMaggio, P. J., & Powell, W. W. (1983). The iron cage revisited: Institutional isomorphism and collective rationality in organizational fields. *American Sociological Review*, *48*(2), 147–160. doi:10.2307/2095101

Dirr, P. J. (1999). Distance and virtual learning in the United States. In Farrell, G. M. (Ed.), *The development of virtual education: A global perspective* (pp. 23–48). Vancouver, BC: The Commonwealth of Learning.

Discipio, T. (2008, September/October). Adapting social networking to address 21st century skills. *Multimedia & Internet @Schools. 15*(5), 10-11.

Doane, W. E. J., & Stefl-Mabry, J. (2009). Trans-generational problem-based Web development learning experience. In Tan, O. S. (Ed.), *Problem-based learning and creativity*. Singapore: Cengage Learning Asia Pte Ltd.

Dolezalek, H. (2004). Comprehensive Analysis of Employer-Sponsored Training in the United States. *Training (New York, N.Y.)*, *41*(10), 20–36.

Doll, C. A. (2005). *Collaboration and the School Library Media Specialist.* Location: Scarecrow Press.

Dolmans, D. H. J. M., De Grave, W., Wolfhagen, I. H. A. P., & van der Vleuten, P. M. (2005). Problem-based learning: Future challenges for educational practice and research. *Medical Education*, *39*, 732–741. doi:10.1111/j.1365-2929.2005.02205.x

Dooley, K. E. (1999). Towards a holistic model for the diffusion of educational technologies: An integrative review of educational innovation studies. *Journal of Educational Technology & Society*, *2*(4), 35–45.

Dooly, L. M., Metcalf, T., & Martinez, A. (1999). A Study of Adoption of Computer Technology by Teachers. *Journal of Educational Technology & Society*, *2*(4), 107–115.

Dowding, K. (1995). Model or Metaphor? A critical review of the policy network approach. *Political Studies*, *43*(2), 135–158.

Du, J., Havard, B., Yu, C., & Adams, J. (2004). The impact of technology use on low-income and minority students' academic achievement: Educational longitudinal study of 2002. *Journal of Educational Research & Policy Studies*, *4*(2), 21–39.

Duhaney, D. C. (2001). Teacher education: Preparing teachers to integrate technology. *International Journal of Instructional Media*, *28*(1), 23–30.

Dunleavy, M., Dede, C., & Mitchell, R. (2008). Affordances and limitations of immersive participatory augmented reality simultaneous for teaching and learning. *Journal of Science Education and Technology*, *18*, 7–22. doi:10.1007/s10956-008-9119-1

Dunleavy, M., & Heinecke, W. F. (2007). The impact of 1:1 laptop use on middle school math and science standardized test scores. *Computers in the Schools*, *24*, 7–22. doi:10.1300/J025v24n03_02

Durrington, V., Repman, J., & Valente, T. (2000). Using Social Network Analysis to Examine the Time of Adoption of computer-Related Services among University Faculty. *Journal of Research on Computing in Education*, *33*(1), 16–28.

Dwyer, D., Ringstaff, C., & Sandholtz, J. H. (1990). Teacher Belief and Practices Part 1: Patterns of Change. Apple Classrooms of Tomorrow, Apple Computer, Inc., 1-10.

Earle, R. S. (2002). The integration of instructional technology in public education: Promises and challenges. *Educational Technology*, *42*(1), 5–13.

Earle, R. (2002). The Integration of Instructional Technology into Public: Promises and Challenges. *Educational Technology Magazine, 42*(1), 5-13. Retrieved from http://asianvu.com/bookstoread/etp/earle.pdf

Eberhardt, D. (2007, September/October). Facing up to Facebook. *About Campus*, 18–26. doi:10.1002/abc.219

Edirisingha, P., Nie, M., Pluciennik, M., & Young, R. (2009). Socialisation for learning at a distance in a 3-D multi-user virtual environment. *British Journal of Educational Technology*, *40*(3), 458–479. doi:10.1111/j.1467-8535.2009.00962.x

Ellison, N., Steinfeld, C., & Lampe, C. (2008). The benefits of Facebook friends: Social capital and college students' use of online social network sites. *Journal of Computer Mediated Communication, 12*(4). Retrieved January 31, 2009, from http://jcmc.indiana.edu/vol12/issue4/ellison.html

Elmore, R. (2002). *Bridging the gap between standards and achievement*. Washington, DC: The Albert Shanker Institute.

Emes, C., & Cleveland-Innes, M. (2003). A journey toward learner-centered curriculum. *Canadian Journal of Higher Education*, *33*(3), 47–70.

Engelbart, D. (1992). T*oward High-Performance Organizations: A Strategic Role for Groupware*. The Bootstrap Institute. Retrieved from http://www.bootstrap.org

Engestrom, Y. E., Engestrom, R., & Vahaaho, T. (1999). When the centre does not hold: The importance of knotworking. In Chaiklin, S., Hedegaard, M., & Jensen, U. J. (Eds.), *Activity theory and social practice (pp. ##-##)*. Aarhus: Aarhus University Press.

Engström, Y. (1987). *Learning by expanding: An activity-theoretical approach to developmental research*. Helsinki: Orienta-Konsultit.

Engström, Y., Miettinen, R., & Punamaki, R. L. (1999). *Perspectives on activity theory*. Cambridge: Cambridge University Press.

Erginel-Sanal, S. (2006). *Developing reflective teachers: A study on perception and improvement of reflection in pre-service teacher education*. Ankara: Ankara, Middle East Tecnical University.

Ertmer, P. A. (1999). Addressing first- and second-order barriers to change: Strategies for technology integration. *Educational Technology Research and Development*, *47*(4), 47–61. doi:10.1007/BF02299597

Ertmer, P. A., Gopalakrishnan, S., & Ross, E. M. (2000). *VisionQuest: Helping teachers achieve technology integration*. Paper presented at the annual meeting of the Society for Information Technology and Teacher Education, San Diego, CA.

Estabrook, L., Witt, E., & Rainie, L. (2007). *Information searches that solve problems: How people use the internet, libraries and government agencies when they need help*. Location: Pew Internet & American Life Project. Retrieved February 13, 2008, from http://www.pewinternet.org/pdfs/Pew_UI_LibrariesReport.pdf

Eve, J., & Brabazon, T. (2008). Learning to leisure? Failure, flame, blame, shame, homophobia and other everyday practices in online education. *Journal of Literacy and Technology*, *9*(1), 36–61.

Evoh, C. J. (2007). ICTs, Secondary Education, and the Knowledge Economy: Exploring the Roles of the Private Sector in Post-Apartheid South Africa. *Journal of Education for International Development*, *1*(3).

Evoh, C. J. (2008). Collaborative Partnerships and the Transformation of Secondary Education through ICTs in South Africa. Unpublished dissertation. The New School University, Country.

Falba, C., Grove, K., Anderson, D., & Putney, L. (2001). Benefits of laptop computers for elementary teachers. *Journal of Research on Technology in Education*, *33*(5), 105–114.

Farmer, J. (2006). The inevitable personal learning environment post. Retrieved March 13, 2009, from http://incsub.org/blog/2006/the-inevitable-personal-learning-environment

Feagin, J., Orum, A., & Sjoberg, G. (Eds.). (1991). *A case for case study*. Chapel Hill, NC: University of North Carolina Press.

Feenburg, A. (1991). *Critical Theory of Technology*. New York: Oxford University Press.

Feiman-Nemser, S. (2003). What new teachers need to learn. *Educational Leadership*, *60*(8), 25–29.

Felix, K. (2008, September/October). AASL study shows schools accept social networking. *Multimedia & Internet @Schools*, *15*(5), 8.

Ferguson, P. (2004). Faculty Beliefs about teaching with Technology. Association for Educational Communications and Technology. *Georgia State University, ERIC, ED485069*, 155–166.

Fichman, R. G. (1992). Information Technology Diffusion: A Review of Empirical Research. Proceedings of the Thirteenth International Conference on Information Systems, Dallas, 195-206. http://citeseer.ist.psu.edu/fichman92information.html

Fincher, C. (1998). Teaching and Technological Innovation: the IHE Perspectives. Georgia University Institute of Higher Education, http://service.uga.edu/ihe/. ED429492.

Fink, L. S. (2009). Research building blocks: Examining electronic sources. *Readwritethink.org*. Retrieved June 24, 2009, from http://www.readwritethink.org/lessons/lesson_view.asp?id=149

Firek, H. (2003). *10 easy ways to use technology in the English classroom.* Portsmouth, HH: Heinemann.

Fishbein, M., & Ajzen, I. (1975). *Beliefs, Attitude, Intention, and Behavior: An Introduction to Theory and Research.* Reading, MA: Addison-Wesley.

Fishman, B. J., Marx, R. W., Best, S., & Tal, R. T. (2003). Linking teachers and student learning to improve professional development in systemic reform. *Teaching and Teacher Education, 19*(6), 643–658. doi:10.1016/S0742-051X(03)00059-3

Fleming, L., Motamedi, V., & May, L. (2007). Predicting preservice teacher competence in computer technology: Modeling and application in training environments. *Journal of Technology and Teacher Education, 15*(2), 207–231.

Flintoff, K. (2007). Digital natives have limits. *Grip, fix, turn [blog].* Retrieved June 1, 2009, from http://gripfixturn.com/2007/03/31/more-on-grip-fix-turn/

Foster, A. L. (2007). Information navigation 101. *The Chronicle of Higher Education Online.* Retrieved March 9, 2007, from http://chronicle.com/free/v53/i27/27a03801.htm

Foucault, M. (1982). The subject and power. In Dreyfus, H. L., & Rabinow, P. (Eds.), *Michel Foucault: Beyond structuralism and hermeneutics* (pp. 208–226). Chicago: The University of Chicago Press.

Fountain, R. (2007). Wiki Pedagogy. *Dossiers Technopedagogigues.* Retrieved April 4, 2007, from: http://www.profetic.org/dossiers/dossier_imprimer.php3?id_rubrique=110

Fowler, F. J. (1995). *Improving survey questions: Design and evaluation.* Thousand Oaks, CA: Sage.

Fowles, J. (1978). *Handbook of futures research.* Westport, CT: Greenwood Press.

Fox, S., Anderson, J. Q., & Rainie, L. (2005). *The future of the Internet.* Washington, DC: Pew Internet & American Life Project. Retrieved March 1, 2005, from http://www2.scedu.unibo.it/roversi/SocioNet/Future_of_Internet.pdf

Frand, J. (2006). The information mindset: Changes in students and implications for higher education. *EDUCAUSE Review, 35*(5), 15–22.

Franklin, C. A. (2008). Factors determining elementary teachers' use of computers. *Principal, 87*(3), 54–55.

Franklin, T., & Van Harmelen, M. (2007). Web 2.0 for content for Learning and Teaching in Higher Education. Bristol: JISC. Retrieved June 24, 2009, from http://www.jisc.ac.uk/publications/documents/web2andpolicyreport.aspx

Freire, P. (1973). *Education for critical consciousness.* New York: Continuum.

Freire, P. (1980). *Pedagogy of the oppressed.* New York: Continuum.

Friedman, V. J., & Antal, A. B. (2005). Negotiating reality: A theory of action approach to intercultural competence. *Management Learning, 36*(1), 69–86. doi:10.1177/1350507605049904

Friedman, V. J., & Rogers, T. (2009). There is nothing so theoretical as good action research. *Action Research, 7*(1), 31–47. doi:10.1177/1476750308099596

Friedman, T. (2005). *The world is flat: A brief history of the twenty-first century.* New York: Farrar, Straus and Giroux.

Friedman, V. J., & Antal, A. B. (2006). Interactive critical reflection as intercultural competence. In Boud, D., Docherty, P., & Cressey, P. (Eds.), *Productive reflection and learning at working* (pp. 120–130). London: Routledge.

Friedman, V. J. (2000, July). *The incubator for social entrepreneurship: Creating partnerships for second order social change.* Paper presented at the Annual Conference of the International Society for Third-Sector Research, Dublin, Ireland.

Fryer, W. (2006). Digital refugees and bridges. *Infinite thinking machine: Ideas to help teachers and students thrive in the 21st century.* Retrieved June 6, 2009, from http://www.infinitethinking.org/2006/10/digital-refugees-and-bridges.html

Fuchs-Kittowsk, F., & Köhler, A. (2002). Knowledge creating communities in the context of work processes. *ACM SIGCSE Bulletin*, *23*(3), 8–13.

Fullan, M. (2001). *Leading in a culture of change*. San Francisco: Jossey-Bass.

Fullan, M. (1999). *Change forces: The sequel*. Philadelphia: Falmer Press.

Fullan, M. (2008). *The six secrets of change*. Somerset, NJ: Jossey-Bass.

Fullan, M. G. (1991). *The new meaning of educational change*. New York: Teachers College Press.

Fullen, M., & Scott, G. (2009). *Turnaround leadership for higher education*. San Francisco: Jossey-Bass.

Galbo, C. (1998). Helping Adults Learn. *Thrust for Educational Leadership*, *27*(7), 13–17.

Gall, M., Borg, W., & Gall, J. (1996). *Educational research: An introduction* (6th ed.). White Plains, NY: Longman.

Garage Games. n.d. (Computer Software) Retrieved January 5, 2006, from http://www.garagegames.com

Garcia, O., Kleifgen, J., & Falchi, L. (2008). *Equity in the education of Emergent Bilinguals: The case of English language learners*. Research Review Series Monograph, Campaign for Educational Equity, Teachers College, Columbia University.

Gardner, T. (2009). Inquiry on the internet: Evaluating web pages for a class collection. *ReadWriteThink.org*. Retrieved June 24, 2009, from http://www.readwritethink.org/lessons/lesson_view.asp?id=328

Garet, M., Porter, A., Desimone, L., Briman, B., & Yoon, K. (2001). What makes professional development effective? Analysis of a national sample of teachers. *American Educational Research Journal*, *38*(4), 915–945. doi:10.3102/00028312038004915

Garrison, D. R. (2007). Online community of inquiry review: Social, cognitive, and teaching presence issues. *Journal of Asynchronous Learning Networks*, *11*(1), 61–72.

Garrison, D. R., Anderson, T., & Archer, W. (2001). Critical thinking, cognitive presences, and computer conferencing in distance education. *American Journal of Distance Education*, *15*, 7–23. doi:10.1080/08923640109527071

Garrison, D. R., & Anderson, T. (2003). *E-Learning in the 21st century: A framework for research and practice*. London: Routledge/Falmer. doi:10.4324/9780203166093

Garrison, D. R., Anderson, T., & Archer, W. (2000). Critical Inquiry in a Text-Based Environment: Computer Conferencing in Higher Education. *The Internet and Higher Education*, *2*(2-3), 87–105. Retrieved from http://communitiesofinquiry.com/. doi:10.1016/S1096-7516(00)00016-6

Garson, D. (2007). Scales and standard measures. Retrieved August 8, 2007, from http://www2.chass.ncsu.edu/garson/pa765/standard.htm

Gaver, B. (2002). Provocative awareness. [CSCW]. *Computer Supported Cooperative Work*, *11*(3), 475–493. doi:10.1023/A:1021277326673

Gay, L., & Airasian, P. (2000). *Educational research: Competencies and analysis and application*. London: Prentice-Hall.

Gee, J. P. (2003). *What video games have to teach us about learning and literacy*. New York: Palgrave Macmillan.

Gee, J. P. (2004, May). *Video games: Embodied empathy for complex systems*. Paper presented at Electronic Entertainment Exposition, Los Angeles, CA.

Geertz, C. (1973). *The interpretation of cultures*. New York: Basic Books.

Geertz, C. (1983). *Local knowledge: Further essays in interpretive anthropology*. New York: Basic Books.

Gefen, D., & Keil, M. (1998). The impact of developer responsiveness on perceptions of usefulness and ease of use: An extension of the technology acceptance model. *SIGMIS Database*, *29*(2), 35–49. doi:10.1145/298752.298757

Genesee, F., Lindholm-Leary, K., & Christian, D. (2006). *Educating English language learners: A synthesis of research evidence*. Santa Cruz, CA: Center for Diversity in Education. doi:10.1017/CBO9780511499913

Gennap, A. V. (1960). *The Rites of Passage*. London: Routledge and Kegan Paul.

Geroski, P. A. (2000). Models of Technology Diffusion. *Research Policy*, *29*, 603–625. doi:10.1016/S0048-7333(99)00092-X

Gibbons, P. (2002). *Scaffolding language, scaffolding learning*. Portsmouth, NH: Heinemann.

Giles, J. (2005). Internet encyclopedias go head to head. *Nature 438*(15), 900-901. Retrieved June 24, 2009, from http://www.nature.com/nature/journal/v438/n7070/full/438900a.html

Gillies, R. M. (2007). *Cooperative Learning: Integrating Theory & Practice*. Thousand Oaks, CA: SAGE Publications.

Gillingham, M. G. (1999). Technology in teacher preparation: Preparing teachers for the future. *Journal of Technology and Teacher Education*, *7*(4), 303–321.

Gilman, T. (2009). Not enough time in the library. *The Chronicle of Higher Education*. Retrieved May 18, 2009, from http://chronicle.com

Gilroy, K. (2001). Collaborative e-learning: The right approach. *DestinatioKM.com White Paper*. Retrieved October 15, 2005, from http://www.destinationcrm.com/articles/default.asp?articleid=1767

Gladhart, M. (2001). Models. Retrieved January 15, 2007, from http://education.wichita.edu/m3/models/teachered/intergrationgrid.htm

Gladwell, M. (2002). *The tipping point: How little things can make a big difference*. New York: Back Bay.

Glot, R., Meiszner, A., & Sowe, S. K. (2007). *FLOSSCom – Using the principles of informal learning environments of FLOSS communities to improve ict supported formal education. Phase 1: Analysis of the informal learning environment of floss communities*. FLOSSCom. Retrieved January 31, 2008, from http://opensource.mit.edu/papers/FLOSSCom_WP2_Phase_1_Report_v070709_1.pdf

Goddard, J., & Cornford, J. (2002). The University, ICTs and Development in the Information Society. In Mansell, R., Samarajiva, R., & Mahan, A. (Eds.), *Networking Knowledge for Information Societies: Institutions and Interventions. City, Country: Delft University Press*.

Gokhale, A. A. (1995). Collaborative learning enhanced crtical thinking. *Journal of Technology Education, 7*(1). Retrieved November 27, 2006, from http://scholar.lib.vt.edu/ejournals/JTE/v7n1/gokhale.jte-v7n1.html

Goodwin-Jones, R. (2003). Blogs and wikis: Environments for on-line collaboration. *Language Learning & Technology*, *7*, 12–16.

Goody, J., & Watt, I. (1963). The consequences of literacy. [reprinted in Goody 1968: 27-68]. *Comparative Studies in Society and History*, *5*(3), 304–345. doi:10.1017/S0010417500001730

Goody, J. R. (1986). *The logic of writing and the organization of society*. Cambridge, UK: Cambridge University Press.

Goody, J. R. (1987). *The interface between the written and the oral*. Cambridge, UK: Cambridge University Press.

Goody, J. R. (1977): *The domestication of the savage mind*. Cambridge, UK: Cambridge University Press Goody, J.R. (Ed.). (1968). *Literacy in traditional societies*. Cambridge, UK: Cambridge University Press.

Grade 8 intermediate level test social studies. Rating Guide. Book 2: Document-based question. June 6, 2007.

Graham, S. (1990). The role of production factors in learning disabled students' compositions. *Journal of Educational Psychology*, *82*, 781–791. doi:10.1037/0022-0663.82.4.781

Graham, S., & Harris, K. R. (2006). Explicitly teaching struggling writers and their classmates strategies for mastering the writing process. *Intervention in School and Clinic*, *41*, 290–294. doi:10.1177/10534512060410050601

Graham, J., & Semich, G. (2006). A model for effectively integrating technology across the curriculum: A three step staff development program for transforming practice. *International Journal of Information and Communication Technology Education*, *2*(1), 1–10.

Graham, J., & Semich, G. (2006). Integrating technology to transform pedagogy: Revisiting the progress of the three phase TUI model for faculty development. Retrieved May 21, 2009, from www.igi.global.com/downloads/excerpts/Reference/IGR4510_F17OA3gb35.pdf

Greene, J. (2002). Civic report: High school graduation rates in the United States. Manhattan Institute for Policy Research. Manhattan Institute. Retrieved September 28, 2008, from http://www.manhattan-institute.org/html/cr_baeo.htm

Gros, B. (2001). Instructional design for computer-supported collaborative learning in primary and secondary school. *Computers in Human Behavior*, *17*(5-6), 439–451. doi:10.1016/S0747-5632(01)00016-4

Gros, B. (2002). Knowledge Construction and Technology. *Journal of Educational Multimedia and Hypermedia*, *11*(4), 323–343.

Gross, T., Stary, C., & Totter, A. (2005). User-centered awareness in computer-supported cooperative work-systems: Structured embedding of findings from social sciences. *International Journal of Human-Computer Interaction*, *18*(3), 323–360. doi:10.1207/s15327590ijhc1803_5

Grossberg, L. (1992). *We gotta get out of this place: Popular conservatism and postmodern culture*. New York: Routledge.

Grosso de Leon, A. (2001). *Higher Educations Challenge: New Teacher Education Models for a New Century*. Carnegie Challenge, Carnegie Corporation of New York.

Grow, G. (1991). Teaching learners to be self-directed. *Adult Education Quarterly*, *41*(3), 125–149. doi:10.1177/0001848191041003001

Guba, E. G., & Lincoln, Y. S. (1994). Competing paradigms in qualitative research. In Denzin, N. K., & Lincoln, Y. S. (Eds.), *Handbook of Qualitative Research* (pp. 105–117). City.

Gulsecen, S., & Kubat, A. (2006). Teaching ICT to teacher candidates using PBL: A qualitative and quantitative evaluation. *Journal of Educational Technology & Society*, *9*(2), 96–106.

Gunawardena, C. N., Lowe, C. A., & Anderson, T. (1997). Analysis of a global online debate and the development of an interaction analysis model for examining social construction of knowledge in computer conferencing. *Journal of Educational Computing Research*, *17*(4), 397–431. doi:10.2190/7MQV-X9UJ-C7Q3-NRAG

Gura, M. (2005). *Recapturing technology for education: Keeping tomorrow in today's classrooms*. Lanham, MD: Scarecrow Education.

Guskey, T. R. (2000). *Evaluating professional development*. Thousand Oaks, CA: Corwin Press.

Guskey, T. R. (1994, April). *Professional development in education: In search of the optimal mix*. Paper presented at the annual meeting of the American Educational Research Association, New Orleans, LA.

Gusky, T. (2003). What makes professional development effective? *Phi Delta Kappan*, *84*(10), 748–750.

Haddad, W. (2007). ICTs for Education: A Reference Handbook. Retrieved October 22, 2007, from http://www.ictinedtoolkit.org/usere/pdfs/ICTs_for_Education_Analytical_Review.pdf

Hagenson, L., & Castle, D. (2003). The Integration of Technology Into Teaching By University College of Education Faculty. In C. Crawford et al. (Eds.), *Proceedings of Society for Information Technology and Teacher Education International Conference 2003* (pp. 947-952). Chesapeake, VA: AACE.

Hagner, P. (2001). Interesting Practices and Best Systems in Faculty Engagement and Support. NLII White Paper, January 25 final report, 1-32.

Hai-Jew, S. (2007). F2F and online "live personalization" of learning and implications for learning object repositories and automated eLearning (A survey and analysis). *Journal of Interactive Instruction Development, 19*(4), 19–39.

Hakuta, K., Goto Butler, Y., & Witt, D. (2000). How long does it take English learners to attain proficiency? *University of California Linguistic Minority Research Institute Policy Report* 2000-1.

Hall, G. E., & Hord, S. M. (1987). *Change in schools*. Albany, NY: State University of New York Press.

Hall, S. (1981). Notes on deconstructing 'the Popular. In Samuel, R. (Ed.), *People's history and socialist theory* (pp. 227–240). Boston: Routledge and Kegan Paul.

Halpern, D. F., & Hakel, M. D. (2003). Applying the science of learning to the university and beyond: Teaching for long-term retention and transfer. *Change, 35*(4), 36–41. doi:10.1080/00091380309604109

Hamdy, A. (2007). ICT in Education in Egypt. In G. Farrell and S. Isaac (Eds.), *Survey of ICT and Education in Africa (Vol. 2) 53 Country Reports*. Washington, DC: InfoDev.

Hanks, R. F. (2002, June). *Environmental and Personal Factors Effecting K-12 Teacher Utilizatio of Technology*. Paper presented at the annual meeting of National Educational Computing Conference, San Antonio, Texas.

Hanneman, R. A., & Riddle, M. (2005). *Introduction to social network methods. Riverside*. CA: University of California, Riverside.

Hara, N., Bonk, C. J., & Angeli, C. (2000). Content analysis of online discussion in an applied educational psychology course. *Instructional Science, 28*, 115–152. doi:10.1023/A:1003764722829

Harada, V. H. (2003). Taking the lead in developing learning communities. *Knowledge Quest: Journal of the American Association of School Librarians, 31*(2), 12–16.

Harasim, L. (1990). *On-line education: Perspectives on a new environment*. New York: Praeger Publishers.

Harel, I. (1990). Children as software designers: a constructionist approach for learning mathematics. *The Journal of Mathematical Behavior, 9*(1).

Harel, I., & Papert, S. (Eds.). (1991). *Constructionism*. Norwood, NJ: Ablex.

Harland, T. (2002). Zoology students' experiences of collaborative enquiry in problem-based learning. *Teaching in Higher Education, 7*(1), 6–17. doi:10.1080/13562510120100355

Harlen, M. (2009). IST673 Wiki Weekly Reflections.

Harp, S. F., & Mayer, R. E. (1998). How seductive details do their damage: A theory of cognitive interest in science learning. *Journal of Educational Psychology, 90*(3), 414–434. doi:10.1037/0022-0663.90.3.414

Harris, J., O'Bryan, E., & Rotenberg, L. (1996). It's a simple idea, but it's not easy to do: Practical lessons in telementoring. *Learning and Leading with Technology, 24* (2), 53-57. Retrieved March 30, 2004, from http://emissary.wm.edu/templates/content/publications/October96LLT.pdf

Hartley, K., & Bendixen, L. D. (2001). Educational research in the Internet age: Examining the role of individual characteristics. *Educational Researcher, 30*(9), 22–26. doi:10.3102/0013189X030009022

Hartzell, G. N. (2001). The implications of selected school reform approaches for school library media services. *School Library Media Research, 4*.

Havelock, E. (1963). *Preface to Plato*. Cambridge, MA: Harvard University Press.

Hawkes, M., & Good, K. (2000). Evaluating professional development outcomes of a telecollaborative technology curriculum. *Rural Educator, 21*(3), 5–11.

Haycock, K. (1997). Working together to improve student achievement, kindergarten through college. *The Educational Record, 78*, 10–18.

Haycock, K. (1999). *Foundations for effective school library media programs*. Englewood, CO: Libraries Unlimited.

Haycock, K. (2003). *The crisis in Canada's school libraries: The case for reform and reinvestment*. Toronto, Canada: Association of Canadian Publishers and Canada Heritage.

Head, A. J., & Eisenberg, M. B. (2009). Finding context: What today's college students say about conducting research in the digital age. *Project information literacy progress report*. Retrieved June 15, 2009, from http://projectinfolit.org/

Headlam-Wells, J., Gosland, J., & Craig, J. (2006). Beyond the organization: The design and management of e-mentoring systems [Electronic version]. *International Journal of Information Management*, *26*, 372–385. doi:10.1016/j.ijinfomgt.2006.04.001

Healy, C. C., & Welchert, A. J. (1990). Mentoring relations: A definition to advance research and practice. *Educational Researcher*, *19*(9), 17–21.

Heer, J., & Boyd, D. (2005). Vizster: Visualizing online social networks. In *Proceedings of Symposium on Information Visualization* (pp. 33-40). Minneapolis, MN: IEEE Press.

Hennessy, S., Ruthven, K., & Brindley, S. (2004). Teacher perspectives on integrating ICT into subject teaching: Commitment, constraints caution and change. *Journal of Curriculum Studies*, *37*(2), 155–192. doi:10.1080/0022027032000276961

Hensler, B. (2008). ACLU sues to protect Broward student's free speech in a Web 2.0 world. ACLU. Retrieved January 31, 2009, from http://www.aclufl.org/

Heppell, S. (2008). Education 2020. *ESCalateNews*, *10*(Spring), 29-31. Retrieved April 27, 2008, from http://www.escalate.ac.uk/4439

Herbert, M. (1998). *Education as a social institution and ideological process*. City, Country: Waxmann Verlag.

Herring, S. C. (2004). Content analysis for new media: Rethinking the paradigm. In *New research for new media: Innovative research methodologies symposium working papers and readings* (pp. 47–66). Minneapolis, MN: University of Minnesota School of Journalism and Mass Communication.

Herselman, M. E., & Hay, H. R. (2003). (ICT) for South African Higher Education Institutions. In InSITE. In *Where Parallels Intersect*. Challenges Posed by Information and Communication Technologies.

Hersey, P., & Blanchard, K. H. (1977, 1982). *Management of organizational behavior: Utilizing human resources*. Englewood Cliffs, NJ: Prentice-Hall.

Hew, K. F., & Cheung, W. S. (2008). Attracting student participation in asynchronous online discussions: A case study of peer facilitation. *Computers & Education*, *51*(3), 1111–1124. doi:10.1016/j.compedu.2007.11.002

Hew, K. F., & Knapczyk, D. (2007). Analysis of ill-structured problem solving, mentoring functions, and perceptions of practicum teachers and mentors toward online mentoring in a field-based practicum [Electronic version]. *Instructional Science*, *34*, 1–40. doi:10.1007/s11251-006-9000-7

Hewitt, J. (2005). Toward an understanding of how threads die in asynchronous computer conferences. *Journal of the Learning Sciences*, *14*(4), 567 589. doi:10.1207/s15327809jls1404_4

Hewitt, J. (2004). An exploration of community in a knowledge forum classroom: An activity system analysis. In Barab, S., Kling, R., & Gray, J. (Eds.), *Designing virtual communities in the service of learning* (pp. 210–238). New York: Cambridge University Press.

Hidi, S. E., & Hildyard, A. (1983). The comparison of oral and written productions in two discourse types. *Discourse Processes*, *6*, 91–105. doi:10.1080/01638538309544557

Hills, M. (2002). Kluckhohn and Strodtbeck's values orientation theory. In Online Readings in Psychology and Culture (Unit 6, Chapter 3). Retrieved 10 July, 2007, from http://www.wwu.edu/~culture

Hiltz, S. R. (1997). Impacts of college-level courses via asynchronous learning networks: Some preliminary results. *Journal of Asynchronous Learning Networks*, *1*(2), 1–19.

Hjorland, B. (2008). Information literacy and digital literacy. *Prisma*, *7*, 4–16.

Hobbs, V. (2004). *The promise and the power of distance learning in rural education*. Arlington, VA: Rural School and Community Trust.

hooks, b. (1990). *Yearning: Race, gender, and cultural politics*. Boston, MA: South End Press.

Hooper, S., & Rieber, L. P. (1995). Teaching with technology. In Orstein, A. C. (Ed.), *Teaching: Theory into practice* (pp. 154–170). Boston: Allyn and Bacon.

Hord, S. M. (1992). *Facilitative leadership: The imperative for change*. Austin: Southwest Educational Development Laboratory. Retrieved April, 11, 2005, from http://www.sedl.org/change/facilitate/

Horrigan, J. (2006). *The internet as a resource for news and information about science*. Location: Pew Internet & American Life Project. Retrieved February 13, 2008, from http://www.pewinternet.org/pdfs/PIP_Exploratorium_Science.pdf

Horrigan, J., & Rainie, L. (2006). *The internet's growing role in life's major moments*. Location: Pew Internet & American Life Project. Retrieved February 13, 2008, from http://www.pewinternet.org/pdfs/PIP_Major%20Moments_2006.pdf

Howard, R.M. (2009). Email to author. June 18, 2009.

Howe, N., & Strauss, W. (1993). *Millennials rising: The next greatest generation*. New York: Vintage Books.

Howell, S. L., Williams, P. B., & Lindsay, N. K. (2003). Thirty-two trends affecting distance education: An informed foundation for strategic planning. *Online Journal of Distance Learning Administration*, *6*(3), 8–26.

Hu, W. (2007, May 4). Seeing no progress, some schools drop laptops. *The New York Times*.

Huff, S., & Malcolm, M. (1985). Information Technology Assessment and Adoption: A Filed Study. *Management Information Systems Quarterly*, *9*(4), 327–341. doi:10.2307/249233

Hughes, T. (2005). *Human-built world: How to think about technology and culture*. Chicago, IL: University of Chicago Press.

Hughes, J. (2005). The role of teacher knowledge and learning experiences in forming technology-integrated pedagogy. *Journal of Technology and Teacher Education*, *13*(2), 277–302.

Hughes, T. (1989). The evaluation of large technological systems. In Bijker, W., Hughes, T., & Pinch, T. (Eds.), *The social construction of technological systems: New directions in the sociology and history of technology*. Cambridge, MA: MIT Press.

Hughes-Hassell, S., & Harada, V. H. (2007). *School reform and the school library media specialist*. Westport, CT: Libraries Unlimited.

Huntley, L., & Greever-Rice, T. (2007). *Analysis of 2005 MAP results for eMINTS students*. Retrieved June 27, 2009, from http://www.emints.org/evaluation/reports/

Hutchings, P., & Shulman, L. S. (1999). The scholarship of teaching: New elaborations, new developments. *Change*, *31*(5), 10–15. doi:10.1080/00091389909604218

Ijsselsteijn, W., Freeman, J., & De Ridder, H. (2001). Presence: Where are we? *Cyberpsychology & Behavior*, *4*(2), 179–182. doi:10.1089/109493101300117875

Ijsselsteijn, W., & Riva, G. (2003). Being there: The experience of presence in mediated environments. In Riva, G., Davide, F., & Ijsselsteijn, W. A. (Eds.), *Being there: Concepts, effects and measurements of user presence in synthetic environments* (pp. 3–16). Amsterdam, Netherlands: IOS Press.

Illinois Technology Standards for All Teachers. (nd). Retrieved June 15, 2009, from http://web54.sd54.k12.il.us/district54/lts/dmoore/techstandards/illtech.htm

Ingersoll, R. M., & Smith, T. M. (2003). The wrong solution to the teacher shortage [Electronic version]. *Educational Leadership*, *60*(8), 30–33.

Inglis, A., Ling, P., & Joosten, V. (2002). *Delivering digitally: Managing the transition to the knowledge media.* London: Kogan Page.

Innis, H. A. (1951). *The bias of communications*. Toronto: University of Toronto Press.

Integrated Postsecondary Education Data System (IPEDS). (2009). Data Center. National Center for Educational Statistics at US Department of Education Institute of Educational Sciences. Retrieved June 1, 2009, from: http://nces.ed.gov/ipeds/datacenter

International Society for Technology in Education. (2008). National Educational Technology Standards for Students: The Next Generation.

International Society for Technology in Education. (2002). *NETS Project*. Eugene, OR: ISTE Publications.

International Society for Technology in Education. (2008). *Technology and student achievement: The indelible link.* Retrieved June 28, 2009, from http://www.iste.org/Content/ NavigationMenu/ Advocacy/Policy/59.08-PolicyBrief-F-web.pdf

ISTE. (2007). The National Educational Technology Standards for Students. The Next Generation. Retrieved January 10, 2008, from http://www.iste.org/net

Jackson, L. A., von Eye, A., Biocca, F., Barbatsis, G., Zhao, Y., & Fitzgerald, H. (2005). How low-income children use the Internet at home. *Journal of Interactive Learning Research*, *16*(3), 259–271.

Jacobsen, D. M. (1998). Adoption Patterns of Faculty who Integrate Computer Technology for Teaching and Learning in higher Education. *ERIC*, *ED428675*, 3–9.

Jacobsen, M. (1997). Bridging the Gap Between Early Adopters' and Mainstream Faculty's use of Instructional Technology. Information Analyses. *Opinion Papers*, *ED423785*, 2–31.

Jaffer, S., Ng'ambi, D., & Czerniewicz, L. (2007). The Role of ICTs in Higher Education in South Africa: One Strategy for addressing Teaching and Learning Challenges. *International Journal of Education and Development using Information and Communication Technologies (IJEDICT)*, *3*(4), 131-142.

Jarmon, L., Traphagan, T., Mayrath, M., & Trivedi, A. (2009). Virtual world teaching, experimental learning and assessment: An interdisciplinary communication course in Second Life. *Computers & Education*, *53*, 169–182. doi:10.1016/j.compedu.2009.01.010

Jarvela, S., Naykki, P., Laru, J., & Luokkanen, T. (2007). Structuring and regulating collaborative learning in higher education with wireless networks and mobile tools. *Journal of Educational Technology & Society*, *10*(4), 71–79.

Jenkins, H. a. (2006). *Confronting the challenges of participatory culture: Media education in the 21st century.* Chicago: MacArther Foundation.

Jenkins, H. (2007). Reconsidering digital immigrants. *Confessions of an Aca/Fan: The official weblog of Henry Jenkins*. Retrieved June 15, 2009, from http://www.henryjenkins.org/2007/12/reconsidering_digital_immigran.html

Jensen, J. F. (1999). From "flatland" to "spaceland": Spatial representation, enunciation and interaction in 3D-virtual worlds. *Webnet Journal*, *1*(1), 44 57.

Jensen, M. (2006). Open Access: Lowering the cost of International Bandwidth in Africa. APC "Issue Papers" Series 2006 October 2006 http://rights.apc.org/documents/open_access_EN.pdf

Jenson, J. (2007). *Policy Unplugged: Dis/Connections between Technology Policy and Practices in Canadian School*. London: McGill-Queen's University Press.

Jocoy, C., & DiBiase, D. (2006). Plagiarism by adult learners online: A case study in detection and remediation. *International Review of Research in Open and Distance Learning, 7*(1). Retrieved April 18, 2007, from http://www.irrodl.org/index.php/irrodl/article/view/242/495

Johnson, D. W., & Johnson, R. T. (1999). Making cooperative learning work. *Theory into Practice*, *38*(2), 67–73. doi:10.1080/00405849909543834

Johnson, D. W., Johnson, R. T., & Holubec, E. J. (2003). *Cooperation in the classroom*. Edina, MN: Interaction Book Company.

Johnson, D. W., Johnson, R. T., & Smith, K. A. (2006). *Active Learning: Cooperation in the College Classroom*. Edina, MN: Interaction Book Company.

Johnson, S. (2009). How twitter will change the way we live. *Time*, *173*(23), 32–37.

Johnson, R. T., & Johnson, D. W. (1994). An overview of cooperative learning. In Thousand, J., Villa, A., & Nevin, A. (Eds.), *Creativity and collaborative learning* (pp. 31–44). Baltimore: Brookes Press.

Johnson, N. L., Clift, R. T., & Klecka, C. L. (2002, August). *Novice Teacher Support Project (NTSP): Following program participants*. Presentation to the Association of Teacher Educators, Williamsburg, VA.

John-Steiner, V., Panofsky, C., & Smith, L. (Eds.). (1994). *Sociocultural approaches to language & literacy: An Interactionist perspective*. New York, NY: Cambridge University Press.

John-Steiner, V. (1996, February). Creativity and collaboration in knowledge construction. Paper presented at National Council of Teachers of English Assembly on Research. Vygotsky Centennial: Vygotskian Perspectives on Literacy and Research. Chicago, IL.

Johnston, J., & Killion, J., et al. (2005). Student satisfaction in the virtual classroom. The Internet Journal of Allied Health Sciences and Practice,*3*.

Jonassen, D., Howland, J., Mara, R., & Crismond, D. (2007). *Meaningful learning with technology* (3rd ed.). Upper Saddle River, NJ: Prentice Hall.

Jonassen, D. H., & Reeves, T. C. (1996). Learning with technology: Using computers as cognitive tools. In Jonassen, D. H. (Ed.), *Handbook of research on educational communications and technology* (pp. 693–719). New York: Macmillan.

Jonassen, D. H. (2000). Revisiting activity theory as a framework for designing student-centered learning environments. In Jonassen, D. H., & Land, S. (Eds.), *Theoretical foundations of learning environments* (pp. 89–122). Mahwah, NJ: Erlbaum.

Jones, A., & Issroff, K. (2005). Learning technologies: Affective and social issues in computer-supported collaborative learning. *Computers & Education*, *44*, 395–408. doi:10.1016/j.compedu.2004.04.004

Jones, A. (2004). *A review of the research literatures on barriers to the uptake of ICT by teachers*. Retrieved from http://www.becta.org.uk/page_documents/research/barriers.pdf

Jorczak, R. L. (2008). *The effects of task characteristics on higher-order learning in online collaborative learning*. Unpublished doctoral dissertation, University of Minnesota, Minneapolis, MN.

Jukes, I., & McCain, T. (2008). Understanding digital kids: Teaching and learning in the new digital landscape. *The Info Savvy Group*. Retrieved October 31, 2008, from http://web.mac.com/iajukes/thecommittedsardine/Articles.html

Kafai, Y., & Resnick, M. (Eds.). (1996). *Constructionism in practice: Designing, thinking, and learning in a digital world*. Mahwah, NJ: Erlbaum.

Kafai, Y. B. (In press). Synthetic play: Teens gaming together and apart in virtual worlds. In Y. Kafai, C. Heeter, J. Denner, & J. Sun (Eds.), *Beyond Barbie and mortal kombat: New perspectives on gender and computer games*. Cambridge, MA: MIT Press. Retrieved May 10, 2008, from http://www.gseis.ucla.edu/faculty/kafai/paper/whyville_pdfs/PAP_kafai_bbmk.pdf

Kafai, Y. B., Fields, D. A., & Cook, M. (forthcoming). *Your second selves: Avatar design and identity play in a teen virtual world.* Paper submitted to DiGRA07. Retreived May 10, 2008, from http://www.gseis.ucla.edu/faculty/kafai/paper/whyville_pdfs/DIGRA07_avatar.pdf

Kale, U., Brush, T., & Saye, J. (forthcoming). Assisting teachers' thinking and participation online. *Journal of Educational Computing Research, 41*(3).

Kanaya, T., Light, D., & Culp, K. M. (2005). Factors influencing outcomes from a technology-focused professional development program. *Journal of Research on Technology in Education*, *37*(3), 313–329.

Kansas State Department of Education. (2008). Regulations and standards for Kansas educators..

Kao, G. Y. M., Lin, S. S. J., & Sun, C. T. (2008). Beyond sharing: Engaging students in cooperative and competitive active. *Journal of Educational Technology & Society*, *11*(3), 82–96.

Karrar, T. (2007). Facebook as a learning platform. Retrieved from http://elearni2007 15ngtech.blogspot.com/2007/10/facebook-as-learning-platform.html

Kauffman, D. (1976). *Teaching the future*. Palm Springs, CA: ETC Publications.

Kaun, K., Arora, P., & Bucuvalas, A. (2007, April). Designing an enhanced web-based civil rights curriculum for Latino English Language Learners. Paper presentation at the American Educational Research Association (AERA) Annual Conference, Chicago, IL.

Kay, R. H. (2006). Evaluating strategies used to incorporate technology into preservice education: A review of the literature. *Journal of Research on Technology in Education*, *38*(4), 383–408.

Kearsley, G., & Shneiderman, B. (1999). Engagement Theory: A framework for technology based teaching and learning. Retrieved January 10, 2008, from http://home.sprynet.com/~gkearsley/engage.htm

Keesey, C. (2009, April 6). From tourists to residents: An exploration of virtual world use in education. *Using Second Life for Teaching and Learning in Higher Education* [Webinar]. Ohio University, City, OH.

Kellner, D. (2006). Technological transformation, multiple literacies, and the re-visioning of education. In Weiss, J., Nolan, J., Hunsinger, J., & Trifonas, P. (Eds.), *The international handbook of virtual learning environments* (pp. 241–268). Dordrecht, Netherlands: Springer. doi:10.1007/978-1-4020-3803-7_9

Kellogg, R. T. (1988). Attentional overload and writing performance: effects of rough draft and outline strategies. *Journal of Experimental Psychology. Learning, Memory, and Cognition*, *14*(2), 355–365. doi:10.1037/0278-7393.14.2.355

Kellogg, R. T. (1990). Effectiveness of prewriting strategies as a function of task demands. *The American Journal of Psychology*, *103*(3), 327–342. doi:10.2307/1423213

Kennedy, G. E., & Krause, K. L. (2008). First year students' experiences with technology: Are they really digital natives? *Australasian Journal of Educational Technology*, *24*(1), 108-122. Retrieved June 14, 2009, from http://www.ascilite.org.au/ajet/ajet24/kennedy.html

Kersley, G., & Shneiderman, B. (1998). Engagement Theory: A Framework for Technology-Based Teaching and Learning. *Educational Technology*, *38*(5), 20–23.

Ketterer, J., & Marsh, G. (2006). Re-conceptualizing intimacy and distance in instructional models. *Online Journal of Distance Learning Administration*, *9*(1). Retrieved April 18, 2007, from http://www.westga.edu/~distance/ojdla/

Kezar, A., & Eckel, P. (2000). Examining the Institutional Transformational Process: The importance of Sensemaking and Inter-related Strategies. *ERIC Clearinghouse*, *ED446720*, 2–46.

Kezar, A., & Lester, J. (2009). *Organizing higher education for collaboration*. San Francisco: Jossey-Bass.

Kim, B., & Reeves, T. C. (2007). Reframing research on learning with technology: In search of the meaning of cognitive tools. *Instructional Science*, *35*, 207–256. doi:10.1007/s11251-006-9005-2

Kinchin, I. (2004). Investigating students' beliefs about their preferred role as learners. *Educational Research*, *46*(3), 301–312. doi:10.1080/0013188042000277359

Kindler, A. (2002). *Survey of the states' limited English proficient students and available education programs and services: 2000-2001 summary report*. Washington, DC: National Clearinghouse for English Language Acquisition.

King, K., & Lawler, P. (2003). Trends and Issues in the Professional Development of teachers of Adults. *New Directions for Adult and Continuing Education*, *98*, 31–37.

King, K. P. (1997). Examining learning activities and transformational learning. *International Journal of University Adult Education*, *36*(3), 23–37.

King, K. P. (1999, Fall). Unleashing technology in the classroom: What adult basic education teachers and organizations need to know. *Adult Basic Education: An Interdisciplinary Journal for Adult Literacy Educators*, *9*(3), 162–175.

King, K. P. (2000, Summer). The adult ESL experience: Facilitating perspective transformation in the classroom. *Adult Basic Education: An Interdisciplinary Journal for Adult Literacy Educators*, *10*(2), 69–89.

King, K. P. (2002). *Keeping pace with technology: Educational technology that transforms* (*Vol. 1*). Cresskill, NJ: Hampton Press.

King, K. P. (2005). *Bringing transformative learning to life*. Malabar, FL: Krieger Publishing.

King, K. P., Melia, F., & Dunham, M. (2005). Update Anytime Anywhere- Finding our way: Better understanding the needs and motivations of teachers in online learning. *International Journal of Information and Communication Technology Education*, *1*(4), 57–70.

King, K. P., & Wright, L. (2003, Summer). New perspectives on gains in the ABE classroom: Transformational learning results considered. *Adult Basic Education: An Interdisciplinary Journal for Adult Literacy Educators*, *13*(2), 100–123.

King, K. P. (1998). *A guide to perspective transformation and learning activities: The Learning Activities Survey*. Philadelphia: Research for Better Schools. Retrieved from http://www.transformationed.com

Kirschner, P., Strijbos, J., Kreijns, K., & Beers, P. J. (2005). Designing electronic collaborative learning environments. *Educational Technology Research and Development*, *52*(3), 47–66. doi:10.1007/BF02504675

Kirschner, P. A., Sweller, J., & Clark, R. E. (2006). Why minimal guidance during instruction does not work: An analysis of the failure of constructivist discovery, problem-based, experiential, and inquiry-based teaching. *Educational Psychologist*, *41*(2), 75–86. doi:10.1207/s15326985ep4102_1

Kirsh, D. (2000). A few thoughts on cognitive overload. *Intellectica*, *1*(30), 19–51.

Kluckhohn, F. R., & Strodtbeck, F. L. (1961). *Variations in value orientations*. Evanston, IL: Row, Peterson and Company.

Knezek, G., & Christensen, R. (2007). Effect of technology-based programs on first- and second-grade reading achievement. *Computers in the Schools*, *24*, 23–41. doi:10.1300/J025v24n03_03

Knobel, M., & Wilber, D. (2009). Let's talk 2.0. *Educational Leadership*, *66*(6), 20–24.

KnowledgeWorks Foundation. (2006). *2006-2016: Map of future forces affecting education*. Palo Alto, CA: Institute for the Future and KnowledgeWorks Foundation.

Knowles, M. (1984). *The adult learner: A neglected Species* (3rd ed.). Houston, TX: Gulf Publishing.

Knowles, M. S. (1980). *The modern practice of adult education: From pedagogy to andragogy* (2nd ed.). Chicago: Association/Follett.

Knowles, M. S. (1984). *Andragogy in action: Applying modern principles of adult learning*. San Francisco: Jossey-Bass.

Knowles, M. S. (1986). *Using learning contracts*. San Francisco: Jossey-Bass.

Kohls, L. R. (1981). *Developing intercultural awareness*. Washington, DC: Sietar Press.

Koster, R. (2000). *The laws of online world design*. Retrieved October 12, 2009 from Raph Koster'sWebsite: http://www.raphkoster.com/gaming/laws.shtml

Koth, C. W., Bradshaw, C. P., & Leaf, P. J. (2008). A multilevel study of predictors of student perceptions of school climate: the effect of classroom-level factors. *Journal of Educational Psychology, 100*(1), 96–104. doi:10.1037/0022-0663.100.1.96

Kotter, J. P. (1996). *Leading change.* Cambridge, MA: Harvard Business School Press.

Kounin, J. S. (1970). *Discipline and Group Management in Classrooms.* New York: Holt, Rinehart and Winston.

Kozma, R. (n.d). Comparative Analysis of Policies for ICT in Education. *International Handbook on Information Technology in Education.* Retrieved October 23, 2007, from http://robertkozma.com/images/kozma_comparative_ict_policies_chapter.pdf

Kozol, J. (1991). *Savage inequalities: Children in America's schools* (1st ed.). New York: Crown Publishers.

Kram, K. E. (1983). Phases of the mentor relationship. *Academy of Management Journal, 26*(4), 608–625. doi:10.2307/255910

Kreijns, K., Kirschner, P. A., & Jochems, W. (2003). Identifying the pitfalls for social interaction in computer-supported collaborative learning environments: A review of the research. *Computers in Human Behavior, 19,* 335–353. doi:10.1016/S0747-5632(02)00057-2

Kreijns, K., Kirschner, P. A., & Jochems, W. (2004). Determining sociability, social space, and social presence in (a) synchronous collaborative groups. *Cyberpsychology & Behavior, 7*(2), 155–172. doi:10.1089/109493104323024429

Krueger, K., Boboc, M., Smaldino, S., Cornish, Y., & Callahan, W. (2004). InTime impact report: What was InTime's effectiveness and impact on faculty and preservice teachers? *Journal of Technology and Teacher Education, 12*(2), 185–210.

Krug, D. H., & Arntzen, J. (in press). Ecologies of learning: Efficacious learning and ICT pedagogical and technological adaptability. In Mukerji, S., & Tripathi, P. (Eds.), *Cases on technological adaptability and transnational learning: Issues and challenges.* Hershey, PA: IGI Global.

Krug, D. (2006). Seeds of possibility: Mentoring K–7 educators' ICT ecology of cognition (pp. 10 - 27).

Kuhlthau, C. C. (1989). Information search process: A summary of research and implications for school library media programs. *School Library Media Quarterly, 18*(1), 19–25.

Kurtz, W. H. (1983). Identifying their needs: How the principal can help beginning teachers. *NASSP Bulletin, 67*(459), 42–45. doi:10.1177/019263658306745908

Kurzweil, R. (2000). *The age of spiritual machines: When computers exceed human intelligence.* New York: Penguin Books.

Kurzweil, R. (2005). *The Singularity is near: When humans transcend biology.* New York: Penguin Books.

LaChapelle, N. (2007). Some foundation for Second Life pedagogy. *Educause* Blog. Retrieved April 7, 2009, from http://www.educause.edu/blog/hireded/somefoundationsforsecondlifepe/167081

Laidler, D. (Ed.). (2002). *Renovating the ivory tower: Canadian universities and the knowledge economy.* Ottawa: C.D. Howe Institute.

Lajoie, S. P. (2000). *Computers as cognitive tools: No more walls (Vol. 2).* Mahwah, NJ: Erlbaum.

Lamb, B. (2004). Wide open spaces: Wikis, ready or not. *EDUCAUSE Review, 39*(5).

Lang, G. (2007, July 25). Current list of universities in Second Life®. Message posted to http://secondliferesearch.blogspot.com/2007/07/current-list-of-universities-in-second.html

Lange, D. (1988). *Tomorrow's Schools: The reform of education administration in New Zealand.* Wellington, New Zealand: The Government Printer.

Langer, A. (2005). *IT and Organizational Learning: Managing Change through Technology and Education.* New York: Routledge.

Lantolf, J. P. (2000). *Sociocultural theory and second language learning.* Oxford: Oxford University Press.

Lantolf, J. P. (2006). Sociocultural theory and Second Language Learning: State of the art. *Studies in Second Language Acquisition*, *28*, 67–109.

Lantolf, J. P., & Pavlenko, A. (1995). Sociocultural theory and second language acquisition. *Annual Review of Applied Linguistics*, *15*, 38–53. doi:10.1017/S0267190500002646

Lapadat, J. C. (2002). Written interaction: A key component in online learning. *Journal of Computer-Mediated Communication*, *7*, 4.

Latour, B. (1987). *Science in Action: How to Follow Scientists and Engineers through Society*. Cambridge, MA: Harvard University Press.

Latour, B. (1992). The Sociology of a Few Mundane Artifacts. In Bijker, W., & Law, J. (Eds.), *Shaping Technology / Building Society Studies in Sociotechnological Change*. Cambridge, MA: MIT Press.

Latour, B. (2004). On Using ANT for Studying Information Systems: A (Somewhat) Socratic Dialogue. In Chrisanthi, A. (Ed.), *The Social Study of Information and Communication Technology Innovation, Actors, and Contexts*. Oxford: Oxford University Press.

Latrobe, K. (1998). *The emerging school library media center: Historical issues and perspectives*. Englewood, CO: Libraries Unlimited.

Laurillard, D. (2002). *Rethinking University Teaching: A Framework for the Effective Use of Learning Technologies* (2nd ed.). London: RoutledgeFalmer. doi:10.4324/9780203304846

Lave, J. (1988). *Cognition in practice: Mind, mathematics, and culture in everyday life*. Cambridge, UK: Cambridge University Press. doi:10.1017/CBO9780511609268

Lave, J., & Wenger, E. (1991). *Situated learning legitimate peripheral participation*. Cambridge, UK: Cambridge University Press.

Lave, J. (1996). Teaching, as learning, in practice. *Mind, Culture, and Activity*, *3*(3), 149–164. doi:10.1207/s15327884mca0303_2

Lave, J. (1988). *Cognition in practice: Mind, mathematics and culture in everyday life*. New York: Cambridge University Press. doi:10.1017/CBO9780511609268

Lave, J. (1992). *Learning as participation in community of practice*. Paper presented at the Annual Meeting of the American Educational Research Association, San Francisco, California.

Lawler, P. A., & King, K. P. (2000). *Preparing for effective faculty development*. Malabar, FL: Krieger.

Lawless, K. A., & Pellegrino, J. W. (2007). Professional development in integrating technology into teaching and learning: Knowns, unknowns, and ways to pursue better questions and answers. *Review of Educational Research*, *77*(4), 575–614. doi:10.3102/0034654307309921

Lawrence, G. (1974). *Patterns of effective in-service education: A state of the art summary of research on materials and procedures for changing teacher behaviors in in-service education*. Tallahassee: Florida State Department of Education. Retrieved from ERIC database (ED 176 424).

Lazarus, B. (2003). Teaching courses online: How much time does it take? *JALN*, *7*(3), 47–54.

Leach, J. (2002). The curriculum knowledge of teachers: A review of the potential of large-scale, electronic conference environments for professional development. *Curriculum Knowledge*, *13*(1), 87–120. doi:10.1080/09585170110115303

Lee, K. M. (2004). Presence, explicated. *Communication Theory*, *14*(1), 27–50. doi:10.1111/j.1468-2885.2004.tb00302.x

Lee, J. (2001). Instructional support for Distance Education and Faculty Motivation, Commitment, Satisfaction. *British Journal of Educational Technology*, *32*(2), 153–106. doi:10.1111/1467-8535.00186

Lee, A. (2006). The wonderful world of wikis. In A. Rolls (Ed.), *The reference shelf: Vol. 78 (2) New media* (pp.148-152). Bronx, NY: The H. W. Wilson Company.

Leh, A. S. C. (2005). Lessons learned from service learning and reverse mentoring in faculty development: A case study in technology training. *Journal of Technology and Teacher Education, 13*(1), 25–41.

Leh, A. (1999). Computer-mediated communication and foreign language learning via telecommunication technology. *Ed-Media: World Conference on Educational Multimedia, Hypermedia, and Telecommunications* Charlottesville, VA, Association for the Advancement of Computing in Education.

Leithwood, K. A., Steinback, R. S., & Raun, T. (1993). Superintendent's group problem-solving process. *Educational Administration Quarterly, 29*(3), 364–391. doi:10.1177/0013161X93029003008

Lektorsky, V. A. (1999). Activity theory in a new era. In Engström, Y., Miettinen, R., & Punamaki, R. L. (Eds.), *Perspectives on activity theory*. Cambridge: Cambridge University Press.

Lenhart, A., Simon, M., & Graziano, M. (2001). *The internet and education*. Location: Pew Internet & American Life Project. Retrieved February 13, 2008, from http://www.pewinternet.org/pdfs/PIP_Schools_Report.pdf

Leonard, L. J., & Leonard, P. E. (2006). Leadership for technology integration: Computing the reality. *The Alberta Journal of Educational Research, 52*(4), 212.

LeTendre, G. K., Baker, D. P., Akiba, M., Goesling, B., & Wiseman, A. (2001). Teachers' work: institutional isomorphism and cultural variation in the U.S., Germany, and Japan. *Educational Researcher, 30*(6), 3–15. doi:10.3102/0013189X030006003

Leuf, B., & Cunningham, W. (2001). *The wikiway: Quick collaboration of the web*. Boston, MA: Addison-Wesley Professional.

Levin, J. (2002). A 2020 vision: Education in the next two decades. *Quarterly Review of Distance Education, 3*(1), 110–117.

Levine, A. (2000). The future of colleges: Nine inevitable changes. *The Chronicle of Higher Education, 47*(9), B10.

Levinson, P. (1999). *Digital McLuhan: a guide to the information millennium*. New York: Routledge.

Levy, S. (2007, August 27). The Facebook effect. *Newsweek*. 8/9, 40-46.

Li, X. (2007). Intelligent agent-supported online education. *Decision Sciences Journal of Innovative Education, 5*, 311–331. doi:10.1111/j.1540-4609.2007.00143.x

Library Services, Minnesota State University, Mankato. (2005). *Program review self-study, 1999/2000-2003/2004*. Retrieved January 10, 2006, from www.lib.mnsu.edu/intx/ProgRev.pdf

Liebowitz, J. (2007). *Social networking: The essence of innovation*. Lanham, MD: The Scarecrow Press.

Lih-Juan, C. (2005). Development of a questionnaire for determining the factors in technology integration among teachers. *Journal of Instructional Psychology, 32*(4), 287–292.

Lincoln, Y., & Guba, E. (1985). *Naturalistic inquiry*. Newbury Park, CA: Sage Publications.

Linden Research, Inc. (2008). What is Second Life? Retrieved January 15, 2008, from http://secondluife.com/whatis/

Linden Research, Inc. (2007) www.secondlife.com

Lipponen, L. (2000). Towards knowledge building: From facts to explanations in primary students' computer-mediated discourse. *Learning Environments Research, 3*, 179–199. doi:10.1023/A:1026516728338

Litterst, G. F. (2005/2006). Your role in music history. *The American Music Teacher, 55*(3), 50–51.

Lobry de Bruyn, L. (2004). Monitoring online communication: Can the development of convergence and social presence indicate an interactive learning environment? *Distance Education, 25*(1), 67–81. doi:10.1080/0158791042000212468

Lombard, M., & Ditton, T. (1997). At the heart of it all: The concept of presence. *Journal of Computer-Mediated Communication, 3*(2), 20.

Longe, O. B., Ogege, F. J., et al. (2005). Students' perceptions of Web-based learning Tools: A case study of the Web course tool (Webct). The African Symposium: An On Line Journal Of African Educational Research, 5(1): 20-27.

Lount, R. B. Jr, Park, E. S., Kerr, N. L., Messe, L. A., & Seok, D. H. (2008). Evaluation concerns and the Kohler effect: The impact of physical presence on motivation gains. *Small Group Research*, *39*(6), 795–812. doi:10.1177/1046496408323215

Loveless, A., Devoogd, G., & Bohlin, R. (2001). Something old, something new….: is pedagogy affected by ICT? In Loveless, A., & Ellis, V. (Eds.), *ICT, pedagogy and the curriculum* (pp. 63–83). London: Routledge/Falmer.

Lowe, C. A. (2000). *The role of the school library media specialist in the 21st century* [Electronic Version]. ERIC Digest.

Lucus, C., & Murray, J. (2002). *New Faculty: A Practical Guide for Academic Beginners*. New York: Palgrave.

Lunenberg, F. (1998). Constructivism and Technology: Instructional Designs for Successful Education Reform. *Journal of Instructional Psychology*, *25*(2), 75–83.

Luppicini, R. (2005). A System Definition of Educational Technology in Society. *Journal of Educational Technology & Society*, *8*(3), 103–109.

MacArthur, C., & Cavalier, A. (2004). Dictation and speech recognition technology as test accommodations. *Exceptional Children*, 71.

MacArthur, C. A., & Graham, S. (1987). Learning disabled students composing under three methods of text production: Handwriting, word processing, and dictation. *The Journal of Special Education*, *21*, 22–42. doi:10.1177/002246698702100304

MacDonald, C. J., & Thompson, T. L. (2005). Structure, content, delivery, service, and outcomes: Quality e-Learning in higher education. *International Review of Research in Open and Distance Learning*, *6*(2). Retrieved April 18, 2007, from http://www.irrodl.org/index.php/irrodl/article/view/235/853

Macedo, D. (2006). *Literacies of power: What Americans are not allowed to know*. Boulder, CO: Westview Press.

Magagulu, C. (2005). The Benefits and Challenges of Cross-Border Higher Education in Developing Countries. *Journal of Higher Education in Africa/RESA*, *3*(1), 29–49.

Maguire, L. (2005). Faculty Participation in Online Distance Education: Barriers and Motivators. *Online Journal of Distance Learning Administration*, *8*(1), 14.

Mahmood, A. K., & Ferneley, E. (2006). Embodied agents in e-learning environments: An exploratory case study. *Journal of Interactive Learning Research*, *17*(2), 143–162.

Major, C., & Palmer, B. (2006). Reshaping teaching and learning: The Transformation of Faculty Pedagogical Content Knowledge. *Higher Education*, *51*, 619–647. doi:10.1007/s10734-004-1391-2

Mania, K., & Chalmers, A. (2001). The effects of levels of immersion on memory and presence in virtual environments: A reality centered approach. *Cyberpsychology & Behavior*, *4*(2), 247–264. doi:10.1089/109493101300117938

Mann, C., & Stewart, F. (2000). *Internet Communication and Qualitative Research: A Handbook for Researching Online*. London: Sage Publication.

Mann, D., Shakeshaft, C., Becker, J., & Kottkamp, R. (1999). *West Virginia's basic skills/computer education program: An analysis of student achievement*. Santa Monica, CA: Milken Family Foundation.

Mantovani, G., & Riva, G. (1999). "Real" presence: How different ontologies generate different criteria for presence, telepresence, and virtual presence. *Presence (Cambridge, Mass.)*, *8*(5), 540–550. doi:10.1162/105474699566459

Margerum-Leys, J., & Marx, R. W. (2004). The nature and sharing of teacher knowledge of technology in a student teacher/mentor teacher pair. *Journal of Teacher Education*, *55*(5), 421–437. doi:10.1177/0022487104269858

Marino, R., & Stuart, G. W. (2005). The validity and reliability of the tertiary student values scale (tsvs). *Medical Education*, *39*, 895–903. doi:10.1111/j.1365-2929.2005.02244.x

Markham, A. N. (1998). *Life online researching real experience in virtual space*. Walnut Creek, CA: AltaMira Press.

Mars, M., & Ginter, M. (2007). Connecting Organizational Environments with the Instructional Technology Practices of Community College Faculty. *Community College Review*, *34*(4), 324–343. doi:10.1177/0091552107300331

Marshall, C., & Rossman, G. (1999). *Designing qualitative research* (3rd ed.). London: Sage.

Martin, R., & Lundstrom, K. (1988). Attitudes of vocational home economics teachers toward computers. *Journal of Vocational Education Research*, *13*, 83–93.

Martin, T., & Schwartz, D. L. (2005). Physically distributed learning: Adapting and reinterpreting physical environments in the development of fraction concepts. *Cognitive Science: A Multidisciplinary Journal, 29*(4), 587-625.

Martler, C. (2008). *Action research: Teachers as researchers in the classroom*. Thousand Oaks, ST: Sega Publications.

Marx, R. W., Blumenfeld, P. C., Krajcik, J. S., & Soloway, E. (1998). New technologies for teacher professional development. *Teaching and Teacher Education*, *14*, 35–52. doi:10.1016/S0742-051X(98)00059-6

Marzano, R. J., Brandt, R. S., Hughese, C. S., Jones, B. F., Presseisen, B. Z., Stuart, C., & Shhor, C. (1988). *Dimensions of Thinking*. Alexandria, VA: Association for Supervision and Curriculum Development.

Mason, R., Pegler, C., & Weller, M. (2004). E-portfolios: An assessment tool for online courses. *British Journal of Educational Technology*, *15*(6), 717–727. doi:10.1111/j.1467-8535.2004.00429.x

Mason, B. (1999, January). Issues in virtual ethnography: Ethnographic studies in real and virtual environments: Inhabited information spaces and connected communities. In K. Buckner (Ed.), Proceedings of esprit i3 workshop on ethnographic studies (pp. 61–69). Edinburgh: Queen Margaret College.

Maurer, M. M., & Davidson, G. S. (1998). *Leadership in instructional technology*. Upper Saddle River, NJ: Prentice Hall.

Maxwell, N., Bellisimo, Y., & Mergendoller, J. (2001, March/April). Problem based learning: Modifying the medical school model for teaching high school economics. *Social Studies*, 73–78. doi:10.1080/00377990109603981

Mazzolini, M., & Maddison, S. (2003). Sage, guide or ghost? The effect of instructor intervention on student participation in online discussion forums. *Computers & Education*, *40*, 237–253. doi:10.1016/S0360-1315(02)00129-X

Mbarika, V. W. A. (2002). Re-thinking Information and Communication Technology Policy focus on Internet versus Teledensity Diffusion for Africa's Least Developed Countries. *The Electronic Journal on Information Systems in Developing Countries*, *9*(1), 1–13.

McClintock, R. (1992). *Power and pedagogy: Transforming education through information technology*. New York: Teachers College, Columbia University.

McClure, R. (2009). (forthcoming). Examining the presence of advocacy and commercial websites in research essays of first-year composition students. *WPA: Writing Program Administration*.

McClure, R., & Clink, K. (2009). How do you know that? An investigation of student research practices in the digital age. *portal. Libraries and the Academy*, *9*(1), 115–132. doi:10.1353/pla.0.0033

McClure, R. (2007). Digital soapboxes: Understanding the growing presence of advocacy and commercial sites on the web. 8.3. *The Journal of Literacy and Technology, 8*(3). Retrieved June 22, 2009, from http://www.literacyandtechnology.org/volume8/no3/JLT_v8_3.htm

McClure, R., & Baures, L. (2007). Looking in by looking out: The DNA of composition in the information age. *Computers and Composition Online*. Retrieved June 22, 2009, from http://www.bgsu.edu/cconline/McClure_and_Baures/

McCombs, B. L. (2003). A framework for the redesign of K-12 education in the context of current educational reform. *Theory into Practice*, *42*(2), 163–167. doi:10.1207/s15430421tip4202_2

McCombs, B. L., & Whisler, J. S. (1997). *The learner-centered classroom and school: Strategies for increasing student motivation and achievement.* San Francisco: Jossey-Bass.

McCutchen, D. (1987). Children's discourse skill: Form and modality requirements of schooled writing. *Discourse Processes*, *10*, 267–286. doi:10.1080/01638538709544676

McCutchen, D. (2006). Cognitive factors in the development of children's writing. In MacArthur, C. A., Graham, S., & Fitzgerald, J. (Eds.), *Handbook of writing research* (pp. 115–130). New York: The Guilford Press.

McDonald, M., & Castleton, G. (2001). *Mentoring in adult learning contexts: Partners in dialogue*. Melbourne, Australia: Australian National Training Authority.

McFadden, A., Marsh, G., & Price, B. (1999). Why do educators embrace high-cost technologies? *Journal of Distance Learning Administration, 2*(3). Retrieved April 18, 2007, from http://www.westga.edu/~distance/ojdla/

McGee, C., Jones, A., Bishop, R., Cowie, B., Hill, M., Miller, T., et al. MacKenzie, K. (2002). *Teachers' Experiences in Implementing the New Zealand National Curriculum*. Wellington, New Zealand: Ministry of Education.

McGregor, D. (1960). *The human side of enterprise*. New York: McGraw-Hill.

McKenzie, J. (2002). Beyond Toolishness: The Best Ways for Teachers to Learn and Put New Technologies to Good Use. *Multimedia Schools*, *9*(4), 34–39.

McLeod, P. L., Baron, R. S., Marti, M. W., & Yoon, K. (1997). The eyes have it: Minority influence in face-to-face and computer-mediated group discussion. *The Journal of Applied Psychology*, *82*(5), 706–718. doi:10.1037/0021-9010.82.5.706

McLuhan, M. (1962). *The Gutenberg Galaxy: The Making of Typographic Man*. London: Routledge & Kegan Paul.

McLuhan, M. (1964). *Understanding Media: The Extensions of Man*. New York: McGraw Hill.

McLuhan, M., & Logan, R. K. (1977). Alphabet, mother of invention. *Et Cetera*, *34*, 373–383.

McLuhan, M. (1957, May). Classrooms without walls. *Explorations*. Retrieved October 10, 2005, from http://www.tcpd.org/Thornburg/Handouts/McLuhan.pdf

Meadows, M. S. (2008). *I avatar the culture and consequences of having a second life*. Berkeley, CA: New Riders.

Means, B., Roschelle, J., Penuel, W., Sabelli, N., & Haertel, J. (2003). Technology's contribution to teaching and policy: Efficiency, standardisation, or transformation? *Review of Educational Research*, *27*, 159–182. doi:10.3102/0091732X027001159

Means, B. (1994). *Technology and education reform*. San Francisco: Jossey-Bass.

Means, B., Toyama, Y., Murphy, R., Bakia, M., & Jones, K. (2009). Evaluation of evidence based practices in online learning: A meta-analysis and review of online learning studies. U.S. Department of Education Office of Planning, Evaluation and Policy Development, Center for Technology and Learning. (ED-04-CO-0040 Task 0006).

Meehan, M. L., & Burns, R. C. (1997, March). *E-mail survey of a listserv discussion group: Lessons learned from surveying an electronic network of learners.* Paper presented at the Annual Meeting of the American Educational Research Association, Chicago, IL.

Meltzer, J., & Hamann, E. T. (2005). *Focus on classroom teaching and learning strategies*. Providence, RI: Education Alliance Northeast and Islands Regional Education Lab, Brown University.

Mentor /National Mentoring Partnership. (2003). *Elements of effective practice* (2nd ed). Retrieved March 31, 2004, from http://www.mentoring.org/common/effective_mentoring_practices/effective_mentoring_practices.adp?Menu=nav_left_resources.adp&Preload=resources

Merriam, S. B. (1998). *Qualitative research and case study applications in education*. San Francisco: Jossey-Bass Publishers.

Merriam, S. B., Caffarella, R. S., & Baumgartner, L. M. (2007). *Learning in adulthood. A comprehensive guide* (3rd ed.). San Francisco, CA: Jossey-Bass.

Merrill, M. D. (2002). First principles of instruction. *Educational Technology Research and Development*, *50*(3), 43–59. doi:10.1007/BF02505024

Merseth, K. K. (1990, April). *Beginning teachers and computer networks: A new form of induction support* [Electronic version]. Paper presented at the annual meeting of the American Educational Research Association, Boston, MA.

Meyer, K. (2003). Face-to-face versus threaded discussions: The role of time and higher -order thinking. *JALN*, *7*(3), 55–65.

Meyer, K. (2004). Evaluating online discussions: Four different frames of analysis. *JALN*, *8*(2), 101–114.

Meyer, J. W., & Rowan, B. (1977). Institutionalized organizations: Formal structure as myth and ceremony. *American Journal of Sociology*, *83*(2), 340–363. doi:10.1086/226550

Mezirow, J. D. (1981). A critical theory of adult learning and education. *Adult Education*, *32*(1), 3–24.

Mezirow, J. (1990). *Fostering critical reflection in adult hood.* San Francisco: Jossey-Bass.

Mezirow, J. (Eds.). (2000). *Learning as transformation*. San Francisco: Jossey-Bass.

Mezirow, J. D. (1990). *Fostering critical reflection in adulthood. A guide to tranformative and emancipatory learning*. San Francisco: Jossey-Bass.

Mezirow, J. (1997). Transformative learning: Theory to practice. In P. Cranton (Ed.). *Transformative learning in action: New Directions in Adult and Continuing Education* (No. 74, pp. 5-12). San Francisco: Jossey-Bass.

Middle Tennessee State University. (2005). Assessment of Instructional Technology Survey. Academic and Instructional Technology Services, http://www.mtsu.edu/~itsurvey

Miller, J., Martineau, L., & Clark, R. (2000). Technology infusion and higher education: Changing teaching and learning. *Innovative Higher Education*, *24*(3), 227–241. doi:10.1023/B:IHIE.0000047412.64840.1c

Miltner, R. (2001, Fall). Where the visual meets the verbal: Collaboration as conversation. *Enculturation* 3(2).

Mims, C., Polly, D., Shepherd, C., & Inan, F. (2006). Examining PT3 projects designed to improve preservice education. *TechTrends*, *50*(3), 17–24. doi:10.1007/s11528-006-7599-5

Min, W. (2001). Information and Communication Technology and Education: Potential for Partnerships. Executive Summary of Proceedings 23 – 27 April 2001, Hong Kong China. http://www.adbi.org/files/2001.04.ess41.information.communication.technology.education.pdf

Minishi-Majanja, M. (2007, August 9-23). Integration of ICTs in Library and Information Science Education in sub-Saharan Africa. Paper presented at the World Library and Information Congress: 73rd IFLA General Conference And Council, Durban, South Africa. Retrieved from http://www.ifla.org/IV/ifla73/papers/083-Minishi-Majanja-en.pdf

Ministry of Education. (2003). *The Digital Horizons: Laptops for Teachers Scheme*. Wellington, New Zealand: Learning Media.

Mischo, W. H., Norman, M. A., Shelburne, W. A., & Schlembach, M. C. (2006). The growth of electronic journals in libraries: Access and management issues and solutions. *Science & Technology Libraries*, *26*(3/4), 29–59.

Mishra, P., & Koehler, M. (2006). Technological Pedagogical Content Knowledge: A Framework for Teacher Knowledge. *Teachers College Record*, *108*(6), 1017–1054. doi:10.1111/j.1467-9620.2006.00684.x

Mitchell, M. (1999). Effects of Faculty Motivation in Distributive Education Environments at Institutions of Higher Education. *ERIC, ED436155*, 269–274.

Mitham, N. (2007, July 11). Age ranges and gender analysis. Message posted to: http://www.kzero.co.uk/blog/?p=887

Moersch, C. (2001). Next steps: Using LOTI as a research tool. *Learning and Leading with Technology*, *29*(3), 22–26.

Molenda, M., & Sullivan, M. (2002). Issues and Trends in Instructional Technology: Hitting the Plateau. *Educational Media and Technology Yearbook*, *27*, 3–13.

Monaghan, J., & Lunt, N. (1992). Mentoring: Person, process, practice and problems. *British Journal of Educational Studies*, *40*(3), 248–263. doi:10.1080/00071005.1992.9973929

Monge, P. R., & Contractor, N. S. (2003). *Theories of communication networks*. New York: Oxford University Press.

Moon, B. (2004). 'Open and Distance Learning for Teacher Education in Africa: Innovation and Change': A Toolkit for Education Policy Makers, Planners and Teacher Educators in Sub-Saharan Africa. *Region Human Development Working Paper Series,* 5. Washington, DC: The World Bank.

Morris, L. (2004). Changing Institutions and Changing Faculty. *Innovative Higher Education*, *29*(1), 3–6. doi:10.1023/B:IHIE.0000035494.75389.83

Morrow, C. A., & Fredin, B. (1999). *Worksite mentoring guidebook: Practical help for planning and implementing quality worksite learning experiences*. Columbus, Ohio: Ohio State Department of Education.

Morrow, R. A., & Torres, C. A. (1994). Education and reproduction of class, gender, and race: Responding to the postmodern challenge. *Educational Theory*, *44*(1). doi:10.1111/j.1741-5446.1994.00043.x

Morse v Frederick 127 S. Ct 2818 (2007)

Moses, P., Khambari, M., & Luan, W. (2008). Laptop use and its antecedents among educators: A review of the literature. *European Journal of Soil Science*, *7*(1), 104–114.

Mullen, C. A., Whatley, A., & Kealy, W. A. (1999). *Co-mentoring support groups in higher education. HE 031 943*. Washington, DC: US Department of Education.

Murphy, E., & Manzanares, M. A. R. (2008). Contradictions between the virtual and physical high school classroom: A third-generation Activity Theory perspective. *British Journal of Educational Technology*, *39*(6), 1061–1072. doi:10.1111/j.1467-8535.2007.00776.x

Myers, C., Bennett, D., Brown, G., & Henderson, T. (2004). Emerging online learning environments and student learning: An analysis of faculty perceptions. *Journal of Educational Technology & Society*, *7*(8), 78–86.

Nagin, C. National Writing Project. (2006). *Because Writing Matters: Improving Student Writing in Our Schools*. San Francisco: Jossey-Bass.

Nakamura, L. (2002). *Cybertypes: Race, ethnicity, and identity on the Internet*. London: Routledge.

National Board for Professional Teaching Standards. (2002b). *Adolescence and young adulthood science for teachers of students ages 14–18+ Portfolio Instructions*. Arlington, VA: NBPTS.

National Board for Professional Teaching Standards (NBPTS). (2002a). *What teachers should know and be able to do*. Arlington, VA: NBPTS.

National Center for Education Statistics. (2004). *The condition of education*. Retrieved February 22, 2009, from http://nces.ed.gov/programs/coe

National Center for Education Statistics. (2009). *High school dropout and completion rates in the United States, 2007*. Retrieved October 8, 2009, from http://nces.ed.gov/pubsearch/pubsinfo.asp?pubid=2009064

National Center for Education Statistics. (2000). *Teachers' tools for the 21st century: A report on teachers' use of technology. (Report No. NCES 2000-102)*. Washington, DC: U.S. Department of Education.

National Center for Education Statistics. (2007). Educational technology in teacher education programs for initial licensure: A statistical analysis report. Washington, DC: U.S. Department of Education. Retrieved June 25, 2009, from http://nces.ed.gov/pubs2008/2008040

National Council of Teachers of English. (2008). The NCTE Definition of 21st Century Literacies. Retrieved June 15, 2009, from http://www.ncte.org/positions/statements/21stcentdefinition

National Council of Teachers of English/International Reading Association. (1996). *Standards for the English Language Arts*. Retrieved June 24, 2009, from http://www.ncte.org/standards

National Partnership for Excellence and Accountability in Teaching (NPEAT). (2000). *Revisioning professional development: What learner-centered professional development looks like*. Oxford, OH: Author. Retrieved April 4, 2009, from http://www.nsdc.org/library/policy/npeat213.pdf

National School Boards Association. (2007). Creating and connecting: Research and guidelines on online social and educational networking. Retrieved January 31, 2009, from http://www.nsba.org/site/docs/41400/41340.pdf

National Telecommunications and Information Administration (NTIA). (1999). Falling through the net. Washington, DC: U.S. Department of Commerce. Retrieved March 25, 2005, from http://www.ntia.doc.gov/ntiahome/fttn99/contents.html

National Telecommunications and Information Administration (NTIA). (2004). A nation online: Entering the broadband age. Washington, DC: U.S. Department of Commerce. Retrieved February 25, 2007, from http://www.ntia.doc.gov/reports/anol/NationOnlineBroadband04.htm

Nelson, L., Sadler, L., & Surtees, G. (2005). Bringing problem based learning to life using virtual reality. *Nurse Education in Practice*, *5*, 103–108. doi:10.1016/j.nepr.2004.05.001

New York City Department of Education, Office of English Language Learners. (2009). The performance of New York City's English language learners. Retrieved February 22, 2009, from http://schools.nyc.gov/NR/rdonlyres/3B377E6B-5E22-4E63-A4DA-2B7FD-14E5D62/57000/ELLPerformanceReport2009.pdf

New York City Department of Education. (2006). The 2005-2006 Annual School Reports. Retrieved July 29, 2007, from http://schools.nyc.gov/daa/schoolreports/

New York State Department of Education. (n.d.). *New York State learning standards*. Retrieved July 30, 2007, from http://www.emsc.nysed.gov/ciai/cores.htm#3ela

New York State Education Department. 89 Washington Avenue, Albany, New York 12234 (http://www.nysed.gov/).

Ngugi, C. (2007). *ICTs and Higher Education in Africa: Status Reports on Information and Communication Technologies (ICTs) in Higher Education in eight African countries*. Cape Town, South Africa: The Centre of Educational Technology, University of Cape Town.

Niess, M. L. (2005). Preparing teachers to teach science and mathematics with technology: Developing a technology pedagogical content knowledge. *Teaching and Teacher Education, 21*, 509-523.

Noam, E. (1995). Electronics and the dim future of the university. *Science*, *270*, 247–249. doi:10.1126/science.270.5234.247

Nonaka, I., & Takeuchi, H. (1995). *The knowledge-creating company: how Japanese companies create the dynamics of innovation*. New York: Oxford University Press.

Northwest Regional Educational Laboratory. (2004) *OPTIC- Observation Protocol for Technology Integration in the Classroom*. Portland, OR: Author. Retrieved June 26, 2006, from http://www.netc.org/images/doc/observation.continuum.doc

O'Shea, P., Curry-Corcoran, D., Baker, P., Allen, D. A., & Allen, D. W. (2007). New Levels of Student Participatory Learning: A WikiText for the Introductory Course in Education. *The Journal of Interactive Online Learning*, *6*(3).

O'Sullivan, E. (1999). *Transformative learning*. London: Zed Books.

Oakley, C. (2008). *Preparing future teachers for 21st century learning: Partnerships that enhance the capacity of pre-service education* [White Paper]. City, ST: Intel Corporation.

Oberlander, J., & Talbert-Johnson, C. (2007, February). *Envisioning the Foundations of Technology Integration in Pre-service Education*. Paper presented at the annual meeting of the Association for Teacher Education, San Diego, California.

Oblinger, D., & Hawkins, B. (2005). The myth about students. *EDUCAUSE Review, 40*(5), 12–13.

Oliver, R. (1999). Exploring strategies for online teaching and learning. *Distance Education, 20*(2), 240–254. doi:10.1080/0158791990200205

Omale, N., Hung, W. C., Luetkehans, L., & Cooke-Plagwitz, J. (2009). Learning in 3-D multiuser virtual environments: Exploring the use of unique 3-D attributes for online problem-based learning. *British Journal of Educational Technology, 40*(3), 480–495. doi:10.1111/j.1467-8535.2009.00941.x

Ong, W. (1982). *Orality and literacy: The technologizing of the word*. London, New York: Metheun. doi:10.4324/9780203328064

Online Computer Library Center. (2006). *College students' perceptions of the libraries and information resources: A report to the OCLC membership*. Retrieved February 24, 2009, from http://www.oclc.org/reports/perceptionscollege.htm

Oreilly, T. (2007). What is Web 2.0?: Design patterns and business models for the next generation of software. *Communications & Strategies, 1*, 17.

Orlich, D. C. (1989). *Staff development: Enhancing human potential*. Boston: Allyn and Bacon.

Orrill, C. H. (2001). Building learner-centered classrooms: A professional development framework for supporting critical thinking. *Educational Technology Research and Development, 49*(1), 15–34. doi:10.1007/BF02504504

Ortiz de Gortari, A. (2007, September). *Second Life® survey: User profile for psychological engagement and gambling*. Paper presented at The Virtual 2007 Conference: Interaction, Stockholm, Sweden.

Ortuno, M. M. (1991). Cross-cultural awareness in the foreign language class: The Kluckhohn model. *Modern Language Journal, 75*, 449–459. doi:10.2307/329494

Osika, E. R., Johnson, R. Y., & Buteau, R. (2009, Spring). Factors influencing faculty use of technology in online instruction: A case study. *Online Journal of Distance Learning Administration, 12*(1). Retrieved June 11, 2009.

Oslin, G.P. (1992). *The story of communications*. Location: Mercer University Press.

Ostlund, B. (2005). Stress, disruption and community: Adult learners' experiences of obstacles and opportunities in distance education. *European Journal of Open, Distance and E-Learning*. Retrieved April 18, 2007, from http://www.eurodl.org/materials/contrib/2005/Ostlund.htm

Owston, R. (2007). Contextual factors that sustain innovative pedagogical practice using technology: An international study. *Journal of Educational Change, 8*, 61–77. doi:10.1007/s10833-006-9006-6

Papert, S. (1991). Situated constructionism. In Harel, I., & Papert, S. (Eds.), *Constructionism: Research reports and essays, 1985-1990* (pp. 1–10). Norwood, NJ: Ablex.

Park, H. S. (2008). The impact of technology use on Hispanic students' mathematics achievement within family and school contexts: Subgroup analysis between English- and non-English speaking students. *Journal of Educational Computing Research, 38*(4), 553–568. doi:10.2190/EC.38.4.d

Park, S., & Kim, K. (2008). The use of pedagogical agent as a tool to improve learning interest: Based on the distinction between individual interest and situational interest. In K. McFerrin et al. (Eds.), *Proceedings of Society for Information Technology and Teacher Education International Conference 2008* (pp. 2777-2781). Chesapeake, VA: AACE.

Parsons, J., & Johnson, T. (1978). *Adults learn differently than children. An examination of an old basic assumption.* Washington, DC: National Inst. of Education. (ERIC Document Reproduction Service No. ED166372)

Partnership for 21st Century Skills. (2004). *The road to 21st century learning: Policymakers' guide to 21st century skills.* Retrieved April 22, 2005, from http://www.21stcenturyskills.org/images/stories/otherdocs/P21_Policy_Paper.pdf

Patton, M. Q. (1987). *How to use qualitative methods in evaluation.* Newbury Park, CA: Sage.

Pea, R. D. (2004). The social and technological dimensions of "scaffolding" and related theoretical concepts for learning, education and human activity. *Journal of the Learning Sciences, 13*(3), 423–451. doi:10.1207/s15327809jls1303_6

Pelgrum, W., & Law, N. (2003). *ICT in education around the world: trends problems and prospects,* Paris: UNESCO International Institute for Educational Planning educational assessment.". *Computers & Education, 37,* 163–178. doi:10.1016/S0360-1315(01)00045-8

Pelz, B. (2004). (My) Three principles of effective online pedagogy. *JALN, 8*(3), 33–46.

Penuel, W., Fishman, B., Yamaguchi, R., & Gallagher, L. (2007). What makes professional development effective? Strategies that foster curriculum implementation. *American Educational Research Journal, 44*(4), 921–958. doi:10.3102/0002831207308221

Peregoy, S. F., & Boyle, O. F. (2005). *Reading, writing and learning in ESL: A resource book for K-12 teachers.* Boston: Pearson Education.

Perraton, H., & Creed, C. (2000, April 26–28). Applying new technologies and cost-effective delivery systems in basic education. World Education Forum, Dakar, Senegal. UNESCO: Paris.

Peterson, P. L. (1990). Doing more of the same: Cathy Swift. *Educational Evaluation and Policy Analysis, 12*(3), 261–280.

Philips, D. C. (1997). How, Why, What, When and Where: Perspectives on Constructivism in Psychology and Education. *Issues in Education, 3*(2), 151–195.

Philips, D. C. (2000). *Constructivism in Education.* Chicago: The University of Chicago Press.

Phillips, R., Bailey, M., Fisher, T., & Harrison, C. (1999). Questioning teachers about their use of portable computers. *Journal of Computer Assisted Learning, 15,* 149–161. doi:10.1046/j.1365-2729.1999.152087.x

Piaget, J. (1970). *Genetic epistemology.* New York: Columbia University Press.

Picciano, A. G. (2002). Beyond student perceptions: Issues interaction, presence, and performance in an online course. *Journal of Asynchronous Learning Networks, 6,* 20–41.

Pilling-Cormick, J. (1997). Transformative and self-directed learning in practice. In P. Cranton (Ed.), *Transformative learning in action: New Directions in Adult and Continuing Education* (No. 74, pp. 69-78). San Francisco: Jossey-Bass.

Pityana, N. B. (2004). Higher Education in South Africa: Future Perspectives. Keynote address at Bill Venter/Altron Literary Awards 2003; Wednesday 7 April 2004, Westcliff Hotel, Johannesburg. http://www.unisa.ac.za/contents/about/principle/docs/AltronAwardsspeech.doc

Pogatchnik, S. (2009). Student hoaxes world's media on Wikipedia. *msnbc.* Retrieved May 13, 2009, from http://www.msnbc.msn.com

Polly, D., & Ausband, L. (in press). Developing higher order thinking skills through WebQuests. *Journal of Computing in Teacher Education.*

Polly, D., & Brantley-Dias, L. (2009). TPACK: Where do we go now? *TechTrends*, *53*(5), 46–47. doi:10.1007/s11528-009-0324-4

Polly, D., & Mims, C. (2009). Designing professional development to support teachers' TPACK and integration of Web 2.0 technologies. In Kidd, T. T., & Chen, I. (Eds.), *Wired for Learning: Web 2.0 Guide for Educators* (pp. 301–316). City.

Polly, D. (2006). *Examining the influence of learner-centered professional development on elementary mathematics teachers instructional practices, espoused practices, and evidence of student learning*. Unpublished Doctoral Dissertation, University of Georgia, Athens, GA. Polly, D. (2008-a). Modeling the influence of calculator use and teacher effects on first grade students' mathematics achievement. *Journal of Technology in Mathematics and Science Teaching, 27*(3), 245-263.

Polly, D. (2008, Month day). Supporting standards-based mathematics in elementary classrooms. Paper presented at the Annual Conference of the School Science and Mathematics Association, Raleigh, NC.

Pomeroy, J. R. (1997). *The rural learning network: A teaching and learning collaborative.* Paper presented at the Annual NREA Convention, Tucson, AZ.

Poole, D. M. (2000). Student participation in a discussion-oriented online course: A case study. *Journal of Research on Computing in Education*, *33*(2), 162–177.

Posner, G. J. (2005). *Field experiences: A guide to reflective teaching* (6th ed.). New York: Allyn and Bacon.

Pough, G. (2009). The remix: Revisit, rethink, revise, renew. *Conference on College Composition and Communication Call for Program Proposals*. Urbana, IL: NCTE.

Pragnell, M. V., Roselli, T., & Rossano, V. (2006). Can a hypermedia cooperative e-learning environment stimulate constructive collaboration? *Journal of Educational Technology & Society*, *9*(2), 119–132.

Prensky, M. (2001). Digital natives, digital immigrants. *Horizon*, *9*(5), 1–6. doi:10.1108/10748120110424816

Prensky, M. (2001). Digital natives, digital immigrants. *On the Horizon, 9*(6). Retrieved April 18, 2007, from http://www.marcprensky.com/writing/Prensky

Prensky, M. (December 2005/January 2006). Listen to the natives. *Educational Leadership, 63*(4), 8-13. Retrieved August 19, 2006, from http://www.ascd.org/cms/objectlib/ascdframeset/index.cfm?publication=http://www.ascd.org/authors/ed_lead/el200512_prensky.html

Primary Research Group. (2009). *The survey of academic libraries, 2008-2009 edition*. Retrieved June 21, 2009, from http://www.primaryresearch.com/content-200902049-Libraries--Information-Science.html

Prince, M. (2004). Does active learning work? A review of the research. *Journal of Engineering Education*, *93*(3), 223–231.

Privateer, P. M. (1999). Academic Technology and the Future of Higher Education. *The Journal of Higher Education*, *70*, 60–79. doi:10.2307/2649118

Project Information Literacy. (2009). *About*. Retrieved June 15, 2009, from http://www.projectinfolit.org

Protesting against new technology – The early days. Cartoon retrieved June 8, 2009. www.inkcinet.com.au/Web/CARTOONS/2007/2007~34

Pryor, B., & Pryor, C. (2005). *The School Leader's Guide to Understanding Attitude and Influencing Behavior*. Thousand Oaks, CA: Corwin Press.

Psycharis, S. (2005). Presumptions and actions affecting an e-learning adoption by the educational system implementation using virtual private networks. *European Journal of Open, Distance and E-Learning*. Retrieved April 18, 2007, from www.eurodl.org

Quinlan, T. (2004). Speech recognition technology and students with writing difficulties: Improving fluency. *Journal of Educational Psychology*, *96*(2), 337–346. doi:10.1037/0022-0663.96.2.337

Raja Hussain, R. M. (2006, September, 9-11). Pedagogy of Engagement Integrating Technology (PoEIT). Paper presented at the Malaysian Educational Technology Association Convention, Johor, Malaysia.

Rajasingham, L. (2005). The virtual university: From turf to surf-same journey different routes. *European Journal of Open, Distance and E-Learning*. Retrieved April 18, 2007, from www.eurodl.org

Raman, M., Ryan, T., & Olfman, L. (2005). Designing knowledge management systems for teaching and learning with wild technology. *Journal of Information Systems Education*, *16*(3), 311–320.

Rea, L. M., & Parker, R. A. (2005). *Designing and conducting survey research: A comprehensive guide*. San Francisco: Jossey-Bass.

Redmond, P. A. (2002). Building a community of practice: A case study of technology augmented mentoring for new teachers. Available from Dissertations and Theses database. (UMI No. 3059402)

Reece, J. E., & Cummings, G. (1996). Evaluating speech-based composition methods: Planning, dictation, and the listening word processor. In Levy, C. M., & Ransdell, S. (Eds.), *The science of writing: Theories, methods, individual differences, and applications* (pp. 361–380). Mahwah, NJ: Erlbaum.

Regan, A. E., & Zuern, J. D. (2000). Community-service learning and computer-mediated advanced composition: The going to class, getting online, and giving back project. *Computers and Composition*, *17*, 177–195. doi:10.1016/S8755-4615(00)00028-1

Reidel, C. (2009, January). Create, collaborate, communicate: Empowering students with 21st century skills. *THE Journal*. Retrieved June 11, 2009, from http://thejournal.com/articles/2009/01/27/create-collaborate-communicate-empowering-students-with-21st-century-skills.aspx

Remedios, L., Clarke, D., & Hawthorne, L. (2008). Framing collaborative behaviors: Listening and speaking in problem-based learning. *The Interdisciplinary Journal of Problem-Based Learning*, *2*(1), 1–20.

Revised generic scoring Rubric for Document-Based Questions (DBQs) on the Grade 8 Intermediate-Level Social Studies Test.

Rhem, J. (1995). Close up: Going deep. *The National Teaching and Learning Forum*, *5*(1), 4.

Richardson, V. (2003). Constructivist Pedagogy. *Teachers College Record*, *105*(9), 1623–1640. doi:10.1046/j.1467-9620.2003.00303.x

Richardson, V. (1990). Significant and worthwhile change in teaching practice. *Educational Researcher*, *19*, 10–18.

Ringstaff, C., & Kelley, L. (2002). *The learning return on our educational technology investment*. San Francisco: WestEd.

Robbins, S. (2008). *Chapter 3 method: Developing the faceted classification*. Retrieved March 8, 2009, from http://www.sarahrobbins.com/RobbinsChapter3Method.pdf

Roberts, F. D., Kelley, C., & Medlin, B. D. (2007). Factors Influencing Accounting Faculty Members' Decision to Adopt Technology in the Classroom. *College Student Journal*, *41*(2), 423–435.

Roberts, A. (2000). Mentoring revisited: A phenomenological reading of the literature. *Mentoring & Tutoring: Partnership in Learning*, *8*(2), 145–170. doi:10.1080/713685524

Robson, C. (2002). Real world research. Malden, ST: Blackwell Publishing.

Rockwell, S. K., Schauer, J., Fritz, S. M., & Marx, D. B. (1999). Incentives and Obstacles Influencing Higher Education Faculty and Administrators to Teach Via Distance. *Online Journal of Distance Learning Administration*, *2*(4), 7.

Rogers, E. M. (1962). *Diffusion of Innovation*. New York: Free Press.

Rogers, E. M., & Shoemaker, F. (1971). *Communication of Innovations: A Cross-Cultural Approach* (2nd ed.). New York: Free Press.

Rogers, P. L. (2000). Barriers to adopting emerging technologies in education. *Journal of Educational Computing Research, 22*(4), 455–472. doi:10.2190/4UJE-B6VW-A30N-MCE5

Rokeach, M. (1973). *The Nature of Human Values*. New York: The Free Press.

Romero, N., Markopoulos, P., van Baren, J., de Ruyter, B., Ijsselsteijn, W., & Farshchian, B. (2007). Connecting the family with awareness systems. *Personal and Ubiquitous Computing, 11*(4), 299–312. doi:10.1007/s00779-006-0089-0

Romiszowski, A. J., & Mason, R. (2004). Computer mediated communication. In Jonassen, D. H. (Ed.), *Handbook of research on educational communications and technology* (2nd ed., pp. 397–426). Mahwah, NJ: Erlbaum.

Roosevelt, M. (2009, Month day). Student expectations see as causing grade disputes. *The New York Times,* 1.

Roschelle, J., Pea, R., Hoadley, C., Gordin, D., & Means, B. (2001). Changing how and what children learn in schools with computer-based technologies. *The Future of Children, 10*(2), 76–101. doi:10.2307/1602690

Rose, G. L. (2003). Enhancement of mentor selection using the ideal mentor scale. *Research in Higher Education, 44*(4), 473. doi:10.1023/A:1024289000849

Ross, E. W., Cornett, J. W., & McCutcheon, G. (1992). Teacher personal theorizing and research on curriculum and teaching. In Ross, E. W., Cornett, J., & McCutcheon, G. (Eds.), *Teacher personal theorizing: Connecting curriculum practice, theory, and research*. Albany, NY: State University of New York Press.

Rourke, L., Anderson, T., Garrison, D. R., & Archer, W. (1999). Assessing social presence in asynchronous text-based computer conferencing. *Journal of Distance Education, 14*(3), 51–70.

Rourke, L., Anderson, T., Garrison, D. R., & Archer, W. (2001). Methodological issues in the content analysis of computer conference transcripts. *International Journal of Artificial Intelligence in Education, 12*, 8–22.

Rovai, A. P. (2002). Building sense of community at a distance. *International Review of Research in Open and Distance Learning, 3*(1).

Roval, A., & Barnum, K. (2003). On-line course effectiveness: An analysis of student interactions and perceptions of learning. *Journal of Distance Education, 18*(1), 57–73.

Rudd, P. (2001, September 20). *School Improvement through ICT: The Case of England.* Paper presented at the CIDREE Seminar: The Use of ICT in Supporting Effective Learning and Teaching. Scottish Education and Teaching Technology Show, SECC, Glasgow, Scotland.

Rudner, L., Garcia, V., & Welch, C. (2006). An evaluation of the IntelliMetric essay scoring system. *The Journal of Technology, Learning, and Assessment, 4*(4). Retrieved April 18, 2007, from http://escholarship.bc.edu/jtla/

Russell, A. L. (1996). Six Stages in Learning New Technology. Proceedings of Selected Research and development Presentations at the 1996 National Convention of the Association for Educational Communications and Technology, ED 397 832, 633-641.

Russo, T. C., & Koesten, J. (2005). Prestige, centrality, and learning: A social network analysis of an online class. *Communication Education, 54*(3), 254–261. doi:10.1080/03634520500356394

Russo, K. W. (Ed.). (2000). *Finding the middle ground: Insights and applications of the value orientations method.* Yarmouth, ME: Intercultural Press.

Sadat, S. (2007). Higher Education Transformation in South Africa Post 1994: Towards a Critical Assessment. *Solomon Mahlangu Education Lecture 2007.* Location: Centre for Education Policy Development. Retrieved June 22, 2009, from http://www.cepd.org.za/files/CEPD_SolomonMahlanguLecture1_Badat_2007.pdf

Sahin, I., & Thompson, A. (2007). Analysis of Predictive Factors That Influence Faculty Members' Technology Adoption Level. *Journal of Technology and Teacher Education, 15*(2), 167–190.

Sahin, I. (2005). Understanding Faculty Adoption of Technology Using the Learning/Adoption Trajectory Model: A qualitative Case Study. *The Turkish Online Journal of Educational Technology, 4*(1). Retrieved from http://???

Salaway, G., & Caruso, J. B. (2007). The ECAR Study of undergraduate students and information technology. Boulder, CO: Educause Center for Applied research.

Salmon, G. (2009). The future from (second) life and learning. *British Journal of Educational Technology, 40*(3), 526–538. doi:10.1111/j.1467-8535.2009.00967.x

Sarama, J., Clements, D. H., Swaminathan, S., McMillen, S., & Gómez, R. M. G. (2003). Development of mathematical concepts of two-dimensional space in grid environments: An exploratory study. *Cognition and Instruction, 21*(3), 285–324. doi:10.1207/S1532690XCI2103_03

Sarason, S. (2004). *And what do you mean by learning?*Portsmouth, NH: Heinemann.

Scandura, T. A., & Williams, E. A. (2001). An investigation of the moderating effects of gender on the relationships between mentoring initiation and protégé perceptions of mentoring functions. *Journal of Vocational Behavior, 59*, 342–363. doi:10.1006/jvbe.2001.1809

Scanlon, E., & Issroff, K. (2005). Activity theory and higher education: Evaluating learning technologies. *Journal of Computer Assisted Learning, 21*(6), 430–439. doi:10.1111/j.1365-2729.2005.00153.x

Scardamalia, M., Bereiter, C., & Goleman, H. (1982). The role of production factors in writing ability. In Nystrand, M. (Ed.), *What writers know: The language, process, and structure of written discourse* (pp. 175–210). San Diego, CA: Academic Press.

Scardamalia, M., & Bereiter, C. (2006). Knowledge building: Theory, pedagogy, and technology. In Sawyer, K. (Ed.), *Cambridge Handbook of the Learning Sciences* (pp. 97–118). New York: Cambridge University Press.

Scardamalia, M. (2002). Creative work with ideas: A luxury? Annual meeting of the American Psychological Association. New Orleans, LA.

Schacter, J. (1999). *The impact of education technology on student achievement: What the most current research has to say*. Santa Monica, CA: Milken Exchange on Education Technology.

Scheid-Cook, T. L. (1992). Organizational enactments and conformity to environmental prescriptions. *Human Relations, 45*(6). doi:10.1177/001872679204500601

Schifer, C. (2000). Faculty Participation in Asynchronous Learning Networks: A Case Study of Motivating and Inhibiting Factors. *Journal of Asynchronous Learning Networks, 4*(1), 15–22.

Schlager, M. S., & Fusco, J. (2004). Teacher professional development, technology, and communities of practice: Are we putting the cart before the horse? In Barab, S., Kling, R., & Gray, J. (Eds.), *Designing virtual communities in the service of learning* (pp. 120–153). New York: Cambridge University Press.

Schneider, R. M., Krajcik, J., & Blumenfeld, P. (2005). Enacting reform-based science materials: The range of teacher enactments in reform classrooms. *Journal of Research in Science Education, 42*(3), 283–312.

Schneider, D. (2009). Personal learning environment. Retrieved March 13, 2009, from http://edutechwiki.unige.ch/en/Persnal_learning_environment

Schoepp, K. (2005). Barriers to Technology Integration in technology-Rich Environment. *Learning and Teaching in Higher Education* [Special issue on Gulf Perspectives], *2*(1). 1-24. Retrieved from http://www.zu.ac.ae/ithe

Schön, D. (1983). *The reflective practitioner: How professionals think in action*. New York: Basic Books.

Schrum, L. (1999). Technology professional development for teachers. *Educational Technology Research and Development, 47*(4), 83–90. doi:10.1007/BF02299599

Schütz, A. (1967). *The phenomenology of the social world*. Evanston, IL: Northwestern University Press.

Schwab, J. J. (1983). The practical 4: Something for curriculum professors to do. *Curriculum Inquiry, 13*(3), 239–265. doi:10.2307/1179606

Scribner, S., & Cole, M. (1981). *The Psychology of Literacy*. Cambridge, MA: Harvard University Press.

Second Life® Education Wiki. (2007). Retrieved from http://www.simteach.com/wiki/index.php?title=Second_Life_Education_Wiki

Seely Brown, J., Collins, A., & Duguid, P. (1989). Situated cognition and the culture of learning. *Educational Researcher*, 18.

Selwyn, N. (1999). Why the computer is not dominating schools: A failure of policy or a failure of practice? *Cambridge Journal of Education*, *29*(1), 77–91. doi:10.1080/0305764990290106

Selwyn, N., & Facer, K. (2007). *Beyond the digital divide: Rethinking digital inclusion for the 21st century*. London, United Kingdom: Futurelab.

Selwyn, N. (2000). Creating a connected community? Teachers' use of an electronic discussion group. *Teachers College Record*, *102*(4), 750–778. doi:10.1111/0161-4681.00076

Sener, J. (2007). In search of student generated content in online education. e-mentor, *4*(21). Retrieved from http://E-mentor.edu.pl/org

Sergiovanni, T. J. (1991). *The principalship: A reflective practice perspective*. Boston: Allyn & Bacon.

Sewell, A. (2002). Constructivism and Student Misconceptions. *Australian Science Teachers Journal*, *48*(4), 24–29.

Shannon, D. (2002). The education and competencies of school library media specialists: A review of the literature. *School Library Media Research, 5*.

Sharan, S. (Ed.). (1990). *Cooperative Learning: Theory and Research*. New York: Praeger Publishers.

Shareski, D., & Winkler, C. A. K. (2005/2006). Are wikis worth the time? *Learning and Leading with Technology*, *33*(4), 6–7.

Shea, P. (2007). Bridges and Barriers to Teaching Online College Courses: A Study of Experienced Online Faculty in Thirty-Six Colleges. [JALN]. *Journal of Asynchronous Learning Networks*, *11*(2), 73–128.

Sheilds, R. (2003). *The Virtual*. London: Routledge.

Sherry, L., Billig, S., Tavalin, F., & Gibson, D. (2000). New insights in technology adoption in schools. *T.H.E. Journal*, *27*(7), 43–46.

Sherry, L., & Gibson, D. (2002). The path to teacher leadership in educational technology. *Contemporary Issues in Technology & Teacher Education*, *2*(2), 178–203.

Shor, I. (1992). *Empowering education: Critical teaching for social change*. Chicago: University of Chicago Press.

Short, J., Williams, E., & Christie, B. (1976). *The social psychology of telecommunications*. London: John Wiley & Sons.

Shotsberger, P., & Vetter, R. (2000). The handheld Web: How mobile wireless technologies will change Web-based instruction and training. *Educational Technology*, *40*, 49–52.

Shulman, L. (1987). Knowledge and Teaching: Foundations of the New Reform. *Harvard Educational Review*, *57*(1), 1–20.

Sid, H., & Malcolm, M. (1985). Information Technology Assessment and Adoption: a Field of Study. *Management Information Systems Quarterly*, *9*(4), 327–341. doi:10.2307/249233

Siebert, C. J., Clark, A., Kilbridge, A., & Peterson, H. (2006). When preserve teachers struggle or fail: Mentor teachers' perspectives. *Education*, *126*(3), 409–422.

Siemens, G. (2004). Connectivism: A Learning Theory for the Digital Age. Retrieved 24th August, 2009, from http://www.elearnspace.org/Articles/connectivism.htm

Silver, E. A., & Stein, M. K. (1996). The QUASAR project: The "revolution of the possible" in mathematics instructional reform in urban middle schools. *Urban Education*, *30*(4), 476–521. doi:10.1177/0042085996030004006

Simmel, G. (1949). The sociology of sociability. *American Journal of Sociology*, *55*(3), 254–261. doi:10.1086/220534

Simmons, W. M., & Grabill, J. T. (2007, February). Toward a civic rhetoric for technologically and scientifically complex places: Invention, performance, and participation. *College Composition and Communication*, *58*(3), 419–448.

Single, P. B., & Muller, C. B. (2001). When email and mentoring unite: The implementation of a nationwide electronic mentoring program. In L. Stromei (Ed.), *Implementing successful coaching and mentoring programs* (pp. 107-122). Cambridge, MA: American Society for Training & Development (ASTD) In Action Series.

Single, P. B., & Muller, C. B. (2003, under review). *Electronic mentoring programs: a model to guide practice and research.*

Single, P. B., & Single, R. M. (2004, in press). E-mentoring and telementoring: Review of research. In F. K. Kochan & J. T. Pascarelli (Eds.), *Technological aspects of mentoring*. Greenwich, CT: Information Age Press. Retrieved on March 31, 2004, from www.uvm.edu/~pbsingle

Single, P. B., Muller, C. B., Cunningham, C. M., Single, R. M., & Carlsen, W. S. (2003, forthcoming). Inter-organizational connections, the value of impartial advisors, and increased self-confidence: Research from a large-scale e-mentoring program.

Singleton-Jackson, J., & Newsom, R. (2006). Adapt, adjust, respond: Perspectives on current trends in American colleges and universities. *Higher Education Perspectives, 2*(1). Retrived April 18, 2007, from http://aries.oise.utoronto.ca/highered/

Slack, J. D. (1996). The theory and method of articulation in cultural studies. In Morley, D., & Chen, K. H. (Eds.), *Stuart Hall: Critical dialogues in cultural studies. City, ST.* Taylor & Francis.

Small, G., & Vorgan, G. (2008). *iBrain: Surviving the Technological Alteration of the Modern Mind.* New York: HarperCollins.

Smith, G. G., Passmore, D., & Faught, T. (2009). The challenges of online nursing education. *The Internet and Higher Education*, *12*(2), 98–103. doi:10.1016/j.iheduc.2009.06.007

Smith, M. K. (1999). Andragogy: The encyclopaedia of informal education. Retrieved June 15, 2009, from http://www.infed.org/lifelonglearning/b-andra.htm

Smith, P. L. H. (1998) *The impact of a computer enhanced instruction staff development program on elementary teachers' self efficacy and outcome expectancy in the use of computers.* Unpublished doctoral dissertation, Georgia State University.

Solomon, G., Allen, N., & Resta, P. (2003). *Toward digital equity.* New York: Allyn and Bacon.

Sorcinelli, M. D., Austin, A. E., Eddy, P. L., & Beach, A. L. (2006). *Creating the future of faculty development: Learning from the past, understanding the present.* Bolton, MA: Anker Publishing.

Sorensen, E. (2005). Networked eLearning and collaborative knowledge building: Design and facilitation. *Contemporary Issues in Technology & Teacher Education, 4*, 444–455.

Soulier, E., & Caussanel, J. (2002). Narrative tools to improve collaborative sense-making. *AAAI Technical Report WS-02-09 Papers from AAAI Workshop, Paolo Bouquet, Chair*. Association for the Advancement of Artificial Intelligence. Menlo Park, California ISBN 978-1-57735-162-7.

Southwest Educational Development Laboratory. (1994). *Staff development and change process: Cut from the same cloth.* Austin, TX: Southwest Educational Development Laboratory. Retrieved April 11, 2005, from http://www.sedl.org/change/issues42.html

Spigner-Littles, D., & Anderson, C. (1999). Constructivism: A Paradigm for Older Learners. *Educational Gerontology*, *25*(3), 203–209. doi:10.1080/036012799267828

Spotts, T. (1999). Discriminating Factors in Faculty Use of Instructional Technology in Higher Education. *Journal of Educational Technology & Society*, *2*(4), 92–99.

Spradley, J. P. (1979). *The ethnographic interview.* Fort Worth, TX: Hartcourt Brace Jovanovich.

Spradley, J. P. (1980). *Participant observation.* New York: Holt, Rinehart and Winston.

Squire, K. (2006). From content to context: Videogames as designed experiences. *Educational Researcher*, *35*(8), 19–29. doi:10.3102/0013189X035008019

Stacey, E. (2001). Quality online participation: Establishing social presence. *Research in Distance Learning*, 138-153. Retrieved October 25, 2005, from www.deakin.edu.au/education/ripvet/conferneces/2000/RIDE/Ch13_Stacey.pdf

Stake, R. E. (1994). Case studies. In Denzin, N. K., & Lincoln, Y. S. (Eds.), *Handbook of qualitative research* (pp. 236–247). Thousand Oaks, CA: Sage.

Stanford Web Credibility Project. (2007). Web Credibility Research. Retrieved June 24, 2009, from http://credibility.stanford.edu/

Stansbury, M. (2009). School of the future: Lessons in failure. *eSchool News*. Retrieved from http://www.eschoolnews.com/news/top-news/?i=58973

State University of New York and New York State Education Department. (2008). Grade 8 intermediate level test social studies. Book 2: Document-based question. June, 4, 2008.

Stefl-Mabry, J. (2004). Learning made real: Collaborative work, shared Assessment. *Knowledge Quest. Journal of the American Association of School Librarians*, *32*(5).

Stefl-Mabry, J., Doane, W. E. J., Radlick, M. S., & Theroux, P. (2007). Redefining schools as learning organizations: A model for trans-generational teaching and learning. *International Journal of Teaching and Learning in Higher Education*, *19*(3).

Stefl-Mabry, J., & Lynch, B. L. (2006). *Knowledge communities: Bringing the village into the classroom*. Lanham, MD: Scarecrow Press.

Stefl-Mabry, J., Powers, J. G., & Doll, C. (2006). Creating and sustaining problem-based partnerships among graduate, undergraduate, and K-12 learners: Opportunities and challenges. *Journal of Educational Technology Systems*, *34*(2), 131–153. doi:10.2190/4DMJ-85B4-GMH7-GEQB

Stefl-Mabry, J., & Lynch, B. L. (2004). A teaching hospital approach to graduate course design and implementation: Authentic project-based curricula and school library media graduate students.

Stefl-Mabry, J., & Powers, J. G. (2004). Learning Pathways Project: Collaborative Multidirectional Learning.

Stefl-Mabry, J., & Powers-Goodall, J. (2005). A model of problem-based learning higher education curricula: Creating learning pathways. The Twelfth International Conference on Learning Faculty of Education at the University of Granada from 11-14 July 2005. *The International Journal of Learning*.

Stefl-Mabry, J., Doane, W. E. J., & Radlick, M. S. (2009, April 13 - 17). *Seen and still not heard: What students voices reveal about teachers and technology.* Paper presented at the American Educational Research Association, San Diego, CA.

Stefl-Mabry, J., Radlick, M., Doane, W. E. J., & Theroux, P. (2007). Redefining schools as learning organizations: A model for trans-generational teaching and learning. *International Journal of Teaching and Learning in Higher Education.*

Stefl-Mabry, J., Theroux, P., J., & Radlick, M. S. (2005). *Examining data from multiple perspectives: A gestalt approach to library information science & educational research.* Philadelphia, PA: Treasure Mountain #12 (AASL Research Group).

Stein, M. K., Grover, B. W., & Henningsen, M. (1996). Building student capacity for mathematical thinking and reasoning: An analysis of mathematical tasks used in reform classrooms. *American Educational Research Journal*, *33*, 455–488.

Steinkuehler, C. (2007, November). Massively multiplayer online gaming as a constellation of literacy practices. *E-learning*, *4*(3), 297–318. doi:10.2304/elea.2007.4.3.297

Steinkuehler, C. (2008). Massively multiplayer online games as an educational technology: An outline for research. *Educational Technology*, *48*(1), 10–21.

Steinkuehler, C. (2005). *Cognition & learning in massively multiplayer online games: A critical approach* (Doctoral Dissertation, University of Wisconsin-Madison, 2005). Retrieved on February 19, 2008, from http://website.education.wisc.edu/steinkuehler/thesis.html

Stephens, A., & Hartmann, C. E. (2002). *Using an online discussion forum to engage secondary mathematics teachers in teaching with technology.* Paper presented at the Annual Meeting of American Educational Research Association, New Orleans, LA.

Strauss, A., & Corbin, J. (1990). *Basics of qualitative research: Grounded theory procedures and techniques* (3rd ed.). Newbury Park, CA: Sage.

Street, B. (1984). *Literacy in theory and practice*. Cambridge, UK: Cambridge University Press.

Street, B. (2005). *Social Literacies: Critical approaches to literacy in development ethnography and education.* London, New York: Longman.

Strickland, J. (2008). How Web 3.0 will work. *HowStuffWorks.com* (March 2008). Retrieved from http://computer.howstuffworks.com/web-30.htm

Strudler, N., Archambault, L., Bendixen, L., Anderson, D., & Weiss, R. (2003). Project THREAD: Technology helping restructure educational access and delivery. *Educational Technology Research and Development, 51*(3), 41–56. doi:10.1007/BF02504517

Sugar, W., Crawley, F., & Fine, B. (2004). Examining Teachers' Decisions to Adopt New Technology. *Journal of Educational Technology & Society*, 7(4), 201–213.

Sulzby, E. (1985). Children's emergent reading of favorite storybooks: A developmental study. *Reading Research Quarterly*, *20*, 458–481. doi:10.1598/RRQ.20.4.4

Sulzby, E. (1996). Roles of oral and written language as children approach conventional literacy. In Pontecorvo, C. (Eds.), *Children's early text construction.* Mahwah, NJ: Erlbaum.

Sulzby, E. (1994). Children's emergent reading of favorite storybooks: A developmental study. In Ruddell, R. B., Ruddell, M. R., & Singer, H. (Eds.), *Theoretical models and processes of reading* (pp. 244–280). Newark, DE: International Reading Association.

Supovitz, J. A. (2001). Translating teaching practice into improved student achievement. In Fuhrman, S. (Ed.), *National Society for the Study of Education Yearbook.* Chicago, IL: University of Chicago Press.

Swain, C. (2006). Preservice teachers self-assessment using technology: Determining what is worthwhile and looking for changes in daily teaching and learning practices. *Journal of Technology and Teacher Education, 14*(1), 29–59.

Swanson, T. (2004). A radical step: Implementing a critical information literacy model. *portal. Libraries and the Academy*, *4*(2), 259–273. doi:10.1353/pla.2004.0038

Sweeney, R. (2006). Millennial Behaviors and Demographics. Retrieved June 25, 2009, from http://www.google.com/url?sa=t&source=web&ct=res&cd=1&url=http%3A%2F%2Flibrary1.njit.edu%2Fstaff-folders%2Fsweeney%2FMillennials%2FArticle-Millennial-Behaviors.doc&ei=5zVESvPABIOENKr-7JkB&usg=AFQjCNEaGFMJ_yjHwMs7TCRtcAK-3p8Y-Eg

Szep, J. (2008, July 7). Technology reshapes America's classrooms. *Reuters.* Retrieved July 20, 2009, from http://www.reuters.com/article/topNews/idUSN254788552008 0707?feedType=RSS&feedName=topNews

Takatalo, J., Nyman, G., & Laaksonen, L. (2008). Components of human experience in virtual environments. *Computers in Human Behavior*, *24*(1), 1–15. doi:10.1016/j.chb.2006.11.003

Tannen, D. (1989). *Talking voices: Repetition, dialogue, and imagery in conversational discourse.* Cambridge, UK: Cambridge University Press.

Tannen, D. (1982). The oral/literate continuum in discourse. In Tannen, D. (Ed.), *Spoken and written language: Exploring orality and literacy* (pp. 1–16). Norwood, NJ: Ablex.

Taylor, T. L. (1999, November/December). Life in virtual worlds: Plural existence, multimodalities, and other online research challenges. *The American Behavioral Scientist*, *43*(2), 436–449. doi:10.1177/00027649921955362

Taylor, E. W. (2000). Analyzing research on transformative learning theory. In Mezirow, J. (Eds.), *Learning as transformation: Critical perspectives on a theory in progress* (pp. 29–310). San Francisco, CA: Jossey-Bass.

Taylor, J. (2001). Fifth generation distance education. *Journal of Instructional Science and Technology, 4*(1). Retrieved April 18, 2007, from http://www.usq.edu.au/electpub/e-jist/docs/old/vol4no1/contents.htm

Tennant, M. (1988). *Psychology and adult learning*. London: Routledge. doi:10.4324/9780203441619

Tharp, R., & Gallimore, R. (1988). *Rousing minds to life: Teaching, learning, and schooling in social context*. New York: Cambridge University Press.

Tharp, R. (1993). Institutional and social context of educational practice and reform. In Forman, E. A., Minick, N., & Stone, C. A. (Eds.), *Context for learning* (pp. 269–282). New York: Oxford University Press.

Thornburg, D. D. (1996). *Campfires in Cyberspace*. USA: Starsong Publications.

Time (1973, July 30). Sweatshops in the sun. *Time*. Retrieved from http://www.time.com/time/magazine/article/0,9171,907638,00.html

Tisdell, E., Strohschen, G., Carver, M., Corrigan, P., Nash, J., Nelsen, M., & O'Connor, M. (2004). Cohort learning online in graduate higher education: Constructing knowledge in cyber community. *Journal of Educational Technology & Society*, *7*(1), 115–127.

Tokin, E. (2005). Making the case for a wild. *Ariadne, 42*. Retrieved June 24, 2009, from http://www.ariadne.ac.uk/issue42/tonkin/

Toledo, C. (2005). A Five-Stage Model of Computer Technology Integration Into Teacher Education Curriculum. *Contemporary Issues in Technology & Teacher Education*, *5*(2), 177–191.

Torrance, M., & Jeffery, G. (1999). *The cognitive demands of writing: Processing capacity and working memory in text production*. Amsterdam: Amsterdam University Press.

Trevor, C. (1991). *A Consultation on Higher Education in Africa: A Report to the Ford Foundation and Rockefeller Foundation, New York*. UNESCO Bangkok. (n.d). Technologies. Retrieved August 3, 2008, from http://www.unescobkk.org/index.php?id=663

Tu, C. H., & McIsaac, M. (2002). The relationship of social presence and interaction in online classes. *American Journal of Distance Education*, *16*, 131–150. doi:10.1207/S15389286AJDE1603_2

Tu, C. H., & Yen, C. J. (2006). A study of multi-dimensional online social presence. In L. W. Cooke (Ed.), *Frontiers in Higher Education* (pp. 77-102). New York: Nova Science Publishers. Wachowski, A., Wachowski, L. (Writer), & J. Silver (Producer). (1999). *The Matrix* [Motion picture]. United States: Warner Brothers.

Turkle, S. (1995). *Life on the screen: Identity in the age of the internet*. New York: Touchstone.

Tursak, M. (2007). *Perceptions of students and instructors about using remote access technology in programming language courses: a case study*. Ankara: Middle East Technical University.

U.S. Department of Education. (2009). U.S. Department of Education study finds that good teaching can be enhanced with new technology [Press Release]. Retrieved June 30, 2009 from http://www.ed.gov/news/pressreleases/2009/06/06262009.html

U.S. Department of Education. (2003). Federal funding for educational technology and how it is used in the classroom: A summary of findings from the Integrated Studies of Educational Technology. Washington, DC: Office of the Under Secretary, Policy and Program Studies Service. Retrieved June 25, 2009, from www.ed.gov/about/offices/list/os/technology/evaluation.html

U.S. Department of Education. (2004). Toward a new golden age in American education--How the internet, the law and today's students are revolutionizing expectations: National Educational Technology Plan. Retrieved June 28, 2009, from http://www.ed.gov/about/offices/list/os/technology/plan/2004/plan.pdf

University College London. (2008). *Information behaviour of the future of the researcher: A ciber briefing paper*. Retrieved January 15, 2009, from http://www.jisc.ac.uk/media/documents/programmes/reppres/gg_final_keynote_11012008.pdf

University of Missouri. (2008). Evaluation, assessment, grading, norming. In *Teaching at Mizzou: A guide for new faculty, graduate instructors and teaching assistants 2008*. Columbia, MO: University of Missouri.

University of the State of New York, State Education Department. 8 Washington Ave. Albany, NY 12234. http://www.nysed.gov/

Use of social network websites in investigations. Wikipedia Retrieved January 31, 2009 from http://en.wikipedia.org/wiki/Use_of_social.netwrok_websites_in_investigations

Vannatta, R. A., & Fordham, N. (2004). Teacher dispositions as predictors of classroom technology use. *Journal of Research on Technology in Education*, *36*(3), 253–271.

Veenman, S. (1984). Perceived problems of beginning teachers. *Review of Educational Research*, *54*, 143–178.

Vella, J., Berardinelli, P., & Burrow, J. (1998). *How do they know they know? Evaluating adult learning*. San Francisco: Jossey-Bass.

Villano, M. (2008). Immersive learning: World teaching. *Campus Technology*. Retrieved January 17, 2008, from: http://www.campustechnology.com/printarticle.aspx?id=57065

Vygotsky, L. S. (1978). *Mind in society*. Boston: Harvard University Press.

Vygotsky, L. S. (1978). *Mind in Society: The Development of Higher Psychological Processes*. Cambridge, MA: Harvard University Press.

Vygotsky, L. S., & Luria, A. (1994). Tool and symbol in child development. In van der Veer, R., & Valsiner, J. (Eds.), *The Vygotsky reader*. Oxford, UK: Blackwell.

Vygotsky, L. S. (1981). The instrumental method in psychology. In Wertsch, J. (Ed.), *The concept of activity in Soviet psychology*. Armonk, NY: Sharpe.

Vygotsky, L. S. (1987). Thinking and speech. In L. S. Vygotsky, R. W.Rieber (Series Eds.), & A. S. Carton (Vol. Ed.), *The collected works of L. S. Vygotsky*. Vol. 1: *Problems in general psychology* (N. Minick,Trans.). New York: Plenum.

Wadhwa, G., Schulz, H., & Mann, B. L. (2006). Effects of anonymity and peer-accountability during online peer assessment. In Mann, B. L. (Ed.), *Selected styles in web-based educational research* (pp. 300–331). Hershey, PA: Idea Group.

Wagner, C. (2004). Wiki: A technology for conversational knowledge management and group collaboration. *Communications of the Association for Information Systems*, *13*, 265–289.

Walker, S. L. (2005). Development of the Distance Education Learning Environments Survey (DELES) for higher education. *The Texas Journal of Distance Learning*, *2*(1), 1–16.

Ward, B. (2008). Blog post title? *Squaredpeg.com* Blog. Retrieved January 31, 2009, from http://squaredpeg.com/index.php/2008/12/18/facebook-pay-attention/

Wasserman, S., & Faust, K. (1994). *Social network analysis: Methods and applications*. Cambridge, UK: Press Syndicate of the University of Cambridge.

Waycott, J., Jones, A., & Scanlon, E. (2005). PDAs as lifelong learning tools: An activity theory based analysis. *Learning, Media and Technology*, *30*(2), 107–130. doi:10.1080/17439880500093513

Weil, E. (2008). Meet your new school library media specialist [Electronic Version]. *Scholastic Administrator*. Retrieved March 12, 2008, from http://www2.scholastic.com/browse/article.jsp?id=3748779&print=2

Weinberg, B. A. (2004). Experience and Technology Adoption. The Institute for Study of Labor (IZA), IZA DP No. 1051, 60pg.

Weller, M. (2007). *Virtual learning environments: Using, choosing and developing your VLE*. London: Routledge.

Wenger, E. (1998). *Communities of practice: Learning, meaning, and identity*. Cambridge, UK: Cambridge University Press.

Wenglinsky, H. (1998). Does it compute? The relationship between educational technology and student achievement in mathematics. *Educational Testing Service Policy Information Center*. Retrieved June 25, 2009, from www.mff.org/pubs/ME161.pdf

Wergin, J. (1994). *Analyzing Faculty Workload*. San Francisco: Jossey-Bass Publishers.

Wertsch, J. (1991). *Voices of the Mind: A Sociocultural Approach to Mediated Action*. Cambridge, MA: Harvard University Press.

Wertsch, J., & Stone, C. A. (1985). The concept of internalization in Vygotskys account of the genesis of higher mental functions. In Wertsch, J. (Ed.), *Culture, communication, and cognition* (pp. 162–179). New York: Cambridge University Press.

Wikimedia Foundation. (2009). Web 2.0. Retrieved June 24, 2009, from http://en.wikipedia.org/wiki/Web_2.0

Wilkerson, L., & Irby, D. M. (1998). Strategies for improving teaching practices: A comprehensive approach to faculty development. *Academic Medicine*, *73*(4), 387–396. doi:10.1097/00001888-199804000-00011

William, M. (2008). *Broadband for Africa: Policy for Promoting the Development of Backbone Networks*. Washington, DC: InfoDev and the World Bank.

Williams, M. (2003). *Making Sense of Social Research*. London: Sage Publication.

Williams, R. (1957). Working class culture. *Universities and Left Review, 2*.

Wilson, T., & Whitelock, D. (1998). Changing roles: Comparing face to face and on-line teaching in the light of new technologies. *European Journal of Open, Distance and E-Learning*. Retrieved April 18, 2007, from http://www.eurodl.org

Wilson-Meddeb, E. J. (2004). *The interaction between speech recognition dictation technology and language use: A sociolinguistic study*. Unpublished doctoral dissertation.Columbia University, New York.

Windschitl, M., & Sahl, K. (2002). Tracing teachers' use of technology in a laptop computer school: The interplay of teacher beliefs, social dynamics, and institutional culture. *American Educational Research Journal*, *39*(1), 165–205. doi:10.3102/00028312039001165

Windschitl, M. (1999). The Challenges of Sustaining a Constructivist Classroom Culture. *Phi Delta Kappan*, *80*(10), 751.

Winiecki, D. J. (2003). Instructional discussions in online education: Practical and research-oriented perspectives. In Moore, M. G., & Anderson, W. G. (Eds.), *Handbook of Distance Education* (pp. 193–211). Mahwah, NJ: Erlbaum.

Wolcott, L. (1997). *Tenure, Promotion, and Distance Teaching: A Study of faculty rewards and incentives*. Information and Technology, Utah State University.

Wolcott, L. (1998). Faculty Issues Pertaining to Institutional Support and Reward Practices in Distance Education. Presented at the annual meeting of the American Educational Research Association, San Diego, CA: Utah State University.

Wolski, S., & Jackson, S. (1999). Technological Diffusion within Educational Institutions: Applying the Technology Acceptance Model. In J. Price et al. (Eds.), *Proceedings of Society for Information Technology and Teacher Education International Conference 1999* (pp. 1718-1723). Chesapeake, VA: AACE.

Wood, D., Bruner, J., & Ross, G. (1976). The role of tutoring in problem solving. *Journal of Child Psychology and Psychiatry, and Allied Disciplines*, *17*, 89–100. doi:10.1111/j.1469-7610.1976.tb00381.x

Woolls, B. (1995). The role of library media services in future schooling: The future of the school library media center. [SLMA]. *School Library Media Annual*, *13*, 54–59.

Work, A. P. A. Group of the Board of Educational Affairs (1997). *Learner-centered psychological principles: A framework for school reform and redesign*. Washington, DC: Author.

World Bank. (2002). *Constructing Knowledge Societies: New Challenges for Tertiary Education*. Washington, DC: The World Bank.

World Bank. (2009). *Accelerating Catch-up Tertiary Education for Growth in Sub-Saharan Africa*. Washington, DC: The International Bank for Reconstruction and Development / The World Bank.

Wulff, S., Hanor, J., & Bulik, R. J. (2000). The roles and interrelationships of presence, reflection, and self-directed learning in effective world wide web-based pedagogy. In Cole, R. (Ed.), *Issues in web-based pedagogy* (pp. 143–160). Westport, CT: Greenwood Press.

Yamada, M. (2009). The role of social presence in learner-centered communicative language learning using synchronous computer-mediated communication: Experimental study. *Computers & Education*, *52*(4), 820–833. doi:10.1016/j.compedu.2008.12.007

Yan, J. (2008). Social technology as a new medium in the classroom. *The New England Journal of Higher Education,* Winter 27-30 22:4.

Yang, S. C., & Liu, S. F. (2004). Case study of online workshop for the professional development of teachers. *Computers in Human Behavior*, *20*(6), 733–761. doi:10.1016/j.chb.2004.02.005

Yang, F., Wang, M., Shen, R., & Han, P. (2007). Community-organizing agent: An artificial intelligent system for building learning communities among large numbers of learners. *Computers & Education*, *49*, 131–147. doi:10.1016/j.compedu.2005.04.019

Yee, N. (2006, June). The demographics, motivations, and derived experiences of users of massively multi-user online graphical environments. *Presence (Cambridge, Mass.)*, *15*(3), 309–329. doi:10.1162/pres.15.3.309

Yildirim, A., & Simsek, H. (2001). *Nitel araştırma yöntemleri* [Qualitative research methods]. İstanbul: Seckin Yayincilik.

Yildirim, A., & Simsek, H. (2006). *Nitel araştırma yöntemleri* [Qualitative research methods]. İstanbul: Seckin Yayincilik.

Yoon, K. S., Duncan, T., Lee, S. W. Y., Scarloss, B., & Shapley, K. (2007). *Reviewing the evidence on how teacher professional development affects student achievement* (Issues & Answers Report, REL 2007–No. 033). Washington, DC: U.S. Department of Education, Institute of Education Sciences, National Center for Education Evaluation and Regional Assistance, Regional Educational Laboratory Southwest. Retrieved December 31, 2008, from: http://ies.ed.gov/ncee/edlabs

Zachary, L. J. (2000). *The mentor's guide: Facilitating effective learning relationships*. San Francisco, CA: Jossey-Bass.

Zayim, N., Yildirim, S., & Saka, O. (2006). Technology Adoption of Medical Faculty in Teaching: Differentiating Factors in Adopter Categories. *Journal of Educational Technology & Society*, *9*(2), 213–222.

Zehr, M. A. (2009, January 8). English-learners pose policy problem. *Edweek*. Retrieved January 15, 2009, from http://www.edweek.org/login.html?source=http://www.edweek.org/ew/articles/2009/01/08/17ell.h28.html&destination=http://www.edweek.org/ew/articles/2009/01/08/17ell.h28.html&levelId=100

Zhao, Y., & Frank, K. (2003). Factors affecting technology uses in schools: An ecological perspective. *American Educational Research Journal*, *40*(4), 807–840. doi:10.3102/00028312040004807

Zhao, Y., Pugh, K., Sheldon, S., & Byers, J. (2002). Conditions for classroom innovation. *Teachers College Record*, *104*(3), 482–515. doi:10.1111/1467-9620.00170

Zhao, S. (2003). Toward a taxonomy of copresence. *Presence (Cambridge, Mass.)*, *12*(5), 445–455. doi:10.1162/105474603322761261

Zhao, Y., & Cziko, G. (2001). Teacher Adoption of Technology: A perspective Control Theory Perspective. *Journal of Technology and Teacher Education*, *9*(1), 5–30.

About the Contributors

Steven D'Agustino is the Director Fordham University's RETC, Center for Professional Development. Dr. D'Agustino's principal research interest is in the integration of technology into instructional environments. He is the author of several articles, grants and presentations in this field. The focus of his work at the University is the access to technology for historically underserved populations. Successful grant-funded programs developed and implemented by Dr. D'Agustino include a 21st Century Community Learning Center, established to provide access to technology to inner-city students and their families, a Title IID educational technology grant that provides technology professional development to NYC public school teachers in the Bronx and a Title IID technology integration grant that provides technology professional development to teachers in charter schools across New York City.

* * *

Dwight W. Allen was the instructor for more than twenty years of the course in which the project described in this book was conducted, until his retirement from Old Dominion University in fall 2007. He worked to develop and refine the Wikibooks project and, though no longer serving as course instructor, remains instrumental in the project's revision and study. He received his AB in History with Distinction, an MA in Humanitics with Honors in 1957 and an Ed.D. in Education in 1959. All degrees were earned from Stanford University.

Jenny Arntzen is a graduate student at the University of British Columbia in the Faculty of Education, Department of Curriculum and Pedagogy. She is currently working on completing her PhD program. She has a Master of Arts degree in Technology Studies Education (2007).Arntzen's research investigates the cultural formations of ICT engagement and pedagogy perspectives. She is interested in the role participants play in forming, and being formed by, institutional experiences. Her research involves asking how learning occurs as phenomenological processes of empathy, enculturation and the formation of consciousness in institutionalized settings. She is particularly interested in the role ICT social learning cultures will play in shaping educational institutions in the 21st century.

Cengiz S. Askun is an instructor in the department of Computer Education and Instructional Technology at the Faculty of Education of The Middle East Technical University, Ankara, Turkey. He is teaching courses on computer literacy, instructional design and material development, computer networks as well as programming languages. His research interests includes online and blended learning environments, use of multimedia in formal and informal learning environments, human-computer interaction and accessibility in online learning environments. Working as either primary investigator or investigator, he has actively participated on various research and community reach projects in which blended learning environments on science and geometry topics were developed for 4-8 grade students.

Simon Atkinson is Director of Teaching & Learning at the College of Education, Massey University, New Zealand. An educational developer and strategist with specialist interests in educational technologies, his research interests focus on tertiary educations strategic response to the impact of technology-enabled communication on cultural interactions and the values of academe. Current work is developing reusable learning designs to maximize engagement with digitally rich resources (DiAL-e Framework - http://www.dia-e.net). He has held a number of senior roles in higher education in New Zealand and the United Kingdom, in e-learning and academic development, with the University of Hull, United Kingdom (2003-2008) and the Open University UK (2001-2003). Simon was a European TEMPUS visiting expert for the Croatian National e-Learning Project – EQIBELT from 2005-2008. He has run capacity development workshop in Kenya, and delivered invited keynotes in Croatia and Estonia on issues of foresight and planning for technology enabled learning.

Suzanne Aurilio leads an emerging technologies program at San Diego State University and works with faculty, academic program directors and instructional staff to infuse technology into the curriculum. Dr. Aurilio's interests and research converge on informal learning in academic and non-academic settings.

Patricia Baia is an Assistant Professor at Albany College of Pharmacy and Health Sciences specializing in pedagogy, professional development and instructional technology. She teaches communication, writing, and general education courses. Dr. Baia's research interest is situated within higher education and includes technology adoption, professional development initiatives, and faculty's commitment to the profession. She is the founder of the Capital District Educational Technology Group and on the Board of Trustees for the Capital District Library Consortium and Schenectady County Community College's Library/Instructional Technology Advisory Board. She resides in Albany, NY with her husband (Kevin) and purposely lives close to her dear family.

Peter B. Baker has been the lead graduate teaching assistant associated with the course described in this chapter since its development began in summer 2006. He received a BA in Literature and Composition from the College of William & Mary in 2005, an MS Ed in General Secondary Education from Old Dominion University in 2007 and is currently a doctoral candidate in Curriculum and Instruction at Old Dominion University.

Holly Lynn Baumgartner has a Ph.D in Rhetoric and Writing and a Masters degree in Culture Studies from Bowling Green State University. She is a professor of the humanities at Mercy College and has taught at the summer programmes for Oxford University, England. Her most recent publication is as co-editor of the book *Hosting the Monster.* Along with Garrick Ducat, she is co-chair of the Mercy College Second Life Learning Community which advocates for the use of immersive learning environments and pedagogies in academic settings as well as coordinates with regional communities to generate and share best practices. She has won numerous awards, such as Mercy College Professor of the Year, and regularly publishes and presents at conferences nationally and internationally.

Kevin Burden is responsible for Post-graduate professional development (PPD) in the Centre for Educational studies, based at the University of Hull. He co-ordinates professional development work for teachers including a variety of evidence-based practitioner programmes focusing on the role of action research for educators. He has undertaken a wide variety of development and evaluation programmes for various UK agencies including Becta, Nesta, the JISC, QIA and the BBC. His research interests lay in the area of professional learning with particular emphasis on the role of technology and social software for collaborative learning. He has worked closely with Simon Atkinson to develop the DiAL-e framework for the effective use of digital resources in teaching and learning and is currently the pedagogic expert for EduTubePlus, an innovative European project developing a video-clips library for use in school (www.edutubeplus.com).

Brian G. Burton is an assistant professor teaching digital entertainment, game development, and mobile application development courses. His research centers on learning and collaboration in virtual environments. Brian has successfully started digital entertainment degrees at multiple universities. During his free time he operates a state of the art online school with his wife Rosemary.

Al Byers is the Assistant Executive Director of Government Partnerships and e-Learning at NSTA. A former science teacher himself, Al's current responsibilities at NSTA include oversight and management of the production, delivery, and evaluation of nearly all e-Learning and blended professional development opportunities provided by NSTA, the world's largest association of science educators.

Evoh Chijioke completed his PhD at the Milano School of Management and Public Policy, the New School University. He is a Teaching Fellow with the New York City Department of Education and an adjunct instructor at the College of New Rochelle, New Rochelle, New York, and St. Thomas Aquinas College, Sparkill, New York. His scholarship connects various complementary issues in collaborative partnerships, Information and Communication Technologies (ICTs) in development, environmental policy/advocacy, educational leadership and public policy analysis.

Nancy K. Gagen Clouse is an adjunct assistant professor in the Phyllis J. Washington College of Education and Human Sciences at The University of Montana. She teaches in the Business and Information Technology Program as well as in the area of instructional technology. Her research interest focuses on best practices of integrating technology for teaching, learning, and professional development. Prior to her work in higher education, she taught high school business education for 11 years in Oregon and Montana.

Bronwen Cowie is an associate professor and director of the Wilf Malcolm Institute of Educational Research, The University of Waikato. Previously she was director of the Centre for Science and Technology Education Research, The University of Waikato. She has directed a number of long-term national research projects including the 6-year Laptops for Teachers Evaluation study and the Curriculum Implementation Exploratory Studies project. She is co-director of the Science Learning Hub. Bronwen has extensive research experience of working with teachers and students in both primary and secondary classrooms. Her research interests include supporting teachers to make more effective use of ICTs for teaching and learning, whole school approaches to curriculum implementation, and formative assessment/ assessment for learning.

William E. J. Doane holds a PhD in Information Science, a Masters degree in Information & Computer Science with a focus on uses of computing technologies to support K-12 education, and a Bachelors degree in Cognitive Science from Hampshire College. His research interests include computer science education research, technology in education, and science education research. Doane participated in a National Science Foundation funded Rural Systemic Initiative in Hawai`i to develop web-based tools to support K-12 teacher collaboration and professional development at a distance. He has extensive experience teaching computer science and information science topics to students from grade school through elderhostel. Doane is also a founding member of ACASE, a professional organization of educators and scientists working to improve education, and is an active member of ACM's Special Interest Group in Computer Science Education (SIGCSE).

Garrick Ducat has an M.Ed in technology education from BGSU. He is the Instructional Designer for Mercy College and is responsible for coordinating the design, development, and evaluation of both credit and non-credit online courses and programs. He has presented at numerous conferences about topics specific to how creative commons licensed materials can be used in academic setting and the use of emerging technologies to facilitate student engagement. Along with Dr. Holly Baumgartner, he is co-chair of the Mercy College Second Life Learning Community which advocates for the use of immersive learning environments and pedagogies in academic settings as well as coordinates with regional communities to generate and share best practices. His most recent research undertaking has focused on the application of humor and parody to enhance student understanding of core course concepts.

Roberta D. Evans is Dean of the Phyllis J. Washington College of Education and Human Sciences, The University of Montana. Roberta supports achievement of the strategic goals of The University of Montana, leads academic departments (Communicative Sciences & Disorders, Counselor Education, Curriculum & Instruction, Educational Leadership, and Health & Human Performance); Nationally-renown centers (Institute for Education Research Services with Montana Safe Schools Center the National Native Children's Trauma Center; Montana Center for Work Physiology and Exercise Metabolism); clinics (The University of Montana RiteCare Speech, Language and Hearing Clinic; CE; CSD); LAB Preschool; and the Montana Virtual Academy.

Joanne Gilbreath is a professor of education in the Department of Innovative Educational Technology and Physical Education at Azusa Pacific University. Focusing on preparing teachers to integrate technology tools and instructional strategies in the classroom, she works with new teachers to meet the needs of 21st century learners. Research areas include the alignment of technology to instructional use in teacher preparation courses, and accreditation and accountability within schools of education. She is a grant screener and evaluator for Hewlitt-Packard's "HP Innovations in Education" grant program for both United States secondary schools, and international higher education institutions.

Ann Harlow is a senior research officer for the Wilf Malcolm Institute of Educational Research, The University of Waikato. She was the researcher for the Laptops for Teachers evaluation. She has extensive experience with collaborative research, national survey work and focus groups. She has undertaken research to explore the nature and role of professional development advisors as they work with individual teachers and with whole schools. Her research interests include the use of ICTs for teaching and learning, particularly the use of an interactive whiteboard in primary classrooms along with collaborative action research to do with teacher professional learning and e-learning.

Caroline Hilk is a doctoral candidate in educational psychology and instructional technology fellow at the University of Minnesota-Twin Cities. In addition to teaching several psychology courses she also works closely with faculty to make effective use of classroom technology, create virtual learning environments, and evaluate the effects of technology on student learning outcomes. She received her master's degree in educational psychology with a thesis examining social presence and student interaction in an asynchronous, computer-supported collaborative learning environment. Her research interests include cooperative learning, creative problem solving, social network analysis and meta-analysis techniques.

Mary Hricko is a Professor, Library & Information Services at Kent State University where she serves as the Library Director at Kent State University Geauga Campus and Twinsburg Center. She has published and presented numerous articles and papers on academic support services and distance education, web accessibility and instructional technology. She has edited three books on online assessment and measurement and is the facilitator of the Web Teaching and Academic Services (WEBTAS) Learning Community. Her current research involves quality assessment for the design and delivery of online instruction and the use of participant web technologies in teaching, learning, and research.

Raja Maznah Raja Hussain is a Professor of Instructional Technology and Director of Academic Development Centre at the University of Malaya, Malaysia. She is responsible for setting the objectives and leading a team of designers and trainers to develop curriculum for training of lecturers in skills related to teaching and learning, coaching, mentoring, supervision of research, project management, counselling and ICT. Her area of specialization and supervision is Instructional Design and Training. She is currently researching on the scholarship of teaching and learning (SoTL) specifically studying strategies to develop personalized learning environment and students' engagement (PLEaSE).

Azad Isik is a computer teacher and an instructional technologist. He is currently working as a software developer and working on a project named Document Management and Workflow Systems (DMWS) at Cybersoft, an IT company in Ankara, TURKEY. He used to work as a computer teacher at METU Development Foundation School in Ankara, Turkey. His main responsibility was to teach computer literacy courses and maintain learning / sharing portal applications as an instructional technologist for five years. He holds an M.S. degree in computer education and instructional technology and the focus of his research comprises the perceptions of his students and teacher colleagues about the use of the learning / sharing portal in educational activities.

James Johnson is the Director of Instructional & Information Technology in the Bayh College of Education at Indiana State University. He received his Bachelor of Science in Computer Science with a Secondary Education certification from Muskingum College. He also holds a Master of Education degree from Ohio University in Curriculum and Instruction with an Education Technology specialty. He is currently a doctoral student at Indiana State University. James has previously worked as a Director of Technology at the K-12 and university levels and has taught graduate courses as an adjunct professor for several universities. He also operates his own business, JohnsonTech Computer Services.

Alister Jones is a professor and the Dean of the School of Education, The University of Waikato. He previously directed the Wilf Malcolm Institute of Educational Research. He has directed a number of long-term national research projects including the Laptops for Teachers evaluation study and the National Schools Curriculum Stocktake Sampling Study. He currently co-directs the Science Learning Hub website development. The Hub aims to make science, in particular the work of New Zealand scientists, more accessible to teachers. His research interests include curriculum development, technology education, teacher pedagogical content knowledge for primary science and technology education and assessment for learning.

Ugur Kale is an assistant professor in Instructional Design & Technology at West Virginia University. He earned his Ph.D. from Indiana University's Instructional Systems Technology Department. He currently teaches courses in instructional design and technology integration. His research focuses on the educational use of emerging technologies for pre-service and in-service teachers. These efforts are extension of his prior experiences, where he worked as a senior research associate and a multimedia developer on federal funded projects involving web-based tools and resources to assist teachers in implementing PBL activities.

Jamie A. Kaufman was a student in the class described in this chapter during the second semester of the Wikibooks project's implementation. Likewise, she has been the lead graduate teaching assistant associated with the course since summer 2007. She received a BS in Human Development from Virginia Polytechnic Institute and State University (Virginia Tech) in 2004, an MS Ed in Elementary Education from Old Dominion University in 2008, and is currently a doctoral student in Curriculum and Instruction at Old Dominion University.

Karen P. Kaun is Co-founder and Executive Director of Knowledge iTrust, a non-profit organization that works in partnership with educational institutions, non-governmental and community-based organizations, and experts from various fields to design, develop, and facilitate technology-infused literacy and applied learning programs that empower individuals and communities. Her doctorate is from Columbia University.

Jennifer J. Kidd has been the instructor of the course described in this chapter since fall 2007. She received a B.A. in Elementary Education from the University of Illinois at Chicago in 1992, a M.S. in General Secondary Education in 1999 and a Ph.D. in Urban Services in 2006, both from Old Dominion University.

Kathleen P. King is professor of education at Fordham University's Graduate School of Education in NYC, president of Transformation Education LLC, and former director of the university's RETC, Center for Professional Development. Dr. King's major areas of research include training, change process, distance learning, transformative learning, new media, diversity issues, and career and technical education. She is an award winning author (17 books), popular keynote and conference speaker, editor, mentor, and consultant. She has been recognized for her research, service, and contribution to the fields of research and publication, and technology innovations in learning. Recent books include *Global Models of Human Performance) (2009, with Wang)*; *Handbook of Evolving Research in Transformative Learning (10th anniv. ed.) (2009); and Podcasting for Teaching* (2nd ed) (2009, with Gura). *Examples of* *the awards she has received for her books and research include those from AERA, ACHE, UCEA, POD Network, and NYACCE.* Through distance technologies Dr. King and her collaborators have reached over 6.3 million learners. Dr. King earned her Ed.D. and M.Ed. from Widener University, Chester, Pennsylvania. She also has a M.A. from Columbia International, Columbia, SC and a B.A. from Brown University, Providence, RI. She may be reached through her website:

Don Krug is a Professor in the Faculty of Education at the University of British Columbia in the Department of Curriculum & Pedagogy and a faculty associate with the Institute for Computing, Information & Cognitive Systems (ICICS), Media and Graphics Interdisciplinary Centre and Centre for Digital Media at UBC. From 1993-2002, he taught at The Ohio State University and held associate faculty appointments with the Advance Computing Center for Art and Design and the Center for Folklife Studies. He was a Fulbright Award recipient in 2000-2001. Krug's research investigates how to develop, design, and use digital media in virtual education spaces (e.g., face-to-face, hybrid, and online learning environments), whether it is a K–16 classroom, an online university course, or professional development seminar. His research involves asking critical questions about the social-cultural conditions of using ICT in education to ensure that human interaction remains part of the process of curriculum and pedagogy.

Daniel R. Lawson is an associate professor and the Program Director in the Department of Doctoral Studies in Education at Azusa Pacific University in Azusa, California. He has a strong background in pre-k--12 education, in curriculum development and administration. His research interests are in strength-based leadership in early childhood education and technology integration in teacher preparation. His most recent publication is an article entitled, A Partnership Experience in Private Schools.

Marina Leight is Director of the Center for Digital Education. She manages and maintains business policy and standards for the Center's many programs, publications, and special events. Prior to joining the Center, Leight was the publisher of the Center's sister division, Converge magazine, an award-winning publication covering technology's impact on education. Leight also headed Government Technology Executive Events. In this position, she produced executive forums, managed strategic relationships and produced customized executive technology events throughout the country. Marina's professional experience has included work as a teacher, corporate trainer as well as managing sales and marketing teams. A professional writer and speaker, Marina received her BA in English and Communications at California State University, Sacramento with graduate work completed specializing in Shakespeare. Marina resides in Folsom, California.

Barbara Martin is a professor in the Educational Leadership and Human Development department at the University of Central Missouri. The focus of her research involves the use of technology in educational settings, social justice issues, and educational leadership.

Randall McClure is Associate Professor and Chair of the Department of Writing and Linguistics at Georgia Southern University. He has authored or co-authored several articles on information literacy and behavior of college students, particularly first-year students enrolled in college English courses. In addition to a forthcoming essay in the collection *Writing Spaces: Readings on Writing* from Parlor Press, his articles on information behavior have appeared in *Computers and Composition Online*, *portal: Libraries and the Academy*, *WPA: Writing Program Administration*, and the *Journal of Literacy and*

Technology. His other interests include online teaching and learning, program assessment, and higher education administration. He also has a textbook for first-year writing forthcoming in 2012 from Pearson Publishing.

Michael C. Mensink is a doctoral candidate in Educational Psychology, Institute of Education Sciences predoctoral fellow in the Minnesota Interdisciplinary Training in Education Research program, and a predoctoral member of the Center for Cognitive Sciences at the University of Minnesota-Twin Cities. His research interests include the general cognitive mechanisms involved in understanding text and multimedia, the influence of attention and interest on learning, and the psychological elements of transportation and presence in literature and technology. He received his master's degree in educational psychology from the University of Minnesota in 2007. More info, including publication downloads and curriculum vitae, can be found at http://www.michaelmensink.com. Michael's contribution to this chapter was funded by the Institute of Education Sciences training grant R305C050059, University of Minnesota PRF# 473473.

Patrick M. O'Shea was the first to envision the project described in this chapter in 2006. He helped to develop the project for initial implementation and has been instrumental in its revision during each subsequent semester. He received a BA in History, an MS in General Secondary Education and a Ph.D. in Urban Services from Old Dominion University. He currently acts as the Directory of the Handheld Augmented Reality Project at Harvard's Graduate School of Education.

M. Yasar Özden is a full time professor at the department of Computer Education & Instructional Technology at the Faculty of Education of The Middle East Technical University, Ankara, Turkey. He is teaching courses on WEB programming, WEB Design, Integrating Technology into Educational Settings and programming languages. He has published several articles in national and international journals. He is actively working on the use of multimedia on the WEB, teacher education through WEB and distance education.

Hae Seong Park is a professor in the Department of Doctoral Studies in Education at Azusa Pacific University. His research interests and publications are in the areas of technology integration in teacher preparation, technology and language minority students, and religiousness, parenting and academic achievement. His most recent publications are an article entitled "The Impact of Technology Use on Hispanic Students' Mathematics Achievement within Family and School Contexts: Subgroup Analysis between English- and Non-English Speaking Students" in *Educational Computing Research* and "Family Religious Involvement, Parenting Practices and Academic Performance in Adolescents" in *School Psychology International*.

Linda B. Pincham is an Associate Professor in secondary and middle school education at Roosevelt University in Chicago, Illinois where she previously served as the Assistant Dean and Certification Officer for the College of Education. Before joining the faculty at Roosevelt, she was the principal of William Ruffner Magnet Middle School in Roanoke, Virginia for three years. Prior to that, she was a middle school assistant principal for eight years in Fairfax County, Virginia. She began her career in education as a middle and high school English teacher for thirteen years. Her research interests include middle school leadership, middle-level education, and recruiting and retention of traditional-aged students to the teaching profession. She has presented nationally and locally on each topic.

Drew Polly is currently an Assistant Professor in the Department of Reading and Elementary Education at the University of North Carolina at Charlotte. He is a former elementary school teacher. His research interests include learner-centered models of professional development to support technology integration and reform-based mathematics instruction.

Michael S. Radlick is an independent researcher and program evaluator emphasizing technology planning assessment and evaluation in schools and public sector organizations. One major area of focus for his research is on K-12 student learning, the use of technology, and the development of information and communications technology (ICT) skills. Prior to over 15 years of independent consulting and research work, he served as the Director of Planning, Evaluation, and Technology for the New York State Education Department for 16 years. Throughout his career in education, he has participated in many national technology efforts, serving on a number of national technology advisory boards and committees, as well as consulting for the Center for Children and Technology at EDC, the International Society for Technology in Education, the RAND Corporation, the US Department of Education, and TERC in Cambridge.

Scott Reid recently received his PhD from the University of Ottawa in Canada. His dissertation was a case study of the adoption of asynchronous online courses by professors at Memorial University of Newfoundland. He works as a Senior Policy Advisor with a Member of the House of Commons in Canada and also teaches courses in change management and politics at Memorial University of Newfoundland. His research interests include the integration of technology into teaching, the politics of technological change, change management and education policy. He lives in St. John's Newfoundland with his wife Shaunna and daughter Katherine.

Greg Sherman is an associate professor of instructional technology at Radford (VA) University where he teaches courses and conducts research on the effective design and use of technology-supported learning environments. Greg has experience as a high school science teacher as well as a professional development consultant for a number of school districts across the United States. More recently, Greg has been working as a consultant with NSTA to design and evaluate various features of the *NSTA Learning Center*.

Joette Stefl-Mabry is an Associate Professor in the Department of Information Studies, College of Computing and Information, and Associate Research Professor in the Department of Educational Theory and Practice, School of Education, University at Albany, State University of New York. She is involved in teacher/librarian training for future educators at the graduate level, and her research interests include: aligning instruction and adapting learning environments to support problem-based learning; social aspects of technology; creating collaborative learning communities; designing instruction that supports learning and social understanding; and the impact of technology on formal and informal learning environments.

David S. Stein received his Ph.D. in adult education from the University of Michigan. He also received an M.S. in community health planning and administration from the University of Cincinnati.. He currently serves as an associate professor in the College of Education and Human Ecology at The Ohio State University. Dr. Stein specializes in adult teaching and learning. He has conducted workshops on principles of adult teaching and has served as a consultant to professional associations and other universities on adult education. Presently, Dr. Stein is researching online learning and its influence on adult learning. He has presented at national and regional conferences on adult learning and has written extensively on how adults learn.

Doug Thomas is a professor in the Educational Leadership and Human Development department at the University of Central Missouri. The focus of his research includes investigation of the middle school level and charter schools.

Larry Tinnerman is an assistant professor of curriculum, instruction and media technology in the Bayh College of Education at Indiana State University where he teaches both undergraduate and doctoral courses in curriculum. He received his Doctorate of Education from Indiana University of Pennsylvania in 2007 in Curriculum and Instruction. He holds a Master of Education degree from Edinboro University of Pennsylvania. Over the past three years, Dr. Tinnerman is a regular presenter at the International Association for the Advancement of Computers in Education (AACE), The New England Educational Research Organization (NEERO), and The Midwest Educational Research Organization (MWERA) conferences. Currently, he consults with the Center for Collaboration and Innovation in Education (CCITE) and is the coordinator for the Scholars Collaborative Partnership social networking community for faculty and graduate students. Dr. Tinnerman also serves as a reviewer for the Early Childhood Education and Teaching Exceptional Children Plus journals.

Constance E. Wanstreet received her Ph.D. in workforce development and education from The Ohio State University. She is an adjunct assistant professor in the College of Education and Human Ecology. Dr. Wanstreet has developed and implemented training programs for adult learners in workplace settings and has served as a consultant to the Ohio Board of Regents. She has presented at national and regional conferences, primarily on how adults learn in online environments.

Helen Easterling Williams is the Dean of the School of Education at Azusa Pacific University. Prior to joining the University, she served as senior assistant dean at the University of Delaware College of Arts and Sciences. Her breadth of professional educational experience includes roles in administration, teaching, counseling and speech and language therapy. Dr. Easterling Williams is an American Council on Education 2004/2005 Fellow. In that capacity, she served at the University of Maryland University College in Adelphi, where she established the Office of Instructional Design and Development, collaborated on a K-16 Early college Program concept paper, prepared an assessment report for the University of Delaware, and provided consultation support to the University of Baltimore. From 1986 through 1997, Dr. Williams served as the Counselor for Special Services, International Students, Computer Sciences, and other technologies.

Sandra R. Williams is an associate professor and director of the Business and Information Technology Program at The University of Montana. Her current research interests include best practices in online teaching and learning, and using technology to improve students' writing. Prior to her academic career, she worked in the field of accounting for more than 15 years.

Index

Symbols

A

B

C

U

V

W

X

Z

Breinigsville, PA USA
07 April 2011
259405BV00007B/6/P

9 781616 928544